FROM FETISH TO GOD

IN ANCIENT EGYPT

E. A. Wallis Budge

DOVER PUBLICATIONS, INC.
NEW YORK

Published in Canada by General Publishing Company, Ltd., 30 Lesmill Road, Don Mills, Toronto, Ontario.
Published in the United Kingdom by Constable and Company, Ltd.

This Dover edition, first published in 1988, is an unabridged and basically unaltered republication of the work originally published by the Oxford University Press, London, in 1934. A few obvious typographical errors have been tacitly corrected.

Manufactured in the United States of America
Dover Publications, Inc., 31 East 2nd Street, Mineola, N.Y. 11501

Library of Congress Cataloging-in-Publication Data

Budge, E. A. Wallis (Ernest Alfred Wallis), Sir, 1857–1934.
From fetish to God in ancient Egypt / E. A. Wallis Budge.
p. cm.
Reprint. Originally published: London : Oxford University Press, 1934.
Includes index.
ISBN 0-486-25803-3 (pbk.)
1. Egypt—Religion. 2. Mythology, Egyptian. I. Title.
BL2441.B82 1988
299′.31—dc19 88-20228
CIP

NOTE

THIRTY years ago I published *The Gods of the Egyptians*, an illustrated work in two volumes which dealt in a general and popular way with the mythology and religion of the dynastic EGYPTIANS. The book was well received and the whole edition was sold out in a few months; the printing of the long series of coloured plates rendered reprinting impossible, and the book can now only be obtained second-hand and at an enhanced price. Colleagues and friends assured me in 1930 that some book of this kind was more needed then than it was in 1900–4 when *The Gods of the Egyptians* was written, especially when the vast amount of new material which had become available for study since 1900 was taken into consideration. They wished me to return to the study and to produce a book which would, as far as possible, deal with the religion of the predynastic portion of Egyptian history, as well as the cults, theological systems, and religions of the dynastic period. The present book is the result of their friendly suggestion. It is divided into two Parts in which I have tried to deal with the main facts of the religious beliefs of the EGYPTIAN from the time when the Egyptian savage filled earth, air, sea, and sky with hostile evil spirits and lived in terror of the Evil Eye, and relied upon every branch of magic for help and deliverance from them, to the moment when the Egyptian nation hailed as their One God, or God One, AMEN–RĀ of THEBES, lord of the thrones of the world.

Part I contains the principal facts about the religious beliefs and thoughts of the EGYPTIANS, and their conception of God and the 'gods', their enneads and triads, the religions and systems of the great cities, &c. Magic, the cult of animals, the cult of OSIRIS, and the ṬUAT, or Other World, are treated at some length.

Part II is devoted to a series of revised English translations of a considerable number of fine hymns; myths, both ritual and aetiological; legends of the gods, and a few miscellaneous texts. The aetiological myths, i.e. those which were invented to account for some existing condition, are of special interest for myths constructed in the same way exist in Babylonian literature. I discussed many of them with SIDNEY SMITH, Keeper of Egyptian and Assyrian Antiquities in the BRITISH MUSEUM, and he has most obligingly drawn up a memorandum on the myths of both kinds, and I have printed this as a preface to the myths translated in Part II.

In the Introduction I have described briefly the results of the study of the ancient Egyptian religion in EUROPE, chiefly in the nineteenth century, and summarized the deductions which I believe may be rightly made from the facts supplied by the monuments and papyri, and the conclusions at which I have arrived. The most important sections of the Introduction are the paragraphs which deal with the results which SETHE has obtained from his exhaustive study of the remarkable hieroglyphic text of the reign of SHABAKA (about B.C. 700) in the BRITISH MUSEUM. For sixty or seventy years this text has been studied, from the time of BIRCH who translated portions of it in his official manuscript catalogue, but it has been reserved for SETHE to bring out the full import of the mutilated inscription. He has proved beyond all doubt that it describes the theological system of the priests of MEMPHIS as it existed under the Old Kingdom some five thousand years ago. The priests of PTAḤ had at that time arrived at the highest conception of God which was ever reached in EGYPT, and their religion was a pure monotheism. They evolved the idea of God as a Spirit, a self-created, self-subsisting, eternal, almighty mind-god, the creator of all things, the source of all life and creation, who created everything that is merely by *thinking*, HORUS being his heart or mind, and THOTH, the Word which gave expression to the thought which 'came into his mind'. Creation was the visible result of the utterances of his mouth. The other gods, e.g. those of HELIOPOLIS, were only the *thoughts* of PTAḤ, the One God. As we work out the details of the text and the scheme of thought underlying them, it becomes clear that the Memphite theology can be fittingly described by the opening verses of the Gospel of St. John:

1. In the beginning was the Word, and the Word was with God, and the Word was God.

2. The same was in the beginning with God.

3. All things were made by him; and without him was not any thing made that was made.

4. In him was life; and the life was the light of men.

When exactly and how the Memphite system of theology came into being is not clear, but there is every reason for agreeing with SETHE that it dates from the time of the founding of MEMPHIS. Purity of religion was not the only motive of the king (probably MENES) who established it as the religion of his kingdom, for it is clear that there was a political element in his mind. He wished to destroy the supremacy of the great and powerful priesthood of HELIOPOLIS, and to reduce their god RĀ to the position of a thought of the mind of PTAḤ. And we may be sure that the wealthy endowments of HELIOPOLIS were not forgotten by the royal reformer of the Egyptian religion. But the EGYPTIANS, when once the material powers of the Memphite cult had declined, rejected the Spirit-god of MEMPHIS, and his religion decayed, and before the end of the Old Kingdom disappeared, as JABLONSKI showed. Under the New Kingdom the cult of PTAḤ was of great importance, and in the hymns to him we find all the titles and powers of the old Spirit-god applied both to him and to AMEN-RĀ, as SETHE has proved convincingly.

A great deal of new light has been thrown on the attitude of the EGYPTIANS towards their gods by the recently discovered CHESTER BEATTY Papyrus No. I which DR. ALAN GARDINER has edited with conspicuous learning and success, and translated. The information to be derived from it seems to me to be of such importance that I have ventured to give a summary of it in Part II, and I am glad to express my obligation to DR. GARDINER, its first editor and translator. In connexion with the Egyptian religion and PLUTARCH's treatise on ISIS and OSIRIS, the attention of students may be called to *Osiris, a Study in Myths, Mysteries and Religion*, by HAROLD P. COOKE, LONDON, 1931. The author gives an accurate translation of PLUTARCH's work, and discusses many points in it which have not been adequately dealt with, if at all, by Egyptologists. His criticisms are to the point, and are to be welcomed, and a great many of his conclusions, especially those which deal with the stellar origin of the Egyptian religion, must be accepted.

The black and white illustrations which are given in Part I explain themselves for the most part, and all spare the reader much verbiage in descriptions. They are taken from tracings and drawings which were made by MR. ANDERSON, an artist who was attached to the departments of Antiquities in the BRITISH MUSEUM, and MR. F. C. COMPTON PRICE, a distinguished lithographer, who prepared the plates for the *Great Harris Papyrus, No. 1* (BRITISH MUSEUM No. 9900) edited by DR. BIRCH, and the second edition of the *Papyrus of Ani* edited by myself. The drawings and tracings were intended to be used in illustrating a dictionary of the Egyptian gods, but the scheme broke down, and as they were my personal property I used many of them in the official *Guides* of the BRITISH MUSEUM and other works. ANDERSON and COMPTON PRICE were masters of their craft, and it is fitting that their names should be remembered. When the War broke out neither of them could find work, and both were too old to join the Army. ANDERSON suffered serious privations and succumbed, but a year or two later, through my friend DR. SHIPLEY, late Master of Christ's, COMPTON PRICE was elected a brother in the Charterhouse. Worthy of remembrance also are MR. NETHERCLIFT who prepared the copies of the SALLIER and ANASTASI papyri for DR. BIRCH'S *Select Papyri* in 1840–1, and MR. BOWLER the lithographer of the early volumes of SIR HENRY RAWLINSON'S *Cuneiform Inscriptions of Western Asia*.

Whilst the manuscript of the present volume was being set in type, and the illustrations were unplaced, I was attacked by an illness which was sufficiently severe to send me into a nursing home. Work of any kind was strictly prohibited, and there was every probability that my enforced idleness would continue for a considerable time. On leaving the home I consulted JOHN JOHNSON, M.A., D.Litt., Printer to the University of OXFORD, and asked his help. He promptly made arrangements which relieved me of most of the reading of proofs, and index-making, and much else, and undertook that the publication of my works which he was then printing should not be delayed through my illness. To their supreme expert skill he and his staff of readers have added efficient sympathy, and it is to them entirely that the appearance of this work at the present time is due. I am glad to have the opportunity of expressing my obligation to them, both official and private, and I offer them my profound gratitude and sincere thanks.

E. A. WALLIS BUDGE

48 BLOOMSBURY STREET
BEDFORD SQUARE, W.C.1
July, 1934

CONTENTS

INTRODUCTION

INTRODUCTION

THE EARLY EGYPTOLOGISTS AND THE EGYPTIAN RELIGION

THE foundation of the popular opinion about the religious beliefs of the ancient EGYPTIANS was laid by the great pioneer of Egyptology E. DE ROUGÉ about the middle of the last century. He stated that the EGYPTIANS believed in One self-existent, supreme, eternal, almighty God, who created the world and everything in it, and endowed man with an immortal soul, which was capable of receiving punishments and rewards. DE ROUGÉ's words were to all intents and purposes a paraphrase of the passage in NEWTON'S *Principia*[1] in which the great scientist expressed his belief in the Unity of the God who is supreme, infinite, omnipotent, omniscient, and absolutely perfect. Who is present always and everywhere. The various works of creation are the product of his ideas, and his existence is proclaimed by them.

Many who read DE ROUGÉ's introduction to his edition of the hieratic text of the *Book of the Dead* concluded that the god of the EGYPTIANS and the God of the HEBREWS had much in common, and that the Egyptian Religion was closely akin to Christianity. And for a considerable time it was generally thought that the *Book of the Dead* was a theological work or treatise on the Egyptian Religion which would prove in detail the supposed identity of the old religion of the Valley of the NILE and that of the HEBREWS. When it was found that the title 'Book of the Dead' was merely a translation of the name given by the ARABS to an inscribed roll of papyrus found in a tomb, and that the text on such a roll was nothing but a series of spells which were intended for the use of the deceased, and not a

[1] Hic omnia regit non ut anima mundi, sed ut universorum dominus. . . . Deus summus est ens aeternum, infinitum, absolute perfectum; sed ens utcunque perfectum sine dominio non est dominus deus. . . . Et ex dominatione vera sequitur deum verum esse vivum, intelligentem et potentem; ex reliquis perfectionibus summum esse, vel summe perfectum. Aeternus est et infinitus, omnipotens et omnisciens, id est durat ab aeterno in aeternum, et adest ab infinito in infinitum; omnia regit, et omnia cognoscit, quae fiunt aut fieri possunt. Non est aeternitas et infinitas, sed aeternus et infinitus; . . . Deus est unus et idem deus semper et ubique. Newton's *Principia*, Lib. III (at the end). The priests of Memphis described their eternal Spirit-god Ptaḥ in much the same terms.

religious composition, some were disappointed, but others clung firmly to their own original opinions. I have heard papers read at the meetings of Societies, e.g. the Syro-Egyptian Society, in which it was asserted by their authors that the religion of the ancient EGYPTIANS was a prototype of Christianity which Almighty God had allowed to come into being in order to prepare the EGYPTIANS for the advent of CHRIST and His Gospel.

THE PUBLICATION OF THE 'BOOK OF THE DEAD'

How far DE ROUGÉ himself held these extreme views is not clear, but it is quite certain now that they were based on a want of information about the true character and contents of the religious texts. The great papyrus rolls containing the Theban Recension of the *Book of the Dead*, and the 'Coffin Texts' from the wooden sarcophagi of the XIth and XIIth dynasties, and the 'Pyramid Texts' of the Vth and VIth dynasties had not been discovered.[1] Men like LEPSIUS, BIRCH, GOODWIN, and CHABAS were still groping their way laboriously through the hieroglyphic texts in their efforts to understand their contents and translate them, and anthropologists had not yet proved that animism, fetishism, and magic were the predominant characteristics of the Egyptian Religion from first to last. That the beliefs of the EGYPTIANS passed through various stages like those of every other primitive people was first proved by EDWARD BURNETT TYLOR (1832–1917) in his *Primitive Culture*, 1871.[2]

THE ONE ONE

DE ROUGÉ was quite correct in saying that the EGYPTIANS believed in One self-existent god, who had given to man a soul which existed after death and suffered punishment or enjoyed rewards of various kinds. On these and several other points the teaching of the Egyptian theologian and the Christian agree in a general way. There is no doubt that monotheism was a tenet of the Egyptian Faith, but it was entirely different from the monotheism of Christian peoples. When the EGYPTIAN called his god 'One', or the 'One One', or the

[1] The photograph of the Papyrus of Nebseni in the British Museum was not published until 1876, and the *Coffin of Åmamu* until several years later. On the funerary papyri which were written between the VIth and XIth dynasties and have recently been discovered at Ṣaḳḳârah see *British Museum Quarterly*, vol. viii, No. 2, p. 76.

[2] See chapters xi–xvii.

'Only One', he meant exactly what he said and what the MUSLIM means to-day when he says, 'There is no god but God'. And that god was the sun in the sky from whom he received light and heat and the food whereon he lived. The EGYPTIAN in his hymns called many gods 'One', but these gods were all forms of the Sun-god, and, as I understand it, he was a monotheist pure and simple as a sun-

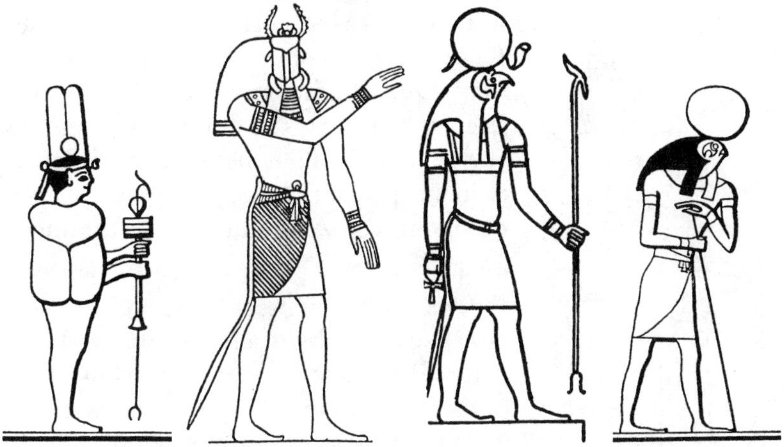

Khepri, the morning sun. Rā, the noon-day sun. Temu (Atem), the setting sun.

Rā, the god One or Only god, in his three chief aspects.

worshipper. It avails nothing to call his monotheism 'henotheism'. A time came when OSIRIS was associated with KHEPRI, the sun at dawn, and with RĀ at noon-day, and with TEMU the setting sun, and the Pyramid Texts make it clear that under the VIth dynasty OSIRIS usurped all the attributes and powers of the 'Sun, the One lord of heaven'. There was, of course, a time when men thought that the Sun-god had no counterpart, no offspring, and no associate or equal. But there must have been some reason why theologians permitted OSIRIS to usurp the position of the god of day; what was that reason?

OSIRIS, THE SON OF PTAḤ OF MEMPHIS AND RĀ OF HELIOPOLIS

In very early times in EGYPT men made the face of heaven a god, and the texts call him the 'great HORUS' or the 'old HORUS'. He had two eyes, the sun and the moon, the former ruled his face by day and the latter his face by night, but each was akin to the other and each formed one of the members of HORUS the Aged, and both existed before the 'gods'. Unfortunately we do not know the words which the earliest EGYPTIANS used for sun and moon, but the sun as a god was called ḤER (or ḤUR, or ḤOR) at a very early period, and OSIRIS was regarded as the god of the moon and the deputy at least of the sun, as we see from the *Book of the Dead*. In chap. ii the scribe ANI addresses OSIRIS in these words: 'Hail, One, rising (or shining) from the Moon! Hail, One, shining from the Moon.' And in chap. viii he says: 'I am the Moon among the gods, I shall not perish', and in chap. xviii he prays that he may 'see the face of the sun (*athen*) and behold the moon *aḥ*  forever'. A passage in chap. xvii throws much light on the relationship which existed between the Sun-god (RĀ) and the Moon-god (OSIRIS) at the beginning of the XVIIIth dynasty. This chapter contains explanations of a number of difficult passages in the text of some documents, and among them is the following:

Ḥer-ur, Horus the Aged.

'I am his (HORUS'S ?) Soul within his two children (twins ?).' The commentator says: 'What is the explanation of this?', and the answer is, 'This [hath reference] to OSIRIS. He entered into ṬEṬU (BUSIRIS) and found there the Soul of RĀ; the one god embraced the other, and divine souls came into being within his children.' Here the Papyrus of ANI stops, but the Papyrus of NEBSENI, which is a much older roll, continues: 'Now his (i.e. HORUS'S) children are ḤER-NEDJ-ḤER-TEF-F[1] and ḤER-EM-KHENT-EN-ARITI.[2] But, according to a variant reading, his two souls which are within his children are the Soul of RĀ and the Soul of OSIRIS, or [his two souls] may be the Soul which dwelleth in SHU and the Soul which dwelleth in TEFNUT, his twin divine Souls which dwell in ṬEṬ-T (BUSIRIS).' In the vignette in the Papyrus of ANI we see RĀ in the form of a hawk with the solar disk on his head, and OSIRIS in the form of a hawk with a human

[1] i.e. Horus the avenger of his father.
[2] i.e. Horus without eyes, or the 'Blind Horus'.

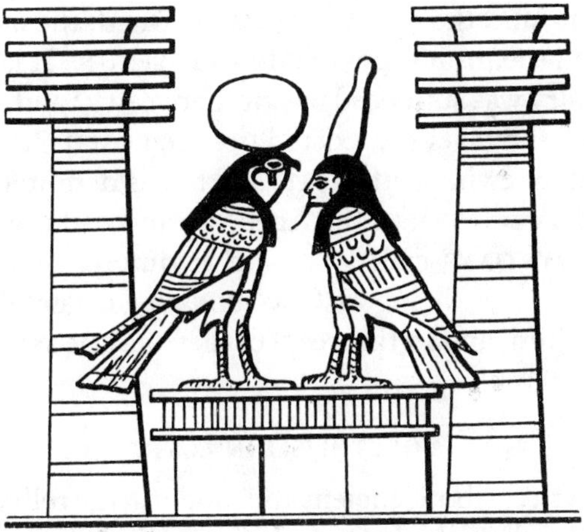

The Souls of Rā and Osiris, the sons of Ḥer-ur, meeting in Busiris.

From the Papyrus of Ani (vignette, chap. xvii).

Shu bearing up the solar disk.

Shu, god of light and the atmosphere.

Tefnut, goddess of damp, mists, dew, rain, &c.

face, with the White Crown on his head, standing on a building between two ṬEṬS. The meaning of this passage seems to be that HORUS the Aged, a bisexual god, produced two children. Some theologians regarded these children as two forms of their father, but others identified them with the Souls of RĀ and OSIRIS, or with the Souls of SHU and TEFNUT. Thus it is clear that OSIRIS and RĀ were twin brothers, and the sons of ḤORUS the Aged, the oldest Sky-god in EGYPT, and the prototypes of SHU and TEFNUT. It is possible that a kind of rivalry was supposed to exist between RĀ and OSIRIS, similar to that which the texts say existed between OSIRIS, the son of GEBB and NUT and his twin brother SET, and this is definitely hinted at in the Pyramid Texts. HORUS the Aged, RĀ, and OSIRIS were names by which the EGYPTIANS called the sun at different periods of their history; the sun was their god 'One', and they never faltered in their allegiance to him, and in this respect they may be said to have been monotheists.

POLYTHEISM IN EGYPT

By many writers, both ancient and modern, the religion of ancient EGYPT has been described as polytheism. Why this has been so it is easy to understand if we remember the large number of Egyptian 'gods' and that those who have attempted to describe them have had no real knowledge of the religious literature of EGYPT. The Hebrew Prophets said many hard things about EGYPT and her idols, and they regarded the latter as abominations and defilements (Joshua xxiv. 14; Ezekiel xx. 7, 8; Ezra ix. 1), but there is no reason for believing that they knew anything about the gods of the EGYPTIANS except by hearsay.[1] It is worthy of note that MOSES, 'who was learned[2] in all the wisdom of the EGYPTIANS', is also said to have 'been mighty in words and in deeds'.[3] The depth of his knowledge

[1] From Ezek. xx. 8 it is clear that many of the Hebrews took Egyptian gods with them when they left Egypt, and Isa. xxiii. 2–4 shows that Jerusalem, personified as Aholibah, was a notorious centre of their cults.

[2] ἐπαιδεύθη, he was trained or educated, Acts vii. 22.

[3] The words of this last portion of the verse in the Acts have a very definite meaning, and they represent a summary of the native Egyptian description of Isis, the great magician goddess. On a stele in Paris (see Ledrain, *Monuments Égyptiens*, Plate XXII f.) she is said to be the mistress of powerful spells, which her cunning tongue and magical power of utterance enabled her mouth to pronounce with correct magical intonation and with such force and effect that her words never failed to bless or to ban. So Moses was mighty in spells and produced great effects by the utterance of them. All that the Bible tells us about Moses indicates that he had studied the various branches of Egyptian magic, and that he was a skilled performer of magical rituals and was deeply learned in the knowledge of the accompanying spells, incantations, and magical formulas of every description. He was saved from death by an Egyptian princess, and was educated either at Court, or under Court influence, and the miracles which he wrought in Egypt, and in the desert, suggest that he was not only a priest, but a magician of the highest order, and perhaps even a Kheri ḥeb of Memphis. At the end of the first forty years of his life, which he

of Egyptian magico-religious ritual is proved by the closeness with which he followed it in constructing the Tabernacle, and in the regulations which he drew up concerning offerings, the equipment of the Tabernacle, and the official dress of the priests. Following the lead given by SIR GARDINER WILKINSON,[1] Mr. H. P. COOKE has pointed out (*Osiris*, p. 103) in detail how great was the debt owed by ISRAEL to EGYPT in connexion with their own worship of God. MOSES even went so far as to declare that YAHWEH, like the God of the EGYPTIANS, was 'One' (Deut. vi. 4).

PLURALITY OF GODS AND ANIMAL CULTS

Every one who has written about the Egyptian Religion has been faced with the difficulty of reconciling the Egyptian monotheistic belief with the cults of several hundred 'gods' and the worship of a score or more of sacred animals. The EGYPTIANS had a foolish habit of adding the hieroglyphic for 'god', 𓊹 or 𓀭, to the name of any creature which seemed to them to possess any unusual faculty or characteristic. The result was that many of the 'gods' were merely local spirits like the pixies and fairies and gnomes of Western nations, or the Jinn, and the Jann, and the Ufarît of the ARABS. We now know that the 'multitude of Egyptian gods' was not as large as has been supposed. Many of the Egyptian gods, and among them the oldest of all, were bi-sexual; thus the oldest of the four gods of CHAOS, NUN, had a female counterpart NUNET, and the female counterpart of RĀ was RĀIT. The so-called Nine gods of HELIOPOLIS really become five, thus: TEM and his female counterpart, SHU–TEFNUT, GEBB–NUT, OSIRIS–ISIS, and SET–NEPHTHYS. If we could only regard the 'great' gods of EGYPT as 'he-shes' (as Mr. COOKE calls them) we should reduce their number by one half. But unfortunately the EGYPTIANS themselves insisted on treating the female principle of every god as

had spent in Egypt among priests, noblemen, government officials, and others, the Egyptians must have regarded him as an Egyptian. Mr. Cooke's remarks (*Osiris*, p. 97 f.) are very much to the point.

[1] *Ancient Egyptians*, ed. Birch, vol. iii, pp. 407 ff. And yet we find Driver writing that the statement in Acts vii. 22 that Moses 'was instructed in all the wisdom of the Egyptians' has no support in the Old Testament itself! How could Moses have performed all the magical deeds related in the Pentateuch unless he had been instructed in every branch of learning, both sacred and profane, and had been educated as a priest and magician?

a separate being and on giving it a special name. The number of the gods might also be reduced in another way, namely by calling each of thirty local forms of HATHOR, each with her special name, simply HATHOR, and the various local forms of ISIS, which could be counted by the dozen, might be treated in the same way. And in his hymn to RĀ, or to some form of him, the worshipper himself addresses him as a being possessing many 'names[1] and aspects' or forms. In the Hymn to AMEN by ḤER and SUTI,[2] AMEN is called 'Glorious Mother of gods and men', the female aspect of the god in this case being emphasized. There is no doubt that the priests distinguished carefully between the 'Great' and 'Little' gods, but it is very doubtful if the middle and lower classes of the people did.

THE NATURE OF THE EGYPTIAN GOD ONE

Whether the Egyptian theologians ever attempted to describe the nature of their One god or to discuss his attributes, as the ARABS did, is doubtful; as no literature dealing with this subject has been found they probably did not. The pictures of the sun, moon, and stars sufficiently indicate the nature of these forms of him, and the blue or green figures of ḤĀPI (the NILE) prove that they identified him as a water-god, but the figures of most of the gods and goddesses only represent anthropomorphized fetishes, and the common sense of the EGYPTIANS must have told them that they were merely imaginary objects. TEMU or RĀ, the great god of HELIOPOLIS, was a material being,[3] and the source whence he came was NUNU, the great primeval abyss of water. Water existed before RĀ and was regarded as the oldest thing in the world, and therefore the 'father of the gods'. The cult of RĀ, i.e. the worship of the Sun-god, was well established at HELIOPOLIS long before the union of the North and the South by MENES. And, as we shall see, it continued to be the most popular of the solar cults in EGYPT until the end of the dynastic period. The Pyramid Texts show that he had recourse to masturbation in order to produce the twins SHU and TEFNUT and the

[1] Compare: 'I am Rā, the creator of the names of his limbs, which came into being in the form of the gods who are in the Hair of Rā,' *Book of the Dead*, chap. xvii.

[2] See the stele in the British Museum, No. 475, line 10.

[3] 'I am Tem in his rising: I am the Only One: I became in Nenu. I am Rā who rose in the beginning. I am the Great God who created himself.' *Book of the Dead*, chap. xvii.

peoples of the SÛDÂN. His cult was gross and material, and the benefits which the EGYPTIANS hoped to receive from him were material, virility, fecundity, robust health, and abundant offspring both human and animal. The cult of the solar disk ATEN was even more material still, although many of its bloodthirsty rites were curtailed or suppressed by AMEN-ḤETEP IV. As men expected RĀ to give them great

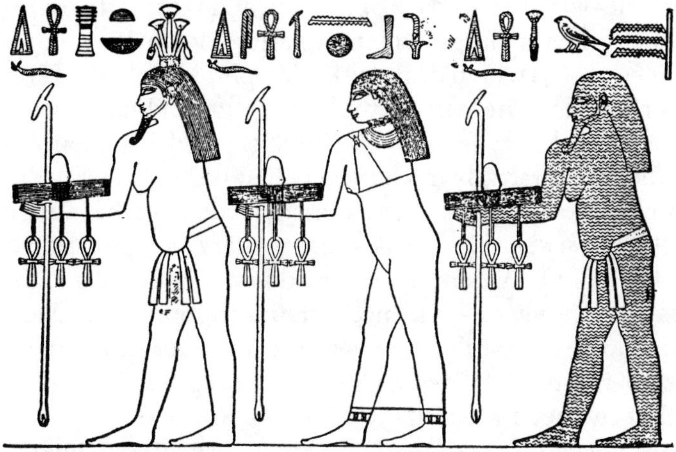

Ḥāpi, the Nile-god, 'giveth life and all stability'. N.B.—He has a woman's bosom.

Nekhebit, a goddess, 'giveth life and power'. She was associated with the Nile of the South.

Uadj-ur, i.e. the 'Great Green' World Ocean, 'giveth life'.

material prosperity on earth, so after death, in heaven, they relied upon him to provide them with divine meat and drink and apparel, and unstinted gratification of their carnal appetites. In no prayer to RĀ can be found a petition by the suppliant for spiritual gifts, or any expression indicating his need of divine help for his soul. During the great festivals when a statue of the god was carried by the priests round the town or through the country the people in crowds appeared before him, for by this act they discharged a religious obligation and, so to say, acquired merit, and they expected the god to give them in return health, strength, virility, and prosperity.

THE THEOLOGIANS OF MEMPHIS

But though the HELIOPOLITANS and those who accepted their dogmas and worshipped RĀ throughout the country were content to worship a material god who had sprung from the water of NUNU, there was under the earlier dynasties a time when the priesthood of MEMPHIS held entirely different views. Thanks to the copy of an inscription made from an ancient archetype in the reign of SHABAKA,[1] much is now known of the doctrines of the priesthood of PTAḤ, a very ancient god of MEMPHIS. An account of the inscription and its contents will be found on pp. 15, 16, and we may therefore call attention to the very important information contained in the section of it (lines 53–64) which deals with Memphite theology. It may be thought that the late date of this inscription militates against its value as an authority for the religion of the Old Kingdom. But it is not the comparatively modern copy that is the authority, but the worm-eaten archetype which was written soon after the founding of MEMPHIS by MENES. Dr. SETHE's commentary and quotations from texts of the Old Kingdom render any doubt as to the age of the *text* untenable. The general evidence of the inscription shows that it was intended to be a great political as well as religious instrument, and Dr. SETHE rightly speaks of its 'political background'. The writer or author intended MEMPHIS to supersede ON (HELIOPOLIS) as the centre of the countries of the Delta and UPPER EGYPT which MENES had united into one kingdom. It is impossible to believe that his aim was simply and solely religious, and that all he wished to do was to depose the Sun-god and disendow his priesthood though the revenues of RĀ must have been very considerable.

THE FETISH PTAḤ

The god chosen by MENES to be the protagonist of TEMU or RĀ of ON was an ancient fetish called PTAḤ, whose cult seems to have been general in the neighbourhood of MEMPHIS. The idol representing this god was in the form of a mummy, with his legs close together, and he appears frequently in this form in the temples and tombs of the New Kingdom. It is possible that PTAḤ was a deified man, who when on earth had been a skilful worker in metals and stones and an engineer.

Be this as it may, the priests of MEMPHIS, interpreting no doubt the instructions of their king, determined to make PTAḤ the source

[1] A Nubian king, the founder of the XXVth dynasty about 712 B.C.

and head of all the gods of EGYPT. They were well acquainted with the Creation Myths current in ON, and how TEMU or RĀ sprang from NUNU, and how the plot of earth on which he first stood, and the well of water in which he first dipped his face was at ON. They first made PTAḤ the predecessor of NUNU, and called him PTAḤ–NUNU, and then the predecessor of TANEN or TUNEN, the oldest Earth-god, and claimed that the plot of earth on which PTAḤ–TANEN first stood was at MEMPHIS. But the nature of PTAḤ was entirely different from that of TEMU or RĀ, for it was spiritual and not material. JABLONSKI pointed out in his *Pantheon Aegyptiorum* in 1750 that many ancient writers regarded PTAḤ as a spiritual being, and LEPSIUS arrived at the same conclusion about a century later.[1] BRUGSCH was convinced that the Egyptian theologians evolved the idea that their Great God was a spirit, and he called him 'der göttliche Urgeist'; and in our own day we find SETHE endorsing the opinion of LEPSIUS.

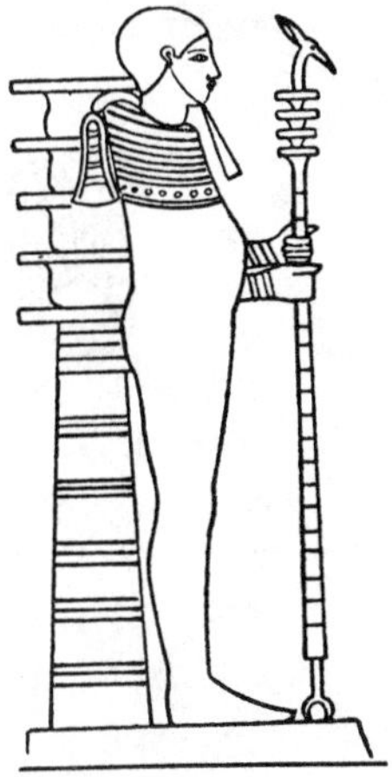

Ptaḥ of Memphis in predynastic form standing by the fetish tree trunk of Ṭeṭu which was associated with the idea of new life, resurrection, and creative energy. He wears the archaic Puntite beard, and a *menat* amulet hangs from his neck behind. He stands on an object which represents the measuring reed (*kanôn*?) of a workman and the symbol of stability is attached to the upper part of his sceptre.

From the text which was rescued from oblivion by SHABAKA we learn that PTAḤ, the Great and Mighty, had eight principal forms among which were PTAḤ–NUN, and PTAḤ–TANEN. He therefore preceded NUN and TANEN in existence and he was their creator, and he created them by an effort of his heart or mind. Thus PTAḤ was the oldest being the priests could imagine, and he was the Eternal Heart or Mind and was self-created. The male part of PTAḤ begot TEM or

[1] 'Ptah wurde nicht mit Ra identifiziert, sondern als eine geistigere Potenz angesehen und als solche in der Memphitischen Lehre wenigstens noch über Rā gesetzt' (*Abhandlungen Berlin. Akad.*, 1851, p. 196). I understand that Dr. Sethe examined the paper squeeze of the inscription of Shabaka in the British Museum, and it seems probable that he derived his view of the spiritual nature of Ptaḥ from it. He was the first Egyptologist to express this view.

TEMU or RĀ, and his female portion was the mother of the Sun-god of HELIOPOLIS. And, like RĀ, PTAḤ was the father and mother of men, and he conceived and fashioned and made the gods. TEM was a form or figure *tat* 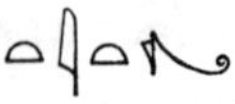 of PTAḤ and was produced by a thought, literally 'what came into the heart (or, mind)'  of

Ptaḥ–Nunu, the god of the great primeval abyss of water, the 'Father of the gods'. On his head are the solar disk, which emerged from him, and the plumes of the older gods.

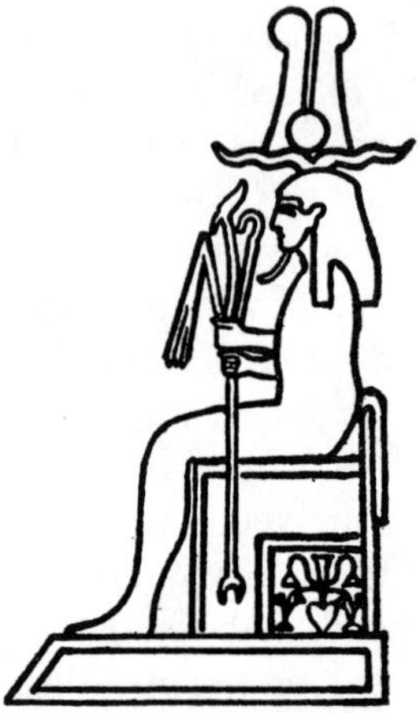

Ptaḥ–Tanen, the oldest Earth-god in Egypt. He wears the crown of Seker, the god of the Ṭuat of Memphis, and holds the triple sceptre. The symbol of the Union of the North and South is seen on his throne which rests on an instrument for measuring.

PTAḤ. TEM produced the gods SHU and TEFNUT by masturbation and self-impregnation, whereas PTAḤ produced the gods by the motions or thoughts of his mind. HORUS, the oldest Sun-god in EGYPT, acted as the heart or mind of PTAḤ, and THOTH, the god of wisdom, as his tongue. What the heart of PTAḤ thought passed on to THOTH who translated it into words, which were uttered by the one great almighty mouth, from which everything which is hath come, and everything which is to be shall come. Though THOTH was the Word-god, his actual creative power was derived from the magical pronouncement by PTAḤ, who alone knew how to utter the words with the correct intonation.

The text continues (l. 54):

'It happened that the heart and the tongue acquired power over all [the other] members, teaching that he (PTAḤ) lived as the governor in every body, and as the tongue in every mouth of all the gods, all cattle, all reptiles, and everything else—at the same time PTAḤ [as heart] thinks, and [as tongue] commands as he wishes.'

The relationship of PTAḤ to TEM is next described:

'PTAḤ's company of the gods are before him as teeth and lips [the teeth] being the seed and [the lips] the hands of TEM. The company of the gods of TEM came into being through his seed and his fingers.[1] But the company of the gods [of PTAḤ] are the teeth and the lips in this Mouth, which assigneth names to all things, and from which SHU and TEFNUT have gone forth.

'The company of the gods [of PTAḤ] create the sight of the eyes, the hearing of the ears, the breathing of the nostrils and make announcement to the heart. [The heart] it is which maketh every information to come forth, and the tongue it is which repeats what the heart has thought out.

'Thus all the gods were created, and TEM and his company of the gods, but every word of the god exists through that which the heart has thought out and the tongue commanded.

'Thus were the KAU-spirits  and the ḤEMSUT-spirits   ordained, and every kind of food and every kind of offering through this word which is thought upon by the heart and permitted to come forth on the tongue.

'[Goodness] is made for him that doeth it; [evil] is made for him that doeth what is hated. Life is given unto him who hath content and death to the transgressor.

'Thus every kind of work and every handicraft, and everything done with the arms, and every motion of the legs, and every action of all the limbs take place through this command, which is planned by the heart (or mind), and is brought to pass by the tongue, and giveth value to everything.

'He created the gods, he made the towns, he founded the Nomes, he set the gods in their shrines, he established the endowments for their offerings, he founded their sanctuaries, he made their bodies to have the forms wherewith their hearts would be content, and the gods went into their bodies of wood of every kind, of stone of every kind, of clay of every kind, and every other kind of substance, which grow upon the back of PTAḤ, in the forms which they had taken.'

All EGYPT existed by and through PTAḤ, and as the 'Overlord of the Two Lands', the theologians called him 'ḤETEPI' 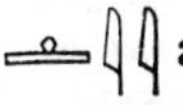 and

[1] Alluding to Rā's act of masturbation.

'KHNEMI' . It is impossible to say what these titles conveyed to the EGYPTIANS, and they must remain, for the present, untranslated. SETHE renders ḤETEPI by 'der Friedliche', offering 'Gnädige' as an alternative translation; 'KHNEMI' he connects with the idea of rejoicing. It is probable that the two words are 'beautiful names' of PTAḤ, just as 'RAḤMÂN' (Merciful) and 'RAḤÎM' (Gracious) are two of the 'beautiful names' of ALLÂH in use among the ARABS.

The inscription of SHABAKA is the most important of all the Egyptian religious texts hitherto discovered, and it removes once and for all from the religion of ancient EGYPT the stigma of gross materialism. The doctrines of the priests of MEMPHIS under the Old Kingdom were of an almost unbelievable spiritual and philosophical character. And they had a broadness and boldness never attained by the religious theories and conjectures of any other of the great priesthoods of EGYPT. To them PTAḤ was a spirit self-created, self-existent, without beginning and eternal. He was the Mind of the universe, the Cause of Causes, whose thoughts had produced every material thing and being in heaven, earth, and the underworld. The gods were merely forms of his thoughts, and he was therefore God alone. Light was an emanation from his heart, his influence pervaded all Nature, through his breath of life every creature lived, and almighty power resided in the Word of his Mouth.[1] That such lofty spiritual conceptions were evolved by the priests of MEMPHIS about 4,000 years before the Christian Era is a matter for wonder.[2]

[1] Jablonski was the first to note that we have the same idea expressed in Hebrews xi. 3. 'The worlds were framed by the word of God, so that things which are seen were not made of things which do appear.'

[2] No. 7 Question in the *Westminster Catechism* is, 'What is God?' The Answer is, 'God is a spirit, infinite, eternal and unchangeable, in his being, wisdom, power, holiness, justice, goodness and truth.' No. 8 Question is, 'Are there more Gods than one?' and the Answer is, 'There is but one only, the living and true God.' If a priest of Memphis had been asked these two Questions 5,500 years ago, his Answers, according to the Shabaka's inscription, would have resembled very closely those in the *Westminster Catechism*. In the large edition of the *Westminster Catechism* the attributes of God are enumerated together with Bible references as authorities. Thus we have: His infinity Exod. iii. 14; Job xi. 7–9; glory Acts vii. 2; blessedness 1 Tim. vi. 15; perfection Matt. v. 48; all-sufficiency Gen. xvii. 1; eternity Ps. xc. 2; unchangeableness Mal. iii. 6; incomprehensibility 1 Kings viii. 27; ubiquity Ps. cxxxix. 1–13; almightiness Rev. iv. 8; Omniscience Heb. iv. 13; wisdom Rom. xvi. 27; holiness Isa. v. 24; justice Deut. xxxiv. 4; mercy and graciousness Exod. xxxiv. 6; unity Deut. vi. 4; 1 Cor. viii. 4. The great Hymn to Ptaḥ at Berlin shows that the same attributes were ascribed to him.

PTAḤ REJECTED IN FAVOUR OF RĀ

It must be said at once that it is extremely improbable that such a highly philosophical system as the theology of MEMPHIS ever became generally popular in EGYPT. It in no way appealed to the working classes and peasants, and few outside the priesthood could ever have understood it. As long as the power of the MEMPHITES was supreme PTAḤ would be regarded as the overlord of RĀ. The cults of the old fetish and cosmic gods continued to flourish, and we need not be surprised that the theology of MEMPHIS was abandoned in proportion as the material powers of the kings of MEMPHIS diminished. Men preferred the worship of anthropomorphized fetishes whose attributes could be easily understood, and whose natures and habits were believed to be very like their own. The position of PTAḤ in EGYPT at that time is well described by JABLONSKI in his *Pantheon*, i, p. 52.[1]

AMEN OR AMEN-RĀ OF THEBES

The only other god who was declared by his priesthood to be of the same nature as PTAḤ and to possess his powers was AMEN of THEBES, whose worship attained its greatest popularity under the New Kingdom. One of the most important series of addresses to him known is contained in a papyrus at LEYDEN, and we owe the hieroglyphic transcripts and translations of the texts to Dr. ALAN GARDINER.[2] From these the following extracts are taken.

I. AMEN's origin. He was self-created and as he fashioned himself none knoweth his forms. He existed first as the EIGHT GODS of KHEMENU (HERMOPOLIS),[3] then he completed them and became ONE . He became in primeval time, no other being existed, there was no god before him, there was no other god with him to declare his form, all the gods came into being after him. He had no mother by whom his name was made, he had no father who begot him, saying, 'It is even myself'. He shaped his own egg, he mingled his seed with his body to make his egg to come into being

[1] He says: 'labentibus tamen annis, honos eius et cultus, ut videtur, frigescere et etiam vilescere coepit. Niligenae, in necessitates urgentes, et praesentia commoda, unice intenti, Deorum illorum, a quibus bona hujus vitae exoptata proxime et immediate expectabant, Solis, Lunae, Nili et similium, cultui totos se consecrarunt, venerationem vero religiosam Mentis aeternae, in loco, coelis omnibus superiori, collocatae, Philosophis relinquendam esse putarunt.'

[2] See *Aegyptische Zeitschrift*, Bd. 42 (1905), p. 12 f.

[3] The head of this Ogdoad was Thoth.

within himself. He took the form of TANEN in order to give birth to the PAUTTI (Companies of the ?) gods.

II. The hiddenness of AMEN. His body is hidden in the Chiefs. He is hidden as AMEN at the head of the gods. AMEN is ONE, he hides himself from the gods and conceals himself from them.

III. His Oneness. His Unity is absolute.

IV. He was a Trinity, i.e. he had three persons, or characters.

Amen-Rā 'king of the gods'.

V. His name. His name is more helpful to a man than hundreds of thousands of helpers. The gods cannot pray to him because his name is unknown to them. The man who utters the secret name of AMEN falls down and dies a violent death. His name is victory.

VI. AMEN as lord of time. He makes the years, rules the months, ordains nights and days. The night is as the day to him. He the One Watcher neither slumbers nor sleeps.

VII. The beneficence of AMEN. He breaks evil spells, expels sicknesses from the bodies of men. He, the Physician, heals the Eye, he destroys the Evil Eye (?), he releases men from hell, he abrogates the Destinies (or Fates) of men at his good pleasure, he hears all petitions and is present immediately he is invoked, he prolongs or shortens the lives of men at will, to the man he loves he adds to what Fate has decreed for him, and to the man who sets him in his heart he is more than millions. He was a Bull for his town, a Lion for his people, a Hawk that destroyed his attackers, and at the sound of his roaring the earth quaked.

From what has been said above it is quite clear that there was a monotheistic element in the Egyptian Religion. The Spirit-god PTAḤ was One, the material god RĀ was One, and AMEN who was claimed by his priests to be both Spirit and Matter was One.

PTAḤ AS GOD OF THE DEAD

The founders of the great city of White Wall or MEMPHIS adopted the ancient fetish of the neighbourhood, and also the guardian spirit or 'god' of the cemetery of MEMPHIS, which from the earliest times must have been of considerable extent. This spirit or 'god' seems to have been called SEKER 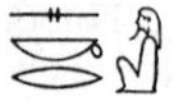 a name which he probably bore in predynastic times. He seems to have been to ṢAḲḲÂRAH what ANPU was to ABYDOS. He was incarnate in a species of hawk.

The derivations of the name which have been proposed are unsatisfactory. In the Pyramid Texts (§ 1712)[1] the determinative of his name is a hawk resting upon an oval, and he is mentioned with MENU. Under the New Kingdom he appears as a hawk-headed mummy, like PTAḤ. SEKER was a very ancient god who was associated with the darkness and decay of the tomb, and

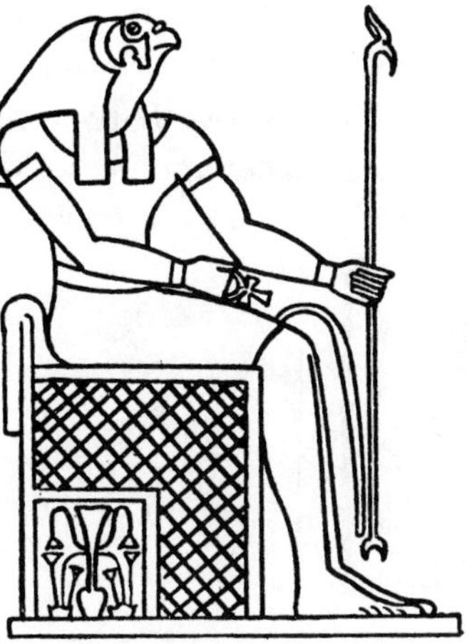

Seker as king of all Egypt.

Seker, the Death-god of Memphis, having assumed the ancient mummy form of Osiris, and the White Crown and plumes of Osiris.

he reposed in the night. The scribe ANI prayed to be delivered from 'the great god who snatcheth away the soul, who devoureth hearts, who feedeth upon offal, the gatekeeper in the darkness and the dweller in the Sekri Boat'. The text continues, 'Who then is this?' And the answer is, 'This is SUTI, or SMAM-UR, the soul of GEBB' (chap. xvii, l. 113). From this it is clear that SEKER was an ancient Earth-god whose abode was as black as night. The Sekri Boat mentioned was a boat which had a high bow terminating in the head of a horned animal; it had three oars. In the centre of it stood a funerary chest with its cover surmounted by a head of a hawk. The chest or coffer stood

[1] He is described as .

upon a base, with ends curved upwards, and the whole construction rested upon a sledge with runners. One of the most elaborate representations of it forms the vignette of chapter lxiv of the Theban Recension of the *Book of the Dead.* The oldest known picture of the Boat of SEKER is found in the Pyr. Texts (§ 138 *c*), where it is called 'ḤENU' ; a later form is , which is applied both to the boat and its god.

THE ḤENU BOAT OF SEKER

Traditions current in the *Book of the Dead* show that the ḤENU Boat played a very prominent part in magical ceremonies at MEMPHIS.

Ebony plaque of Ṭen Semti Ḥesepti a king of the Ist dynasty. In the upper register the king, wearing the double crown , is seen performing a ceremonial dance of worship, in the presence of a god (Osiris ?). In the middle register he is drawing along the Ḥenu Boat as an act of worship. (British Museum No. 32650).

The rubric of chapter lxiv says that the chapter was 'found' in the masonry under the shrine of ḤENU during the reign of SEMTI (ḤESEP–TI), a king of the Ist dynasty, and a figure of it is cut on the wooden tablet which was made for ḤEMAKA, the royal chancellor of this king. The shrine in the ḤENU Boat probably contained a fetish (hawk ?) which was symbolic of the Night-sun. The cult of SEKER was very ancient, and even in early dynastic times he had many sanctuaries in LOWER EGYPT (see LANZONE, *Mitologia*, p. 1117). On the great festival days of SEKER his boat was placed on the sledge whilst magical ceremonies were performed by the high-priest of

MEMPHIS, the UR-KHERP-ḤEM, and it was drawn round about the sanctuary in solemn procession. The revolution of the sun and other celestial bodies seems to have been symbolized by this act, but no information on the subject is supplied by the texts.

The Ḥenu Boat.

SEKER was one of the oldest gods of the dead in EGYPT, and probably the most important on the west bank of the NILE. The priests prefixed the name of PTAḤ to his name to indicate that he, like all the other gods, was a creation of a thought of PTAḤ, and that PTAḤ was the god of the dead as well as the living. Now the text of SHABAKA states that OSIRIS was drowned at MEMPHIS, and that his body was brought into the City and buried there. The fame of OSIRIS as the god of the land of the dead (ṬUAT) and the judge of the dead was well established long before MEMPHIS was built, and the HELIOPOLITANS admitted the claims of his priests, and included OSIRIS and his brother and two sisters among their Great Company of the Gods. But according to the theology of MEMPHIS these four deities were only forms of the thoughts of PTAḤ, and thus PTAḤ became the One God of the dead, or perhaps the Death-god of all EGYPT.[1] The Pyramid Texts prove that under the VIth dynasty OSIRIS usurped the position of RĀ as the One God of heaven, and it is clear that through the progress of his cult towards the south, the fame of PTAḤ-SEKER suffered eclipse. At a later date, probably soon

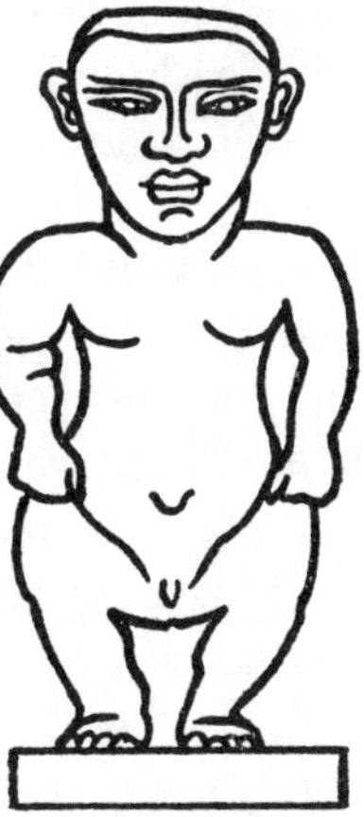

Ptaḥ–Seker–Asar.

[1] According to the Papyrus of Ani (chap. xv, sheet 19) a form of Ptaḥ, viz. Ptaḥ–Seker–Tem was worshipped in Heliopolis.

after the city of ABYDOS became the centre of the cult of OSIRIS, the name of OSIRIS was added to PTAḤ–SEKER, and PTAḤ–SEKER–ASAR appears in the texts. He is represented as a squat male figure, like a pigmy, with a very large head on which rests a beetle, and thick limbs. Originally he probably represented the human embryo. His cult was very general under the New Kingdom, as the numerous painted wooden figures of him which exist by the score in our great museums testify. The figure stands on a pedestal on one side of which is a rectangular cavity which contains a small roll of inscribed papyrus. Before the figure is a model of a funerary coffer which covers a portion of the body of the deceased mummified; figures of the hawk of SEKER often decorate the coffer.

EGYPTIAN POLYTHEISM

The highly philosophical and religious beliefs which are outlined in the inscription of SHABAKA were not generally accepted by the EGYPTIANS. Although the priests, some of whom were undoubtedly sincere seekers after God, proclaimed the existence of a self-created, self-existent, and eternal Spirit God, or Eternal Mind, and many of the people, no doubt, subscribed to this doctrine, their innate love of their fetish spirits and gods, and their invincible conservatism, when it came to giving practical expression to their own personal views, made them choose visible creatures and things for their objects of worship. What CHAMPOLLION-FIGEAC wrote in 1839 is undoubtedly correct: 'The Egyptian religion is a pure monotheism, which manifested itself externally by a symbolic polytheism' (*L'Égypte*, p. 245, col. 1). And TIELE believed that the Egyptian religion 'was polytheistic, and that it developed in two opposite directions: in the one direction gods were multiplied by the addition of local gods, and in the other the EGYPTIANS drew nearer and nearer to monotheism.'[1]

The study of the iconography of the gods of EGYPT often brings a smile on our faces and sometimes even produces a kind of contempt for what appears to be puerile in it. But we may be sure that every detail in the forms and equipments of the gods had a very real meaning when they were first drawn, and, in my opinion, if we

[1] *Hypothesen omtrent de wording van den Egyptischen Godsdienst*, Amsterdam, 1893, p. 25.

only knew what that meaning was, we should cease to smile. It is clear in many cases that the original meanings had been forgotten, and that the scribe or artist himself was as ignorant about them as we are. The form of one god the EGYPTIANS made no attempt to indicate in stone or wood, viz. ḤĀPI the Nile-god. In the 'Address of Thanksgiving' which is commonly called a 'Hymn to the NILE',[1] it is said of him, 'He cannot be figured in stone, he is invisible, he hath neither servants nor ministers, he cannot be brought forth from [his] secret places, it is unknown where he is, he is not to be found in ornamented sanctuaries, there is no habitation which will contain him, he cannot be imagined in thy heart.'

The native myths and legends of the gods of EGYPT show that at a very early period men regarded them as a class of beings who were in many respects like themselves, who possessed the same virtues and vices as themselves, and committed acts of folly like men and women. The lapses of the gods and goddesses, moral or otherwise, did not stir men to anger, but did provoke men to regard them with a sort of kindly and good-humoured ridicule. Proof of this is furnished by the great hieratic papyrus which Dr. GARDINER has recently published. This contains what I believe to be the 'book of words' of a play, 'The Contendings of HORUS and SET', which may rightly be described as 'a Mythological Drama'. The narrative is slight, but the speeches of all the actors are given at length, and a connected story can be constructed. This play represents the gods assembled as a Court of Justice with RĀ as chairman, and they have to decide a simple issue, viz. whether the son of OSIRIS, the youthful cripple HORUS, is to succeed to his father's office, or whether it is to be given to his bold, handsome and free-living uncle (or brother) SET. RĀ is in favour of SET, but many of the gods are not. They lose their tempers, contradict and insult each other, and wrangle together like the members of a local or municipal Miglis in EGYPT at the present day. The delay of the Law is laughed at,[2] and the indecision and vacillation of the gods is made clear. The gross social customs of a bygone age are pilloried in the story of the criminal assault which SET made on HORUS whilst they were occupying the same couch, and in the account of the obscene relations which existed between

[1] For the hieratic text see Birch, *Select Papyri*, pl. xx f.

[2] The case had been before the gods for 80 years.

ISIS and her son HORUS. The ribaldry of NEITH, the whorish behaviour of HATHOR, the daughter of RĀ, the lasciviousness of SET, the quarrel of SET with the gods when he threatened to slay them one by one, the quarrel of HORUS with ISIS when he cut off her head, the impudence of BABAI, the bribery of ĀNTI the ferryman, &c., are all lightly but clearly brought out. The gods adjourn and change the site of their Court, but come to no decision, for they ignore the advice of the old gods, and the evidence which they ask for and obtain from them, and snub their referees. Finally, forgetting their precarious position, they address disparaging words in their letters to OSIRIS, but his reply is so menacing that they fulfil straightway his command to make HORUS his successor, and give SET a position in the sky where he can act as the god of thunder. This play makes good reading and is a thoroughly 'human document', but it is difficult to think that those who saw it played would find their reverence for the gods increased.

THE EGYPTIAN MYSTERIES AND MAGIC

The Egyptian word *sheta* , var. 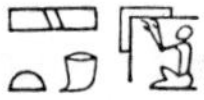, means something which is hidden or secret, or unknown, or cannot be seen through or understood, a secret, a mystery. Matter possessed *shetau akhet* , 'hidden properties'; rituals, spells, religious texts and pictures were *shetaut neter*  'divine mysteries'; (SHETAI)  was the 'hidden god' or the 'incomprehensible god', and there were gods whose forms, and faces and bodies and souls were 'hidden'. Egyptian literature is full of 'mysteries', and Mysteries, Magic, and the cult of OSIRIS form the three great outstanding features of the Egyptian Religion from first to last. The 'mysteries' which are spoken of by HERODOTUS, PLUTARCH, and IAMBLICHUS concerned OSIRIS, and those described by APULEIUS referred mainly to ISIS, but the priests of every great god in EGYPT celebrated mysteries which concerned their god alone, and probably each priesthood had its own special mysteries whereby the sinner was comforted and the sick man healed. The texts make it quite clear that one of the fundamental characteristics of the EGYPTIAN was his love for the drama; words alone did not satisfy him, he must have actions. Among the earliest examples of religious drama may be mentioned the 'Book of Opening of the Mouth', and the 'Book of the Liturgy of Funerary Offerings'. In the first work the ritual acts and the spells are enumerated which were believed to have the effect of enabling the deceased to breathe, think, speak, walk, &c., in spite of the fact that his body was bound round tightly with the funerary swathings. In the second work, the object of which was to maintain the life of the deceased in the Other World, the KHERI ḤEB or chief priestly magician presents to a statue of the deceased a long series of offerings of meat, drink, unguents, wearing apparel, &c. As he presents each he repeats a spell, the effect of which was supposed to transmute the object into something which could be used by the deceased in the Other World. Every act in every 'mystery' had originally a special signification, or was symbolic of some well-known happening. Eventually the *meanings* of such actions were forgotten in many cases, but the repetition of the actions never ceased.

The Mysteries of OSIRIS and ISIS were a series of Miracle Plays in which all the events of the life, death,[1] mummification, resurrection, and enthronement of OSIRIS as king of the Other World and god of the dead were reproduced mimically.[2] At ABYDOS all these 'mysteries' were directed by a chief priest (or KHERI ḤEB) who was, of course, a learned man, and he was assisted by a number of priests of the various lower grades. In some of the acts the public were allowed to take part, and thus the performance of the OSIRIS cycle of 'mysteries' tended to the edification of all classes. In the late temples at DENDERAH, ESNA, EDFÛ, and PHILAE, certain chambers were set apart for the performance of the 'Mysteries' of ISIS, and at SAÏS there were several chambers in which the 'Mysteries' of the ancient Virgin Mother-goddess NEITH were celebrated.

The *Book of the Dead* shows that some of its chapters or spells were 'great mysteries'. In the rubric, chap. clxii, which is called the 'Book of the Lady of the Hidden House', is described as a 'book of very great secrets', . And the reciter

[1] The Memphites said he was drowned, and the Heliopolitans that he was killed in battle, but no representation of the murder of Osiris has been found.

[2] For pictures and descriptions see Mariette, *Dendérah*, Paris, 1880, tom. iv; Budge, *Osiris and the Egyptian Resurrection*, London, 1911, vol. ii, pp. 21 ff.; and Moret, *Mystères*, pp. 20 ff.

of it is ordered 'to allow no one to see it', for it is an abominable thing for an outsider to know it, and it must be hidden. In the text of the chapter the spell is described as a 'very, very great protection', 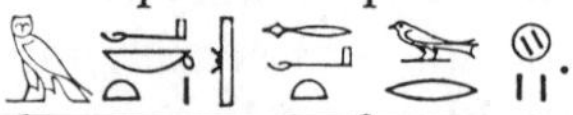. Chapter clxxxix was not to be recited in the presence of any one except the dearest friend of the reciter and the priest (KHERI ḤEB). And no one was to be allowed to approach the chamber during the recital, for 'this book is a very real mystery, ; never let the ignorant person or any one whatsoever look upon it'. And one of the rubrics to chapter cxxxvii states expressly, that 'the things which are done secretly  in the hall of the tomb are the mysteries of the ṬUAT and types of the mysteries of KHERT NETER  '.

In these rubrics, and many others, nothing is said as to *why* the chapters were 'great mysteries', or *why* no man except father or son or priest was to be allowed to hear them read, or to see the rituals performed. It would be natural to prevent any one seeing the drawing or picture of the vignette, because it lessened the risk of the Evil Eye falling on it. It was a simple matter to insert an amulet in each wall of the mummy chamber and to light four lamps or 'blazing torches', and then to extinguish them in four vessels filled with the milk of a white cow. But what, naturally, we want to know is, how this ritual grew up, and what it was based upon, and if it had any deeper, special meaning, which was known only to the priests, and what that meaning or doctrine was. I feel sure that every lighted torch, and every vessel of milk, and every amulet represented events in the history of the Four Sons of HORUS, and OSIRIS, and the Eye of HORUS, and RĀ, and that these events were known to the priests who based esoteric doctrines upon them. The deceased acquired life and happiness in the ṬUAT not from the material lamps and vessels of milk, but from the esoteric powers which the priests, through knowledge of them, could bring into operation for his benefit. Surely no ritual with its accompanying spells could be a 'mystery' unless some esoteric doctrine or wisdom lay behind it, which was known only to the priest.

HERODOTUS believed that the priests possessed secret doctrines which were unknown to the laity, and PLUTARCH, who on this point was well instructed and informed, asserts the same thing. The GREEKS could not have used the word 'mysteries' to describe what the texts call *shetat* or *seshetat*, i.e. the secret rituals in the cults of the Egyptian gods, unless they had definite knowledge of the character of the cults. And the knowledge of the *shetat* and their meaning and history can never have been known to the people generally, for to them even the hieroglyphs on the temple walls and in the funerary papyri were unfathomable 'mysteries'. The pictures of the bull's skin hanging on a pole before OSIRIS, and the skin of a certain ape, and the ḤENU Boat were accepted by the laity as sacred objects, which could be used for their benefit, but the doctrines of prolonged life, renewed birth, and resurrection which were connected with these objects could never have become parts of popular religious knowledge. Undoubtedly the priests of the higher grades possessed esoteric knowledge, which they communicated orally to those who were their equals or successors, but it is tolerably certain that they did not commit it to writing; and the only inscription of the kind is that which SHABAKA had recopied (see pp. 15, 16) from a decayed archetype on papyrus or wood.

The Eye of Horus, i.e. the right eye of Ḥer-ur (Horus the Aged), or the sun. Because of its great power it was separated from the god by the later Egyptian theologians and regarded as an independent god. Here the Udjat is made to be the head of an ancient kneeling god.

The two vignettes from the Theban *Book of the Dead* well illustrate the difficulty of the subject.

No. 1, Chapter CLXVIII

In the upper register we have the rising of RĀ from the waters of NUNU, and figures of the god seated in his two boats of the day, and his ṬUAT boat. All these suggest that the 'mystery' of the vignette has something to do with birth, or rebirth, or resurrection. In the lower register we have a woman seated in the act of bringing forth a child; ANUBIS holds her hand and gives her

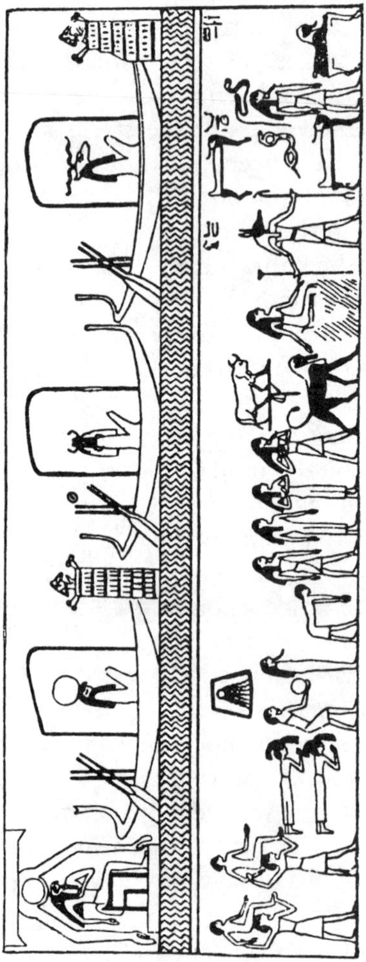

No. 1, Chapter CLXVIII

virility and strength. The man-headed sphinx is the god TEMU or PTAḤ, the bull on a standard is for sacrifice. Between two mummies and a sphinx stands the old god DJESER-TEP . Next we have a priest (?) followed by four women, then the name of an ancient god above a mummy, and two wailing women and two men bringing two human beings for sacrifice. There is no doubt that the vignette represents the ceremonies connected with birth, but it is impossible to give a clear description of the exact meaning of every figure in it. NAVILLE and MORET have failed to do so, and I cannot.

No. 2, Chapter CLXXXII

Here, in the centre, we have the 'august SĀḤ, i.e. the mummy of MUT-ḤETEP, with NEPHTHYS, MESTHA and QEBḤ-SENU-F at the head, and ISIS, ḤĀPI, and ṬUA-MUT-F at the feet. Above are a group of six ancient animal gods: SEBEK with a serpent; a dog-god, SET, and a bull-god holding crocodiles or lizards; ANUBIS; and a serpent god, also with a crocodile. Below are KHNEMU, GEBB, and SHU holding serpents; a gazelle (?) -god with knives; a baboon with a knife; and a hawk-god. It is clear that all these gods are performing a ritual for the benefit of the dead, but of the ideas which underlie it we know nothing. Only the priest who composed the vignette could explain its esoteric meaning. Only one thing is quite certain, and that is that the ritual here represented is very ancient, probably predynastic.

THE KHERI ḤEB AND THE SUBORDINATE PRIESTS

The staff of a large temple consisted of (1) the 'servants of the god' 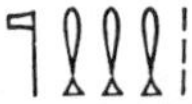 who had a chief known as the '*Mer*  -ḤEMU-NETER'; (2) A 'father of the god'  *Atef neter*; (3)  *Uāb*, i.e. the washer and dresser of the god; (4) The temple scribe 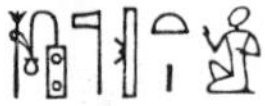; (5)  = 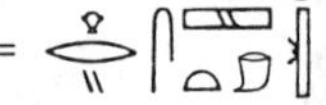 *Ḥeri sesheta*, i.e. 'He who is over the mysteries or secrets'; (6) The  *Kheri ḥeb*, i.e. 'the holder of the papyrus roll or book'. Of these the KHERI ḤEB was undoubtedly the most learned. The texts show that his knowledge of the ancient literature of EGYPT was very great, that he was well acquainted with the regulations which governed the celebration of festivals, and that he arranged and directed all the services and ceremonial observances in connexion with the dead. He was, of course, a master magician, and was learned in every branch of magic, both White and Black. It goes without saying that the KHERI ḤEB of MEMPHIS or ON or THEBES, or in fact of any great town, would be, necessarily, a man of outstanding natural ability and that his power would be very great. All the 'mysteries' connected with his god, including the god's secret name, would be known to him. It is possible that the scribe of the temple might have some knowledge of the same, but it is unlikely that all the grades of priests had knowledge of the most profound mysteries. The SEM (or SETEM), the AMMI-AS, the AMMI-KHENT, and other priests who assisted the KHERI ḤEB in performing the mysteries of the 'Opening of the Mouth', and the MESENTIU or 'handicraftsmen' thoroughly understood the staging of the mysteries, but it was the KHERI ḤEB who, as the 'wise' one, directed the proceedings, and was the master of them all. The learned magician who was sent to PHARAOH to expel a devil from the daughter of the king of BEKHTEN was chosen from the PER-ĀNKH, or College of Scribes and Magicians, because he was 'deeply instructed in his heart and possessed skilful fingers'.[1] This shows that some of the priests were experts in the mysteries which were manipulated with the hands. The view that all the priests possessed equal knowledge of the 'mysteries' is shown to be wrong by the incident recorded in Exodus vii. 10 f. AARON cast down his rod[2] before PHARAOH and it became a serpent, and the Egyptian magicians cast their rods down and they also became serpents, but AARON's rod swallowed up the rods of the magicians. In other words AARON's knowledge of Egyptian magic was greater than that of JANNES and JAMBRES, and he knew the master spell which they did not.

Osiris seated in judgement.

It may be urged that any priest who could read the hieroglyphic or hieratic texts could learn all that there was to learn about the 'mysteries', and but one instance is known in which an attempt has been made to hide the meaning of some of the texts in the Judgement Hall of OSIRIS. In the VIth section of the *Book of Gates* we see OSIRIS seated in judgement on a pedestal with nine steps, and a pair of scales balanced on the figure of a mummy. In front of him is the baboon-associate of THOTH standing in a boat and driving away the black pig, symbolic of SET who blinded the eye of RĀ or HORUS. Above, in the upper left-hand corner, is a figure of ANUBIS. In the space above the pedestal, and on the side of the pedestal itself are several short inscriptions in hieroglyphs which can only be read if unusual phonetic values are given them. CHAMPOLLION first noticed this fact and called this manner of writing 'enigmatic' (*Monuments*, p. 272). Though several scholars have studied these inscriptions,[3]

1 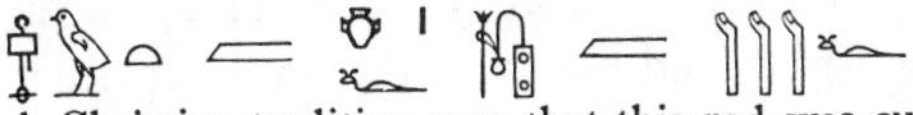 Bekhten Stele, line 10.

2 A Christian tradition says that this rod was cut from the Tree of Good and Evil in Paradise, and that it swallowed up the serpent of Pôzdî, the Sorceress. Solomon of Al-Baṣra devotes a whole chapter (xxx) of the *Book of the Bee* to the rod of Aaron.

3 See Goodwin, *Aeg. Zeit.*, 1873, p. 138; Renouf, ibid., 1874, p. 101; Lefébure, *Records of the Past*, vol. x, p. 114.

no satisfactory translations of them have as yet been published. There must have been some good reason for the use of 'enigmatic' writing in these inscriptions, but what it was is unknown.

MAGIC

It is impossible to doubt that the most powerful of all the beliefs in the minds of the EGYPTIANS, in every period of their history, was the belief in the power of *Ḥeka*, a word which by common consent is now translated by 'magic' (see p. 113.) The primitive savage possibly had a vague idea that somewhere a great and almighty spirit or god existed, but he soon made up his mind that this being paid no attention to terrestrial affairs, and he peopled earth, air, sky, and sea with legions of spirits, most of whom were unfriendly to man. The oldest cult of these formed the foundation of magic. The wants of the Egyptian savages were relatively few and may perhaps be summed up in three words—food, women, and progeny; and his early mysteries, ritual, and drama were devoted to providing himself with these fundamental necessaries for existence. The night struck terror into his soul, for it deprived him of light, heat, and movement, and a very real fear of darkness fills the mind of the modern Egyptian peasant and even people of the effendi class. The belief in magic promptly produced the magician and witch-doctor; and their successors, by means of their natural ability and astuteness, developed systems of magic, whereby the predynastic and dynastic EGYPTIANS, and their Muslim and Christian descendants, have become the bond-servants of magic. Some authorities say that the Egyptian Religion was developed from magic, and others that Egyptian magic was the Egyptian Religion in a state of decay or was developed from it, but these views seem to me to be incorrect.

Relying on the evidence of the Egyptian texts we find that the heart of TEMU, or RĀ, was only able to assume a material form by the application of magic to his name (see p. 117). *Ḥeka* enabled him to transmute his name into a material body, and ever after the name was the equivalent of the person who bore it. What this name was is not said. As long as the 'hidden' or secret name was unknown to any except the god himself nothing could harm him. Thus the 'One god eternal and everlasting' only existed by the help of magic. In the paintings and reliefs we see that every god carries the object ☥ in his right hand, and he who has it not is no god. The phonetic value of the hieroglyph is *ānkh̩* and the meaning given to it is 'life', but the exact meaning which it had in the mind of the EGYPTIAN five or six thousand years ago is unknown, and what exactly the object represented by ☥ was is also unknown. It was probably a very ancient fetish of special importance and signification, and it may be assumed that it was connected with some fertility cult and the human organs of generation. The Egyptian sage tells us (see p. 119) that RĀ created *Ḥeka* or magic in order to help man, which can only mean that he transferred to man some of his own power and nature, reserving his own 'hidden' or secret name for his own special use. Then we find in the religious literature abundant proof that the EGYPTIAN used the magic which his god had given him to coerce and outwit his benefactor. The Egyptian Creation-myths make it clear that TEMU or RĀ employed *Ḥeka* in constructing heaven, earth, and the underworld, and then *Ḥeka* assumes the form of *divine* magic, and has something of the character of the 'wisdom' (*khochmâh*) which is so often mentioned by SOLOMON as the helper of God at the Creation (Prov. viii. 22 f.). If this be so we may wonder if *Ḥeka* is correctly translated by 'magic'.

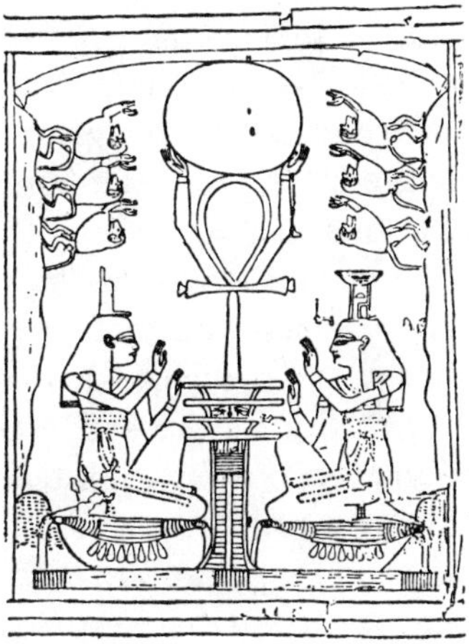

The solar Disk supported by the Ka or arms of 'Life' rising out of the fetish tree Ṭeṭ. Isis and Nephthys salute the Disk as it rises, and the morning stars in the form of baboons sing praises to it.

THE MAGICIANS OF THE OLD KINGDOM

The EGYPTIANS used magic largely in all their daily affairs, but it was developed greatly in connexion with the dead. Magical spells were recited during the making of the mummy, and amulets of various kinds were inserted between the swathings. Spells were written on the mummy and on the sides of the coffin and outer walls of the tombs, and amulets were inserted in the walls and floor of the tomb to prevent the entrance of evil spirits. And the rolls of papyri inscribed with many scores of spells and magical drawings proclaim the importance which the EGYPTIANS assigned to funerary magic. The magicians employed by the people generally, and the great KHERI ḤEBS of the temples, lost no opportunity of increasing their power and influence. The magician DJADJAMĀNKH in the reign of KHUFU (IVth dynasty) used spells which made one half of the water in a lake to lift itself up and place itself on the other half; the normal depth of the water in the lake was 12 cubits, and the depth of water when the one half of the lake was piled on the other, was 24 cubits. The magician TETA cut off the heads of geese and the head of an ox and then rejoined them to their bodies; the geese cackled and the ox rose up on his feet.[1] One of the questions addressed by the king to TETA the magician was unable to answer, but he volunteered some information which made the king very sad because it showed him that the days of his dynasty were coming to an end. In this case TETA played the part of a prophet, but it is certain that his prophecy was based on more than an intelligent anticipation of events.

THE FLUID OF LIFE

During the performance of some of the great religious ceremonies the magician had to represent the king, and acquired almost divine power. The 'Divine Service'[2] which was performed daily in the great temples of ABYDOS, THEBES, MEMPHIS, and elsewhere was supposed to be directed by the king who went to the temple to 'see his father', i.e. OSIRIS, or RĀ, or HORUS, or PTAḤ, and to receive from the god the measure of the divine life-essence without which he could not perform his duties satisfactorily in the temple. When the king arrived at the hall of the sanctuary two of the solar-gods and their female counterparts received him and placed his royal crowns, the White  and the Red , upon his head. The chief god of the temple received the king and stood up and embraced him, or remained

[1] See Erman, *Die Märchen des Papyrus Westcar*, Berlin, 1890.

[2] 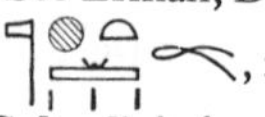, i.e. 'things of the god done into writing'. See A. Moret, *Le Rituel du Culte divin journalier en Égypte*, Paris, 1902.

seated and took the king upon his knees. Then the king turned his back to the god who straightway began to make magical passes[1] down it, from the nape of his neck to the lower vertebrae. By these passes the magical life-essence *sa ānkh̩* or *sa en ānkh̩*, of the god was transferred to the body of the king. This life-essence

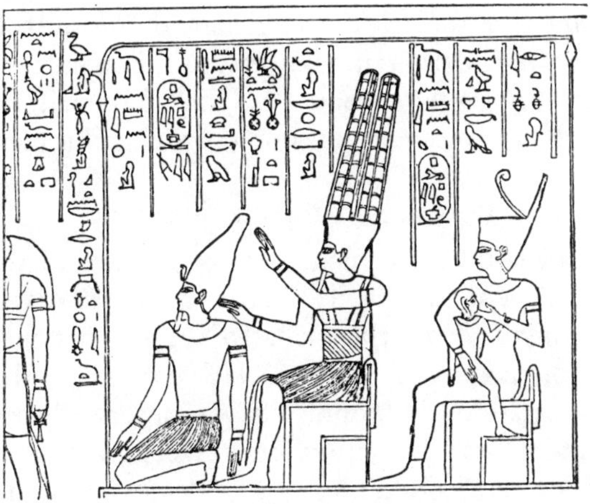

Amen-Rā making magical passes over the king's back, and saying, 'I stablish thy rising as king of the South and the North on the throne of thy father Rā'.

The goddess Amenit seats the king on her knees and gives him her breasts, saying, 'Suckle thyself with the milk of both my breasts'.

was derived from RĀ or from the older sun-god HORUS, and the king having received it was able to transfer it to his statues, being now the counterpart of RĀ. The king then either seats himself on the knees of one of the goddesses, ISIS, or HATHOR of SEKHMIT, or is drawn thereon by the statue, and the goddess turns her breast to him so that he may draw milk therefrom into his mouth. When this ceremony is completed the king becomes a god, the son of a god, and receives all the magical powers of the gods. He can now perform effectively all the ceremonies which are connected with the 'giving of life' to the god, and the receipt of the same from the god. This interchange of 'life' between the god and the king was

1 *setep sa.*

the basic idea which lay beneath all the worship of the gods.[1] Now it was manifestly impossible for the PHARAOH to minister as the high-priest at the celebration of the long service in the temple daily, but the service had to be held, and whenever the king was absent, 'the great priest of the day' became his deputy. The introductory ceremonies of purification, consecration, &c., were then performed upon him, and thus the priestly magician became the son of the god and was endowed with divine powers. And on such occasions he was as great, if not greater than, the king. The priestly magicians throughout EGYPT were not slow in recognizing this fact.

THE MAGICAL CULT OF OSIRIS

The cult of OSIRIS, the most striking feature of the Egyptian Religion, was essentially magical. After a comparatively rapid but victorious progress from the Delta to ABYDOS, his cult flourished throughout the country from the XIIth dynasty to the middle of the Ptolemaic period. Its popularity was deservedly great because it promised to all its adherents the resurrection of the dead, and a renewed life of indefinite duration after death, and it did away with the monopoly of gods and kings in heaven. The followers of OSIRIS were helped in every way, for apart from the teaching of the priests the great 'Book of Coming Forth by Day' provided them with all the spells and with directions for using them which would enable them to find their way to the kingdom of the god. OSIRIS was raised from the dead, and his mortal body reconstituted and revivified by magic, and those who wished to live with him in felicity in the underworld after death could attain their wish by employing the means which had been used on his behalf by the gods. Myriads of EGYPTIANS died believing in Osirian magic, but there is no evidence that they regarded OSIRIS as a Saviour, or that they hoped to inherit a new life after their death through any merit of his sufferings and death. The idea of OSIRIS as a Sacrifice offered up for his followers or as a Redeemer finds no expression in the texts; it can never have entered the minds of the EGYPTIANS.

In the hymns to OSIRIS very little reference is made to him as the *Judge* of the dead, but he is frequently called the Ruler of the world

[1] 'Cet échange de la vie donnée et rendue du dieu au roi, et réciproquement, est le fond même du culte égyptien': Moret, op. cit., p. 99.

and of Agert (the Underworld). He is 'King of kings, Lord of lords, and Prince of princes, the king of eternity, the lord of everlastingness, whose existence continueth through millions of years' (Papyrus of ANI, sheet 2). 'His majesty strikes with terror the hearts of the gods. They come to meet him with bowed backs, and their bodies retreat when they see him arrayed in the majesty of RĀ' (Papyrus of HUNEFER, sheet 3). 'In his name of OSIRIS terror of him is very great' (Papyrus of ANI, sheet 2).

OSIRIS AND THE WEIGHING OF HEARTS

It is not easy to decide what part OSIRIS was supposed to take in the 'Great Judgement' of the dead, and a doubt arises in the mind about the accuracy of the Judgement Scene which appears in the great papyri of the *Book of the Dead.* ANUBIS performs the actual work with the Great Scales, and THOTH accepts the report of the Baboon-god his deputy, and registers it on his palette. The gods confirm THOTH's report, and the deceased is led into the presence of OSIRIS who assigns to him an estate in his kingdom. Now many texts speak of the terrible DJADJAU who judge the dead, but these are not represented in the large funerary rolls of papyrus. In fact the picture indicates that the deceased by means of a spell as old as the Ist dynasty has overcome any opposition which they or the SHENIT might offer, and by a formal denial of guilt, and the profession of an impossible degree of innocence, has persuaded OSIRIS and the Great Company of the Gods, that he has crushed sin within himself (see p. 297) and brought before them the absolute righteousness which the Law demanded. Thus magic enabled a man, according to the priests of OSIRIS, to hoodwink or deceive the gods and obtain the reward of the righteous. The Code of OSIRIS, which is based on one still older, permitted a man to believe that he could by his own works, make himself fit to receive whatever reward OSIRIS could give him, and that all he had to do was to find some means of escape from the condemnation of the implacable and absolutely impartial DJADJAU. If we are to regard the passive figure of OSIRIS as a mere symbol of death or the eternal Death-god, then we may consider the scene of the 'Weighing of the Heart' as a picture of the result of a successful gamble of the deceased with the gods. Or the picture may represent the attempt made by the priests of OSIRIS to provide means by which *every* follower of OSIRIS, however great a sinner, might escape

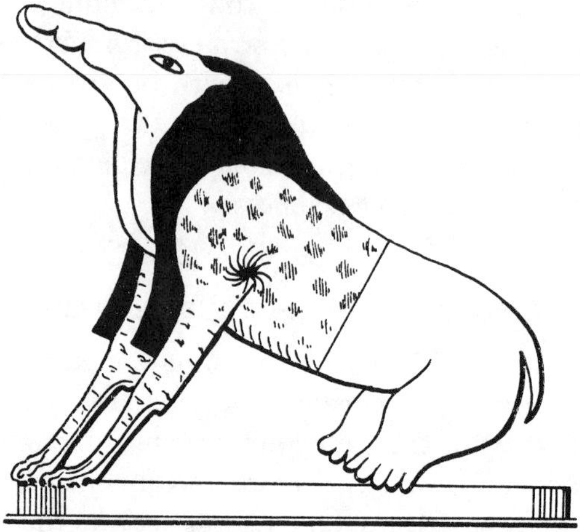

Am-Mit, the composite monster one-third crocodile, one-third lion, and one-third hippopotamus.

The scribe Ani about to move a piece on a draught-board, his wife Tutu apparently advising him.

The souls of Ani and his wife seated on their tomb. On the stand before them is a libation vessel of water and flowers.

from the jaws of ĀM-MIT, the Eater of the Dead, who destroyed both the souls and bodies of those whose evil deeds outnumbered his good deeds.[1]

[1] From the Tale of Khamuas (see Griffith, *Stories of the High Priests of Memphis*, Oxford, 1900, p. 46 f.) we learn that : (1) Those whose good deeds outnumbered his evil deeds became gods of Amenti and their souls went to heaven. (2) Those whose evil deeds outnumbered their good deeds were delivered over to Am-mit and were annihilated. (3) Those whose good and evil deeds were equal in number

But the need of the EGYPTIAN for spells and amulets and talismans and magical pictures, was not ended when he became a BA and entered the kingdom of OSIRIS. He could only effect his transformations with the help of spells, and magical names were absolute necessities to him if he would traverse in safety the region between this world and the next. Hostile beings menaced him on all sides, and the river of liquid fire in the ṬUAT had to be crossed. In the first section of the vignette of chapter xvii in the Papyrus of ANI, we see the scribe seated in a bower with a draught-board before him. His right hand is raised above the board, and he seems to be hesitating where to move the piece he holds in it. His wife is seated behind him, and her right hand is raised as if she is warning him against the move which he is proposing to make. It has been suggested that ANI is playing a game of draughts with his wife, but I believe that he is really playing a game with some unseen adversary, and that his wife is helping him and suggesting to him to be careful. Gods and men alike played at draughts. 'HERMES played at draughts with the Moon and won the 72nd part of each one of her lights, out of which he composed five days' (PLUTARCH). And SETNA played at draughts with NENEFERKAPTAH, and lost three games of 52 points.[1]

CONCLUSIONS

The path of the man who sets out to write an account of the religious beliefs of the Ancient EGYPTIANS is strewn with difficulties, some of which are insuperable. A vast mass of funerary and religious literature has been published and is available for study, but it is insufficient for the purpose of the historian of the Egyptian Religion, because it was all written during the dynastic period. We have no first-hand knowledge of the predynastic magical cults and religions, and the only documents that give us any information about them were written chiefly in the dynastic period. These cults were

became followers of Seker-Osiris. Prof. Griffith thinks that the high moral idea represented by the Demotic story 'shows the mark of influences such as those of Christianity'. Every honest sinner had a chance of salvation.

[1] The pieces on the board are called 'dogs' in the Demotic text (Griffith, *Stories of the High Priests of Memphis*, p. 31). In connexion with this we may note the set of draughtsmen in the British Museum (Nos. 24668 f.), ten having heads of Bes, the god of pleasure and jollity, and seven with heads of Anubis, a very ancient god of the dead.

formulated thousands of years ago by natives of the NILE valley and the Delta, and being of a non-African race we can never recover the exact meaning which the primitive EGYPTIANS gave to the words they used to express their religious feelings. And rituals and spells, which we regard as foolish, must have represented to them the profoundest wisdom and been held in the greatest reverence. Such being the facts no account of the Egyptian Religion which existed between say 10000 B.C. and the beginning of the Christian Era can ever be more than approximately correct. Using such material as we have, the following conclusions may be drawn:

1. The Egyptian Religion stands alone; nothing exactly like it is known. Certain rituals and beliefs find counterparts in the religions of the SUMERIANS, BABYLONIANS, and ASSYRIANS, but it cannot properly be said that the MESOPOTAMIANS borrowed from the EGYPTIANS or the EGYPTIANS from the BABYLONIANS. The truth is, as SIDNEY SMITH has pointed out, that in the fourth millenium B.C. the peoples of Western ASIA and the EGYPTIANS had arrived at much the same level of a civilization which was derived from a people who lived more to the East. In some matters the ASIATICS and EGYPTIANS thought alike and expressed their thoughts in much the same kind of way; in others they did not, and each people acted independently. And the actions and beliefs of each people were at times modified by climatic and geographical conditions. Attempts have been made to show that the Egyptian Religion owed much to the religion of the HEBREWS. That distinguished scholar, the late A. H. SAYCE—alas that the word 'late' must be written!—after reading SETHE's monograph on the god AMEN of the 'hidden name', found an Egyptian equivalent for the early chapters of the Book of Genesis. We might as well say that the story of the Flood given in the Book of Genesis is derived from the story of the Flood by which OSIRIS intended to blot out all mankind, as told in chapter clxxv of the Theban Recension of the *Book of the Dead*.[1]

[1] On the other hand, as Sir Gardner Wilkinson observed, 'Many of the religious rites of the Jews bear a striking resemblance to those of Egypt' (*Ancient Egyptians*, ed. Birch, vol. iii, p. 411 f.). Mr. H. P. Cooke (*Osiris*, p. 103) has rightly emphasized this fact, and there is little doubt that this result is due to Moses who possessed an expert knowledge of the Egyptian Religion, and was a 'high-grade priest'. Manetho says that Moses was himself a priest, and Josephus held this opinion (*Contra Apion.*, i, pp. 238–50). According to the latter, the rebel Hebrews, determined on revolt, gathered together at a certain place, and appointed as their leader a priest of

2. Among the many cults of the predynastic EGYPTIANS the oldest is that of the stars, but the EGYPTIANS never became astronomers, although they had knowledge of some of the 36 Decans under the Old Kingdom, and compiled lists of observations of stars of a scientific character.[1] The forms which they gave to the Signs of the Zodiac and the 36 Decans were derived from the GREEKS. But at a very early period the EGYPTIANS were masters of the arts of astrology which was mingled with the cults of evil spirits, devils, the disembodied souls of the dead, &c. They made groups of stars around which they cast forms of men and animals and reptiles, and they firmly believed that the destinies of men were decreed by them. Then arose the men who cast nativities and constructed horoscopes, and told fortunes, and the astrologer, who was of course an expert magician, became a power in the land. The earth and all beings on it reacted to the motions of the stars—so it was believed, and this belief remained unchanged century after century, and was adopted by the COPTS, i.e. the EGYPTIANS who embraced Christianity. In the Pyramid Texts SAḤ, i.e. ORION, is called the 'father of the gods'  (§ 408 *c*), and among these gods were the Five Planets MERCURY, VENUS, MARS, JUPITER, and SATURN. Prog-

Heliopolis called Osarsiph. He drew up a constitution for them, and framed a code of laws, and when he had definitely thrown in his lot with them, this priest of Heliopolis changed his name from Osarsiph to Moses. Now Osarsiph is quite a good Egyptian name and its meaning is clear 'Osiris+child' 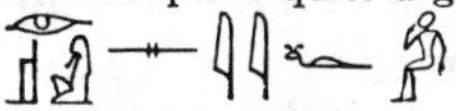 (or, 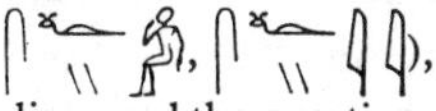), i.e. the Osiris-child, or the 'child of Osiris'. Mr. Cooke has discussed the question as to whether the great Hebrew was first called Osarsiph and later Moses or vice versa (p. 99), and like him I prefer the opinion of Manetho who had full access to all the documentary evidence available to that of modern critics. Moses and Aaron his brother and Miriam his sister were Egyptians, though the offspring of Hebrews domiciled in Egypt. There is little doubt that Aaron and his sister were well-educated, and though in a lesser degree they were no doubt learned in all the wisdom of the Egyptians. Aaron was probably a member of one of the guilds of priests, and was in any case admirably fitted to be the first high-priest of the Hebrews and the spokesman of Moses (Exod. iv. 14, 16, 27). He was likewise a skilled magician, for his rod became a serpent (Exod. vii, 10), and he brought on Egypt the plagues of frogs, lice, and flies (Exod. viii. 5, 17, 24). His sympathy with the cult of animals led him to make the golden calf (Exod. xxxii. 4) to gratify those who still clung to Egyptian beliefs. Miriam 'the prophetess' (Exod. xv. 20) had probably been a singing woman in one of the temples, and it is clear that she knew how to lead a choir of women, and to direct antiphonal singing accompanied by the beating of timbrels and dancing.

[1] Burchardt, *Zeit. für Aegypt. Sprache*, vol. xxxvii, p. 12, and Spiegelberg, ibid., vol. liii, p. 113 f.

noses derived from the planets were accepted unquestioningly.[1] The magician alone could annul the decrees of the planets and the great constellations. The draught-board, which seems to have been introduced into EGYPT from BABYLONIA,[2] was used in connexion with astrology, and later the dead made use of it when playing against MEḤEN the serpent-god and protector of the Sun-god. Still later it again assumed an astral character. The early EGYPTIANS called the pieces 'dancers', the Demotic writers 'dogs', and the ARABS also 'dogs' (*kilâb*). The board is said to have been invented by THOTH, and also by ALEXANDER the Great.

3. The cult of sacred animals, birds, reptiles, &c., was one of the most important features of the Egyptian Religion. It was based on the idea that certain animals possessed divine powers, and this remained unchanged and undiminished from the time of the first occupation of the NILE valley by men until after the occupation of EGYPT by the ROMANS. The ROSETTA STONE records (lines 3 f.) that PTOLEMY V provided endowments for APIS, MNEVIS, and all the other sacred animals on a greater scale than any of his predecessors. He furnished their temples with all the necessary equipments, and provided animals for sacrifice, and libations, and everything which was necessary for the celebration of their festivals. And he built a magnificent temple for APIS, giving gold and silver for its decoration, and he supplied grain in vast quantities. Admiration and fear were the basic reasons for the cults of animals of birds, beasts, reptiles, and fishes. The bull and the ram represented strength and virility; the cow, fertility; the jackal, cunning; the lion, leopard, panther, and crocodile, savage strength; the cobra and the scorpion, powers fatal to man; the goose, fertility; the scarab, new life; the baboon, wisdom; and many birds were admired and protected for their beauty.

4. Magic played so great a part in the life of the EGYPTIANS of all periods that it is difficult to define the Egyptian Religion as any-

[1] See Boll, *Sternglaube und Sterndeutung*, Leipzig, 1919, p. 105; and Brugsch, *Thesaurus*, p. 819 f.; and Brugsch, *Aegyptologie*, pp. 323–40.

[2] See the valuable article by Pieper, 'Ein Text über das ägyptische Brettspiel', in *Zeit. für Aegypt. Sprache*, vol. lxvi (1931), pp. 16–33. It is clear from the vignette showing Ani playing draughts that he was playing with some very definite object. The squares of the draught-board may represent the fields of the sky or the divisions of the Underworld, and Ani may be playing to gain access to these unhindered. On the other hand, he may be playing against Fate.

thing but magical. We may call the magic in use among living men 'black' or 'profane', and that employed in connexion with the dead as 'white' or sacred', but the fact remains that it was universally believed that the power of magic could, and did, modify and annul the power of the gods, who themselves could not exist without it. Every great hymn insists that heaven, earth, and the Underworld and all in them were made by the god One, but the destinies of men were ruled by magic. The true lord of the world was the experienced magician before whom every one had to bow down—gods, and the living, and the dead. I can see no evidence in the texts that Egyptian magic ever developed into religion, although there must have been men among the priests who possessed religious instincts and who sought and found the true God. The aim of most of the priesthoods of EGYPT was to acquire and possess knowledge of magic.

5. The 'Mysteries' formed a very important feature in the cult of every god, and it seems that some of them, i.e. the rituals and spells, were common to all of them. The ordinary 'mysteries' which were connected with the welfare and future of the dead were probably as well understood by the better-educated portion of the laity as by the priests. But it is clear that many of them possessed a significance which only the KHERI ḤEB knew, and this is specially true of the 'mysteries' which came into being in the Old and Middle Kingdoms. There must have been a progressive development in the 'mysteries', and it seems as if some of them were entirely unknown under the Old Kingdom. It is impossible to doubt that these were 'mysteries' in the Egyptian religion,[1] and this being so, it is impossible to think that the highest order of the priests did not possess esoteric knowledge which they guarded with the greatest care. Each priesthood, if I read the evidence correctly, possessed a 'Gnosis', a 'superiority of knowledge', which they never did into writing, and so were enabled to enlarge or diminish its scope as circumstances made it necessary. It is therefore absurd to expect to find in Egyptian papyri descriptions of the secrets which formed the esoteric knowledge of the priests. Among the 'secret wisdom' of the priests must be included the knowledge of which day was the shortest of

[1] See the classical authorities quoted by Hopfner in his *Fontes Historiae Religionis Aegyptiacae*, Bonn, 1922 (Index, p. 875).

the year, i.e. the day when OSIRIS died[1] and the new Sun began his course, and the day when SIRIUS would rise heliacally, and the true age of the moon, and the days when the great festivals of the year were to be celebrated. This knowledge, of vital importance to the whole country, must always have been the monopoly of the priests.[2]

6. There is no doubt that the EGYPTIANS included monotheism among their dogmas, but it is impossible to say when their theologians evolved it. Two forms of it existed, a higher and a lower. The higher is the monotheism of PTAḤ of MEMPHIS, the spirit God, the Eternal Mind, who existed before everything else, and created matter by thought; and the lower is the monotheism of RĀ of HELIOPOLIS. But the African monotheism of 3800 B.C. or earlier, though not to be compared with that of modern Christian people, is a remarkable spiritual achievement. The 'monotheistic MOSES', as Mr. H. P. COOKE calls him, must have known of it, and the verse in Deut. vi. 4,[3] 'Hear, O ISRAEL: the Lord our God is One' (see also Mark xii. 29, 32), may be connected with his teaching of ISRAEL in the desert.

7. Of the earliest phases of the cult of OSIRIS in the predynastic period nothing is known; it is probable that OSIRIS was not his original name, for the view that the name of OSIRIS is of Babylonian or Sumerian origin has much to recommend it. The texts suggest that OSIRIS and ISIS were stellar deities (SIRIUS and VENUS?), and SET may have been a hostile star (or, perhaps, SAḤ (ORION) of the northern heavens). OSIRIS, though eclipsed temporarily by SET, came to

[1] See Wiedermann, *Das Alte Ägypten*, Heidelberg, 1920, p. 368.

[2] Concerning sacerdotal mysticism Iamblichus says (I. xi, Taylor's translation): 'For of the things which are perpetually effected in sacred rites, some have a certain arcane cause, and which is more excellent than reason; others are consecrated from eternity to the superior genera, as symbols; others preserve a certain other image, just as nature, which is effective of invisible reasons, expresses certain visible formations; others are adduced for the sake of honour, or have for their end some kind of similitude, or familiarity and alliance; and some procure what is useful to us, or in a certain respect purify and liberate our human passions, or avert some other of those dire circumstances which happen to us.' For the Greek text see Parthey, *Jamblichi de Mysteriis Liber.*, Berlin, 1857, p. 37. The German translation by Hopfner (*Über die Geheimlehren von Jamblichus*, Leipzig, 1921) removes many difficulties in understanding the Greek text.

[3] Compare Deut. iv. 39; 'I [am] the Lord, and [there is] none else', Isa. xlv. 6, 14; 'I [am] God, and [there is] none else; I [am] God, and [there is] none like me', Isa. xlvi. 9; So also St. Paul 'to us one God', 1 Cor. viii. 6; 'Verily thou [art] a God that hidest thyself, O God of Israel', Isa. xlv. 15. Compare the hymn to Amen in Part II of this book in which he is said to 'hide' himself and to have a 'hidden' name.

life again. Or OSIRIS may have been the Year-god, or the Moon-god, or the NILE-god, but the dying year is followed by a new year, and the waning moon by a new moon, and the fallen NILE by a new NILE-flood. OSIRIS never represented death final and absolute. The pre-dynastic EGYPTIANS also made him an ancient king of EGYPT, and his death and resurrection, and the sorrows of ISIS his widow, and the fight of HORUS, his son, begotten after his death,[1] were promptly made the subjects of numerous religious dramas at the great popular festivals. The cult of OSIRIS destroyed the king's monopoly of heaven, and favoured the burial of the dead without mutilation, and promised every man renewed life after death. Towards the close of the Middle Kingdom the cult of OSIRIS became firmly established in UPPER EGYPT, and it became the popular cult of the people generally. Early in the XVIIIth dynasty the scene of the Last Judgement appears in the great papyri of the *Book of the Dead*, and in them the 'Great Scales' are represented for the first time. The idea of this seems to have been that the actual material heart of a man would be weighed, and not moral or immoral actions only. Perhaps the existance of LIBRA in the Babylonian Zodiac became known in EGYPT. The Code of OSIRIS (see p. 297) is based on an older document. The cult of OSIRIS is from first to last magical, and it was this characteristic which endeared it to the people generally. The use of magical means, under the direction of the priests, enabled a man to justify himself before OSIRIS, and even to believe that he had killed sin in himself, and that his whole life had been righteous 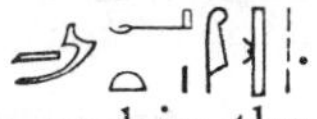. There are many passages in the hymns to the gods, and in the magical spells of the *Book of the Dead* (which in later times became prayers), which show that many of the scribes were truly religious

[1] The Greek magical papyri say that when Isis discovered that Osiris had committed adultery with her sister Nephthys, she gave vent to a 'mighty shriek which shook the universe', and she went and tore the bands off her marriage bed. She complained to Thoth about her treatment by Osiris, and he promised to supply her with the means of winning back the affections of her husband. Violent emnity existed between Set and Osiris, and Set avenged himself by casting Osiris into the river where he lay for three days and three nights being devoured by the fish. Isis found the body and dragged it out of the water, and found that the phallus of Osiris was non-existent. Isis found it at length and placed it on the body, and the virile power of Osiris was so great that he begot Harpokrates forthwith. After this figures of Osiris as an ithyphallic mummy became common in Egypt. See Hopfner in *Archiv Orientální* or *Journal of the Czechoslovak Oriental Institute*, Prague, April 1931, No. 1, p. 122 f.

men and had truly spiritual aspirations and yearnings. They were conscious of their sins and longed to be free from guilt before their god, even after they had offered up the statutory sacrifices and oblations. This fact is clearly proved by *The Teaching of Amen-en-apt* (ed. Budge, London, 1924). But their highest and best spiritual ideas and conceptions were overshadowed by their ineradicable belief in magic. The wheat was choked by the tares. This either checked their growth or wholly prevented their development into a religious system which would have enabled them to commit their souls and bodies in absolute confidence and freedom into the hands of Almighty God, the Everlasting Father and Maker of All. From first to last the EGYPTIAN believed that the performance of ritual ceremonies, coupled with ceremonial personal cleanliness, produced holiness. 'I am pure. I am pure. I am pure', says the scribe NU. 'I have washed my front parts with the water of libations, I have cleansed my hinder parts with drugs which make wholly clean, and my inward parts have been washed in the liquor of *maāt*. There is no single member of mine which lacketh righteousness.' Such a condition of body and mind induced emotions which secured for a man life after death in a state of perpetual bliss, and were his only means of obtaining immortal life and salvation. His belief was due to the emotions stimulated as we have seen by ritual ceremonies, in other words to religious mysticism, otherwise called magic sacramentalism, which killed true religion in EGYPT generally. Bishop BARNES says rightly, 'In theory we may separate religion from magic. It is doubtful . . . if primitive man ever made the separation: at any rate, as every close observer knows, the vitality of magical beliefs in present day religion is great' (*Scientific Theory and Religion*, p. 546). But, on the other hand, let us never forget that the priests of MEMPHIS more than five thousand years ago proclaimed the existence of a self-created, self-subsisting, and eternal Creator, who was a Spiritual Essence, and thus doing they abandoned the cult of the fetish in favour of the worship of God.

PART I

I

THE RELIGIONS OF ANCIENT EGYPT

THE most cursory perusal of the religious texts of every period of Egyptian History will convince the reader that from first to last the EGYPTIAN was a very religious man. But it will also show him that many religions flourished simultaneously in EGYPT, and that as the EGYPTIAN advanced in civilization he unhesitatingly changed his religious views. Which, then, of these religions was the 'Egyptian Religion'? The early Egyptologists talked and wrote about the religion of EGYPT which was revealed to them by a limited number of papyri and inscriptions upon stone monuments, and they spoke of the 'Egyptian Religion' as we speak of Judaism, Christianity, and Muhammadanism (i.e. Islâm), not realizing how greatly they were hampered by their imperfect knowledge of the Egyptian language. It is now evident that there never existed in EGYPT a form of religion which was generally accepted and practised throughout the country. And there is reason for thinking that in the earliest period the EGYPTIANS had no religion of any kind, and only an elaborate system of magic which satisfied their elementary spiritual needs, and at a later period became not only the foundation of all the various schemes of religion which came into being, but formed the larger and most important part of each of them in the minds of the people. This is not to be wondered at, for the texts written in the dynastic period prove that the EGYPTIAN in every period of his history was a lover of the drama. The ceremonies, or rituals, were performed in connexion with the utterance of spells and the recital of words of power, i.e. magical formulae, and he was content to believe that their efficacy was at least as great as the magical or holy words.

Even with the help of the large amount of material with which the scribes and priests of the dynastic period have provided us, it is by no means easy to describe accurately all that the EGYPTIANS believed in respect of the future life during that period. It is more difficult still, nay, it is impossible, to give even in outline a connected account of the various stages of the beliefs of the predynastic

EGYPTIANS from the time when they worshipped the stars and the sun and moon, animals, fetishes or idols, evil spirits, &c., to the period when they adopted the cult of OSIRIS. It is tolerably certain that the predynastic period lasted several thousands of years, but who shall say how many? Our old friend the 'general reader' must be necessarily greatly disturbed in mind when he compares the systems of chronology proposed by the various Egyptologists. According to Dr. BREASTED, MENES began to reign about 3400 B.C., and according to Sir FLINDERS PETRIE about 5500 B.C., the difference between the two dates being 2,100 years. Such views are so widely divergent that nothing can well reconcile them (H. P. COOKE, *Osiris*, p. 165). Either we have not sufficient information to decide which authority is correct, or we have misinterpreted such facts as we have. One or the other authority may be right, but I believe that both are wrong. LEPSIUS and BIRCH thought that MENES began to reign about 3800 B.C., following MANETHO fairly closely, and their opinion is undoubtedly sound and sane.

The flints which have been collected from the deserts on the banks of the NILE in EGYPT and the Egyptian SÛDÂN show that there was both a Palaeolithic and a Neolithic period in EGYPT, but of the former we possess nothing but its flints, and of the latter such remains as we have belong to the two or three centuries which immediately precede the dynastic period. It is futile to attempt to assign a date for the beginning of the predynastic period, but our greatest authority on flints is inclined to think that the Neolithic period began about 10000 B.C. There is absolutely no authority for the statement, which has appeared in various papers, that there was a civilization in EGYPT as early as 15000 B.C. The remains of the latter part of the Neolithic period which are now in the great collections preserved in LONDON, PARIS, BERLIN, AMERICA, and EGYPT, were found in UPPER EGYPT, and owe their existence to the dryness of the soil in which they were buried. In LOWER EGYPT, i.e. the Delta, the annual NILE flood has destroyed not only the bodies of its predynastic inhabitants but also their works.

The monuments prove that towards the close of the Neolithic period the EGYPTIANS had reached a comparatively high state of civilization. EGYPT was divided into two parts, each of which was ruled by a king, a fact which the evidence of the PALERMO STONE makes certain. The southern part or kingdom included that portion of the NILE valley which lies between ÂL-KÂB and CAIRO, and the northern part or kingdom was formed by the Delta. Each kingdom was divided into provinces, which we know as Nomes, and each nome acknowledged a tutelary deity. We have no written records to help us in finding out what the religious beliefs of the predynastic EGYPTIAN were, for the art of writing was unknown to him until almost the close of the predynastic period. But many of his 'gods' were adopted by the Heliopolitan theologians of the early centuries of the dynastic period, and their fundamental doctrines were based upon predynastic beliefs which were well established and had been current throughout the Delta for hundreds of years. The priests of HELIOPOLIS were not skilful theologians, and their own carelessness as well as the ignorance of their scribes produced a system of theology which defies unravelling and systematization. The proof of these statements is provided by the religious and funerary inscriptions which are found inside several of the royal pyramids at ṢAḲḲÂRAH, and were engraved on the walls of their corridors and chambers for kings of the Vth and VIth dynasties. The texts are often quoted in this book as the 'Pyramid Texts', or Pyr. §, followed by the number of the paragraph. Various sections, or groups of paragraphs, were written at different periods; the oldest were composed in the predynastic period and the youngest was drafted under one or other of the five kings for whom the compilations were made, that is to say, about one hundred and fifty years later. It is evident in some paragraphs that the scribe did not know the meanings of the texts he was drafting, but then this is not to be wondered at, for many of the words in the oldest paragraphs had become obsolete. Many passages refer to primitive star-worship, many more to the worship of animals and natural objects, and references to animistic cults and fetish-worship are not uncommon, and confusion of ideas and contradictions are not rare. In the oldest of the five Pyramid Texts the predominant god is RĀ, the Sun-god, but in the latest, the god-incarnate OSIRIS, giver of everlasting life, the beloved of the people generally as opposed to the Court and its officials, has usurped his power and attributes and position.

As the first edition of the Pyramid Texts was not published until the 'eighties of the last century, the early Egyptologists knew nothing of their contents and so were led into error when they formed their opinions of the character of what they called the 'Egyptian Religion'. They had no idea that there was more than one religion in EGYPT, and they never realized the number and variety of the changes which took place in the religious beliefs of the EGYPTIANS as they advanced from the cults of spirits and fetishes to the conception of a self-created god who was the creator of the universe. Moreover, they had no clear idea of the Heliopolitan system of theology which was already well established under the Old Kingdom, and the discoveries at ABYDOS and elsewhere which revealed the state of civilization of the EGYPTIANS towards the end of the Neolithic period had not been made.

THE EGYPTIAN RELIGION ACCORDING TO THE EARLY EGYPTOLOGISTS

CHAMPOLLION-FIGEAC, relying on information supplied by his brother,[1] the great CHAMPOLLION, wrote: 'The Egyptian religion is a pure monotheism which manifested itself externally by a symbolic polytheism' (*Égypte*, PARIS, 1839, p. 245, col. i). The Vicomte E. DE ROUGÉ, who had spent many years in the study of the Egyptian monuments in the Museum of the LOUVRE, published a summary of his views on the Egyptian Religion in his famous *Notice sommaire des monuments Égyptiens exposés dans les galeries du Musée du Louvre*, PARIS, 1855, and in the *Revue Archéologique*, PARIS, 1860, p. 72. He was convinced that the ancient religion of EGYPT was monotheistic, because the EGYPTIANS believed in the existence of 'One Great God', the Θεὸς εἷς of IAMBLICHUS (see PARTHEY, *Iamblichi de Mysteriis Liber*, BERLIN, 1857, p. 261 f.). DE ROUGÉ wrote:

'The unity of a supreme and self-existent being, his eternity, his almightiness, and external reproduction thereby as God; the attribution of the creation of the world and of all living beings to this supreme God; the immortality of the soul, completed by the dogma of punishments and rewards; such is the sublime and persistent basis which, notwithstanding all deviations and all mythological embellishments, must secure for the beliefs of

[1] Champollion died leaving the great work which he had begun unfinished; his *Panthéon Égyptien* was to have filled several volumes, but only the plates were printed.

the ancient Egyptians a most honourable place among the religions of antiquity.'

And DE ROUGÉ held these same views nine years after ('Conférénce sur la Religion des anciens Égyptiens', in *Annales de Philosophie Chrétienne*, 5ième Série, PARIS, 1869, tom. xx, pp. 325–37).[1] DE ROUGÉ'S views were shared by CHABAS and PIERRET,[2] and THÉODULE DEVÉRIA in FRANCE. The last-named had studied intensively for many years the great collection of Egyptian funerary papyri in the LOUVRE. He was engaged in preparing a summary of the notes on the religion of EGYPT and her gods which he had made whilst writing his *Catalogue des Manuscrits Égyptiens conservés au Musée Égyptien du Louvre*, PARIS, 1881, but he died in JANUARY 1871, and Egyptology suffered a great loss. No other scholar had such a wide and competent knowledge of the PER-T-EM-HRU or, *Book of the Dead*. DE ROUGÉ'S views on the monotheistic character of the Egyptian Religion was shared by MASPERO for several years, but an article by RICHARD PIETSCHMANN, entitled 'Der aegyptische Fetishdienst und Götterglaube' (in the *Zeitschrift für Ethnographie*, BERLIN, 1878, Band X, pp. 153–82), caused him to alter his whole attitude towards the religious ceremonies and beliefs of the EGYPTIANS. In his later works he never missed an opportunity of showing how greatly the dynastic theologian borrowed from his savage, or half-civilized, predynastic predecessor. BIRCH'S views on the subject are given in the little book *Egypt* (vol. iii of *Ancient History from the Monuments*, LONDON, 1880, p. x), in which he says: 'The idea of a single self-existent deity was indeed stated in the hymns and prayers addressed to certain gods, who are said to have animated or produced all beings, or to have been the universal and animating principle of nature. At a later period the eight great gods were considered different[3] in the colleges of THEBES and MEMPHIS.' The most strenuous supporter of the old Egyptian dogma of the Unity

[1] 'La croyance à l'Unité du Dieu suprème, à ses attributs de Créateur et de Législateur de l'homme, qu'il a doué d'une âme immortelle; voilà, les notions primitives enchâssées comme des diamants indestructibles au milieu des superfétations mythologiques accumulées par les siècles qui ont passé sur cette vieille civilisation.'

[2] See *Le Panthéon Égyptien*, Paris, 1881, p. 4.

[3] He means that the names of the eight gods (ogdoad) of Thebes were different from those of the eight gods of Memphis; curiously enough, he omits to mention the eight gods of Heliopolis and Hermopolis.

or Oneness of God was H. BRUGSCH, who collected from Egyptian texts of all periods a number of extracts[1] in which the power and attributes of God the Creator are clearly expressed. It need hardly be said that this God had many names. The extracts are very instructive and informing, and I have given a rendering of many of them later on in this book.

[1] See *Religion und Mythologie der alten Aegypter*, Leipzig, 1885, pp. 96–9.

II

PREDYNASTIC CULTS: ANIMISM; FETISHISM; GODS AND GODDESSES OF FETISH ORIGIN; THE CULTS OF ANIMALS, BIRDS, REPTILES, ETC.; THE ANTHROPOMORPHIZATION OF FETISHES; THE CULT OF MEN GODS; IDOLS; FABULOUS ANIMALS; NOME FETISHES

ANIMISM

ONE of the oldest forms of religion in the predynastic period was what is now called ANIMISM. This included the worship of the souls of men, especially of those who were dead, the worship of incorporeal spirits who govern the natural world and who for good or evil direct or interfere with the affairs of men. The worship of the souls of the dead, commonly called ANCESTOR-WORSHIP, was based upon the anxiety of the living (1) to obtain the goodwill and favour and help of the souls of their dead relations and friends, and (2) to avert any and every kind of evil which the dead souls might have the power to inflict upon their living kinsfolk and friends and connexions. Primitive man believed that all animate and many inanimate objects possessed qualities which resembled those of his mind and soul, and that these qualities could detach themselves from the bodies in which they were living. Once separated from their own bodies, these qualities, or as they are commonly called 'spirits', were supposed to have the power of taking any form they pleased. It was believed that such spirits were always watching for opportunities to enter into and occupy the bodies of men and animals, and when they did so they completely changed the character of his actions and general life, and produced disease, usually of a most malignant kind, and death. Disembodied spirits were generally divided by their worshippers into various classes or groups, and the groups had different names and were supposed to possess special dwelling-places and powers.

The spirits of natural objects were supposed to be able to abandon the objects in which they usually dwelt, and to take human or animal forms. The greater number of them were held to be foes of men, and to be the causes of every disaster and calamity which took place. Some of them were so evil that they assumed the forms of the holy souls of the dead in order to carry out their nefarious designs, and they were thought to disguise themselves in the forms of the generous and friendly spirits who, if not helpers of man, did nothing to injure him. The spirits of nature directed the motions of the heavenly bodies and produced thunder, lightning, earthquakes, disastrous floods, and all calamities. Usually it was some disaster which revealed their presence, but at a very early period men began to regard as dwelling-places dear to them certain animals, birds, reptiles, trees, woods, hills, and mountains which became objects of fear, reverence, and worship. Primitive man regarded all nature as an aggregate of animated entities, and every happening in his daily life, and the actions of animate and inanimate objects he attributed to the operation of some spirit. There were, however, among the nature spirits a number who were distinctly favourable to man, and when these were identified attempts were made to retain their favour and protection permanently by means of gifts and offerings, and by the use of magical drama and spells. At a later period benevolent spirits of this kind became 'gods', and magicians claimed to possess powers which would make them the servants of his clients. The number of the evil spirits who were believed to exist by the EGYPTIAN is beyond count, and the dread and terror of them filled the minds of men in every period of Egyptian history. It was thought that the EVIL EYE which belonged to a malevolent man had the power to detach itself from that man and to put on a special form, and so was enabled to do evils unimaginable.

The religious texts show that gods as well as men were ever in danger from their spirit enemies, and gods, like men, only maintained themselves in safety by the use of magical ceremonies and spells. Animism must have preceded the magical cults of the predynastic EGYPTIANS, and it, in its turn, was succeeded by the cults of animals, birds, reptiles, trees, &c., which after animism formed the predominant part of the later religion of the EGYPTIANS. The great merit and importance of it in connexion with religious beliefs consisted, in the fact that it embraced a qualified TOTEMISM and FETISHISM and prepared the way for the higher classes of spirits to become 'gods'. In its highest form it probably gave solace and comfort to many religious though uninstructed men.

FETISHISM

All the authorities agree in saying that the word FETISH is derived, through the French, from the Portuguese *feitiço*, which in its turn, comes from the Latin *factitius*, but the views which are current as to what FETISHISM is are divergent and in some cases absolutely contradictory. There seems to be no doubt that there are several kinds of fetishism, but the ancient Egyptian form of it is best described by E. B. TYLOR, GOBLET D'ALVIELLA, and R. H. NASSAU. According to TYLOR fetishism 'is the doctrine of spirits embodied in, or attached to, or conveying influences through, certain material objects' which become 'vessels or vehicles or instruments of spiritual beings'.

. . . 'To class an object as a fetish demands explicit statement that a spirit is considered as embodied in it or acting through it or communicating by it, or at least that the people it belongs to do habitually think this of such objects; or it must be shown that the object is treated as having personal consciousness and power, is talked with, worshipped, prayed to, sacrificed to, petted or ill-treated with reference to its past or present behaviour to its votaries' (*Primitive Culture*, vol. ii, pp. 144, 145).

GOBLET D'ALVIELLA (*Hibbert Lectures*, LONDON, 1891) defines fetishism as the 'belief that the appropriation of a thing may secure the services of the spirit lodged within it'. And an object becomes a FETISH when spirits penetrate into it, and so make it the vehicle or organ of their own personality. He carefully distinguishes between the talisman or amulet and the fetish, for in the former the spirits act on inanimate things from without, using them as implements, while in the latter the spirits are embodied in a concrete object. On AFRICAN fetishism see NASSAU, *Fetishism in West Africa*, LONDON, 1904. This work contains the best and fullest account of West African Fetishism which has hitherto appeared.

GODS AND GODDESSES OF FETISH ORIGIN

Among the gods and goddesses of fetish origin may be mentioned the following:

NET, the NEITH of the Greeks. The centre of her cult was SAÏS in the Western Delta in the Vth nome of LOWER EGYPT. The oldest form of her name is  (see Pyr. § 489). Some think that this hieroglyph represents a shuttle and would connect her name with 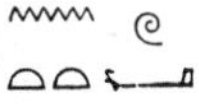

Net (Neith) Lady of Saïs, wearing the Crown of the North and holding in her hands a bow, two arrows and the symbol of 'Life'.

Hathor as the star-bespangled Heaven-Cow, wearing the plumes of Rā, her father, and the solar disk encircled with a cobra from the mouth of which hangs the symbol of power 

Hathor in the Heaven-Tree providing the deceased with food and drink.

Bronze *menat* amulet showing the different forms of Hathor.

Neḥemāuit, i.e. 'Sweeper away of oppressed', a form of Hathor and a counterpart of Thete.

ntt, to weave. But she might have woven spells as well as flax, and she may have been a goddess of magic. But in later times she wears on her head , i.e. crossed arrows, or or . The crossed arrows, which with a shield form the badge of the Vth nome, suggest that she was a goddess of the chase (DIANA of the GREEKS), but what do and really represent? It seems that originally

The Cow-goddess Hathor, Queen of the Underworld, appearing out of the funerary mountain of Western Thebes.

Hathor, Queen of the gods, wearing the head-dress of Mut, the horns of Isis, the disk of Rā, and the feather of Shu.

she was a Cow-goddess for she is identified with HATHOR and ISIS; the object probably represents some part of her body, but the scribes did not know what it was. She was the Virgin-mother of the Sun-god, and the 'Mother-goddess' of the Western Delta.

The Cow-goddesses HATHOR and NEḤEMĀUIT are often seen wearing solar and lunar disks on their heads, and these refer to their solar or lunar origin. But they sometimes wear the object here roughly outlined ; in the centre opening is a cobra, and on each side is a cobra ready to strike.[1] The ancient scribes did not know what HATHOR's fetish object represented, and they drew a funerary building guarded by cobras. The name HATHOR *Ḥet-Ḥor* means the 'House of Horus', a name of that portion of the sky which is called QEBḤU (Pyr. PEPI I, l. 593). Originally HATHOR was a form of

[1] See Lanzone, *Mitologia*, pls. 317, 318.

the great World-Mother, who was 'the mother of her father, and the daughter of her son', and also the wife of the chief of the Nine Gods.[1] Gods and goddesses could have seven aspects or forms, and hence we have the Seven HATHORS in the *Tale of the Two Brothers*, and the *Papyrus of Nesi Amsu* (BRIT. MUS. Papyrus, No. 10188, and see BUDGE in *Archaeologia*, vol. lii). HATHOR dwelt in the great Tree

Meskhenit, one of the four goddesses of the birth-chamber.

Renenit, the celestial cobra nurse who suckled the Pharaohs.

of Heaven and supplied the souls of the dead with celestial food (*Book of the Dead*, chaps. lii, lxiii A, lxviii, and lxxxii. 7).

The goddess ANIT and her sister goddesses TANENIT, MESKHENIT, and others wear on their heads the object here outlined; this is probably an attempt to represent the *vulva* of a cow, which we find in flint in the form of; it was then used as an amulet. MESKHENIT had four forms and all were goddesses connected with the birth chamber and birth stool and birth stones, and they were able to predict the futures of children when newly born. Their husband was SHAI who was regarded as the personification of Luck, Fate, and Destiny. The word *Shai* means 'what is ordained', like the Arabic ḲISMAT.

The goddess SESḤAT is often represented by the

[1] See Brugsch, *Mythologische Inschriften*, Leipzig, 1884, p. 801.

hieroglyph here given ; and her name appears under the form of . She is depicted in the form of a woman wearing a leopard skin and holding a writing-reed and a scribe's palette in her

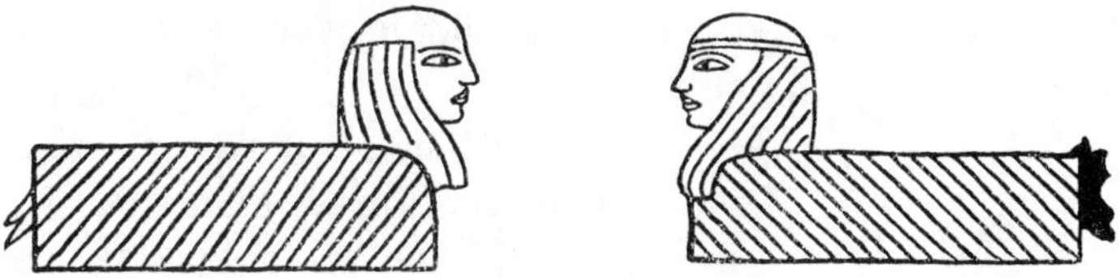

The Two Birth Stones.
(הָאָבְנָיִם Exodus i, 16).

Sesheta.

Isis as a bird of prey with her fetish-symbol on her head.

Nephthys with her fetish-symbol on her head.

hands. She was the celestial librarian and is called the 'lady of books' . She dwelt by the Tree of Heaven, and as the Remembrancer of the gods wrote down on the leaves of the tree the deeds and duration of life of every man and every god. (See LANZONE, op. cit., pl. 360 and p. 1068.) The later EGYPTIANS did not know what her fetish was, and they called her SEFKH-T ĀBUI. Some modern writers in trying to describe her fetish call it a pair of cow's horns inverted over a star, but the so-called star is really a flower.

Over the heads of figures of ISIS and NEPHTHYS we often see the names of these goddesses, viz. or ISIS and NEPHTHYS.

These names I believe to be misrepresentations of their fetishes, which the scribes failed to identify.

The dynastic drawings of gods sometimes supply indications of their fetish origins, and among such may be mentioned:

1. SEPṬ, a god of the XXth nome of LOWER EGYPT who is called 'Lord of the East', 'Smiter of the MENTIU', 'Lord of slaughter', and 'Warrior of EGYPT'. For pictures of him see LANZONE, pls. 356, 357. His oldest title is 'SEPṬ of the teeth (or tusks)' (Pyr. § 201 *d*). The sign is, no doubt, a picture of the original fetish of the god, which was a tooth or a tusk of some savage animal or bird which in dynastic times had become extinct. He was worshipped as HORUS the Elder at PER-SEPṬ (SAFṬ AL-HANNAH in the WÂDÎ TÛMÎLÂT, the GOSHEN of the HEBREWS) where grew the famous *Kesbet* trees which are mentioned in the Pyramid Texts (§ 1476 *c*).

Horus of the Eastern Desert; a form of Sepṭ.

2. MIN or MENU a hieroglyph which was formerly read AMSI and KHEM;[1] he usually appears in the form of an ithyphallic man. His paternity is claimed for many gods, RĀ, OSIRIS, SHU, KHEPRI, ISIS, &c. His worship was universal in EGYPT and NUBIA but the centre of his cult was KHEMMIS[2] (PANOPOLIS) and COPTOS. He was the tutelary god of all nomads and hunters, and the whole of the Eastern Desert as far as the RED SEA was his domain. The oldest statues of MIN, which were originally painted black, represent him as a man standing upright and holding a huge phallus in his left hand; in his right hand is a whip (?). The great antiquity of these statues is proved by the fact that the legs are not shown singly, but are close together; they are carefully described by CAPART, *Les*

[1] How these forms came into being is explained by Sethe, *Urgeschichte*, p. 39, note 3.

[2] Khemmis = Khem Min, i.e. the 'shrine of Min'; from this comes the Arabic name of the city Akhmîm.

Débuts de l'Art, p. 257, and compare SETHE, *Urgeschichte*, p. 17. MIN was the god of procreation and fertility *par excellence*. In drawings of the dynastic period his hand and whip are raised above his head (LANZONE, pl. 332), and he is called the 'god of the lifted hand'. The hieroglyph for the god's name is composed of two parts, viz. and the standard ; the first represents the fetish of MIN, but what that object was we do not know. The form of the fetish found on

Menu, the god of 'the lifted hand', wearing plumes. A late form.

Round temple of Menu with a streamer flying from the roof.

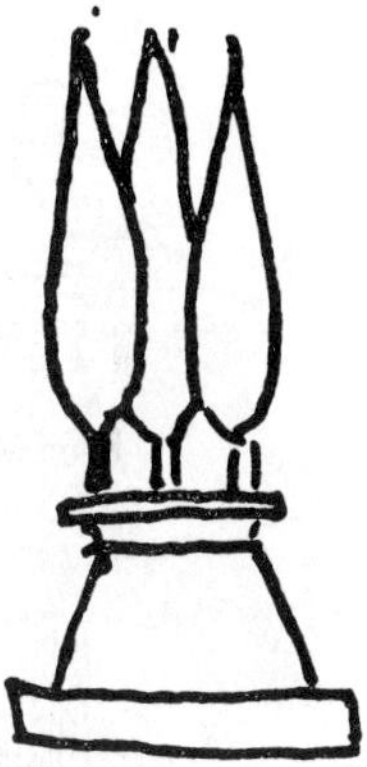

A grove of Menu where phallic rites were performed.

predynastic objects is something like the rough drawings here given 1. . 2. . The character of the god suggests that the fetish was in some way connected with coition, and the second form may represent the union of the male and female organs of generation. A fetish of the same form exists in CHINA and JAPAN at the present day. The worship of the phallic god AAḤES (or RAḤES)[1] of COPTOS seems to have been merged in that of MIN. The 'god-house' or temple of MIN was round,[2] and resembled the churches in ABYSSINIA, and the dwelling-houses in the Egyptian SÛDÂN. The drawings of it show that the building was built among trees, which recall the 'groves' of the Bible. A number of small trees or shrubs are seen near the temple, and these probably represent

[1] See on this name Sethe, *Urgeschichte*, p. 39.

[2] See Lefébure, 'Les Huttes de Cham', in *Muséon*, tom. xvii, 1898, pp. 193 ff., 349 ff.

plants possessing the properties of aphrodisiacs. According to a note by Dr. GARDINER (*Contendings of Horus and Set*, p. 22) these plants were lettuces.

The cult of MENU or MIN in his special character as the god of virility and generation was widespread in EGYPT and was far

Osiris, the Aged One, holding the crook of rule and the whip, crowned with the Ṭeṭ and horns, solar disk, plumes, and cobras.

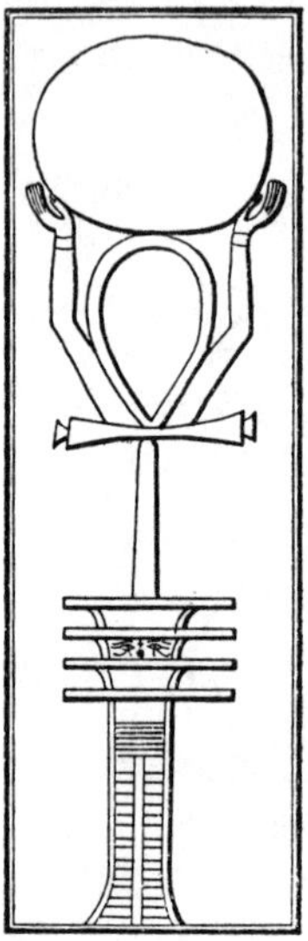

The solar disk raised by Ānkh from out of the fetish-tree of Osiris.

more important than has hitherto been recognized. His public festivals were numerous and the king and his Court-officials assisted at them, for the maintenance and growth of the population were believed to depend wholly upon the favour of this god. Statues of the god were carried in procession through the towns, and mystery plays were performed, and the lower classes made the festivals of MENU excuses for orgies and debauches and the gratification of unbridled lust. The festivals of MENU appear to have been more popular than those of OSIRIS. The priesthood of MENU was a very powerful body, and they condoned sexual excesses, and appear to have made prostitution a religious profession. The cult of the god has been elaborately treated by

H. GAUTIER in 'Les Fêtes du dieu Min', and 'Le Personnel du dieu Min' in P. JOUQUET, *Recherches d'archéologie, de philologie et d'histoire*, tom. ii and iii.

3. The hieroglyph 𓊽 *Teṭ* undoubtedly represents a fetish, which was worshipped at BUSIRIS and MENDES in the Delta at a very early period, and later became associated with the cult of OSIRIS. According to PLUTARCH the fetish was a hollow tree trunk, which restored to life the dead who were placed in it. OSIRIS was identified with the ṬEṬ (or *Ded*) and the 'setting upright of the ṬEṬ' formed a very important act in the drama of the resurrection of OSIRIS. The ṬEṬ is one of the four great fetishes or amulets given in the Papyrus of ANI (chap. clv) and the text suggests that, under the New Kingdom, it was in some way connected with the backbone of a man. The text is clear: 'Rise thou up, O OSIRIS, thou hast thy backbone. O Still-heart, thou hast the tendons of thy neck and back. Set thou thyself upon thy base: I will set water under thee.' The fetish object 𓊽 became very popular as an amulet throughout the dynastic period, and models of it in gold, crystal, porcelain, gilded wood, &c., were laid on and inside the body, and worn by the living as ornaments. The ornamentations of some of these suggest that the original fetish was a tree trunk girt about with metal bands.[1]

4. Another fetish object is represented by the hieroglyph 𓎬 *Tjet*. Models of it in our museums are made of red stone, red paste, or reddish porcelain and fine carnelian, in accordance with the rubric of chapter clvi of the Theban *Book of the Dead*. A coloured drawing of the object forms the vignette of this chapter, and the text reads, 'The blood of ISIS, the spells of ISIS, the magic (𓎛𓂓𓏛𓏥 *ḥekau*) of ISIS, are mighty to protect this great one (i.e. the deceased), and to fetter him that would do to him what is an abomination'. The rubric says that if the TJET be dipped in water wherein *ānkham* plants have been steeped, and tied to the neck of the deceased on the day of his burial, it will be as the fluid of life to him, and he shall have the

[1] In the volume dedicated to Prof. Ll. Griffith by his friends, Dr. Schäfer has put forward another explanation of the 𓊽, but it does not seem to me to be convincing, *Djed-Pfeiler, Lebenszeichen*, &c. The drawings he gives certainly seem to represent the tops of trees, or branches of trees, or of a single tree, and this takes us back to the *erica* spoken of by Plutarch. The original fetish was, I believe, connected with the genitalia of a man, but the later people did not know what it was.

power of traversing all heaven and earth. But care must be taken to tie the object to his neck secretly, for any unauthorized onlooker might steal away its magical powers. The real value of the object

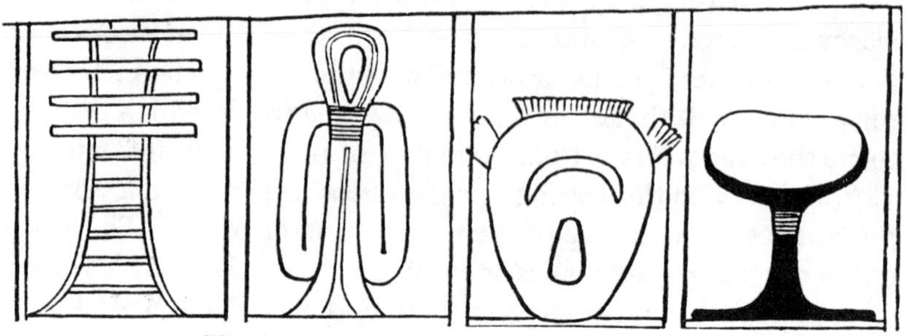

The four great fetishes in the Papyrus of Ani.

1. Osiris. 2. Isis. 3. The heart. 4. The object of the head-supports.

The Tjet personified as a female (the Sky-goddess Nut).

to the EGYPTIAN was that it possessed the power of the blood of ISIS, probably the menstrual blood, and I believe that it represents that portion of the body of the goddess whence came the blood. In a drawing reproduced by LANZONE (pl. 151) a goddess is seen rising out of the TJET in exactly the same way as we see OSIRIS growing out of the 𓊽. Dr. SCHÄFER thinks that the TJET 𓎬 is the female equivalent of 𓋹 ĀNKH, and thinks it may have been a 'Kultbild'.

THE CULTS OF ANIMALS, BIRDS, REPTILES, ETC.

The worship of animals formed an integral part of all the religions of the EGYPTIANS in every period of their history. Various reasons are given for this by modern writers. (1) Animals were worshipped because they were strong, or swift, or virile, or cunning, or pretty, or because they could be useful for domestic service. (2) Animals were worshipped because men feared them. (3) Animals were worshipped by the EGYPTIANS as a religious duty, because they were believed to be the abodes of the spirits of divine and other beings. It is pretty certain that every animal or bird or creature which was an object of worship possessed some special mark or characteristic which distinguished it from all others of its class. Thus the black bull of APIS had a white triangular blaze on his forehead, the figure of an eagle (vulture or hawk?) on his back, the figure of a beetle on his tongue, and he had double hairs in his tail (HERODOTUS, iii. 28). According to AELIAN (*De Nat. Animalium* xi. 10) APIS could be distinguished by twenty-nine distinct marks, which were known to the priests. The MNEVIS Bull of HELIOPOLIS, and the BACHIS Bull, and the Bull of KAKAM no doubt also possessed special marks, or characteristics, or qualities.[1] The same was the case with the Ram of MENDES and the hawks which were believed to be incarnations of the spirit of the Sun-god. Greek and Roman travellers and historians described the Egyptian worship of animals as a 'ludicrous and gross superstition'. The prophet ISAIAH included sacred animals among the idols which were to be 'moved' when the Lord came to EGYPT (xix. 1). The Egyptologist cannot give a summary of the reasons which made animal worship such an important part of the great mixture of beliefs which formed the so-called 'Egyptian Religion', for the texts say nothing about them. But it is wholly wrong to say, as some have done, that animal worship was a product of the period of decadence in EGYPT when men had either lost or forgotten their belief in the One God, and were in consequence giving themselves over to the grossest forms of superstition, and debased symbolism, and the chaotic welter of beliefs which were engendered by the materialism of the day. Like the cult of OSIRIS animal worship

[1] See Wiedermann, 'Quelques Remarques sur la Culte des animaux en Égypte', in *Muséon*, tom. vi. 2, pp. 113–28.

No. 1

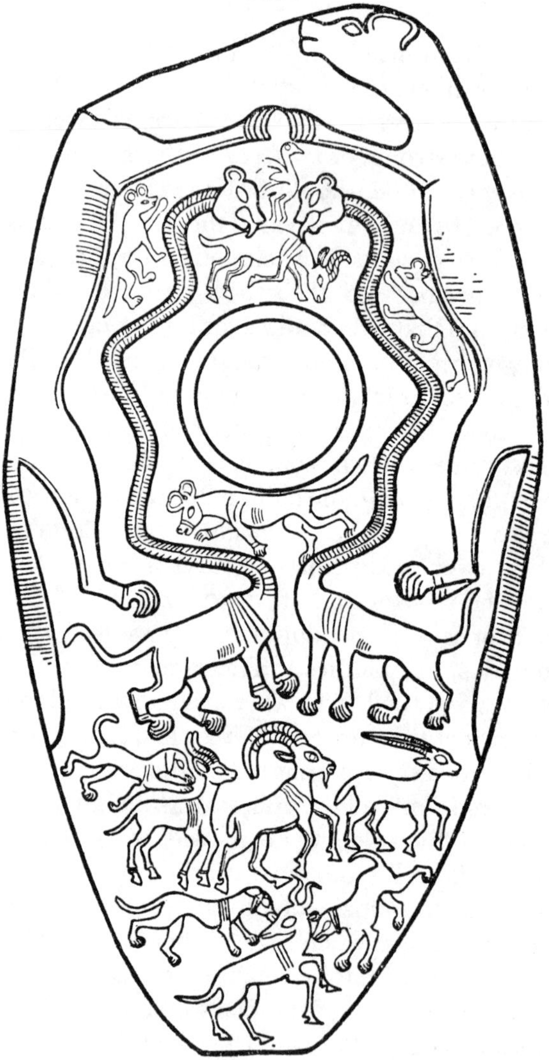

Obverse.

was a form of the religion of the people, and like magic it was ineradicable from their beliefs.

The outline drawings printed on pages 68, 69, 70, and 71 are of special interest in connexion with the study of the representations of animals on the Egyptian monuments, for they are made from the

No. 2

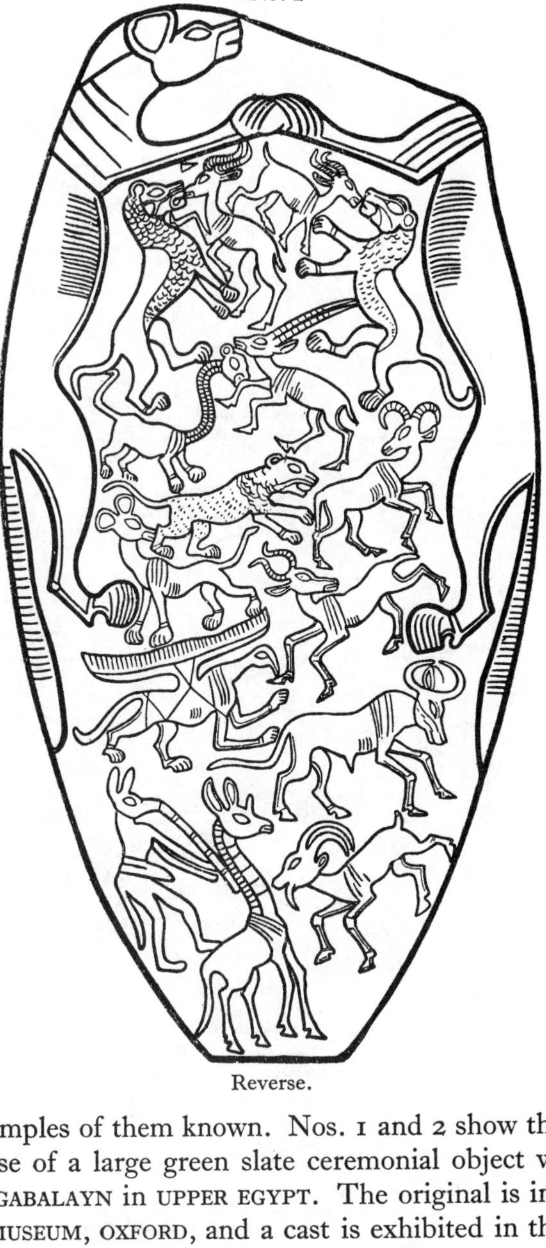

Reverse.

oldest examples of them known. Nos. 1 and 2 show the obverse and reverse of a large green slate ceremonial object which was found at GABALAYN in UPPER EGYPT. The original is in the ASHMOLEAN MUSEUM, OXFORD, and a cast is exhibited in the BRITISH MUSEUM (No. 35715). *Obverse.* The absurdly elongated necks of

No. 3

Obverse.

two animals (giraffes ?) enclose a circular hollow, and at each edge of the object, in high relief, is a hunting-dog (?) with a bushy tail. The long-necked beasts are biting into a horned animal, and between their heads is an ostrich. In the field below lions are seen attacking oryxes and other horned animals. *Reverse*. Here, on

No. 4

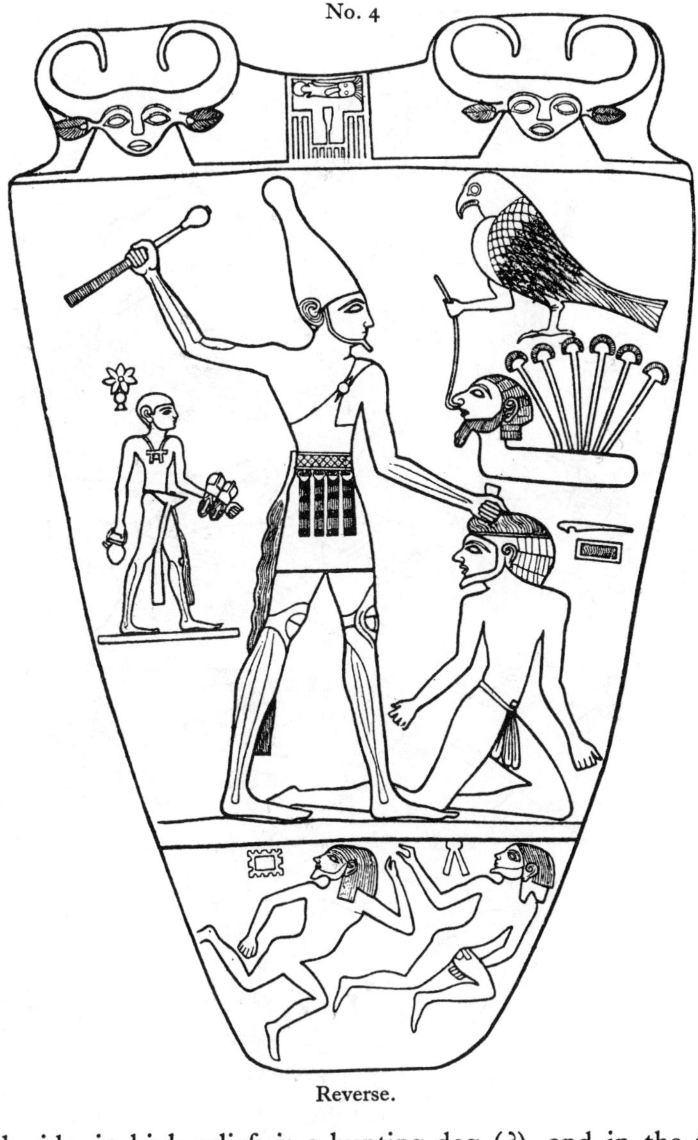

Reverse.

each side, in high relief, is a hunting dog (?), and in the field are seen lions attacking several kinds of horned beasts, wild goats gazelle, oryxes, a giraffe (?), a vulture (?), &c. All these animals were found in the deserts of UPPER EGYPT; no Sûdânî animal, elephant, rhinoceros, hippopotamus, crocodile, baboon, is

No. 5

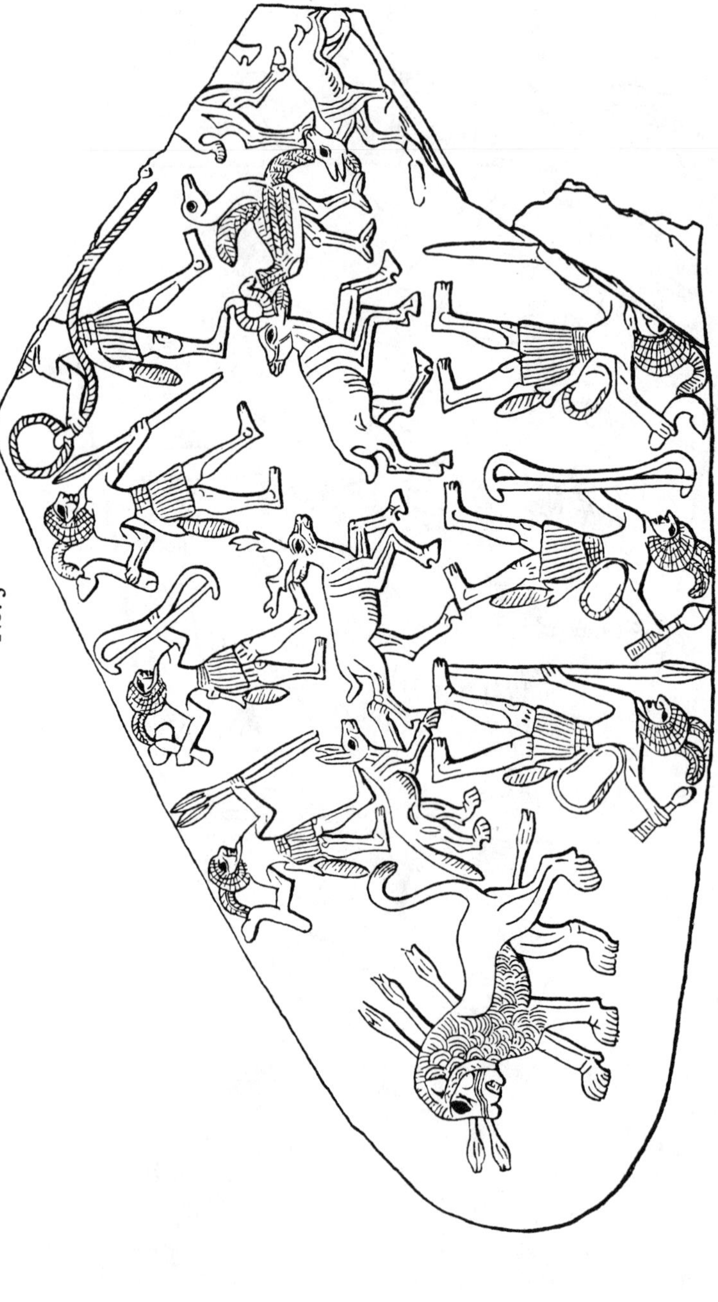

A hunting scene of the early dynastic period. The hunters, wearing feathers in their hair, and tails, are armed with boomerangs, double-headed axes, spears, bows and arrows, and a lasso, and are helped by dogs. The creatures hunted are lions, antelopes, oryxes, ostriches, &c. The original green slate object is in the British Museum, No. 20700.

represented. Nos. 3 and 4 were drawn from the original in the EGYPTIAN MUSEUM in CAIRO. On the *obverse* are: (1) The king's name, NĀRMER, between two heads of HATHOR. (2) The king going to inspect decapitated enemies. (3) Men lassoing lions (?). (4) A bull (i.e. the king) knocking down the walls of town. On the *reverse* are: (1) The king's name between two heads of HATHOR. (2) The king clubbing to death captives. Behind him is his sandal bearer, and before him the hawk of HORUS, the capturer of 6,000 captives; he holds the leader by a chain in his nose. (3) Dead enemies.

Serapis, from a relief at Meroë.

Sacred Animals

The principal sacred animals were:

The Bull APIS, in Egyptian ḤAP , was worshipped at MEMPHIS as an incarnation of OSIRIS and the second life of PTAḤ. SEKER, the god of the underworld of MEMPHIS, was united to OSIRIS, who had become ASAR-ḤAP, i.e. SARAPIS[1] or SERAPIS, and thus the Bull of MEMPHIS became PTAḤ–SEKER–ASAR, the triune god of the resurrection. AELIAN says (xi. 10) that the cult of APIS was established by MENA (MENES), and MANETHO says the Bull of HELIOPOLIS was established by KA-KAU (IInd dynasty).[2] HERODOTUS in speaking of EPAPHOS (iii. 28), i.e. APIS, makes a mistake about the blaze on the forehead of APIS the bull. He says that it was a white and four-sided λευκὸν τετράγωνον, but on the bronze figures of APIS in our museums (e.g. BRITISH MUSEUM, No. 54482) the blaze is triangular. For statements about APIS see PLINY, viii. 72, AMMIANUS MARCELLINUS, xxii. 14, STRABO, xvii. 31, DIODORUS, i. 85, PLUTARCH, *De Iside*, § 56. The APIS bulls were buried with great pomp and ceremony in the Serapeum at ṢAḲḲÂRAH.[3]

[1] Serapis was identified by the Greeks with Pluto or Hades; his worship only ceased when his great temple at Alexandria was destroyed as a result of the Edicts of Constantine the Great and the Emperor Theodosius.

[2] Cory, *Ancient Fragments*, p. 112.

[3] For a detailed account of this building see Mariette, *Mémoire sur la Mère d'Apis*, Paris, 1856.

The Bull MNEVIS, in Egyptian NEM-UR, was worshipped at HELIOPOLIS as the 'Living Sun-god', and the repetition

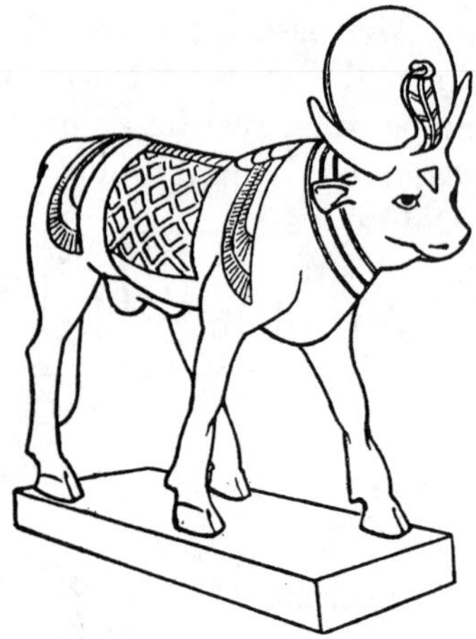

The Apis Bull of Memphis.

The Mnevis Bull of Heliopolis.

A Bull Star-god.

Meḥ-urit.

Bull-god, a form of Rā.

of the lives of both RĀ and OSIRIS. He was either black, like APIS, or piebald. AELIAN states (xii. 11) that BOCCHORIS brought a wild bull to attack MNEVIS, but its horns became entangled in the branches of a persea tree, and it was gored to death by the holy Bull.

The Bull BKHA, in Egyptian, the BACIS, or BASIS, or PACIS of the GREEKS, was probably black and was famed for his strength, violence, and pugnacity. The centre of his cult was HERMONTHIS of the South (ARMANT), some ten miles to the south of THEBES, and he was the incarnation of MENTU, the War-god of the town. AELIAN calls him 'ONUPHRIS', which is probably a garbled form of UN-NEFER, a title of OSIRIS. He was likewise the 'living soul of RĀ', and 'Bull of the Mountains of the Sunrise and Sunset'. In late times ASAR (OSIRIS) was added to his name, and so we have the form ASAR-BAKHA, i.e. OSIRIS-BKHA. The figure of a vulture was seen on his back,[1] and the colour of his hair changed with every hour of the day.

The Bull of MIN, name unknown, was white and was worshipped at KHEMMIS, i.e. (AKHMÎM), and COPTOS.

The Bull of the city of KA-KAM, i.e. the 'city of the Black Bull', was black, but details of his markings are lacking.

The worship of the bull was common in EGYPT and the SÛDÂN at all periods. The dynastic EGYPTIANS and the ROMANS made war on the MENTIU, or 'Cattle men', of NUBIA, who were the ancestors of the BAḲḲÂRA, or 'Cattle breeders', of the northern SÛDÂN at the present day.

The Ram, or Goat, was worshipped at many places in EGYPT, for the EGYPTIANS in all periods admired its strength, virility, and activity. STRABO, quoting PINDAR (xvii. 1. 19), says that the sacred rams of HERMOPOLIS, LYCOPOLIS, and MENDES had intercourse with women. DIODORUS regarded (i. 88) the cult of the ram or goat as identical with that of PRIAPUS, and he ranges the goat with the PANS and SATYRS. The ram these writers refer to is the famous 'Ram of MENDES', the cult of which was re-established by KA-KAU (IInd dynasty). Now 'MENDES' is a garbled form of the name of the city of the Ram in the Delta, viz. BA-NEB-ṬEṬ, which means both the 'Ram lord of ṬEṬ' and the 'Soul, lord of ṬEṬ'. The city of ṬEṬ was called BUSIRIS by the GREEKS, so the animal worshipped there was both the 'Soul, lord of BUSIRIS' and the 'Ram lord of BUSIRIS'. There is no confusion here in reality. The word for 'ram' was *ba* and the word for 'soul' was also *ba*. The fact is that in predynastic times the

[1] See the drawing by Lanzone, *Dizionario di Mitologia*, Pl. 70.

cult was animalistic, and that in dynastic times the ram was made to be the soul of OSIRIS. In later times the Ram of MENDES had four

The Ram of Mendes (Ba-neb-Ṭeṭ).

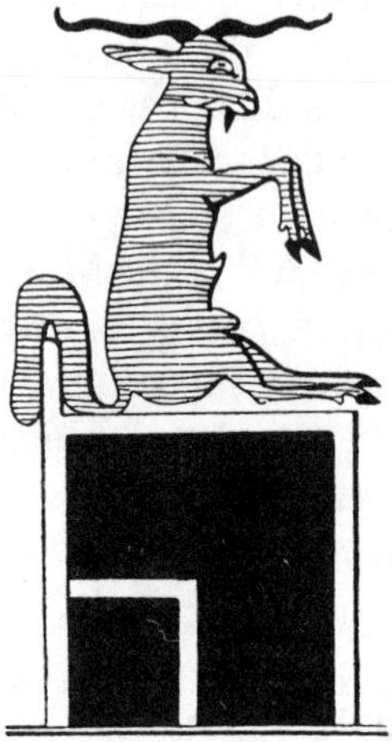

The Ram of Mendes (Ba-neb-Ṭeṭ).

The four-headed Ram of Mendes.

Khnum, the Ram-god of the First Cataract.

heads, and it then was supposed to contain the souls of RĀ, SHU, GEBB, and OSIRIS. When the Ram died the the whole city went into mourning, and he was buried with great pomp and ceremony at public expense. ḤĀT-MEḤIT, a dolphin goddess, was the consort of the Ram of MENDES, and PTOLEMY II rebuilt his temple and enthroned two rams.

Another kind of ram, the name of which was KHNUM in the predynastic speech, was worshipped in UPPER EGYPT; in form he was something like the Kudu. The Khnum became extinct before the rise of the Middle Kingdom.

Ḥat-Meḥit.

Dog-god in the Ṭuat.

Anubis the warrior.

The Lion worshipped at LEONTOPOLIS had special marks and characteristics; his consort was 'MAI-ḤESA' (i.e. the 'fierce eyed'), the MIYSIS of the GREEKS, and she was worshipped at BUBASTIS. The 'Lion temple' near WÂD BA-NAGAʿ shows that the cult of the lion existed on the island of MEROË. SHU and TEFNUT had lion-forms.

The Hare, in predynastic Egyptian *Unu* (i.e. 'the springer up'), was held to be a form of RĀ and, with the title UN-NEFER, a form of OSIRIS. The centre of the cult of the Hare-goddess was HERMOPOLIS.

The Dog was worshipped at CYNOPOLIS; he is often confounded with ANUBIS, the Jackal-god ('dog-headed' ANUBIS).

The Jackal was a very sacred beast, and the Jackal-god ANUBIS conducted the souls of the dead to the Field of Celestial Offerings. In later times he became the apothecary of the gods, and embalmed the dead and reconstituted their bodies. The centre of his cult was CYNOPOLIS, where dogs were worshipped; *anpu* may have been the predynastic word for dog.

The Wolf was worshipped at LYCOPOLIS, a frontier city which marked the end of the THEBAÏD on the north. The Wolf-god UP-UATU, i.e. the 'Opener of the Roads', assisted his colleague in guiding the dead to the Elysian Fields. The centre of his cult was at SAUT, a city in UPPER EGYPT, the modern ASYÛṬ. HORUS and SET were supposed to have lived there in the forms of

Anubis taking the mummy into its tomb. Behind the god are the Benu bird and the soul of the deceased as a man-headed hawk.

wolves. See DIODORUS, i. 88, and MACROBIUS, *Saturnalia*, I. 19, and CHABAS, *Le Calendrier*.

The Fox was, of course, well known to the predynastic EGYPTIANS, but nothing is known about him; the COPTS call the animal *bashor*, but the hieroglyphic form of this word for fox is unknown to me. In BRIT. MUS. papyrus No. 10016, we see a fox standing up and playing a syrinx for a flock of goats to march to; another fox acts as fugleman.

The Ass appears in a vignette in the *Book of the Dead* where he is being attacked by the serpent HAI; he may be a form of the Sun-god, and a symbol of virility. But in a hymn in the Papyrus of ANI (Pl. 1, l. 14) the deceased says: 'May I appear on earth, may I smite the Ass, may I crush the serpent-fiend SEBAU, may I destroy ĀPEP.'

The Pig was an accursed beast and was associated with SET. A black pig smote the eyes of HORUS and blinded him, and the passage of a black pig over a tile defiled it. See *Book of the Dead*, chaps.

The three-headed Lion-god worshipped at Meroë.

From a relief at Wâd Ba-Naga'.

cxii and cxiv. In the *Book of Gates* the black pig is seen in a boat being driven away by a baboon. See also HERODOTUS, ii. 47; HORAPOLLO, ii. 37; and AELIAN, *De Nat. Animalium*, x. 16.

The deceased defending the Ass from the serpent Hai.

Ass-gods in the Ṭuat.

The Wild Cat (*Felis vereata maniculata*) was domesticated at a very early period. The EGYPTIANS[1] called it *Mau* and admired it for its virility, strength, ferocity, and agility. The animal

[1] The Copts transcribed the old name and called the cat *emou*. The Arabs have *ḳiṭṭ*, plur. *ḳiṭāṭ*, probably from the Greek κάττα.

was sacred to the goddess BAST, or UBAST, the centre of whose cult was BUBASTIS (TALL BASTAH) in the Eastern Delta. The cat of BAST was distinguished by special markings and colours. Little girls were often called 'Mai-sheri', i.e. Pussy. The cat appears in mythological scenes, and is sometimes RĀ himself; he killed the serpent of darkness and cut off his head (*Book of the Dead*, chaps. xvii, l. 18 f., and lxxv. iii. 13). A specially sacred cat was kept in the temple of NEITH at SAÏS. The sacredness and popularity of the cat is attested by the scores of mummied cats and cat cases which are found in our Museum. The toy cat, with a movable jaw, in the BRITISH MUSEUM (No. 15671) is a very interesting object.

Bast of Bubastis.

The Ichneumon, the slayer of snakes and destroyer of the eggs of crocodiles, was no doubt protected by the predynastic peoples as the ferret and weasel are to-day. Many good bronze figures of it are to be seen in the BRITISH MUSEUM, e.g. Nos. 6770, 26158, 11590, 29602, 35091, &c. The EGYPTIANS called it *khatru*, and this word is preserved in Coptic (*khatoul*) and is found in some of the Aramean dialects. The modern ARABS call it *Ḳutt Far'ûn*, i.e. 'PHARAOH's Cat'. As a god the ichneumon was called SHEṬ or SESHEṬ, and he was the incarnation of TEMU, the setting sun, and was regarded as the Ka of ANU (HELIOPOLIS). (See NAVILLE, *Goshen*, Pl. 7, No. 1, and BRUGSCH, *Aegyptologie*, p. 389.)

The Shrew Mouse, or Mygale, was an incarnation of HORUS; for figures of it see BRITISH MUSEUM, Nos. 1604, 26335.

The Hedgehog, like the Mygale, was used in medicine. The EBERS Papyrus speaks of 'The hackles of the hedgehog mixed with oil' (Plate 92). Lamps and bottles were often made in the form of the hedgehog (BRITISH MUSEUM, Nos. 4764, 29362, 15475).

The Leopard was regarded as a 'Typhonian' animal, and its skin formed an important part of the dress of the priests. In the SÛDÂN the people believe that leopards are often possessed by the spirits of thieves and robbers.

The Panther, that is to say, the Sûdânî panther, i.e. 'panthers of the South', was greatly prized, and panthers formed part of the tribute of KÛSH to EGYPT.

The Black Pig of Set being driven away in the Judgement Hall of Osiris.

The deceased spearing the Black Pig of Set.

The Lynx, in Egyptian, *Mafṭet*. He is often mentioned in religious texts.

The Baboon was an incarnation of THOTH, whom he assisted in restoring the eye of the Sun-god, i.e. the moon, to its place in the face of RĀ. The baboon represented THOTH in the Judgement Hall of OSIRIS, and watched the weighing of the heart of the deceased with scrupulous care. He is also called ASṬEN or ASṬES.

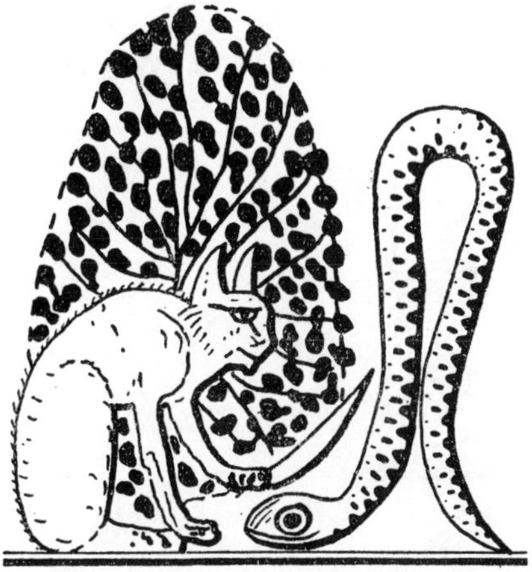

The Cat by the Persea tree slaying the Serpent of Darkness.

The Cat, the ally of Rā

The Cat by the Persea tree slaying the Serpent of Darkness.

The Elephant can hardly have been a regular inhabitant of EGYPT, but the NUBIANS must have known him well, and hunted him, if not for meat, for his tusks. The dynastic EGYPTIANS called him *abu*  and this was probably his name in predynastic times. The island opposite SYENE bore the same name, perhaps because of the ivory market in the vicinity, or because the shape of the island resembled that of the elephant. The GREEKS translated the name by ELEPHANTINE. The town at the junction of the BLUE and WHITE NILES was called 'KHURṬÛM', i.e. 'elephant's trunk', because its contour resembled that of the trunk of the elephant. Figures of the elephant appear on the sculptures at MEROË and MAṢAWWARÂT, but he never has a man's body.

The Ichneumon, sacred to Temu of Heliopolis.

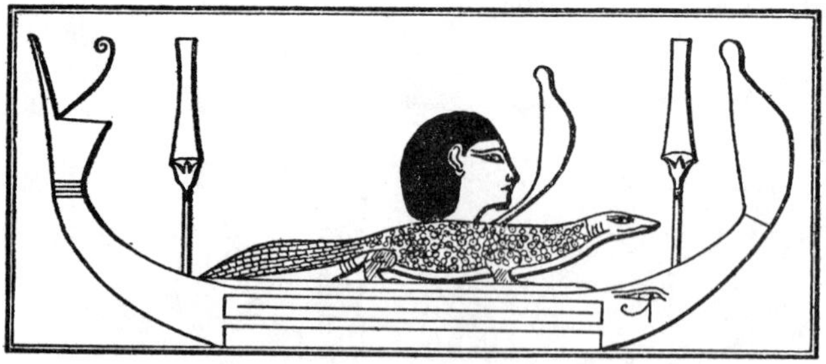

The Ichneumon in the Ṭuat.

The Hippopotamus was common in the Delta in very early times, and she appears in the *Book of the Dead* as a friendly goddess (see Papyrus of ANI, Pl. 37). Her names were APET, RERET, TA-URIT, SHEPUT, &c. A large number of blue- or green-glazed porcelain figures of the hippopotamus have been found in the tombs,[1] but what their purpose was is not known. PALLADIUS (fourth century) reports that a hippopotamus came and ate up a whole crop of the monastery, but after ABBÂ BENUS had ordered the beast to depart in the Name of CHRIST, it retreated and was never more seen.

The Mouse, Rat, Weasel, and Porcupine have always been well

[1] See *Revue de l'Égypte Ancienne*, tom. ii, p. 216 f.

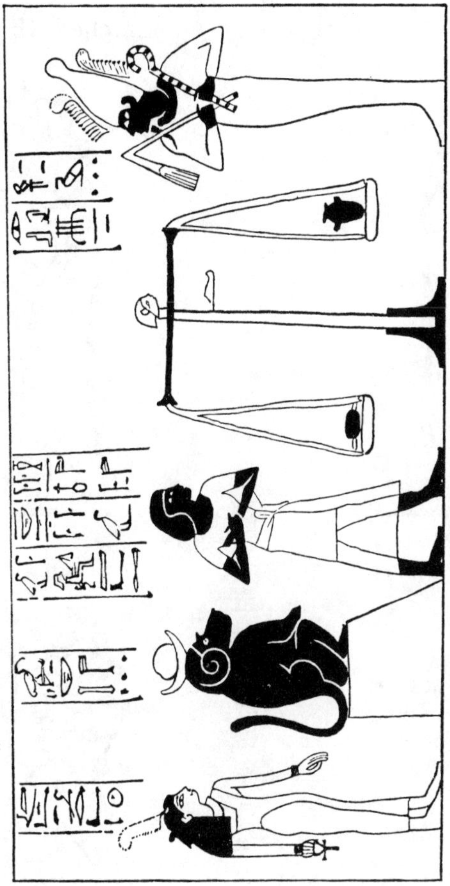

The oldest representation of the baboon watching the weighing of the heart; he is here called 'Thoth, lord of the words of the god' (Papyrus of Nebseni).

known in EGYPT, but there is no evidence that they were regarded as sacred animals.

The Bat. A model of a bat, with outstretched wings, in green

The Hippopotamus.
The Warrior-goddess.

As a form of Hathor.

The Set animal.

The god Set.

stone was found at JABALAIN in UPPER EGYPT; it is now in the BRITISH MUSEUM (No. 21901).

The Oryx was a 'Typhonian' animal and was regarded as a form of SET. HORUS conquered SET, and the oryx, with a figure of the hawk of HORUS on his back, became the badge of the XVIth nome of UPPER EGYPT. The Christian Fathers of EGYPT always associated horned animals of the oryx class with the Devil, and they thought that evil spirits often assumed the form of the common goat.

The SET animal who appears in the texts under the following forms: , , and . Strictly speaking, this animal should be described in the paragraph dealing with fabulous animals, like the SEFER and the SEKA. The god SET was the father and author of all evil, and the animal here represented was believed to be the form in which he appeared on earth. Many Egyptologists have tried to identify this animal and all have failed. WIEDEMANN and others thought he was the okapi, although naturalists had already shown this view to be hopelessly wrong.

From Sethe, *Urgeschichte*, p. 72.

SCHWEINFURTH thought he was a pig (KEES, *Horus and Set*, 1921, p. 26). MASPERO saw in him a bad drawing of the jerboa, and VON BISSING held that he was the giraffe. NEWBERRY, in an elaborate and learned article, declared that he was the wart-hog. The cult of SET was very ancient, for , i.e. the SET animal with a dagger sticking in his head, was the badge of the XIth nome of UPPER EGYPT. The predynastic EGYPTIANS worshipped him, and their descendants preserved him as the badge of a nome for 'old sake's sake'; but they drew him with a knife driven into his head to indicate that as an object of worship his day had passed. Another name for SET was SHA, and SETHE has shown (*Urgeschichte*, p. 46) that this is preserved in the name of the chief town of the nome, SHA-ḤETEP. According to KEES (pp. 40, 41), the home of the cult of SET in the XIth nome was at ḤEN-T .

What appears to me to be the true identification of the animal was made by DR. SCHÄFER, who says that the beast was a hunting-dog of a species which was extinct in historic times like the ram of KHNEMU. Proof of this, in my opinion, is supplied by an ivory magical wand (?), or 'throw stick', in the BRITISH MUSEUM (No. 18175), the obverse and reverse of which are reproduced on p. 88. On this we have figures of a series of predynastic gods, but the drawings

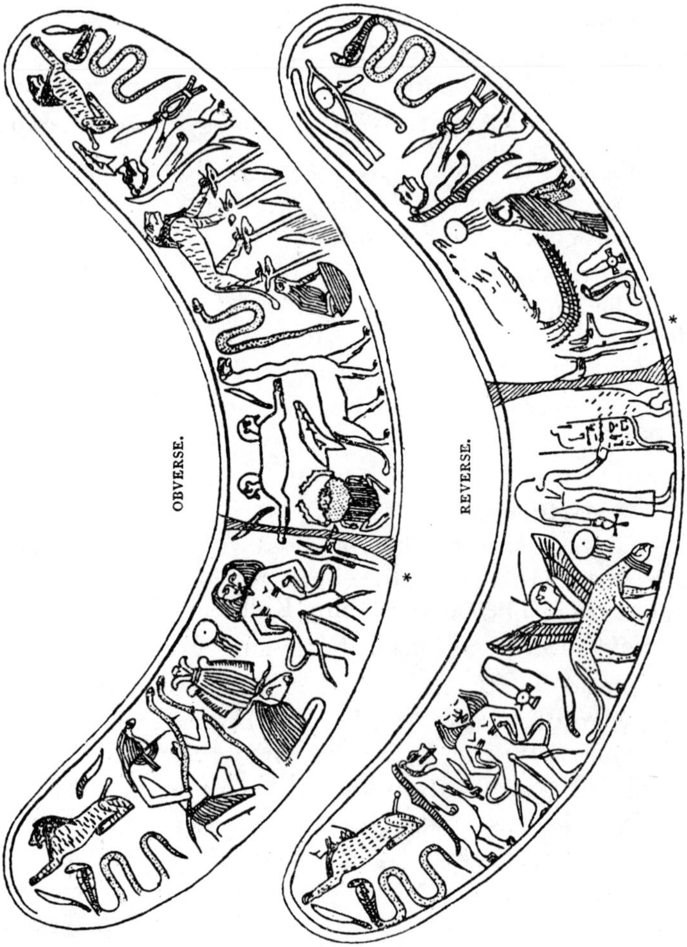

The head of Set is shown by the asterisk.

of knives scattered about in the field indicate that the animals were no longer worshipped. On the obverse are cut: (1) Two lions, *couchant*. (2) A lion with each paw resting on the head of an oryx. (3) A lion, *couchant*, with the head of a man at each end of his body (the god AKER?). (4) A lion-headed giraffe. (5) A hippopotamus standing on her hind-legs. (6) A frog on a bowl or basket. (7) The heads of two crocodiles. (8) A large beetle. (9) A man grasping a serpent in each hand (prototype of BES?). (10) The fetish ,[1] i.e. the solar disk with rays falling. (11) The head of the ram of KHNEMU. (12) A snake-headed man grasping a serpent in each hand. (13) And on the left side of the beetle is the head of a dog with prick ears. This is repeated on the reverse. The long nose and the shape of the head of this dog show clearly that this is not the dog sacred to ANUBIS. The head and neck of the dog on the wand are those of the well-known hunting-dog, the 'Salûḳî', but although this dog does not keep his ears pointed or his tail erect when he is lying down, no one who has ever lived in tents with ARABS who keep Salûḳîs, and seen him frequently, can fail to identify the SET animal with the Salûḳî. The Salûḳî is marvellously fleet and he literally tears his prey in pieces.[2] The ARABS call him 'Kalb Salûḳîyy'.[3] DOZY (*Dictionnaire*, p. 676) says that he is like 'limier' of the FRENCH and the 'sleuth-hound' of the SCOTS. That SET was a god of the chase is proved by the relief in which we see him teaching the king to shoot with the bow and arrow (LANZONE, Pl. 376). A gilded bronze figure of SET in which the dog's head is mounted on a human body is in the BRITISH MUSEUM (No. 30460).

Sacred Birds

The Benu, or Bennu, , was a bird of the heron class, with long crest feathers. He was an incarnation of the sun, and he created

[1] Some read this sign *Tua* and say that this sign represents a bearded human chin. Others say that Tua was a god of whom Borchardt found a picture in human form (*Grabdenkmal des Königs Sa'ḥu-re'*, Pl. X). See  in Petrie, *Royal Tombs*, vol. i, pl. XIII, No. 2. The Barber-god who shaved Pepi was called Tua-ur 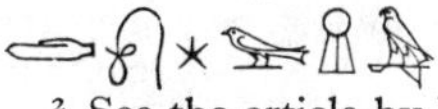.

[2] See the article by Daumas in *Revue de l'Orient l'Afrique*, vol. xiii, p. 168 f.

[3] The fem. is Salûḳiyyah.

himself from the fire which burned at dawn on the top of the holy persea tree in HELIOPOLIS. He sprang from the heart of OSIRIS, and in him was the 'essence of every god' (*Book of the Dead*, chap. lxxxiii). The GREEKS identified him with the PHOENIX, an eagle-like bird with red and gold wings, which came from ARABIA. See HERODOTUS, ii. 75; and LANZONE, Pl. 70. The cult of the bird seems to have been of Heliopolitan origin.

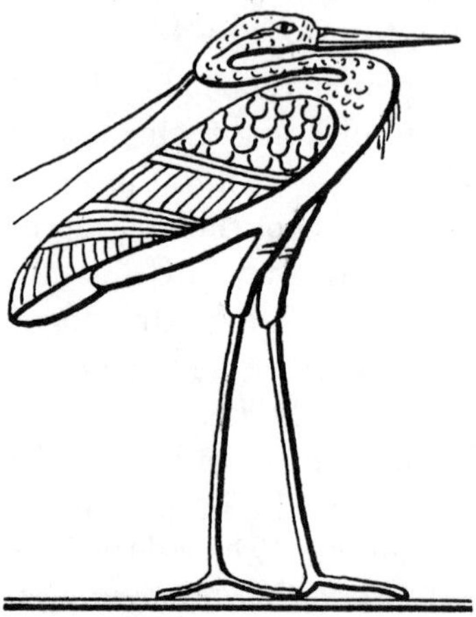

The Benu bird.

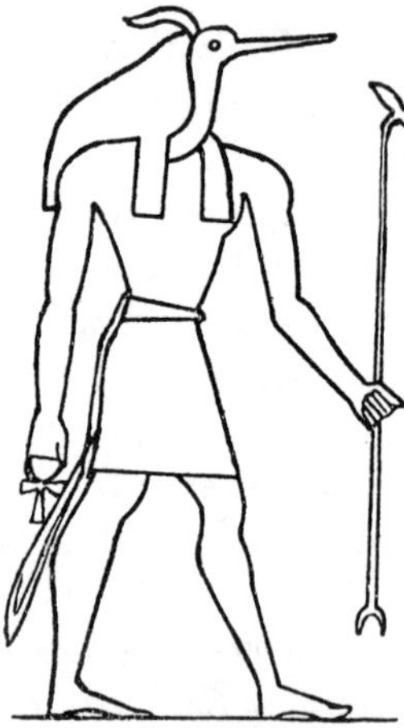

The god Benu.

The Hawk  was worshipped in EGYPT from the earliest times. He was the incarnation of the Spirit of Heaven, and the sun and moon represented his eyes. The centre of the cult of the hawk in LOWER EGYPT was ṬEMA-EN-ḤOR, the modern DAMANHÛR, and in UPPER EGYPT, HIERAKONPOLIS. The texts mention the Golden Hawk which was four cubits in breadth, and had the head of a Benu; this was the PHOENIX[1] of the GREEKS. The 'Divine Hawk' (*Book of the Dead*, chap. lxxviii) was the offspring of TEM or ATEM, and was the incarnation of the One God and of HORUS, the son of OSIRIS; 'millions of years serve him, and millions of years hold him in fear'. The human-headed hawk 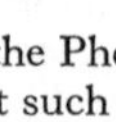 was the symbol of the soul. On the hawk

[1] It has been said that the Phoenix is mentioned in the Septuagint version of the Book of Job (xxix. 18) but such is not the case. The passage reads, 'My age shall continue ὥσπερ στέλεχος φοίνικος as the stem of a palm tree, I shall live a long while'.

generally, see STRABO, xvii. 47; DIODORUS, i. 83; HERODOTUS, ii. 65; AELIAN, x. 24.

The Vulture, which the predynastic EGYPTIANS called *mut*; this word is preserved in the name of the goddess MUT of THEBES. The seat of the cult of the Vulture-goddess NEKHEBIT was NEKHEN

Scene cut on a stone bowl found by Mr. Quibell at Kôm al-Akhmar giving very ancient representations of the Hawk of Horus and the Vulture of Nekhebit. The Vulture is standing on a signet ring, within which are the signs B SH (Besh), and tying together a lotus and papyrus plant, indicating the union of the two Egypts. Besh (i.e. Bedjau) was the personal name of king Khā-sekhem.

The goddess Nekhebit with cobra-headed sceptre.

(EILEITHYASPOLIS) in UPPER EGYPT. According to AELIAN (ii. 46) no male vultures existed, and the females were fecundated by the south or south-east wind.

The Eagle; no details of its cult (if it had one) are known.

The Heron. See *Book of the Dead* (vignette, chap. lxxxiv).

The Swallow, was sacred to ISIS (see *Book of the Dead*, chap. lxxxvi).

The Goose was sacred to AMEN-RĀ. The Goose-god was identified with GEBB the Earth-god. The Cosmic Egg was laid by the Goose-goddess SER-T, who in the *Book of the Dead*, chap. liv, is called KENKEN-UR, the 'Great Cackler'.

The Ibis was the bird of THOTH. The centre of its cult was

KHEMENU (HERMOPOLIS), the city of THOTH. The great ibis-sanctuary, the 'Ibeum', was situated about 25 miles to the north of HERMOPOLIS. On the ibis generally see AELIAN, x. 29; HERODOTUS, ii. 75; DIODORUS, i. 83; PLUTARCH, *De Iside*, § 75; and HORAPOLLO, i. 10. 16.

The Ostrich was probably worshipped in the predynastic period, or in some way held in reverence by the primitive EGYPTIANS, for the unbroken shells of the eggs of ostriches have been found in pre-

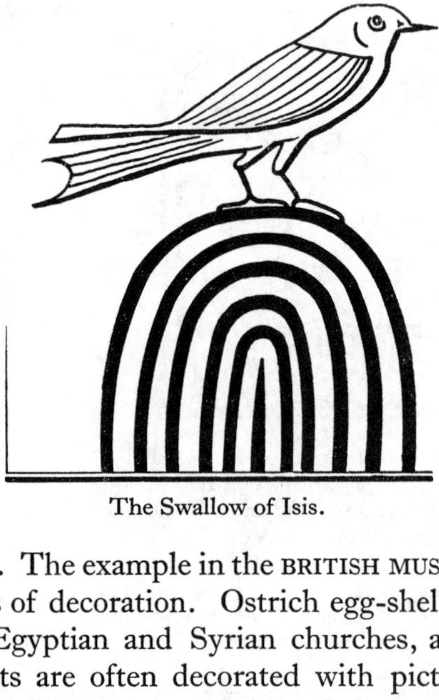

The Swallow of Isis.

dynastic tombs. The example in the BRITISH MUSEUM (No. 36377) has on it traces of decoration. Ostrich egg-shells are often seen suspended in Egyptian and Syrian churches, and in mosques. Predynastic pots are often decorated with pictures of rows of ostriches. The oldest representation of the ostrich is found on the green slate objects from GABALAYN (see p. 68.).

Sacred Reptiles, Insects, &c.

The Turtle or Tortoise  was venerated, but why cannot be said. There are in the BRITISH MUSEUM three green stone figures of turtles of the predynastic period (Nos. 23061, 36367, 37913); and two wooden figures from the tomb of THOTHMES III (Nos. 1416, 20704); and two turtle shells (Nos. 46602, 46603). The Turtle-god was called APESH and SHETA. The fourth sign of the Zodiac is called *shetau* .

The Turtle-god.

Sebek, the Crocodile-god, wearing the horns, disk, uraei with disks, and plumes of solar gods.

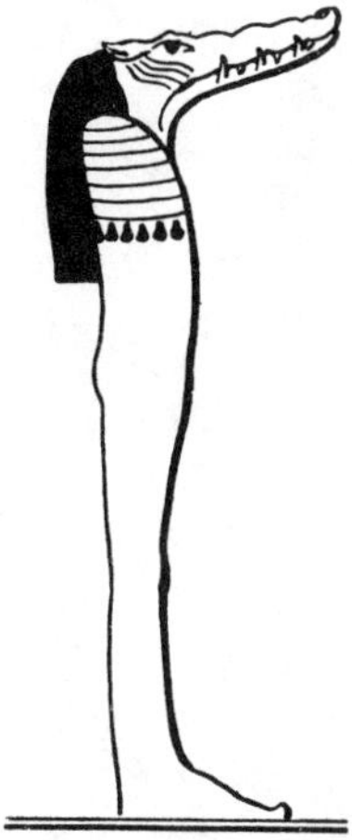

Sebek, the Crocodile-god.

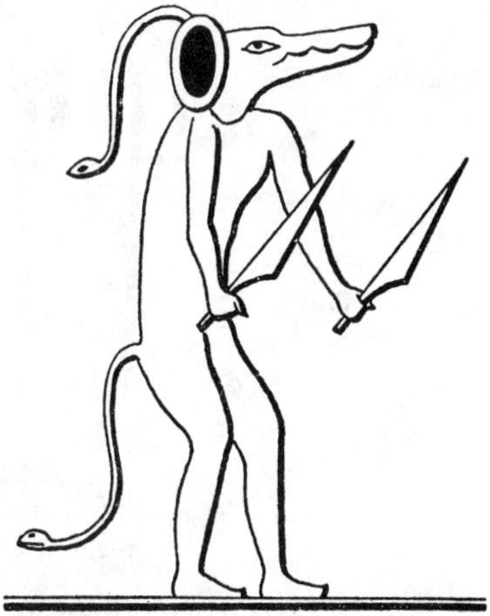

The belligerent crocodile of the Ṭuat with the solar disk. The streamer indicates the antiquity of the figure.

The Crocodile seems to have been called *sebek* by the predynastic EGYPTIANS, and the later Crocodile-god bore the same name . The dynastic EGYPTIANS called the beast *msuḥ* the χάμψαι of HERODOTUS. For a list of his shrines see

LANZONE, *Dizionario*, pp. 1033–6; and see the accounts of the crocodile by STRABO, xvii. 38; HERODOTUS, ii. 68; DIODORUS, i. 35; AELIAN, x. 21.

The Cobra or Asp, the URAEUS of the GREEKS; in Egyptian *Ārā-t*

The Cobra-goddess of Lower Egypt.

The Cobra-goddess of Upper Egypt.

Urt-ḥekau, the Cobra-goddess of magical spells.

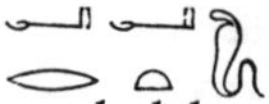. It was worshipped in very early times, and was regarded by the dynastic EGYPTIANS as a sign of sovereignty and royalty. The disk of RĀ had a cobra coiled round it .

The Horned Viper or Cerastes was represented by the hieroglyph . It was exceedingly venomous and greatly feared; only the female has horns. The ARABS know the reptile as *ḥayy bil-ḳurûn*, i.e. the snake with horns.

The Snake. Many snakes were known to the EGYPTIANS, and

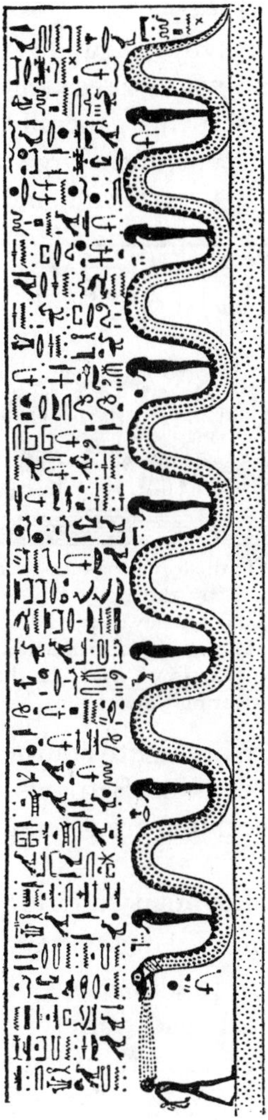

Kheti, the fire-spitting serpent of the Ṭuat.

many of them were harmless and were regarded as friends and protectors. Among these was SA-TA who is mentioned in the *Book of the Dead* (chap. lxxxvii). He was a symbol of new life and resurrection, and renewed youth, ideas suggested by the annual sloughing of the skin by serpents generally. The *Book of Gates* mentions a fire-spitting serpent, and a large number of mythological serpents AQEBI, SETHRA, ABTA, SETHU, and others. The serpent

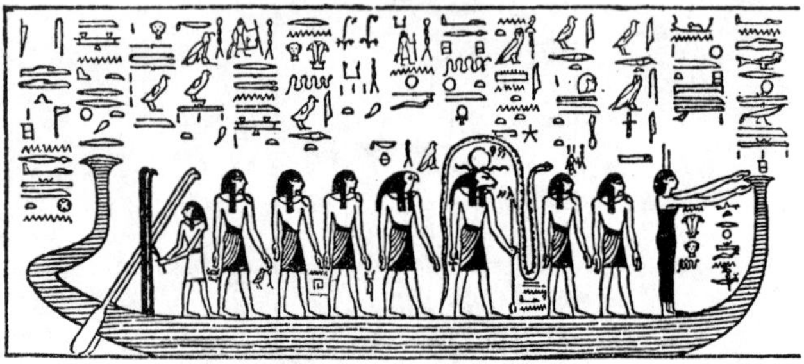

The Sun-god of night in the form of a ram-headed man standing under a canopy formed by the body of the serpent Meḥen, sailing through the Ṭuat on the river of the Ṭuat. His crew consists of Isis, Sia, Ḥeka, the god of magic, Horus of Heken, Ka-Maāt, Neḥes (the 'look-out') and Ḥu the steersman who directs the magical steering-pole. From *The Book of Gates*.

MEḤEN protected RĀ during his nightly journey through the Underworld. The names of the Nine Serpents which protected the Underworld of SEKER (MEMPHIS) are given in chap. x of the *Book of the Dead*.

The Scorpion. Several Egyptian words have a scorpion for determinative; and two of them, *uāt* and *djart*, have been preserved in Coptic. In all periods of Egyptian history the scorpion, especially the small black variety which is common in the SÛDÂN, has been held in fear, and regarded with terror. It was an incarnation of the goddess SERQIT, who seems to have been of Nubian or Sûdânî origin. The centre of her cult was the town named after her which was called by the GREEKS 'PSELCHIS'; it was situated near DAḲḲAH, and its site is marked by the village of KUSHTAMNAH. The goddess appears in the Pyramid Texts under the form (TETA, l. 206). Her character was evil, and she was associated with SET or TYPHON, and the baleful stars of the North Pole; but when ISIS was wandering about in the Delta she had as a bodyguard the Seven Scorpions.

The Frog, was the symbol of fertility, fecundity, and

Serqet in her serpent-boat which was propelled by a crocodile.

The black scorpion with emblems of 'life' and 'eternity'.

The Frog-goddess providing 'life' for newly fashioned children.

Serqet.

birth and renewed life and resurrection. The four gods who lived in the primeval ocean of NUNU had the form of frogs. One of the oldest centres of the cult of the Frog-goddess ḤEQET was near the island of ELEPHANTINE, where the QERTI or caverns through which the NILE entered EGYPT were situated; she was the wife of KHNEMU, the great god of the First Cataract and Controller of the Nile. She presided over the birth of kings and queens, probably as midwife. She assisted OSIRIS to rise from the dead, and among the Egyptian Christians the frog was the symbol of the resurrection. When KHNEMU became a potter god ḤEQET supplied the life wherewith he animated the gods and men whom he fashioned on his wheel.

Sacred Fishes

The texts mention about sixty kinds of fish, that is to say words which have a fish for their determinative. The cult of certain kinds of fish must have existed in very early times, for a green stone model of the cuttle-fish, dating from the predynastic period, has been found (BRIT. MUS. No. 24319). The *Book of the Dead* says that two fish, the ABṬ and the ANT, acted as pilots to the Sun-god. The dolphin[1] was worshipped at MENDES as the consort of the Ram of MENDES; she was called ḤĀT-MEḤIT. The latus, or 'fighting fish', was worshipped at ASNA. The fish which according to PLUTARCH (*De Iside*, § 18) swallowed the phallus of OSIRIS when SET hacked his brother in pieces, was a species of *mormoyrus*, and was worshipped at OXYRHYNCHUS (BEHNESA). According to STRABO (xvii. 2. 4) the fishes worshipped by the EGYPTIANS were the OXYRHYNCHUS, LEPIDOTUS, LATUS, ALABES, CORACINUS, CHOERUS, PHAGRUS, SILURUS, CITHARUS, THRISIA, CESTREUS, LYCHNUS, PHYSA, the BOUS (Bull-fish), and the large shell-fish which emit sounds like wailing.[2] The Eel was worshipped at ASNA and was mummified.

Sacred Insects, &c.

The Bee or Hornet (?).

The Beetle, *khepr*[*e*]*r*, commonly known as *Scarabaeus sacer*, of the species *Ateuchus Aegyptiorum*. Concerning the life of the beetle see FABRE, *The Sacred Beetle*, LONDON, 1919; BUDGE, *The Mummy*, 2nd ed., CAMBRIDGE, 1925, p. 274 f., and for the views of the Christian Fathers about it as a symbol of Christ see T. HOPFNER, *Fontes Historiae Religionis Aegyptiacae*, BONN, 1922.

[1] The dolphin was the badge of the XVIth nome of Lower Egypt.

[2] For shells of mother-of-pearl oysters inscribed with royal names see British Museum, Nos. 15423, 20754, 27723, &c.

The Toad (?) .

The Āpshait a kind of beetle (?). See *Book of the Dead*, chap. xxxvi.

The Mantis (?) *bebait*. See *Book of the Dead*, chaps. lxxvi and civ.

The Āpshait attacked by the deceased.

The Grasshopper *sanḥemu* (Pyr. PEPI. II, l. 860).

The Rat or Mouse *pennu*.

Sacred Trees

The Aser tamarisk. The coffin of OSIRIS was a trunk of this tree, and the BENU bird perched on its branches.

The Persea, Asheṭ . The Sun-god rose daily at HELIOPOLIS out of this tree which was guarded by a fierce Cat. See *Book of the Dead*, chap. cix.

The Sycamore-fig, Neht . It was the abode of NUT and HATHOR.

The Olive tree, Beqt , the abode of HORUS.

The Lotus, Nehebt . RĀ and NEFER-TEM sprang from a lotus flower.

Many animate and inanimate objects possessed a medical as well as a religious value. This is proved by the prescriptions found in the EBERS Papyrus, which was written about 2000 B.C. Among other ingredients we find the oil, hide, and fat, and nails of the hippopotamus; the oil, fat, and excrement of the crocodile; the oil, hair, uterus, and excrement of the cat; the blood and horns of the oryx; the blood, fat, head, hoofs, oil, liver, seed, teeth, testicles, and excrement of the ass; the oil, blood, intestines, egg, &c., of the goose; the blood of the bat; the case of the beetle; the eyes, blood, gall, fat,

Rā rising from the lotus flower of heaven.

teeth, and excrement of the pig; the oil and eggs of the ostrich; the blood and excrement of wasps; the berries, leaves, seeds, and oil of plants which are too many to mention.

THE ANTHROPOMORPHIZATION OF FETISHES

When exactly the predynastic EGYPTIANS began to give human forms to the objects which they worshipped cannot be said, and the reasons for their doing so are not very clear. It was probably due to the natural development of their religious ideas as they advanced in civilization. It may have been due to some external influence, and if it was that influence came from the east, and neither from the south the (SÛDÂN) nor west (LIBYA). From time immemorial the caravans from the east passed through the VIIIth nome of LOWER EGYPT in the Eastern Delta, by the way of SUCCOTH (TJKUT), where stood the famous temple of TEM or ATEM (the PITHOM of the Bible), to

HELIOPOLIS. These caravans not only brought new and strange merchandise into EGYPT, but the caravan men were to all intents and purposes missionaries who carried into EGYPT news of the civilizations of INDIA, ELAM, SUMER, and BABYLONIA and SYRIA, and the half-savage EGYPTIAN was the gainer. They made their way into EGYPT by way of SYRIA and PALESTINE.

There is no doubt that the changes which the EGYPTIANS made in the forms of their gods took place before the union of the northern and southern countries under MENA or MENI. But it is incomprehensible that instead of giving them human heads, they gave them with very few exceptions the *bodies* of men and women. Thus SEBEK becomes a crocodile-headed man, UP-UATU a wolf-headed man, ANPU a jackal-headed man, KHNEMU a ram-headed man, and UBASTIT, SEKHMIT, PAKHIT, &c., lioness-headed women. The HORUS gods, with the exception of HORUS of EDFÛ, became hawk-headed men. THOTH an ibis-headed man, MUT a vulture-headed woman, SET, the god of evil, appears as a man with the head of a hunting-dog. ḤĀPI the Nile-god, becomes a man with the breast of a woman and a cluster of Nile plants  on his head. SERQIT becomes a woman with a scorpion on her head, GEBB becomes a man with a goose (or gander) on his head, and so on. The only goddess represented full-faced is the Syrian goddess QEṬESH 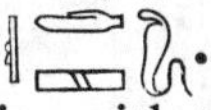. OSIRIS, PTAḤ, and MIN or MENU are represented as mummies with the legs close together. In the case of fetish gods and goddesses they are often given complete human bodies, but they have on their heads drawings of the original fetish objects. NUT is seen with a pot of water , or , NEITH with a solar eye , or crossed arrows , or a shuttle (?) .

THE CULT OF MEN GODS

The god TEM, or TEMU, or ATEM is always represented in the form of a man and with a man's head; although the ichneumon was sacred to him he is never seen wearing the head of that animal. And it is interesting to note that in a drawing of the Boat of the Sun with its divine crew, TEM appears in the form of a man, whilst RĀ is symbolized by a disk, and KHEPRI as a beetle, and ḤARAKHTI as a hawk's head (see LANZONE, Pl. 398). LEFÉBURE thought (*Trans. Soc. Bibl. Arch.*, ix, p. 135) that he was the *first* man among the EGYPTIANS who was believed to become divine, and that he was the first *living* man-god known to them. OSIRIS, of course, was a dead man deified, but he has his own special form as a mummy, as said above. LEFÉBURE boldly asserted that TEM was 'a manifestation of God in human form', but the texts do not support this view. We now know that TEM was a name given by the priests of HELIOPOLIS to the god who created himself and the universe, and that it was a purely artificial name meaning something like 'the complete one'. Another title of God

Tem, wearing the double crown, seated within the solar disk in his boat.

was NEB-ER-DJER, i.e. 'Lord to the Limit', i.e. God Universal.

There seems to be little doubt also that the great god of MEMPHIS, PTAḤ, , was originally a great handicraftsman and worker in metals who was deified. And it is very probable that many of the local 'gods' were deified men.

IDOLS

Every Egyptologist has noted that certain hieroglyphs have sometimes attached to them a whip , or a feather, or a knife, or are mounted on some object or building. Thus we have , i.e. a jackal lying on the top of a building with a feather stuck in his back,[1] or , the jackal lying on a building without a feather. Or the animal may be shown on a standard, as in the Pyramid Texts, thus . Also we have the crocodile lying on a building ; or a vulture on a bowl or basket with a whip attached to its back ;

[1] See Petrie, *Royal Tombs*, Part 1, Pl. XXIX, No. 86.

or a hawk with a whip attached to it ; or a serpent on a standard with a feather attached to it ; or the ram of KHNEMU on a standard  with his name  attached; or a cobra on a bowl ; or a lion on a bowl with  attached ; or a frog on a bowl .

In his recent work[1] SETHE has attempted to give a reason for the appearance of the whip, feathers, &c. He thinks that these hieroglyphs so treated were not intended to represent divine creatures, but were *Cultus pictures*. He suggests that the creatures represented were no longer regarded as operative gods, and that the preservation of pictures of them was due to the religious conservatism of the EGYPTIANS. Cultus figures in wood and stone are also known, e.g.  *ākhem*.

FABULOUS ANIMALS

The following fabulous animals are found in tombs, &c., of the dynastic period:

1. The SEFER-T .[2] He had the head of an eagle, and the body of a lion from which grew two wings. We learn from the Pyramid Texts (§ 517 *a*) that he was a kind friend to the dead king UNAS.

2. The SEDJA[3]  had a leopard's body and a serpent's neck.

3. The SAG . The forepart of the body is that of a lion, and the hind-part that of a horse. It has a hawk's head, and the straight tail ends in a tuft like that of a lotus flower. It wears a collar, its sides are striped, and it has eight teats.[4]

4. The SHA  has long square ears, and a straight stiff arrow-like tail. This is clearly a hunting-dog, probably the Salûḳî or 'oriental greyhound', which never carries its tail in this position. See above, p. 89.

5. The ĀM-MITU , the 'Eater of the Dead'. He has the head of a crocodile; the forepart of his body is that of a lion, and his hind-quarters are those of a crocodile .

[1] *Urgeschichte*, p. 7.
[2] See Newberry, *Beni-Hasan*, ii. Pl. IV.
[3] Champollion, *Monuments*, tom. iv, Paris, 1845, Pl. 382.
[4] Rosellini, *Monumenti Civili*, Pl. XXIII, No. 4.

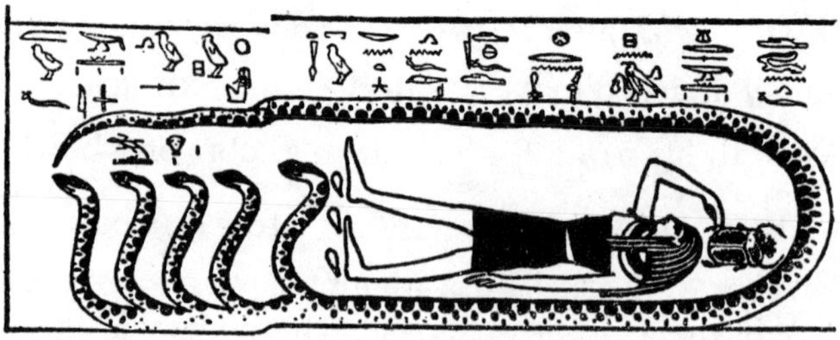

The Sun-god of night surrounded by the five-headed serpent of 'Many Faces'. On his head is the beetle of Khepri the the rising sun of the following day.

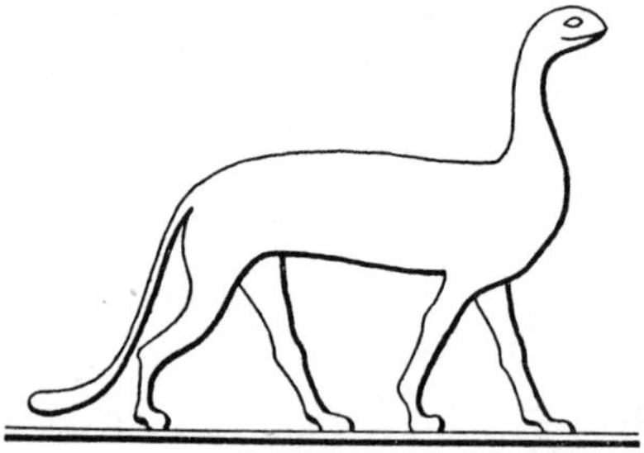

A fabulous animal of the Eastern Desert. The Sedja (?).

A god of magic, name unknown.

6. The winged leopard, with the head of a man growing out of his back.[1]

7. The SEBA serpent  with twelve human heads growing out of his back.

8. The SHEMTI serpent  with four heads and four pairs of human legs at each end of his body (*Book of Gates*, lx).

[1] Seen on the ivory wand (?) described above.

9. The BATA serpent  with four human bodies and four pairs of human legs at each end of his body (Ibid. lx).

10. The KHEPRI serpent 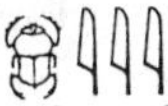 with a pair of human legs at each end of his body; the feet of each pair of legs are turned in the opposite direction (ibid. lx).

In the Book of AMMI ṬUAT we have several examples of winged and many-headed serpents, which the artist invented to amuse himself and to add to the mystery of the texts he was writing.

NOME FETISHES

There is good reason for stating that EGYPT was divided up into 'counties', which the classical writers called nomes, in the predynastic period, and the list of the nomes with the sacred animals and fetishes, which according to dynastic texts[1] were worshipped in them, may here be given.

The number of the nomes is variously given by classical writers. STRABO (xvii. 1. 37) gives 27, DIODORUS (i. 54) gives 36, and HERODOTUS (ii. 164) only says that EGYPT was divided into nomes. According to PLINY (v. 9) there were eleven nomes in the THEBAÏD; OMBITES, APOLLOPOLITES, HERMONTHITES, THINITES, PHATURITES, COPTITES, TENTYRITES, DIOSPOLITES, ANTAIOUPOLITES, APHRODITOPOLITES, and LYCOPOLITES.

Near PELUSIUM were: PHARBAETHITES, BUBASTITES, SETHROÏTES, and TANITES.

On the road to the Oasis of JUPITER AMMON (SÎWAH) were the Arabian and Hammonian nomes.

The other nomes were: OXYRYNCHITES, LEONTOPOLITES, APHRIBITES, CYNOPOLITES, HERMOPOLITES, XOÏTES, MENDESIUM, SEBENNYTES, CABASITES, LATOPOLITES, HELIOPOLITES, PROSOPITES, PANOPOLITES, BUSIRITES, ONUPHITES, SAÏTES, PTENETHU, PHTHEMPHU, NAUCRATITES, METELITES, GYNAECOPOLITES, MENELAITES, HERAKLEOPOLITES (on an island), ARSINOÏTES, MEMPHITES, and OASITES (two nomes). In all forty-one nomes. The Egyptian lists show that the

[1] See Dümichen, 'Geographie des alten Aegyptens' (in Meyer's *Geschichte*), Berlin 1887; J. de Rougé, *Géographie ancienne de la Basse-Égypte*, Paris, 1891; and the list in Erman, *Aeg. Handwörterbuch*, Berlin, 1921, p. 229, and see the series of valuable remarks on the history of the nomes in Sethe, *Urgeschichte*, §§ 38–68.

nomes were forty-two in number, twenty-two in UPPER EGYPT and twenty in LOWER EGYPT. We may note in passing that the Assessors in the Judgement Hall of OSIRIS were forty-two in number, and that each of them represented a nome.

The nome usually included a large town and the estates, vineyards, plantations, &c., which formed its suburbs, and the predynastic EGYPTIANS gave to such a region the name of *ḥesp* 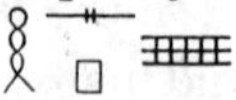. The dynastic EGYPTIANS called it *tash* 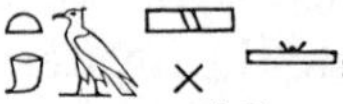, a word which is preserved in Coptic (*tôsh* or *toash*), and *sep-t* 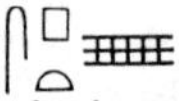. The determinative represents a plot of arable land with its irrigation channels. The first dynastic list of nomes was probably drawn up in, or soon after, the reign of MENA, the founder of White Wall or MEMPHIS.

Upper Egypt

1. 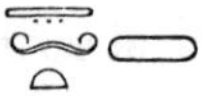 TA-STI. — ELEPHANTINE. Its god was KHNEMU, an ancient Ram-god.

2.  later  UTHES-ḤER. — APOLLINOPOLIS MAGNA. (EDFÛ). Its god was ḤER-BEḤUṬ-T.

3.  later  NEḲHEN. — Originally the blazon of HIERAKONPOLIS, but later of EILEITHYASPOLIS. (AL-KÂB). The god of the former was a hawk, and of the latter, a vulture.

4.  later  UAS-T. — THEBES. Its god was firstly MENTHU of ARMANT, and secondly AMEN. The blazon is an ancient fetish sceptre with a feather attached to show that its cult was obsolete.

5.  . . . . COPTOS[1] (ḲUFT or GUFT). The old god of the nome was AAḤES, who was later identified with MIN. The gods of this blazon are probably gods of ḲÛS.

6.  . . . . . TENTYRA (DENDERAH). Its goddess was HATHOR.

7.  later  . . . . . DIOSPOLIS PARVA (HU). The town was called HE-T SEKHEMU, i.e. 'House of the sistrum', its goddess being HATHOR.

8.  later  TA-UR. ABYDOS. The old god was the jackal-headed KHENTI AMENTIU, 'Governor of those in the West'. The box held the head of OSIRIS.

9.  later  KHEM (?). PANOPOLIS (AKHMÎM). Its god was MIN.

10.  or  UADJ-T. TEBU[2] (ABUTIG). Its dual god was ĀNTIUI.

11.  later  (?) . . . . . HYPSĒLĒ SHA-SEHETEP (SHUTB). Its god was SET.

[1] An attempt to show why the two hawks became the blazon of Coptus is made by Sethe, *Urgeschichte*, p. 26 f. *N.B.* The old form of the standard is .

[2] On the double-god of this city Āntiui , or  see Brugsch, *Dict. Géog.*, p. 866, and Sethe, op. cit., p. 42. The identification of Tebu with Aphroditopolis seems to be incorrect.

12. [1] . . . . .

This nome formed part of the ANTAIOUPOLITES nome, and its capital was ANTAIOUPOLIS which the EGYPTIANS called TU-QA (the modern KAU AL-KABĪR). Its god was HORUS who was called ĀNTI , or .

13. ATF-KHEN-T.

LYCOPOLIS (ASYÛT).[2] Its god was UP-UATU.

14. ATF-PEḤUT.

CUSAE (AL-KUṢĪYAH). Its goddess was HATHOR.

15. later UN-T.

KHMENU, the Greek HERMOPOLIS (AL-ASHMŪNÊN). Its god was THOTH, the head of the eight primeval gods.

16. later MA-ḤEDJ.

HEBNU, HIBIU (ZĀWIYAT AL-MAITÎN). Its god was HORUS, the vanquisher of the oryx (a type of SET), and he is seen on the animal's back.

17. . . . . .

CYNOPOLIS (AL-KES). Its god was ANUBIS–HORUS.

[1] The mountain of the horned viper. Its capital was called by the Greeks *Nu-t ent-bak*, 'Town of the hawk' (Hierakonpolis).

[2] The frontier town of Upper Egypt on the north, and probably a garrison town. The old form of the name suggests to Sethe the meaning of 'Watcher.' The Heptanomis began with the name of Thoth. The nomes of the Heptanomis were:—Hermopolites, Cynopolites, Oxyrhynchites, Aphroditopolites, Crocodilopolites, Herakleopolites, Memphites.

18.  later  SEPA (?). — HIPPONUS. Its god was ANUBIS–HORUS.

19.  UABU-T. — PER-MEDJ-T, OXYRHYNCHUS (BEHNESA). Its god was SET (?).

20.  later  NĀR-T KHEN-T. — HERAKLEOPOLIS ('AHNĀS). Its god was ḤER-SHEFIT, a form of HORUS.

21.  NĀR-T PEḤU-T. — NILOPOLIS. Its god was KHNEMU.

22.  later  . . . . . — APHRODITOPOLIS (ATFÎḤ). Its goddess was HATHOR.

Lower Egypt

1. 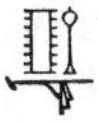 ANEB-HEDJ. — MEN-NEFERT (MEMPHIS). Its god was PTAḤ.

2.  or  later  TUAU. — SEKHEM LATOPOLIS. Its god was ḤER-UR (the Old HORUS).

3.  . . . . . — NU-T ENT HĀP. APIS. Its ancient god was HORUS, later its goddess was HATHOR, i.e. the 'House of Horus'.

4, 5.  later
- 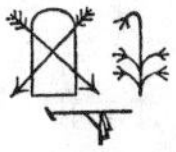 . . . . .SHMĀ. — PROPOSIS. Its god was SEBEK (?).
-  . . . . . MEḤ. — SAÏS. Its goddess was NEITH.

6.  later  . . . . . — KHASU-T XOÏS. SAKHĀ. Its god was a wild bull, later it was AMEN–RĀ.

7, 8.  later {  Western ..... METELIS. Its god was (?)
 Eastern ..... PER-ATEM (PITHÔM). Its god was TEM. }

9.  later  ĀNDJ-TI. — PER-ASAR. BUSIRIS. Its ancient god was ĀNDJ-TI, but later OSIRIS.

10.  later  KAM-UR. — ATHRIBIS (near BANHA). Its ancient god was a 'Great Black Bull'. Later it was HORUS KHENTI-KHATI.

11.  (late form) HESEBU..... — CYNOPOLIS. Its ancient god was a species of bull.

12.  TEB-NETER. — SEBENNYTUS. Its ancient god was the 'Divine Calf'. Later AN-ḤER (ANOURIS) and the Lioness goddess MEḤI-T were worshipped in this nome.

13. 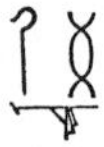 (late form) ḤEQ-ĀNDJ. — ANNU, ON, HELIOPOLIS. Its latest god was RĀ.

14.  later  ..... — ZOAN, TANIS. Its god was HORUS.

15.  ..... — HERMOPOLIS PARVA. Its god was THOTH.

16.  ..... — MENDES. Its ancient goddess was ḤĀT-MEḤIT the Dolphin goddess, but later the great god of the city, the RAM, the Lord of ṬEṬU, BA-NEB-ṬEṬ, whence the name of MENDES.

17.  BEḤUT-T. — DIOSPOLIS PARVA, DAMANHÛR. Its god was HORUS.

18.  AMU-KHENT. — BUBASTUS TALL-BAṢṬAH (ZAḲĀZIḲ). Its goddess in late times was the cat-headed goddess BAST, or UBAST.

19.  AMU-PEḤU.[1] — TANIS, later PELUSIUM. In late times its goddess was UADJIT.

20.  . . . . . — ARABIA. The modern ṢAFṬ AL-HANNAH, in Egyptian 'House of the *Nebes* tree'. This suggests that the original god of the district was a Tree-god. In dynastic times its god was SEPTU.

The first forms of the blazons, or badges, of the nomes given in the above lists are taken from the Pyramid Texts as edited by SETHE, which means that they were the official forms as recognized by the priesthood of HELIOPOLIS in the Vth and VIth dynasties. It must not be assumed that the blazons represent exactly those which were used by the predynastic EGYPTIANS, for there is evidence to show that, in many cases, they do not. The religion of the predynastic inhabitants, both of the DELTA and of UPPER EGYPT, had many phases which even the dynastic EGYPTIANS could not trace, and we, even with our fuller knowledge, can only guess at them. Looking at the blazons given above we see that they consist chiefly of animals, viz. the bull, the cow, the calf, the cow's head, the lion and lioness, the

[1] The XVIIIth and XIXth nomes were originally one, and the XIXth was the older portion of it. The royal child in the blazon who was called Imti was the god of Amtt, a city the ruins of which have been found at Tall Nabashah, near Tanis.

leopard, the SET animal, the wolf, the dog, the cat, the hare, the oryx, the jackal, and the crocodile, and it is easy to understand why the cult of animals was so dear to the EGYPTIANS right down to the Roman period. The cult of the hawk was general, and it is certainly one of the oldest cults in EGYPT.

III

MAGIC THE FOUNDATION OF THE EGYPTIAN RELIGIONS. MAGICAL RITUALS AND SPELLS DESCRIBED. THE MAGICIAN, HIS POWERS AND WORKS

KHATI 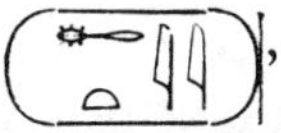, a king of the IXth (?) dynasty wrote a book of Admonitions, i.e. Religious and Moral Precepts, for the use of his son MERI-KA-RĀ , and of this a copy made under the XIXth dynasty has come down to us.[1] In § xxviii of this work the king enumerates the great things which God, of whom to him RĀ of HELIOPOLIS was the symbol, has done for man, and in lines 136–8, he says, 'He made for them the ḤEKAU to fight against (or to repulse) the power of [untoward] happenings and visions (or dreams) by night as well as by day.'[2] The word ḤEKAU is connected with *ḥeka*[3]  which is by the general consent of Egyptologists translated by 'magic'. The ḤEKAU of our text is probably to be rendered 'magician'; for spells, incantations, exorcisms, 'words of power', &c., were called *ḥekau*  or . In a text of a much later period[4] ḤEKA is spoken of as a god who was created by the Sun-god RĀ at a time when nothing else existed, and thus he was coeval with God. According to this statement ḤEKA or magic was believed by the EGYPTIANS to be older than religion. It is certainly open to doubt whether the word 'magic' is the correct translation of ḤEKA, because we can never recapture the *exact* meaning which the EGYPTIANS of any period attached to the word; they probably had no

[1] See Golénischeff, *Les Papyrus Hiératiques Nos. 1115, 1116A, and 1116B de L'Ermitage Impérial à St. Pétersbourg*, 1913; and Gardiner, *Journal of Eg. Arch.* vol. i, pp. 22 ff.

[2] 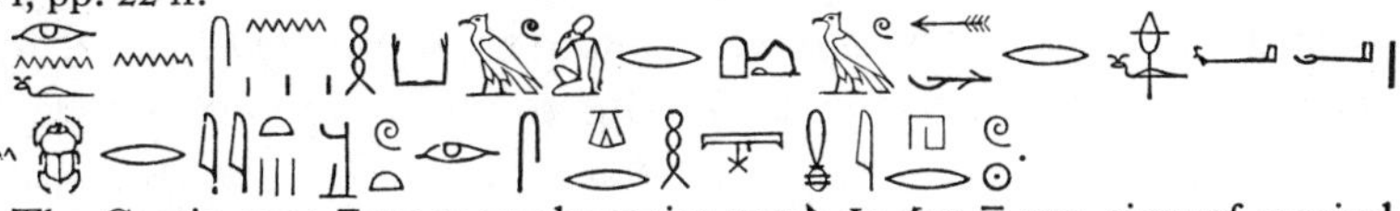

[3] The Coptic ϩⲓⲕ ; ⲣ̄ϩⲓⲕ to work magic; ⲣⲉϥϯ ⲫⲁϩⲣⲓ ⲛ̄ ϩⲓⲕ giver of magical drugs.

[4] Lacau, *Textes religieux*, Paris, 1910, No. 78.

clear idea themselves when they used the word. But on the whole 'magic' must be regarded as a fairly good rendering of ḤEKA, and it is supported by the Sahidic version of the Coptic translation of the *Acts of the Apostles*. The Greek text (viii. 9) describes SIMON the sorcerer by μαγεύων and this is rendered in the papyrus Codex Oriental, No. 7594, fol. 71*b* by ⲉⲩⲣⲉϥⲣ̅ ϩⲓⲕ,[1] 'he worked ḤEKA'. In verse 11, his workings in magic are spoken of as ταῖς μαγείαις, and the Coptic equivalent is ⲛ̅ ⲙⲛ̅ⲧⲙⲁⲅⲟⲥ.[2] Thus the authority for rendering ḤEKA by 'magic' is as old as the third century of our era, but whether the ritual acts and magical formulae of SIMON were Persian or Egyptian in character is not clear.

But what was Egyptian Magic, and what was its relation to the religions of EGYPT? The true answer to these questions is difficult to ascertain, for Egyptologists as well as anthropologists hold opinions on the subject which are generally diverse and sometimes flatly contradictory. The early Egyptologists did not trouble themselves about Egyptian Magic, and no mention of it is made in the index to the last edition of WILKINSON'S *Ancient Egyptians*, LONDON, 1878. BRUGSCH believed that the magical texts of EGYPT had no value for Egyptology except for the information which they afforded scholars who were working on the writing and language of EGYPT.[3] And there is no discussion of magic in his *Religion und Mythologie*, LEIPZIG, 1888.

ERMAN says, 'Magic is a barbarous offshoot of religion, and is an attempt to influence the powers that preside over the destiny of mankind' (*Egyptian Religion*, LONDON, 1907, p. 149). He cannot regard the religious rites and ceremonies of the EGYPTIANS, and their prayers, as magic: thus, according to this scholar, religion is older than magic, but proof of his statement is wanting. WIEDEMANN thought that 'magic was the power which regulated the common relations of superior beings and their dealings with men. It gave movement and power to men, to the dead, and to the gods. The real master of the world was the magician who knew the magical formulas to which all beings were bound to submit' (*Das alte Aegypten*, HEIDELBERG, 1920, p. 411). But this is only another way of

[1] This fact was noted by Tattam (*Lexicon Aegyptiaco-Latinum*, Oxford, 1835, p. 682.)

[2] See Budge, *Coptic Biblical Texts*, London, 1912, pp. 162, 163.

[3] *Die Aegyptologie*, Leipzig, 1897, p. 77.

giving religion priority over magic. GARDINER thinks that the EGYPTIANS might have described all their actions as either ordinary or magical. Ordinary actions were the simple ways of coping with inanimate objects and living beings which were suggested by habit, mother wit, or acquired skill. When these failed the EGYPTIANS achieved their ends by means of an art which they called ḤEKA. Whenever mysterious, miraculous knowledge was required to effect a purpose, that was ḤEKA; ḤEKA was something different from the technique and practices of everyday life, since it postulated special powers in its user, and always made a greater or less demand upon faith. (See the article 'Magic' in HASTINGS's *Encyclopaedia*, vol. viii, p. 262.) GARDINER does not regard as ḤEKA actions performed for the benefit of the dead or those connected with the worship of the gods; thus he makes a clear distinction between magic and religion.

MORET distinguishes between natural power and magical power, and points out that while the priest prays or entreats, the magician commands. Experience showed that force was more efficacious than prayer, and it followed as a matter of course that among primitive peoples the magician had greater authority than the priest (*La Magie*, PARIS, 1906, pp. 241 ff.). The whole question of Egyptian magic has been carefully discussed by CLEMEN ('Wesen und Ursprung der Magie' in *Archiv für Religionspsychologie*, Bande II, III, 1921, pp. 108 ff.), who, although he decides that the views of HUBERT and MAUSS, JEVONS, FRAZER, TYLOR, GRESSMAN, and many others are all wrong, is unable to say definitely what Egyptian magic really was. After a careful discussion of the views of previous scholars who have tried to define magic, Dr. F. LEXA of PRAGUE says, in his *La Magie dans l'Égypte Antique*, PARIS, 1925, p. 17, that MAGIC is the active operation (or principle) which tends to produce the effect of which the connexion with this action cannot be explained subjectively by the law of causality; and he carefully distinguishes magic from superstition.

The writers who have tried to explain the *origin* of magic have come to no agreement on the subject. Some ascribe to it an animistic origin, but this view is not supported by the texts. ERMAN, with the view of explaining how the belief that the powers that preside over the destinies of man could be influenced by man, says, 'On one occasion it appears that a prayer has been heard by the deity, on another it is apparently ignored; thus the idea naturally arises that the words in which the prayer was uttered on the first occasion must have been specially acceptable to the god. This construction is therefore accepted as the most effective, and becomes a formula which is regarded as certainly successful, and able to control destiny' (*Religion*, p. 148). This explanation seems, to the present writer, to be erroneous, for assuredly man performed magical rites, and recited magical spells long before he formulated the idea of a being to whom he could pray. A repeated perusal of all the statements made by scholars, and more particularly by Egyptologists, has convinced me that their authors have overlooked the fact that the primitive EGYPTIANS who first performed magical rites and used magical words were absolute savages. Their thoughts and ideas are not only unknown to us, but can never be known to us.

It is useless to attempt to ascertain whether their magic was the parent of the religion of their descendants in dynastic times, or whether it was a 'barbarous offshoot' of the early forms of that religion, for it is pretty certain that in the earliest period of their history they had no religion at all, as we understand the word. They, no doubt, evolved the idea of the existence of ḤEKA, and probably made use of that very word, but what exactly ḤEKA was has not yet been found out. Our knowledge of Egyptian magic is derived entirely from texts of the dynastic period, and although, fortunately, they tell us what ḤEKA could do, they only suggest dimly what ḤEKA was. In my opinion ḤEKA was a something which formed a very essential part of a divine being or god. It made a god or its possessor superior in power to every being who did not possess it. By it alone a god was able to exist, and to do the work which he did. It was not his life, but it was the source of his life, and it may be compared to the *mâna* of the peoples of the South Seas. Its possession was absolutely necessary for a god if he wished to continue his existence, and in times of danger he relied on it for effective help, and he made use of it also whenever he wished to do any special piece of work. In the Egyptian Creation Legend[1] NEB-ER-DJER the Creator of the world and of all in it says, 'I was One by myself for

[1] In British Museum Papyrus, No. 10188. Published with hieroglyphic transcript and translation by Budge, *Hieratic Papyri in the British Museum*, London, 1910. First Series.

they (i.e. the gods) were not born and I had not produced SHU and I had not produced TEFNUT. I brought my own mouth, my name [being] ḤEKA' (i.e. the magical power came into being, &c.).
 [1]

This suggests that the ḤEKA was the utterance of the god's own name by the god, and that the Creator existed before the Creation in name only. In another passage the god says, 'I found no place on which to stand, I used a spell in my heart (or mind)'  , and so formed the *designs* of the material objects which subsequently came into being. Thus it is clear that the Creator employed ḤEKA in creating himself and in performing his creative acts, and that it was connected with his own name[2] and heart. ḤEKA could be made operative by its possessor through any member of his body, and it could be bestowed by him on a friend. It was as much a part of the body of its possessor as the KA; like Taste and Touch it could be personified, thus  and under certain conditions it was possible to steal ḤEKA from a human being, living or dead. As the gods made use of it in creating themselves we may perhaps assume that it was older than they, and if so, where did it exist, and whence came it? As there was nothing in existence except the primeval abyss of water, and NEB-ER-DJER in the form of KHEPRI came out of that water possessing ḤEKA, ḤEKA must have had its being in the primeval water and operated therein or therefrom as a creative force. The ancient theologians of MEMPHIS would, no doubt, have traced the origin to ḤEKA to PTAḤ, the Eternal Mind, the great *Causa Causarum*. Our word 'magic' will serve as a general description of the rites and spells of the primitive Egyptian savage, but it does not describe ḤEKA, the supernatural mainspring of his rites and spells.

The primitive savage employed his rites and spells for his own benefit or that of his neighbours. His chief object was to defeat the evil spirits wherewith he believed himself to be surrounded, and to

[1] i.e. I uttered my own name from my mouth as a word of power.

[2] We may note that the Abyssinians believed that the Three Persons of the Trinity existed in the waters of the primeval ocean, which had been their abode for ever; but they existed in *name* only. Each Person assumed His Personality only after reciting His own name. See *Book of the Mysteries of Heaven and Earth*, edited by Perruchon (Paris, no date).

render himself immune from their attacks, and the diseases sent by them. He wished to be able to overcome his foes, whether wild animals or men, to obtain offspring, to protect his family and property, and almost above all to destroy the evil influence of the dead, whom he feared with a deadly fear. The dynastic EGYPTIANS adopted many of the rites and spells of their predecessors, the predynastic savages, and employed them in their cult of the dead, and in their worship of their gods. Thus magic and religion became mingled, and it was this fact which made W. MAX MÜLLER write:

'It is, however, very difficult to state where religion ends and magic begins; and to the Egyptian mind magic was merely applied religion. . . . The very naïve Egyptian spirit, which was so unable to distinguish between the material and the supernatural, and the excessive formalism of the worship give us the impression that the whole religion of the NILE-land had a strongly magical character. The *Book of the Dead*, with its directions how to find a way to OSIRIS, what to say before him, what words to recite, and what mysterious names to give to the guardians of his realm, presents a close approximation to magic; yet, after all it is no secret knowledge, but is open to all who can read, and therefore, does not fall under the modern definition of sorcery; neither did the EGYPTIANS themselves consider it magical' (*Egyptian Mythology*, p. 198).

In this passage MÜLLER assumes that magic is degenerated religion, but all the available evidence contradicts this assumption. It may be that magic and religion grew up side by side, but if this was so, magic in primitive times outgrew religion. The equivalent of the modern 'witch doctor', or as we might call him 'the servant of ḤEKA', assuredly preceded the 'servant of the god', though in the dynastic period a man might be 'priest of ḤEKA' as well as 'priest of HORUS'.[1]

From the above it is clear that there were three kinds of magic in EGYPT and certain rites and spells were common to all of them: (1) The magic used by men who tried to get by its means what they could not obtain by ordinary means and methods. (2) The magic used by men to prevent the return of the dead to this world, and to thwart the designs of the evil spirits of the dead. (3) The magic which was used by men to procure the goodwill and favour of the gods, and to obtain immortal life with OSIRIS. It is probable that there existed at various times in the dynastic period learned and

[1] See the example quoted by Gardiner (Hastings's *Encyclopaedia*, vol. viii, p. 263).

educated men who knew how to discount the works of magic, and who were earnest seekers after God. Such would, from the innate conservatism of their minds, tolerate 'White', i.e. Religious, Magic, and utterly condemn and abominate what we call 'Black', i.e. Pagan, Magic. As long as magic was used to benefit men or their neighbours, or the dead and the gods, it was regarded with favour by the

The Kheri ḥeb endowing a statue of the scribe Ani with power to think, breathe, and use his limbs in spite of the funerary bandages. The ram-headed staff conveyed the magician's power to the head of the statue. The typical magician's box and several of its instruments are seen between the deceased and the magician. It is possible that the ebony rod of the magician became ultimately the symbol for 'god'.

EGYPTIANS. But when, as in the case of the man who made magical figures with the view of destroying RAMESES III, it was used with a felonious, or evil, or murderous intent, the punishment meted out to the offender was death.

ḤEKA was made by RĀ for the benefit of mankind (see p. 113), and every man who possessed it made use of it in the way he pleased. But in primitive times there soon appeared among men the equivalent of the modern 'medicine man' or 'witch doctor', who was able to convince his fellows that he was a master of ḤEKA and that by its use he could procure for them everything they desired. Then, as now, the witch doctor being bribed by adequate gifts would use his professed powers to work good or evil. His successor in the dynastic period was the KHERI ḤEB 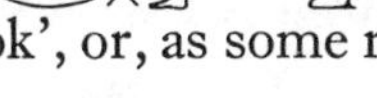 or 'possessor of the book of the ritual, or service book', or, as some render it, 'ritual priest'.

He was the greatest of all the priests, and directed the magical services in the temples and the religious services for the dead. He possessed the art of writing, itself a magical achievement, and could read; he was a theologian and was also well versed in the contents of the books of magic and the *Book of the Dead*; like MOSES, he was learned in all the wisdom of the EGYPTIANS; he was a practical and practised magician, and director of all magical ceremonies which, when performed by him, became religious rites; he was skilled in the art of the physician; and after periods of fasting from meat, wine, and women, the will of the gods was disclosed to him, and the gift of prophecy bestowed upon him. Tradition ascribed to the KHERI ḤEBS who flourished under the kings of the Old Kingdom very great powers. UBANER made a figure of a crocodile in wax seven spans long, and recited a spell over it, and when it was thrown into the river it became a crocodile seven cubits long, and swallowed a man. Seven days later the magician recited a spell, and the crocodile came up out of the water with the man inside him. When the magician took up the crocodile in his hands it turned at once into a harmless wax crocodile; when commanded the wax crocodile leaped out of the magician's hand into the water, and became a living crocodile and swam away with the young man, whom he devoured. Another KHERI ḤEB called DJADJAMĀNKH divided the waters of a lake into two parts, and made the one part rise up and place itself on top of the other part. Another called TETA cut off the head of a goose and then reunited it to its body, and he reunited the decapitated head of an ox to its body by means of his spells. A lion tied with a rope was brought to TETA, and when he had said a spell over the lion he removed the rope, and the lion came and followed TETA, like a dog, with his rope trailing behind him on the ground. TETA also possessed the gift of prophecy and foretold correctly the downfall of the dynasty of the king to whom he had exhibited his skill in the working of magic.[1]

The high-priests of MEMPHIS, HELIOPOLIS, and THEBES were always learned men, and the knowledge of magic and theology possessed by them was alike exhaustive and thorough. Among the learned men of the Old Kingdom ḤERṬAṬAF and IMḤETEP deserve

[1] See the stories in the Westcar Papyrus in Berlin edited and translated by Erman.

special mention. The former was the son of king KHUFU (CHEÔPS) and his name is mentioned in the rubrics to chapters XXX B and lxiv of the *Book of the Dead* as the discoverer of ancient religious texts. The latter flourished in the reign of king DJESER and was a great physician, magician, and architect. He was worshipped as a

Djeḥuti or Thoth, ibis-headed wearing a composite crown composed of the horns of Khnemu, the White Crown, and the plumes of the solar gods. He is known as , the 'Word-god'.

Thoth restoring to Horus the Eye Udjat , which Set had either blinded or swallowed.

god by the EGYPTIANS, and the GREEKS regarded him as the founder of the science of medicine.

The greatest of all magicians was THOTH, the mind and tongue of RĀ. He was the inventor of writing and of the arts and sciences, and the author of the great book of magic which the EGYPTIANS regarded as the source of all their knowledge of magic. He taught the goddess ISIS the spells whereby she restored OSIRIS to life after his murder by SET, and expelled the poison from the body of her son HORUS after he was stung by the scorpion sent by SET. When OSIRIS committed adultery with NEPHTHYS, ISIS complained to THOTH and implored him to right her wrong, for she was childless. When ISIS discovered the phallus of OSIRIS which had been cut off from him by SET,

THOTH assisted her to rejoin it to the body of OSIRIS and supplied her with the magical power which caused it to perform its normal functions and to make her pregnant. The result of the embrace of OSIRIS was ḤER-PA-KHARṬ or HARPOKRATES. He was likewise the master physician, and he healed the eye of RĀ after it had been damaged and blinded by SET, who took the form of a black pig, and

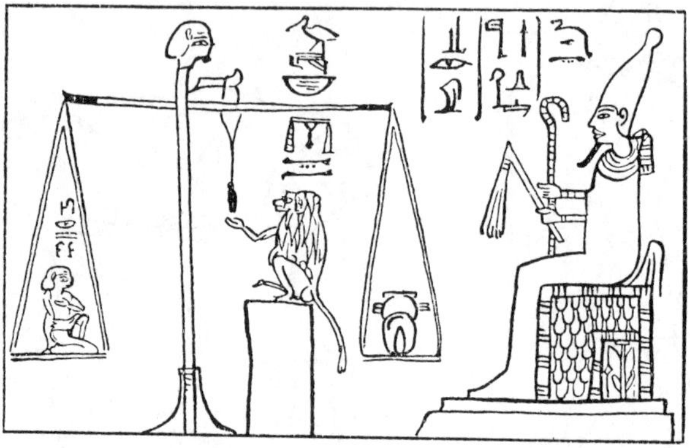

One of the oldest drawings of the Weighing of the Heart from the Theban *Book of the Dead.* Here the Scales are actually Osiris. Nebseni is in one pan and his heart in the other. The Baboon who performs the weighing is called 'Thoth, Lord of the Scales of the Two Lands'. Osiris, seated and passive, is called 'Great God, Governor of Eternity'. This is the Vignette of chapter XXX B.

he restored it to its original place in the face of RĀ. The great learning of THOTH enabled him to fathom all mysteries, especially those connected with the minds of men. Hence his position as scribe and advocate in the Judgement Hall of OSIRIS when men's hearts were weighed in the Great Scales. His counterpart among goddesses was ISIS, who knew everything which was in heaven and upon earth. She knew spells of every kind, and she possessed the tones of voice necessary, and the modes of utterance, which made them effective. With voice and word she bewitched alike gods and men. She aspired to become the mistress of the universe and to enjoy the position and powers of RĀ, but she did not know his hidden and secret name by means of which he maintained his position in the heavens. Fair means failing her, she made a model of a reptile possessing a deadly poison, and by her magic endowed it with power sufficient to kill RĀ if it bit the god. She placed this model by the side of the path over which RĀ journeyed daily, and when he passed the reptile bit him with such terrible results that RĀ began to die, and the gods were powerless to help him. ISIS appeared and told him that she alone knew how to expel the poison from his body, and that she would do so if he would reveal his secret name to her. His agony was so intense that RĀ at length revealed his name to her. When ISIS recited her spells over RĀ the poison flowed out from his body and he recovered. The possession of the secret name of RĀ made ISIS more powerful than ever. The story of the fights between HORUS and SET recently published by DR. GARDINER shows that HORUS possessed great magical powers, which he, no doubt, inherited from his mother ISIS.

Among men probably the greatest magician known was KHĀMUAS, the KHAMOIS of SYNCELLUS, the son of RAMESES II by his wife MEḤUSEKHT, who succeeded in getting possession of the *Book of Magic* which THOTH had written with his own hand. This contained two great spells which, the book claimed, gave to him who knew them extraordinary powers on earth and in AMENTI (the Underworld). By the first he could bewitch heaven, earth, hell, mountains, and seas, and could understand the speech of the birds of the heavens and the creeping things of the earth, and see the fish in the ocean. The knowledge of the second gave the man in AMENTI power to resume the form which he had upon earth, and to see RĀ shining in the sky and surrounded by his company of gods, and the moon ....[1] SA-ASAR, the son of KHĀMUAS, was also a great magician, and it is said that he could read the contents of a roll of papyrus without unrolling it. An official of SA-AMEN called HOR, the son of PANESHE, was also greatly learned in magic. He went into the temple of HERMOPOLIS and having made offerings to THOTH that god appeared to him and told him where to find the great *Book of Magic*. The Ethiopian sorcerers had sent their sorceries to EGYPT intending to spirit away PHARAOH to ETHIOPIA. But as HOR had bound amulets on PHARAOH the sorceries of ETHIOPIA were powerless to carry him off. When HOR heard this from PHARAOH he determined to do to the governor of ETHIOPIA what the governor had tried to do to PHARAOH. He had a large quantity of pure wax brought to him and made a

[1] See Griffith, *Stories of the High Priests*, p. 20.

model of a litter and models of four men to carry it. Then he recited spells over all these, and so endowed them with life, and he ordered them to go to the SÛDÂN (NEḤES), and to bring the Viceroy to the presence chamber of PHARAOH. When there they were to give the Viceroy a beating with sticks, five hundred strokes, and then to carry him back to the SÛDÂN. All this was to be done in six hours. The wax figures set out by night with the litter and accompanied by the sorceries of HOR they travelled through the clouds straight to ETHIOPIA. They seized the Viceroy, brought him to EGYPT, administered the five hundred strokes with sticks, and then carried him back to ETHIOPIA within the six hours.[1] The following morning the Viceroy assembled his nobles, and showed them his back, and they saw the weals and wounds which the sticks had made on it; and seeing them they uttered loud cries of horror. The Viceroy sent for his chief sorcerer, who was also called HOR, and cursed him by AMEN, the Bull of MEROË, and commanded him to save him from further disgrace and suffering at the hands of the Egyptian sorcerers. HOR promptly prepared amulets and bound them on the Viceroy and so protected him.

NEKHT-NEB-F (NECTANEBUS), the last native king of EGYPT, was also a great magician, and he was able to foretell the future. On various occasions he made wax models of his own sailors and ships, and soldiers and horses, and also of the ships and their crews and of the cavalry men and their horses, of the Persians and other enemies. Usually the crews of the Egyptian ships sank the ships of the enemy, and the EGYPTIANS defeated the enemy, and NECTANEBUS reigned undisturbed for some years. But then there came a day when his scouts brought news of the coming to EGYPT of huge armies from many hostile nations, and he became afraid. Retiring to his secret chamber in the palace he brought out his case of magical appliances, the wax and the ebony staff, &c. And he made models of his own ships and those of the enemy, and set them on the water in a tank, and the ships of the enemy sank his ships, and the soldiers of the enemy overthrew his soldiers. And the gods informed him that his rule was ended. Without more ado he collected all the treasure he could lay his hands on and fled from EGYPT to MACEDON, where he set up as a fortune-teller and practical magician. The story

[1] Griffith, *Stories*, p. 59 f.

of his further adventures is told in the Greek text of the pseudo-CALLISTHENES.

The primitive or savage magician made use of his ḤEKA or magical power on every possible occasion without much regard to sense or reason. His chief aim was to protect himself and his women and beasts generally from sickness, disease, and death, and to enable him to avert calamity, destruction, and death at the hands of his enemies. In dynastic times the magician sought to obtain good results by performing certain acts and by reciting certain spells or incantations. On special occasions he purified himself by rigorous fasting and ceremonial ablutions and by putting on rudimentary articles of dress, e.g. a belt or bandlet or fillet, or the skin of an animal, generally that of a leopard, which was believed to facilitate his intercourse with the denizens of the world of spirits and enhance his powers.

The magician sometimes assumed the character and name of some god or some supernatural being with the idea of causing inanimate objects to obey his will or to terrify the spirits of evil; thus we find in the texts the magician or priest declaring, 'I am THOTH', 'I am RĀ, 'I am Fire, the son of Fire'. Often he calls upon the gods to help him and informs them that if they do so the offerings made to them will be increased, and their own powers likewise; but if they do not they will suffer in every way. Libations will cease because the NILE will dry up; the sun, moon, and stars will become eclipsed; the earth will become a ruin, and the heavens be done away. The magician and priest both claimed their right to immediate obedience on the part of all things animate and inanimate because they had obtained possession of the 'great and terrible names', and since the name of a person was that person, and the name of a thing was that thing, the owners of those great and terrible names were their vassals. For, as we have seen above, the name of a god produced the ḤEKA by which he lived. And because the gods had at certain times performed rites by ḤEKA and recited their names, and so produced a marvellous result, the magician assumed that by a repetition of those rites and those names, they would obtain a repetition of the results which the gods arrived at. This is the idea underlying all forms of SYMPATHETIC MAGIC.

The magician made his powers effective at a distance by the use of amulets which had various forms and by means of figures or models of human beings and animals, &c. Certain stones were believed to contain ḤEKA, and to these the magician transferred some of his own ḤEKA by means of touch, or the recital of names of power and magical spells; or by writing or engraving spells upon them. Thus in the *Book of the Dead* we have models of the *scarabaeus sacer* and the GOLIATH beetle, and the heart made of various kinds of stones and each having its magical formula, the head rest, the UDJAT or Eye of RĀ, the ṬEṬ (DED), the ṬJEṬ, the vulture, the pectoral, the UADJ sceptre, &c., and some of these were tied to the necks of mummies. In dynastic times the *shabti* (chap. vi), i.e. a figure of a bearded mummy, was made, by means of the spell written upon it, to do work for the deceased in the Underworld; whether it took the place of the victim slain during funerary murders (the *tekenu*) is not certain. The figures of representatives of the four pillars of HORUS,[1] and the four clay troughs, and the four blazing torches, and the four amulets set up, or mud bricks, had very special importance in one religious ceremony described in the rubrics to chapter cxxxvii A, the object of which was to make the deceased become the equal of OSIRIS. No man might be present during the ceremony except the father or son of the magician, or priest, and the priest must be clean of body and ceremonially pure, and he must have fasted for some days from meat, fish, and women. This ritual was a very old one, and both it and the spells dated from the time of KHUFU (CHEÔPS) whose son ḤERṬAṬAF found them written on a papyrus which was hidden in a coffer in the temple of the goddess UNNUT in HERMOPOLIS, i.e. the city of THOTH. The papyrus had been written by THOTH himself (see the rubrics to chap. cxxxvii A).

Figures of animals and men played a prominent part in religious magic and in what we may call Black Magic. Under the XVIIIth dynasty and onwards the EGYPTIANS believed that a host of infernal beings infested the eastern parts of the heavens with the view of preventing the sun from rising. The leader of the gang was called ĀPEP or ĀPEPI, and he is depicted in the *Book of Gates* in the form of a monster crocodile. He took the place which SET had occupied under the Old and Middle Kingdoms, and was believed to cause thunder and lightning, hurricanes, sand storms, rain storms,

[1] Their names had to be written on their shoulders.

eclipses, fog, mist, and darkness. With the view of preventing the happening of such calamities the priests made large models of crocodiles which were burnt at stated intervals in the great temple

The monster serpent Āpep and his ally the crocodile Seshsesh lying in wait to prevent the rising of the Sun-god at dawn. They are being attacked by the *ābebutiu* or 'harpooners' of Rā with the help of , an ancient god with the ears of an ass, and by a series of goddesses who are working magic with ropes. The monsters become paralysed temporarily and the sun rises, but they renew their opposition the following morning.

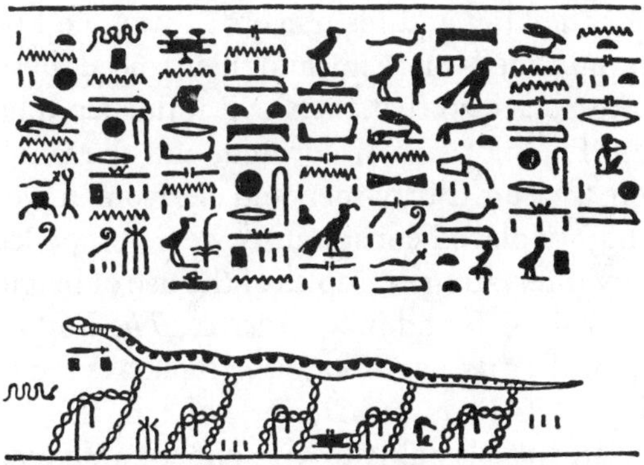

Āpep pegged to the earth and fettered by Gebb the Earth-god and his company of gods.

of AMEN RĀ at THEBES. The wax crocodile with his name cut on his back was brought forward and gashes were made in his back, his skull was smashed, his vertebrae were severed with a knife, his legs were cut off, and the figure was reduced to a ruin. Then a fire was kindled, and the fragments of the crocodile were cast into it, and men defiled them with urine and crushed them to nothingness with their left feet. Meanwhile the priest recited spells of curses over the crocodile, and the ritual and the spells were repeated whenever any appearance in the sky, either by day or by night, suggested that ĀPEP was the cause of it.

The use of figures in Black Magic is commonly known as *envoûtement*, which means the act of making a figure of wax (or of mud, or any other substance) of a certain person as exact as possible as regards face (the Latin *in+vultus*) and form and special characteristics, with the intention, after having performed upon it certain baleful acts and ceremonies, of making the person represented by the wax figure to suffer all the pains and indignities which the magician inflicts on the wax figure. Whilst the magician is attacking the wax figure he repeats spells and incantations which he believes will effect the transmission of aches, and pains, and sufferings to the human being wheresoever he may be. But *envoûtement* could be practised with a good as well as a bad object. The oldest example of the use of wax figures with an evil object is that mentioned in *Le papyrus judiciare de Turin* (PARIS, 1868). Several of the officials and ladies of the *harîm* of RAMESES III employed a magician called HUI to make wax figures of the king and his officers in wax, and to write their names and certain spells on them, and they caused these to be introduced into the palace so that their evil influence might hurt and kill the king. The plot was discovered, and the ringleaders were tried for high treason. Forty men and six women were executed, and several highly placed conspirators were compelled to commit suicide. Many interesting examples of the use of magical figures in modern times will be found in ELWORTHY, *The Evil Eye*, LONDON, 1895, pp. 53–6. For its use among the HEBREWS see GASTER, 'The Sword of Moses', in *Texts and Studies*, vol. i, p. 324, No. 68.

The magician was also able to give effect to his magical powers by means of spells and incantations written on papyrus or linen; compare the picture of the two boats of RĀ (*Book of the Dead*, chap. cxxx), and the pictures of the gods of the Great ENNEAD (chap. cxxxiv), and the pictures of the DJADJAU (chaps. cxliv and cxlviii), and the pictures of the gods of the winds (chap. clxi); see also the rubrics to chaps. clxii, clxiii, clxiv, &c. And protective power could be transferred to both large and small stone monuments, e.g. the so-called CIPPI of HORUS, and the great METTERNICH STELE (see p. 496). In addition to the Drama of the Wanderings of ISIS in the Delta which is inscribed on the latter stele, there are cut figures of hundreds of gods, and vignettes of magical scenes and magical amulets.

Among the equipment of the magician was a rod made of ebony. NECTANEBUS, the magician-king, used one when he worked magic, and tradition says that the magicians who were present with MOSES when he stood before PHARAOH had rods. The rod of MOSES[1] not only brought victory to the ISRAELITES, but had the power of the water-diviner for when he struck the rock with it the waters gushed forth. The Sumerian god NINGISHZIDA, the son of NINAZU, the master physician, also had a rod of office and power.

The great power and influence of the physician was most evident to the people when he was acting in the character of the physician. The patient assumed that he possessed complete knowledge of drugs and medicines, but it was the spells of the magician which gave them their effects in the human body. For many centuries the magic, religion, and the healing art were intimately associated, and the magician, theologian, and physician were usually found in one and the same man. Any man could perform magical ritual and recite spells, but it was only the man of learning who, according to popular belief, could be relied upon to produce satisfactory results. The greater his learning the stronger his magic. When RAMESES II (?) wanted to dispatch a magician-priest to drive out the devil from his wife's sister in BEKHTEN he summoned his officials and told them to produce not only a *Rekhi Khet* 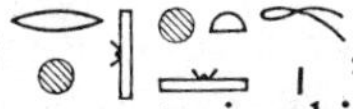, i.e. one who knew things [of magic], but a priest who was trained in mind and whose fingers were instructed in writing and in the manipulation of magical instruments, , and who was an associate or scribe of the 'House of Life'  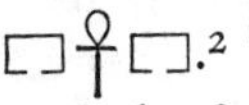.[2] The trained magician-priest knew how to choose the day and the hour most suitable for his operations, and he knew the position of certain heavenly bodies in the sky. He knew what tone of voice to adopt, and when to entreat and when to threaten the spirits or the gods. He knew also whether a spell was to be said four times or seven times. FOUR and SEVEN are magical numbers and

[1] See Exod. iv. 4, 20, vii. 20; Num. xx. 11. The 'rod of God', Job xxi. 9.

[2] The Prince of Bekhten had only asked for a *Rekhi Khet*; see the Bekhten Stele, line 10.

each is found in many religious and magical texts. Thus we have the Four altars, the Four lamps or blazing torches, the Four birth-places at ABYDOS, the Four doors of heaven, the Four rudders, the Four vessels of blood, the Four vessels of milk, the Four mud bricks, the Four pillars or sons of HORUS, the Four spirits, the Four glorious gods, the Four cardinal points, &c. Examples of Seven are: the Seven HATHORS, the Seven ĀRITI, the Seven cows and their bull, the Seven gods of the Lake of Fire, the Seven souls of RĀ, the Seven-headed serpent, the seventy-seven gods, the Seventy eyes, the Seventy ears, and the Two and Forty (i.e. 7×6) assessors of the Hall of Judgement.

It goes without saying that the profession of the magician, religious or otherwise, must have attracted to it many men who were charlatans and impostors. The ritual acts of such 'quacks' would be only clumsy imitations of those of the KHERI ḤEB, and their spells, as we see from the HARRIS Magical Papyrus, consisted of strings of meaningless words. Such men brought discredit on the profession of the magician, and caused it to be banned by the ecclesiastical authorities, and cursed by the ignorant. The KHERI ḤEB and his fellows regarded their profession as important for mankind, and the fact that they associated the ancient rituals and spells as integral parts of religious worship proves that they wished to remove magic from the hands of the charlatans and obtain a position for it as a religious science; for as such did they look upon their learning and knowledge, with an authority commensurate with the great antiquity of magic. The will of the gods and their help could only be obtained by an ascetic life and by ceremonial purity. The KHERI ḤEB and his assistants also had to be free not only from acts of sin, but also from every kind of impurity, for the best results of their works and words could only be obtained by those who possessed 'pure minds in pure bodies'. And even the priestesses who sang the dirges of OSIRIS were not allowed to officiate until the hair of their bodies had been removed. And similarly all the objects used in the ritual had to be fresh and new, water, papyrus, earth, metals, &c.

As time went on and the spiritual development of the EGYPTIANS advanced, the importance of magic, except for religious purposes, seems to have declined, and in the funerary papyri of the Persian and Ptolemaic periods nearly all the old spells are wanting. The various sections of chapter cxxv and the great vignette illustrating the weighing of the heart before OSIRIS were retained, and sometimes the text of an old hymn was added. Many of the funerary papyri of these periods contain copies of texts which though of a funerary character are entirely different from those of the *Book of the Dead*, e.g. the 'Book of Breathings', the Book 'May my name flourish', the 'Book of traversing eternity', &c. But there is no evidence that the class of magic which the people employed for the everyday matters of life fell into disuse. There is little doubt that much of it was absorbed by the Gnostics, and those who used ḲABBÂLÂH, and the EGYPTIANS who embraced Christianity.

The Pyramid Texts (ed. MASPERO and SETHE) contain many spells, both magical and religious, used under the Old Kingdom; those in use under the Middle Kingdom are inscribed upon the great rectangular coffin from AL-BARSHAH and elsewhere (see the *Coffin of Amamu*, ed. BIRCH, and the group of texts published by LACAU in the *Recueil*, vols. xxi ff.). Many of the religious spells, with directions for the ritual acts, will be found in the Theban Recension of the *Book of the Dead* (ed. BUDGE). Another interesting set of spells and incantations is given in the HARRIS Magical Papyrus (ed. BUDGE, *Hieratic Texts in the British Museum*, Series I). On Egyptian Magic generally see LEXA, *La Magie dans l'Égypte Antique*, 3 vols., PARIS, 1925, and the authorities quoted by him. How the old Egyptian Magic was adopted by the EGYPTIANS who embraced Christianity (i.e. the COPTS) is well illustrated by DR. M. KROPP, *Ausgewählte Koptische Zaubertexte*, 3 vols., BRUXELLES, 1931. For a description of Egyptian Magic of all periods see GARDINER in HASTINGS'S *Encyclopaedia*, vol. viii, p. 262 f. Much light has been thrown on Graeco-Egyptian Magic by DR. T. HOPFNER in his *Griechisch-Ägyptischer Offenbarungszauber* (LEIPZIG, 1921) 'mit einer Darstellung des griechischsynkratistischen Daemonenglaubens und der Voraussetzungen und Mittel des Zaubers überhaupt und der magischen Divination im besonderen'. This is a very valuable work, but it should have been printed in type, for the writing is very small, the lines are long, and the page is large. DR. HOPFNER has also published many important articles in connexion with Greek Magic, and his article *Mittel- und Neugriechische Lekano-, Lychno-, Katoptro- und Onychomantien* is of the greatest interest.

No. 1

The 'All-god' of the magician took the following forms. He was supposed to make in himself the powers and forms of the principal ancient cosmic gods, and in him was ascribed the attributes of all the gods of heaven, earth, and the Ṭuat. All the great Typhonic animals are enclosed in the oval bound by the body of a snake on which he stands. No. 1 is reproduced by Hopfner from an object in the Leyden Museum, *Ae id.* 311 (see p. 213) and No. 2 (*see opposite*) from an earthenware amulet published by Von Bissing, *Kultus d. alt. Aeg.* Tafel 22.

No. 2

The following are specimens of spells:

I. Get thee back, thou Crocodile fiend MĀKA, son of SET!

Thou shalt not lash with thy tail, thou shalt not snatch prey with thine arms, and thou shalt not open thy mouth!

The water shall turn into a sheet of fire before thee.

The glare of the seventy and seven gods is in thine eye.

Thou art fast fettered in the windings of the serpent NAIT, the great lady of the god SAR (?)

Thou art fast fettered with the four fetters of metal from the South, which are in the bows of the divine Boat of RĀ. Hail!

Stand thou still, MĀKA, son of SET! Behold me! I am AMEN, the Bull of his mother.

Rubrical directions: Write these words over a figure of the god AMEN, having four faces on one neck. The figure shall be depicted on a piece of earthenware, and a crocodile shall be drawn under his feet, and the Eight Gods of HERMOPOLIS shall be on his right hand and on his left to perform unto him praises.

II. A water enchantment . . . a veritable mystery of the House of Life.

'Egg of the water which is poured out upon the earth. Existing ONE of the Eight Gods of KHMENU (HERMOPOLIS), Chief of the heavens, Chief in the ṬUAT, Dweller in the Nest, President of

MERDJESDJES. I have come forth with thee from the water. I have risen up with thee from out of the divine Nest. I am the god MENU of COPTOS.'

Rubrical direction: This spell shall be recited over an egg of dung, which shall be placed in the hand of a man in the bows of a boat. If anything appeareth on the water cast the egg on the water.

III. 'I am the chosen one of millions of years, he who cometh forth from the ṬUAT, whose name is not known. If his divine name be cut on the bank of the river it will slice it away, and if on the earth it will cause a fire to break out. I am the god SHU, in the form of RĀ. I have my seat in the Eye of the Father. If that which is on the water openeth its mouth, or worketh violence with its arms, I will cause the earth to fall into the water. The South shall become the North, and the earth likewise.'

Rubrical direction. Recite the above four times, and [place] in the hand of the man a drawing of the UDJAT (i.e. the Eye of RĀ), with a figure of the god AN-ḤER in it.

IV. 'Come unto me, O Image of the god of millions of years. I am the Wind, the Sun, the Only One. I was conceived yesterday and I was born to-day. Whosoever knoweth his divine name shall be like him that hath seven and seventy eyes given unto him, and like him that hath seven and seventy ears given unto him. Come thou unto me! Grant that my voice may be heard as is heard the voice of the Great Cackler (i.e. the Earth-goose which laid the Cosmic Egg) during the night. I am BĀH (i.e. the god of the Inundation) the Prince, I am BĀH the Prince.' [Recite this four times.]

Magical names to be used as ḤEKA:

1, 2. ATIR-ATISAU. ATIRKAHA-ATISAU.
3, 4. SMAUIMATEMU-ATISAU. SMAUTANEMUI-ATISAU.
5. SMAUT-TEKAIU-ATISAU.
6. SMAUT-TEKA-BAIU-ATISAU.
7. SMAUT-DJAKARAJA-ATISAU.
1. TĀUARHASA-QINA-HAMA.
2, 3. SENNFET-TA. BATHETET.
4, 5. SATITAUI. ANRAHAKATHĀ-SATITAUI.
6. HAUBAIRHURU (?)
7. HAARI.

The above are taken from BRITISH MUSEUM Papyrus No. 10042 (HARRIS, 501).

The following extracts from GRIFFITH and H. THOMPSON, *The Demotic Magical Papyrus of London and Leiden*, LONDON, 1904, vol. v, p. 45 f. illustrate the ritual and spells which were in use in the Roman Period in EGYPT.

(3) You go to a dark clean recess with its face open to the south and you purify it with (4) natron water, and you take a new white lamp in which no red earth or gum-water has been put and place a clean wick (5) in it and fill it with real oil after writing this name and these figures on the wick with ink of myrrh beforehand; (6) and you lay it on a new brick before you, its underside being spread with sand; and you pronounce these spells over the lamp again another seven times. You display frankincense in form of (7) the lamp and you look at the lamp; and you see the god about the lamp and you lie down on a rush mat without speaking (8) to any one on earth. Then he makes answers to you by dream. Behold its invocation. Formula[1] (9) Ho! I am MURAI, MURIBI, BABEL, BAOTH, BAMUI, the great AGATHODAEMON, (10) MURABHO, the . . . form of soul that resteth above in the heaven of heavens. (11) TABOT, BOUEL, MOUIHTAHI (?), LAHI, BOLBOCH, I, AA, TAT, BOUEL, YOHEL,[2] the first servant (12) of the great god, he who giveth light exceedingly, the companion of the flame, he in whose mouth is the fire that is not quenched, the great god who is seated (13) in the fire, he who is in the midst of the fire which is in the lake of heaven, in whose hand is the greatness and the power of god; reveal thyself to me (14) here to-day in the fashion of thy revelation to MOSES, which thou didst make upon the mountain, before whom thou thyself didst create darkness and light, (15)—I pray thee that thou reveal thyself to me here to-night and speak with me, and give me answer in truth without falsehood; for I will glorify thee (16) in ABYDOS, I will glorify thee in heaven before PHRE, I will glorify thee before the Moon, I will glorify thee (17) before him who is on the throne, who is not destroyed, he (= thou) of the great glory. PETERI,[3] PATER,[3] ENPHE,[3] (18) O god who is above heaven, in whose hand is the beautiful staff, who created deity, deity not having created him. Come down [in]to me (19) into the midst of this flame that is here before thee, thou of BOUEL,[3] and let me see the business that I ask about (20) to-night truly without falsehood. Let it be seen (?), let it be heard (?), O great god SISIHOOUT, otherwise said, ARMIOOUTH, come (21) in before me and give me answer to that which I shall ask about, truly without falsehood. O great god that is on the mountain (22) of ATUKI (of GABAON), KHABAHO,

[1] On the margin is written: Behold the spells which you write on the wick; Bakhukhsikhukh, *and figures*.

[2] Each of these ten names is written twice.

[3] Written twice.

TAKRTAT, come in to me, let my eyes be opened to-night for any given thing (23) that I shall ask about, truly without falsehood . . . this voice (?) of the LEASPHOT, NEBHET . . . LILAS.' Seven times: and you lie down (24) without speaking.

[Preparation of magical unguent.] The ointment which you put on your eyes when you are about to inquire of the lamp in any lamp-divination: You take some flowers (25) of the Greek bean; you find them in the place of the garland-seller, otherwise said, of the lupin-seller; you take them fresh and put them (26) in a *lok*-vessel of glass and stop its mouth very well for twenty days in a secret dark place. After twenty days, if you (27) take it out and open it, you find a pair (?) of testicles in it with a phallus. You leave it for forty days and when you take it out (28) and open it, you find that it has become bloody; then you put it on a glass thing and put the glass thing into a pottery thing (29) in a place hidden at all times. When you desire to make inquiry of the lamp with it at any time if you fill your eyes with this (30) blood aforesaid, and if you go in to pronounce a spell over the lamp you see a figure of a god standing behind (?) the lamp, and he speaks (31) with you concerning the question which you wish; or you lie down and he comes to you. If he does not come to you, you rise and pronounce his compulsion. (32) You must lie down on green reeds, being pure from a woman, your head being turned to the south and your face being turned to the north, and the face of the lamp being turned northwards likewise.

(33) *insert above*—'I pray thee to reveal thyself to me here to-night and speak with me and give me answer truly concerning the given matter which I ask thee about.'

The All-God in embryo.
(From a magical papyrus.)

IV

ANCIENT EGYPTIAN THEOLOGICAL SYSTEMS AND DOGMAS

THE WORD FOR GOD

THE hieroglyph most commonly used by the EGYPTIANS to express God, 'god' (i.e. idol), and any being or thing which was supposed to possess supernatural power or powers was 𓊹, which I believe represents a slice of stone inserted in a groove at one end of a stick, or tied to the upper end of the stick. In one or two instances a sort of lacing is seen covering the lower half of the stick, and this probably indicates the cord or leather thong which was twisted round the handle to help the user or wielder of the axe to get a better grip. Some authorities hold that 𓊹 represents a flag.[1] A star ⋆ and a hawk 𓅃[2] were also used to express God. Another view is that it represents the principal magical instrument used in some cult. The phonetic value of 𓊹 is NTR 𓈖𓏏𓂋 or NTHR 𓈖𓍿𓂋. How the word was pronounced we know not,[3] and its meaning is unknown. Various etymologies for the word have been proposed, WIEDEMANN

[1] Recently an entirely different view has been put forward by Miss M. A. Murray in the volume of papers presented to F. Ll. Griffith, p. 312, where 𓊹 *nether* is defined as a 'pole on which a piece of cloth has been wound for religious purposes'. She rejects the first letter 𓈖 from 𓈖𓍿𓂋 and then goes on to connect 𓍿𓂋 with a Coptic word meaning 'willow' and, presumably, thinks the 𓊹 represents a willow rod with a rag tied to the end of it. Had it been argued that the rod represented the *ebony* rod of the magician, with some object attached to the top of it (compare the ram's head on the rod used in 'opening the mouth'), something might be said for the suggestion, but as it is the theory is too fantastic. The matter is really a simple one: 𓊹 represents a fetish object. The Egyptian scribes did not know *what* the object was—NOR DO WE! And until the texts describe it we shall never know.

[2] Thus we have sing. 𓊹, ⋆, 𓅃, 𓅆, 𓊹𓀭, 𓊹𓅆 = god; plur. 𓊹𓏥, 𓊹𓀭𓏥, ⋆⋆⋆, 𓅃𓅃𓅃, 𓅆𓅆𓅆; fem. 𓊹𓏏, 𓊹𓏏𓐍, 𓊹𓏏𓐍𓁗, 𓅃𓏏; plur. 𓊹𓏏𓐍𓏥, 𓊹𓏏𓐍𓁗𓏥, 𓊹𓆗𓆗𓆗.

[3] The Coptic has *noute* or *nonte*, god, *entêr* gods, and *entore* and *entheri* goddess.

connected it with *nedjer* 'to strike', and RENOUF with the Coptic word *nomte* 'strength', 'power'.[1] The adjective *ntri* suggests one probable meaning. A king's son is called *sefi netri* , and the seed from which he sprung *mu netri* . In these cases the obvious meaning of *netri* is something like 'divine' or 'holy'. Applied to animals NETRI might mean 'sacred'. When the EGYPTIANS spoke of *Pa neter* they seem to have turned the word for God into a proper name.

IDEAS OF GOD, THE ONE GOD

The EGYPTIANS called the creator of the universe UĀ , i.e. One, or UĀ NETER , i.e. One God. In many texts he is called 'Only One' . He is also called , i.e. 'Only One without a second'. Now in a Hymn to RĀ (Papyrus of ANI, sheet 1) the god TA-TUNEN is called One, 'the creator of men and women' . In another hymn (HUNEFER, sheet 1) RĀ is called 'the equipped one coming forth from the primeval abyss of water. In the *Book of the Dead* (chap. clxxiii) the deceased says to OSIRIS, 'I praise thee, Lord of the gods, god One, living in truth'. The princess NESI-KHENSU glorifies AMEN-RĀ, saying, 'August Soul which came into being in primeval time, the great god living in truth, the first Nine Gods who gave birth to the other two Nine Gods, the being in whom every god existeth One One, , the creator of the kings which appeared when the earth took form in the beginning, whose birth is hidden, whose forms are manifold, whose germination cannot be known'. From this passage it is clear that AMEN-RĀ was also the 'One One'. In the *Book of the Dead* (chap. ii) the deceased says, 'Hail One! rising up from the Moon. Hail One! shining from the Moon.'[2] The 'One' is, of course, RĀ, the Sun-god, and the Moon is

[1] , Spiegelberg, *Wörterbuch*, p. 77.

[2] Compare Plutarch, *De Iside*, § 43, and see H. P. Cooke, *Osiris*, London, 1931, p. 39.

OSIRIS. AMEN-HETEP IV says in his hymn to his god ATEN , i.e. the solar disk, the physical body of the Sun-god,

'Thou art One alone [but] there are millions of life in thee.
God One, there is no other [possessing] his powers and attributes.'

But whether the god addressed be called TA-TUNEN, or RĀ, or AMEN-RĀ, or ATEN, it is always the Sun-god, or his home the sun which is in the mind of the worshipper. There was only one sun to the EGYPTIAN, and his name mattered nothing to the devout worshipper. We need not be surprised that OSIRIS is called 'god One', for he was the night-sun, an aspect or form or phase of RĀ the day-sun.[1] From one point of view the EGYPTIANS were from first to last monotheists, and their One God was the Sun.

The monotheism of the EGYPTIANS may even be compared to that of the HEBREWS and ARABS. The HEBREWS proclaimed YAHWEH to be 'One' (Deut. vi. 4). 'The LORD he is God, there is none else beside him' (Deut. iv. 35). 'See now that I, even I, am he, and there is no god with me' (Deut. xxxii. 39). 'I am the LORD, and there is none else, there is no God beside me' (Isa. xlv. 5). The MUḤAMMADANS say, 'ALLÂH is One, the Eternal (AṢ-ṢAMAD); He begetteth not, neither is He begotten, and there is not any one like unto him (Kur'ân, Sûrah cxii). The titles and epithets applied to this One God prove that he was believed to be self-produced, self-existent, almighty, eternal, omniscient, and omnipresent, just, righteous, merciful, good, and gracious. He ruled the universe which he created by means of his ministers or messengers, or angels, who obeyed his decrees and carried out his works.

SET THE DEVIL AND GOD OF EVIL, 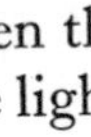

The first day of creation, that is the day when the sun rose on this world, was followed by the night; when the light from the sun

[1] An interesting example of the use of Uo, 'One', is found in Pyr. § 293, where the dead king Unas is called 'One, the Bull of heaven', .
And the goddess Neith is called 'God One', .

ceased to shine, the face of the sky became black, and all was darkness. It is probable that the darkness was regarded with as much fear and terror by the EGYPTIAN, i.e. African savage, as it is by his descendants to-day, and as the night alternated with the day, he regarded it as a powerful opponent of the day. The sun appeared every day, but so did the night; the day was good, the night was evil. The nights were made less evil by the moon and the stars, but the waning of the moon, and the period when it was invisible, convinced him that the darkness was an implacable foe of the light. To the face of the Sky-god by day the name of ḤER or HOR was given, and the night face of the god was called SET ,[1] or , and each was regarded as the implacable foe of the other. Later SET symbolized all that was evil in the material world, the desert, storms, thunder, floods, the sea, &c., and he was regarded as the personification of moral evil, wickedness of every kind, and sin. The creature in which he was incarnate was the so-called 'SET animal' (see above, p. 87). SET, like the One One God, had many names,[2] and he had many captains and servants and followers which were known as the 'sons of SET', the MESU BEṬESH, or 'children of rebellion', the 'SMAIU', or 'slaughterers', the 'ṬESHERU', or 'Red Devils', &c. These occupied themselves in opposing and thwarting the decrees and works of the One God, and there are hints in the texts that SET and his fiends and devils engaged in battle against the Creator of the world and of them. According to Rev. xii. 7 MICHAEL the Archangel inflicted a serious defeat on the rebel army, and many accounts of the battle exist in Christian Apocryphal works. For further remarks about SET and his history see pp. 207–11.

THE GENESIS OF THE MATERIAL ONE GOD AND THE EGYPTIAN COSMOGONY

The Pyramid Texts contain a certain amount of information concerning the genesis of the Creator of the World and the cosmogony,

[1] The form on the Palermo Stone is .

[2] A list of these names in his character as Āpep will be found at the end of Brit. Mus. Papyrus No. 10188. See 'The Papyrus of Nesi Amsu' in *Archaeologia*, vol. lii, there published with a transcript of the hieratic text, and an English translation. The complete hieratic text is published by Budge. *Hieratic Papyri*, Series I (British Museum).

but a tolerably full account of these matters is given in the papyrus of NESI-AMSU in the BRITISH MUSEUM (No. 10188). This document was written in the 12th year of the reign of ALEXANDER IV, the son of ALEXANDER THE GREAT, i.e. about 311 B.C., but many of the myths and traditions which are preserved in it belong to the early period of the Old Kingdom, and some of them were current in the predynastic period. The work given in the papyrus is entitled the 'Book of knowing the *Kheperu* (i.e. the creations, or generations) of RĀ and the overthrowing of ĀPEP' , and the two versions of the legend of the genesis of RĀ, are sandwiched in between the chapters of a service book of the temple of AMEN-RĀ at THEBES. Under the New Kingdom, if not very much earlier, the EGYPTIANS believed that all the fiends of darkness, led by ĀPEP the Arch Crocodile-devil, and counterpart of SET, attacked the Sun during the darkest hours of the night, and exerted all their powers in order to prevent his rising in the sky at dawn. But RĀ, aided by his magical powers, pursued his course to the place of sunrise, and hurled the fiery darts of his rays into ĀPEP and his fiends, and paralysed them and made them impotent. The fight between Light and Darkness, i.e. HORUS and SET, and the fight between the Sun-god and the Crocodile-devil went on daily for neither the god nor the devil gained a final victory. Hence the ancient view that RĀ and SET were equal opposite powers.

The legend in the papyrus is supposed to be recited by NEB-ER-DJER ,[1] the 'Lord to the limit', that is to say by TEMU the 'All-Lord' or Sun-god of HELIOPOLIS, after he came into being. He says:

> I was the Creator in KHEPRI.[2]
> I created the Creator of creations,
> the Creator of all creations.
> Subsequently I created multitudes of creations
> which came forth from my mouth.'

When NEBER-DJER took the form of KHEPRI nothing existed except a vast mass of watery matter, or an abyss of slime, the 'ultimate slime', which, as we learn from the older texts of the cosmogony, was shapeless, black with the blackness of the blackest night. The

[1] Neb-er-djer is, like Temu, a purely artificial name.

[2] The Sun-god was called Khepri in the morning at sunrise, Rā at midday, and Temu at sunset.

bulk of this mass was agitated or heaved from time to time and became billowy, and above it there was a sort of vapour or wind. The god of this liquid mass was NUNU ; he was bisexual or hermaphrodite and the name of his female counterpart was NUNET or NUNIT; one part of him is represented by a frog and the other by a snake.

NEBER-DJER continues:

Heaven (or the sky) had not been created.
The earth had not been created.
The children of the earth [and] reptiles had not been fashioned in that place
I raised [them] up[1] from NUNU from a state of helpless inertness.
I found no place[2] there whereon I could stand,
I formed a spell in my heart, I laid a foundation by MAĀT (physical Law?)
I made forms of every kind.[3]
I was one by myself, for I had not then evacuated under the form of SHU, and
I had not then passed water under the form of TEFNUT.
There existed no other who worked with me.
I laid a foundation in my own heart (or mind).
Many creations of creations came into being from the creations of the offspring from the creations of their children.
I thrust my phallus into my closed hand,[4]
I made my seed to enter my hand.
I poured it into my own mouth.
I evacuated under the form of SHU,
I passed-water under the form of TEFNUT.

The meaning of the next two lines is not clear to me, but they seem to indicate that some calamity befell the Eye of the great god, and it was only restored to him by SHU and TEFNUT after a long period. Having produced these two gods from his own body the god declares:

I became from god one god[s] three.

[1] Or, I rose up with them, or among them.

[2] According to one view this standing-place was at Heliopolis, and according to another it was at Khemenu (Hermopolis).

[3] Or, I worked under every kind of form.

[4] The variant text has 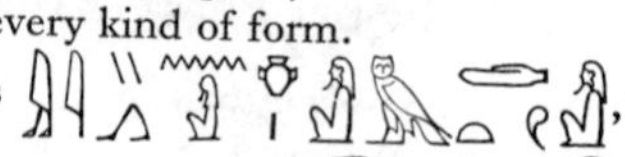, 'came to me my heart (or mind) from my hand', assuming that  and not  is the correct reading.

NEBER-DJER continues:

They brought to me my eye,

Following on after these things, I united (or gathered) together my generative members, and I shed tears over them, and men and women straightway came into being from the tear drops which came forth from my eye.[1]

The text mentions a second eye, the Moon, which the god seems to have produced from his first eye, that is to say the Sun. On the first eye, the Sun, he 'bestowed the uraeus of fire', and this eye was wroth when it discovered that there was a second eye in the face of the god. The moisture and heat which were produced by TEFNUT and SHU, respectively, and the water of REM, the greater eye of the god, caused herbs, plants, trees, and creeping things to come into being, and under the influence of the Moon they flourished and multiplied exceedingly. The Moon took up its place in the face of the god and 'it ruleth the whole earth'. SHU and his female counterpart TEFNUT produced GEBB, the Earth-god, and NUT, the Sky-goddess; and GEBB and NUT produced OSIRIS and ISIS, SET and NEPHTHYS, and the eyeless HORUS.

With the appearance of SHU and TEFNUT, the 'twin lion-gods' as they are called,[2] the first great act of creation was performed; the darkness of the abyss of NUNU, or CHAOS, was destroyed, and SHU and TEFNUT filled the space above NUNU. The earth took the place of NU and divided the space (or sky) which was above it from that which was below it. SHU was light, heat, and air, and TEFNUT was mist, cloud, and rain. The upper sky was said to rest on four pillars, the 'pillars of SHU' , and the sky was *Shuit* 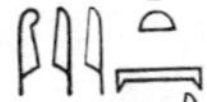 'the raised up place'. The source of SHU was the solar disk ATEN . Some have identified the vapour or wind which hung over the abyss of NUNU with SHU, the giver of the principle of life in the living, and the cause of the revivification of the dead OSIRIS. And BRUGSCH went so far as to say that SHU was the spiritual Pneuma in the higher sense (*Religion*, p. 431).

1 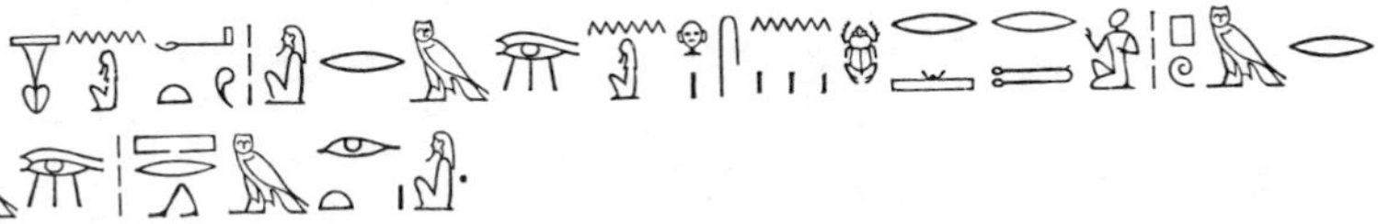

2 

The method by which the Sun-god produced SHU and TEFNUT would probably not surprise a semi-savage people like the predynastic EGYPTIANS, but it is a curious fact that their dynastic descendants took pains to commemorate the masturbation of the god[1] TEMU. And in the *Book of Gates* where the four great races of men are described, viz. the MEN (i.e. the EGYPTIANS), the ĀMU, the THEMEHU, and the NEḤESU or 'Blacks', the writer is careful to point out that the SÛDÂNÎ people were produced by the masturbation of RĀ. In the *Book of the Dead* (chap. cxxv) masturbation is held to be a sin, and yet TEMU is shown to be guilty of it.

In the second version of the story of the Creation the god KHEPRI is made to say, 'I fashioned myself out of the *pautt*' (i.e. the divine plasma of which the gods were made, or protoplasm). 'My name is AUSARS, the *pautt* of *pautiu*'. It is possible that AUSARS may be a transcription of 'OSIRIS'. In another interesting variant KHEPRI says, 'I made my creations therein (i.e. NUNU) by that Soul (Ba) [which] I raised up therein out of inactivity'.

THE THEOLOGICAL SYSTEM OF HELIOPOLIS, THE CITY OF THE SUN

The geographical position of ANU or HELIOPOLIS, made it in predynastic times the most important city in EGYPT. It was the terminus of many caravan routes from the east, north-east, and south-east, and the starting-point for caravans going into LIBYA and NUBIA, and countries farther to the south, and its temples waxed rich through the offerings of merchants and travellers. It was a great central market and men of many nationalities gathered there for business purposes, and many foreign languages must have been spoken in its bazârs. Besides all this its importance as a religious centre was so great that the teachings of its priesthood influenced, if not actually controlled, the religious beliefs of the EGYP-

[1] See Pyr. § 1248. 

TIANS down to the very close of the dynastic period. There was a well at HELIOPOLIS which was most holy, for tradition said that the Sun-god bathed his face in its waters when he rose on this earth for the first time.[1] And the first piece of ground which was created was held to be at HELIOPOLIS. Still more important for HELIOPOLIS was the belief that the 'NILE of the North' rose at HELIOPOLIS,[2] or at least by the neighbouring city of KHERI-ĀḤA , which stood on the east bank of the NILE, probably between the Arab capitals of CAIRO and FUSṬÂṬ. The name KHERI-ĀḤA means 'the city where there was a battle', and the battle referred to was that which took place between HORUS and SET. The GREEKS called the city 'BABYLON' because the sound of its name in Egyptian P(ER)-ḤAPU-L'ŌN, i.e. 'House of the NILE of ON', resembled the sound of the name of BABYLON in MESOPOTAMIA (see SETHE, *Urgeschichte*, p. 91, note 6). Somewhere in the city of KHERI-ĀḤA stood the Temple of ḤĀPI (the NILE) 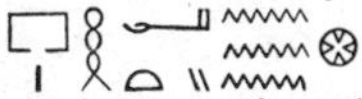, which the GREEKS called NILOPOLIS. Here there must have existed a flight of steps or a wall by which the height of the NILE during its annual rise might be measured. There seems to be a reference to this building in the Papyrus of NU (*Book of the Dead*, chap. cxlix, Aat 14) where we have 'ḤĀPI cometh with [his] water, he standeth still (or mounts up) at that earthwork (?) of KHERI-ĀḤA' 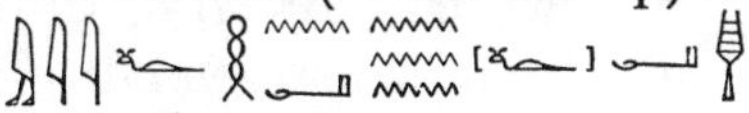
.

The priests of HELIOPOLIS were the richest and most influential and powerful theocratic body in EGYPT, and they set to work at a very early period to classify the gods and arrange them in groups. But it is not easy to understand their system of grouping which seems to be quite artificial and inconsequential. They divided the gods into three groups, each supposed to contain nine gods, PESDJ NETERU 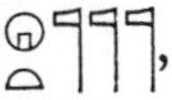, or . Or we have

The Great Nine  Pyr. § 177.

[1] Christian tradition asserted that the Virgin Mary washed our Lord's clothes in the water of this well; the Virgin's Well is close to the Virgin's Tree at Maṭariyaḥ and the Arabs call it 'Ain ash-shems, i.e. Well of the Sun.

[2] The 'Nile of the South' arose at Elephantine, at the Qerti.

The Little Nine 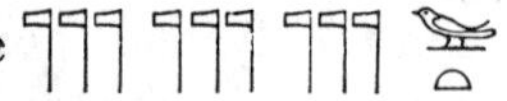 Pyr. § 178.

and these two Nines appear as

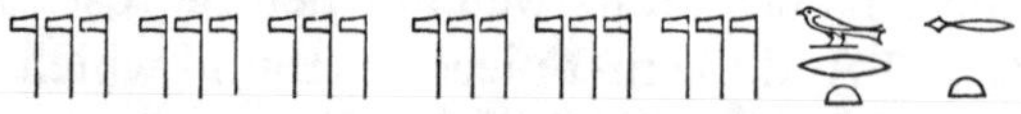

'the great and mighty double nine gods' in connexion with the souls of HELIOPOLIS (Pyr. § 1689 *c*). Elsewhere it is said that when the dead king has become NĀU, the Bull of the Nine Gods, and hath devoured the Seven Cobras on Seven necks, he giveth commands to his Seven, and the three times nine gods

hear his commands and obey him (Pyr. 511 *c*).

But according to the Pyramid Texts (Pyr. § 167) the Ennead or 'Nine' could contain more than nine gods thus:

1. TEM. 2. SHU. 3. TEFNUT. 4. GEBB. 5. NUT.
6. ISIS. 7. SET. 8. NEPHTHYS. 9. THOTH. 10. HORUS.
11. The Great Nine. 12. The Little Nine. 13. RĀT.

Another 'Nine' includes:

1. Dweller in ON.
2. Dweller in ANDJET.
3. Dweller in ḤET SERQ KA-ḤETEP.
4. Dweller in SEḤ-NETER, (?) dweller in KAP.
5. Dweller in ḤEDJ-PAR.
6. Dweller in SAḤ (OSIRIS).
7. Dweller in ṬEP.
8. Dweller in ḤET-UR-KA.
9. Dweller in UNU of the South.
10. Dweller in UNU of the North.

And in another place the 'Nine' includes:

1. TEM.
2. SHU.
3. TEFNUT.
4. GEBB.
5. NUT.
6. OSIRIS.
7. OSIRIS KHENTI AMENTI.
8. SET of OMBOS.
9. HORUS of EDFU.
10. RĀ.
11. KHENTI ARITI.
12. HORUS.
13. UADJAT.[1]

[1] In the Salt Papyrus (BRITISH MUSEUM Salt 825, or 10051) the 'Nine' are: Rā, Shu, Tefnut, Gebb, Nut, Horus, Isis, Nephthys.

The passage in Pyr. § 1655 shows that the canonical Great Nine of HELIOPOLIS were

1. TEM 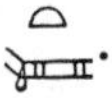.
2. SHU .
3. TEFNUT .
4. GEBB .
5. NUT .
6. OSIRIS 
7. ISIS .
8. SET 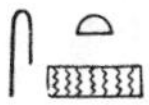.
9. NEPHTHYS 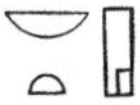.

We have seen that the self-created god was bisexual, and as we must assume his offspring to have been the same, the 'nine' becomes a company of five cosmic gods, viz. TEM the SHU and his female counterpart Heat, Light, and Moisture, GEBB and his female counterpart the Earth and Sky, OSIRIS and his female counterpart the Seed of Life and Vegetation, SET and his female counterpart Darkness and Decay. If we are to assume that OSIRIS and ISIS and SET and NEPHTHYS were separate deities, then it is difficult to understand why they were grouped with five cosmic gods. And the matter is further complicated when different forms of the myth of OSIRIS tell us that OSIRIS begot ANUBIS his son by NEPHTHYS, whom he mistook for his wife ISIS, and that OSIRIS after his death begot a son by ISIS. When the priests of HELIOPOLIS were formulating their theological system, the worship of the Hawk-god, the Old HORUS, and the worship of OSIRIS, the man who raised from the dead by magic, were common in the Delta, to say nothing of the cult of NEITH of SAÏS in the Western Delta and that of UBAST or SEKHMET in the Eastern Delta. And there must have been some form of worship of the fetish or man PTAḤ in the region where, at a later period, MEMPHIS was built. Judging by the Pyramid Texts the priests of HELIOPOLIS borrowed very largely from the religious beliefs of the predynastic EGYPTIANS, some of which they misunderstood or misrepresented. Their power was due chiefly to their wealth and political importance, and not to their religious teaching. Their cult of RĀ was based upon that of HORUS, and it was essentially materialistic in character. It was adopted by the royal and official classes, but long before the downfall of the Old Kingdom it was thrust aside by the ever-increasing popularity of the cult of OSIRIS. Though the priests of RĀ succeeded in placing three of the sons of a priest of RĀ of SAKHABU on the throne they, like the priest of AMEN at THEBES at a later date, failed to maintain themselves in the position which they had usurped.

TEM, an old solar god, was, it was claimed, the son of NUNU, or primeval chaos; his inferiority to RĀ was made known by the priests of HELIOPOLIS, who prefixed the name of their god RĀ to his, and often called him RĀ-TEM. The name TEM is probably connected with *temm* 'to be complete'. He was a form of the setting sun, and was depicted in the form of a man wearing the double crown, and holding the sceptre of royal authority and the sign of 'life' *ānkh*. This sign, commonly called the *crux ansata*, I believe represents one or more of the generative organs of ISIS only, for the *genitalia* of OSIRIS are represented by.[1]

The Ichneumon-god, a form of Tem, who was thought to be incarnate in the ichneumon.

SHU, the Σῶς of the GREEKS, was in turn a nature power, a cosmic god, a king, and a theological abstraction. He was the light of the sun, heat, dryness, and air. He is seen wearing on his head one or more feathers, , or the hind-quarters of a lion; he and TEFNUT were often represented by a lion and a lioness. SHU supported heaven, and many figures represent him kneeling with his arms raised holding up the sky with the sun in it. The four pillars of heaven are one of his symbols. The shrine of SHU and TEFNUT was in the city of KHERI-ĀḤA, which lay between HELIOPOLIS and BABYLON (FUSṬÂṬ). Their sanctuary of MENSET was divided into two parts: SHU dwelt in Upper MENSET and TEFNUT in Lower. The GREEKS knew the sacred settlement as LEONTOPOLIS. The tears of SHU and TEFNUT, who were said to weep copiously, when they fell on the ground they were changed into incense-bearing plants (*Eg. Hier. Papyri*, ed. Budge, vol. ii, Plate XXXI, col. 2). From these plants

[1] See the interesting note in H. P. Cooke's *Osiris*, p. 54.

the CHRISTIANS pressed out an oil which formed the χρῖσμα used by the COPTS in ceremonies of consecration. For the legend of the reign of SHU see Part II, p. 438.

TEFNUT, the female counterpart of SHU, was the moisture and damp generative heat of heaven, and, as some say, rain and clouds. But there may have been a second goddess of this name, for we have a god TEFEN and a goddess TEFENT in the text of UNAS (l. 453, Pyr. § 317 *a*). As a solar goddess she wears the disk with a cobra on her head. We have seen that the Sun-god had trouble with his eye, and late texts say that his eye left him and went to NUBIA where it took the form of a savage-lioness or a lynx. When the god heard this he sent the NUBIAN god ARI-ḤEMS-NEFER, a form of SHU, and THOTH to bring the eye back. They took the form of baboons and very soon found the eye in BU-GEM,[1] near the Mountain of the Sunrise, where OSIRIS was born. THOTH worked his magic on the eye and brought it back to the Sun-god and restored it to his face. The baboons led the rejoicings, and they and their companion baboons hymn the sun at dawn daily; they are represented in the vignette to chapter xv of the *Book of the Dead*. The oldest triad in EGYPT was formed by the Sun-god and GEBB the Earth-god and NUT the Sky-goddess. This was probably displaced by the priests of HELIOPOLIS who substituted for it the triad of the Sun-god, SHU, and TEFNUT. In any case, the restoration of the eye of the Sun-god by THOTH seems to refer to the restoration of some religious dogma or belief.

GEB, or GEBEB,[2] , , , , , the Κῆβ of the GREEKS, was the Earth-god, who made OSIRIS, king of the North (LOWER EGYPT) and SET, the king of the South (UPPER EGYPT). The earth formed his body. His female counterpart was NUT, , , , , , , , the Sky-goddess. As a bisexual god GEBB produced the Great Egg out of which came the sun under the form of the phoenix[3] (so HERODOTUS, ii. 73). He is

[1] See Junker, 'Der Auszug der Hathor-Tefnut aus Nubien' (*Abhandl. K. Preus. Akad.*, Berlin, 190).

[2] See Sethe in *Aeg. Zeit.*, Bd. xliii, p. 14.

[3] He means the Benu bird (see Brugsch, *Religion*, p. 577).

called the 'Great Cackler' , and he cackled before he laid his egg (*Book of the Dead*, chaps. liv-lix). He is always depicted as a man with a gander on his head. In a Ritual text found in the pyramids it is GEBB who is asked to give a royal offering and not the king (Pyr. § 218 *b*).[1]

From the earliest times GEBB was called by a title which was given to no other god, viz. ERPĀT NETERU , or ERPĀT of all the gods . In Pyr. § 1645 we have

GEBB, the mouth wise, ERPĀ of the gods.

There was a shrine of GEBB at BATA in HELIOPOLIS (?), in which hoes were presented as offerings, and one to NUT called ḤET-SHENAT ; the site of the latter is unknown. Another earth-god called AKER is mentioned in Pyr. § 796 *b*, and he had a lion's head at each end of his body. There is a curious reference to GEBB and NUT in the *Book of the Dead*, chaps. xxxi and lxix. The deceased says: 'I am OSIRIS, who shut in his father GEBB and his mother NUT on the day of the great cutting (or slaughter).' BRUGSCH thought that this cutting referred to the act of self-mutilation of OSIRIS on the part of RĀ which is mentioned in chap. xvii, l. 61. The gods sprang from the drops of blood which dripped from the phallus of RĀ.[2]

NUT, 'daughter of RĀ, Lady of heaven, Queen of the gods', appears in the form of a woman with a waterpot on her head, or a pear-shaped vessel or object which resembles the uterus, which was probably her fetish. HATHOR, MUT, NUBIT, APIT, TAURIT, ḤEQIT, and other goddesses were forms of NUT. According to one legend NUT brought forth her five children at one time, but according to another each of the five children was born on one of the five epagomenal days of the year . OSIRIS on the first day (unlucky); HORUS on the second day (lucky or unlucky); SET on

[1] See Sethe, *Dramatische Texte*, Leipzig, 1928, p. 209.

[2] Brugsch, *Religion*, p. 581. He compares the punishment which Kronos inflicted on his father Uranus.

the third day (unlucky); ISIS on the fourth day (lucky[1]); NEPHTHYS on the fifth day (unlucky).

The remaining members of the Great Ennead of HELIOPOLIS, OSIRIS-ISIS, and SET-NEPHTHYS, are the family of GEBB, which his female counterpart NUT produced at a single birth. They are discussed in another chapter.

[1] A beautiful festival of heaven and earth.

V

EGYPTIAN THEOLOGICAL SYSTEMS AND DOGMAS—*Continued*

THOTH, THE GOD OF WISDOM, AND HIS COMPANY OF GODS

THOTH, in Egyptian DJḤUTI[1] , is the Θῶυθ or Θῶυτ of the GREEKS, and his name commonly appears under the form of , i.e. an ibis mounted on a raised standard. Little is known about the origin of THOTH, and the meaning of his name has not yet been satisfactorily explained. A very ancient legend makes THOTH to be the son of HORUS, whose seed had been introduced into the body of SET by means of lettuce (?) leaves. The seed of HORUS germinated and produced THOTH, who came forth from the forehead of SET. Another version says that SET brought forth a gold disk from his forehead, which THOTH seized and placed on his own head as an ornament. The old form of the legend was rejected by the author of the 'Contendings of HORUS and SET' published by DR. GARDINER.[2] SETHE regards the name DJḤUTI as an 'anonyme Herkunft-bezeichnung' and thinks that it means 'he who is from DJḤUT'.[3]

THOTH is depicted as an ibis-headed man, and he holds the sceptre and  common to all gods. As a chronographer he wears the full lunar disk in a crescent; as a god of the dead (OSIRIS) he wears the ATEF crown  with horns, cobras, solar disk, &c. As the Moon-god AĀḤ 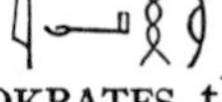 he has the form of a mummy, with the lock of hair of HARPOKRATES, the crescent and full moon, and the sceptres, &c. of OSIRIS . He appears also as a baboon and an ibis. In dynastic times THOTH was the registrar and secretary of RĀ and OSIRIS; he kept the accounts of the god of day, and acted as remembrancer of the Sun-god of night, OSIRIS. He invented writing and the science of numbers, and ordered the movements of the celestial bodies, and

[1] Dialectic variations are , , ; for others see Boylan, *Thoth*, Oxford, 1922.

[2] *Chester Beatty Papyrus No. 1*, London 1931, pp. 22, 23.

[3] *Urgeschichte*, § 13.

governed times and seasons. In the earliest times he was probably a star-god, and maintained equilibrium in the heavens. He may have been a member of the triad PTAḤ–HORUS–THOTH, later RĀ–HORUS–THOTH, and OSIRIS–HORUS–THOTH. THOTH was the Word-god as well as the heart of PTAḤ of MEMPHIS, TEM of HELIOPOLIS, and the throat of AMEN-REN-F, i.e. he whose name is hidden. At the utterance of THOTH the sun appeared out of chaos, and light flooded the world; everything was created by the utterances of THOTH. Among the titles of THOTH are: Governor of years; Computer of the time of life; Deputy of RĀ; and Governor of the living star-gods. 'White Disk', as he is called made the night beautiful, and his unhurried but never-resting march across the heaven of night won for him the titles 'Bull of heaven', 'Bull of AMENTI', and 'Bull among the stars'.

The greatest work of THOTH was bringing back the missing eye of RĀ and restoring it to its place in his face. SET swallowed the eye both of RĀ and his predecessor HORUS, but he was compelled to vomit it (Pyr. §§ 39, 118). HORUS hacked off the testicles of SET (Pyr. § 594). A title of THOTH was , 'the bringer back of it', i.e. the eye, and it is possible that this title belonged originally to AN-ḤER , a very ancient god of ABYDOS. As the 'filler' of the eye of the moon on the day of full moon THOTH was called 'The Filler' .

The oldest seat of the cult of THOTH was UNU-RESU 'UNU of the South' the capital of the Hare nome, i.e. the XVth nome of UPPER EGYPT; the GREEKS called it HERMOPOLIS. There THOTH was regarded as the head of an Ogdoad, or company of eight primeval gods, four gods who were frog-headed, and four goddesses who were serpent-headed. Hence the city was called KHEMENU , i.e. the 'City of the Eight'.[1] Here was, the priests said, the first plot of ground upon which the Sun-god first stood. Originally KHEMENU, or a part of it, was the centre of the cult of

[1] Or , or . This is the Ashmûnên of the Arabs.

the hare, which was the blazon of the nome, but this was set aside, and the part of it which was sacred to THOTH became the most important. This is clear from the fact that the GREEKS called the city HERMOPOLIS, i.e. the city of HERMES or THOTH, and it was well known as 'the House of the Ibis', and the 'House of THOTH'. At one time a group of five gods, of which nothing is known, was worshipped there and its chief god was called 'Great god among the Five'; but this chief can have been neither OSIRIS nor THOTH. In an inscription on the wall of the temple of AMEN built by DARIUS at KHÂRGAH we read of 'HORUS, the Five living Souls who live in NENU'.[1] In the HARRIS Papyrus mention is made of 'Five great gods' who came forth from KHEMENU when there was no heaven and no earth, and SHU (the Sun) had not sent out his light.[2] There is no evidence which would prove that THOTH was the chief of these Five Gods, but the texts show that Five Gods were worshipped at one time in KHEMENU and Eight Gods at another, and that THOTH was the head of the Eight Gods.[3]

According to the Pyramid Texts (§ 445) the Eight Gods with TEM were:

1. NAU. 2. NUNET.
3. AMEN. 4. AMENT.
5. TEM and 6, 7. RURU-TI (lion and lioness gods).
8. SHU. 9. TEFNUT.

In the temple at KHÂRGAH we have:

1. NENU. 2. NENUT.
3. ḤEḤU. 4. ḤEḤUT.
5. KEKUI. 6. KEKUIT.
7. GERḤ. 8. GERḤET.

Nos. 1 and 2 are the primeval abyss, the World Ocean, and the NILE of heaven and earth.

[1] See Brugsch, *Reise*, pl. 14.
[2] Budge, *Hieratic Papyri*, i, p. 35.
[3] See Brugsch, *Religion*, p. 443, and Maspero, *La Mythologie*, p. 257, and Sethe, *Amun und die Acht Urgötter*, Berlin, 1929.

Nos. 3 and 4, 5 and 6, 7 and 8, represent some attribute of the ocean, the penetrating power of water, storm, &c., and mist, fog, or darkness. In AMEN and AMENT of the Pyramid Texts SETHE sees the wind that blew over NUNU, and identifies it with the spirit of God which hovered over the waters.

The following were dogmas of the priests of HERMOPOLIS:

1. THOTH was the mind and intelligence and reasoning power of the self-created, self-subsistent god. He was the spirit and soul of the primeval ocean. He was light and life and gave life to man.

2. Four gods and four goddesses assisted THOTH in ruling NUNU. These were NUN and NUNET, HUH and HUHET, KUK and KUKET, and AMEN and AMENT.

3. These gods created the mound at HERMOPOLIS on which the Sun-god stood.

4. These gods created the Sun and assisted him to take his stand on the mound of HERMOPOLIS.

5. The eight gods were the oldest gods in EGYPT, and they were the fathers and the mothers of the Sun.

These views were diametrically opposed to the teachings of the priests of HELIOPOLIS, and probably strife broke out between the rival Colleges of Theology. The theology of THOTH was of a highly spiritual character, and his character and attributes are well described by the opening words of St. John's Gospel: 'In the beginning was the Word, and the Word was with God, and the Word was God. The same was in the beginning with God. All things were made by him; and without him was not any thing made that was made. In him was life; and the life was the light of men.' We may note in passing that the Nine gods of Creation in Egyptian have very much in common with the Creation gods of the SUMERIANS. The similarity between the two Companies of gods is too close to be accidental. It would be wrong to say that the EGYPTIANS borrowed from the SUMERIANS or the SUMERIANS from the EGYPTIANS, but it may be submitted that the litterati of both peoples borrowed their theological systems from some common but exceedingly ancient source.

In later dynastic times the character of THOTH as a god of creation became somewhat obscured. Very special emphasis was then laid upon the fact that he was regarded as the author or inventor of the hieroglyphic system of writing, *meṭu neter*, i.e. 'the words of the god'. The *Book of the Dead* (chap. lxviii. 11) shows that there existed a special 'Book of THOTH' and that copies of sections of it were made for use in temples and elsewhere. It was these copies, which were referred to by the GREEKS when they spoke of the 'Hermetic Books' of the EGYPTIANS. THOTH was the founder of Egyptian Literature, and as such was called, 'Prince of books'. He was the 'original Lawgiver'. He enunciated the laws which governed the motions of the heavenly bodies, and was the god of the first month of the Egyptian year. He was the repository of all learning, both sacred and profane, a profound linguist, a skilled physician, and he was the Master of ḤEKA, or 'Magic'. From first to last he was the UR-ḤEKAU, whose 'word' on all things was absolute and final. Like ANUBIS (ANPU) he was a great god of the dead long before men began to compose the myth of OSIRIS. He produced order in heaven and earth, and pacified and reconciled gods and men. He struck the balance between Day and Night when the world began, and as the 'Judge of the two fighting gods', UP REḤḤUI, i.e. HORUS and SET, he maintained peace in heaven and earth.[1] He was the 'scribe of Truth' and the 'judge of Truth', and his impartiality and righteousness were absolute. The 'Lord of Truth', he 'rested on Truth'. How THOTH was regarded by the gods is well illustrated by the following extract from the Pyramid Texts (§ 1521):

'TAU, father of the gods, and SHU and TEFNUT, and GEBB and NUT, and OSIRIS and ISIS, and SET and NEITH, and all the gods in heaven and upon earth, and in the lands (?) and [those who] are in the south and the north, and the west and the east, and [those who] are in the nomes of HORUS, and those who are in the Sanctuaries of HORUS, are content with the great and mighty WORD, which hath come forth from the mouth of THOTH concerning OSIRIS. [It is sealed with] the seal of life, the seal of the gods.'

[1] He was the 'Pacifier' Seḥetpi *par excellence.*

Elsewhere (Pyr. § 155 *b*) THOTH's Word was 'SET is a liar, OSIR right' .

The large vignette of the Judgement Scene in the Theban funera papyri of the New Kingdom shows that the judgement of the dea had practically passed from the hands of OSIRIS to THOTH. It is THOTI who is the Warden of the Scales , and the Overseer of the Scales , and the examiner of the beam of the Scales whilst OSIRIS sits motionless. And it is his verdict of 'Maā Kheru' , i.e. 'True of voice (or word)', which was accepted by the jury of the gods and their spokesman OSIRIS, son of ISIS, and by OSIRIS himself.

Curiously enough very few texts refer to the paternity of THOTH, and he might almost be regarded as a sort of MELCHISEDEK, 'without father and without mother' among the gods of EGYPT. But there is one mention of his father in the Papyrus of NU (*Book of the Dead*, chap. cxxxiv, l. 6) where we have

THOTH, son of ANER,[1] coming forth from the two ANERS.[2]

An ancient myth seems to be referred to in this passage.

In Ptolemaic and later times THOTH was called 'Great Great' which the ROSETTA STONE, l. 19, rendered by ΜΕΓΑΣ ΚΑΙ ΜΕΓΑΣ.

He is also called Great Great Great and , i.e. the 'great Great Great Great'. For some time it was thought that this form was the original of the Greek name for THOTH Τρισμέγιστος (TER MAXIMUS). The name of THOTH followed by the sign for 'great' repeated eight times has been found in a Demotic papyrus,[3] and the god is called 'Lord of KHEMENU, the great god'. KHEMENU, the HERMOPOLIS of the GREEKS, was the city of the eight primeval gods of chaos (see *supra*, pp. 17, 153). Prof. GRIFFITH transcribes by $2a$, and the eight signs for 'great' by $(2a)^3 = 8$, i.e. 'twice great' cubed = Τρισμέγιστος.

[1] Variant in Nebteni .

[2] Variant in Nebteni .

[3] Griffith, *Stories of the High Priests*, pp. 48, 58, 184.

THE TRIAD OF MEMPHIS

.e triad was PTAḤ, who was originally a fetish
.d in the form of a mummied man with his legs un-
.e MIN, OSIRIS, and KHONSU. He has short side-whiskers,
.ite beard, and at the back of his neck hangs a *menat*,

Ptaḥ as guardian of one of the Ārits of Osiris (Papyrus of Ani).

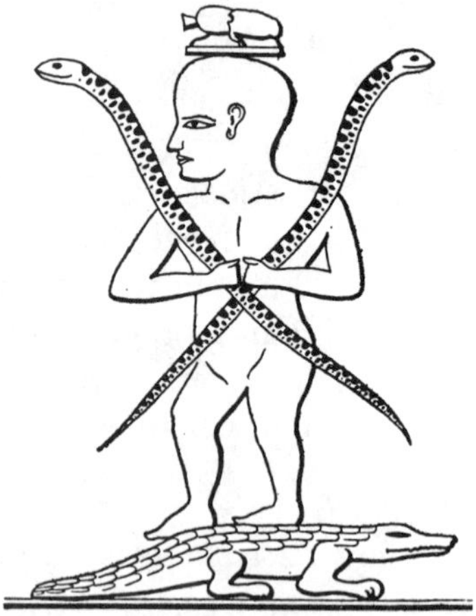

Ptaḥ of the magicians lord of all primal and creative matter, and master of the great serpent gods of Upper and Lower Egypt.

symbol of virility and fertility. His hands project through his funeral wrappings, and he holds in them , and the symbol of ISIS , or , and . He stands on the pedestal of MAĀT . He sometimes wears a disk with horns , or a disk between feathers , and he wears a fillet with a streamer flowing behind him. BRUGSCH and others connected his name with the word *pt[a]ḥ*, to engrave, and the texts support this view for he was the patron god of all artisans and workers in stone and metal, and even wielders of the artist's brush and crayon. When MENA built ANEB-HEDJ , or , or White Wall, i.e. MEMPHIS, on the left bank of the NILE about twenty miles to the south of the modern CAIRO, he turned the district into a nome, and the local fetish acquired very great importance. One of the commoner names of the city of White Wall is ḤE-T KA PTAḤ, 'House of the Ka of PTAḤ', the whole city being regarded as the temple of the god. From this name some think the Greek word for EGYPT, AIGUPTOS, is derived. The name MEMPHIS Μέμφις appears to be derived from MEN-NEFER, the tomb of OSIRIS.

The texts of the dynastic period agree in associating PTAḤ with the oldest fetishes and gods of EGYPT. Thus we have:

PTAḤ NUNU, i.e. Ptaḥ-Chaos.

PTAḤ ḤĀP, i.e. Ptaḥ-Nile.

PTAḤ TENEN, i.e. Ptaḥ-Earth.[1]

PTAḤ ATEN, i.e. Ptaḥ-Solar disk.

He is also associated with the gods of the dead, i.e. PTAḤ–ASAR (OSIRIS), PTAḤ–SEKER,[2] PTAḤ–SEKER–ASAR, and even PTAḤ–SEKER–TEM, i.e. PTAḤ–SEKER, and the setting, i.e. dying, sun. As PTAḤ–TENEN the god is united with the still more ancient Earth-god GEBB. As such he is no longer represented as bald-headed, but he wears on his head a pair of horns between which is the solar disk, and behind them rise two high plumes. This crown resembles that of OSIRIS, the great god of BUSIRIS, and it was the badge of the old nome of ABYDOS (TENI, Greek THIS, THINIS). SETHE suggests (*Urgeschichte*, § 222) that as MENA, the founder of MEMPHIS, came from ABYDOS, he may have wished his god to have some visible resemblance to the god of his home in the south. And as he saw the stone walls of his city rising up out of the flooded fields round about him, he may have realized that he was emulating the example of his god who raised up the land from out of the waters of the primeval abyss.

SEKHMET, or (in Pyr. § 262), was the female counterpart of PTAḤ and the mother of NEFER-TEM,

[1] Var. or .

[2] Seker was the ancient god of the dead of Memphis. The Arab name for the necropolis Saḳḳârah is probably derived from Seker.

, and I-EM-ḤETEP , the ʼΙμούθης of the GREEKS. She is depicted as a woman with the head of a lioness, or a crocodile, or the UDJAT .[1] In one aspect she was the female counterpart of

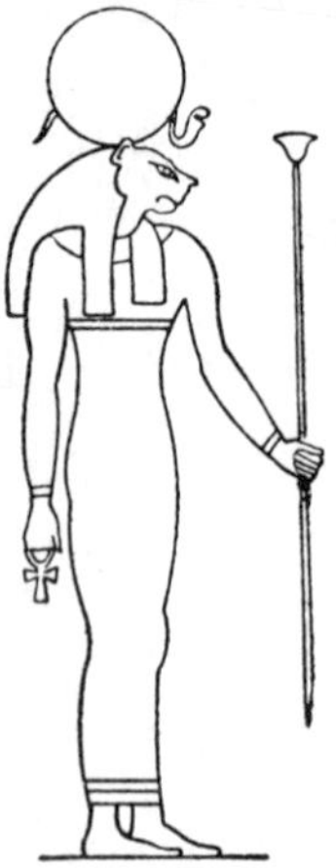

Sekhmet (Sekhmit).

Nefer-Tem.

I-em-ḥetep (Imouthes).

Sekhmet-Ubastei-Rā.

MIN, for her right arm is raised, and she holds a knife, and her body has the form of the ithyphallic MIN. The name SEKHMET means 'mighty one', and is derived from 'to be strong'. As a cosmic goddess she was the fierce, scorching, pulverizing heat of the sun's rays and was called the Eye of RĀ . In the form of the cobra and with the name of MEḤENIT she guarded

[1] Lanzone, Pls. 63 and 64.

the head of her father RĀ. She was identified with the Fire-goddess NESERIT, and UADJIT, or BUTO, and PEKHAT and UBASTIT; the latter appears as a cat-headed woman. A late tradition says that the worship of SEKHMET, SHU, and TEFNUT was introduced into EGYPT from BUGEM, a country in the SÛDÂN. The extraordinary triad of SEKHMET–UBASTI–RĀ mentioned in the *Book of the Dead* (chap. clxiv) is probably of Sûdânî origin. UBASTI was in one character a benevolent goddess and akin to HATHOR.

NEFER-TEM appears as a lion-headed man holding and or a lotus flower with plumes on it. On his head he wears a model of his old fetish object made of a lotus supporting two plumes, with two *menats* (i.e. fertility amulets) suspended from the stalk. The lotus proclaims his connexion with the sun, and the archaic form of his body with MIN. In Pyr. § 266 we read that 'King UNAS riseth like NEFER-TEM from the lotus at the nostrils of RĀ'. In the *Book of the Dead* (chap. lxxxi) the deceased says, 'I am that holy lotus coming forth from the light god, the watcher at the nostrils of RĀ'.[1] See also chapter clxxiv. 19.

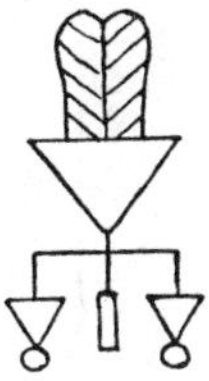

I-EM-ḤETEP, or IMOUTHES, usurped the place of NEFER-TEM in the triad of MEMPHIS under the New Kingdom. His temple called the 'House of I-EM-ḤETEP' stood near MEMPHIS, and as the GREEKS called it τὸ 'Ασκληπιεῖον they must have regarded him as a master physician like their own AESCULAPIUS. The building stood near the SERAPEUM and is mentioned in the *Ritual of Embalmment*.[2] In a Greek inscription found at PHILAE he is called the son of TENEN (Earth-god), 'mighty one of miracles, giver of life to all men, maker of times and seasons, who cometh to all who invoke him; who giveth sons to the childless, the great *Kheri ḥeb*, the Image and Likeness of THOTH'.[3] We now know that I-EM-ḤETEP was the Wazîr or Prime Minister of DJESER, the first king of the IIIrd dynasty. He was a great physician and magician, a wise and far-sighted scholar, and a great architect. It was he who planned and built the 'house of stone' which MANETHO attributes to TOSOR THOS (DJESER) and the

1 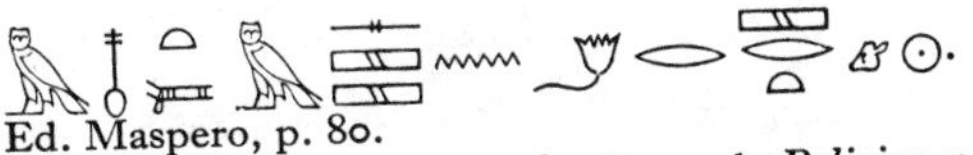

2 Ed. Maspero, p. 80.

3 See Brugsch, *Theraurus*, p. 783; Brugsch, *Religion*, p. 527, Sethe, *Imhotep*, p. 95 f.

so-called 'Step Pyramid'. The deification of I-EM-ḤETEP, whose name does not occur in the Theban *Book of the Dead*, probably took place under the XXVIth dynasty.

AMEN OF THEBES AND HIS COMPANY OF GODS

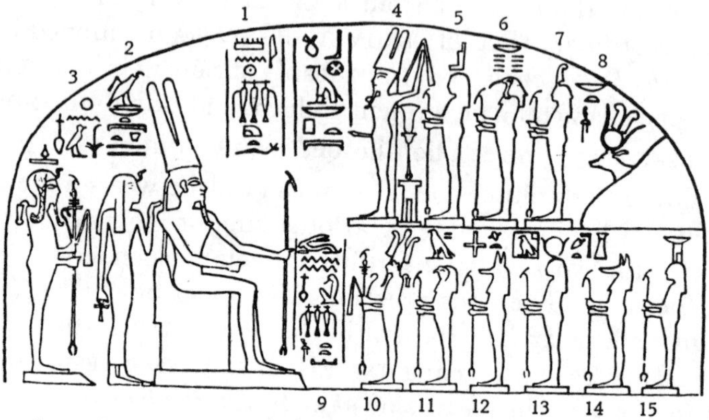

1. Amen-Rā at the head of the Southern Apt (Luxor), the lord of heaven, and his gods; 2. Mut, Lady of heaven Mistress of the World. 3. Khonsu, Nefer-ḥetep. 4. Min with symbol and temple. 5. Isis. 6. Neb Khemenu (Thoth). 7. Maāt. 8. The Lady of Amenti (Hathor (3)) 9. Osiris. 10. Un-Nefer-Khenti-Amenti. 11. Horus of the Two Horizons. 12. He of the embalmment chamber. 13. Ḥet-Ḥer (Hathor). 14. Governor of the house of the physician. 15. Nephthys.

AMEN OF THEBES AND HIS FETISH

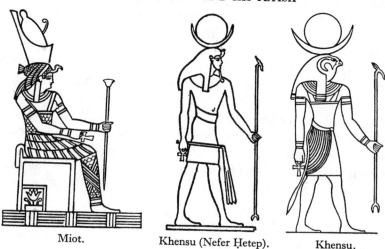

Miot.

Khensu (Nefer Ḥetep).

Khensu.

AMEN, MUT, AND KHONSU

AMEN[1]-AMENET[2] is one of the oldest gods of EGYPT, for this bi-sexual god is one of the four primeval gods[3] who lived in the watery abyss of NUNU, and who were worshipped in the Hare-city, which became the city of THOTH and was called by the GREEKS HERMOPOLIS. The name AMEN is derived from *Amen* , 'to hide', or 'to be hidden'. The texts make it quite clear that the EGYPTIANS understood the name to mean, 'hidden', 'unseen', 'invisible', perhaps even 'unknown', 'unknowable'. In hymns to AMEN we have, 'He hideth his name from his children in this his name of AMEN'; 'he maketh himself to be hidden'; 'the One AMEN who hideth himself from men, who shroudeth himself from the gods, his colour (i.e. personal appearance) is not known.' A common name for the god is 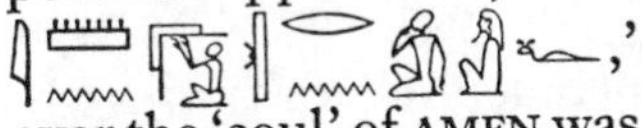,' AMEN-REN-T 'hider of his name'.[4] Moreover the 'soul' of AMEN was hidden or unseen. In the LEYDEN papyrus he is called 'BAI', i.e. 'the being who is endowed with a soul', and this Hidden Soul raised up his head from NENU when nothing else existed. Thus from this point of view he was the Soul-god of Creation, who, though the source of all life, was himself invisible. SETHE, quoting demotic texts, says that AMEN represented the πνεῦμα or breath of life, but not the atmosphere ἀήρ, though he may have been the Wind-god *par excellence*. And he was identified with the Sphinx-god of GÎZAH, who protected the temples from the sand-storms of the desert. Other texts show that AMEN was the breath which is in everything, and AMENET was the North Wind. All this is quite probable as far as AMEN–AMENET are concerned, but it is permissible to wonder if AMEN of the NENU is to be identified with the local god of THEBES. The early Egyptologists thought that AMEN of THEBES was the hidden and creative power of creation, and identified him with MIN or MENU, the ithyphallic god of generation, virility, procreation, and fertility. It is difficult to see in him the Soul-god of the universe, or the 'Spirit of God [which] moved on the

1 Variously read Amon, Amun, Amonu, and Amunu.

2 Or Amaunet.

3 These were Nenu and Nenet, Hehu and Hehet, Kaku and Keket, and Amen and Amenet. See Pyr. § 446.

4 A serpent god called 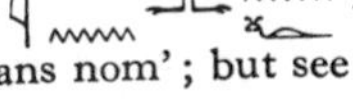 is mentioned in Pyr. §§ 399, 434; Masters translated 'le dieu sans nom'; but see Sethe, *Amun*, § 182.

face of the waters'. The home of the Theban AMEN may have been HERMOPOLIS, and it is probable that the princes of THEBES adopted him as their god after their conquest of the princes of HERAKLEOPOLIS, and they were able to call themselves 'Kings of the Two Lands, the North and the South', i.e. of all EGYPT.

Of the early history of THEBES very little is known. The district round about formed a nome 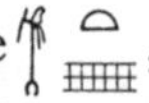,[1] and the city itself was called 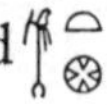. Then it became 'the city of AMEN' 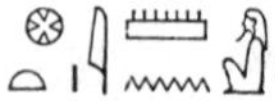, or 'the city UAST of AMEN . In this we have the No of Ezek. xxx. 16 and the No Amon of Nahum iii. 8. The GREEKS called the city 'DIOSPOLIS', the city of JUPITER, whom they identified with AMEN. The capital of the nome of THEBES was ANI 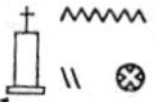 which lay on the west bank of the NILE about eight miles to the south of the modern LUXOR. The god of the city was a sacred bull called MENTU . The GREEKS garbled the name of the city and produced 'HERMONTHIS' (STRABO), the COPTS followed with 'ERMENT', and the ARABS with 'ARMANT'. The character of the god was changed after the war, and the god of procreation became a mighty war-god. The princes of THEBES showed their respect for him by including his name in their own personal names, e.g. MENTU-ḤETEP.

As the result of his excavations at KARNAK, G. LEGRAIN thought that the MENTU-ḤETEPS built a sanctuary at THEBES, on the site of an ancient temple which could be traced back to the IIIrd dynasty. Be this as it may, at the beginning of the XIIth dynasty AMEN had usurped the position of MENTU as the War-god, and like him was called the 'Strong Bull'. The kings of the XIIth dynasty built a temple of AMEN called AP-T ASUT 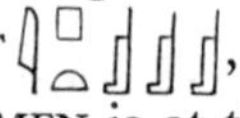, and their first king called himself 'AMEN-EM-ḤET', i.e. 'AMEN is at the forefront'. The glory and fame and power of AMEN grew with the victories of the various kings, and his priests called him 'King of the gods', and suggested that he existed before EGYPT came into being.[2] They next added RĀ to his name, and as AMEN-RĀ, and pictures of him show him wearing all the symbols of the power and sovereignty of the Sun-god.

[1] The badge of the nome was written originally , the sceptre being a fetish; the feather and short string were additions.

[2] See the title 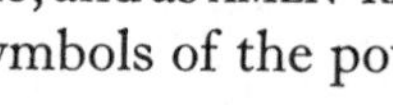 aptly quoted by Sethe, *Amun*, § 14.

Like OSIRIS, MIN, and KHONSU he appears in mummied form with his legs close together, and he wears streamers, and is called FAI Ā, 'he of the sacred arm'; KA-MUT-F, 'Bull of his mother' (the Καμῆφις of the GREEKS), and QAI-SHUTI, 'he of the lofty plumes'.

The forms of AMEN as a wind-god and as the ithyphallic MIN were carefully distinguished, and the temple of the former was in the Northern Apt, i.e. KARNAK, and that of the latter in the Southern Apt, i.e. the modern temple of LUXOR. The fetish origin of the cult of MIN is proved by an object which was discovered there by G. LEGRAIN. This was a small portable shrine decorated with figures of a lion and a sphinx, and containing the upper part of a figure of MIN, who is seen emerging from an object which DARESSY believed[1] to be a model of the umbilicus. This shrine was carried through the city in festival processions of the god, so that those who wished could pray to it for offspring and touch it in order to obtain special assistance. The cult of MIN was general at COPTOS and AKHMÎM in the earliest times, and probably at THEBES also, and there is little doubt that AMEN usurped the form and powers of MIN as he did those of the War-god MENTU. And political and commercial considerations probably influenced the priests, who wished to attract a large portion of the trade of COPTOS, the terminus of the great caravan road from the RED SEA to the NILE.

The animal sacred to AMEN was the *sheft* ram probably because of its virility, and pugnacity, and handsome appearance. He is known to naturalists as *Ovis platyura aegyptiaca*, and he belonged to the fat-tailed species of sheep. He was introduced into EGYPT under the Middle Kingdom, by which time the ram of KHNEMU (*Ovis longipes aegyptiaca*) had become extinct.[2] The spirit of AMEN dwelt in the RHNI or Ram-sphinx of which so many statues are seen in the Avenue of Criosphinxes (TA-MA-T RHN-T) at THEBES.[3] No drawing of an anthropomorphized RHNI seems to be known.[4] The text quoted by

[1] *Annales du Service*, tom. ix, p. 64 f.

[2] See the monograph by Lepsius in *Aeg. Zeit.* Band xv, pp. 8 ff.

[3] See Lanzone, Pl. 23, where 'the beautiful Rhni' is figured.

[4] But Amen is once seen crocodile-headed (Lepsius, *Denkmäler*, iii. 188).

SETHE (*Amun*, § 35) states that R[E]H[E]N was the life of AMEN .

The bird sacred to AMEN was the *smen* goose , which connects AMEN in some way with GEBB, the Earth-god. But it is more probable that it was the virility and fecundity of the bird which caused it to be associated with AMEN. AMEN is often seen in the

The boat of the Sun-god of might with the god under the guardianship of the serpent Meḥen setting out to sail down the river of the Ṭuat to revisit and to refresh the denizens of all the Underworlds of Egypt. Khepri, the Sun-god of the following day is seen in the bows.

Books of the ṬUAT holding a serpent-shaped sceptre, which was originally a fetish. The serpent represented was KAM-AT-F , 'He who hath finished his moment', and he was supposed to enshrine the real soul of AMEN.

Under the XVIIIth dynasty THEBES became not only the capital of EGYPT, but the metropolis of all the known world. The native Kingdom of EGYPT included a portion of the NILE valley 1,700 miles long, and a very large portion of western ASIA. AMEN became the 'Lord of the thrones of the world', his solarization became complete under THOTHMES III, his treasury was overflowing with the wealth obtained from foreign conquests, and his priesthood formed the greatest and most powerful theocracy ever known in EGYPT. The title by which the god was honoured was AMEN-RĀ 'King of the gods' , AMEN-RĀ NESU NETERU, which the GREEKS transcribed by 'Αμονρασωνθήρ.

The Book *Ammi Ṭuat* and the *Book of Gates* show that AMEN-RĀ sailed down the river of the ṬUAT nightly, and gave renewed life and air for a short time to the denizens of all the Underworlds of the dead. But it is a remarkable fact that the name of AMEN is not found in any of the oldest copies of the Theban Recension of the *Book of the Dead*. Therefore the god had no real jurisdiction in the kingdom

Amen-ḥetep IV and his wife adoring Atem and receiving blessings from the many hands of the god.

of OSIRIS. He does appear in copies of the Saïte and Ptolemaic periods, and in chapters clxii–clxv he is called 'Lord of the phallus, Bull Scarab, god of many names'. These chapters are probably of Nubian origin, for the cult of AMEN was firmly established at NAPATA in the tenth century B.C.

AMEN-ḤETEP IV, commonly known as AKHUNATEN, attempted to substitute the cult of the material disk of the sun ATEN for that of

AMEN, but the opposition he met with was so general and powerful that he abandoned THEBES, and founded a new capital, AKHUT ATEN, farther to the north. The result of his rule, or rather want of rule, was disastrous for EGYPT for she lost most of her Asiatic colonies during his short reign. After his death the cult of AMEN was speedily restored, and it continued to flourish under the XIXth and XXth dynasties. Little by little the priests of AMEN usurped the power and authority of the last RAMESSIDS of the XXth dynasty, and finally the high priest of AMEN proclaimed himself king of EGYPT. Though astute priests they were failures as kings, and finally they forsook THEBES and fled to NAPATA, where they founded a new house for AMEN-RĀ, and the cult of the god flourished. The priests again made a mistake, for they interfered so much in the affairs of the kingdom that they were at length suppressed by the NUBIANS. The centre of government was removed to MEROË, the capital of the island of MEROË, and there the cult of AMEN flourished until the BLACKS from the south conquered the island. The victory of ÊZÂNÂ, king of ETHIOPIA, and his campaigns in the south practically destroyed all Meroitic civilization. DARIUS established the cult of AMEN in the oasis of KHÂRGAH in the fifth century B.C., and the temple of AMEN (JUPITER AMMON at SÎWÂH) was famous in the days of ALEXANDER THE GREAT. The priests of AMEN adopted the old dogma of the priests of RĀ of the IVth dynasty and declared that AMEN became incarnate by the queens of EGYPT, and that the kings of EGYPT were his sons, and Queen ḤATSHEPSUT his daughter. Through this dogma ALEXANDER THE GREAT became master of EGYPT without striking a blow.

The priests of AMEN were never tired of proclaiming the greatness and majesty of AMEN, but the texts especially, the hymns, show that the EGYPTIANS generally held other views about him and that they ascribed to him the character of a compassionate and gracious god, who was long-suffering and of great goodness. Therefore they appealed to him, as to a loving father, in their troubles and sicknesses, being persuaded that the human side of him could feel, sympathize, and understand their difficulties. To these he was merciful, kind, gracious, and forgiving. He protected the weak against the strong, and the oppressed against the oppressor. He honoured the humble, strengthened the weak, healed the sick, fed the poor and needy, protected the orphan, relieved the widow, and assisted every one who called upon his name in their distress. He answered prayers and gave to every man his heart's desire. And when he dealt with men as their judge, he showed himself to be just, impartial, incorruptible, and righteous; the offender and the sinner were punished, and the righteous were rewarded. Like the

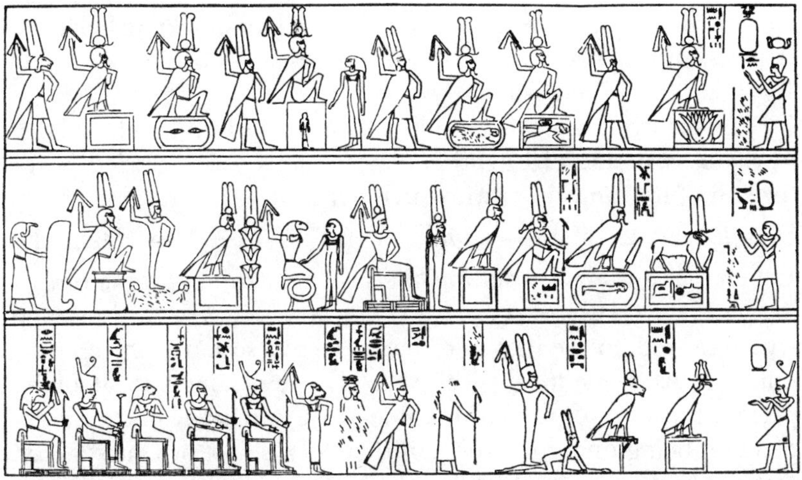

Here I reproduce from Brugsch's *Reise* a drawing of three rows of the gods of Khârgah which shows how a purely phallic character had been ascribed to many of them, I spent four days at Khârgah examining the reliefs and trying to reconstruct the names, but many were beyond recognition.

God of the HEBREWS, AMEN was a 'jealous' god, and the apostate, the backslider, and the swearer of false oath, were abominations to him. From many passages it is clear that to obtain AMEN's help a man had to admit his own foolishness and to express and to show humility, and the texts show that he did so in much the same words as the Psalmist (Ps. lxxiii. 22), 'So foolish was I, and ignorant: I was as a beast before thee'.[1] But the EGYPTIAN does not seem to have known repentance in our sense of the word, although it is possible that he realized the importance of a 'broken and contrite heart' when appealing for help to AMEN.

A few years ago DR. K. SETHE published a remarkable thesis entitled *Amun und die Acht Urgötter von Hermopolis*, BERLIN, 1929,

[1] See Erman, *Denksteine aus der thebanischen Gräberstadt*, pp. 1086–110.

in which he maintains that if a prototype for the presentation of the God of HEBREWS and CHRISTIANS alike ever existed, it can only be found in AMEN-RĀ, the king of the gods. The various stages of his argument are most skilfully arranged and developed, and he supports his statements by quotations from texts of all kinds and periods. These proclaim the width and depth of his reading, and even those who reject his main conclusions must admit that he has sustained his thesis with consummate skill, and acknowledge the deftness of this master hand of the craftsman whose knowledge of Egyptian texts is unrivalled.

All the evidence collected by SETHE proves undoubtedly that in the later period of Egyptian history AMEN was regarded as the 'breath of life' and the spirit which permeated and vivified everything. He was the *suḥ en ānkh* , 'der Hauch des Lebens', and the πνεῦμα of the GREEKS. SETHE thinks that the creating wind which was over the waters of NUNU and the spirit of God which moved on the face of the waters have so much in common that YAHWEH is identical with AMEN. He points out that, at a later period, the spirit of God of the Book of Genesis became an independent being under the form of the Holy Ghost of Christianity, just as the Eye of the Sun became separated from the Sun and developed into an independent deity. But there is no need, in my opinion, to seek for a prototype of the Spirit of God in EGYPT or elsewhere, for the fundamental conceptions of the HEBREWS in respect of the Creation were entirely different from those of the EGYPTIANS. A distinguished German Assyriologist found the prototype of the Holy Ghost in the Babylonian tablets, but the discovery was rejected by every one. The angriest critics of his 'discovery' were his own colleagues.

Again, SETHE compares the ark of AMEN with the Ark of the Covenant of the HEBREWS and assumes that each contained nothing but air. YAHWEH, like AMEN, the 'unseen', being represented therein by the empty air. Little is known about the origin of the Ark of the Covenant, which may have been the badge of a single tribe, perhaps that of JOSEPH. But in the days of MOSES it was a national shrine into which, by God's command (Exod. xxv. 16, 21) he placed the Two Tables of the Law (Deut. x. 2). The first Ark, no doubt, contained something besides air, and one naturally assumes that that something was a sacred stone or fetish of some kind. But this something was superseded by the stone tablets of the Law. The ark to which the writer of the Epistle to the HEBREWS (ix. 4) refers contained a gold pot of manna, AARON'S rod that budded, and the tables of the Law. This widespread Hebrew tradition must have been based upon some historical fact. In any case there is no evidence that the HEBREWS believed that the 'unseen' air represented YAHWEH. Another question arises: Why should not AMEN-AMENET indicate that some quality or attribute was unseen and therefore unknowable? If HUH and HUHET, and KUK and KUKET represent some quality or attribute of NUN, why should not AMEN-AMENET do the same? And AMENET of NUN, and AMENET, the old Theban goddess, were probably two entirely distinct persons.

AMENET, the old Theban goddess, seems to have been a form of NEITH of SAÏS, and she is said to have given birth to RĀ, and to AMEN-RĀ. She was bi-sexual and was associated with MIN. NEITH-AMENET, AHAT-AMENET, and ISIS-AMENET were all fertility goddesses who were worshipped in the Delta long before the old AMEN and AMEN-RĀ, king of the gods, were domiciled in THEBES. Her cult was suppressed in favour of that of MUT, an ancient local goddess of THEBES.

MUT, Lady of ASHERU , was a local vulture-goddess of THEBES; *mut* was the predynastic[1] name for 'vulture', but it became a proper name only when the priests of AMEN made her the second member of their triad. Her sanctuary lay near the lake still existing at KARNAḲ, and she was worshipped under the form of a woman with the whole body of a vulture for her head. Her common titles are UR-T  'the Great' and USER-T  'the Mighty'. She was the mother, wife, and daughter of AMEN, and the mother of KHONSU. She was self-produced. 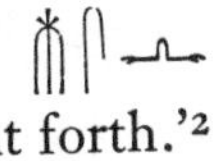  'She brought forth, but was not herself brought forth.'[2] She was perhaps akin to the goddess MU-T  who is mentioned in the Pyramid Texts (UNAS, l. 181). For pictures of her

[1] The common dynastic word for vulture is  *nert*.

[2] Brugsch, *Recueil*, i, Bl. 39.

see LANZONE, Plates 37 and 38, and *Book of the Dead*, chap. clxiv (vignette).

KHONSU [1] was the third member of the triad of THEBES. He was a form of the Moon-god, and was the 'Runner' who scoured the skies. His chief sanctuary was at THEBES, but he was worshipped in many places. Two forms of him are known:

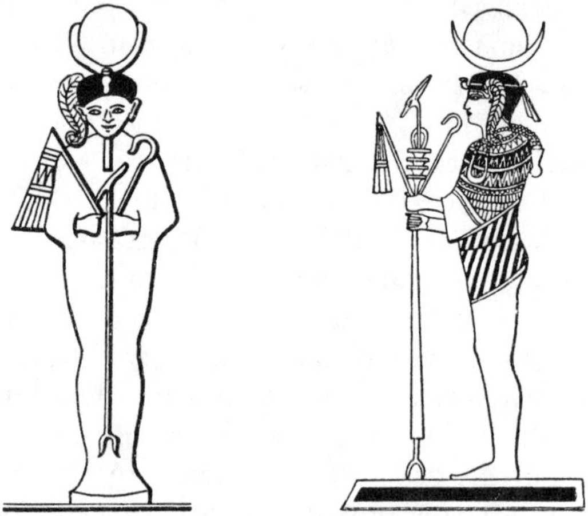

Khonsu the chronographer.

(1) KHONSU, the 'maker of destinies in THEBES', and (2) 'KHONSU NEFER-ḤETEP'. As the crescent moon he was called KHONSU-PA-KHARṬ, 'KHONSU the child', and as the full moon KHONSU ḤUNNU 'KHONSU the strong youth'. Under the influence of the former women conceived, cattle multiplied their young, the germ grew in the egg, and all throats were filled with fresh air. He was a source of generation like ATEN, AMEN, RĀ, and MIN, and was called the 'Bull of his mother' (KA-MUT-F). He appears as a mummied man, like PTAḤ and OSIRIS, with the crescent and full moon on his head. A *menat*, symbol of virility, hangs from the back of his neck, and he holds the fetish symbols of OSIRIS and ISIS, and .[2] He shared

[1] A goddess is also known.

[2] See Lanzone, Pl. 341, for his special form with hawk's heads, &c.

with THOTH the duties of the celestial chronographer and 'reckoned time'. KHONSU-PA-ARI-SEKHERU had authority over all evil spirits. For the legend of his journey to BEKHTEN see Part II, pp. 487–90.

THE TRIAD OF ELEPHANTINE

KHNEMU, the first member of the triad, usually appears in the form of the flat-horned ram, the animal which was sacred to him. He was one of the oldest gods in EGYPT and his name is really the predynastic word for ram, which was taken over by the dynastic EGYPTIANS. He appears in Pyr. § 445 as, and he is often depicted as a ram-headed man. He was originally the local god of the First Cataract, then he was identified with NENU, and was said to bring the NILE into EGYPT from the great World Ocean through two caverns (the QERTI) on the island of ELEPHANTINE. There he divided the river into two parts, and sent one part to the north and the other to the south. A text at DENDERAH (MARIETTE, *Dendérah*, tom. iv, p. 81) speaks of four rivers, which, like the four rivers in Genesis, flowed to the east, west, south, and north. But only two goddesses of the Inundation are known, MERT of the South and MERT of the North. In the texts written under the New Kingdom KHNEMU is called:

'Builder of men, maker of the gods, the Father who was from the beginning.[1]
Maker of the things which are, creator of the things which shall be, the source of things which are, father of fathers, mother of mothers.[2]
Father of the fathers of the gods and goddesses, lord of the things, created by himself, maker of heaven, earth, the Ṭuat (Underworld), waters [and] the mountains.[3] Supporter of the sky on its four pillars, raising it up to all eternity.'[4]

1 . Brugsch, *Religion*, p. 290.

2  Ibid.

3 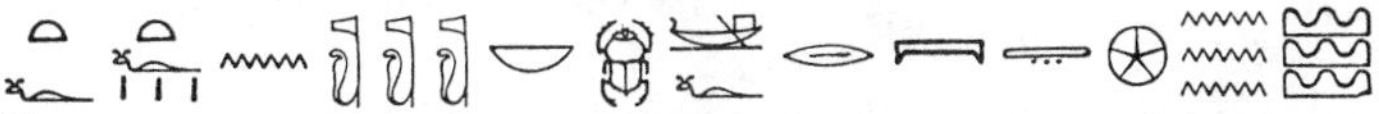 Ibid. p. 291.

4 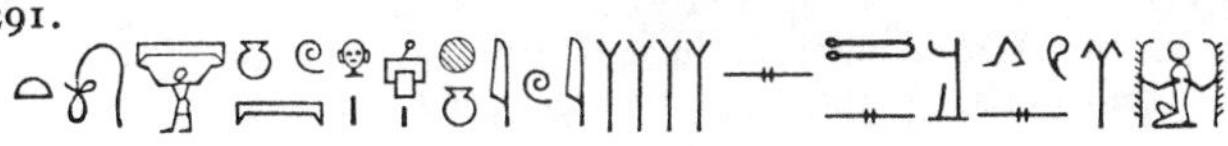 Ibid.

Sometimes KHNEMU has four rams' heads and as such he was called 'SHEFT-ḤAT'; the heads signify that he was the god of ELEPHANTINE, LATOPOLIS, HE-T-URT, HYPSELIS, HERMOPOLIS, and THMUIS. The centres of his cult were at ABU, ELEPHANTINE, and the island of SENMUT, the modern BIGGA, when he lived as the vicar or deputy of ḤĀP-UR, the NILE of heaven.[1]

Mer, god of the whole Inundation.

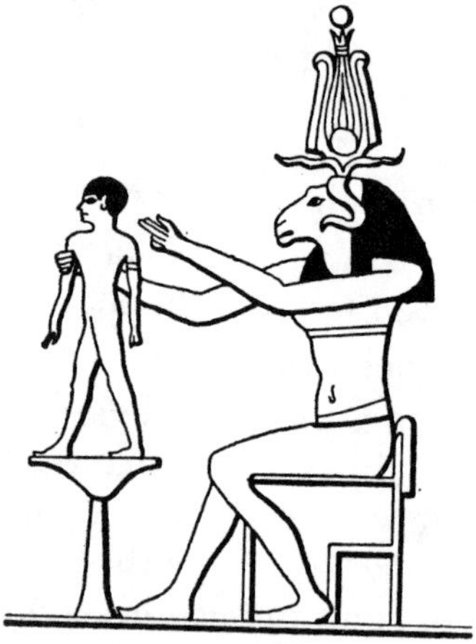

Khnemu, the Potter.

KHNEMU and PTAḤ were the architects of the universe, and they carried out the works of creation as planned by THOTH, and under the direction of THOTH and MAĀT. KHNEMU, like RĀ, OSIRIS, HATHOR, and other deities, existed in seven forms or characters; pictures of them are sometimes seen on the walls of the temples of the late period and their names are:

1. KHNEMU NEḤEP, KHNEMU the Potter.
2. KHNEMU KHENTI-TAUI-NETERU, i.e. KHNEMU, Prince (or Governor) of the Two Lands of the gods.
3. KHNEMU SEKHET-ASH-F, i.e. KHNEMU, 'Weaver of his light'.

[1] For the legend of the terrible seven years famine which took place in the reign of Djeser, a king of the IIIrd dynasty, because Khnemu failed to provide the waters for the annual Inundations, see the translation in Part II, pp. 480–6.

4. KHNEMU KHENTI-PER-ĀNKH, i.e. KHNEMU, Prince of the House of Life.

5. KHNEMU NEB-TA-ĀNKHTT, i.e. KHNEMU, Lord of the Land of Life (i.e. the tomb).

6. KHNEMU KHENTI-NEDJEMDJEM ĀNKH, i.e. KHNEMU, Prince of the House of the Life-joys (?)

7. KHNEMU NEB, i.e. KHNEMU, the Lord.

In the Ptolemaic period the ancient character of KHNEMU as the god of the First Cataract and as a water-god in general was forgotten, and he became known as KHNEMU the Potter, who is seen depicted as a ram-headed man seated behind a potter's wheel, which he works with his foot, and fashioning a man. He is accompanied by THOTH who holds a palm branch with notches on which he marks the number of years which the man, then being fashioned, is to live.

SATET or SATI

SATET, or SATI, was the second member of the triad of ELEPHANTINE, and she usurped the position of the Frog-goddess ḤEQET who was the oldest feminine counterpart of KHNEMU. She appears in the form of a woman with a vulture (?) head-dress, and she wears the White Crown and a pair of horns of an unusual sort. She carries a bow and arrow and her name appears to be connected with 'to shoot', to 'pour out water', &c. She was probably a local goddess of the chase, who became a goddess of the Inundation. Her horns[1] suggest a connexion with ISIS of the Dog-Star (SIRIUS), though she was the HERA of the GREEKS (BRUGSCH, *Religion*, p. 299). Her original home was the island of SÂḤEL (now engulfed in the ASWÂN Dam) and she was probably of Sûdânî origin. Her cult at ELEPHANTINE is very ancient for we read in the Pyramid Texts (PEPI, i, l. 297) 'GEBB leads him (i.e. the king) through the doors of heaven, and the goddess SETHET washeth him in the water of the four vases of purification in AB

[1] Sethe thinks (*Urgeschichte*, § 28) that they may be the horns of an antelope, but she is never seen with an animal's head.

(ELEPHANTINE)'. And the deceased says, 'I was in AB  in the temple of SATITT' (*Book of the Dead*, chap. cxxv. i).

ĀNQET 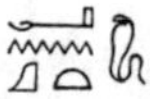 was a Sûdânî water-nymph originally, and she is depicted as a woman wearing a crown of feathers (red parrot's?). She seems to have been a sort of concubine of KHNEMU, and all her attributes were obscene. She had a shrine on the island of SÂḤEL,[1] and a temple of PHILAE, where she was called 'Lady of heaven, Queen of the gods'. The GREEKS identified her with HESTIA.

[1] On the connexion of Min with this island see Sethe, *Urgeschichte*, § 204.

VI

THE FAMILY OF GEBB AND NUT

THE group of gods and goddesses of which OSIRIS was the eldest and most important form a family which must be considered as a whole. Although the grouping is very ancient it is nevertheless artificial, and it is probable that in the earliest times the fetish ancestors of these gods had little or nothing about them which suggested actual relationship. Each of the group shared with various nature-gods certain attributes and powers, but it was their character as a human family which endeared them to the EGYPTIANS of all periods, and made all the other gods seem to be of comparatively little importance. The dynastic EGYPTIANS knew nothing about the history of OSIRIS in the predynastic period, and for this reason made him in turn a solar-god, a water-god, a god of the moon and of the stars, an animal-god, a vegetation-god, a man-god, a god of all living beings and things, and a god of death and the dead. As the god of the dead possessing power to keep alive and to slay, and as the giver of resurrection to the dead and eternal life, during the whole of the dynastic period at least, he was held to be the Death-god *par excellence*. And at the same time the EGYPTIANS thought of him as a man, with twin sisters and a twin brother and a son or nephew, and as the 'eldest of five children who were brought into the world by their mother at the same time'.

Many Egyptian texts suggest that the EGYPTIANS in the later period of their history regarded OSIRIS as a king who had once reigned over their country with great success, and foreign historians like PLUTARCH confirm this view. PLUTARCH, who was born at CHAERONEIA in BOEOTIA and flourished about the middle of the first century after CHRIST, wrote a now famous treatise on OSIRIS in which he appears to have summed up the ideas about OSIRIS and his family which were current in his day. Many of the facts described in his work are supported by statements found in hieroglyphic and hieratic texts, but even though he had no exact knowledge of the most ancient views of the religion his work has considerable value. Some parts of it contain details that suggest that he may have been a priest. A good edition of the Greek text of his treatise, *De Iside et Oriside*, together with a Latin translation, will be found in DIDOT's edition of his *Scripta Moralia*,[1] tom. i, p. 429 f.; the following is a short summary of its contents.

OSIRIS was the son of RHEA (NUT) and CHRONOS (GEBB), and was born on the first of the five epagomenal days of the year. He became king and devoted his whole life to improving the condition of his people. He taught them agriculture, and the worship of the gods, and he drew up a code of laws for their use. Having improved the condition of his own subjects, he left EGYPT and toured about the world and taught all nations to follow the example of his own subjects. He never forced men to accept his views, but argued with them and appealed to their reason. He taught men by means of hymns and songs accompanied by musical instruments. During his absence his wife ISIS administered the kingdom, but her work was sorely hampered by the machinations of TYPHON (SET), her twin brother and also brother-in-law, who devoted himself to making changes in the existing state of things, and counteracting her efforts. When OSIRIS returned to EGYPT TYPHON (SET) determined to remove him and to take to wife ISIS with whom he was violently in love. He, and a certain Ethiopian queen called ASÔ,[2] and seventy-two other persons, banded themselves together and concocted a plan to destroy OSIRIS. They made a chest or coffer which would fit the body of OSIRIS, and placed it in a banquet hall, and at a banquet one night, they called upon the assembled guests one by one to try to get into the coffer. Many attempted to do so and failed, but OSIRIS succeeded in getting into it, and found that it fitted him exactly. Whilst he lay there the conspirators rushed to the box, seized the cover and nailed it on the box, and thus OSIRIS became their prisoner. They melted lead and poured over the coffer, or, perhaps, covered it with sheets of lead. And then they dragged the coffer to the NILE and cast it in. The murder of OSIRIS took place on the 17th day of the month of HATHOR[3] (i.e.

[1] The most accurate English translation of the work known to me will be found in H. P. Cooke's *Osiris. A Study in Myths, Mysteries, and Religion*, London, 1931.

[2] See Cooke, *Osiris*, p. 34.

[3] This day is marked as triply unlucky 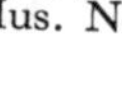 in the Calendar of Lucky and Unlucky Days (Papyrus Sallier IV, Brit. Mus. No. 10184). And on this day the

NOVEMBER[1]) in the 28th year either of the reign or life of OSIRIS, when the Sun was in SCORPIO. The river carried the coffer northwards and it floated out to sea by the Tanitic mouth of the NILE, which was in the north-east of the Delta near PELUSIUM. When ISIS heard of the murder of her husband she cut off a lock of hair and arrayed herself in mourning apparel, and then set out to find the coffer. Some children had seen the coffer being thrown into the NILE, and they told her that it had floated out to sea by the Tanitic mouth of the NILE. Before she continued her journey, she sought for and found ANUBIS, the son of OSIRIS by NEPHTHYS, and made him her guard.

The waves carried the coffer to the Syrian sea-coast and cast it up at BYBLOS (the modern JUBAIL), and as soon as it came to rest a large Erica tree (tamarisk?) sprang up and surrounded the coffer on all sides. The king admired the tree greatly and had it cut down, and of that portion of the trunk which enclosed the coffer he made a pillar for his palace. As soon as ISIS received the news of the children she set out for BYBLOS, and when she arrived she sat down by the royal fountain, and spoke to no one except the queen's maidens who came to question her. To these she replied graciously, and she dressed their hair, and by her contact with them she transferred to them the wonderful perfume of her body. On the return of the maidens to the palace the queen perceived the odour which they had derived from ISIS, and learning whence it came she sent and invited ISIS to the palace, and appointed her nurse to one of her children. The queen was called ASTARTE (i.e. ISHTAR, or ASHTORETH[2]) and the king's name was MALAKANDROS (read MELEK-KARETH[3]). ISIS gave the child a finger to suck instead of the nipple of her breast, and night by night she burned away in fire the mortal parts of his body; meanwhile she herself took the form of a swallow[4] and flew round and round the pillar containing her husband's body. ISIS at length revealed herself to the queen and begged her to give

Lamentations of Isis and Nephthys were recited everywhere from Saïs in the North to Abydos in the South.

[1] Mr. Cooke thinks (*Osiris*, p. 19) late in September.

[2] Or Saosis, or Nemanous, whom the Greeks identified with Athenais.

[3] i.e. 'king of the city' (Melkarth).

[4] Chapter lxxxvi of the *Book of the Dead* provided every deceased person with a spell which would enable him or her to take the form of a swallow. See the vignette in the Papyrus of Nebseni.

her the pillar of the roof. This the queen did, and ISIS opened the pillar and took out the coffer. Then she anointed the pillar with choice unguents, and swathed it in linen and gave it back to the king, who sent it to the temple of BYBLOS where it was worshipped by the people. ISIS took the coffer and placed it in a boat and sailed to EGYPT, and having hidden it in a certain place she went to visit her son HORUS at BUTO[1] [in the VIth nome of LOWER EGYPT]. The coffer was discovered by TYPHON, the murderer of OSIRIS, who burst it open and broke up the body of OSIRIS into fourteen parts, which he scattered about the Delta. ISIS set out in search of these pieces, and she found them all save one, i.e. the member of OSIRIS, which TYPHON cut off from the body and cast into the NILE, where it was swallowed by a fish.[2] ISIS made a model of the phallus of OSIRIS which was duly honoured. OSIRIS returned to earth and encouraged his son HORUS to fight TYPHON, and HORUS made ready to do so.[3] The fight lasted for three or more days, and HORUS was the victor; with the help of HERMES (THOTH), he proved his legitimacy to the gods, and succeeded OSIRIS on the throne of EGYPT. Subsequently ISIS consorted with OSIRIS, and the result of the embrace was HARPOKRATES.

DIODORUS of AGYRIUM in SICILY, who was probably a contemporary of PLUTARCH says (Book I, chap. 11) that OSIRIS and ISIS were two great and eternal gods, and were the Sun and the Moon; they were the children of CHRONOS and RHEA, who gave birth to five gods, each god being born on one of the five epagomenal days, viz. OSIRIS, ISIS, TYPHON, APOLLO, and APHRODITE. Some identify OSIRIS with BACCHUS and ISIS with CERES. OSIRIS became king and abolished cannibalism, and taught men agriculture, and introduced vine-growing into his country. OSIRIS had a scribe called HERMES (in Egyptian THOTH) who gave names to things hitherto unnamed, and he invented arithmetic, sculpture, music, and astronomy. OSIRIS determined to go into other countries and to teach men the art of vine-growing, and how to cultivate wheat and barley. When he set out he took with him a large army, and he committed the administration of his kingdom to ISIS, and gave her THOTH to be

[1] I omit the paragraph dealing with the terrified child who fell into the sea.

[2] The lepidotus, phagrus, and oxyrhyncus fishes had all fed upon it.

[3] I omit the passage mentioning the horse and the lion.

her assistant, and HERCULES his kinsman to command the soldiers. He took with him also APOLLO (HORUS?), ANUBIS, MACEDO (UP-UATU?), and PAN (MENU), and musicians and singers, and marched into ETHIOPIA. There he taught agriculture, and built cities, and established a river NILE conservancy, and dug canals which were equipped with flood-gates and regulators. He marched into INDIA via ARABIA, planted the ivy plant in NYSA, hunted elephants, and returned to EGYPT with his army. He was the world's great benefactor, for he taught men what to eat, and he was rewarded with immortality and was worshipped as a god. OSIRIS was murdered by his brother TYPHON, who broke the body into twenty-six pieces, and usurped the throne of EGYPT. ISIS and her son HORUS avenged the murder of OSIRIS, and HORUS ascended the throne of his father. ISIS succeeded in finding twenty-five parts of the body of OSIRIS, and with the help of wax and aromatic gums and spices, she reconstructed the body and handed it over to the priests for burial. She set apart the revenues of one-third of the country of EGYPT to form an endowment fund for the maintenance of the worship of OSIRIS. It is clear that she wished to associate the worship of OSIRIS with the cult of a certain beast which they maintained, for she stipulated that they were to pay to it the same veneration which they were to pay to OSIRIS, and when it was dead to worship it as sincerely as they did OSIRIS. This the priests agreed to do, and they dedicated the bull to OSIRIS, and made lamentation over the tombs of the APIS Bull of MEMPHIS and the MNEVIS Bull of HELIOPOLIS, as they did over the tomb of OSIRIS. ISIS also caused models of the missing part of the body of OSIRIS (i.e. the phallus) to be made and distributed among the temples, where they were worshipped and held in great veneration.

ISIS devoted the rest of her life to works of charity and the welfare of her people; she was buried at MEMPHIS or PHILAE, and was numbered among the gods. She discovered many medicines, and was greatly skilled in the art of healing. She restored many 'incurables' to robust health, she made the lame to walk and the blind to see, and invented a medicine which raised the dead to life. Her son HORUS was killed by TITANS, who threw his body into the water, but having administered this medicine to him, he not only came to life again but became immortal. He learned the arts of physic and divination from ISIS, and used them for the benefit of mankind.

JULIUS FIRMICUS MATERNUS, who flourished early in the fourth century A.D., misunderstood several parts of the history of OSIRIS and ISIS and thought that ISIS was the wife of TYPHON who, finding that ISIS was in love with OSIRIS slew him. TYPHON dismembered OSIRIS and scattered his limbs along the banks of the NILE, but ISIS and her sister NEPHTHYS and ANUBIS found them, and buried them, and made a figure of OSIRIS which was worshipped as OSIRIS in the temples. The murder and dismemberment of OSIRIS were commemorated annually with universal weepings and wailings and extravagant lamentations. After a few days the mourning ceremonies were suspended, and an announcement was made to the effect that all the members of the body of OSIRIS had been found and rejoined, and then universal rejoicings became the order of the day. MATERNUS thought that wheat was the seed of OSIRIS, that ISIS was the earth, and TYPHON heat.

MACROBIUS (fifth century) thought that OSIRIS was the sun and ISIS the earth. Now, of the classical writers PLUTARCH was the best informed as far as the legend of OSIRIS and ISIS is concerned, but he seems to have made a serious mistake in stating that the coffer containing the body of OSIRIS was taken to BYBLOS. The NILE carried it down to the papyrus swamps in the Eastern Delta, and there ISIS sought for it. Now *byblos* is a well-known word for the papyrus plant, and the scribe confused it with the Greek name of JUBAIL on the Syrian coast.

PLUTARCH was right to describe OSIRIS as a god, but there is no evidence that he was ever a king of EGYPT. The GREEKS never realized that OSIRIS represented a fusion of many gods, and that his cult in the Roman period was a mixture of many cults, some of them dating from the earliest times of the predynastic period. He may be described as the god *par excellence* who assumed a material form and flourished and decayed and died and lived again. He represented, and was, the sun which dies in the evening and rises the following morning, and as the Moon he might be regarded as the Night-Sun or Sun-god of Night. The story of the dismemberment of OSIRIS and the scattering of his members about the Delta is probably a late form of a legend concerning the dismemberment of the moon during the period of her waning, or the break-up of the Sun-god of day at eventide, and the scattering of his members which in the forms of stars and constellations are strewn about the night sky. He was also the great Sky-tree, out of which the sun rose, and the Moon, which waxed and waned, and promptly renewed itself. Indeed, he is often called the Moon, and because of this some Egyptologists have asserted that the two pre-eminent gods of the EGYPTIANS were the Sun and the Moon, i.e. RĀ and OSIRIS. OSIRIS was also a form of ORION the giant, and the Bull, and the Morning Star, and SIRIUS, and the embryonic Sun-god in the constellation of ARGO. He even became the ferryman of RĀ, and the Ladder of RĀ. He was also the Year-god, a fact proved by the 365 lamps which were lighted at DENDERAH,[1] and the 365 trees which were planted round his temples. He was the god of the Great Ocean which surrounds the whole world, and therefore of the NILE which flowed out of it into EGYPT. He himself is the water of the NILE which exudes from his body (for he was drowned therein at MEMPHIS). OSIRIS was the source of all vegetation and was in every green plant and herb, and as the god of the harvest and of all grain crops, he passed into the bodies of all who consumed them, both man and beast. His body formed the Circle of the TUAT, which existed at all times in the great primeval NU or NUNU, or abyss, and here he reigned as king of the dead. OSIRIS enshrined within himself all the cosmic gods or gods of nature, but the EGYPTIANS worshipped him because he had himself been raised from the dead, and they believed that he was able to give them resurrection and new and eternal life. And he was in the form of every being and thing which is born and dies. From first to last he was the Sun, for he was older than RĀ, and what the myth of OSIRIS really means to describe is his annual course through the heavens as the creator and sustainer of them all. But the cult of OSIRIS was essentially different from the cult of RĀ, for from first to last it was a great, perhaps the greatest work, of all the works of the priesthoods of all EGYPT.

[1] See Budge, *Osiris*, vol. ii, p. 28.

OSIRIS THE FETISH AND HIS NAMES

There is good reason to believe that the god who in dynastic times was appointed by the Great Council of the Gods assembled in HELIOPOLIS to be the god and judge of the dead, was originally a mere fetish, and that the seat of its cult was in a city which was the capital of a nome on the DAMIETTA arm of the NILE in the Eastern Delta. The oldest god of the nome known to us was called ĀNDJ-TI, the determinative being a hawk standing on a perch and having two feathers on his head (Pyr. § 614 *a*). But in the parallel passage in M. 422 he is represented thus:

He has two feathers on his head, a streamer hangs from the back of his head, in his right hand he holds the shepherd's crook, and in his left an instrument which may be a 'flicker' or a whip. A straight line serves for the body of the god, and the standard on which it rests is fixed in the sign for nome. In another passage he is called 'dweller in ĀNDJ-T[I], great overlord of his marshes', (Pyr. § 182 *a*). Both the nome and its god were called 'ĀNDJ-TI', The shepherd's crook and the 'flicker' indicate that the Delta contained herds of cattle (probably the ancestors of those which AMEN-ḤETEP III hunted there) and flocks of sheep and goats. The exact purpose of the streamer which is attached to the god's head is unknown, but we see it attached to the heads of the gods MENU and AMEN; it probably refers in some way to the air or wind. Now the capital of the nome of ĀNDJ-TI was ṬEṬU (or DEDU) and there in some form or other the fetish of ANDJ-TI was worshipped. What its form was no one can say, but it was probably a trunk of some tree which had bands of metal round it and possibly some other ornamentation. It may have contained some sacred object used in the cult, or it may have been kept hollow. The dynastic EGYPTIANS called this tree trunk ṬEṬ (or DED), and its simplest form in the hieroglyphic inscriptions is. The principal ceremonial acts of the cult consisted in 'setting up the ṬEṬ', i.e. raising it into a standing position. If the trunk was kept empty it is possible that sick folk, and the dead, were placed in it so that the former might receive renewed health, and the latter renewed life. In some way the ṬEṬ was supposed to give health and life to all who touched it, and many drawings show that the ṬEṬ was the god himself whether he was called ĀNDJ-TI or OSIRIS (see Budge, *Osiris*, vol. i, p. 51 f.)

The drawing on p. 110 shows that the head of ĀNDJ-TI rests on top of a pole, or it may be a slim tree trunk, instead of a body in human form, and so the fetish may have been a magical life-giving rod or pole. In a vignette in the Papyrus of ANI the symbol of life ☥ is seen rising out of the top of the ṬEṬ, and from this two arms project upwards and support the solar disk (Budge, *Osiris*, p. 51). This seems to connect the ṬEṬ with the bare tree trunk or pole of the ASSYRIANS which is discussed by SIDNEY SMITH in his *Early History of Assyria* (p. 123 f.). At the New Year Festival in ASSYRIA metal bands were fastened round a bare tree trunk, and fillets were attached to it with the view of assisting the revival of Nature in the New Year. The SYRIANS and PALESTINIANS performed magical ceremonies with bare tree poles, and the HEBREWS had their *ashêrâh*,[1] which was either a bare pole or a sacred tree of some sort. In fact the pole or tree or the trunk figures prominently in all the religions of all the peoples in the eastern MEDITERRANEAN, e.g. in CRETE, EGYPT, and ASIA MINOR. Now the sacred tree of ASSYRIA was associated with the cult of ASHUR whose symbol, the winged solar disk with the god himself sitting inside it, is often seen over the tree. In the case of the ṬEṬ, the head of the sun-god either as a young man or the 'Aged of Days' projects from the top of the ṬEṬ and wears a crown formed by a pair of horns, similar to those of the ram of KHNEMU, and the two feathers or plumes of the god ĀNDJ-TI. Sometimes the solar disk is added. Now ASHUR was believed by the ASSYRIANS to have been killed or died and to come to life again at the New Year. And he was so close a counterpart of MARDUK of BABYLON, the son of BÊL, that in later times, when they adopted the Creation Epic which describes the exploits of MARDUK, the chief alteration they made in the text of it was to substitute ASHUR for MARDUK. Much is known about the death and resurrection of MARDUK, and, in its general features, the story of MARDUK as told in the cuneiform texts of BABYLON, and later in those of ASSYRIA, runs

[1] A symbol of a god or goddess which was set up near an altar (1 Kings xvi. 33). One such was burnt by Gideon (Judges vi. 25–30).

on substantially parallel lines with that of OSIRIS as it is found in the hieroglyphic inscriptions. And the ṬEṬ resembles the tree sacred to ASHUR. Thus myth and ritual coincided in EGYPT and ASSYRIA, and it is only reasonable to seek for a common origin of both in the two countries.

It may be argued that the myth of MARDUK belonged to some older god, but even if it did, it does not affect the relation of MARDUK, ASHUR, and OSIRIS. All over western ASIA and in EGYPT there must have been legends of gods or divine beings who were either murdered or killed and rose again, long before the later local gods, whose names are known to us, came into being. The same kind of story was probably told about MARDUK, ASHUR, and OSIRIS, and the circumstances which produced these gods were probably the same. Popular tradition in EGYPT made out that OSIRIS was a mere human being and a king, and that he was murdered by his brother SET, who coveted not only his kingdom but his wife also. But such things have happened in every country from time immemorial, and it is possible that the BABYLONIANS and the ASSYRIANS told similar stories of the predecessors of MARDUK and ASHUR.

We have seen that the centre of the cult of the god ĀNDJ-TI, the pole-god or tree-god, was at ṬEṬU, a city on the DAMIETTA arm of the NILE in the Eastern Delta, a little south of west of the cities which in dynastic times were called MENDES and TANIS. This city is called 'The House of OSIRIS, the lord of ṬEṬU',[1] and the reach of the river which flowed by it was known as 'the river of OSIRIS'.[2] In dynastic times the nome of which it was the capital was called by the GREEKS BUSIRITES, and it was then regarded as the IXth nome of LOWER EGYPT. The Greek name for the city of ṬEṬU was BUSIRIS, which is derived from the Egyptian 'PA-ASAR' or 'PER-ASAR', i.e. the 'House of OSIRIS'. Thus it was no longer the city of ĀNDJ-TI but of OSIRIS, and the chief god of the city was OSIRIS, or of his fetish pole the ṬEṬ. We must now try to find out what caused the change in the name of the city, and with that object in view we must consider the *name* of OSIRIS.

'OSIRIS' is the Greek form of the name which is written in hieroglyphs with the signs 𓊨𓏤, 𓊨𓁹, 𓊨𓁹𓀭, 𓁹𓊨, 𓁹𓊨𓀭, 𓁹𓊨𓀭,

[1] [hieroglyphs]

[2] [hieroglyphs]

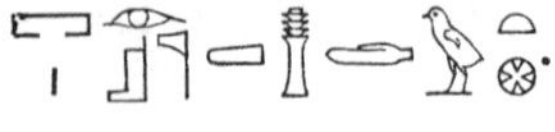

, 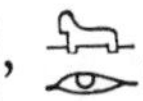, , &c.; these are read AS-AR or AS-ARI. In the Ptolemaic period we have , 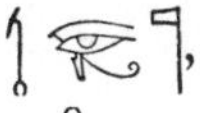, or , which are to be read US-ARI. Other forms are SER , USER , USRI , ASARS 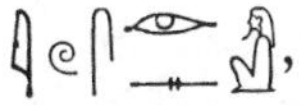, from which probably comes the Greek OSIRIS. Other late forms of the name are: , , , , &c. The Coptic form OUSIRI shows that the *u*-sound predominated at the beginning of the name in the Ptolemaic and Greek periods, just as MUSLIMS to-day often pronounce the name of God ULLÂH, instead of ALLÂH.

Ancient as well as modern writers have been puzzled about the meaning of the name OSIRIS , AS-AR. The upper sign is the picture of a seat or chair, and the lower sign represents the human eye. DIODORUS thought that OSIRIS meant 'many eyes' (i. 11), and PLUTARCH took the same view (§ 10). JABLONSKI and LEEMANS connected the name with two Coptic words meaning 'working much' (*Panthéon*, ii. 7; *Horapollo*, p. 243); SHARPE connected it with the Coptic words for 'crying overmuch' (*Eg. Mythology*, p. 7); BRUGSCH assumed that the oldest form of the name was US-IRI, and believed that it meant 'die Macht, die Kraft des Augapfels' or 'Kräftig ist der Augapfel'. These meanings, however, offer no equivalent for the sign , a throne, or seat. SETHE regards OSIRIS as a pet name (*Urgeschichte*, § 94) and renders it by 'the seat of the eye' ('Sitz des Auges'). ERMAN approves most of the forms 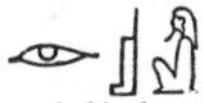 and  and thinks that the name means 'maker, or establisher, of a throne'. None of these explanations has been accepted by Egyptologists generally, and it is tolerably certain that all are wrong.

A suggestion was made several years ago that ASAR, or OSIRIS, was not an Egyptian name at all, and that it was derived from ASARI, a title of the god MARDUK of BABYLON, the son of EA. At the time the idea seemed far-fetched, and it was not accepted generally. But in recent years many facts have been brought to light which support the suggestion, and which show that OSIRIS usurped the position which the old god ĀNDJ-TI held in the nome of ĀNDJ-TI, and that, under the Old Kingdom, ĀNDJ-TI and OSIRIS were regarded as identical gods. This fact indicates that at one time at least the cult and ritual of the one god had much in common with the other, but the cult and ritual of OSIRIS were also identical with the cult and ritual of ASHUR of ASSYRIA and MARDUK of BABYLON. Each of the three was a god who had died and risen again, and at the New Year Festival in the three countries ceremonies were performed in connexion with a bare pole or tree trunk. The pole or tree trunk was dressed and decorated and adorned with the object of assisting the spring vegetation. The knowledge of all this was common property in the three countries, for it was carried from one country to the other by the caravans. Much of the early civilization in the Delta was derived from BABYLONIA and SYRIA; it did not come directly across that 'great and terrible' desert, by way of SYRIA and PALESTINE. The knowledge of 'the chthonian deity ASARI, the son of EA, who was begotten in the underworld *duku* where the sweet waters lay'[1] was brought to EGYPT by foreigners who were followers of his cult, and they found that the cult of ĀNDJ-TI was similar to their own. Thus we may assume that, under circumstances of which we know nothing, they found a way to establish the cult of ASARI in the nome of ĀNDJ-TI. This result was probably arrived at by peaceful means or by arrangement. That it took place in very early times there is no possibility of doubting, for the cult of OSIRIS and his holy family were established in the Delta long before the reign of MENA and the unification of the Two Lands.

We may now compare the cuneiform characters for ASARI, i.e. MARDUK, and the transcription of them into hieroglyphs. The group of wedges which are read ASARI is  and it is composed of two distinct characters, viz.  and . The first has the well-known meaning of 'tent', or 'dwelling', or 'resting-place', and the second has the meaning of 'eye', and is placed inside the sign for 'tent'. The two signs by which these are transcribed in Egyptian are , a seat or throne, and an eye. Now the sign  is followed in the text by two other cuneiform characters, viz. ; these form a title of ASARI and are read in Sumerian LU DUG, and they mean 'good man or being'. Thus we have 'ASARI, the good being'. But we find in the Egyptian texts that one of the principal titles of OSIRIS is UN-NEFER 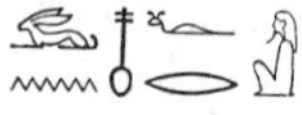, i.e. the 'Good

[1] See Sidney Smith, *Early History of Assyria*, p. 175.

Being', and it seems clear that this title is the Egyptian translation of the cuneiform . Thus there is little doubt that the Egyptian AS-AR is the equivalent of the Babylonian ASARI.

THE ICONOGRAPHY OF OSIRIS

In the earliest times OSIRIS was regarded as a god, and probably the son of a god, who had died and risen from the dead. But in the period immediately preceding the Union of the Two Lands, there is little doubt that the EGYPTIANS believed that he was a good and just king of EGYPT who had been murdered by his brother, and had risen from the dead. He and the four deities who were born with him formed a sort of 'holy family', the members of which were endued with human attributes. The blazon of the IXth nome of LOWER EGYPT (BUSIRITES) gives us a representation of the old god of the nome ĀNDJ-TI, but we possess no drawing of OSIRIS made in the predynastic period or under the Old Kingdom. The body of ĀNDJ-TI is represented by a bare pole, but this is not the case with OSIRIS for he usually appears in the form of a mummy, like MENU, AMEN, and PTAḤ, in fact a sort of conventional idol. Sometimes his body is given the form of the ṬEṬ .[1] The head-dress of ĀNDJ-TI consisted of two plumes , and these appear in the crown of the ṬEṬ or OSIRIS, but fastened above a pair of horns . Why these horns appear is not clear; above them we sometimes have the solar disk . The crown composed of horns, disk, and feathers is called the 'Atef' crown , but it is usually associated with SEKER, the god of the underworld of MEMPHIS. From ĀNDJ-TI OSIRIS also borrowed the pastoral crook or sceptre , and the object , about which there has been so much unconvincing discussion, but which was probably a kind of whip, or 'flicker', or 'whisk', which the ancient EGYPTIANS used in driving herds of cattle. When the ṬEṬ takes the place of OSIRIS it is given human arms and in its right hand it holds the and in the left the pastoral crook . In

[1] What this hieroglyph represents exactly is unknown. I believe it to be a faulty drawing of the fetish object which was associated with the tree trunk Ṭeṭ. And in my opinion this fetish was a portion of some organ or of the bony structure of the human body which was connected with reproduction, in other words it was a fertility fetish.

many pictures the two plumes of ĀNDJ-TI are placed one on each side of the White Crown of UPPER EGYPT , thus . We may note that the streamer which is attached to the head of the nome-god ĀNDJ-TI is not reproduced in the drawings of OSIRIS.

Though the operations of OSIRIS were manifold and there was no realm in the kingdom of Nature in which his influence was not predominant, none of the representations of him which we find in papyri and on stelae shows us the god in motion or making any movement. He is always a passive figure, and is usually seated on a chair-like throne or a seat which resembles a funerary coffer. As a cosmic god he appears as a motionless director or observer of the actions of his servants who fulfil his will, and it was as the almighty and everlasting Judge of the Dead that the EGYPTIANS loved to represent him. In the Papyrus of NEBSENI in the BRITISH MUSEUM he, the Eternal Judge 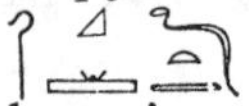 is seen seated on a throne decorated with symbols of the union of UPPER and LOWER EGYPT. The throne rests on a reed mat, which is laid on a flat pedestal shaped like the hieroglyph of *maāt*  meaning 'justice', 'law', truth'. He is in mummy form, and wears the White Crown of UPPER EGYPT . From his chin hangs the long narrow projecting Puntite[1] beard, and he holds in his hands the pastoral crook and flail or whip.

He is seated under a canopy, which is like the top of a funerary coffer and is supported by two columns having lotus-like capitals. Above is a row of bunches of grapes, which illustrates the connexion of the god with the vine.[2] In painted papyri (e.g. the Papyrus of IUAU, Plate 1) OSIRIS wears a long white garment which extends from his neck to his ankles, and his crown is white, with a red feather on each side of it. The body of the god is of an earthy-red colour; in the Papyrus of ANI (Plate 4) it is painted green, which is probably intended to indicate that OSIRIS was the Ancient of Days. Elsewhere (HUNEFER, Plate 5) the throne of OSIRIS is set above a lake out of which grows a lotus plant; on this stand the four sons of OSIRIS (MESTA, ḤĀPI, ṬUAMUTEP, and ḲEBḤSENUF), who are often confounded with the four sons of HORUS. The goddesses of the

[1] Punt was a country far away to the south in the Sûdân.

[2] Diodorus says (i. 15) that Osiris was the first to plant the vine and to teach men to drink wine.

northern and southern inundations of the NILE sometimes stand before him with their arms raised in adoration. According to tradition OSIRIS was drowned by SET in the NILE, and henceforth he became god of the NILE, in fact a cosmic god. The plinth of the throne was ascended by means of a stairway. The plinth should have nine steps, one for each god of the 'Company of

Osiris in his shrine (Papyrus of Hunefer.

OSIRIS', but in the Papyrus of NERI-TA-NEB-ASHRU the throne of OSIRIS is formed by five rectangular blocks which diminish in size as they go upwards. The same papyrus shows that the throne was guarded by a huge serpent. In some papyri OSIRIS is accompanied by a fetish in the form of a pied bull's skin fastened to a bare pole which stands upright in a pot; this skin was used by the god ANUBIS who performed with it ceremonies of rebirth for the god, and for his votaries, and was used as such under the Old Kingdom. The reliefs at ABYDOS show that OSIRIS existed in seven forms; 1. OSIRIS of ṬEṬU (BUSIRIS). 2. OSIRIS NEDJṬIS wearing the crown of SEKER. 3. OSIRIS KHENTI-AMENTI. 4. OSIRIS KHENTI PER-SEPEN. 5. OSIRIS KHENTI AMENTI NEB ḤERI-MESEN. 6. OSIRIS KHENTI ḤET-A-AST.

7. OSIRIS NEB-MER-NEFERT. No. 1 wears the plumes (?) of ĀNDJ-TI, and his hands are outside his swathings. No. 2 wears the crown of SEKER, and Nos. 3 to 7 wear the White Crown and have their hands inside their swathings.

Important forms of OSIRIS were:

ASAR-AĀḤ , OSIRIS the Moon-god. He appears in the form of a mummy with the crescent moon holding the full moon on his head.

ASAR-SAḤ 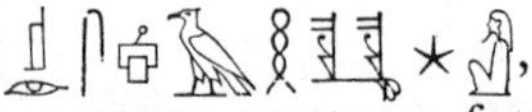, OSIRIS-ORION.

ASAR-ḤER or OSIRIS-HORUS, a form of the rising sun.

ASAR-RĀ or OSIRIS-RĀ.

ASAR-HERAKHTI-TEMU, or OSIRIS with the rising and setting sun and TEM.

ASAR-NEB-ḤEḤ 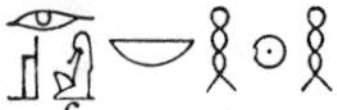, OSIRIS, lord of eternity, who appears in the form of a mummy with the head of a Benu-bird, or phoenix.

ASAR-NUB-ḤEḤ , OSIRIS, gold of eternity.

ASAR-GEBB , OSIRIS Earth-god.

ASAR-TA-NEB-ṬEṬ , OSIRIS and the Ram of MENDES.

ASAR-TUA , OSIRIS the Begetter.

THE DISMEMBERMENT OF OSIRIS

An old Memphite tradition says that OSIRIS was drowned in the NILE, and with this statement PLUTARCH agrees, but he goes on to say that the body of OSIRIS was recovered by ISIS and hidden by her in a secret place. TYPHON discovered the body, and hacked it in pieces, which he scattered about the country or along the banks of the NILE. PLUTARCH believed that OSIRIS was a very ancient king who had been murdered, and there is no doubt that the EGYPTIANS themselves had believed the same thing for thousands of years. And, of course, there may have been a king, or knight, who had reigned over some portion of the Eastern Delta in prehistoric times, although we know nothing about him. It is quite clear that the story of the murder and dismemberment of this king OSIRIS is substantially the same as that which was told by the predynastic theologians who turned this king OSIRIS into the god OSIRIS, because he had risen from the dead. In the Pyramid Texts OSIRIS is a god with whom the dead kings mentioned in the texts are identified, and there are many allusions to his dismemberment. Thus we have, 'Thou hast thy heart, OSIRIS, thou hast thy feet OSIRIS, thou hast thy arms, OSIRIS. The heart of UNAS is to him, his feet are to him, his arms are to him' (UNAS, l. 476). 'Hail! Hail! rise up, thou TETA! Thou hast received thy head, thou hast embraced thy bones, thou hast gathered together thy flesh' (TETA, l. 287). 'The goddess KHNEMET-URT cometh to thee. She breatheth (?) on thee, she speaketh words of power, thou movest. She giveth thee thy head, she presenteth to thee thy bones, she gathereth together thy flesh, she bringeth to thee thy heart in thy body' (PEPI i, l. 109). The reconstitution of the body of OSIRIS was effected by HORUS and his four sons, and ISIS, and NEPHTHYS, and GEBB, and NUT also assisted. HORUS gave the god his Eye and gave him life in his name of ĀNDJ-TI and restored to him the use of all his members, and 'opened his mouth' for him with his little finger (PEPI i, l. 59).

The exact number of pieces into which the body of OSIRIS was cut is doubtful; PLUTARCH says *fourteen*, but the hieroglyphic texts give both *fourteen* and *sixteen*, and in one case eighteen. The eighteen are as follows:

1. Head.
2. Eyes.
3. Ears.
4. Nose.
5. Mouth.
6. Jaws.
7. Beard.
8. Lips.
9. Tongue.
10. Body.
11. Neck.
12. Hands.
13. Nails and ankles.
14. Belly.
15. Shoulders.
16. Genital organs.
17. Backbone.
18. Feet.[1]

[1] See the *Book of making the Spirit of Osiris* (ed. Pierret, p. 17).

The list giving sixteen members reads:

1. Head . 2. Feet . 3. Bones 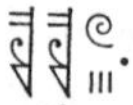. 4. Arms . 5. Heart . 6. Interior . 7. Tongue 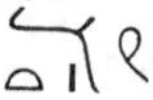. 8. Eye . 9. Fist 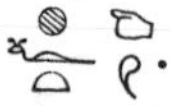. 10. Fingers 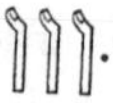. 11. Back 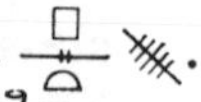. 12. Ears . 13. Loins . 14. Body 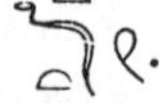. 15. Ram-faced head 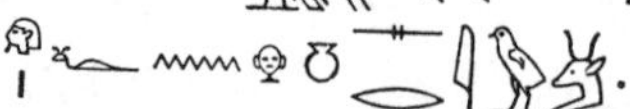. 16. Hair 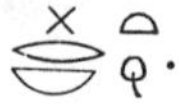.

The head was buried at ABYDOS, his left eye in LOWER EGYPT, his eyebrows at PELUSIUM, his jaw-bones at FĀKET, parts of his head at ḤET-GAR, his neck in the Delta, an arm and the right leg at ATE-RAUI SHEMĀ, his left leg at MEḤET, his coccyx at HELIOPOLIS, his thighs at ḤET-ḤER-ATEB, a foot at NETERT, his heart in USEKH-MEḤT, his phallus at ḤET-BENNU, and a part of his back at PA-PESṬ-NETERU. The sixteen sanctuaries in which the members of OSIRIS were buried were in (1) ṬEṬU (BUSIRIS). (2) ABYDOS. (3) White Wall (MEMPHIS). (4) NUBIA. (5) HERAKLEOPOLIS. (6) KUSAE. (7) ATEF-KHENT. (8) SAÏS. (9) MEḤTET. (10) AMU. (11) SMA-BEḤT. (12) REAQIU. (13) HEN. (14) NETERT. (15) BAḤT. (16) KAKAM. [17. DENDERAH.][1] In the late period, i.e. in Graeco-Roman times, the sanctuaries of OSIRIS were forty-two in number, for each nome possessed its central shrine of OSIRIS which was called a 'Serapeum', or a place where SARAPIS was worshipped. But this happened because OSIRIS-KHENTI-AMENTI was identified with SARAPIS who was not OSIRIS himself, but only a dead APIS Bull which had become an OSIRIS.

ASAR-ḤAP 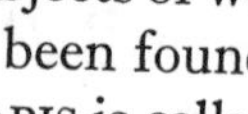. Here we have the name of OSIRIS coupled with that of the Bull APIS, and the original form of the Greek SERA-PIS, or SARAPIS, Σάραπις. The cult of the APIS Bull was established at MEMPHIS, and the cult of the MNEVIS Bull at HELIOPOLIS, by KAKAU, a king of the IInd dynasty, but there is no doubt that both bulls were objects of worship in predynastic times. In inscriptions which have been found in the great APIS mausoleum (Serapeum) at ṢAḲḲĀRA APIS is called the 'life of OSIRIS, the lord of heaven, TEM [with] his two horns [in] his head' ,[2]

[1] See V. Loret in the *Recueil*, tom. v, p. 85. See also the list published by Brugsch (*Aeg. Zeit.*, 1881, pp. 79 ff.).

[2] See Mariette, *Le Sérapéum*, Paris, 1882, p. 125 f.

and he is said to give life, strength, and health, to the nostrils of the king for ever. Elsewhere we have the form ḤAP-ASAR, and the special titles of OSIRIS are given to him thus: 'great god, KHENTI AMENTI, the lord of everlasting life'. The inscription in which these words occur was written in the period of the XVIIIth dynasty, and it is therefore clear that about 1300 B.C. some of the funerary attributes of OSIRIS were ascribed to APIS, or that in some way the functions of the two gods were identical. At MEMPHIS, where PTAḤ was the head of the great triad of that city, APIS is called the 're-newed life of PTAḤ' 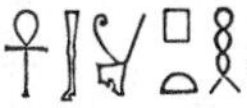, and the 'second' or 'deputy' of PTAḤ , and the 'son of PTAḤ 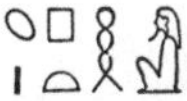. In Ptolemaic times the centre of the cult of SERAPIS was ALEXANDRIA, where it is said to have been established by PTOLEMY SOTER. This king wished to find some god who could be worshipped both by GREEKS and EGYPTIANS in ALEXANDRIA, and one who could be regarded as the characteristic god of the Ptolemaic dynasty in EGYPT. PLUTARCH says (*De Iside*, § 28) that whilst he was meditating on this matter he had a dream in which a colossal statue of a god appeared to him, and a voice told him to remove the statue from the place where it was to ALEXANDRIA. He had never seen a god in this form, and he knew neither the place where it stood, nor the name of the god represented by the statue. One day he described the statue which he had seen in his dream to his councillor SOSIBIUS, who at once said that he had seen a similar statue at SINOPE. PTOLEMY wanted to have the statue brought from SINOPE to ALEXANDRIA, but the inhabitants of the city refused to let it go. When negotiations had continued for three years, the SINOPIANS remaining obdurate, the statue of its own accord moved itself to the harbour, and embarked on a ship, and arrived at ALEXANDRIA in safety after a voyage which lasted three days. PTOLEMY placed the statue in the Serapeum which he built at ALEXANDRIA, and the Greek priests told the people that it was the god HADES or PLUTO and the EGYPTIANS called it ASAR-ḤAP or SERAPIS. And GREEKS and EGYPTIANS alike worshipped it as the god of the Underworld. SERAPIS is represented in the form of bull-headed man who stands with his legs separated. On his head is the crescent moon holding the full moon in it, and above it are two large plumes, like those of AMEN. On his breast is a pylon-shaped pectoral with two cobras, one at each end. And he grasps with both hands the sceptre, the flail or whip, and the pastoral crook 𓋾; under the head of the sceptre are 𓊽 and 𓋹.

In the annexed drawing we have a scene in which a noble of Memphis of the late Ptolemaic Period (?) is making an offering to the gods of Memphis. It is taken from the sculpture on the funerary stele of the official, in the British Museum. The gods represented are Osiris, Sarapis, bull-headed, Isis, Nephthys, Ḥer-nedj-tef, Anubis, I-em-ḥetep 'the son of Ptaḥ', and Amentet, the mother of the gods'. The form of Sarapis here given is that generally found at this period. The words 'king of the gods, lord of eternity, and governor everlasting' apply to Osiris and not Sarapis.

On the decadence of the cult of OSIRIS see the section on ISIS (pp. 199–205). Some extremely interesting questions relating to the Graeco-Egyptian religions have been discussed at great length and with characteristic learning by SETHE in 'Sarapis und die sogenannten Κάτοχοι des Sarapis', (*Abhandl. der Gesellschaft der Wissenschaften zu Göttingen*, Phil-hist. Kl. N.F. Bd. xiv, Nr. 5). He has cleared up several difficulties.

OSIRIS MAKER OF A FLOOD

Mention of OSIRIS as the maker of a Flood is made in the funerary composition entitled the 'Chapter of not dying a second time', which forms chapter clxxv of the Theban Recension of the *Book of the Dead*. It is of unusual interest because it contains neither spells nor prayers, and there is no mention of magical names such as we find in chapter cxxv; in it we find short conversations between the deceased and certain gods, and dialogues between the gods. Two copies of it exist: one in the Papyrus of ANI, in the BRITISH MUSEUM (No. 10470, sheet 29) and the other is the Papyrus of RĀ, in the museum at LEYDEN;[1] the text of the former was written at THEBES under the XIXth dynasty, and the text of the latter at MEMPHIS under the same dynasty.

The chapter opens with the words, 'What is it that hath happened to those who have become like the children of NUT? They have fought fights, they have upheld strifes, they have done evil, they have created hostilities, they have made slaughter, they have caused trouble and oppression. Verily in all their doings they have made the great to become feeble in all our works. O Great THOTH, declare strongly that what TEM hath commanded shall be performed. Thou shalt not see iniquity, thou shalt not be pained, for their years are nothingness, and their months are drawing to an end, even whilst they are working mischief.

'I am thy writing palette, O THOTH, and I have brought unto thee thine ink-jar. I am not one of those who work iniquity in their secret places; let not evil happen unto me.'

The text continues: 'Hail, TEM! What kind of place is AUGERT (the Underworld) whereto I have come? There is neither water nor air in it. It is an unfathomable abyss, it is dark with the blackest darkness, and a man wandereth about helplessly therein. There is [no] life whatsoever therein, and no rest of the heart, and the pleasures of love cannot be enjoyed therein. But let the glory of the beatified be given unto me instead of water and air, and the satisfying of the pleasures of love be given unto me instead of cakes and

[1] See Naville, *Todtenbuch*, Bd. i, and *Proceedings of Society of Bibl. Arch.* for December 1904. Translations of the text of Ani have been made by Renouf and Budge, and the Leyden text by Naville.

ale. The god TEM hath decreed that I shall see thy face, and that I shall not suffer from the things which pained thee. May every god transmit his throne to thee for millions of years. Thy throne hath descended to thy son HORUS, and TEM hath decreed that his course shall be among the holy princes. Verily he shall rule from thy throne, and he shall be the heir of the Dweller in the Lake (or Island) of Fire. Verily it hath been decreed that in me he shall see his counterpart (or likeness), and that my face shall look upon the face of the Lord TEM.'

The deceased then says to TEM, 'My Lord, what shall the duration of my life be?' (or What length of life hath been decreed for me?). TEM replies, 'It hath been granted by the Princes (i.e. the Old Gods) that thy life shall endure for millions of millions of years, and thy period of existence shall be prolonged for millions of years. This I have given to thee.'

Then THOTH, being the tongue of the Great God declares that, acting for the Lord TEM, he is going to make a Flood. He says: 'I am going to blot out everything which I have made. This earth shall enter into (i.e. be absorbed in) the watery abyss of NU (or NUNU) by means of a raging flood, and will become even as it was in primeval time. I myself shall remain together with OSIRIS, but I shall transform myself into a small serpent which can neither be apprehended nor seen.' The word used for 'flood' is *ḥuḥu*  and some of its forms are used to describe the annual inundation of the NILE. The meaning is clear. The NILE of EGYPT comes from the World Ocean NUNU. Each year the river swells and rises, and waters the country, and then it sinks and diminishes having done no lasting harm. But one day the NILE will rise, and cover all EGYPT with water, and drown the whole country; then, as in the beginning, there will be nothing to be seen except water. OSIRIS will then sail over the water in a boat like RĀ, and he will travel to the Island of Fire where HORUS is established on the throne of his father OSIRIS. Certain passages in the mutilated version of the chapter in the LEYDEN Papyrus suggest that the destruction of all mankind was decreed by TEMU, and that it took place.

ISIS

ISIS, in Egyptian , , or 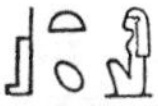 *As-t*, was either the female counterpart of the bisexual god OSIRIS, or a fetish goddess who was worshipped in some town near BUSIRIS, the seat of the cult of OSIRIS. The hieroglyph which stands for her name, 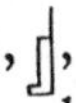, represents a 'seat' or 'throne', but it is probably an inaccurate drawing of her fetish object. At all events it symbolized something quite different from her canonical amulet . The priests of HELIOPOLIS made ISIS the sister-wife of OSIRIS, but like her twin-sister NEPHTHYS she is a shadowy creature as a goddess, and the arrangement of the triad OSIRIS—ISIS–NEPHTHYS is purely artificial. There is no mention of her resurrection, and no tomb of her is known. She usually appears in the form of a woman with her fetish sign on her head. As a form of every one of the great goddesses she has many different kinds of head-dress and head adornments. Her names are many.[1] It is tolerably certain that there was a portion of every temple reserved for the celebration of the mysteries of ISIS, but the first great temples dedicated to ISIS were built under the XXXth dynasty and in the Ptolemaic period. The greatest was begun by NECTANEBUS II, and continued by PTOLEMY II PHILADELPHUS and completed by PTOLEMY EUERGETES I. It stood in PER-ḤEBÎT (i.e. the House of ḤEBÎT, a form of HORUS), and was known to the GREEKS as the 'Iseion', and to the ROMANS as 'Isidis Oppidum'. Its ruins lie at BAHBIT AL-ḤIGÂRA, near MÎT ʿASSÂR, on the road between ṬANṬA and DAMIETTA in the Eastern Delta. It was a large and magnificent temple, granite, both red and grey, being used freely in its construction. Here the triad OSIRIS–ISIS–HORUS was worshipped until the sixth century of our era.

The home of ISIS in the heavens was SEPT 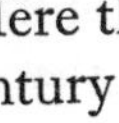 SIRIUS, the Dog-star), whilst OSIRIS dwelt in SAḤ 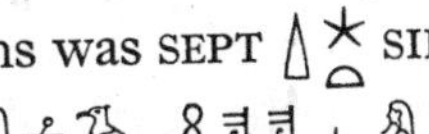 (ORION). Her name AMENIT 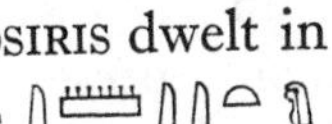 shows that she had an abode in the Underworld, where she directed all the affairs of the 'household of the dead'. Under the New Kingdom she was known as the 'goddess of many names',[2] and among such are: 'great goddess,

[1] See the list in Brugsch, *Thesaurus*, p. 773.

[2] See Brugsch, *Thesaurus*, pp. 102, 217–19.

existing from the beginning. Divine One. Only One. Greatest god and Queen of all gods, goddesses, and women. The prototype of all beings. The Female RĀ. The Female HORUS. The Eye of RĀ. The Star-crown of RĀ–HORUS. Queen of the DEKANS. Creator of the sunrise. Lady of the North Wind. The vomiter of fire. The blazing flame. The filler of the ṬUAT with good things. The

Forms of Isis as queen of Sothis (the Dog-star), and regent of the heavenly bodies and controller of seasons, Other goddesses appear in these forms.

bestower of life. The Lady of bread. The Lady of beer. The Lady of abundance. The Lady of joy. The Lady of love. Beautiful, mighty, and beloved One. Mistress of spells. Weaver and fuller. First royal wife of RĀ. Her father's wife.' As Queen of all EGYPT she, like the PHARAOHS, wore the Crowns of the South and the North, .

But the form of the myth of OSIRIS and ISIS which was most popular in dynastic times was that which represented her as the faithful and devoted wife who was made a widow by the murder of her husband, and was then persecuted by her brother-in-law, who wished to possess both her person and her kingdom. The distraught queen flying in deadly fear from SET, and her successful attempt to obtain a son from her dead husband, appealed to the imaginations of the EGYPTIANS, and some of the versions of the legends current in the dynastic period have come down to us. It seems that when OSIRIS was murdered ISIS had no child, and this was a sore grief to her because there was no one to inherit her husband's kingdom, and it was bound to fall into the hands of SET, the murderer. How she managed to obtain a son who would be the lawful heir to the throne is described both in the Pyramid Texts, and on a stele in PARIS.[1] The version given in four copies in the Pyramid Texts (§ 630) reads:

'ISIS and NEPHTHYS work magical protection for thee,—behold their lord is in thee—in the city of SAUT, in thy name of "NEB-SAUT" (i.e. Lord of SAUT); behold their god (NETER) is in thee in thy name of "NETER". They adore thee, depart not from them in thy name of "TUA-NETER" (i.e. Morning Star). They present themselves before thee; be not angry in thy name of "DJENTERU".[2] Thy sister came to thee rejoicing because of her love for thee. Thou didst set her on thy phallus, thy seed came forth into her, she became great with child like the Star SEPTET (i.e. SOTHIS, SIRIUS, the Dog-star). HORUS–SEPTET came forth from thee in [the form] of HORUS, dweller in the star SEPTET. Thou gavest him a spirit in his name of "Spirit dweller in DJENTERU". He avenged thee in his name of "HORUS, the son who avenged his father".'

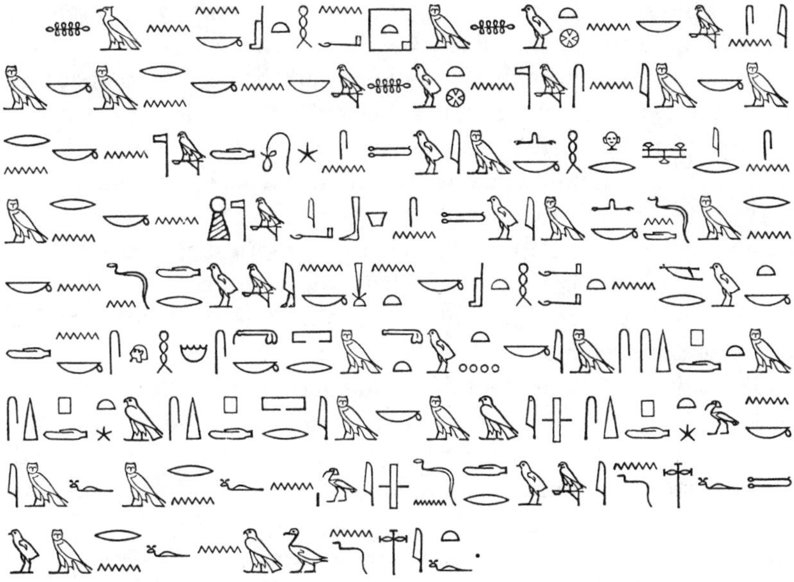

[1] See Chabas, *Rev. Arch.*, 1867, p. 65; Ledrain, *Monuments*, Pl. XXII.

[2] The god of the solar ship called Djenteru.

The translation of the version given on the stele in PARIS reads:

'Thy sister ISIS acted as a protectress to thee. She drove thine enemies away. She averted seasons [of calamity], she recited formulae with the magical power of her mouth, [being] skilled of tongue and never halting for a word, being perfect in command and word. ISIS the magician avenged her brother. She went about seeking him untiringly. She flew round and round over the earth uttering wailing cries of grief, and she did not alight on the ground until she had found him. She produced light from her feathers, she made air to come into being by means of her two wings, and she cried the death cry for her brother. She made to rise up the inert members of him whose heart was at rest. She drew from him his essence, and she made therefrom an heir. She suckled the child in solitariness, and none knew where his place was, and he grew in strength, and his arm increased in strength in the house of GEBB.'[1]

Among other legends of ISIS worthy of special interest are: (1) How she caused RĀ to be poisoned and succeeded in obtaining from him the secret name by which he ruled. (2) How she watched the fight between her son HORUS and SET, and incurred the wrath of HORUS. (3) How she wandered about the Delta with seven scorpion goddesses, and how with the help of THOTH she restored to life HORUS who had been stung to death by a scorpion of SET. Translations of these are given in Part II of this work.

In the latter part of the dynastic period the cult of ISIS became specialized, and in the mythical history of her life on earth the writers of mythological dramas and miracle plays found abundant and most suitable material for their purpose. Dramas of the 'Mysteries of ISIS' became very popular not only in EGYPT but in neighbouring countries, and they gave the priests good opportunities for imparting religious instruction to the people. By their means too they were able to place before all classes of men popular forms of their most esoteric doctrines.

The cult of ISIS won ground in many of the countries to the north of EGYPT, and representations and drawings of the goddess are found in PHOENICIA as early as the sixth century B.C. ADONIS and ASHTORETH were confused with OSIRIS and ISIS, and traces of this

[1] In the latter extract the resuscitation of Osiris is attributed wholly to Isis, who renewed life in the god so that she might obtain from him a son. In the magical papyri Isis is made to have procured a phallus, whether the god's or a dummy is not clear, but it was the god's virility which made it reunited to his body and effect her purpose.

confusion appear in PLUTARCH's *De Iside*.[1] Figures of ISIS appear on coins of TYRE,[2] and figures of SERAPIS on the coins of GÂZA[3] and BOSTRA,[4] OSIRIS was worshipped at TEIMA in ARABIA as early as 500 B.C.[5] The cult of SERAPIS and ISIS passed into ASIA MINOR, and into several islands of the MEDITERRANEAN, e.g. CYPRUS, RHODES, SAMOS, CHIOS, LESBOS, DELOS, CRETE, &c., and many parts of GREECE, e.g. THESSALY, EPIRUS, MEGARA, CORINTH, ARGOS, &c., contained shrines to the god and goddess. The group of OSIRIS, ISIS, NEPHTHYS, HARPOKRATES, and ANUBIS were well known in MALTA in the second century B.C., and CATANIA in SICILY was a centre for the cult of Egyptian gods. There were many temples of ISIS in southern ITALY, and the remains of statues of Egyptian gods found in REGGIO, PUTEOLI, POMPEII, and HERCULANEUM prove that the gods represented were worshipped in these cities. In the first century B.C. ISIS was one of the most popular goddesses in the city of ROME. Her temples were filled with altars, statues, lavers, obelisks, &c., brought from EGYPT, and orders of priestesses were endowed in order to perform the 'Mysteries of ISIS', and other Egyptian miracle plays, in the great temples of the Eternal City.[6] From ROME the cult of ISIS spread to SPAIN and PORTUGAL, to GERMANY, to GAUL, and SWITZERLAND, and by way of MARSEILLES to north AFRICA. As ISIS was identified with many other Egyptian and Nubian goddesses in EGYPT so in foreign lands she was given the attributes of SELENE, DEMETER, or CERES, APHRODITE, JUNO, NEMESIS, FORTUNA, PANTHEA, &c. In the *Golden Ass* of APULEIUS of MADAURA[7] ISIS says to LUCIUS:

'The whole earth worships my godhead, one and individual, under many a changing shape, with varied rites, and by many diverse names. There the PHRYGIANS, first-born of men, call me "mother of the gods that dwell in PESSINUS"; there the ATHENIANS, sprung from the soil they till, know me as CECROPIAN MINERVA; there the wave-beaten CYPRIANS style me VENUS of PAPHOS; the archer CRETANS, DIANA of the hunter's net; the SICILIANS, with their threefold speech STYGIAN PROSERPINE; the ELEUSINIANS, the ancient goddess CERES. Others call me JUNO, others BELLONA, others HECATE, others

1 Scholz, *Götzendienst*, pp. 226–52.
2 Imhoof, *M. Gr.*, p. 443.
3 Reichardt, *Num. Chron.*, 1862, p. 122.
4 Leake, *N.H.*, p. 35.
5 Noldske, *Sitzungsberichte*, 1884, p. 813 f.
6 For the literature see the article 'Isis', in Roscher, *Ausführliches Lexicon*, col. 400.
7 See H. E. Butler's translation, Oxford, 1910 (Bk. XI, 2 f.).

the RHAMNUSIAN, but those on whom shine the first rays of the Sun-god as each day he springs to new birth, the ARII and the ETHIOPIANS and the EGYPTIANS mighty in ancient lore, honour me with my peculiar rites, and call me by my true name of "ISIS the Queen".'

In a remarkable Greek inscription which was found in duplicate, one on the island of IOS and the other on the island of ANDROS, the goddess ISIS is made to describe her own power and attributes. The inscription was dedicated to ISIS, SERAPIS, and ANUBIS by a man whose name is wanting.

AN INSCRIPTION IN WHICH THE GODDESS ISIS DESCRIBES HER OWN ATTRIBUTES AND POWERS

For the Greek texts see F. HILLER DE GAESTRINGEN in *Inscriptiones Graecae*, vol. xii, fasc. v, part I, BERLIN, 1903.

Translation

'I am ISIS, the mistress of every land.

'I was taught by HERMES (the Egyptian THOTH), and by his aid I found out demotic letters, so that all things should not be written with the same letters.

'I laid down laws for mankind, and I ordained things which no one hath the power to change (the Egyptian goddess SESHETA).

'I am the eldest daughter of KRONOS (Egyptian GEBB).

'I am the wife and sister of OSIRIS the king ().

'I am she who governeth the star of KUON (the Dog-star, Egyptian).

'I am she who is called Divine among women (Egyptian).

'For me was built the city of BUBASTIS (Egyptian).

'I divided the earth from the sky.[1]

'I marked out clearly the paths of the stars.

'I prescribed the course of the sun and moon. (In Egyptian MAĀT the female THOTH.)

[1] She is Tefnut, , the wife of Shu, who lifted up the Sky-goddess from the embrace of Gebb, the Earth-god.

'I found out the labours of the sea (MAĀT, who piloted the boats of the Sun).

'I made justice mighty (one of the two  in the Hall of OSIRIS).

'I brought together woman and man (as HATHOR?)

'I made women carry their babes into the tenth month.

'I ordained that parents should be beloved by their children.

'I punish those who feel no love for their parents.

'I, by the aid of my brother OSIRIS, put an end to anthropophagy.[1]

'I revealed initiations to mankind.

'I taught men to honour the statues of the gods.

'I founded sanctuaries of the gods.

'I overthrew the sovereignties of tyrants.

'I compelled women to accept the love of men.

'I made justice more mighty than gold and silver.

'I ordained that truth should be accounted beautiful.

'I founded marriage contracts for women.

'I appointed separate languages for GREEKS and for foreigners.

'I made virtue and vice to be distinguishable by instinct.

'I imposed the obligation of an oath on those [who would swear] unjustly.'

The cult of ISIS was succeeded in EGYPT and neighbouring countries by that of the VIRGIN MARY and the Child JESUS and pictures and figures of both are said to have been made in EGYPT in the fifth century of our era.

HORUS, SON OF ISIS, SON OF OSIRIS

HORUS, son of ISIS, son of OSIRIS, was the third member of the triad of OSIRIS–ISIS–HORUS. He was begotten by OSIRIS after his death as already stated. His uncle SET declared him to be illegitimate and endeavoured to wrest from him the heirship of the kingdom. HORUS engaged in battle with him to avenge his father's death, and so obtained the title of ḤER-NEDJ-ḤER-TEF-F  . The HELIOPOLITANS made a distinction be-

[1] It is tolerably certain that the primitive Egyptians were cannibals, and that they only ceased to be so when they learned how to grow cereals. Cannibalism is still practised in some parts of Africa.

tween HORUS, the Sun-god, and HORUS, the son of ISIS, but eventually they were merged, and HORUS, son of ISIS, became a solar god.

Horus of Beḥut-t or Horus, son of Osiris, or Horus, son of Isis.

Horus and Rā in Ṭetu, but the hawk with the solar disk is really Ḥerur the 'Old Horus'.

Osiris, grasping 'life' in each hand, emerging from the coffer which his sons have protected.

The four gods who are commonly called the 'sons of HORUS' were AMSET (man-headed), ḤĀPI (baboon-headed), ṬUA-MUT-F (jackal-headed), and QEBḤ-SENU-F

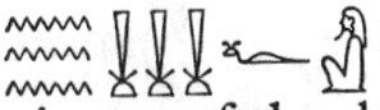 (hawk-headed). They were supposed to guard the viscera of the dead which were placed in four pots (Canopic jars). HORUS, son of ISIS, was a friend and protector of the dead, and his so-called 'sons' were friendly to the dead. Originally they were solar beings and had no connexion whatsoever with OSIRIS.

SET 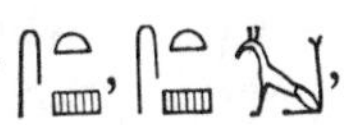, SUTI , SUTEKH 

SET, the Σήθ of PLUTARCH, or TYPHON, was, according to the HELIOPOLITANS, the son of GEBB and NUT, and twin brother of OSIRIS, ISIS, and NEPHTHYS. SET, however, was one of the oldest gods of EGYPT, and represented the dark half of the face of ḤER-UR, the ancient Sky-god, that is to say, the night as opposed to the day. He was probably also a star. He was incarnate in the so-called 'SET animal', a kind of hunting dog which became extinct in EGYPT before the close of the dynastic period. In very early times SET became the god of evil as well as the blackness of night; everything good was associated with the daylight, and everything bad by the darkness of night. A very ancient legend states that GEBB the Earth-god divided EGYPT between these two equal and opposing gods, and gave the south to SET and the north to HORUS. The capital of the kingdom of HORUS was ṬEMA-EN-ḤER[1] 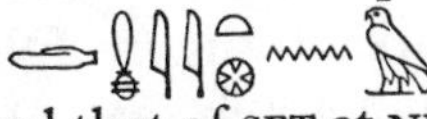, i.e. 'the City of HORUS', in the western Delta, and that of SET at NUBIT[2] 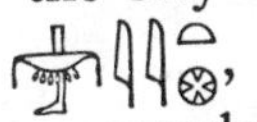, which is about thirty miles north of SYENE. HORUS governed wisely and justly, and SET ill and unjustly. GEBB was displeased, and taking SET's kingdom from him handed it over to HORUS. Thus the ancient quarrel between HORUS and SET began. SET was associated with all kinds of 'Typhonic' animals, the red ass, the black pig, the wild boar, the serpent, the hippopotamus, the crocodile, the turtle, the scorpion, &c. Before birth SET was violent and impatient, and he came into the world by bursting through the side of his mother.[3] SET was usually successful in his fights, but on one occasion HORUS carried away his testicles.[4]

1 The modern Damanhur.

2 The Ombos of the Greeks, and Kôm Ombo of the Arabs.

3 Plutarch, § xii, and Cooke, *Osiris*, p. 113. The sons of Cain could only be born via the umbilicus; see *Book of Enoch*, ed. Charles; Budge, *Cave of Treasures*, p. 91; Budge, *Queen of Sheba*, p. 88.

4 , *Book of the Dead*, chap. xvii, l. 66 f.

PLUTARCH says (§ 62) that TYPHON was called SETH ( ), BEBO ( ), and SMY ( ). Thus the identity of SET and TYPHON.[1] Elsewhere (§ 30) PLUTARCH says that SET was held in the greatest contempt, and that the EGYPTIANS do all they can to vilify and affront him. Under the HYKSOS the cult of SET obtained a great vogue at AVARIS, the HYKSOS capital, where he was called both NUBTI and SUTEKH . The men of AVARIS identified him with BAAL , BĀR, and RESHPU. , gods of war and the chase. The HYKSOS king of AVARIS, APAPA, regarded him as his chief god, and under dynasties XIII–XVII he appears to have been the national god of the Delta. Under the XIXth dynasty he became 'great god, lord of heaven'. This is amply proved by the figures in the BRITISH MUSEUM, Nos. 18191, 22897, and 30460. A remarkable figure (No. 16228) of AMEN-HAR-POKRATES has the head of a ram (AMEN) and the head of the SET animal, with prick ears.

Reshpu, a Canaanite god.

The texts show that SET was at all times the antagonist of the solar gods (1) HORUS the Elder, (2) RĀ, (3) OSIRIS, and (4) HORUS, son of HORUS, son of OSIRIS.

1. His first fight was in the sky where he and the seven stars of the Great Bear attacked HORUS the Sun-god. The constellation was called 'MESEḲHTI' (Pyr. § 458), i.e. the 'Fighter', and ranked with the never-setting stars . Later it was called the 'Thigh' and was depicted as an oval bull-headed object or by a whole ox. Another name of it was the 'Great Club'. An ally of his was the Hippopotamus goddess APIT. The Seven Stars were regarded as a symbol of ill luck. Showers of meteorites and shooting-stars were probably thought to represent attacks and

[1] From this name the Arabic *Ṭawfân*, 'storm', 'deluge', 'whirlwind', seems to be derived.

SET by RĀ, and eclipses as successful assaults of SET on HORUS on the Moon. The Seven Stars of the PLEIADES became in the dynastic period the Seven HATHORS who predicted men's fates and destinies. There is little doubt that many of the oldest dynastic gods and goddesses were stars or constellations in the predynastic period. OSIRIS himself, under an old forgotten name, may have been both Sun and Moon, and his merging into SERAPIS suggests that in very remote times he may have been the Zodiacal TAURUS or even ALDEBARAN.

2. Under the New Kingdom the place of SET was taken by ĀPEP or ĀPEF, a name preserved in the Coptic **ⲁⲡⲱⲫ, ⲁⲫⲟⲡⲓ** and **ⲁⲫⲱⲫⲓ**, i.e. the 'Giant'.[1] He is probably of Babylonian origin. He appears in the form of a huge serpent, and a crocodile-devil[2] was his chief ally. He tried daily to destroy the Sun-god at birth. The monster was attacked by OSIRIS (?) in the form of a prostrate man with a pair of ass's ears.[3] The voice of ĀPEP traversed the ṬUAT. He was accompanied by 'the sons of rebellion' MESU BEṬSHET, SEBA, NEḤA-ḤER 'Stinking Face', and the 'Worm'.

3. SET brought a series of charges against OSIRIS, and the case was tried by the great gods in the heavenly HELIOPOLIS. THOTH, the scribe of the gods, acted as advocate for OSIRIS, and obtained for him the verdict *Maā kheru*, i.e. true of voice, or speaker of the truth. SET was proved to be the liar.

4. SET next tried to destroy HORUS, the son of ISIS, the son of OSIRIS, i.e. HORUS the Child (the 'Ἁρποκράτης of the GREEKS), and caused him to be stung to death by a scorpion. The child was restored to life and when he became a man he engaged in a series of fights against SET which lasted for eighty years. Great light has been thrown upon these fights by the important hieratic papyrus CHESTER BEATTY Papyrus No. 1. This papyrus was found at THEBES, and is thought to have been written during the reign of RAMESES V, about 1160 B.C. The name of its

1 In the Coptic Bible this word translates γίγας: see Crum, *Coptic Dict.*, p. 21.

2 Sheshers.

3 See *Book of Gates*, sections ix and x.

author is unknown, for though the scribe NEKHT-SEBEK is mentioned on the obverse, DR. GARDINER regards this as a 'clumsy insertion over an erasure', and as an 'impudent usurpation'. The text has been admirably edited and translated by DR. GARDINER, who has also given us a careful introduction and many notes.[1]

This papyrus tells at considerable length the story of the 'Contendings of HORUS and SET', and is a valuable document from every point of view, and it is one of the most important mythological works which has come down to us. It is evident that the author was well acquainted with the theological literature of EGYPT of all periods, but he has not produced a work which can be regarded either as religious or devotional. On the contrary, from first to last, he treats the gods with good-humoured ridicule. The gods were called upon to decide whether HORUS, a frail child, should succeed to the throne of his father OSIRIS. This was claimed by SET, the murderer of OSIRIS, and the evil and foul-minded persecutor of ISIS, the widow of OSIRIS, and a twin sister of SET himself. The gods meet, they talk, they consult local gods, they adjourn more than once, and for eighty years they shilly-shally and cannot make up their minds. Meanwhile HORUS and SET carry on their 'contendings', and sometimes one is victorious and sometimes the other. The coarse and disgusting incidents mentioned bring the composition into line with the native plays which I have seen acted at ṬANTA, FUSṬÂT (OLD CAIRO), ḲANNA, and at various places in the SÛDÂN at the festivals celebrated in honour of the Birthday of the Prophet (MULID AN-NABI) and other festivals. In his work the author describes the gods in exactly the same way as Baron CORVO,[2] when he describes the Deity, the Trinity, the Virgin and Child, and the Saints, as viewed by the Italian peasant in the middle of the last century. The narrative is very interesting, and the way in which the author leads up to the climax when OSIRIS suddenly threatens the gods with death unless they make his son HORUS king of EGYPT is wholly unexpected. And the end of SET is ludicrous, for though having terrorized the gods for eighty years, and he is non-suited, as a *solatium* a position is given to him in the sky where he can make

[1] A. H. Gardiner, *Description of a Hieratic Papyrus*, London, 1931, and *Later Egyptian Stories*, Brussels, 1932.

[2] See *In His Own Image*, London, 1924, by F. W. Serafino Austin Lewis Mary Rolfe; born 1860, died 1913.

the thunder to frighten men! A brief summary of the contents of the CHESTER BEATTY Papyrus No. 1, based upon DR. GARDINER'S translation, is given in Part II of this book.

NEPHTHYS

NEB-T ḤET, i.e. the 'Lady of the House', commonly known as NEPHTHYS was the female counterpart of SET in dynastic times, but in the predynastic period she was probably, like ISIS, a local fetish goddess who became a sort of 'housekeeper' or concubine of OSIRIS. She was said to be the mother of ANPU, , i.e. ANUBIS, but the father of ANUBIS was OSIRIS and not SET. In the Pyramid Texts (§ 1521) NEITH is spoken of as the wife of SET, and according to Pyr. § 489 he had two wives . She appears in the form of a woman, but she took at times the form of a kite (?) (*Book of the Dead*, chap. xvii), and that of a heron (MANETHO, *Dendérah*, iv, pl. 81). In late times she was identified with MAĀT and other goddesses, and she assisted at the Judgement, and was a friend to the dead. As the 'Lady of Books' she composed many dirges which she sang with ISIS at the festivals of OSIRIS. For specimens see Part II of this work.

Maāt.

ANPU, COMMONLY CALLED ANUBIS

ANPU, or INPU, , or , or was probably the predynastic name of the animal which we now identify as the ordinary jackal of the deserts. On funerary stelae ANUBIS is depicted as a man-god with the head of what is now generally thought to be a jackal, but in some drawings the head might well be that of a jackal, or wolf, or dog; in the small funerary figures the head often resembles that of a fox. He was a sacred animal in the nome of THIS (ABYDOS) at a very early period and, judging by the number of places in which his cult was observed in dynastic times, his worship must have been universal. It is possible that in his original form he was a star. The jackal lived, and still lives, in the open desert or in hills and mountains in the desert some miles from towns and villages, and he became associated with the dead because of his habit of prowling among the tombs. The EGYPTIANS seem to have attributed to the jackal a kind of human intelligence for in the Pyramid Texts (UNAS, l. 207) these words are addressed to the dead king: 'Thy hands are TEM, thy shoulders are TEM, thy body is TEM, thy back is TEM, thy hind-quarters are TEM, thy legs are TEM, thy face is like that of the Jackal (ANUBIS)'. To King PEPI I it is said, 'Thou receivest thy face like the jackal ' (§ 896), and the king's form is hidden like the Jackal's  . When the anthropomorphization of the gods took place in EGYPT, the Jackal-god came into being, and he was given the titles of KHENTI AMENTIU  (Pyr, § 57 *d*) and KHENTI QA-T AMENTT  (§ 157 *b*), i.e. 'Prince, or Chief, of the West', and 'Prince of the hill of the West'. He was also 'Prince of the Divine Hall 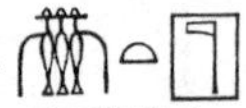 (§ 896 *c*).[1] The Nome-Lists show that the blazon of the XVIIth nome of UPPER EGYPT was  or ANUBIS, but it does not follow that CYNOPOLIS, the capital of that nome, was the original seat of the cult of ANUBIS. If, as SETHE thinks, a feather stuck in the back of the jackal's body indicates that the animal was no longer worshipped, and that figures of him had become merely sacred images, the antiquity of his cult must be very great, and probably far older than that of OSIRIS. One of the commonest titles of OSIRIS is 'KHENTI AMENTT', or 'KHENTI AMENTIU', i.e. 'Prince of the West' (where the dead dwelt), or 'Prince of those who are in the West' (i.e. the dead), which was usurped by him from ANUBIS. A house, i.e. temple, of ANUBIS is mentioned in Pyr. § 1995 *b*, where we have, 'Thy heart in thy body cooleth thee in the House of thy father ANPU',[2] but where that house was situated is not stated. One of the chief shrines of ANUBIS was at TURA  on the east bank of the NILE near BABYLON of EGYPT.

In dynastic times ANUBIS was said to have assisted ISIS and HORUS

[1] ANPU became the name for, or title of, princes  Brugsch, *Thes.* 1281.

[2] .

in mummifying the body of OSIRIS, and it was he who provided the unguents and medicaments which were necessary for the purpose; he may be regarded as the apothecary of the gods. In the papyri of ANI and HUNEFER, ANUBIS stands at the door of the tomb and embraces the mummy of the deceased, and takes it over for transfer to his kingdom. In the papyrus of NEBSENI (chap. cli B) ANUBIS 'the dweller in UT'[1] (UHET ?) is seen laying his hands on the mummy of the deceased, as if in protection, and he says, 'I have come to protect OSIRIS'. But most important of all his offices was that of the 'Guardian of the Scales', that is the Scales in which the hearts of the dead were weighed in the Hall of Judgement of OSIRIS. Originally he alone was the Judge of the Dead, but that exalted office was usurped by OSIRIS when he adopted the titles of ANUBIS. 'Prince of the West' and 'Prince of those who are in the West'. But from first to last it was ANUBIS who watched the pointer attached to the beam of the Scales, and decided whether or not the equilibrium of the heart and the feather of MAĀT was perfect. In fact the fate of the deceased depended upon his report, for THOTH the Registrar accepted it without demur, the jury of the gods adopted it, and on it HORUS, the son of ISIS, based his statement to OSIRIS. In some of the vignettes of the weighing of hearts ANUBIS is seen dragging a man to the Scales and in others the standard of the Scales terminates in the head of a jackal, that is ANUBIS. In the papyrus of ANI (chap. xxvi) ANUBIS is seen giving a necklace and a pectoral to ANI, and in the papyrus of NEBSENI, ANUBIS is seen giving back to the deceased his heart after he had weighed it. NEBSENI prayed to the god, saying, 'Make my thighs strong that I may be able to stand on them'.

ANUBIS took care of the bodies of the dead, and guided their souls across the stony western desert to the place where the Paradise of OSIRIS was situated. In this work he was assisted by a fellow god called UP-UATU, i.e. the 'Opener of the roads'.[2] It has

[1] . The first meaning of seems to be 'skin', 'hide', then funerary equipment, e.g. the swathings of a mummy. Finally it means Anubis himself and his skin. Moret quotes Pyr. Text (§ 574) . Anubis was the embalmer and the Ut was embalmment in general.

[2] Pyr. § 126 has .

been thought that ANUBIS and UP-UATU were only two forms of the same god, but this view is contradicted by the vignette to chapter cxxxviii of the *Book of the Dead*, where it is clear that one jackal on

Anubis, the divine embalmer completing the laying out of the embalmed mummy.

Anubis taking the mummy of Hu-nefer to the tomb.

his standard represents the North and the other the South, one being ANUBIS and the other UP-UATU. ANUBIS was the SEKHEM-EM-PET or 'The Power in heaven', and was the son of OSIRIS, and UP-UATU was the SEKHEM TAUI, i.e. 'Power of the Two Lands', and was a form of OSIRIS himself.

ANUBIS was held by the priests of HELIOPOLIS to be the last member of their Ennead or Nine gods, and was said to be the son of SET and NEPHTHYS. This view suggests that in very early times ANUBIS was a cosmic god and that he represented some phase of the darkness of night, and therefore the West where the dead dwelt became a suitable kingdom for him. PLUTARCH refers (§§ 44, 61) to his celestial character thus:

'By ANUBIS they understand the horizontal circle, which divides the invisible part of the world, which they call NEPHTHYS, from the visible, to which they give the name of ISIS; and as this circle equally touches upon the confines of both light and darkness, it may be looked upon as common to them both, and from this circumstance arose that resemblance, which they imagine between ANUBIS and the Dog, it being observed of this animal, that he is equally watchful as well by day as night.'

He goes on to compare ANUBIS to HECATE, a deity common both to the celestial and infernal regions. He thinks that ANUBIS means Time. Referring to OSIRIS as the 'common Reason which pervades both the superior and inferior regions of the universe', PLUTARCH says that it is called both ANUBIS and HERMANUBIS (i.e. ), the first name expressing relationship to the superior, as the latter, to the inferior world. APULEIUS mentions (bk. xi) the two faces of the Dog ANUBIS, 'the one being black as night and the other golden as the day'.

HOR, HORUS , AND THE HORUS GODS

The cult of HORUS was one of the oldest cults in ancient EGYPT and it was general in the Delta at least in prehistoric times; he was originally a fetish god and was worshipped under the form of a hawk. At a very early period in dynastic times he absorbed the attributes of many other hawk-gods in every part of EGYPT. The Greek and Coptic forms of the name (Ὧρος, ϩⲱⲣ[1]) show that the vowel in the name had the sound of *o* or *ô* in Ptolemaic and Roman times. *Hor* was probably the early Egyptian word for the actual bird, but some think it was connected with the word for 'face',  or  *ḥra*, i.e. the 'face' [of the heavens]. Others again connect it with *ḥer-t*  'what is above', the 'sky', 'heaven'. In this face

[1] Many Egyptian Christian monks were called 'Hôr'.

the sun was the right eye, and the moon the left eye, and each was called the 'Eye of HORUS'. And there was a form of the Face of HORUS with no eyes, i.e. the moonless night. The Pyramid Texts speak of the hair, or tresses, of this Face 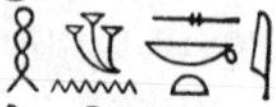, , and the Four Gods, the Children of HORUS 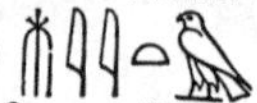[1] had their abodes therein. Their sceptres formed the four pillars of heaven  and supported the sky.[2]

The original home of the cult of HORUS was in the Western Delta  (UNAS, l. 293) and in that portion of it which was at a later period known as the IIIrd nome of LOWER EGYPT.[3] The capital of this nome was AAM-T , or the 'House of the Lady of the palm trees', which is marked by the ruins at KÔM AL-ḤIṢN,[4] near the modern town of DAMANHÛR. The Lady referred to was the cow-goddess SEKHAT-ḤER ,[5] a nurse of HORUS, who was perhaps originally a forest goddess and who changed herself into a cow, i.e. HATHOR, so that she might protect the child HORUS from SET. The original temple of HORUS was at BEḤṬ-T, a few miles from AAM-T, which was at a later period called TEMAIT-EN-HOR, i.e. the 'Town of HORUS' 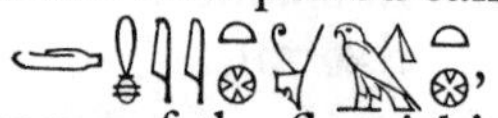, and the name is preserved in the Arabic name of the flourishing town of DAMANHÛR. At a very early period the EGYPTIANS changed the fetish character of HORUS into that of a sun-god, and his cult travelled eastwards and absorbed many local cults of hawk-gods, and all LOWER EGYPT acknowledged his power. The priests of HELIOPOLIS received him as sun-god, and adopted him, and in his Heliopolitan form he became RĀ ḤARAKHTI  or 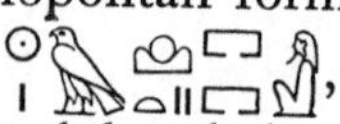, i.e. 'RĀ HORUS of the two horizons'. The priests insisted that their great sun-god RĀ should have precedence, and they added HORUS to their Ennead. They gave him a position by himself as 'god number ten',[6] and in late dynastic times the hawk of HORUS represented the number 10, just as the ibis, the symbol of THOTH of the City of the

[1] Pepi I, ll. 595, 600.
[2] Maspero, *Mythologie*, p. 227.
[3] Libya Mareotis.
[4] Petrie, *Naukratis*, vol. ii, p. 78.
[5] See the references quoted in J. de Rougé, *Géog. Ancienne de la Basse-Égypte*, Paris, 1891, p. 13 f.
[6] , , F. Wolff quoted by Sethe, *Urgeschichte*, § 121.

Eight Gods (KHEMENU), represented the number 8.[1] But it is quite possible that every god had a special number attached to him as every god had in BABYLONIA.

The priests of HORUS took every advantage which the spread of the cult of their god gave them, and long before the union of the Delta and UPPER EGYPT they succeeded in making the people believe that their god was incarnate in the reigning king, and they gave him a special name which indicated that he was the 'living HORUS'. When the whole of the Delta acknowledged the supremacy of HORUS among the gods, they turned their attention to UPPER EGYPT, and made plans for carrying the cult of their god far to the south. They watched their opportunity, and making some kind of rebellion in UPPER EGYPT their excuse the warriors of HORUS sailed up the river and conquered the men of OMBOS and gained a great victory over their god SET. The story of this conquest is told in the inscriptions on the walls of the Ptolemaic temple which now stands at EDFÛ, and was built on or near the site where the warriors of HORUS built a temple to commemorate their victory. (For the translation of the inscriptions see Part II, p. 467.) This temple was, naturally, dedicated to HORUS of BEḤṬ-T, that is to say HORUS of the town of BEḤṬ-T in the Western Delta. But though the cult of HORUS of BEḤṬ-T was thus transferred by conquest to a town in UPPER EGYPT, the priests of HORUS did not call that town 'BEḤṬ-T' of the South, but gave it the name of 'TJEB-T' 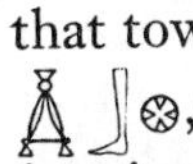,[2] a name which is preserved in Coptic,[3] and in Arabic (ADFÛ, UDFÛ). SETHE thinks that this name was connected with the word *ṭeba*,[4] 'to exchange', 'to barter', 'to give something in the place of', and that the EGYPTIANS regarded it as a 'substitute' (Ersatz)[5] for BEḤṬ-T in the Delta. The GREEKS called the town

Horus of Edfû spearing a hippopotamus.

[1] See Brugsch, *Aegyptologie*, p. 327.

[2] The full form  is given by Gardiner (*apud* Sethe), § 148.

[3] In Sahidic ⲁⲧⲃⲱ, in Bashmuric ⲑⲃⲱ. Spiegelberg, *Kopt. Wörterb.*, 206.

[4] In Coptic ⲧⲱⲱⲃⲉ.

[5] *Urgeschichte*, § 148.

'APOLLINOPOLIS MAGNA', because HORUS, the Sun-god, whom they identified with APOLLO, was worshipped there.

In late times the EGYPTIANS called it BEḤṬ-T, and often made no attempt to show whether it was the northern or the southern town to which they were referring. The symbol of HORUS of BEḤṬ-T was a winged solar disk with 'variegated plumage',[1] and pendent uraei, and the wings were extended at full length after the manner of the flying beetle, the symbol of KHEPRI, a form of the Sun-god in the early morning, or at dawn. The victory of the followers of HORUS over SET and his men of OMBOS was perpetuated in dynastic times by the addition of a third name in the king's titulary, which he adopted as the successor and living representative of HORUS of NUBTI, i.e. HORUS of OMBOS. The cult of HORUS continued to increase, and the god absorbed the attributes of other ancient hawk-gods and especially those of the ancient double city of PE-TEP (BUTO) in the Delta, and NEKHEN, or HIERAKONPOLIS, in UPPER EGYPT near the modern town of AL-KÂB.

Many forms of HORUS are mentioned in the texts, e.g.:

1. ḤER-UR, i.e. 'HORUS the Elder', was originally the Face of heaven by day. He appears in the form of a hawk-headed man, or hawk-headed lion. Several shrines were dedicated to him, but probably only after he was identified with RĀ and other solar gods. At KÔM OMBO he was the head of a triad, and his female counterpart was TASENT-NEFERT, and their son P-NEB-TAUI. He was the Ἀρωῆρις of the GREEKS.

2. ḤER-P-KHARṬ, i.e. 'HORUS the Child'. He was the Ἁρποκράτης of the GREEKS. He is represented as a man child, and seated, owing to weakness in his legs and feet; he wears a lock of hair, symbolic of youth, on the right side of his head, and a finger of his right hand is thrust in his mouth.[2] As the successor of OSIRIS, both as god and human king, he wears the triple crown with feathers and disks, or the united crowns of the South and North. His solar character is proclaimed by the solar disk and plumes

[1] feathers of different colours.

[2] (Pyr. 663) 'Horus the Child, the babe [with] his finger in his mouth'

.[1] His name distinguishes him from ḤER-UR, and he was a cosmic god, and a form of the rising sun; he probably represented the earliest rays of the luminary. Seven forms of him are known: (1) ḤER-RĀ-P-KHARṬ of HERMONTHIS (Southern ON). (2) ḤER-SHU-P-KHARṬ-P-Ā, son of SĀBA and ANIT. (3) SMA-TAUI-P-KHARṬ, son of HATHOR. (4) ḤER-P-KHARṬ, the dweller in ṬEṬ-T (BUSIRIS). (5) AḤI, the son of HATHOR of DENDERAH. (6) ḤEQA-P-KHARṬ, son of SEKH-MIT. (7) ḤER-ḤENNU.[2]

Harposerato.

3. ḤER-MERTI who appears as a hawk-headed man wearing the horns of KHNEM and the solar disk encircled by a cobra. In his hand are the Udjati , or eyes of the sun and moon. He is a form of MIN-AĀḤ . ATHRIBIS was a centre of his cult. In Pyr. § 1211 we have and .

4. ḤER-AN-MUT-F , 'HORUS, the pillar of his mother', a local form of HORUS BEḤṬ-TI (i.e. HORUS of EDFÛ). Little is known of the ceremony at EDFÛ in which this HORUS played a prominent part.

5. ḤER-NUBTI . He is depicted as a hawk seated on an antelope, which, according to BRUGSCH,[3] commemorates his victory over SET. In late times this was the blazon of the XVIth nome of UPPER EGYPT.

6. ḤER-KHENTI-KHAT , of ATHRIBIS or Xoïs. He is depicted in the form of a crocodile-headed man wearing the horns of KHNEM and a triple crown and plumes.[4]

7. ḤER-KHENTI-AN-ARITI or , 'HORUS without eyes',[5] i.e. when neither sun nor moon was visible.

[1] In Lanzone, pl. 328, he is seen in a box which rests on the back of a lion.
[2] Brugsch, *Dict. Géog.*, p. 348.
[3] *Religion*, p. 664.
[4] Lanzone, p. 622, pls. 17; Brugsch, *Religion*, p. 606.
[5] Or perhaps 'Horus, Chief of the one who is without eyes' (§ 771).

8. ḤER-AKHTI , or , or , or , i.e. 'HORUS of the two horizons', the horizons of the sunrise and sunset. He was a sun-god like RĀ, but the priests of HELIOPOLIS made his name to follow that of RĀ, thus RĀ-ḤER-AKHTI. His name is joined to that of KHEPRI, the rising sun, and that of TEMU, the setting sun. He is usually depicted with the head of a hawk, and he wears the solar disk of RĀ with its cobra. Once he appears as a double man with a head having two hawk-faces, one looking right and the other left; above these is an udjat , which shows that the double figure is the sun-god.[1] The Sphinx at GÎZAH was called ḤER-EM-AKHT , i.e. 'HORUS on the horizon'; the GREEKS called it Ἅρμαχις. The inscription of THOTHMES IV says that the god of the Sphinx, whom he calls ḤERAKHTI-RĀ-TEMU-KHEPRI, appeared to the king and asked him to free his image from the sand in which it was buried.

9. ḤER-SMAI-TAUI , 'HORUS, the uniter of the Two Lands', i.e. EGYPT, the Ἁρσομτοῦς of the GREEKS. The centre of his cult was DENDERAH. He is often depicted as a man, but he is sometimes given the head of a hawk or serpent. He is said to have sprung into being out of a lotus flower, which blossomed annually at dawn in the abyss of NU on New Year's Day. He was held to be the son of HATHOR.[2]

10. ḤER-ḤEKENU , 'HORUS of Praises', the son of BAST (or UBAST); little is known about his functions. He was originally a star-god and he appears in the form of a lion.

11. ḤER BEḤUṬ-T . A great solar-god and war-god, who is depicted as a hawk-headed man whose weapons were a bow and arrows and a marvellous spear the head of which was the head of a hawk bearing on it a triangular spear-point. His principal shrines were at MESEN , QEM-BAIUS , PHILAE, and TJEB-T, a town or village in the Tanite nome in the Eastern Delta. An outline of the history of the god and his conquests in UPPER EGYPT has already been given (see above, p. 106). For the story of his fight with SET, see Part II of this work.

[1] Lanzone, pl. 229 ff.

[2] Lanzone, pl. 259.

12. ḤER-SA-AST-SA-ASAR 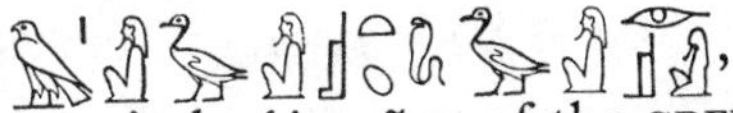, 'HORUS, the son of ISIS, the son of OSIRIS', the 'Αρσιῆσις of the GREEKS. He was begotten by his father after his death and was brought forth by ISIS in the papyrus swamps of the Delta. For the story of his death through the bite of a scorpion sent by SET, and the translation of the inscriptions on the METTERNICH stele, see Part II, p. 491. For a summary of the narrative of the fights between HORUS and SET as related in the CHESTER BEATTY Papyrus No. 1, see Part II, p. 444.

HORUS, the son of ISIS, performed a very important part in the ceremony which took place after the hearts of the dead had been weighed by ANUBIS in the Great Scales. It was he who introduced the righteous dead into the presence chamber of OSIRIS, and reported to that dread god the verdict of THOTH, which had been confirmed by the Great Company of the gods, and petitioned him to assign them homesteads in his kingdom, where they were to rank with SHEMSU-ḤERU . In none of the variant versions of the Judgement Scene do we find the place of HORUS, son of ISIS, as introducer of the dead, taken by any other god. HORUS, the son of ISIS, was ever the friend of the dead, and the foe of their foes.

The texts show that the difference between HORUS, son of ISIS, and the other HORUS-gods was not carefully distinguished. He appears in the form of the babe HARPOKRATES seated on a lotus, and like HORUS of BEḤṬ-T he stands on a hippopotamus into which he is driving a spear. Sometimes he has the form of a hawk-headed lion, and, besides the forms, the attributes of many gods were ascribed to him. Thus with ANPU,[1] or ANUBIS, he becomes ḤER-EM-ANPU, i.e. 'HORUS as ANUBIS', who is probably the HERMANUBIS mentioned by PLUTARCH (*De Iside*, § 61). This dual god is represented in the form of a wolf-headed man, and has the form of ANUBIS, 'the opener of the roads of the South',  and UP-UATU 'the opener of the roads of the North' 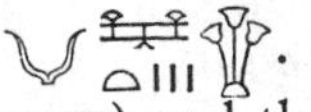. The former is the Power  of the Two Lands (i.e. EGYPT) and the latter the Power of Heaven (*Book of the Dead*, chap. cxlii, § iv, 24, 25). HORUS, son of ISIS, is identified with HORUS, the slayer of men, the god of HEBNU,[2] the

[1] More probably Up-uatu, one of the two wolf-gods.

[2] Its ruins lie near Minya at Zâwiyat al-Maitîn.

metropolis of the XVIth nome of UPPER EGYPT, who was a form of HORUS of BEḤṬ-T.

13. ḤER-NETJ-ḤER-AT-F , 'HORUS, the avenger of his father'. Whilst ISIS was bringing up her son HORUS she never ceased to encourage the idea which he had of fighting SET, the murderer of OSIRIS, and killing him. When HORUS became a man he attacked SET and many fights between HORUS and SET took place. In the end HORUS conquered his uncle SET, just as his ancestor HORUS the Elder had done. The young HORUS as the avenger of his father was a very popular god among the EGYPTIANS.

14. ḤER-SEPṬ . The god SEPṬ was worshipped in the XXth nome of LOWER EGYPT , which is commonly called the 'ARABIAN'. His fetish was some object in the form of , which was probably a pointed weapon; his cult was absorbed by HORUS, whose hawk took the place of the old native fetish. He appears in the form of a man wearing on his head , or two plumes, or the solar disk, or a hawk with two plumes on his head . He was called 'lord of the East', the 'god of battles', the 'smasher of the MENTIU' , i.e. the savage tribes of the Eastern Desert and ARABIA, 'Bull, trampler on the MENTIU', 'lord of battles', the 'strengthener of EGYPT and the protector of the gods'.[1] As the 'lord of battle' 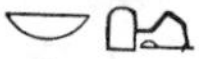 he is depicted in the form of a hawk-headed lion with the tails of a lion and a hawk. In his hands, which are those of a man, he holds a bow and a club, and on his head are a disk and plumes. His temple was PER-SEPṬ and near it was a famous grove of Nebes trees;[2] hence its name 'Seat of Nebes trees' 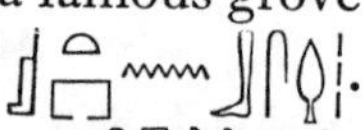. His wife was a form of HATHOR and was called SEPTIT 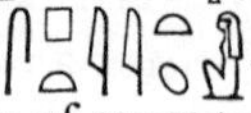. In the *Book of the Dead* the deceased assumes the name of SEPṬ to help him drive away the Crocodile of the South (chap. xxxii), and attacks the foes of NEB-ER-TJER (chap. xvii, l. 30), and his slaughtering house 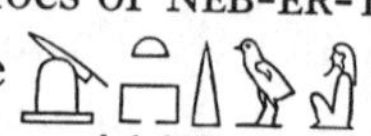 is mentioned in chap. cxxx.

In the Pyramid Texts the following forms of HORUS are men-

[1] See Naville's description of the throne found by him at Saft al-Hanna.
[2] The *Cordia Sebestena*, or *Zisyphus Lotus* W. (Brugsch, *Religion*, p. 567).

tioned: ḤER in his name of AMI-ḤENU; HORUS in his name of 'He who is in the ḤENU Boat' (§ 138); ḤER-KHENTI-PERU (§ 133); ḤER-TESHER-ARITI, HORUS, red of eyes (§ 253); ḤER-KHESBETJ-ARITI, HORUS, blue of eyes (§ 253); ḤER-ṬUATI, HORUS of the ṬUAT (§ 148). In the Theban *Book of the Dead* are mentioned the following forms of HORUS: HORUS—great-of-hearts; HORUS—the-sustainer; HORUS—dweller-in-hearts-dweller-in-the-belly; HORUS—dweller-in-the-Disk (i.e. the Sun); ḤERU-EM-KHEBIT, HORUS—on-the-look-out-stand (); HORUS—traverser-of-millions-of-years, HORUS—Prince-of-millions-of-years, ḤER-SKHAI, ḤER-SESHEṬ-ḤRA, ḤER-SHUTI; HORUS—of-the-two-plumes, and ḤER-KHENTI-MEN-ATF (Pyr. § 1719). A late form of HORUS was known as 'HORUS of the Three Hundred', and he was depicted as a quadruple animal, part lion, part crocodile, part ichneumon, and part hippopotamus. HORUS was identified with several of the planets. As JUPITER he was called UPSH the 'Illuminer' (Pyr. §§ 362 *b*, 1455 *a*) and ḤER-TEHEN (i.e. the scintillating star); as SATURN he was ḤERU-KA, 'HORUS the Bull'; as MARS he was ḤER-TESHER or the 'Red HORUS'.

The METAL-WORKERS (or BLACKSMITHS) OF HORUS. In the legend of the conquest of UPPER EGYPT by HORUS of BEḤṬ-T it is stated that the men who fought under HORUS were armed with weapons made of metal. The sculptures on the walls of the temple of EDFÛ illustrating the legend show that each man carried in his right hand a metal weapon, head downwards, and in his left hand a metal weapon. HORUS himself is seen spearing a hippopotamus, and holding the animal with a double chain which he grasp with his left hand. ISIS also holds in each hand a chain by which the beast is fettered. These men were called *mesniu* or *mesentiu*, , i.e. 'smiths'[1] but recent writers prefer to translate the

[1] The Coptic ⲃⲉⲥⲛⲏⲧ which Crum translates by 'smith' (*Copt. Dict.*, p. 44). Spiegelberg quotes an Egyptian word (*Wörterbuch*, p. 19).

word by 'harpooners'. HORUS is often called 'HORUS of MESEN city', and 'he of MESEN'. A chamber in the temple of EDFÛ was called *mesent*, and this may have been a place set apart there for the use of harpooners or smiths. The weapon with which HORUS fights and which he drives into the head of the hippopotamus is at first sight a very long spear with a sharp-pointed triangular head, . But some of the drawings of it which have been discussed by SCHÄFER (*Aeg. Zeit.*, Bd. XLI, p. 69) show that it must have had an unusual shape and some peculiarities which the artist did not reproduce accurately. The EGYPTIANS called the weapon *māba*, which is written in Pyr. § 1212. The three signs mean 'thirty' and have the phonetic value of *māb*, and these are followed by a picture of the weapon itself. Judging by the picture of it in LEPSIUS, (*Denkmäler*, Bd. IV, bl. 35) it had three points, i.e. tangs, or perhaps barbs, or recurved hooks, which when withdrawn tore the flesh of the man or animal into which the weapon had been driven. Such recurved hooks are mentioned in Pyr. § 1212 where they are called *bun* , and are said to belong to the *ḥenbu* or harpoons of RĀ

Horus of Beḥuṭet spearing the hippopotamus with the help of Isis.

Horus of Deḥuṭat and Isis fettering the hippopotamus at Edfû.

which have the three hooks at each end. The hooks of PEPI'S harpoon are said to be like the Lynx-god MAFṬ-T 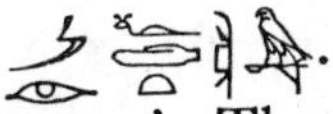.

The ḤERU-SHEMSU or 'servants (or followers) of HORUS'. These beings are mentioned in Pyr. § 1245 under these forms: 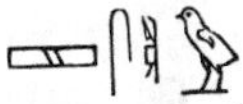 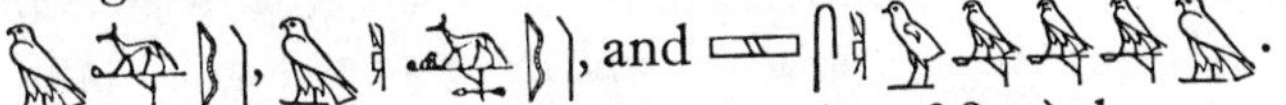. In some of the sections of the Pyramid Texts (e.g. § 897) the name of SHEMSU-ḤERU is followed by a stand across the upright support of which a club is drawn, and on it stands a jackal; next to this we have a bow and a curved stick or boomerang. It seems certain that the 'servants of HORUS' who used weapons like the club, or mace, and the bow and the boomerang lived in the prehistoric period, and that at first they were either the companions of HORUS of BEḤṬ-T during his successful campaign at EDFÛ in UPPER EGYPT or the kings who were his immediate successors in that country. But the jackal on the stand is hard to explain, for the jackal on a stand was the blazon of the XVIIth nome of UPPER EGYPT (LYKOPOLITES or CYNOPOLITES?). In connexion with this difficulty SETHE[1] refers to Pyr. § 2011 where it is said that HORUS of NEKHEN (HIERAKONPOLIS) gives his 'spirits'  the jackals  to assist the dead king. Thus it seems that the spirits of HORUS of NEKHEN had a different form from that of the spirits of HORUS of the city of P[E][2] in the DELTA, where they were depicted as hawk-headed men. This was natural enough, for in the earliest times, when PE was called 'TJBĀUT',[3] the fetish god of the city was some kind of large bird of prey. The cult of HORUS, the great Hawk-god or Falcon-god, displaced that of the older bird, and the remains of the old name of his city are probably preserved in the second part of the name of PE-TEP.

But whatever may be the solution of the difficulty it seems quite clear that the 'spirits of NEKHEN' and the 'spirits of PE' are not to be identified with the SHEMSU-ḤERU or 'Followers of HORUS'. The spirits of NEKHEN and PE must be the old kings of those cities, and

1 *Urgeschichte*, § 191, n. 1.

2  This was the name of one half, probably the modern half, of the city called by the Greeks Buto; the other half was called Tep 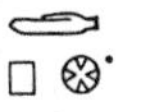.

3 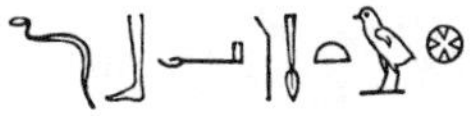

the Followers of HORUS, the kings who were identified with HORUS. The whole subject has been carefully considered by SETHE (*Untersuchungen*, iii. 16) who discusses the reasonable views of KEES in his *Urgeschichte*, § 192, note 2.

TETRADS of HORUS-gods. In the Pyramid Texts there are several references to groups of four 'spirits', and four HORUS-gods, and four gods who were the sons of GEBB, and four gods who were the sons of ATEM and NUT, and four gods who became the sons of HORUS and OSIRIS. The four oldest HORUS-gods were HORUS of the horizon, HORUS OF SHESMET, HORUS of the East, and HORUS of the gods (Pyr. §§ 1083, 1086). These were evidently the four eldest spirits , each with his sceptre, who are attached to the tresses of HORUS, and who stand in the eastern side of heaven and announce the beautiful name of the deceased to RĀ, and turn away the evil one NEHEBKAU[1] from him. And these were, no doubt, the four , or long-haired (or bearded, or bewigged) gods, who stand in the eastern quarter of the sky, and prepare the two rafts for RĀ (Pyr. § 1206). We read of another group of four gods 'who rejoice, and have jet-black hair, and sit under the shadow of the shrine (?) of the god QAṬJ ' (Pyr. § 1105), and of yet another group of four (Pyr. § 1141) who are over the Lake of KENSET (NUBIA). In Pyr. § 1092 we are told that the four spirits of HORUS who are with the deceased king are called ḤĀPI, ṬUAMUTEF, AMSET, and QEBḤSENUF. And thus the sons of HORUS have become the sons of OSIRIS or his son HORUS, that is to say purely funerary gods. We find them again in Pyr. §§ 2078, 2079, where they are preparing a ladder and setting it up for the deceased king to ascend to heaven. Another group of four HORUS-gods is mentioned in Pyr. §§ 1257, 1258, namely, HORUS of SHETA, HORUS lord of PĀT (i.e. men), HORUS of the ṬUAT, and HORUS lord of the Two Lands. The Pyramid Texts also speak of the deceased king being 'one of the four gods, the

Neḥebkau.

1 , Pyr. § 340.

children of GEBB, who traverse the South and the Land of the North, who stand by their sceptres, who are perfumed with *ḥatt* perfume, and draped with *atma* apparel, who live on figs, and drink wine' (Pyr. § 1510). Yet another group of four gods is known, and these are said to be the 'sons of TEM and the sons of NUT', who neither suffer decay nor corruption' (Pyr. § 2057).

The ancient Horus-tetrad in its latest purely funerary form.

VII

HATHOR AND THE HATHOR-GODDESSES

HATHOR was so intimately connected with HORUS that an account of her must follow here. The cow was one of the oldest sacred animals of EGYPT, and the worship of the Cow-goddess was wellnigh universal in EGYPT. The Cow-goddess who is best known to us was called ḤET-ḤOR or ḤAT-ḤOR, which means the 'House of HORUS', the Hawk-god, and the compound hieroglyph which represents her name is a house or temple with a hawk inside it . The house was the sky, i.e. the eastern portion of it, and the hawk is the sun-god, who was born there daily. The great antiquity of her cult is illustrated by a flint model of the head and horns of a cow dating from the predynastic period, now in the BRITISH MUSEUM (No. 32124). This object has special interest when considered in connexion with the blazon or nome-sign of DIOSPOLIS PARVA, the VIIth nome of UPPER EGYPT. This, according to its oldest form, was the skull of a cow which was hung up or placed on the top of a pole in front of the door of the predynastic 'god-house' or temple . In the dynastic period, probably under the Middle Kingdom, the scribes either did not know what the old blazon represented, or they were dissatisfied with it, and as a result they substituted the sign , i.e. a sistrum above a woman's face. The EGYPTIANS called the town where the cow's head in this form was exhibited before the temple, 'House of the Sistrum' (of HATHOR). Now in many texts we find the name of HATHOR written ḤAT-ḤERT 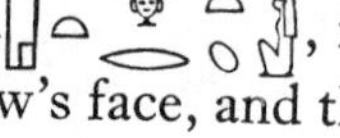, i.e. 'House of the Face', the allusion being to the cow's face, and this form of her name is probably older than .

From representing a portion of the sky, or even its whole face, HATHOR in the form of a cow came to represent heaven in its entirety, which was then held in its place by her four legs, and these marked the four cardinal points. Under the Old Kingdom she had a male counterpart who is mentioned in the Pyramid Texts as the 'Bull of RĀ' (§ 470 *ab*). He had four horns, one in the west, one in the east, one in the south, and one in the north. As the goddess of heaven HATHOR was associated with the Sun-god RĀ, and she appears as his wife and, curiously enough, is described as his eye. She was identified with ISIS, and so became the mother of HORUS, and in short with every great goddess in EGYPT. As a woman HATHOR was the World-Mother, and she symbolized the great power of nature which was perpetually conceiving and creating, and bringing forth and rearing in all things, both great and small. She was the 'mother of her father, and the daughter of her son', and the mother of every god and goddess, and as a result she was Lady of Heaven, Earth, and the ṬUAT, i.e. Underworld. She was the friend and protectress of all pregnant women, and their sympathetic midwife and nurse, and the ally of all lovers and beautiful women. She was as good to the dead as she was to the living, and the deceased found in her a helper and protectress, for she was present in the ṬUAT every night when the sun passed through it on his way from the western horizon to the place of sunrise in the east. The texts suggest that there was one portion of the ṬUAT or AMENTT which was specially set apart for her as a Paradise wherein she received the righteous, and the vignettes of the *Book of the Dead*, and cognate works represent her standing knee-deep among masses of luxurious vegetation, overshadowed by the Celestial Tree of RĀ.

In every local Company of gods she had an honoured place, and she always became the chief female counterpart of the head of the Company or Triad into which she had been allowed to enter as a guest. The EGYPTIANS compiled a list of all the great goddesses who were regarded as forms of HATHOR, and this shows that shrines wherein she was worshipped existed in all the great towns of UPPER and LOWER EGYPT. Of a great many of these goddesses very little is known, certainly not enough to justify us in giving a paragraph to each, and therefore a mere list of them is here given. She was identified with:

SATET and ĀNQET in the triad of KHNEMU in ELEPHANTINE.

TA-SENT-NEFERT 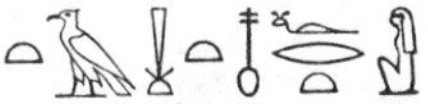 in OMBOS (KÔM OMBO).

BEḤUṬET , in APOLLINOPOLIS MAGNA.

NIT, NEBUT 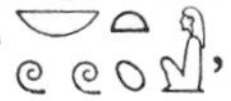, and MENHIT [1] in LATOPOLIS.

[1] A lioness goddess.

MUT and NEKHEBET[1], in EILEITHYIASPOLIS.

RĀT-TAUI-T and THENENET in HERMONTHIS.

MUT and AMENTHET[2] in THEBES.

ḤEQET in APOLLINOPOLIS PARVA.

Uadjit.

ISIS and ANIT in COPTOS.

SESHETA in DIOSPOLIS PARVA.

MEḤIT and TEFNUT, and AAKHUT and MENḤIT in THIS (ABYDOS).

ISIS and KHENTI ABTETT in PANOPOLIS.

ḤEQET and ĀNTAT in APHRODITOPOLIS.

NIT, and UADJIT and SEKHMET in HYPSELIS.

MAĀT and ISIS in HIERAKONPOLIS.

MUT and SESHETA in LYCOPOLIS.

SEKHMET and MAĀT in CUSAE.

NEHEMĀUAIT, and SESHETA, and MEḤURT in HERMOPOLIS.

ḤEQET and ASHET in IBIU.

PAKHTH at the SPEOS ARTEMIDOS.

ANPET in CYNOPOLIS.

UADJIT in ALABASTRONPOLIS.

ANTAT and MER-SEKHENT in HERAKLEOPOLIS MAGNA.

RENPET (the year goddess) in CROCODILOPOLIS.

KHERSEKHET in PTOLEMAÏS.

ISIS and TEP-AḤET in APHRODITOPOLIS.

[1] The great and very ancient Vulture-goddess of Nekheb. She often carries a ring with a bezel in one claw.

[2] Perhaps a goddess of Lower Egypt, then usually regarded as the wife of Amen.

UBASTET[1] and RENPET in MEMPHIS.

NEB[T]-UAREKHT-ĀAT in LATOPOLIS.

USERT and ḤEQET in PROSOPIS.

NIT (NEITH) in SAÏS.

URT-UPSET-SHEPSET (?) in Xoïs.

ISIS in CANOPUS; UADJIT in BUTO.

TEFNET in PER-TEM (PITHOM).

TAIT in BUSIRIS.

AKHUIT (?) in ATHRIBIS.

ṬEṬET-SAT-RĀ, ḤERT, the female HORUS.

NESERT a fire goddess, IUSĀSET.

NEBT-ḤETEP, MENAT, REPIT.

KHENT-ABTET in SELE.

NEḤEMĀUAIT, TEFNET, and ISIS in HERMOPOLIS.

ḤAT-MEḤIT in MENDES.

MUT, TEFNET, and KHENT-ABTET in DIOSPOLIS.

UBASTET in BUBASTIS.

ISIS and UADJIT in AMM-T.

SEPTIT and KHEKHSIT in the nome of SEPṬ (ARABIA).[2]

The cult of HATHOR was followed in some of the large towns in SYRIA, e.g. BYBLOS, and in SINAI, and certainly in the islands at the head of the First Cataract, and in LOWER NUBIA. The reputation of some of the HATHORS was greater than that of others, and the most important of them were held to be seven in number. The SEVEN HATHORS of DENDERAH were represented in the form of young and beautiful women in close-fitting tunics, who wore vulture-head-dresses and cows' horns and the solar disk on their heads, and carried tambourines in their hands. They were goddesses of love and pleasure, and in fiction they appear as a group of benevolent

[1] The cat-headed and lioness-headed goddess of Bubastis; the site of her city is marked by Tall Baṣṭa, near Zaḳāziḳ. Her temple Par Ubasṭet is mentioned in Ezekiel xxx. 17 under the form of Pibeseth.

[2] See Brugsch, *Mythologische Inschriften*, Leipzig, 1884, p. 801 f.; Lanzone, *Mitologia*, p. 875.

fairies who have the power of foretelling the destinies of those whom they are pleased to visit. Thus in the *Tale of the Two Brothers* having looked upon the beautiful maiden whom KHNEMU by the order of the Company of the gods, had created to be the wife of BATA, they said, 'Her death will be caused by the knife', and it was so.[1] And they also prophesied an unpleasant death, either by a snake or a crocodile or a dog, for the 'predestined prince'.[2] In the *Litanies of Seker* the specially important HATHORS were twelve in number, one for each month of the year.

HATHOR was associated with the rise of the NILE preparatory to the annual Inundation, and under the form of SOTHIS, the Dog-star SIRIUS, , she appeared near the sun in the second half of JULY. When RĀ entered his boat she, both as his wife and daughter, went with him and took up her place on his forehead like a crown. As the child of NUT she was called 'KHNEMET ĀNKH'.[3] She is mentioned frequently in the *Book of the Dead*, and always as a friend and protectress of the deceased. She is a sympathetic witness of the weighing of his heart, she encouraged the deceased to fight ĀPEP (chap. xxxix), his eyes were to become the eyes of HATHOR (i.e. the sun and moon); she provided him with food from the heavenly palm tree, and she made him to seat himself under the shadow of the great Heaven-Sycamore-Fig-tree (chaps. lii, lxiii A, lxviii); and admitted him to her own bodyguard of heavenly beings (chap. 103). In the *Ritual of Mummification*[4] it is said that when the embalmer was going to swathe the face of the dead body with the 'swathing of HATHOR', he recited the words, 'HATHOR shall make thy face perfect among the gods, she shall make thy thighs large among the goddesses, she shall open thine eyes that thou mayest see each day, she shall provide a spacious place for thee in AMENTET, she shall make thy voice to prevail over the voices of thine adversaries, and she shall make thy legs to walk with ease in AMENTET in her name (i.e. by virtue of her name) of 'HATHOR, Lady of AMENTET'.

For the important part which HATHOR played in the destruction of mankind by the command of RĀ, see Part II of this work.

[1] For the text see Birch, *Select Papyri*, ii, Pl. IX, l. 8.
[2] For the text see Budge, *Hieratic Papyri*, vol. ii.
[3] Brugsch, *Mythol. Inschriften*, p. 844.
[4] Maspero, *Mémoire sur quelques Papyrus du Louvre*, Paris, 1875, p. 104.

A large number of figures of miscellaneous 'gods' are given in the papyri of the later priests of Amen, and they are placed on them to illustrate the forms of Amen-Rā who are alluded to in the 'Addresses to Amen-Rā'. The figures are wholly artificial in character, and many have no names, and many different 'gods' are given the same name. A number of examples without names are given on p. 234.

GODS AND GODDESSES WHOSE EXACT FUNCTIONS ARE UNKNOWN

VIII

GODS—COSMIC, STELLAR, BORROWED, AND FOREIGN

THE cult of the cosmic gods and adoration of the powers of Nature must have been, in some form or other, coeval with the existence of men in the Valley of the NILE. Without water, heat, and grain the primitive EGYPTIAN found that he could not live, and without light he could neither work nor move about. The dynastic texts state that NUNU, that is to say the primeval collection of water, was the 'Father of the Gods'. This abyss of waters existed, apparently, from all time, and no scribe ever conceived how it came into being; at all events the texts are silent on the matter. This NUNU or (Pyr. § 132 *c*), or or was ruled over by four frog- and serpent-headed bisexual deities, and the chief of them, NENU-NENET, permitted the waters which formed the NILE to flow, under his direction, from out of his storehouse into EGYPT. On the gods of this abyss see p. 483. The principal cosmic gods were:

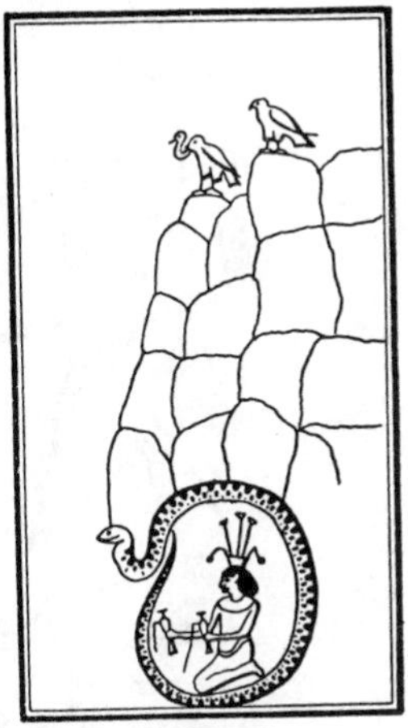

The Nile-god in his cavern under the mountains near Philae.

1. The NILE, in Egyptian, ḤEP, ḤEPR, ḤĀPR, ḤĀPI; these forms probably represent a predynastic word for 'river'. The origin of the Greek Νεῖλος seems to be doubtful. The priests thought that the 'NILE of the North' rose at KHERI-ĀḤĀ near the modern FUSṬÂṬ, and the NILE of the South at SILSILAH. Later, the sources of the NILE were said to be at ELEPHANTINE. The EGYPTIANS knew nothing about the true sources of the NILE, and the annual flooding or Inundation. ARISTOTLE (*Meteorologicorum* (I. viii. 1 *a*) and ERATOSTHENES (276–196 B.C.) had some knowledge of the great lakes in central AFRICA, and of the influence of summer rains on the same. ARISTOCREON, CAECILIUS BION, and

DALION possessed much knowledge about the NILE and its course from the great lakes, and they were regarded as authorities on the geography of north-east AFRICA by PLINY (*Hist. Nat.* v. 9; vi. 35). PTOLEMY, the geographer, believed the three great central lakes to be the two sources of the NILE. The NILE-god is represented in the form of a man painted green or blue, with a cluster of aquatic

Scene symbolizing the Union of Upper and Lower Egypt. The Nile-gods of the South and North tying stems of the lotus and papyrus round the symbol of 'union' (*sma*).

plants on his head; he is sometimes seen pouring out water from libation vases (see LANZONE, Pl. 198). In the Papyrus of ANI (chap. xvii) the two lakes UADJ-URA and MAĀT represent the sources of the NILE, and the NILE-god has his hands stretched out over them. The god standing close by with the emblem for 'year' on his head is probably the ancient Year-god. The two great festivals of the NILE took place one in the middle of JUNE and the other in the middle of AUGUST. During the first of these the goddess ISIS was supposed to shed tears into the NILE to make the river rise. The night when this took place was called 'Gerḥ-en-ḥatuiy', and the ARABS describe the night as 'Lailat al-Nuḳṭah', the 'Night of the Tear Drop'. The great HARRIS Papyrus No. 1 (ed. BIRCH, LONDON, 1876, Pl. 37 f.) proves that the EGYPTIANS made great gifts to the NILE at the time when it was due to rise.

RAMESES III had statues and figures of the NILE-god made in gold, silver, lapis-lazuli, malachite, iron, copper, tin, lead, stone, and wood, and 5,098 statues of the NILE-goddess made in wood, and he

Rā the Sun-god of Heliopolis.

Rā, the War-god of Hermonthus, later adopted by the Thebans as Amen-Rā.

Khepri in his boat.

had spells written on 272 'books of the NILE' and cast into the river during the thirty-one years of his reign.

2. The Sun, of which three principal forms were recognized: (1) KHEPRI , the sun at dawn, or the rising sun. (2) RĀ , the noon-day sun. (3) TEM, (Pyr. § 135) , or ATEM the sun at the end of the day. KHEPRI appears as a beetle or a man with the head of a beetle *Kheprer* . The predynastic people saw some connexion between the *scara-*

baeus sacer which rolled or pushed its egg-ball over the ground, and the great beetle of the sky which rolled the ball of the sun across the heavens. The beetle of KHEPRI is seen with a ball before him and a ball behind him; the former is the sun of to-day and the latter the sun of yesterday. He is mentioned in the Pyramid Texts (§ 366), was associated with HORUS (LANZONE, Pl. 329), and the Great and Little Companies of the gods were in his body (Papyrus of ANI, chap. xvii, l. 116). The fundamental ideas connected with KHEPRI were rebirth and renewed life, hence the thousands of amulets of the scarab; and he protected the dead (*Book of the Dead*, chap. xxx B and lxiv) as far back as the time of SEMTI, the fifth king of the Ist dynasty. KHEPRI sailed across the sky in a boat called MANDJET 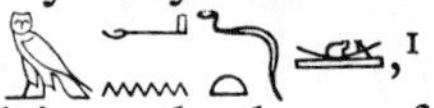,[1] the boat of the rising sun; at noon he changed into the boat of the setting sun, MESKETT 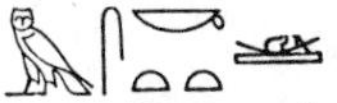 or SEKTET 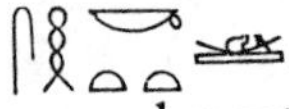.[2]

TEM or ATEM seems to have been a predynastic name for the sun, which was adopted by the priests of ON. On the other hand, it might mean 'he who has come to an end'; he usually appears as a man. A legend states that he was once attacked by a huge serpent, and as he could not destroy it he changed himself into an ichneumon, in the form of which he appears twice.[3] See also p. 81.

3. The Moon, in Egyptian, AĀḤ 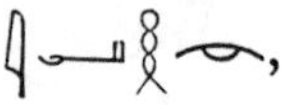, 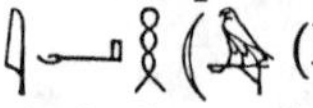 (Pyr. § 1104). The Moon-god appears as a man in the archaic form of PTAḤ, MIN, OSIRIS, &c., i.e. with his legs closed together. On his head is the 'young moon with the old one in its arms' , he wears the lock of hair of youth, and a cobra above his forehead. Behind his neck hangs the *menat* 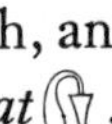, on his breast is the symbol of fecundity, in his hands he holds , and he stands on  *maāt* 'law' or 'truth'. His old fetish object is shown in LANZONE, Pl. 36. He sailed over the sky in a boat, viz. the 'Boat of millions of years'. Often the god is called AĀḤ DJḤUTI 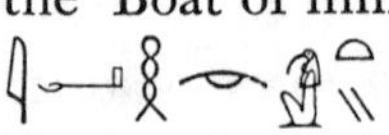 or , and a baboon-god called  is seen bringing back the udjat , i.e. the stolen or damaged Eye of RĀ. The name of the baboon was ASṬEN

[1]  Pyr. § 211. [2] 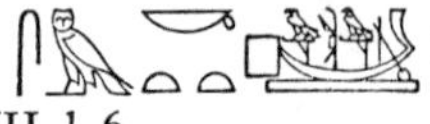 Pyr. § 210.

[3] See Naville, *Goshen*, Pl. VI, l. 6, and Pl. XVII, l. 6.

or ASṬES, and he assisted THOTH in the Judgement. The Moon-god of THEBES was called, i.e. the 'Traveller' or, 'Runner', goose.

4. The Earth-god GEBB, appears sometimes as a goose, and sometimes as a goose-headed man. In the papyri his body is covered with little patches of green to indicate his character as a god of vegetation.

5. The Sky-goddess, or female counterpart of GEBB, was NUT, whose old fetish object was a, probably symbolizing a human uterus. She usually appears in the form of a woman carrying the same emblems of rank as the other goddesses. The Sky was represented by, i.e. a flat plate of something supported by a projection downwards at each end; this something may have been thought to be brass or stone. The two supports of the sky were Mount BAKHAU in the east and Mount MANU in the west. There was a northern support called UPT-TA, as BRUGSCH pointed out, like a tent pole. The moon and sun moved under the plate but the stars were hung in it like a lamp, and the stars were called 'lamps'. It was decided at length that the sky had four pillars and that during rain-storms the sky slipped down the pillars. Thunder was called 'Voice of the sky'. The inscriptions in the papyri illustrating the nightly descent of the Sky-goddess to receive the embraces of GEBB shows that both GEBB and NUT were regarded as bisexual. Under the New Kingdom NUT appears in the form of a very handsome cow, the body of which is strewn with stars.

6. The Four Winds. These were supposed to be stored in the

QEBIU or, i.e. 'the Cooler' or North wind, belonging to OSIRIS. Coptic ⲕⲃⲱⲟⲩ,

SHEHEBUI, i.e. 'the Heater' or South wind, belonging to RĀ, Coptic ϣⲁⲑⲉⲣⲁ,

ḤENKHISESUI (?), the East wind, belonging to ISIS.

ḤEDJIUI, the West wind, belonging to NEPHTHYS.

The four winds were kept by THOTH in four chambers of the

sky, and he kept shut or opened the doors at will. See *Book of the Dead*, chap. clxi.

THE FOUR ELEMENTS AND THEIR GODS

Earth	GEBB		Fire	RĀ	
Air	SHU		Water	ASAR	.

THE FOUR RUDDERS OF THE BOAT OF RĀ

1. North Rudder SEKHEM NEFER .
2. West Rudder TEBEN-SEMU-TAUI .
3. East Rudder KHU(?)-ḤER-AB ḤE-T ASHEMU,  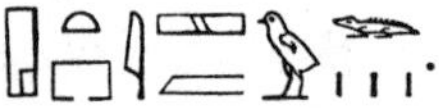.
4. South Rudder KHENTI-ḤER-AB ḤET-ṬESHERU 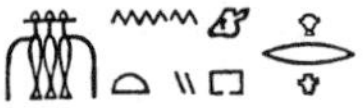 .

The names mean:

1. Beautiful Power.
2. Revolver, Guide of the Two Lands (EGYPT).
3. Light god, dweller in the Temple of the ASHEMU.
4. Governor dweller in the Temple of the Red Gods.

THE FIXED STARS AND PLANETS

The predynastic EGYPTIANS believed that the stars of heaven governed the destinies of men, and there seems to be little doubt that the astrologer and his craft existed in the NILE valley from time immemorial. The little knowledge of the subject which we possess is derived from texts of the dynastic period.

The Pyramid Texts contain many proofs that the EGYPTIANS possessed an elementary knowledge of astronomy, and that they had given names to many prominent stars. They divided heaven and earth into four parts, and the Thirty-six Dekans of heaven had their counterparts in the Thirty-six Nomes on earth (BRUGSCH, *Aegyptologie*, p. 321). They divided the whole company of the stars into two great groups, the Northern and the Southern:

1. AKHEMU SEKU, i.e. 'the stars that never set or fail'. These are commonly known as the circumpolar stars.

2. AKHEMU URTU, the 'stars that never rest', or the southern stars.

The circumpolar stars vary in number; twelve of them towed the Boat of the Sun through the ṬUAT at night. They did constant homage to the god of heaven (Pyr. § 1155 *c*) and they were the ministers and followers of OSIRIS (§ 749 *e*). According to the text of UNAS (§ 491 *b*) this king had a special servant, for we read, 'UNAS hath sent his unresting messenger'. The most important of all the fixed stars was SEPṬET or, or SIRIUS, the Dog-star, which the GREEKS called SOTHIS. The EGYPTIANS discovered that when on one or other of the days which would be the equivalents of July 19 and 20 of the Julian Calendar, SIRIUS rose heliacally (i.e. with the sun), in the eastern sky, the inundation or flooding of the NILE began. In other words this rising of SIRIUS marked the beginning of the year, and by it the priests were able to regulate the agricultural operations of the country. In the Pyramid Texts SEPṬET is called 'the Year' (§ 965 *b*). As the dominant star of the heavens SOTHIS was identified with HATHOR, and she is therefore depicted as a cow with a star between her horns and lying in a boat. SEPṬET was the 'Queen of the Year' and she was the first of all the DECANS.[1] One aspect of her was identified with ORION, and her head bandlet is mentioned in Pyr. § 1048 *b*.

THE CONSTELLATIONS

The constellations known to the EGYPTIANS were few. The most important were:

1. SAḤ, i.e. ORION, 'the fleet-footed, long-strided god, pre-eminent in the Land of the South' (i.e. the SŪDĀN) (Pyr. § 959 *e*). He was the 'Father of the gods',[2] and was identified with

[1] The Egyptians seem to have sometimes confounded Sepṭet with the Horus-god of the eastern desert Sepṭu (Pyr. § 1534 *c*).

[2] (Pyr. § 409 *c*).

HORUS and OSIRIS, and was distinguished by a 'great star' on his shoulder (Pyr. § 882 *b*). His female counterpart SAḤ-T seems to have been included among the 'Souls of HELIOPOLIS' (*Book of the Dead*, chap. xxiii, ANI, l. 5). He was associated with SEPṬET, and in late times was confounded with CANOPUS. He

The deceased addressing Ḥer-f-ḥa-f.

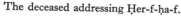

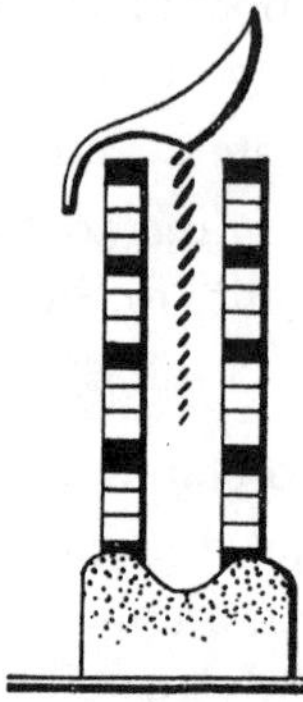

The block of slaughter of the god Shesmu.

is depicted in the form of a god who holds a sceptre in his right hand, and in his left hand, which is extended, is a star; and he is looking backward in the act of running. The texts show that he was a celestial ferryman, and it is probable that he was the prototype of the ferryman with his face turned behind him who is seen in the *Book of the Dead*.[1] On the other hand, ḤER-F-ḤA-F is called the 'Doorkeeper of OSIRIS' (Pyr. § 1201 *a*).

2. The PLEIADES. This constellation was unknown to the early dynastic EGYPTIANS, but in the Ptolemaic period attempts were made to identify the SEVEN HATHORS (see p. 232) with them, because they were regarded to all intents and purposes as the FATES of classical mythology. The PLEIADES[2] were known to be in the Sign of the Bull, and in the vignette to chapter cxlviii of the *Book of the Dead* we have the SEVEN COWS of HATHOR and their BULL.

3. The constellation represented by the XVIth Decan is important because its chief star was the abode of the god SHESMU

1 'Looks behind him', Also *Ma-ha-f*.
2 The Copts called them ϭⲓⲏⲙⲟⲩⲧ.

or (Pyr. § 403). The hieroglyph for his name is a wine-press, and in Pyr. § 1552 *a*, he is said 'to come bearing water and wine'. But he was known to the later theologians as the headsman or executioner of OSIRIS, who hacked in pieces the bodies of the damned. He was depicted in the form of a lion-headed man. His female counterpart had the head of a lioness, and was called SHESEMTET or SEBSHESEN.

4. THE GREAT BEAR. This constellation was identified with SET, the god of evil, and it had various names, e.g. 'the Thigh [of the Bull]', MESEḲHTI, i.e. the Slaughterer (Pyr. § 458 *c*); it is our URSA MAJOR. In the illustration on the right is the Hippopotamus-goddess (No. 1) called by the various names ḤESAMUT, RERET (i.e. the Pig), SHEPUT, APET, and TA-URET (i.e. the 'Great'). On her back she carries a crocodile, a matter not easy to explain. The object on which her foreleg rests is a mooring post, and because of this she is sometimes called MENT URET, i.e. the 'Great Mooring Post' (Pyr. § 794 *c*). She was originally the Sky-goddess, and assisted as midwife or nurse at the birth of the Sun-god.

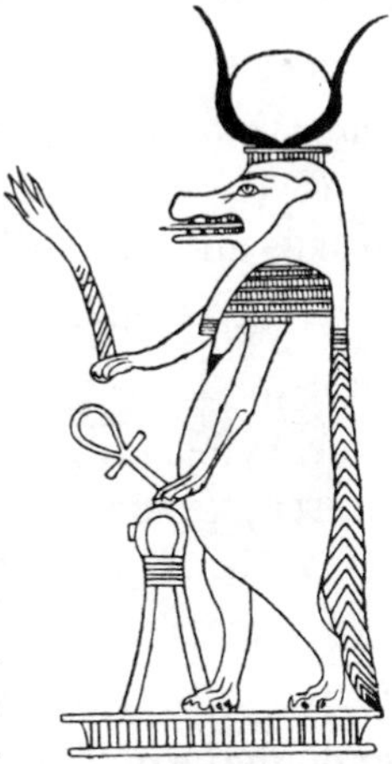

The friend of the dead.

5. ĀN, the 'Repulser', or ṬUA-ĀNNU (Pyr. 1098 *a*) a name of HORUS as the warrior-god who is attacking the Bull. He was supported by the Four Sons of HORUS, ḤEP, ṬUAMUTF, MESTI, and QEBḤSENUF.

6. A god wearing the solar disk and gripping the Bull's tail. Name unknown.

7. A god spearing the crocodile SERSA (No. 9).

8. A HORUS-god.

9. The Scorpion-goddess SERQET in the form of a woman; she was a morning star.

10. The constellation of the LION, perhaps the representation of the star NEKHEKH (Pyr. § 332 *c*).

THE PLANETS

1. JUPITER was called the star of the south or UPESH-PET 'the light-scatterer of the sky' (Pyr. § 1455). The god of this planet has not been identified.

2. SATURN, 'the star of the west traversing heaven' was called ḤOR-KA-PET, 'HORUS, Bull of Heaven'. In later times he was known as 'HORUS the Bull', or the 'HORUS Bull'. He is depicted as a bull-headed hawk. The god of this planet was HORUS and he was bull-headed.

3. MARS, 'the star of the east of heaven', was called ḤOR-ṬESHER, the 'Red HORUS'. He was said 'to journey backwards in travelling', and he was also known as 'ḤAR-AKHTI', 'HORUS of the Two Horizons'. The god of this planet was RĀ; he had the head of a hawk with a star above it.

4. MERCURY was called SEBGU or SEBEG. He is depicted in the form of a man with a star above his head. Curiously enough the god of this planet is SET, the god of evil. In the *Book of the Dead* a staircase, or stepped pedestal, is under the charge of SEBEG.

5. VENUS, the Evening Star, was called SEB-UĀTI (Pyr. § 251 *b*), and the god of this planet was ISIS. In the late period she is depicted as a two-headed woman, one wearing and the other. She was probably the evening equivalent of NETER ṬUAU, the 'god of the dawn' or Morning Star, which was also called 'HORUS of the ṬUAT, or Underworld' (Pyr. § 1207 *a*) and the 'star sailing over the Great Green' (i.e. the MEDITERRANEAN, § 1720 *c*). Though the Morning Star was masculine he is spoken of as having given birth to the dead king (Pyr. § 929 *b*) and to ORION, ṢEḤ (Pyr. § 820 *e*). The Morning Star was the ferryman of OSIRIS, or the Soul of OSIRIS, i.e. the Benu bird, which the GREEKS identified with the Phoenix.

THE THIRTY-SIX DECANS

The EGYPTIANS divided the sky into thirty-six sections which they called 'Bakiu' and the GREEKS 'Decans'. Each Decan had its spirit or god, and corresponded to ten days of the vague or wandering year of 360 days. The five epagomenal days were dealt with separately. This Decan belt was superseded in Graeco-Roman times by the ZODIAC which was introduced into EGYPT from BABYLONIA via GREECE. It contained Twelve Signs, to each of which was attached three stars. Each god was provided with a boat. A handy list of the names of the Decans in hieroglyphs and GREEK will be found in Budge, *Gods of the Egyptian* vol. ii.

THE STAR-GODS BEHIND SOTHIS AND ORION

These were: (1) SHETU . (2) NESRU . (3) SHEPET . (4) APSEDJ . (5) SEBSHES (6) UASH-NETER .

The funerary texts mention several star-gods who were undoubtedly very ancient, but about whose origin and attributes the dynastic EGYPTIANS knew as little as we do. Among these are:

HAPHAP who appears in the form of a man wearing the Atef Crown (CHAMPOLLION, *Monuments égyptiens*, II. lxxxiv); he is mentioned in the *Book of Traversing Eternity*, l. 70.

ḤEQES , who was a guide and protector of mariners and seafaring folk in general; he is mentioned in the Pyramid Texts (§ 452).

SUNTJ . This star-god is often mentioned in the Pyramid Texts (§§ 1019, 1250, &c.), and is always referred to as the traveller who strides or sails across the sky. In one text (N. 1110) he is said to 'sail over heaven nine times in the night'.[1] Beyond this nothing is known about him.

THE ZODIAC

The knowledge of the Signs of the Zodiac was brought into EGYPT by the GREEKS, who adopted them from the BABYLONIANS. The COPTS, i.e. the EGYPTIANS who embraced Christianity, adopted

1 .

them, and the names under which they appeared at the time of the Roman Emperors are made known to us by four Coptic ostraka, a Coptic papyrus, and a wooden tablet. These names are discussed and published by SPIEGELBERG in the *Aegyptische Zeitschrift*, Bd. 48, p. 147 ('Die ägyptische Namen und Zeichen der Tierkreisbilder in demotischer Schrift'). The first sign is the Sheep (i.e. Ram), and the second *pa ka* the Bull. The third is *na ḥtre* =  (two men clasping hands) = GEMINI. The fourth is *pa kenhḏ* (or *genhḏ*) which is a kind of scarab or beetle and not a crab (CANCER). The fifth is *pa-me* = LEO, and is represented either by a lion  or a knife . The sixth is *tarpi* (compare Θρῖφις in an inscription) = VIRGO. The seventh is *ta aḥi* which means 'the horizon', and the picture represents the solar disk or the horizon . This is a mistake for the Balance 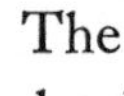, and cannot be explained. The eighth is *taḏl*, i.e. the Scorpion. The ninth is *pa ent atḥ* 'he who draws a bow', i.e. SAGITTARIUS. The tenth is *pa ḥer ānkh* = CAPRICORNUS. The eleventh is *pa mu*, i.e. the 'waterman' = AQUARIUS, and the twelfth is *na tebte*, i.e. 'the fishes' = PISCES.

That the dynastic EGYPTIANS under the XVIIIth dynasty possessed considerable knowledge of astronomy is proved by the description which MR. WINLOCK gives of the ceiling in the tomb of SENMUT, the great architect of Queen ḤATSHEPSUT, which he has recently discovered. He says:

'The real gem of the little room in the tomb of SENMUT is its ceiling. We have the heavens mapped out above us in one of the best and one of the earliest astronomical charts yet found, drawn by the most skilful penmen of the mid-XVIIIth dynasty. In the centre of the northern hall appears the bull-headed constellation "MESKHETIU"—our Great Bear—and the circumpolar star groups. Across the sky the twelve[1] ancient monthly festivals are drawn, each in a circle with its norm of 24 hours, and below, the celestial bodies of the northern sky pass in procession. Opposite, in the southern skies, ORION stubbornly turns his face away from the smiling SOTHIS, who chases after him beckoning fruitlessly year after year. Above them in turn come the lists of the Dekans with the name of HATSHEPSUT herself introduced among the heavenly beings. We have here an earlier and finer celestial chart even than that in the tomb of King SETI, and one which no future study of Egyptian astronomy can neglect.'

[1] The Copts celebrated monthly the festivals of the Virgin, St. Michael the Archangel, &c.

Sheep (Aries).

Bull (Taurus).

Twins (Gemini, Shu and Tefnut).

Scarab (Cancer).

Lion (Taurus).

Tarpi (Virgo).

Scales (Libra with Harpokrates in disk).

Scorpion.

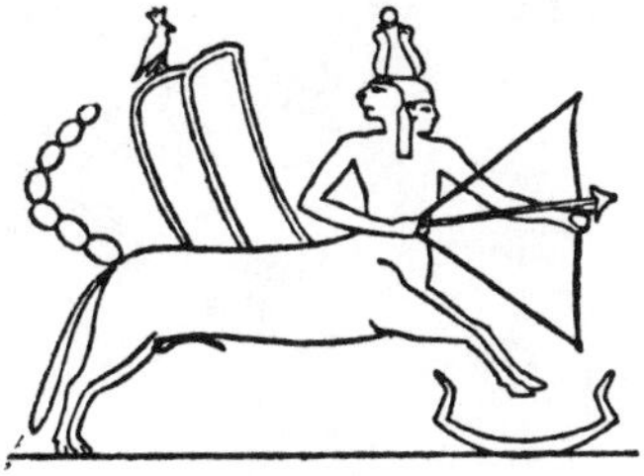

Sagittarius.

Capricornus.

The Nile god Aquarius with the sources of the South and North Nile.)

Pisces.

We may note too the wooden inner coffin of ḤER-NEDJ-TEF-F, a prophet of AMEN and other gods at THEBES. Painted on the inside are figures of the gods of the constellations and planets, the Signs of the Zodiac, the Decans and several scenes from the *Book of Gates*. See the *Guide to First, Second, and Third Egyptian Rooms*, LONDON, 1924, p. 133. No. 4. Date from 500–350 B.C. Number of coffin 6678.

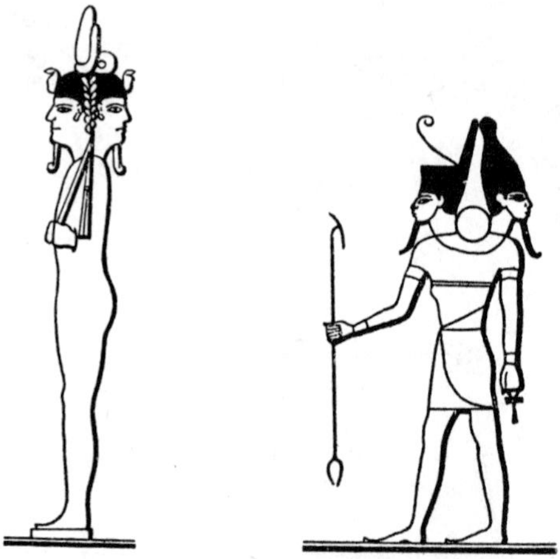

GODS of Yesterday and To-day.

IX

IMPORTED FOREIGN GODS AND GODDESSES

THE greater number of the gods of EGYPT worshipped in dynastic times are of Nilotic origin, even though the fundamental conceptions concerning them and the forms of their worship differed very considerably from those which were current in the predynastic period. The original homes of many of the gods were in countries to the south of EGYPT, and the funerary ceremonies which were performed in UPPER EGYPT under the Middle and New Kingdoms prove that their place of origin was in the south. From the south came all the great animal gods, and the animistic or religious views of the peoples of the south, that is the regions which we now call LOWER and UPPER NUBIA and the EGYPTIAN SÛDÛN, influenced greatly the inhabitants of UPPER EGYPT and the Delta. The EGYPTIANS, like many other Orientals, appear to have been tolerant of alien gods, and when it was alleged that any of these possessed powers and attributes similar to any of their native gods, they accepted them and gave them Egyptian forms. The home of the new Egyptian gods who appear in human form was PALESTINE and SYRIA. Though up to the time of AMASIS I, the first king of the XVIIIth dynasty, PALESTINE was to all intents and purposes a foreign country, communication by means of caravans between it and the Eastern Delta was frequent. And there seems to be no doubt that many of the inhabitants of both countries were of a mixed origin—Egyptian and Semitic. Even in the earliest times the caravan men and merchants exchanged a great deal more than merchandise, and constant intercourse between SEMITE and EGYPTIAN in ON (HELIOPOLIS) and other towns on the eastern frontier of the Delta made each familiar with the manners and customs and religion of the other. The EGYPTIAN gained more than the SEMITE by the intercourse, but nothing that the latter told him made him abandon his cult of animals, birds, reptiles, &c., or relinquish his age-old beliefs in the powers of his fetishes. The religions of the ASIATIC and AFRICAN had little in common, but the moral culture of the former and his skill in business and trafficking were superior to those of the latter.

The EGYPTIANS did not begin to adopt Palestinian and Syrian gods until they had taken possession of both countries and built forts on the sea-coast, and principal towns, that is to say not until about 1600 B.C. The foreign gods who appealed most to them were those who were identified with war and the chase, and in some parts of UPPER EGYPT the Mother-goddess of WESTERN ASIA and the 'naked goddess', and ASHTORETH found worshippers. The principal Syrian gods adopted by the EGYPTIANS were:

1. BĀR 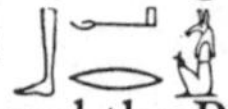 = BA'AL, the god of the CANAANITES and PHOENICIANS, and the Babylonian god BÊL MARDUK. The determinative of his name shows that the EGYPTIANS identified him with SET, the god of evil, but all the same they regarded him as a terrible god of war, whose help was invaluable. At the battle of KADESH RAMESES II raged like MENTHU, the War-god of ARMANT and THEBES, and 'he girded on his armour and grasped his spear, and like BĀR in the height of his wrath, he leaped upon his horse, and charged the host of the KHETA'. The principal seat of the cult of BĀR in EGYPT was TANIS (ZOAN), but we do not know how the EGYPTIANS represented him in their pictures. The centre of the cult of BA'ALATH or BĒLTIS, the female counterpart of BĀR, was JUBAIL or BYBLOS, and the EGYPTIANS identified her with HATHOR, who was called the 'Lady of KIPU[NA]' and 'Mistress of UA[UA-T].' The inscriptions also mention a BĒLTIS of DJAPUNA, who may be the female counterpart of BA'AL ṢEPHŌN (Exodus xiv. 2), but not necessarily of BĀR, and the ASSYRIANS mention this god and BAAL SAMEME and BAAL MALAGI.[1]

2. RESHPU  was the god of lightning, fire, and of the pestilence which follows in the train of war. His name is derived from the Phoenician *reshef*, or *reshep*, 'fire-bolt', 'thunder-bolt'. The centre of his cult in EGYPT was at ḤE-T RESHEP. He is represented as a man wearing a head-covering like the White Crown of EGYPT, from which the head and neck of a gazelle appears. This may indicate that he was a god of the chase, but it is more likely that some species of gazelle was his sacred animal. His armour consisted of a shield and spear, which he carries in his left hand, and a battle-axe of the Egyptian type which he wields above his

[1] Müller, *Asien und Europa*, p. 315.

head in the right hand. He is associated with MIN and the naked-woman goddess called KENT on a stele in the BRITISH MUSEUM (p. 252 No. 10), and he was identified with SHULMANU, an Assyrian god of battles.[1] The EGYPTIANS called him 'the everlasting, eternal great god, the lord of valour, the president of the Company of the gods, the lord of heavens, governor of the gods'.

3. ATUMA, , a Syrian god who has been identified with the EDŌM mentioned in the Bible (Ezekiel xxv. 14); he had a female counterpart of the same name.[2]

4. SUTEKH  a god of the KHETA who was identified by the EGYPTIANS with the god SET. It is clear from the treaty which RAMESES II made with KHETA-SAR, the prince of the KHETA, that SUTEKH was worshipped in many places in northern SYRIA, ARENNA, KHIREPU (ALEPPO), REKHA-SUA, &c.

5. NUKARĀ  is perhaps the Babylonian NIN-GAL; no Egyptian picture of her is known.

6. AMIT (?) 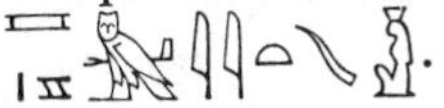. Details of her form and attributes are wanting.

7. ĀNTAT . A Syrian War-goddess who is represented as a woman wearing the Egyptian Crown of the South with plumes, and armed with spear, shield, and battle-axe. A sanctuary for her was built at THEBES in the reign of THOTHMES III. She may be akin to the goddess ĀNTHRETJU  mentioned in the great Hittite treaty.

8. ASTHART , i.e. 'ASHTORETH', a Semitic goddess of war who was in EGYPT regarded as a form of HATHOR, ISIS, and other goddesses, and at a late period she appears as a lioness-headed woman wearing a disk on her head, and holding a whip (?) in her right hand, standing in a chariot and driving her team of four horses over prostrate foes. The centre of her cult in EGYPT was APOLLINOPOLIS MAGNA (EDFÛ). The EGYPTIANS learned to employ the horse in war from the SEMITES of the Eastern Desert, and their knowledge of the value of the animal for military purposes, and their use of him in war, is not older than about 1700 B.C. In the

[1] On Shulmanu see Sidney Smith, *Early History of Assyria*, p. 340.

[2] Müller, *Asien und Europa*, p. 316.

relief on the temple at EDFÛ the goddess is called 'lady of horses, lady of the chariot', but this title is not an old one.

9. KENT 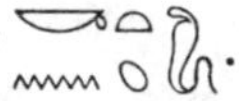. See the following paragraph.

10. QEṬESH 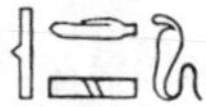 or QETSHU . A Syro-Phoenician goddess, the personification of love and beauty, who was in EGYPT identified with HATHOR and ISIS and other moon-goddesses. She is represented as a naked woman, full-faced and standing on a lion. She has the head-dress of HATHOR, which in one case is surmounted by the full moon resting in the crescent moon; in her right hand she holds a bunch of flowers, and in her left a serpent.[1] On the stele in the BRITISH MUSEUM she is called KENT, and on the stele in TURIN QETESH, and in the inscription on each she is said to be the 'lady of heaven, the mistress of all the gods, the eye of RĀ, without a second'. The name QEṬESH is perhaps connected with the Hebrew *kādēsh*,[2] a temple-prostitute, a harlot, and if it be so, we may regard her as the harlot of the gods. The gods MIN and RESHPU who are seen with her on the stele in the BRITISH MUSEUM probably represent the lovers of the goddess.

11. ĀSIT 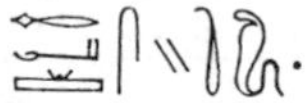. An equestrian War-goddess who bore a spear and shield. MÜLLER thought she was the female counterpart of the god USOOS (*sic*), who wore skins and could be propitiated by means of blood offerings. That she was a goddess of the Eastern Desert is proved by a stele which was found near the temple at RADĀSĪYAH, on the road to the gold-mines of JABAL ZĀBARĀ.[3]

12. ĀNAT . A Syrian War-goddess who appears in the form of a woman wearing a lofty crown with plumes, and bearing a spear and shield and battle-axe (MÜLLER, *Asien und Europa*, p. 306). See the lower register on the stele in the BRITISH MUSEUM.

The oldest Nubian or Sûdânî gods known to us are:

1. ṬEṬUN, a War-god who, in the form of a bird of prey standing on a crescent-shaped perch  (?), is seen on objects of the early

[1] Lanzone, Plates 191 and 192.

[2] The licentiousness of her rites is indicated by such passages as Gen. xxxviii. 1, 2; Deut. xxiii. 18; Num. xxv. 1; Hos. iv. 14.

[3] i.e. the emerald mines on the western side of the Red Sea.

dynastic period found at ABYDOS[1] and at HIERAKONPOLIS.[2] He is mentioned several times in the Pyramid Texts and his name is always followed by a bird as a determinative, thus,  (§ 803 *c*),  (§ 994 *d*). The second determinative shows that in the VIth dynasty his cult, in EGYPT at least, was antiquated or obsolete. In the Pyramid Texts he is called the 'young man of the South who cometh forth from TA-STI (NUBIA)', and he brings to the dead king the sweet-smelling incense which is used for the gods (§ 1718 *a*). Elsewhere he is one of the four gods who carry the ladder by which king PEPI is to ascend into heaven (§ 1718 *a*). The earliest Egyptian picture we have of ṬEṬUN is found in the little temple of KHNEMU which THOTHMES III built at SEMNAH in the Second Cataract. There he appears as an ordinary god-king of EGYPT, bearded and holding  and . The address to ṬEṬUN is made by the priestly official KENEMTEF i.e. the 'wearer of the leopard's skin', who is here called 'AN-MUT-F', as in the Pyramid Texts  (§ 1603). In the papyrus of ANI (pl. XII) we have a picture of AN-MUT-F wearing the leopard skin.[3]

2. BES , called by the GREEKS Βησᾶς. The oldest mention of this god's name appears to be in the Pyramid Texts (§ 1768 *c*), where mention is made of the 'tail of BES' . And the oldest representation of him is found on the magic wand (?) which is figured on p. 88. He is usually depicted in the form of a dwarf with a huge bearded head, protruding tongue, flat nose, shaggy eyebrows and hair, large projecting ears, long thick arms, and bowed legs, and a tail. He sometimes wears round his body the skin of an animal of the panther tribe, and on his head he has a crown with high plumes, much resembling the head-dress of the goddess SATET, a member of the triad of ELEPHANTINE. His pygmy form and his head-dress prove that he was of Sûdânî origin. There is no doubt that his cult was very ancient. He is usually represented, both in drawings and statues, full-faced, like the naked goddess QEṬESH. He appears as a dancer; as a musician he played

[1] Petrie, *Royal Tombs*, vol. i (objects of the time of Mena).

[2] Quibell, *Hierakonpolis*, Plates 19, 26, and 34.

[3] In the *Book of the Dead* (chap. xcii) we read, 'I am Horus Nedj-tef-f. I am An-atf-f. I am An-mut-f', &c.

the lyre and the harp, and probably acted as tribal singer; as a soldier he wears a short military tunic with belt, and he holds a short sword in his right hand and a shield in his left. He symbolized the jolly, good-natured, happy-go-lucky Sûdânî man, who loved, and still loves, good eating and good drinking and pleasure,

Bes the baboon.

Bes the harper.

jollity, feasting, and amusement of every kind, and was equally ready to make love and to fight his enemies. Figures of BES are found carved on the handles of mirrors and stibium tubes, and on the head-rests or pillows of mummies, which shows that he was closely associated with happiness and restfulness; his ugly, grinning face provoked mirth and laughter and drove away evil spirits and influences.[1] He was also a slayer of serpents and all kinds of noxious animals. In the reign of THOTHMES I we find him associated with the hippopotamus-goddess TA-URT, or APET, and both are seen in the birth-chamber in which Queen ḤATSHEPSUT is about to be born; apparently he was also regarded as a friend of children. But the dwarf or pygmy must have been connected with some very ancient religious Sûdânî belief. King ASSA (Vth dynasty) sent a high official to the 'Land of the Spirits' in the SÛDÂN, and he brought back to him a pygmy, to dance the 'dance of the god' before him. Another official ḤER-KHU-F also brought back a pygmy

[1] See the group of pictures of the god given by Lanzone, Pls. LXXIII f.

who was sent to PEPI II (VIth dynasty) at MEMPHIS. In the Pyramid Texts three of the kings are identified with the 'dwarf of the dance of the god who made merry the heart of the god' (§ 1189 *a*). As is well known, dancing in the SÛDÂN, as elsewhere, was considered to be an act of worship, and we may note that THOTHMES III danced before the goddess HATHOR. The attributes of BES were greatly modified under the New Kingdom (see *Book of the Dead* (chap. cxlv, § xxi),[1] and he seems to appear as the 'Aged of Days' on the METTERNICH stele (see the illustration in Part II). The name BES survives in Coptic as 'BĒSA'. The female counterpart of BES was called BESET or BESIT.

PTAḤ–SEKER, one of the oldest gods of EGYPT, is represented in the form of a dwarf, with a beetle on the crown of his head. Now the beetle is the symbol of 'new life' and 'birth', and it is probable that the figure of PTAḤ–SEKER represents the *human embryo* immediately before birth.

Less well-known Sûdânî gods are:

ARI–ḤEMS–NEFER 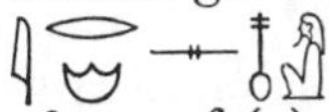, a local god of the district of PHILAE. He has the form of (1) a lion-headed man wearing the Crowns of the South and North, with the cobra, and (2) a man seated on a throne and wearing the Atef crown.

MERIL 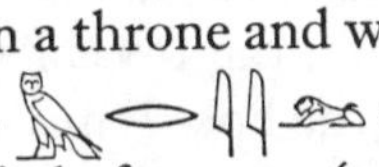 or MERUL , the third member of the triad of TELMES (TALMIS), the site of which is marked by the modern village of KALĀBSHAH in NUBIA, about 35 miles south of ASWĀN. A text quoted by BRUGSCH (*Dict. Géog.*, p. 954) speaks of his coming from the 'Land of the god', i.e. the region of southern ARABIA and the African coast as far as SOMALILAND. His cult was probably very ancient. Once he appears naked, except for a pectoral, and a neck-chain with a heart amulet attached .[2]

AAḤES 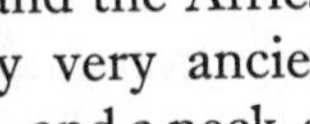 is called in the Pyramid Texts (§ 994) 'Regent of the land of the South', which in early times probably meant the region between JABAL-SILSILAH and ASWĀN or KALĀBSHAH. ṬEṬUN, who is mentioned in the same paragraph, is called 'Regent of TA-STI', that is all NUBIA and KŪSH.

Under the heading of borrowed gods must be mentioned

[1] He is probably to be seen in the monster shown in the vignette of chap. xxviii.

[2] See Brugsch, *Religion*, p. 290 f.; Lauzone, *Dizionario*, p. 958 f.

KHNEMU, who together with his two female counterparts, SATEL and ĀNQET, formed the great triad of ELEPHANTINE. The name KHNEMU, or KHNUM, is the predynastic name for the special kind of ram which represented his incarnation. In the earliest times KHNEMU was a water-god, and the god *par excellence* of the First Cataract. His chief shrines were there, and he controlled the NILE and its annual inundation. As such one of his names was QEBH or the 'god of cool water'. Among his many titles we find the following:

1. Fashioner of men, maker of the gods, the Father who was in the beginning.

2. Maker of things, the things which are, the definer of the things which shall be, the source of things which shall come into being, the Father of Fathers, the Mother of Mothers.

3. Father of the fathers of the gods and goddesses, lord of what cometh into being from himself, maker of heaven and earth and the ṬUAT (i.e. Underworld), and of water and of the mountains.

4. Raiser up of heaven upon its four pillars and the supporter of the same in the firmament for ever.

5. KHNEM, lord of PHILAE, the living divine Ram of RĀ, the great god, dweller in the first of the nomes, the fear of whom is great as possessor of the four ram's heads, the holy Ram of RĀ.[4]

The principal object of the care of KHNEMU was the First Cataract, but this was entirely forgotten at a later time when the priests transferred his seat of power to SHA-SEHETEP, ESNEH, ABYDOS, and HERAKLEOPOLIS.

King DJESER was sorely distressed because there had been very low NILES for the past seven years. All stores of grain and provisions had been consumed, there was nothing left to eat, and men were collapsing in the streets and dying, and children and old men were perishing. The king sent an envoy to MATER (?), governor of NUBIA, asking him to tell him where he could find the god or goddess of the NILE, so that he might appeal to him or her for help. MATER informed him that the NILE entered EGYPT through the two caves, the QERTI, on the island of ELEPHANTINE, and that the 'couch' of ḤĀPI was there. The keeper of these caves was KHNEMU, and he was the doorkeeper who withdrew the bolts so that the water might enter the NILE. The king, it seems, journeyed to the south, and made offerings in the temple of KHNEMU, and the god himself appeared to him and said: 'I am the Creator, and I protect thee and thy body. I am the self-created god, I am the primeval water, I am the NILE and I rise at my pleasure. I am the Almighty, the father of the gods, and the ruler of men. I am SHU the landlord of the earth.' And he complained that men had neglected his worship and his shrine. The king issued a decree ordering the repair of the temple, and assigned endowments to it, and the god promised that hereafter the NILE should rise annually as in days of old.

An-ḥer. Among foreign gods we may place An-ḥer of Abydos whose cult and attributes were usurped by Osiris.

In the *Book of the Dead* (chap. XXX B) the deceased refers to KHNEMU as the 'knitter together and strengthener' of his body; and he claims to be KHNEMU of KÔM OMBO (chap. xxxvi); and says that his house had been built for him by the goddess SESHETA and KHNEMU (chap. lvii); and in the vignette of chap. clxvii we see KHNEMU, KHEPRI, and HORUS (or RĀ) each sitting in his boat.

The form of the name of KHNEMU was changed in late times, for on the walls of the pyramid tomb of 'MURTEK' at MEROË we have KNUFI, and from this are derived the forms KHNEPH (Greek Κνήφ), KHNOUPHIS, &c. The name KHNEMU is spelt by the Gnostics KHNOUBIS, KNOUPHIS, and even KHNOUMIS. But the Gnostics did not regard him as a water-god, but as a sort of Agathodaemon, and they represented him as a huge serpent with the head of a lion, surrounded by a crown of seven or twelve rays. The green stone amulets on which this serpent and his name are engraved were magical and medicinal rather than spiritual agents; and they were expected to give the wearers health, wealth, prosperity, and long life. The old water-god KHNEMU gave men all these when he gave EGYPT year by year a high NILE.

The triad of which KHNEMU was the head formed part of the Company of gods of ELEPHANTINE which consisted of SATET,

ĀNUQET, ḤĀPI, GEBB, NUT, OSIRIS, ISIS, HORUS, and NEPHTHYS. But we know that another goddess ought to have been mentioned, viz. ḤEQET, the Frog-goddess,[1] for she is kneeling before KHNEMU, and as he is fashioning two men on his potter's wheel that goddess is providing 'life' for them.

[1] She is mentioned in the Pyramid Texts (§ 1312 *c*).

X

MEMPHITE THEOLOGY AND THE GOD PTAḤ-TENEN

IN a hymn to the god PTAḤ-TENEN, written in hieratic character and published by LEPSIUS (*Denkmäler*, vi. 118), we find a list of titles which were given to the god by the theologians of the XIXth or XXth dynasty. The hymn begins:

'Homage to thee, O PTAḤ-TENEN, thou great god whose form is hidden. Thou openest thy soul, thou wakest up in peace, O Father of the fathers of all the gods, thou PTAḤ of heaven. Thou illuminest it with thy two Eyes (i.e. Sun and Moon) and thou lightest up the earth with thy brilliant rays in peace.

'Thou art the begetter of men and the fashioner of their lives, and the creator of the gods.

'Thou passest through eternity and everlastingness, thy forms are multitudinous, thou hearest the prayers which men address to thee.

'Thou didst build up thine own members, and fashion thy body when the heavens and the earth were unmade, and when the waters had not come forth.

'Thou didst knit together the earth, thou didst assemble thy members, thou didst embrace thy body, and thou didst find thyself in the condition of the One who made his seat, and who moulded the Two Lands.

'Thou hadst no father to beget thee, and no mother to give birth unto thee; thou didst fashion thyself without the help of any other being, and thou didst come forth fully equipped.

'Thou existest (?) in thy aged son RĀ, thou destroyest the night and scatterest the darkness by the two Eyes of PTAḤ-TENEN (i.e. the sun and moon).

'Thy feet are on the earth, and thy head is in the heights above in thy form of "Dweller in the ṬUAT". Thou bearest up the work which thou hast made, thou supportest thyself by thine own divine strength, and thou holdest thyself up by the vigour of thine own hands.

'Thy feet are on the earth, thy head is in the heights, in thy becomings (or creations) as "Dweller in the ṬUAT". . . . Heaven is above thee, the ṬUAT is beneath thee.

'The words come forth from thy nostrils, and the celestial waters from thy mouth, and the staff of life (i.e. grain) cometh forth on thy back. Thou makest the earth fruitful, gods and men have abundance, and they see the cow-goddess MEḤURIT in thy field.

'When thou restest darkness cometh; and when thou openest thy two eyes, beams of light are produced. . . .

'Thou art the Great God who hath stretched out the heavens, who maketh his disk to revolve in the body of NUT, and to enter into the body of NUT in thy name of "RĀ". Thou art the moulder of gods, and men, and everything which is produced, thou art the creator of all lands, and countries, and the Great Green Sea in thy name of KHEPER-TA . Thou art the Bringer of ḤĀPI 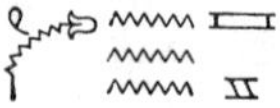 from his source, making to flourish the staff of life.

'Thou makest the staff of life (i.e. grain) to flourish, thou makest the grain which cometh forth from thyself in thy name of NU the Aged 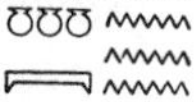 . Thou makest fertile the watery mass of heaven, and makest water to appear on the mountains to give life to men and women in thy name of "ARI-ĀNKH" (Life-Maker).

'Thou art the Babe born daily, the Aged One on the limits of eternity, Aged One traversing eternity, Lord of the Hidden Throne, himself being hidden, Hidden One whose form is unknown, Lord of years, giver of life at will.'

If we were to judge by the above extracts alone, we should have to admit that the EGYPTIANS regarded PTAḤ-TENEN much as we do TEM or RĀ or AMEN, or any other ancient solar god. Nearly all the above series of passages are found in hymns to other gods, whom the EGYPTIANS declared to be self-created, self-existent, almighty creative Powers. But there is one point in which this hymn differs from the other hymns, viz. the mention by the worshipper of PTAḤ-TENEN's aged son RĀ 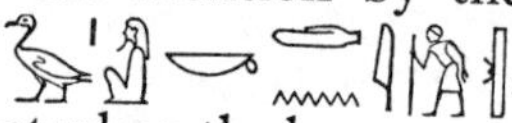, 'thy son aged (or venerable)'. This shows that when the hymn was composed PTAḤ-TENEN was held to be the predecessor of RĀ, and that the god of MEMPHIS was older than the sun-god of HELIOPOLIS. This agrees with MANETHO's statement that HEPHAESTUS (VULCAN) was the first king of EGYPT, and HELIOS, the son of HEPHAESTUS, the second (CORY, *Ancient Fragments*, p. 111, and *The Old Egyptian Chronicle*, p. 136).

All the passages from the hymn quoted above justify us in assuming that the EGYPTIANS regarded PTAḤ-TENEN as a purely material god, but among comparatively modern investigators the first to prove that the assumption of the dynastic theologians was wrong was P. E. JABLONSKI. This writer, who was undoubtedly a very learned man, set out to discuss and describe the character of the gods of EGYPT, and to come to some conclusion about the ancient Egyptian religion. He collected a large number of passages referring to them in the works of classical writers, and he attempted by means of a somewhat limited knowledge of Coptic to explain their names.[1] Many of his conclusions and derivations are wholly incorrect, but he arrived at one very important fact, viz. that among the gods of EGYPT there were some Beings who were invisible and who possessed spiritual natures.[2] To him belongs the credit of calling the attention of scholars to the fact that the EGYPTIANS believed in a spiritual origin for the universe, and that they associated the Eternal Mind and Spirit with PTAḤ, the most ancient god of MEMPHIS, and regarded him as the source of all that is and of all that shall come into being. Many of JABLONSKI'S remarks show that he had arrived at a true conception of the characters of the Egyptian gods, and that the statements of classical writers on these subjects contained more accurate information than Egyptologists generally have admitted. In the first half of the last century LEPSIUS suggested that PTAḤ's nature was spiritual in character, but it is possible that he had read JABLONSKI's work and approved of his view. BRUGSCH was well acquainted with the 'Pantheon Aegyptiorum', for in his *Die Aegyptologie*, LEIPZIG, 1891, p. 167, he speaks of it as 'einem auch heute noch brauchbaren Werke'. From it he may have derived his ideas about an Egyptian πνεῦμα, which he discussed in his *Religion und Mythologie*, published six years earlier. I cannot find that CHAMPOLLION, or DE ROUGÉ, or CHABAS viewed the Egyptian gods as other than material beings or things.

We owe our knowledge of what the Memphite system of theology was to an inscription cut on a large black basalt slab, now preserved in the BRITISH MUSEUM.[3] It was presented to the Museum in 1805 by EARL SPENCER, who obtained it from the ruins of the great

[1] See his *Pantheon Aegyptiorum: de diis eorum commentarius*, Frankfort, MDCCL.

[2] Spiritum aliquem ingenitum, aeternum, omnibus rebus quae existunt prius, qui omnia creaverit, omnia conservet, omnia contineat, omnia permeet atque vivificet, qui fit spiritus totius mundi, hominum vero custos et benefactor', *Prolegomena*, xlvi.

[3] In the old register of objects in the Egyptian Galleries it was numbered 135. Dr. Birch numbered it in his manuscript catalogue 498. This number is preserved in the *Guide to the Sculptures* (London, 1909), but its running number is 797 (p. 220).

temple of PTAḤ at MEMPHIS. The slab was set up as a stele, but was thrown down from its pedestal and was probably walked on by many generations of men or it may have formed part of a wall; a large portion of the hieroglyphic inscription has been obliterated. The unusual arrangement of the text provoked curiosity, and SAMUEL SHARPE[1] published an inaccurate copy of it in his series of inscriptions. The manuscript catalogue made by Dr. BIRCH about the middle of the last century contains a careful copy of many sections of the parts of the inscription which are legible, and to these BIRCH added translations. He made out the true character of the inscription and its date, and in passages like that which describes how OSIRIS was drowned at MEMPHIS he was successful. But he failed to connect the passages in their right sequence. GOODWIN translated[2] a part of the text, and two young students, BRYANT and READ,[3] published comments on the stele. The arrangement of the text was puzzling. BIRCH thought that it was to be read both horizontally and perpendicularly. BREASTED discovered that the text was intended to be read not in the usual way, i.e. *towards* the hieroglyphs, but in a retrograde direction, and published a running translation of the whole text.[4] Several years later the text was republished by ERMAN,[5] who dissected it and analysed its contents with characteristic skill. In 1928 SETHE published what may be regarded as the final edition of the hieroglyphic text with elaborate notes and a German translation, and a most instructive introduction.[6] The text is here dissected and analysed, and the difficulties are handled in a thoroughly efficient manner and explained by an unparalleled wealth of quotations from texts of all periods. The treatment of the contents of the text is unusual, but

[1] *Egyptian Inscriptions from the British Museum and other sources*, London, 1837–41.

[2] 'Upon an Inscription of the reign of Shabaka' (in Chabas, *Mélanges égyptologiques*, Chalon-s-S., 1873 (Sér. 3, tom. i, pp. 247–85).

[3] Read, F. W., and Bryant, A. C., 'A Mythological Text from Memphis' in *Proceedings Soc. Bibl. Arch.*, London, 1901, vol. xxiii, pp. 160–87, and vol. xxiv, pp. 206–16. In the latter volume see a paper by Breasted, p. 300.

[4] Breasted, 'The Mythological Text from Memphis again' (*Proc. Soc. Bibl. Arch.*, vol. xxiv, p. 300).

[5] 'Ein Denkmal memphitischer Theologie' (in the *Sitzungsberichte d. König Preuss. Akad.*, Berlin, 1911, pp. 916–50).

[6] 'Dramatische Texte zu altägyptischen Mysterienspiegeln' (in *Untersuchungen zur Geschichte und Altertumskunde Ägyptens*, Band X, Leipzig, 1928).

very satisfactory. It shows that SETHE not only possesses supreme philological skill, but also a personal religious instinct which has enabled him to read between the lines, and to tell us what the old priest of MEMPHIS really wanted his readers to understand. No other document contains such a full account of the greatest and oldest of all the religious mysteries of the EGYPTIANS, and their esoteric teachings, and none shows more clearly that the 'wisdom of the EGYPTIANS' alluded to by St. PAUL was not an empty thing. The fundamentals of the theology of MEMPHIS are laid bare, and they show that more than five thousand years ago one priesthood at least had been able to formulate the belief that the God who had made Himself and heaven and the earth, and who was the creator of gods as well as men and animals and all that exists, was a Spirit and the Eternal Mind of the universe. And SETHE has shown that the inscription on the stele of MEMPHIS is in reality the libretto of a drama or stage-play which was probably acted when certain important festivals were celebrated at MEMPHIS. Various gods and goddesses in it make speeches, and here and there explanatory remarks are added by unnamed beings. It is in short a sort of religious Miracle-play such as the EGYPTIANS have always loved, and which finds its modern equivalent in the Miracle-plays which are performed on the Birthday of the Prophet (MULID AN-NABI) in all the great towns of EGYPT and ARABIA.

The opening lines of the stele of MEMPHIS state that it was copied from an archetype (written on papyrus or engraved upon wood) which was so worm-eaten that portions of the text were lost. This worm-eaten document was found in the great temple of PTAḤ in MEMPHIS, and the new copy was engraved upon the slab of hard black stone by the command of the Nubian king SHABAKA, the founder of the XXVth dynasty about 712 B.C., who offered it as a votive offering to PTAḤ of MEMPHIS. At first sight it might be thought that a text written at the end of the VIIIth century B.C. has little value in considering the Creation Myths which were already in existence when the union of the Two Egypts took place under MENA and his immediate predecessors. But the archetype must have been written, as the language of the copy proves, in the early part of the dynastic period, say about 4000 B.C. The first part of the text deals with speculations or theories about primitive religion in EGYPT, and the second (lines 53–64) contains a definite statement about the religious system which MENA (?) intended to become current in his newly founded city of MEMPHIS. This second part had, as SETHE pertinently observes (*Dem. Texte*, p. 5), a 'political background'. The founder of MEMPHIS intended his city to supersede HELIOPOLIS as the centre of the kingdoms of the North and South. He determined that his form of religion should oppose fundamentally the system current in HELIOPOLIS, and either to kill it or absorb it. He adopted the local fetish and provided him with a suitable ancestry. His priests adopted the ancient legend of a primeval abyss-god NUNU , and his female counterpart NUNET, or NENET , and made PTAḤ the Eternal Mind which produced them.

The first section of the text contains statements of historical facts, with explanatory remarks on them. TEMU says that PTAḤ (or PTAḤ-TENEN 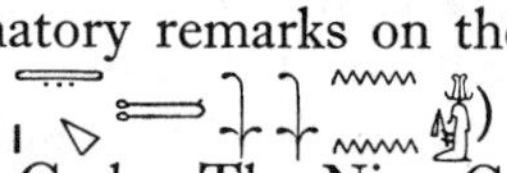) begot himself, and gave birth to the Nine Gods. The Nine Gods assembled in order to judge HORUS and SET. GEBB the Earth-god forbade them to quarrel, and they made SET king of UPPER EGYPT in the place where he was born, viz. SU .[1] And GEBB made HORUS king of LOWER EGYPT in the place where his father [OSIRIS] was drowned, viz. PESESH-T TAUI 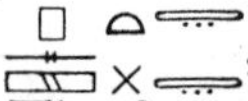, i.e. 'The Half (or Halfway place) of the Two Lands'.[2] The frontier town between the two kingdoms was 'AIAN  in the eastern half of the Memphite nome, near the quarries of TŪRAH. Then GEBB told each brother to depart to the place to which he had been appointed; but it grieved GEBB that the portion of HORUS should only equal that of SET. Then (i.e. much later) he gave HORUS, his son's son, all his inheritance, and HORUS united the kingdoms of the South and the North and became king of all EGYPT, and established himself in the Nome of the Wall 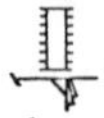, i.e. MEMPHIS.

TEMU, the great god of HELIOPOLIS, was the head of the Nine Gods of that great ancient city, and from l. 48 f. we find that the priesthood of MEMPHIS made PTAḤ the head of the Ennead of

[1] This town was probably situated on the northern frontier of Upper Egypt.
[2] A place in the Memphite nome.

MEMPHIS. Of the eight forms of PTAḤ only four are preserved in SHABAKA'S inscription, viz. (1) 'PTAḤ, who is seated on the Great Throne' , which perhaps refers to the piece of land which he caused to come into being in the primeval abyss. (2) PTAḤ NENU , the FATHER, who begot TEMU. (3) PTAḤ-NAUNET[1] , the MOTHER,[2] who brought forth TEMU. (4) PTAḤ, the GREAT, the Heart and Tongue of the Nine Gods, . These four forms are of special interest, for they show that the priests of PTAḤ proclaimed that their god was certainly the father and mother of TEMU, the head of the Great Company (i.e. Nine) of the gods of HELIOPOLIS, and that he was also the heart and tongue of a Company of gods. If PTAḤ was the father and mother of TEMU he existed in the primeval waters of NENU, and it is probable that his Eight Forms really represented the Eight Primeval Gods of HERMOPOLIS, and that PTAḤ himself was a predecessor or prototype of THOTH. In any case, the priests of PTAḤ maintained in these words their belief that their Company of Gods was the oldest in EGYPT.

From lines 53 and 54 (SETHE, p. 50) it is clear that they claimed a very great deal more than that for their god, for they said that TEMU himself came into being as the *result of a thought* (or idea, or some mental motion) of PTAḤ. Through his heart HORUS came to PTAḤ, and through his tongue THOTH came to PTAḤ. Moreover, PTAḤ, the great and mighty god, made all the gods and their KAU or vital invisible personalities, to inherit his powers. It follows, then, that the gods of the Company of PTAḤ were very different from those of the Company of TEMU of HELIOPOLIS, for they were products of the *spirit* of PTAḤ, and not of the *body* as were the gods of the Company of gods of HELIOPOLIS. The origin of the latter is clearly described in a passage in the Pyramid Texts: SHU and TEFENT owed their existence to an act of masturbation on the part of TEMU in the city of HELIOPOLIS. Writing on the gods of EGYPT

[1] Originally Naunet, but later Nunet or Nut , or . In the earliest times she was the goddess under the earth.

[2] Ptaḥ is actually called the pregnant god .

more than eighty years ago LEPSIUS pointed out that 'PTAḤ was never identified with RĀ, and that he was always regarded as a Spiritual Force (*eine geistige Potenz*), and as such was, at least in the teaching of MEMPHIS, set above RĀ'.[1] This highly spiritual conception of PTAḤ was arrived at by thinking men in the Delta, in the early part of the dynastic period, and shows how very far the EGYPTIANS had travelled in their religious beliefs from the savage theogony of the Heliopolitan sages.

The text (l. 54) goes on to say that the heart and tongue of PTAḤ acquired power over all the other members of the Divine Company, that PTAḤ was the heart in every body, and the tongue in the mouths of all gods, all men, all cattle, and all creeping things, and by thinking with the heart, and commanding with his tongue, whatsoever hath life liveth according to his will.

The Nine Gods of PTAḤ are before him as teeth and lips. The teeth are the seed and the lips are the hands of TEMU. The Nine Gods of TEMU exist through the seed and fingers of PTAḤ. The Nine Gods of PTAḤ are the teeth and lips of this mouth which giveth names to all things, and from which SHU and TEFENT have gone forth.

The Nine Gods have created the sight for the eyes, the hearing for the ears, and the breath for the nose, so that they may make announcements to the heart. The heart it is which arrangeth for every piece of information to come forth, and it is the tongue which reproduceth that which the heart hath thought out. And so the KAU (i.e. male) spirits were made, and the ḤEMSUT (i.e. female) spirits[2] were ordained, through the decrees which were thought out by the heart, and have come forth by the tongue, and they create all food and all provisions. And so righteousness is given unto him that doeth what is beloved, and unrighteousness unto him that doeth what is hated. In short 'Good to the good' and 'evil for the evil' There is no mixture. And life is given unto him that doeth what maketh for peace, and death unto the evil doer (or transgressor). And thus all works and all handicrafts are done (or carried on)—the working of the arms, the walking of the legs, the movements of

[1] Aptly quoted by Sethe, p. 51.

[2] . On the word and its determinative see Sethe, op. cit., p. 62.

the limbs—according to this decree which is decided upon by the heart, and is brought forth by the tongue, and maketh the significance (or importance) of all things.

It came to pass that it was said, He who made TEMU, he who caused the gods to come into being from PTAḤ, TA-TENEN it is who created the gods. All things have proceeded from him, provisions and food, the provisions of the gods, and every kind of good thing. And it will be found and understood that his power is greater than that of the other gods. And so it cometh to pass that having made all things, and all divine words, PTAḤ is content.

The text then goes on to say that it was PTAḤ who createth and maintaineth the local gods: He createth the gods, he maketh [their] towns, he foundeth their nomes, he placeth the gods on their shrines, he maketh to be regular and permanent their offerings, he foundeth their sanctuaries, he establisheth their bodies to the satisfaction of their hearts. And thus the gods enter into their bodies which are [made of] various kinds of wood, and various kinds of stones, and various kinds of earth (i.e. clay, lime, &c.), and other substances, which grow on him,[1] in which they have taken [their] forms.

Then all the gods and their KAU gathered themselves together to PTAḤ in MEMPHIS, the seat of all life, to ḤETPI KHNEMI,[2] i.e. the 'Gracious one', and the 'Kind Protector', the Lord of the Two Lands (i.e. EGYPT). The 'Great Throne' is the granary of PTAḤ-TENEN, (or TANEN), which rejoiceth the heart of the gods who are in the HOUSE of PTAḤ,[3] the Lady of all life, from which the means of subsistence for the Two Lands would be provided. MEMPHIS was to become this granary because OSIRIS was drowned there. It happened that OSIRIS was drowned in his water whilst ISIS and NEPHTHYS saw his drowning take place. They looked on him and were astonished at him. HORUS commanded ISIS and NEPHTHYS to grasp him without delay and to rescue him so that he might not sink. They turned the head straightway (?), and so permitted him

[1] Ptaḥ being an Earth-god, like Gebb.

[2] 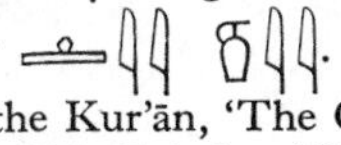. The titles seem to mean something like the two titles of Allâh in the Kur'ān, 'The Compassionate, the Merciful'. According to Sethe, *Hetpi* = 'der Friedliche' or 'Gnädige', and Khnemi suggests the idea of 'rejoicing'.

[3] In fact 'the asylum of the universe'.

to reach land. He entered in through the secret doors in the splendour of the lords of eternity, with the strides of him who riseth up (or shineth) in the horizon on the ways of RĀ in the Great Throne (i.e. MEMPHIS). He uniteth himself to the Court-quarter [of the city], and maketh himself a counterpart of the gods of PTAḤ-TENEN, the lord of years. So OSIRIS came into the land of the 'House of the Prince' on the north side of the land which he had reached. His son HORUS came forth and rose up as king of UPPER EGYPT and as king of LOWER EGYPT in the arms of his father OSIRIS and the gods who were before him [and the gods] who were after him.[1]

The importance of the inscription which SETHE has elucidated with such skill in connexion with the religion of the ancient EGYPTIANS cannot be overestimated. That the theologians of MEMPHIS who lived in the early years of the dynastic period should have been able to conceive of the existence of a Creator who was a spirit, and whose mere thoughts produced the 'gods' and whose tongue named (i.e. produced) everything in earth, air, sea, and sky, is a very remarkable fact. When MENES built the White-walled MEMPHIS and set up in it the temple of PTAḤ and the tomb of OSIRIS, he not only founded a great city but established a highly spiritual religion and the cult of a god of the dead, who promised his worshippers resurrection from the dead and immortality. PTAḤ is mentioned in many places in the Theban *Book of the Dead*, and always as a friend and protector, and he 'opened the mouth' of the deceased as he did that of the gods (chap. xxiii).

In connexion with the dead PTAḤ has two forms: (1) PTAḤ–SEKER  and (2) PTAḤ–SEKER–ASAR . Of the early history of SEKER nothing is known, but there is little doubt that he was an early fetish god, who was worshipped under the form of a hawk. He appears on the monuments in the archaic form of a mummy (like PTAḤ, and OSIRIS, and MIN), with the head of a hawk;

[1] Thus Memphis received the Nile-god and Isis, his female counterpart, and Memphis became the Granary of Egypt. Note that the head-dress of Tanen 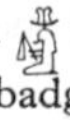 is similar to that of Āndj-ti of Busiris. The horns and plumes were the blazon or badge of the nome of This in which Menes was born; it seems that there was some connexion between This (Abydos) and Memphis. Under the XIIth dynasty the birthplace of Menes became the centre of the cult of Osiris.

seated or standing he holds , , and with both hands. He became the god of the Other World and the necropolis of MEMPHIS (the modern ṢAḲḲÂRAH) at a very early period, and his fetish was enclosed in a hawk-headed shrine which was fixed in a boat-shaped sledge with runners. One end of the sledge was very much higher than the other, and was made in the form of the head of an oryx (?). The sledge was called ḤENNU and it seems that this sledge was drawn round the sanctuary of SEKER at dawn on the days of the festivals of the gods. The ceremony of setting the shrine on its sledge was performed under the direction of the High Priest of MEMPHIS, whose official title was UR-KHERP-ḤEM , i.e. the 'great chief of the hammer (or chisel)'. The ceremony of drawing the ḤENNU round the sanctuary was observed as late as the Ptolemaic period, for PTOLEMY EUERGETES is seen with the cord of the sledge in his hand. In the *Book of the Dead* (chap. xvii, l. 113 f.) SEKER (or SEKRI), the deceased, prays to be delivered from the 'great god who seizeth the soul, and devoureth hearts, and liveth upon offal (or corruption), the guardian of the darkness, and the god of the Seker Boat. In answer to the question, 'Who is this?' the answer is, 'It is SUTI or SMAM-UR, the soul of GEBB'. The name PTAḤ–SEKER shows that SEKER is the name of a very old and very important god of the dead, and that the priests prefixed PTAḤ to it in the same way as they added it to NUN, ḤĀPI, and other ancient gods. They also prefixed 'PTAḤ–SEKER' to TEMU, the great solar god of HELIOPOLIS, to show the pre-eminence of the god of the dead of MEMPHIS, and his antiquity.

PTAḤ–SEKER–ASAR form the remarkable triad of PTAḤ the Creator, SEKER the god of the dead of MEMPHIS (ṢAḲḲÂRAH), and OSIRIS the god of the dead of ABYDOS, or of the nome of THIS in UPPER EGYPT. He is represented in the form of a squat child, or perhaps embryo, with a large bald head like PTAḤ, and thick limbs. On the top of his head he usually has a beetle, but sometimes he is seen wearing horns and plumes. He represents the creative power of KHEPRI, who is symbolized by the beetle. Faience figures of this triune god represent him standing on crocodiles, but the reason for his association with them is not clear. Under the New Empire PTAḤ–SEKER–ASAR figures were made of wood and mounted on pedestals which contain small rolls of inscribed papyri or mummified portions of the bodies of the deceased persons, whose names are inscribed upon them.[1] Texts of the later period show that the APIS Bull was identified with PTAḤ.

THE DECLINE OF THE CULT OF PTAḤ

The cult of PTAḤ represented a protest against the materialistic character of the other forms of the Egyptian Religion, but its highly religious and philosophic conceptions were not acceptable to the people generally; it was at once too great and too simple for them. They were not ready to accept 'eine geistigere Potenz' (LEPSIUS), or a 'göttliche Urgeist' (BRUGSCH), for it left nothing for their imaginations to work on, or their minds to grasp. And many would regard the idea of a spiritual Cause of Causes as a mere product of priestly theorizing. As long as the kings of MEMPHIS held the predominant power in the land the cult of PTAḤ flourished, but under the IVth dynasty the priesthood of RĀ of HELIOPOLIS developed the cult of their god with great success, and the sun-temples of ṢAḲḲÂRAH prove how great that success was. The cult of OSIRIS was making its way into the Upper Country, and the worship of PTAḤ, the Eternal Mind, decayed, and on the downfall of the Old Kingdom at the end of the VIth dynasty, suffered final eclipse.[2] The peculiar *spiritual* character of PTAḤ was not claimed by any of the later priesthoods of EGYPT for their god.

[1] Several of these are described in the British Museum *Guide to the Fourth, Fifth, and Sixth Egyptian Rooms*, London, 1922, p. 28. The pedestals of such figures often have the form of ▭, i.e. *maāt*, like those of Ptaḥ.

[2] Jablonski writes (*Pantheon*, i, p. 52) 'labentibus tamen annis, honos eius et cultus, ut videtur, frigescere et etiam vilescere coepit. Niligenae, in necessitates urgentes, et praesentia commoda, unice intenti, Deorum illorum, a quibus bona hujus vitae exoptata proxime et immediate expectabant, Solis, Lunae, Nili, et similium, cultui totos se consecrarunt, venerationem vero religiosam Mentis aeternae, in loco, coelis omnibus superiori, collocatae, Philosophis relinquendam esse putarunt.' See also Sethe in *Dram. Texte*, p. 51 (note).

XI

OSIRIS THE RIVAL OF RĀ

WHEN the union of the 'Two Lands', i.e. UPPER and LOWER EGYPT, was completed by MENA, the priests of HELIOPOLIS formed the most powerful ecclesiastical body in the country. The cult of HORUS flourished at TEMAI-EN-ḤER, the cult of NEITH at SAÏS, the cult of PTAḤ at MEMPHIS, and the cult of OSIRIS at BUSIRIS, but the cult of the Sun-god of HELIOPOLIS was the greatest of all cults, and the priests of HELIOPOLIS were the richest and most powerful. The position of OSIRIS as king and judge of the dead was firmly established in the minds of all the people in the Delta; his kingdom was placed in the ṬUAT  which was commonly supposed to be situated somewhere under the earth. According to the Papyrus of ANI (chap. clxxv) it was a place airless, waterless, and lightless; there dwelt alike the beautiful and the damned. By a decree of the old Earth-god GEBB the kingdom of OSIRIS was placed in the west, where the dead Sun-god of day passed the night. The priests of HELIOPOLIS assigned the boat, or boats, of their Sun-god RĀ to be the final abode of the sun-worshippers, where there never could be any darkness or gloom of night. They would be ever in the light, and would live on light, and array themselves in light, and share the existence of RĀ. The solar cult was adopted by the king and his Court, and by the high officials of all classes; in fact it was the cult of the Egyptian aristocracy. The heaven of RĀ was placed by his priests in the stars and in the sky. Through some unknown impulse under the IVth dynasty the priests of OSIRIS modified their views and stated that their ṬUAT was situated in the sky, and that their god OSIRIS was its king. Hence OSIRIS and RĀ became rivals, and in spite of strenuous resistance on the part of the priests of RĀ the Osirians made good their claim for their god. They transferred the ṬUAT or ṬAT  from the earth to the sky, perhaps to NUT  or nether heaven mentioned in Pyr. § 149 *b*. The 'imperishable stars' of RĀ[1]

[1] , Pyr. § 749 *e*.

became 'the followers of OSIRIS'. The 'fields of heaven become green' through OSIRIS, who was the NILE, who was drowned in the river. And OSIRIS becomes the host of the souls of the dead kings in the place of RĀ. OSIRIS also seized the ferry-boat of RĀ, and he commanded its steersman ḤER-F ḤA-F to go and fetch king PEPI (Pyr. § 1201 *a*). RĀ constructed a Ladder for the use of his followers, but this also OSIRIS seized, and he him-

Ḥer-f Ḥa-f.

self went up into heaven by means of it. This 'Ladder of the god' (Pyr. § 971) was set up and held in possession by RĀ and the Old HORUS (Pyr. § 472), or by HORUS and SET, and it was carried by IAḤES and ṬEṬUN, gods of NUBIA, and SEPṬ of the Eastern Delta (Pyr. § 994). Finally OSIRIS himself becomes the Ladder, and souls ascended by him into heaven.[1]

On the other hand, we find passages in the Pyramid Texts which show that RĀ asserted his authority (§ 350 *a*) and associated OSIRIS with the dead, from whom the king had to be protected (§ 251 *b*). The 'Four Sons of HORUS' who are always seen in connexion with OSIRIS in the funerary papyri were originally solar gods, and had nothing to do with OSIRIS. As solar gods they may have been the 'four gods, the sons of GEBB' (Pyr. § 1510) or the 'sons of TEM, the children of NUT', who never see corruption (Pyr. § 2057). We also find that OSIRIS is grouped with 'HORUS of the gods', HORUS of SHESMET , and HORUS of the East (Pyr. §§ 1085 and 1086).

[1] See the picture of this Ladder in the Papyrus of Ani, sheet 22.

The Pyramid Texts prove that OSIRIS usurped the position of RĀ before the downfall of the Old Kingdom. Under dynasties VII–XI the cult of OSIRIS made its way southwards with great rapidity, and under the XIIth dynasty it was established as firmly at ABYDOS as it had been at BUSIRIS. The birth-place of OSIRIS is unknown, and there are doubts about the place where he met his death. The Pyramid Texts say that he was killed by SET at NEṬIT , a village or district 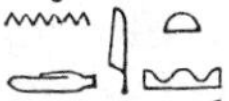 (Pyr. § 1008 *c*) near ABYDOS; the text on the stele of SHABAKA says he was drowned at MEMPHIS. On the other hand, he is called 'the dweller in ANU' (HELIOPOLIS, Pyr. § 181 *a*). For many centuries the EGYPTIANS believed that OSIRIS was buried at ABYDOS, and a late tradition asserts that he was buried at PHILAE.

The old name of the district of ABYDOS was 'TA-UR' 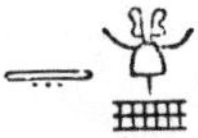, i.e. the 'Great Land' (Pyr. § 627 *b*) otherwise . Later the second sign was written  which resembles closely , the old symbol of the eastern kingdom of ṬEṬU (BUSIRIS). The two feathers of the oldest sign recall those of ĀNDJ-TI (see above, p. 268) the old symbol of ṬEṬU (BUSIRIS). And the forms  and  recall the streamer of the symbol ĀNDJ-TI. The object under the pair of horns was the coffer which contained the head of OSIRIS, and as this is found in the Pyramid Texts it seems that the belief that ABYDOS contained the tomb of OSIRIS was well established under the Old Kingdom. The cenotaph of OSIRIS found by AMÉLINEAU, though not early, has its own special significance and importance.[1] The priests of OSIRIS made their god usurp all the powers and attributes of the very ancient Jackal-god ANPU, whose titles were KHENTI AMENTT, , i.e. 'Foremost one of AMENTT' (the Underworld) and KHENTI BAIU AMENTIU , 'Foremost one of those who are in AMENTI' (i.e. the West, the realm of the dead). OSIRIS also usurped the position of AN-ḤER 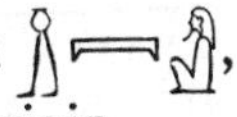, an ancient Sky-god of the district, probably of LIBYAN origin.

Under the patronage of the kings of the XIIth dynasty OSIRIS attained to a position of power and importance hitherto unknown;

[1] *Le Tombeau d'Osiris*, Paris, 1899; also *Les Nouvelles Fouilles*, Angers, 1893.

he became the great Ancestor-god of the country, and his career as the national god of EGYPT began about that time. On stelae of this period (Middle Kingdom) OSIRIS is called 'Governor of AMENTI', 'Lord of Life', 'Prince of Eternity', and the texts say, 'that the souls of the dead flocked to ABYDOS in order to be blessed by the god and to eat bread with him.[1] A considerable number of facts about the annual OSIRIS Miracle play which was performed at ABYDOS have been given us by the high official I-KHERT-NEFERT; the following description has been compiled from the inscription on his stele.

THE OSIRIS DRAMA WHICH WAS PERFORMED ANNUALLY AT ABYDOS

The performance of this drama was the principal event of the year at ABYDOS, and in it an attempt was made to reconstruct the history of the tragedy of the death of OSIRIS, and illustrate his resurrection. The opening scene represented OSIRIS setting out in his Neshmet Boat to attack SET, his brother. The procession was headed by one who represented UP-UATU  (i.e. the 'Opener of the ways'), a very ancient god of ABYDOS who was incarnate in a jackal or wolf, and was held to be the son of OSIRIS. Behind him came the boat containing the figure of the god, and a company of priests, some of whom made magical passes to keep away enemies from the divine boat, and behind them came the crowd. The boat was attacked by a mob of people who acted the part of enemies of OSIRIS, but UP-UATU repulsed them, and the procession moved on again. Soon after this a great mob of men, armed with sticks and cudgels, attacked OSIRIS, and they were met by another great mob of men, similarly armed, but they were defenders of OSIRIS, and a sort of free fight took place. This fight was intended to represent the battle which took place in prehistoric times between the followers of OSIRIS and those of SET. This sham fight often degenerated into a serious fight in which many heads and limbs were broken. After a time OSIRIS was missed, for he was not in his boat, and no one knew what had become of him, or

[1] See Lepsius, *Denkmäler*, Bd. II, pl. 135, and the excellent monograph on the text by Schäfer in Sethe, *Untersuchungen*, Bd. IV, No. 2, Leipzig, 1904.

whether he was dead or not. Then a man specially chosen was supposed to set out with a party of assistants in search of OSIRIS, whether living or dead. The search was supposed to last three days, and meanwhile the fight between the rival factions was renewed at frequent intervals. And loud cries of lamentation resounded throughout the town, for crowds of weeping women who beat their faces and breasts bewailed the loss of OSIRIS, and also the wounds and other injuries which were inflicted on their husbands and sons during the fight.

The search for OSIRIS was successful, and the official I-KHERT-NEFERT says that he traced the god by his footsteps. In due course he came to the place where OSIRIS was lying dead on a dyke at NEṬIT whereon he had been cast by SET, who had killed him. But ANUBIS had already found the body. According to an ancient legend in the Pyramid Texts the body of OSIRIS was found by the goddesses ISIS and NEPHTHYS, who had taken the form of swallows or some other kind of bird, and their cries were so loud that they attracted the attention of the gods of PE-TEP, a city in the Delta.[1] In the OSIRIS Drama women played the parts of ISIS and NEPHTHYS. For some reason the Neshmet Boat of OSIRIS was not available for transporting his body to ABYDOS, but ISIS appealed to THOTH for help, and THOTH was sent in a boat to take the body of OSIRIS to the town. A model of the boat of THOTH containing a figure of THOTH seated in a shrine was carried along in the procession. Scenes connected with the mummification of OSIRIS were acted by players who represented ISIS and NEPHTHYS, HORUS and THOTH, and ANPU (or ANUBIS), the apothecary of the gods. ISIS recited the spells which she had been taught by THOTH. NEPHTHYS assisted in swathing the body together with the official priests, and ANUBIS produced the necessary unguents and medicaments. When the mummy was ready for burial I-KHERT-NEFERT provided the boat called 'KHĀ-EM-MAĀT' which was to take it to the tomb. This boat had a cabin shrine, and in it sat the god arrayed in his splendid apparel, which likewise was produced at the cost of I-KHERT-NEFERT. Then the pious official says, 'I directed the ways of the god to his tomb in PEQER'. The exact position of PEQER, or rather of the tomb of OSIRIS, is not known, but the position of the great

[1] This suggests that Neṭit was in the Delta.

plain of ABYDOS which contained the tombs of several of the kings of the Ist dynasty lies about a mile and a half from the great temple of OSIRIS. This is called by the ARABS, UMM AL-KA'ĀB, i.e. 'Mother of pots', because of the large quantity of ancient Egyptian pottery which has been found there. Among the tombs of the Ist dynasty found there was one of a king whose name sign was in 1900 read 'KHENT', and it seems certain that the EGYPTIANS of the XVIIIth dynasty believed this tomb to be that of OSIRIS. The EGYPTIANS of a later period thought the same, for they placed there the cenotaph of OSIRIS which was discovered by AMÉLINEAU.

The next great scene in the OSIRIS Drama was the avenging of the murder of OSIRIS. Legend declared that a great fight between the followers of OSIRIS and those of SET had taken place in very early times, and that the enemies of OSIRIS were routed with great slaughter; OSIRIS himself was killed. Later, when HORUS, the son of OSIRIS, had grown up, he collected an army and set out to take vengeance on SET and his followers. In the fight which followed the SETITES were defeated with great slaughter, and many prisoners were taken. These prisoners were beheaded, and their blood was used for watering the ground of the sanctuary of OSIRIS. In the OSIRIS Drama a sham fight took place. I-KHERT-NEFERT played the part of HORUS, the avenger of his father, and he and his men attacked those who played the part of the SETITES and routed them, and he says, 'I avenged UN-NEFER on the day of the Great Battle. I overthrew all his enemies on the dyke of NEṬIT'. The last and greatest scene of all represented 'OSIRIS KHENTI AMENTI, the Lord of ABYDOS' returning to his palace or temple as a 'living god', and seated in his Neshmet Boat. ISIS, HORUS, ANUBIS, and other gods were believed to have reconstituted the body of OSIRIS in the chamber of embalmment, and the Old HORUS and his Four Sons to have revivified that body. It follows as a matter of course that the OSIRIS Drama was performed in many of the capitals of the nomes of EGYPT, and it is probable that wherever a shrine of OSIRIS existed the priests took care to have some scenes of the play acted by the people generally. A list of these shrines is preserved in the Papyrus of NU (sheet 15), and in the Papyrus of IUAU (Plate IX). In the OSIRIS Drama briefly described above I-KHERT-NEFERT acted as the 'Chief of the Mysteries' and played the part of the Old HORUS throughout. He ends his inscription with these words: 'I caused him [i.e. OSIRIS] to set out in the Boat which bore his Beauty. I made the hearts of the dwellers in the East to expand with joy, and I caused gladness to be in the dwellers in the West, when they saw [his] Beauty as it landed at ABYDOS bringing OSIRIS KHENTI AMENTI, the Lord of ABYDOS to his palace.'

XII

THE JUDGEMENT OF THE DEAD, AND THE WEIGHING OF THE HEART BEFORE OSIRIS

WRITERS on the religion of ancient EGYPT from MASPERO downwards have never failed to point out that even at the highest stage of its development it was little better than that of a half-civilized or semi-barbarous people. And they have claimed that owing to the unconquerable belief of the EGYPTIANS in the power of magic, and the efficacy of magical rituals, and ceremonies, and formulae, and their cult of sacred animals, and fetishes, and purely cosmic gods it possessed little or no ethical or moral influences upon the minds and characters of those who were its closest adherents. But in saying this they have said too much, and fortunately this fact can be easily proved from the earliest inscriptions of the Old Kingdom. We can only *assume* that the predynastic EGYPTIANS possessed what we call a 'moral sense', because, as they could not write, they have left no written records to enable us to speak with certainty. But the Pyramid Texts make it clear that the ideas of 'right and wrong', and 'truth and falsehood', did not suddenly spring into existence in the minds of the EGYPTIANS as the result of the union of the Two EGYPTS, and that even the predynastic EGYPTIANS never lacked them. From time immemorial in EGYPT moral goodness, right-doing, and righteousness in word and deed were held to be pleasing both to gods and men, and wrong-doing of every kind was displeasing to the gods and was detested by men. In the Memphite Code of Religion which must have been drawn up soon after the founding of MEMPHIS by MENES we have the following:[1]

He who doeth that which is loved, to him life is given, the possessor of peace.
He who doeth that which is hated, to him death is given, the possessor of transgressions.

A somewhat similar idea is expressed in the phrase 'To the doer of sin sin is given; righteousness is given to him who cometh there-

[1] Sethe, *Dram. Texte*, p. 64.

with' (DÉVAUD, quoted by SETHE); in other words, 'sin to the sinner, righteousness to the righteous'.

The EGYPTIAN, who was a keen student of his own interests, whether material or spiritual, decided at a very early period that if he lived a righteous life here upon earth it would not only assist him in temporal affairs, here and now, but would stand to his credit in the hereafter. There is no reason to think that the EGYPTIAN was satisfied or thought that the mere exercise of the virtues and the living of a righteous life would have no beneficial result for him in the world to come. Viewing such evidence as we have it seems that the EGYPTIAN at this period possessed a feeling, which was born with him and was an integral part of his spiritual nature, of reverence, or even fear, of a great unknown God to whom he felt it to be his natural duty to worship. In all periods the AFRICAN has always believed that such a Being existed, but that He was too great and too remote to trouble about human affairs. Attached to this belief was an unconquerable feeling that his life would not end with the death of the body, and that he would either continue or renew his life in some unknown place indefinitely. The pyramids and funerary temples which line the western bank of the NILE from ṢAḲḲÂRAH southwards are proofs not only of his invincible craving for immortality, but also of his deep-seated consciousness of and reverence for the Being Whom he called NETER or NETHER. Under the Memphite religion the spirituality of the EGYPTIAN'S religion reached a height which was rarely reached and never added to under the Middle and New Kingdoms, and it left an indelible mark on his architecture, sculpture, arts, and handicrafts.

Even under the Old Kingdom attempts seem to have been made to distinguish between NETER (𓊹𓏤 God) and NETER Ā (𓊹𓉻 Great God) and the cosmic gods like RĀ. In the Pyramid Texts two great cosmic gods are often referred to and are sometimes mentioned by name, i.e. RĀ and OSIRIS; the latter was, probably, in the predynastic period a star-god, or even a solar god. Men, including the king, and gods were subjected to some kind of examination in respect of their moral qualities, and were judged in a celestial court by a supreme judge. As the Pyramid Texts reflected the beliefs and theology of ON (HELIOPOLIS) that supreme judge was, at the beginning, RĀ, but long before the end of the Vth dynasty his supremacy was challenged by the votaries of OSIRIS. Whoever the judge was, he was held to be almighty, righteous, and just. As the actual personification of righteousness and justice all moral worth and virtue were associated with him who dwelt in righteousness and whose every action was directed by MAĀT[1]. The fundamental idea underlying this word seems to be 'straight', 'straightness', and hence what is straight, what is right, rectitude, integrity, uprightness, genuineness, true, truth, righteousness, law, both moral and physical. The divine or heavenly judge lived, reigned, ruled, and judged by MAĀT, or as we may say the LAW. His attribute of absolute impartiality was personified under the form of the goddess MAĀT 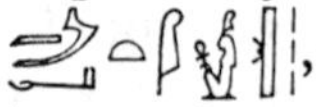, or , or , who was the equivalent of our 'JUSTICE'. She appears as such in Pyr. § 1774 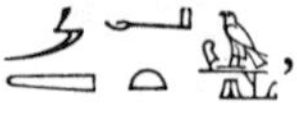, wearing the feather of MAĀT.

The primitive EGYPTIANS assigned to this righteous Judge a court in which he sat and tried cases and delivered his judicial decisions. The day on which a trial took place was called 'the day of the hearing of words'  (Pyr. § 1027), and a right or 'true decision'  is mentioned in Pyr. § 1776. The Memphite theologians speak of a celestial court which preceded that of RĀ or OSIRIS, for they tell us that the Earth-god GEBB sat in judgement on the quarrel between SET and HORUS; he decided that SET was to rule over UPPER EGYPT, and HORUS over LOWER EGYPT. SET refused to accept this ruling and continued to bring charges and accusations against HORUS and OSIRIS, for he wished to be the king of all EGYPT. Finally the whole kingdom was given to OSIRIS, and OSIRIS's son HORUS inherited it, and SET was transferred to the sky, where he became the god of storms and thunder. Now we do not know where 'the Great god' held his court, or to what kind of tribunal the kings mentioned in the Pyramid Texts had to submit, but in several passages we have definite proofs that they ascended into heaven *because of* their moral worth and religious excellence.

[1] The oldest form of *maāt* is 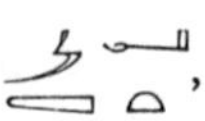, but in later times we find  instead of . It is possible that  may represent some tool or object used in measuring by artisans, and so it may be the equivalent of our foot rule or the old measuring reed.

When a man gained his case in a court of law on earth, and the verdict was given in his favour, he was declared to be *maā kheru* 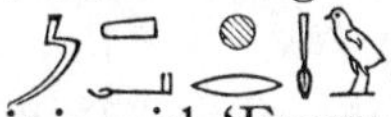, i.e. 'true of voice, or word'.[1] Thus of MERIENRĀ it is said, 'Every god taketh the hand of this MERIENRĀ in heaven, or the sky, and conducteth him to the house of HORUS which is in the cool water (*qebhu*); his KA is *maā kheru* 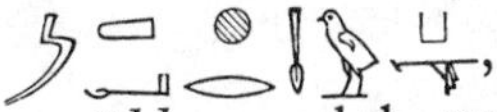, before GEBB' (Pyr. § 1327). Again, 'This PEPI is *maā kheru* and the KA of this PEPI is *maā kheru*' (Pyr. § 928). As HORUS is said to be '*maā kheru*' (Pyr. § 2089) and also that his four sons 'live in *maāt*' (Pyr. § 1483) it would seem that even the Sun-god was judged in a celestial court, and that by virtue of his acquittal his sons acquired some special degree of righteousness. In Pyr. § 815 a mention is made of an *ānkhet* of *maāt* , on the top of which is HORUS. Apart from being declared *maā kheru*, i.e. 'true of word, or voice', the king had to possess *maāt* and the loyal reverence of a vassal for the god. In Pyr. § 1219 it is said, 'Grant thou this PEPI to sit down by his *maāt*; this PEPI standeth up by his *amakh*, i.e. reverent devotion. This PEPI standeth up, he is master of *amakh* before thee, as HORUS was master (or carried off) the house of his father out of the hand of the brother of his father (i.e. uncle) SET before GEBB'.

The EGYPTIANS of the Old Kingdom expressed the idea of 'sin' by the word *asfet* ; and the following words: 'UNAS hath come into the Island of SASA (i.e. Fire); UNAS setteth truth (*maāt*) therein in the seat of *asfet*' (Pyr. § 265), show clearly that *asfet* means the exact opposite of *maāt* or truth, and may be translated by 'untruth, lies, falsehood, evil, sin, rebellion, fault, deceit', &c. In later texts the ASFETTIU , or , are the rebel fiends of the ṬUAT or rebellious men and women disloyal alike to God and man. A god called ATER ASFET 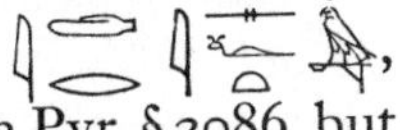, i.e. 'Destroyer of rebellion, or sin', is mentioned in Pyr. § 2086, but nothing is known of his functions or his genesis. Details of the actual process of judging the king are wanting in the Pyramid Texts, and no mention is made of the weighing of the heart in

[1] Or 'truth-speaker'; these words are often translated 'triumphant'. They indicate that the other party in the case was a liar.

the Great Scales in presence of the Judge. The first *pictorial* use of the Scales is in the Theban papyri. As already said it is natural to assume that the Judge was RĀ, the Sun-god. But there are passages in which it is said that it is OSIRIS who acts as Judge. MAĀT, or truth, is closely associated with RĀ, and each of his two boats was called MAĀT (Pyr. § 1785), and the goddess MAĀT was the daughter of RĀ, but in Pyr. § 1520 we have 'OSIRIS hath risen up (or is crowned), holy in the SEKHEM, exalted in the Lord of MAĀT'. And in Pyr. § 964 it is said:

> PEPI cometh to thee, the Lord of Heaven,
> This PEPI cometh to thee, OSIRIS.

And the power and overlordship of a god who must be OSIRIS is described in these remarkable words: 'Thou carriest heaven in the palm of thy hand, thou hast laid down the earth as the place of thy sandal';[1]  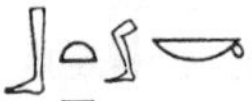 (Pyr. § 2067).

From what is said above it is clear that under the Vth dynasty the EGYPTIANS had in their minds the idea of a celestial court in which their kings were tried by a just Judge, and that their moral worth had to be recognized by that Judge and his assistants before they were admitted into heaven. In other words it was recognized that kings, as well as men, were held to be responsible for their actions. Whether the Judge, the 'Great God', was RĀ or OSIRIS, or even the 'god of the city', mattered little, for men believed that 'The God (NETER) judged the right'.[2] The 'Maxims of PTAḤ–ḤETEP' contain many references to a god (NETER) who, although his ways were inscrutable, nevertheless, paid heed to the moral behaviour of men, and loved obedience and hated disobedience. A man is warned by PTAḤ–ḤETEP not to terrify men because God is hostile to such, and a 'good son is declared to be a gift of [that] God'. How far people in general made their lives to conform to the teachings of such moralists as PTAḤ–ḤETEP is not easy to decide. The common law running in every community in EGYPT prevented men from overt acts of violence, robbery, and murder, and any

[1] Compare Isa. lxvi. 1, 'The heaven *is* my throne, and the earth *is* my footstool'; see also Acts vii. 49.

[2] 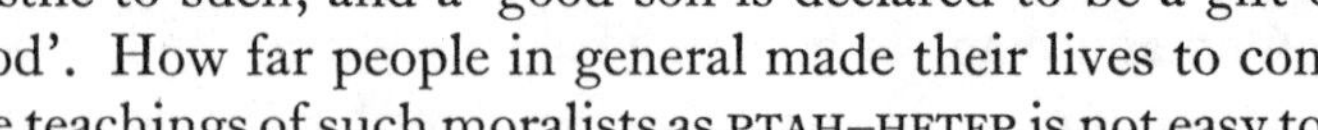

breaches of the laws which protected the irrigation works and temple property would be promptly dealt with by the police.

One high official PEPI-NEKHT has left us in his inscription[1] a valuable statement showing what he considered to be a highly moral life, and he tells us *why* he led that life. After one of the lists of his titles he describes himself as a devotee or reverer of the 'Great god', without giving that god a name. PEPI-NEKHT was a caravan master of SUN-T (SYENE) and a great overlord of the region of the First Cataract. He made two very successful campaigns in NUBIA on behalf of King PEPI II (VIth dynasty) and he led a punitive expedition into the country by the RED SEA in order to obtain the body of a high official who was killed by the natives whilst he was building a ship in order to sail to the land of PUNT, to the south of EGYPT. He says:

'I speak what is good, repeating what is liked (or generally approved of). I never at any time uttered anything harmful to a man of power (or one in authority) [causing him] to attack any people, in order that it might be of advantage to me before the Great God. I gave bread to the hungry man, and clothing to the naked man. I never decided a case wherein two brothers were concerned in such a manner as to strip a son of the possessions of his father. I was one who was the beloved of his father, the favourite of his mother, and the beloved of his brethren and his sisters.'[1]

Here we have a pleasant description of one of the old feudal lords of ELEPHANTINE and SYENE, and who was, like MEKHU and SABEN, a keeper of the 'Gate of the South', i.e. the EGYPTIAN SÛDÂN. From this it is easy to visualize the enterprising Master of Caravans, capable, resourceful, and courageous, who, although he had a considerable armed force at his disposal, managed his business with discretion and tact and by means of the soft word and courteous behaviour avoided friction with his equals, neighbours, and subordinates. And he was, moreover, a God-fearing and a charitable man, and like the old independent shaykhs of ASYÛT and MINYAH of our own times kept open house where the poor and the destitute might come at any time of the day and obtain food, and find a place to sleep at any hour of the night. As to his personal morality, it was probably no different from that of the Egyptian official of all periods, that is he kept a *harîm* and his dealings with women were

[1] For the hieroglyphic text see Sethe, *Urkunden des Alten Reichs*, ii, p. 132.

of a promiscuous character. The ancient EGYPTIANS never held the views about chastity and continence which are common among modern Western peoples, but their devotion to sexual pleasures was due more often to the craving for children than to personal love of voluptuousness. Plurality of wives and concubines was the result of the views which the EGYPTIANS, in common with many African peoples in all periods of their history, held about the segregation of pregnant wives and the long period which they gave to the suckling and rearing of their children during the first two years after their birth. Polygamy and concubinage were never regarded as breaches of moral or religious law, and the EGYPTIANS in their life after death were held to be entitled to possess wives, just as they were supposed to eat and to drink and to hunt animals and snare fish and birds. But we hear nothing of such wives producing offspring.

The inscription in the pyramid of UNAS affords a good example of the manner in which sexual indulgence was regarded by moralists and priests under the IVth dynasty. In § 265, *b* and *c*, it is said, 'UNAS cometh to the Island (or Lake) of SASA.'[1] UNAS giveth *Maā* (i.e. law or justice) therein in the place of *asfet* (i.e. lawlessness or injustice or sin)'. In this Island, or Lake, or City riots and rebellion had broken out among the souls who were condemned to live there because their supply of food had not been provided according to the god's decree. In making UNAS establish law and order therein the scribes made him the substitute of RĀ, the righteous judge and a representative of high moral not to say religious worth. Yet in another passage (§ 123 *a–c*) it is said, 'UNAS hath had union with MUIT' . UNAS hath smelled the odour of ISIS. . . . UNAS hath had union with a maiden . . . she hath given food to UNAS, and hath served him as a wife on this day'. The priests were thus ready to provide the newcomer into heaven with a wife who was also able to provide him with refreshments. In yet another passage (§ 510 *a–d*) this king of moral worth is

[1] 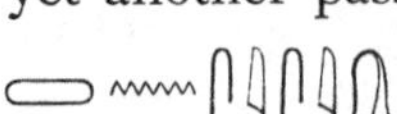. In the later texts we find that the Lake of Serser (*sic*) 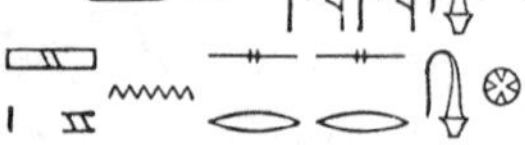 (Budge, *Egyptian Heaven and Hell*, ii. pp. 228–31) was a region of fire in which a certain number of souls had been condemned to live by Rā.

described as 'a man of seed' , in fact a 'stallion of a man', and the text goes on to say, 'He carries off women from their husbands to the place he willeth whensoever he hath a mind to do so'. On the other hand, there was some place in the Underworld where sexual pleasures were not to be obtained. The scribe ANI in chapter clxxv of the Theban *Book of the Dead* complains to TEMU that he has arrived in some region where there was no water and no air; it was a deep, vast place shrouded in thick darkness wherein no love-making could be indulged. He prays that glory may be given to him instead of water, air, and love-making, and says that he prefers peace of heart to cakes and beer.

In addition to the Pyramid Texts and such moral writings as the *Maxims of Ptaḥ-Ḥetep* it is probable that a work similar in character to the Coffin Texts and the Theban *Book of the Dead*, and divided into chapters, existed under the Old Kingdom. This view is supported not only by the mention of certain 'Chapters' in the Pyramid Texts themselves (e.g. The 'Chapter of the Righteous', which was recited by RĀ himself), but by statements in the rubrics of chapters lxiv and XXX B. The rubric of the former chapter in the Papyrus of NU says that it was found in the foundations of the shrine of ḤENNU in the reign of SEMTI-ḤESEP-TI (Ist dynasty) by a master-mason who carried it away as a marvellous object which had never before been seen. The rubric of chapter XXX B states that it was found in the city of KHEMENU (HERMOPOLIS) inscribed on a slab of metal, in letters of real lapis-lazuli, in the reign of MENKAURĀ (MYCERINUS, IVth dynasty), by prince ḤERṬAṬAF, the son of KHUFU (CHEÔPS). Chapter XXX BB forms the prayer which the deceased prays when he stands by the side of the Scales of Judgement in the Hall of the MAĀTI goddesses in the presence of OSIRIS. This prayer was cut on the base of the green stone scarab (the so-called 'Heart Scarab') which, mounted in copper with a silver ring for attachment, was laid either on the breast of the deceased or placed inside his body by the heart. The scarab and the text engraved on it were regarded as forming a most powerful amulet.

The monuments and literature of the dynastic EGYPTIANS proves beyond all doubt that the belief that they would be judged after death existed in some form or other in their minds from the remotest period of their history. At first it was vague and undefined, but as they advanced in civilization and culture it assumed a very definite form, and the more definite and certain it became, the more it ruled their lives and regulated their actions. The 'Teaching of King KHATI' in no uncertain words urges a man to live and act in such a way that he will be able to prove to the god of the Judgement that he is a righteous man, and to justify himself by showing that he has learned the Law, and has carried its precepts into practice. A man must remember that everything on earth lasts for a little time only and passes away speedily. And all men pass away. Speak with discretion and wisdom, for words are mightier than any act of war; rule righteously, render justice to gentle and simple alike. Rear up monuments in honour of God, and thereby will thy name be perpetuated. Visit the temple regularly, eat there, and contribute liberally to the offerings and sacrifices made there. Give according to thy means. Fulfil the Law and deal justly with all men for thereby shalt thou abide on the earth.[1] [Remember] the DJADJAU who judge transgressors.

Green stone 'heart-scarab' inscribed with the opening words of Chapter XXX B of the Theban *Book of the Dead*. It was made for the royal-scribe Nekht-Amen (British Museum).

'Let it be known to thee that there will be no compassion in them on the day of the judgement of the evil-doing man, at the hour when the ordinnances are being carried into effect. It is an awful thing for the sinner to be made to recognize the sin which he hath committed. Fill not thy heart (or mind) [with the thought of] the length of [thy] years, for the DJADJAU look upon a whole lifetime as an hour, their opportunity [for doing this is] after death, and they set his (i.e. a man's) qualities before him like a wall (?). Moreover, existence there is for ever. He who putteth aside from him [the remembrance of] this [fact] is a fool. If the man who attaineth to this hath

1 

committed no sins his existence there is like that of NETER (i.e. God, or the God), and he marcheth on like the Lords who are everlasting.'

This description of the searching character of the Judgement is found in paragraph xiii of the 'Teaching which King KHATI wrote for his son MERIKARĀ' (IXth or Xth dynasty) and nothing like it is found in the texts of the Middle or New Kingdoms. The god referred to is, of course, OSIRIS, who already under the Old Kingdom was recognized as the 'great god, the lord of the judging of words',[1] the 'great god, the lord of MAĀT',[2] i.e. the Righteous or Just God, and the 'lord of heaven'. The Pyramid Texts (§ 954) show that this Just God possessed registers of the deeds of men which were carefully kept by THOTH and SESHETA, and according to these records the hearts of men were judged.

After the downfall of the Old Kingdom the cult of OSIRIS increased greatly, and its votaries, and perhaps missionaries, made their way into UPPER EGYPT, where their doctrine seems to have found great favour. The cult of OSIRIS did away with the exclusive character of heaven, which was no longer a home for the gods and the kings who were the incarnations of the Sun-god on earth, and it offered a life after death to every follower of OSIRIS. The doctrine of OSIRIS was perhaps greater as a moral than a purely religious force, but it was greater still as an edict of the priesthoods. The people generally loved to think of OSIRIS as having once lived and reigned upon earth, and the many myths dealing with his murder and death, and the persecution of his wife by SET, and his triumph after his trial in the Judgement Hall of the great gods, appealed both to their imaginations and their religious sentiments. The dramatized versions of such myths which were enacted during the great Osirian[3] festivals were, it would seem, the most popular forms of amusements for the people; the only festivals which approached them in popularity were those of the god MENU. The resurrection of OSIRIS was the distinguishing feature of the cult of the god. He was the first-fruits of the dead, and every worshipper of OSIRIS based his hope of resurrection and a life after death upon the resurrection of OSIRIS.[4] No other cult offered the EGYPTIAN

1 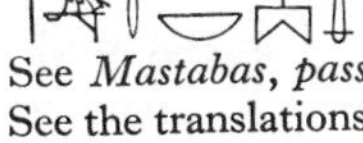 Mariette, *Mastabas*, p. 230.

2 See *Mastabas, passim.*

3 See above, chapter xi.

4 See the translations in Part II, of this work.

such rewards as OSIRIS could give, for it attached great importance to the value of his material body as well as the substantial rewards of a resurrection and a life after death which would be prolonged indefinitely.

In things material as well as spiritual the EGYPTIAN was never slow to seek his own advantage. The cult of OSIRIS also gave a man the power of securing resurrection and a future life by means of his own efforts. The moral obligations of the cult were patent to all, and by performing such obligations a man was able to *justify* himself, and, as it were, to insist on receiving the promised rewards. The more a man's life and works and words conformed to the Code of OSIRIS, the greater was his power to *justify* himself. All this is made clear and certain by chapter cxxv of the Theban Recension of the *Book of the Dead*. The essentials for justification were truth, justice, and honesty in word and deed. The votary of OSIRIS was allowed to use magic, so dear to every EGYPTIAN, in his endeavours to effect the preservation of his material body and the attainment of life after death. Magical names and words of power, magical drawings, amulets, magical ritual and spells, the cult of OSIRIS permitted the use of all these. The cult of OSIRIS was so popular that it developed into a social system, and became what might be called the 'Religion of EGYPT'.

With the materials at present available it is impossible to construct a connected history of OSIRIS, and to describe the growth of the various phases of the life of the god. Such evidence as we have suggests that at one time or another he was regarded (1) as a star-god, (2) the home or abiding place of the Eye of HORUS (i.e. the Old HORUS, or the sun in the daytime), (3) a celebrated local fetish in the Eastern Delta, (4) the god of the NILE and therefore the source of all vegetation and the food of man and beast, (5) the Sun-god *par excellence*, (6) a deified king of all EGYPT and successor of the Old HORUS, ḤER-UR, &c. But it was the myths which grew up about the events in the life of OSIRIS, the old king of EGYPT, which formed the foundation of the widespread and popular cult of OSIRIS, and made it to travel and establish itself in every place from one end of EGYPT to the other, literally from the MEDITERRANEAN to ELEPHANTINE. The EGYPTIANS had no doubt about the place of the birth of OSIRIS, viz. BUSIRIS, where he was given the insignia of the great god of the nome, but opinion among them was sharply divided as to the place of his death and the manner of it. According to Memphite doctrine he was drowned near MEMPHIS, and according to a widespread tradition at ABYDOS he was slain near that city, and was found lying dead on the bank at NEṬIT. Under the Old Kingdom his tomb was said to be both at MEMPHIS and ABYDOS,[1] and in later times the priests of PHILAE declared that OSIRIS was

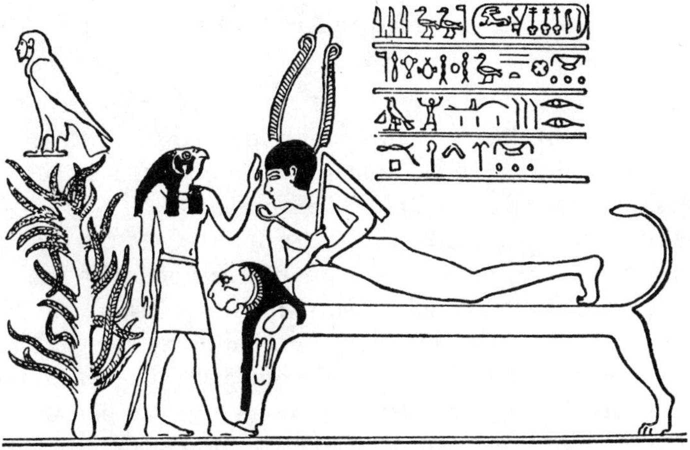

The resurrection of Osiris as shown at Abydos.

buried on their island, and many towns claimed to possess relics of him in their sanctuaries. Egyptian theologians did not value accuracy of detail as regards facts which we should regard as essential, or vital, for they had no means of arriving at the truth.

The establishment of the cult of OSIRIS at ABYDOS was the sign that all the EGYPTIANS recognized the god as the final arbiter of their fate after death, and as the greatest god of the kingdom of the dead.

The conception of a judgement after death is, as we have seen, very, very old, but no representation of OSIRIS, the Righteous Judge, sitting in judgement, older than the XVIIIth dynasty, is extant. The Pyramid Texts contained no illustrations or vignettes, and there is no picture of any such thing on the painted and inscribed coffins of the XIth and XIIth dynasties from BARSHAH and else-

[1] He was also called the 'Dweller in Annu' (Heliopolis), Pyr. § 191.

where. We owe the pictures of the Last Judgement of the EGYPTIANS entirely to the great and learned priests and scribes of the early period of the XVIIIth dynasty, who collected and edited the chapters which form the PERT-EM-HRU, i.e. the '[Book of] Coming Forth by Day', commonly known as the Theban Recension of the *Book of the Dead*. The hall in which the gods sat in judgement on OSIRIS in primitive times was presumably set in high heaven, but in the Papyrus of NEBSENI (sheet 30) it appears in the form of a long chamber which is called the Hall of the MAĀTI goddesses 'USEKHT-ENT-MAĀTI' 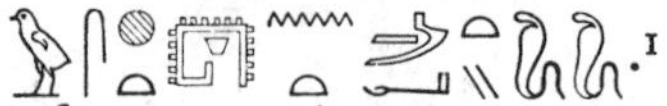.[1] These goddesses represented the Law of UPPER and LOWER EGYPT respectively, and were the Eyes of the Lord of the City (or district) of MAĀT. The main door of the Hall had the magical name of KHERSEK-SHU, and each of the leaves of the door had a magical name, NEB-MAĀT-ḤERI-TEP-REṬUI-F and NEB-PEḤTI-THES-MENMEN-T. Over the cornice of the Hall is a frieze, and in the centre of it is a god with his hands extended over the solar pools called 'Millions of Years', and 'Great Green Lake',[2] which are mentioned in chapter xvii of the Theban *Book of the Dead*. On each side of the god are: (1) a baboon seated before a pair of scales; (2) thirteen feathers symbolic of MAĀT 𓆄 and thirteen cobras 𓆗 arranged alternately; (3) A baboon seated before a pair of scales of unusual form, 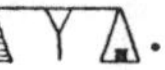. One pan of the scales contains a square weight (?), but the object in the other pan, (which exactly counterbalances this weight (?)), has not, as yet, been identified. The baboon is the companion and servant of THOTH, the secretary of PTAḤ, RĀ, and OSIRIS. By one leaf of the door stand the two MAĀTI goddesses, each holding a sceptre and the 𓋹 *ānkh*;[3] on the head and sceptre of each is 𓆄, the symbol of Law and Truth.

[1] Originally they may have been Uadjit of Pe-Ṭep and Nekhebit of Hierakonpolis, near the modern town of Al-Kâb.

[2] It has been suggested that these pools or lakes show that the Egyptians had some vague knowledge of the existence of the great Central African Lakes.

[3] Many attempts have been made by Egyptologists and others to identify the objects represented by 𓋹, 𓎬, and 𓊽, but hitherto none has, in my opinion, been satisfactory. The first of these, 𓋹, which is read *ānkh* undoubtedly means 'life'. Every god carries it, and it seems as if the possession of it gave its possessor divinity, or something like it. Recently it has been stated that 𓋹 and 𓎬, which it is generally admitted is a symbol of Isis, are one and the same thing, that is they are interchange-

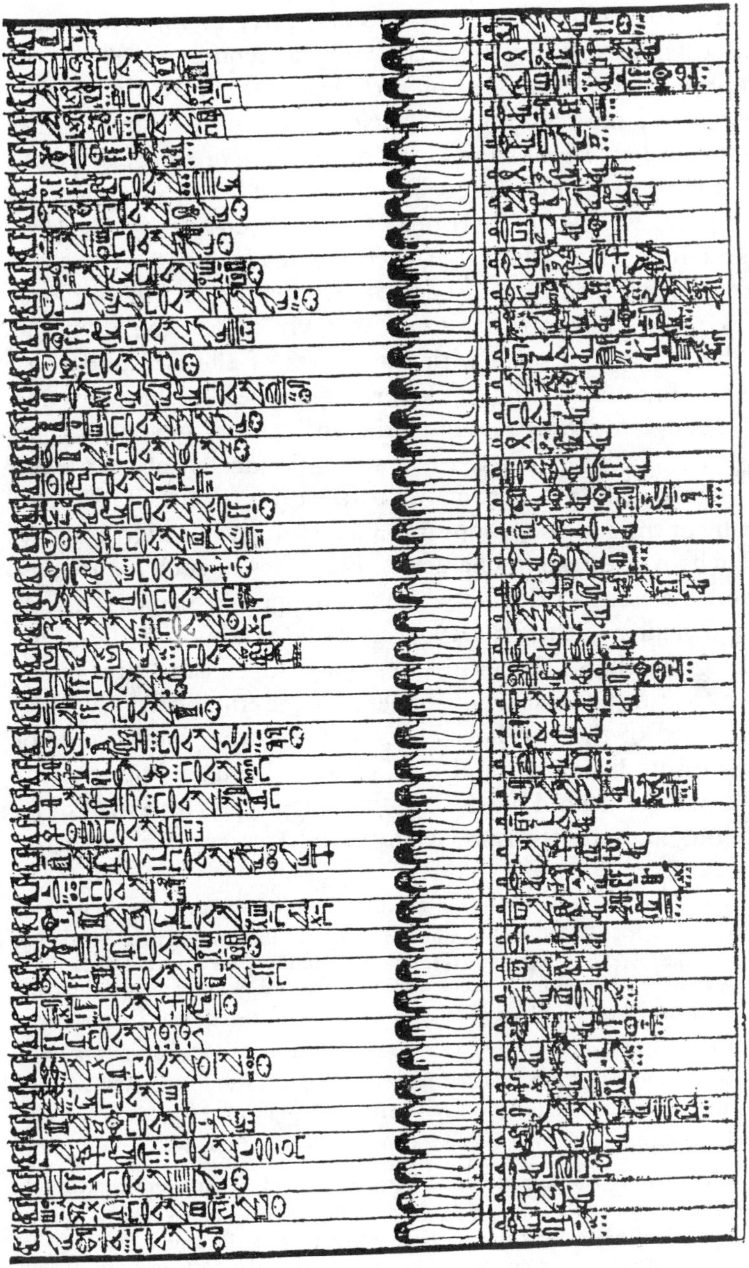

The Forty-two Assessors (Judges) enumerated in chapter cxxv, Part II of the Theban *Book of the Dead*. This section is generally known as the Negative Confession.

Across the Hall of MAĀT are two and forty mummied human forms, each having 𓆄 on his head, which are commonly supposed to represent the 'Assessors of the Dead'; they are thought to have been Nome-gods, or very ancient gods, or ancestral spirits. The text of Part II of chapter cxxv of the *Book of the Dead* makes it quite clear that a man had to justify himself before each of these Assessors as well as before OSIRIS. Curiously enough the declarations of innocence which the deceased made before OSIRIS are identical with those he made before the Assessors, and in the oldest copies of the Theban *Book of the Dead*, viz. those of NEBSENI and NU, they are given once with the names of the two and forty Assessors and once without. According to one text these two and forty beings 'made prisoners of the wicked and devoured their blood on the day when the characters (or deeds) of men were investigated in the presence of UNEN-NEFER' (i.e. OSIRIS). The names of many of the Assessors appear to be nick-names, and in any case to be wholly artificial in character. Examples of such names are: Him-of-the-long-stride; He-who-is-enveloped-in-flames; Divine-Nose (meaning THOTH?); Devourer-of-the-shadows-of-the-dead; Stinking-members; Him-with-eyes-like-flints; Flame-advancing-and-retreating; Crusher-of-bones; Flame-intensifier; White-teeth; Lord-of-the-two-horns, &c. On the other hand, some of the Assessors bear names of mythological beings who are mentioned in the Pyramid Texts, e.g. ḤER-F-ḤA-F, the ferryman of RĀ and OSIRIS, and DJESER-TEP-F. Many of the Assessors are associated

able. This I do not believe. In the *Book of the Dead* 𓎬 forms the vignette of chap. cxlvi, which is a spell and was intended to give the deceased the protection of Isis, and the blood of the goddess is specially mentioned. As the amulet inscribed with this chapter is always made of some red material, it is clear that in the XVIIIth dynasty it symbolized the blood of Isis. It has been suggested that 𓊽 represents a bundle of reeds, and it may at one time have represented the twigs of the erica tree mentioned by Plutarch. But 𓊽 is the vignette of chapter cxlv, and the text connects it with the backbone of Osiris, and not with any bundle of reeds. It is futile to overlook the mention of blood in connexion with 𓎬 and of the backbone of Osiris with 𓊽. It seems to me that the three signs 𓋹, 𓎬, and 𓊽 represent three fetish objects which the scribe could not identify, and we cannot identify them. There is, in my opinion, good reason for believing that they are inaccurate drawings of the generative organs of the human body, male or female, or portions of them, and each of them probably had a more or less phallic character.

with well-known towns or localities, and with each of them a particular sin is mentioned. It is quite clear that the deceased had to justify himself before a great company of two and forty gods who represented as a body all EGYPT.

The forty-two declarations made by the deceased that he had not committed such and such sins form what may be called the Religious and moral 'Code of OSIRIS', and indicate that the man who could not make them truthfully could never expect to enter the Kingdom of OSIRIS. These declarations were always drawn up in tabular form. From the fact that the great priestess NESI-TA-NEBT-ASHER added to her copy of the Theban *Book of the Dead*, which is written throughout in the hieratic character,[1] a copy of them written in hieroglyphs, we may perhaps assume that in the tenth century B.C. the tabular form was regarded as a powerful amulet. The hieroglyphs being the writing of the god THOTH, the greatest of divine magicians, added to the efficacy of the words—at least so it was always believed in ancient EGYPT. The declarations are all couched in the same form. The deceased addressed the Assessor by his name, and mentioned his place of abode, and then categorically denied that he had committed the sin which was an abomination to the Assessor. Example: 'O USEKH-NEMMAT, coming forth from ANNU (HELIOPOLIS), I have not committed sins,  *asfet*'. In some papyri a figure intended to represent the Assessor is inserted after the name of his town (see the Papyrus of ANHAI). Because the words 'I have not' occur in each declaration the early Egyptologists gave to this section of chapter CXXV the name of 'the Negative Confession'. But this is a misnomer, for as a matter of fact the deceased confesses nothing; on the contrary, he makes a very definite statement by which he intends to justify himself before the Assessor.

In many of the Theban papyri the figures of the two and forty Assessors are entirely omitted, and the small vignette shown on p. 122 has developed into a large picture in which the great act of the judgement of the dead, viz. the weighing of the heart, is depicted in full detail (see p. 304). In the Papyrus of ANI the gods of the Company of HELIOPOLIS and a few others are seen seated in the

[1] i.e. the Greenfield Papyrus in the British Museum.

upper register. In the papyrus of ANHAI we find two Companies of the gods, the Great and the Little. At the inner end of the Hall of judgement OSIRIS is seated in a shrine, being embraced by ISIS and the shadowy NEPHTHYS. The shrine has the form of a funerary coffer, from which one side has been removed. The shrine is approached by means of a short stairway. OSIRIS wears sometimes the White Crown, with a feather on each side of it, and sometimes the Atef Crown ; he has short side-whiskers and from his chin hangs a long plaited characteristic African beard, probably of Sûdânî origin. Round his neck is a string of beads and amulets, and at the back of his neck is the *menat* amulet 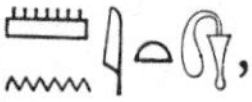, an emblem of physical well-being, virility, &c. The white body of OSIRIS is covered with a painted pattern, which some have described as 'scale work', but which probably represents a design made by tattûing, cicatrization, or painting. OSIRIS is seated on a funerary coffer, which is sometimes made to rest on a stream of water, the celestial NILE, and in front of him are the Four Sons of HORUS standing on a lotus flower which grows out of the water. OSIRIS sits motionless and apparently does nothing except watch the actual weighing of the hearts of the dead, but when the righteous, or justified, are presented before him, either by HORUS or the MAĀT goddesses, he is supposed to assign to them the estate or homestead in his kingdom which he considers them fit to receive.

The Scales of Judgement consist of an upright pillar set in a socket having a peg in the form of an ostrich feather fixed in one side of it near the top. The feather symbolizes MAĀT, the Law or Truth, From this peg, suspended by a cord, hangs the Beam of the Scales with the two pans, each of which is attached to it by two cords. In the right pan is the feather of MAĀT, or a figure of the goddess  and in the left the heart which is to be weighed. On the top of the pillar of the Scales we see: (1) the head of the goddess MAĀT, or the head of ANPU (ANUBIS), or the head of an ibis, the symbol of THOTH, (2) a figure of a baboon, an animal associate of THOTH, which sometimes bears this god's name. The actual weighing of the heart was usually performed by the jackal-god ANUBIS, the son of SET and NEPHTHYS, who in dynastic times held in respect of the judgement of the dead the place which his father SET held during the trial of

OSIRIS before the Company of the gods at HELIOPOLIS. ANUBIS may be regarded as the 'devil's advocate', and the care which he displays in scrutinizing the position of the pointer of the Scales, and his obvious anxiety lest the heart should gain any advantage to which it was not legally entitled, make it quite clear that the deceased could expect no favour from him. Close to the Scales stands the ibis-headed god THOTH with his writing reed and palette on which he registers the result of the weighing as reported to him by his associate, the lynx-eyed baboon, whose vision nothing escapes. The object of the strict watching of the beam of the Scales by ANUBIS and THOTH was to make sure that it did not incline either at one end or the other, and so make the Law outweigh the heart, which would then become 'light on the Scales', or the heart outweigh the Law. In all the papyri the beam of the balance is represented as strictly horizontal, which seems to show that the deceased was not expected to perform more than the Law demanded.

Close to the Scales sits the composite monster ĀM-MIT  , the 'Eater of the Dead' which had the head of a crocodile, the body of a lion, and the hind-quarters of a hippopotamus. He was believed to eat the hearts which were light on the Scales, and were condemned in the judgement or damned. In the Papyrus of ANI the deceased in human form is seen watching the weighing of his heart. Near him stands his soul in the form of a man-headed hawk 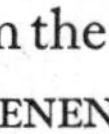 and close by is a rectangular object with a human head at one end of it. This may represent the box in which some important member of ANI's body was placed after his birth, or it may represent the 'birth stone' on which he dropped when he fell from his mother's body.[1] As supporters or friends of ANI we see close to him the god SHAI 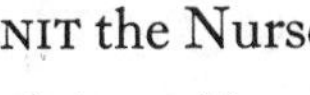, and the two goddesses MESKHENIT and RENENIT. SHAI was the god of luck, fate, and destiny, and unless he possessed other attributes it is difficult to account for his presence here. It is possible that he represented ANI's 'guardian angel'. MESKHENIT was the goddess of the childbirth bed and the birth chamber, and RENENIT the Nurse-goddess presided over the suck-

[1] In the Papyrus of Anhai two objects of this kind are represented, the one being called Shai and the other Renen.

ling and nurture of ANI. SHAI and the two goddesses do not appear in any other picture of the Judgement Scene. Whether they represented a belief which was held by ANI alone and not by the other learned scribes who were his contemporaries cannot be said.

As to the meaning of the whole picture various opinions are current. Some think that it has a devotional character and others regard it as a magical picture which was intended to secure a verdict of 'true of voice' for the deceased from the gods of judgement. The large size of the picture and its prominent place in all the great funerary papyri clearly indicate the predominance which the Judgement of OSIRIS occupied in the minds of his votaries. For the man who was cast out of the Hall of MAĀT condemned could have no lot or portion in the kingdom of OSIRIS with the beatified. The care which ANI displayed in the construction of the Judgement Scene and its unusual feature suggest that it is the expression of the 'trembling hope' of a righteous man and belief in the absolute justice and impartiality of OSIRIS and his ministers. The length of chapter cxxv together with its supplementary texts also indicates the vital importance of the Judgement and the consuming desire of the EGYPTIAN to obtain the rewards which OSIRIS bestowed upon the righteous.

The first part of the chapter contains a hymn of praise to OSIRIS KHENTI AMENTI, which the deceased said when he entered the Hall of Judgement. But before he was allowed to enter he was obliged to tell its guardian, ANUBIS, the name of the door and of the two leaves of the door; and in addition he was compelled to enumerate the various acts of worship which he had performed in a number of holy places. Then in the Hall, addressing OSIRIS, he said:[1]

'Homage to Thee, O Great God, Lord of the city of MAĀTI, I have come unto Thee, O my Lord, and I have brought myself hither that I may gaze upon Thy beauties (or beneficence).

I know Thee, I know Thy Name, I know the name[s] of the Forty-two gods who are with Thee in this Hall of MAĀTI, who live as the warders of sinners [and] who swallow their blood on that day of reckoning up the characters (or dispositions of men) in the presence of UN-NEFER[2] (i.e. OSIRIS). In truth 'REKHTI-MERTI-NEB-MAĀTI' is Thy Name.

[1] I follow the text of the Papyrus of Nu.

[2] i.e. the good or beneficent Being.

Verily I have come unto Thee, I have brought unto Thee MAĀT (i.e. TRUTH, or the LAW), I have crushed for Thee SIN.[1]

1. I have not acted sinfully towards men.
2. I have not oppressed the members of my family.
3. I have not done wrong instead of what is right.[2]
4. I have known no worthless folk.
5. I have not committed abominable acts.
6. I have not made excessive work to be done for me on any day (?).
7. I have [not made] my name to go forth for positions of dignity.
8. I have not domineered over servants.
9. I have not belittled god [or the God].
10. I have not filched the property of the lowly man.
11. I have not done things which are the abominations of the gods.
12. I have not vilified a servant to his master.
13. I have not inflicted pain (or caused suffering).
14. I have not permitted any man to suffer hunger.
15. I have not made any man to weep.
16. I have not committed murder (or slaughter).
17. I have not given an order to cause murder.
18. I have not made men and women to suffer calamities.
19. I have not purloined the oblations in the temples.
20. I have not defrauded the gods of [their] cakes (or offerings).
21. I have not carried off the cakes of the AAKHU (the dead?)
22. I have not committed sodomy.[3]
23. I have not polluted [the sacred waters of the god of my city].[4]
24. I have not made light the bushel.
25. I have not filched from, nor added to, an estate.
26. I have not encroached upon the fields [of others].
27. I have not added to the weights of the scales [to cheat the seller].
28. I have not diminished the weight of the pointer of the scales.
29. I have not snatched away milk from the mouth[s] of children.
30. I have not driven away the cattle from their pastures.
31. I have not snared the geese in the preserves of the gods.

[1] i.e. I have eliminated sin from myself for (or through?) Thee.

[2] There are variant readings.

[3] Or, I have not lain with a man who is a lier with a man.

[4] The words in brackets are from the Papyrus of Amen-neb.

32. I have not fished with bait made of the bodies of fish.
33. I have not stopped water when it should run.
34. I have not made a cutting in a canal of running water.
35. I have not extinguished a fire when it should burn.
36. I have not neglected the times for the chosen offerings.
37. I have not driven away the cattle from the farms of the gods.
38. I have not obstructed the god in his comings forth (or appearances in processions).

I am washed. I am washed. I am washed. I am washed. My purity (?) is the purity of that great BENU which is in ḤENSU (i.e. HANES, HERAKLEOPOLIS). For I am that Nose of the Lord of the Winds (i.e. THOTH), who maketh all mankind to live, on the day of the filling of the UDJAT (i.e. full moon) in ANNU (HELIOPOLIS) in the second month of the season of PERT, the last day [in the presence of the Lord of this land]. I have seen the fullness of the UDJAT (i.e. full moon) in ANNU. Evil shall not happen to me in this land, in the Hall of MAĀTI, because I know the name[s] of these gods who are therein [who are the followers of the Great God].

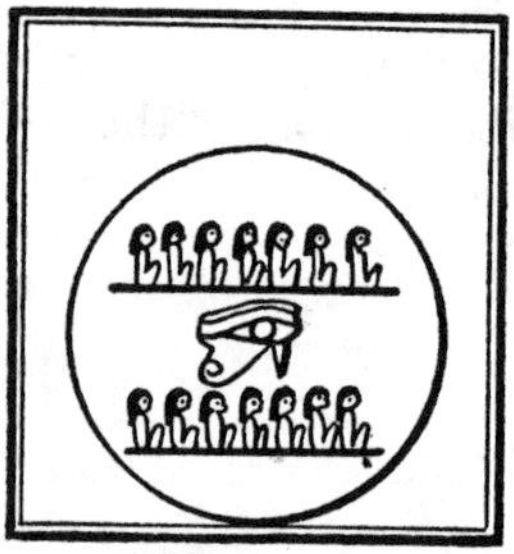

The Udjat or Full Moon containing its 14 days 𓂀.

Following the above declarations in all the great funerary papyri comes the so-called 'Negative Confession' already mentioned.

THE 'NEGATIVE CONFESSION'

from the Papyrus of NU.

1. Hail, USEKH-NEMMAT, coming out from ANNU (HELIOPOLIS), I have not committed sin.
2. Hail, HEPT-SHET, coming out from KHER-ĀBA,[1] I have not robbed.
3. Hail, FENTI, coming out from KHEMENU (HERMOPOLIS).
4. Hail, AM-KHAIBIT, coming out from QERRTI (ELEPHANTINE ?), I have not committed thefts.

[1] This city stood between Heliopolis and the Babylon of Egypt (Fustât).

5. Hail, NEHA-ḤER, coming out from RE-STAU,[1] I have not slain men and women.
6. Hail, RUTI (SHU-TEFNUT), coming out from heaven, I have not diminished the bushel.
7. Hail, ARITI-F-SHET, coming out from SEKHEM, I have not defrauded.
8. Hail, NEBA, coming out and retreating, I have not plundered sacred property.
9. Hail, SET-QESU, coming out from ḤENSU (HERAKLEOPOLIS), I have not uttered falsehood.
10. Hail, KHEMI, coming out from the Hidden Sanctuary, I have not robbed with violence.
11. Hail, UADJ-NESERT, coming out from HE-T-KA-PTAḤ (MEMPHIS), I have not blasphemed (or cursed god or man).
12. Hail, ḤER-F-ḤA-F,[2] coming out from TEPHET-DJAT, I have not carried away food (?).
13. Hail, QERTI, coming out from AMENT, I have not uttered slanders (or words of backbiting).
14. Hail, TA-RET, coming out from the night, I have not eaten my heart.
15. Hail, HEDJ-ABEHU, coming out from TA-SHE (the FAYYÛM), I have not invaded [on the property of others].
16. Hail, UNEM-SNEF, coming out from the chamber of the block of slaughter, I have not slain a sacred bull.
17. Hail, UNEM-BESKU, coming out from the MĀBET chamber, I have not laid waste ploughed lands.
18. Hail, NEB-MAĀT, coming out from the city of MAĀTI, I have not played the eavesdropper.
19. Hail, THENEMI, coming out from UBAST (BUBASTIS), I have not set my mouth in motion [for mischief].
20. Hail, ĀNTI, coming out from HELIOPOLIS, I have not been wroth without a cause (?).
21. Hail, TU-TUT-F, coming out from the nome of ĀNDJ-T,[3] I have not lain with a lier with men.
22. Hail, UAMEMTI, coming out from the chamber of slaughter, I have not masturbated.

[1] The Underworld of Memphis.
[2] The ferryman of Rā and Osiris.
[3] The ninth nome of Lower Egypt; its capital was Busiris.

23. Hail, MA-ANTEF, coming out from PER-MENU, I have not lain with the woman of a man (i.e. another man's wife).
24. Hail, HERI-SERU (?), coming out from NEHAT, I have terrified no man.
25. Hail, NEB-SEKHEM, coming out from GAUI (?), I have not made hot my mouth.[1]
26. Hail, SHEṬ-KHERU, coming out from URIT, I have not made myself deaf to the admonitions of MAĀT (i.e. the Law).
27. Hail, NEKHEN, coming out from HEQA-ĀNDJ (HELIOPOLIS), I have made no man to weep.
28. Hail, KENEMTI, coming out from KENMET, I have reviled no man.
29. Hail, AN-ḤETEP-F, coming out from SAU-T (SAÏS), I have not acted truculently (or with unnecessary violence).
30. Hail, SER-KHERU, coming out from UNSI (?), I have not hurried my heart (i.e. judged hastily, or acted without due thought and consideration).
31. Hail, NEB-HERU, coming out from NEDJF-T, I have not attacked the . . . I have not . . . of the god.
32. Hail, SREKHI, coming out from UTHEN-T, I have not multiplied speech overmuch (?).
33. Hail, NEB-ĀBUI, coming out from SAU-T (SAÏS), I have not acted deceitfully, countenancing evil (or wickedness).
34. Hail, NEFER-TEM, coming out from HE-T-KA-PTAḤ (MEMPHIS), I have not spoken treasonably about the king.
35. Hail, TEM-SEP, coming out from ṬEṬU, I have not fouled water.
36. Hail, ARI-EM-AB-F, coming out from TEBU, I have not made high my voice.
37. Hail, AHI, coming out from NU, I have not blasphemed the god.
38. Hail, UADJ-REKHIT,[2] [coming out from SAU-T], I have not committed acts of arrogance (or 'stinking deeds').
39. Hail, NEHEB-NEFER-T, coming out from his temple, I have not thrust myself forward pridefully.
40. Hail, NEHEB-KAU, coming out from his sanctuary, I have not increased my possessions except through my own property.
41. Hail, DJESER-TEP, coming out from his shrine, the god of the city hath not been cursed through me,

[1] i.e. I have avoided irascibility and swiftness to wrath.

[2] Var. Hedj-rekhit.

42. Hail, ĀN-Ā-F, [coming out from AUGERT], I have not belittled the god of [my] city.

The texts of the 'Negative Confession' found in the other papyri of the XVIIIth dynasty give many variants, many of which are due to the mistakes or misunderstanding of the scribes, and it is impossible to say what the oldest version really was. And the reader must note that the translations of some of the declarations can only be regarded as suggestions as to the meaning of them, for it is clear that some of them are expressed idiomatically, and that others are in the technical language of the law court.

The title of chapter cxxv states that the deceased was to make his declarations of innocence when he entered the Hall of OSIRIS, and when he had done this we may assume that the actual weighing of his heart, which was the seat of his mind and his soul, took place. Though he declares his absolute freedom from the taint of sin, and claims unhesitatingly that he has fulfilled the Law of OSIRIS, he found it necessary to recite a prayer which is found in the Judgement Scene in all the large illustrated copies of the Theban Recension of the *Book of the Dead*, and also forms chapter XXX B of that work. This prayer shows that he was afraid that his declarations of innocence would not be sufficient to ensure his success in the Judgement unless they remained unchallenged by the Assessors and other judges of OSIRIS. This prayer is usually entitled, 'Chapter of not allowing the heart of a man to be repulsed in KHERT-NETER' (i.e. the Underworld), but in the Papyrus of IUAU the deceased is ordered to recite it as a 'magical spell' 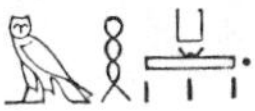. The prayer in the Papyrus of NU opens with the words.

'[O] My heart of my mother, [O] my heart of my mother, my heart (or bosom) of my coming into being.

Let no one stand up against me (i.e. contradict, or gainsay, me) in my righteousness (?).

Let no man cause me to be repulsed by testifying against me.

Let no one of the DJADJAU-Judges cause me to be repulsed,

Make no turning aside from me[1] before the Guardian of the Scales (i.e. ANUBIS).

Thou art my KA in my body, the god KHNEMU[2] who knitteth together and strengtheneth my members.

1 Or 'Incline not against me'.

2 The Potter-god who moulded man on a potter's wheel.

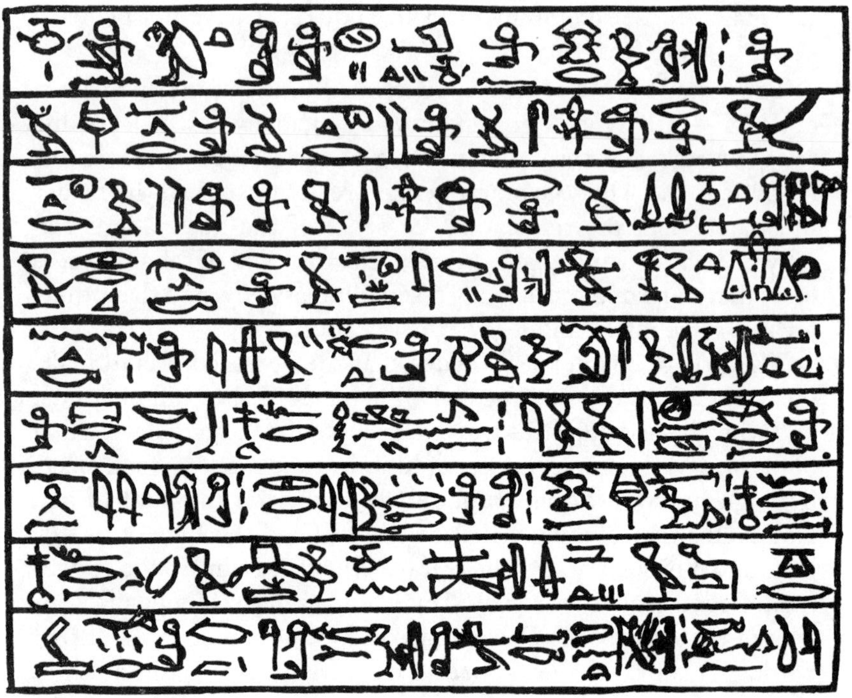

The text of the spell which form chapter xxx B of the Theban *Book of the Dead*. It was in common use in Egypt from the fourth dynasty to the Roman Period. It is addressed both to the heart and the breast of the mother of the deceased.

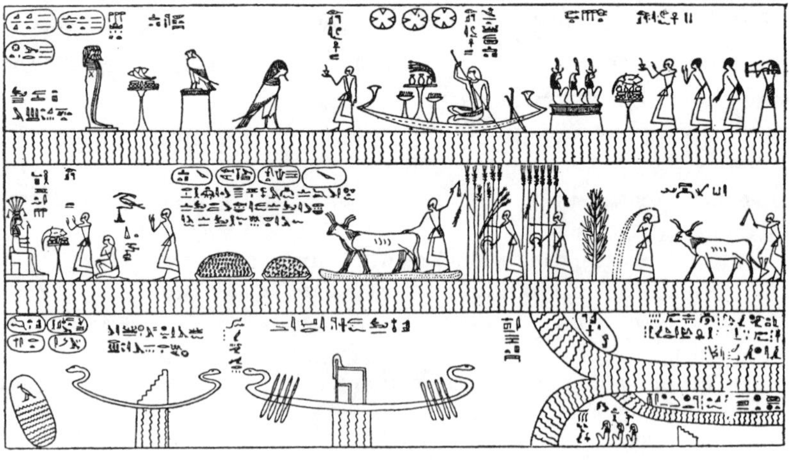

The region where the beatified dwelt in the Ṭuat.

Come forth to the happiness whereto we go.
Let not the SHENIT,[1] who fashion men and women, make my name to stink.
Let there be for us a good (or happy) stability, [and] a good hearing with joy of heart at the weighing of words.
Let not lies be told about me by the side of the Great God [the Lord of AMENTET].
Verily distinguished shalt thou be rising as one true of word (or in triumph[2]).'

This magical spell is very old, and some of the rubrics of chapter xxx B and chapter lxiv of the Theban *Book of the Dead* say that it was known in the time of SEMTI (1st dynasty), and others connect it with the time of MYCERINUS (IVth dynasty). The oldest copy of it known to us was found on the sarcophagus of KHNEM-NEFER, a wife of one of the MENTHU-ḤETEP kings (XIth dynasty); see the transcript of the hieratic text of the sarcophagus in the BRITISH MUSEUM (No. 10553).[3] It is found engraved in hieroglyphs on the large green stone 'heart scarab', and it was written in funerary papyri during the Ptolemaic and Roman periods. It is certainly as old as the dynasties in EGYPT and was therefore in use for at least three thousand years. Few spells or prayers in the world's history have had so long a life.

According to the pictures in the papyri the actual weighing of the heart was a comparatively simple matter. In one pan of the Scales a symbol of MAĀT (i.e. the Law or Righteousness) was placed, and in the other the heart of the deceased. ANUBIS held the pointer of the Scales with the keen attention of the 'devil's advocate', and the Baboon of THOTH took care that ANUBIS did nothing which would tell against the heart. No words are put into the mouth of the Baboon, but four short lines of hieroglyphs are given over the head of ANUBIS and they contain an admonition to himself. The text[4] is broken in one or two places but means something like 'Direct thy face, O judge of the pointer of the Scales make it straight'. In the Papyrus of ANHAI[5] the equivalent text reads,

[1] Another group of divine officers of Osiris. [2] From the Papyrus of Nebseni.
[3] It is published in *Hieratic Papyri*, vol. i, ed. Budge.
4 
5 

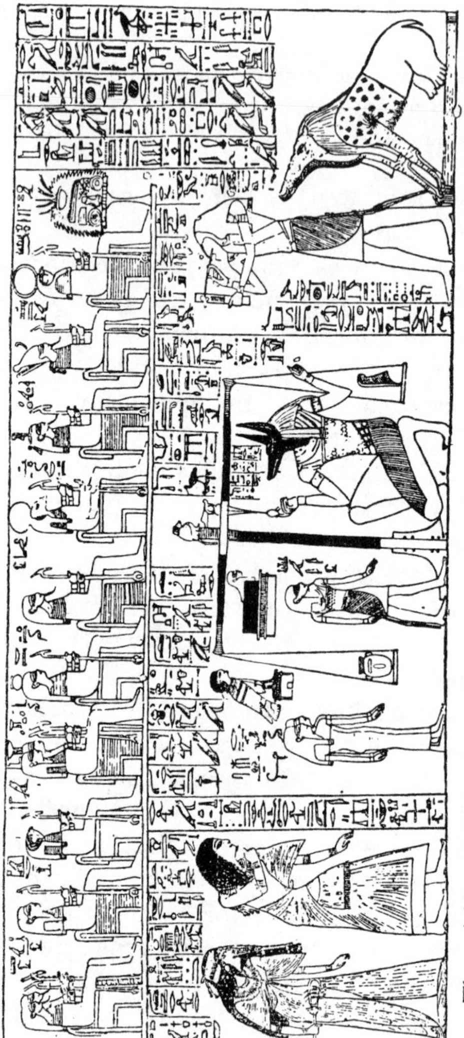

The weighing of the heart of Osiris Ani by Anubis and Asten with Thoth as Registrar and Great Company of the gods of Heliopolis as witnesses, according to the Papyrus of Ani.

'Direct thy face, [O] judge, to the heart (or the middle) of the Scales'.

The Scales showed that the heart of the deceased counterbalanced exactly the feather of MAĀT, and THOTH, the righteous scribe of the gods, who also had been watching the weighing of the heart, was satisfied that ANI was a man without sin, and he reported this fact to the 'Great Company of the Gods' who are before OSIRIS, saying, 'Hear ye this word (i.e. decision). The heart of OSIRIS ANI hath been tried according to the strict requirements of the Law. His soul (BA) hath stood as a witness for him. His character is righteous[1] on the Great Scales, no wickedness (or defect) of his hath been discovered. He hath not purloined the offerings in the temples. He hath done harm to none by his actions. And he vilified no man with his mouth whilst he was on the earth.'

The Great Company of the Gods of THOTH, the dweller in KHEMENU (HERMOPOLIS), accept the verdict of THOTH, and say to him, '[We] endorse emphatically these [words] which have come forth from thy mouth. The scribe ANI, the speaker of the truth, is righteous. He hath committed no evil deed. He hath planned no evil and done nothing to injure us.[2] ĀM-MIT (i.e. the Eater of the Dead) shall not be allowed to have any power over him. Let there be given unto him cakes, [and] appearance before OSIRIS, [and] a lasting estate in SEKHET-HETEPET (the Elysian Fields) like unto that [which is given to] the SHEMSU-ḤERU (Followers of HORUS).'

The deceased having satisfied THOTH and the gods that he has justified himself by his works is ready to enter into the august presence of OSIRIS and to make the final declaration of his righteousness to the Great God himself. His introduction is performed by HORUS, the son of ISIS who was begotten by OSIRIS miraculously after his death. In the portion supplementary to the Judgement Scene we see HORUS, who is wearing the double crown of UPPER and LOWER EGYPT clasping the left hand of ANI with his right hand and addressing OSIRIS. With his left hand raised HORUS says: 'I come before thee, UN-NEFER. I bring unto thee OSIRIS ANI. His heart is righteous [having] come forth from the Scales. He is not evil before any god [and] any goddess. THOTH hath him in accordance

[1] Or, 'his case is correct, according to the evidence of the Great Scales'.

[2] He has always treated us with the proper reverence and respect.

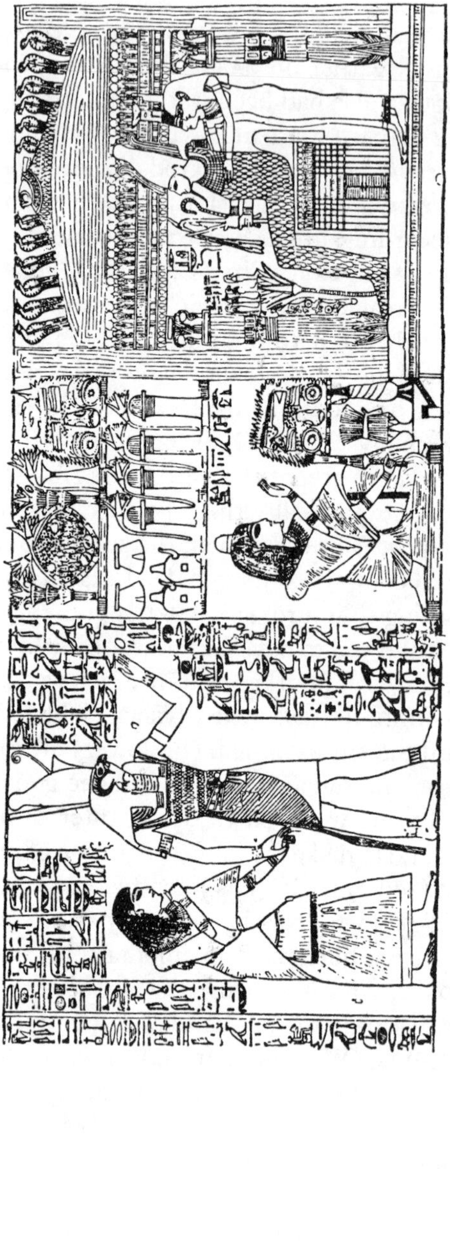

Horus, the son of Isis, reporting the favourable result of the weighing of Ani's heart to Osiris and leading him into the presence of the god to adore him and to receive the reward given to the Followers of Horus.

to the written orders which the Company of the Gods uttered in respect of him; a great righteous witness (?). I pray thee that there may be given unto him bread-cakes [and] beer [and] a coming forth (or appearance) in the presence of OSIRIS. Let him be like the Followers of HORUS.'[1]

The last section of the scene shows us ANI arrayed in elaborate festal attire and surrounded with offerings, kneeling before OSIRIS. His right hand is raised, and he says to OSIRIS: 'Verily (or behold) I am in thy presence, O Lord of AMENTT. There is no sin in my body. I have not uttered falsehood knowingly, or had a double motive (?). Grant thou that I may be like unto those on whom thou hast shown favour, and who are among thy followers, viz. OSIRIS, greatly favoured by UN-NEFER, beloved one of the Lord of the Two Lands (i.e. the King), the real royal scribe loving him—ANI, whose word is truth before OSIRIS.' What answer OSIRIS returned to the deceased it is impossible to say, but according to the papyri he made none. It is difficult to understand what part he played in the Judgement, unless it was that of a passive onlooker. It was THOTH who decided that the heart in the Scales was righteous, and it was the Great Company of Gods who accepted his report and decreed the reward which the BA (i.e. soul) of the deceased was to receive in the Field of Offerings. We read nothing about the consultation of the registers of the doings of men which were kept by OSIRIS; he asks no questions, and allows the gods to assign an estate in his kingdom to the deceased, together with an adequate supply of food and drink, without making any sign, either of approval or disapproval.

The evidence on which an explanation of this fact could be based is at present wanting. We must note too that it is the Great Company of the Gods who decree that the deceased is not to be molested by the Eater of the Dead. But an incident recorded in the CHESTER BEATTY Papyrus, No. 1[2] proves that there was another side to the character of OSIRIS, which was quite different to that which he is made to assume in the funerary papyri. In answer to a letter sent

[1] In the Papyrus of Hu-nefer the equivalent text reads, 'Her-nedj-tef-f, the beneficent heir of Un-Nefer says, "Behold, I am bringing up the Osiris Hu-nefer. He hath been reckoned up in the Scales, and the weight of the pointer remained in its [usual] position".'

[2] See Gardiner's edition, Oxford, 1931, Pl. XV.

to him by RĀ ḤARAKHTI concerning the fight between HORUS and SET, OSIRIS replied that his son HORUS must not be defrauded of his inheritance of the throne of EGYPT, and he reminded RĀ ḤARAKHTI that it was he (OSIRIS) who gave strength to the gods, who made to grow the barley and millet on which gods and men lived and that no other god or goddess could do the like. When the answer of OSIRIS was read out before RĀ ḤARAKHTI and his Company of gods in Xoïs, promptly RĀ ḤARAKHTI replied, and in terse language told OSIRIS that even if he had never come into being or been born, the barley and the millet would still have existed. OSIRIS answered and commended the work which RĀ ḤARAKHTI had done, and his invention of the Company of the Nine Gods, but pointed out that meanwhile Justice had been allowed to sink into hell. And OSIRIS goes on to say that the land in which he lives is filled with 'savage-faced messengers'[1] who fear neither god nor goddess. And he adds, 'I will dispatch them and they shall bring the heart of any one who doeth evil deeds, and they shall abide here with me. What matters it that I repose here in the West whilst all [of you] are outside? Who is there among them (i.e. you) stronger than I?' Thus OSIRIS claims to be the source of life in gods, men, and animals, and the mightiest of the gods, who owe their very existence to the goodwill of OSIRIS.

In connexion with the speech of THOTH to the gods we may note that he mentions the fact that the BA (soul) of the deceased has testified on his behalf. This suggests that the BA watched carefully the doings of the man in whose body it lived because any evil deeds committed by the man would endanger his success in the Judgement Hall, and destroy its own chance of a renewed life in the Kingdom of OSIRIS. If this was so, a man was bound to secure the approval of his actions by the BA to prevent it from testifying against him at the Judgement. The BA, then, acted as a kind of conscience.

1 

THE SPEECH OF THE DECEASED WHOSE HEART IS RIGHTEOUS AND WITHOUT SIN,[1] WHEN HE ENTERS INTO THE PRESENCE OF THE GODS OF THE UNDERWORLD

(*Papyrus of* NU, sheet 24)

Greetings and reverent salutations to you, O ye gods, who dwell in this Half of MAĀTI!

I, even I, know you. I know your names. Let me not fall down by your knives of slaughter. Carry ye not forward my defect to this god in whose following ye are, let not my time [of trial] come through you. Declare ye any righteousness in the presence of NE-BER-DJER, because I have worked (or cultivated) righteousness in TA-MERA[2] (i.e. EGYPT). I have not cursed (or blasphemed) the god. Let not my time [of trial] come through the king who is in his day.

Greetings and reverent salutations to you, O ye gods, who dwell in this Hall of MAĀTI, who have no evil [and] no lies in their (i.e. your) bodies, who live upon righteousness, and nourish yourselves upon righteousness in the presence of HORUS, who dwelleth in his divine Disk.[3] Deliver ye me from BABA ,[4] who liveth on the intestines of the great ones on that day of the GREAT Reckoning . Grant ye to me the favour that I may approach you.

I have not committed sin, I have not done evil, I am guiltless of iniquity, I have not borne [false] witness;[5] therefore let not action be taken against me. I have lived upon righteousness, I have nourished myself upon righteousness. I have performed the admonitions (or behests) of men, and the commandments which afford pleasure to the gods. I have gratified (or pacified) the god by [performing] his will.

I have given bread to the hungry man, water to him that was

1 

2 Literally, the land of the inundation (annual flooding).

3 Horus, dweller in the Sun.

4 Or Babai , a Heliopolitan god said to be the first-born son of Osiris.

5 Or, I am not a professional witness who could be hired.

athirst, apparel to him that was without garments, and I have provided a boat for the mariner whose boat had foundered.

I have offered up divine oblations to the gods, and *per-t er kheru* (i.e. funerary offerings which appear after the recital of a spell) for the AAKHU (i.e. the beatified dead). Therefore be ye my deliverers, therefore be ye my protectors, utter ye not the report of a matter [which shall tell] against me in the presence of the [Great God].

I am washed clean as to my mouth [and] my hands and arms also.

Let there be said unto him (i.e. me) by those who shall see him (i.e. me), 'Come, come, in peace!' (i.e. Welcome! Welcome!) because I have heard that Great Word which the SĀHU[1] spake with the CAT  in the Temple of ḤAPT-RE.[2] I have testified to ḤER-F-ḤA-F[3] and he gave a decision (?) concerning me. I have seen the things over which the Persea Tree spreadeth within RE-STAU. I am an adorer (?) of the gods, I knew the affairs of their bodies. I have come advancing to testify righteous things [and] to make the Scales stand upright in AUGERT (the Underworld).

Hail thou who art exalted on his (i.e. thy) standard, thou Lord of the Atef Crown who makest thy name to be 'Lord of the Winds', deliver thou me from thy divine messengers who shoot forth calamities and cause disasters to come into being, whose faces are without covering, for I have performed (or made) righteousness for the Lord of Righteousness.

I have cleansed my breast (or my fore-parts) with libations, my hinder parts are purified with the things which make clean, and my inward parts have been in the Pool of Righteousness. There is no member of my body lacking righteousness. I have purified myself in the Pool of the South, I have rested in the City of the North in the Field of the Grasshoppers, wherein the mariners of RĀ bathe at the second hour of the night, and the third hour of the day. The hearts of the gods are gratified after they have passed over it, whether it be by night, or whether it be by day.

And they say unto me, 'Let him come forward'. And they say unto me, 'Who, then, art thou?' And they say unto me, 'What is

[1] A class of the beatified dead.

[2] i.e. the god with the gaping mouth; of this myth nothing is known.

[3] The ferryman of Rā.

thy name?' I am he who is provided with foliage; 'Dweller in his olive tree' is my name. And forthwith they say unto me, 'Pass on', and I passed on by the city to the north of the olive tree. [They say unto me,] 'What didst thou see therein?' [I replied,] 'The Leg and the Thigh.' What didst thou say unto them? [I replied,] 'I saw rejoicing in the countries of the FENKHU 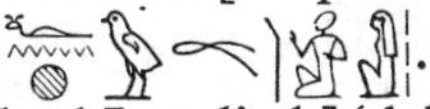.'[1]

And what did they give unto thee? [And I replied,] 'A burning lamp and a sceptre of crystal.'

And what didst thou do therewith? [And I replied,] 'I buried them in the furrow (or bank) of MAĀT with the things of the night.'

And what didst thou find on the bank of MAĀT? 'A sceptre of flint the name of which is "Giver of winds".'

And what didst thou do with the burning lamp and the sceptre of crystal after thou hadst buried them? 'I recited words over them and I dug them up. I extinguished the lamp, I broke the sceptre [of crystal], I made a lake of water.'

'Come then,' [said they] 'and enter in through the door of the Hall of MAĀTI, for thou knowest us.'

The bolts (?) of the door say, 'We will not let thee pass by us unless thou tellest us our name'. [I replied,] 'Weight of the tongue of Scales of the place of righteousness is your name.'

'I will not let thee enter in', saith the western *ārit* (lintel?) of this door, 'unless thou tellest me my name'. [I replied], 'Gift (?) of that which beareth up righteousness is thy name.'

'I will not let thee enter in', saith the eastern *ārit* of this door, 'unless thou tellest me my name.' [I replied,] 'Gift (?) of wine is thy name.'

'I will not let thee pass over me', saith the earth of the floor (i.e. threshold) of this door, 'unless thou tellest me my name.' [I replied,] 'Ox of GEBB is thy name.'

'I will not open to thee', saith the bolt of this door, 'unless thou tellest me my name.' [I replied,] 'SAH-EN-MUT-F (i.e. Flesh of his mother) is thy name.'

'I will not open unto thee', saith the socket of the fastening of the door, 'unless thou tellest me my name.' [I replied,] 'Living Eye of SEBEK,[2] the Lord of BAKHAU,[3] is thy name.'

[1] These have been identified by some writers with the Phoenicians.

[2] The Crocodile-god.

[3] The East or region of the Sunrise.

'I will not open unto thee',[1] saith the guardian leaf of this door, 'unless thou tellest me my name.' [I replied,] 'Shoulder of SHU, the protector of OSIRIS is thy name.'

'We will not let thee enter in by us', say the posts of this door, 'unless thou tellest us our name.' [I replied,] 'Children of the Cobra-goddesses is your name.' They say, 'Thou knowest us; therefore pass in.'

'I will not let thee tread upon me,' saith the floor of this Hall of MAĀTI, 'for I am a *ger* and I am pure. I know not the names of thy two feet wherewith thou wilt tread upon me; therefore tell me what they are.' [I replied,] 'BESU-KHAS (?) is the name of my right foot, UNPEP-T HATHOR is the name of my left foot.' [The floor saith,] 'Thou knowest me; therefore pass in.'

'I will not announce thee', saith the Porter at the door of the Hall of MAĀTI, 'unless thou tellest me my name.' [I replied,] 'Discerner of the heart, searcher of the inward parts is thy name.' [The Porter saith,] 'Now will I announce thee. But who is the god which dwelleth in his hour? Declare thou [his name.' I replied,] 'ĀU-TAUI[2](?) [is his name].'

[The Porter saith,] 'Who is this ĀU-TAUI?' [I replied,] 'He is THOTH.'

THOTH saith, 'Come! But why hast thou come?' [I replied,] 'I have arrived and I press forward in order to be announced.'

[THOTH saith,] 'In what condition art thou?' [I replied,] 'I am cleansed from evil offences, I am protected from the curses (?) of those who live in their days; I am not among them.' [THOTH saith,] 'Now will I announce thee. Declare unto me who is he whose heaven is [made] of fire, whose walls are [surmounted by] living cobras, and the floor of whose house is a stream of water. Who, I say, is he?' [I replied,] 'It is OSIRIS.' [THOTH saith,] 'Advance now, verily thou shalt be announced [to him]. Thy bread shall be the Eye of RĀ, thy beer shall be the Eye of RĀ, and the funerary offerings which shall be brought to thee upon earth shall be the Eye of RĀ.'

RUBRIC. The rubric is important and explains why the Judgement Scene was given such prominence in the great funerary

[1] Nebseni adds, 'and I will not let thee enter in by me'.

[2] i.e. Remembrancer of the Two Lands (Egypt).

papyri. The text of it in the Papyrus of NU reads ON THE MAKING OF AN ILLUSTRATION OF WHAT SHALL HAPPEN IN THE HALL OF MAĀTI.

This Chapter shall be said [by the deceased] after he is cleansed and purified,[1] and when he is arrayed in apparel, and is shod with sandals of white leather, and his eyes have been painted with antimony, and he hath been anointed with unguent of *ānti* (myrrh), and when he hath offered oxen, and geese, and incense, and cakes, and ale, and green herbs (or vegetables).

And behold, thou shalt draw a picture of this in colours upon a new tablet (or plaque) which hath been moulded from earth whereon neither a pig nor any other animal hath trodden. And if thou doest this book (or written spell) upon it [in writing] the deceased shall flourish, and his children shall flourish, and his name shall never fall into oblivion, and he shall be as one who filleth the heart (i.e. prime favourite) of the king and of his princes. Bread, cakes, sweetmeats, wine, and joints of meat shall be given unto him upon the altar of the Great God. He shall not be turned back at any door in AMENTT, he shall accompany the kings of UPPER and LOWER EGYPT, and he shall be in the retinue of OSIRIS continually for ever.

[1] i.e. with water, natron, and incense.

XIII

THE OSIRIAN PENITENT

TAKEN together the three parts of chapter cxxv of the *Book of Dead* make it quite clear that the EGYPTIAN, having by magical means obtained admission to the Judgement Hall of OSIRIS, intended to justify himself to OSIRIS and his Assessors by proving that he had obeyed not only the commandments of the Law, but also the admonitions of men. He said, 'I bring you the Law (i.e. Righteousness), I have destroyed sin in me.' The catalogue of the sins and offences of which he proclaims himself innocent is very comprehensive, and he practically declares that he has satisfied the demands of the Common Law, the Civil Law, the Religious Law, and obeyed the commandments of the god of his city and the king. It is difficult to understand how any man could have such an exalted idea of his own moral worth, and his temerity in seeking to impose upon OSIRIS, the All-knowing, is a thing to be wondered at.

But the *Book of the Dead* proves that there existed among the followers of OSIRIS many men who were fully conscious of their sins and wickednesses, and who expressed their contrition with no uncertain voice. The so-called 'Negative Confession' as we have it in the XVIIIth dynasty papyri is probably a reduction of a very much older set of declarations of sinlessness which the king was supposed to recite when, after death, he appeared in the presence of RĀ and the other gods. These declarations of moral worth were probably first used by the kings of the Old Kingdom, but after the triumph of the cult of OSIRIS over that of RĀ, and the democratization of heaven, they were usurped by the nobles and scribes, and others. In the Ptolemaic period they form the principal text in funerary papyri.

We have seen how NU the great steward of the keeper of the King's Seal declared before OSIRIS that he brought righteousness with him and that he had destroyed sin in himself; we may now consider the text which follows chapter cxxv in his papyrus, it has no title but is commonly known as chapter cxxvi. The vignette shows us a rectangular lake, and the sign 𓈗 together with the sign for 'fire', which projects from each side, shows that it is a lake of boiling water or fire. At each corner a baboon is seated. The text, which is put into the mouth of NU, contains a very clear expression of consciousness of sin and an earnest prayer for absolution. NU says:

'Hail, ye four Baboons who sit in the bows of the Boat of RĀ, who make to advance righteousness to NEB-ER-DJER, who judge my poor estate and my strength, who make the gods to be pacified by the flame of your mouths, who give holy offerings to the gods, and sepulchral meals to the AAKHU,[1] who live upon righteousness, and feed upon righteousness of the heart, who are innocent of lies, whose abomination is sin.

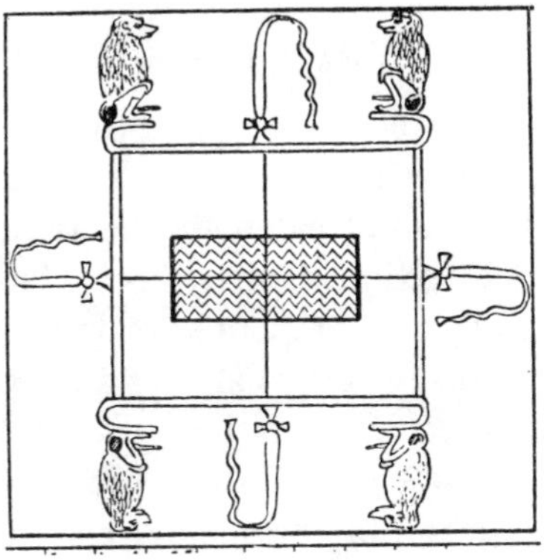

The Four Baboons at the lakes of fire or boiling water.

'Destroy ye my wickednesses, put ye away my sin, let no transgression of mine have existence before you. Grant ye that I may make a way through the AMMḤET,[2] let me enter into RE-STAU,[2] let me pass through the secret chambers of AMENTT. O grant that cakes, and ale, and sweetmeats (?) may be given unto me as unto the living AKHUS, and grant that I may go in and come out [at will] from RE-STAU.'

[The Four Baboons make answer, saying:] 'Come, for we have destroyed thy wickedness, and we have put away thy sin, and no transgression of thine doth now exist before us. Enter thou therefore, into RE-STAU and pass through the secret chambers of AMENTT. Cakes, ale, and sweetmeats shall be given unto thee, and thou shalt go in and come at thy pleasure, even as do those who have had favour shown to them [by the god]. And thou (i.e. thy name) shall be proclaimed each day in the horizon.'

The above prayer makes it clear that the deceased was conscious of his shortcomings and sins. He was afraid that if the gods

[1] A class of the beatified dead.

[2] A section of the Underworld.

decided that he was to be punished he would not become a BA, or beautiful soul, in the Underworld, and would not partake of the spiritual food of the gods and their followers. There is not one word about *repentance* for sins committed in the prayer of the deceased; his only anxiety concerned the possible loss of the reward of the righteous.

It seems that there is no word in Egyptian which is the exact equivalent of *repentance*, but in one or two passages the words *ām ab* , that is, 'to eat, or swallow, the heart', may possibly be correctly translated by 'to repent'. Thus in the 'Negative Confession' the deceased says, 'Hail, TA, coming out from the night, I have not eaten my heart.' The only possible meaning of this declaration seems to be, 'Hail, TA, coming out from the night, I have never repented of [any deed which I had committed]', that is to say, I was always sure that I had done the right thing. In chapter cxii of the *Book of the Dead* we have the myth which describes the injury which SET did to the Eye of HORUS, and when HORUS told RĀ what SET had done, the text adds *ām ab-f* 'he ate his heart'. It is not until towards the end of the New Kingdom that the hymns and funerary stelae contain any very clear references to repentance or any expression of the EGYPTIAN's consciousness of his sins. But even then the upper classes clung to the use of the old declarations of innocence and claimed a reward for their works. 'I have worshipped thee, O RĀ-TEM, therefore do thou for me what I desire', says the lady MUT-ḤETEP, and NEKHTU-AMEN in their hymns to the Sun-god. In the hymns to AMEN and other gods there is abundant evidence that the religion of EGYPT had become 'humanized', and that men had cast aside the ancient royalist and feudal forms of it. They confessed that they were sinners, and confessed their reliance upon the power and the goodness of their God, and prayed to him day and night in forms of words which came not from the formal, official language of an olden time, but from their hearts, and they used the language current in their day among people generally. They believed that their prayers were heard, and relied upon their God to guide them, because they regarded him as the one almighty, infallible, just Judge, the gracious Lord of the universe, the Overlord of the gods, and the great

Shepherd of his flock, that is to say mankind. In an inscription published by ERMAN[1] a worshipper of AMEN-RĀ says, 'O AMEN-RĀ, I love thee, I have filled my heart with thee. I have no haunting fear in my heart, for thy words, O Amen, prevail.' The 'Maxims of ANI' and the 'Teaching of AMEN-EM-APT' advise men to assist regularly at the appointed festivals of God, to present to him gifts and offerings, to frequent his temple and to sit therein and pray to him with a fervent heart, but with few words; for emotional, noisy expressions and much speaking were held to be abominations to 'the God'. And to sit silent in the sanctuary was also regarded as true worship, which God saw and would reward accordingly. From first to last the EGYPTIANS knew quite well that it was their words and deeds upon earth which decided their fate at the Judgement. The belief that good came to the good and evil to the evil remained unchanged from the days of the Memphite theologians of the Old Kingdom to the Roman period, even as SA-ASAR declared, 'These things are established (?) for ever'.[2]

[1] *Zeitschrift für Aeg. Sprache*, Bd. XLII, p. 106.
[2] Griffith, *Stories of the High Priests*, p. 50.

XIV

THE LIFE BEYOND THE GRAVE

We are justified in assuming that among the EGYPTIANS of the Palaeolithic, Neolithic, and Dynastic periods there existed many who believed that the death of their bodies would not terminate their existence, but would mark the beginning of another period of living. It is often stated in books that the EGYPTIANS believed in immortality, but it is clear that at one period some EGYPTIANS thought that the life which they hoped to inherit after the death of the body might be terminated by a second death, for chapter clxxv of the Theban *Book of the Dead* is entitled, 'The Chapter of not dying a second time'. What the men of the Palaeothic period thought about death can never be known, for neither inscriptions nor tombs of theirs, if they constructed any, have come down to us. Their chiefs were probably buried on the edge of the cultivated land, and at no great distance from the alluvial deposit which formed the banks of the NILE. If the graves were shallow, they probably heaped stones and sand over them to protect their occupants from the cheetahs, hyenas, and jackals. Important men were probably buried under the floors of their huts, or *tukuls*, as they are to-day in the Egyptian SÛDÂN, but the bodies of the poor and of those who were in the position of slaves, or serfs, were probably cast out into 'the bush' or the desert. The jackals and the ants quickly disposed of them as they do in many places in the SÛDÂN to-day. It is quite certain that comparatively few of the EGYPTIANS of the Palaeolithic period were 'buried', and as from first to last the dead were always feared by the living, the bodies of the dead would be got rid of as quickly and effectively as possible. A competent authority states that the end of the Palaeolithic period may be placed at from 10,000 to 12,000 years before CHRIST, and that its beginning was not later than about 15000 B.C.

A little more is known about the religious and funerary beliefs of the EGYPTIANS during the late Neolithic and Archaic periods, i.e. from about 10000 to 6000 B.C., and that little is derived from the graves which EUROPEANS and natives have excavated in UPPER EGYPT and NUBIA. These graves are found usually on the outermost border of the alluvial deposit on the banks of the NILE, and are of various shapes and sizes. They usually take the forms of shallow pits and shallower pans, and the dead are laid in them on their left sides with their legs bowed and the knees drawn up close to the chins, and their arms are bent upwards with the hands spread out before their faces. Some lie on a reed mat and are wrapped in pieces of coarse matting, and others are swathed in skins of animals. With some numbers of flint tools and weapons are found, wood saws, knives of various shapes, spear-heads, borers, scrapers, amulets, axe-heads, maces, &c., and many contain bowls, platters, vases, and cups in earthenware and hard stone. And food made of various kinds of grain is often found in some of the vessels. These graves prove that the EGYPTIANS who made them believed that though the dead bodies of their kinsfolk and friends were lying there in the ground close to their villages, some part, or parts, of the dead were still alive. They assumed that they would need food, therefore they offered bowls of grain, &c.; they would have to fight wild beasts or living beings who were hostile to them, therefore they offered them weapons wherewith to fight, spear-heads for their hunting-spears, scrapers to scrape the hair off the pelts of the animals they killed, stone figures of the animals which the living thought the dead would meet, and amulets of flint, the crocodile, horns of animals, Nile-fish, &c. But where were these hypothetical enemies and beasts to be found? We can only assume that the EGYPTIANS thought that their dead were going to have their being in some region or country which closely resembled EGYPT. One thing is very certain: they did not want the dead to come back to EGYPT, for if they did, they would need food and so consume the stores of the living, and perhaps even kill them. To make certain that the dead could not return to their old haunts the neolithic EGYPTIANS at one time dismembered the bodies of the dead, and many of the dead have been found with their heads and hands and feet cut off from their bodies. At one period the dead were partially cremated, and their bones scattered about in the grave.

The graves which were made by the EGYPTIANS after they had acquired the art of writing, contain proofs that their makers were slowly ascending the steps of the ladder of civilization, and that they possessed the rudiments of a religion. They retained the beliefs of their ancestors of the Old Stone Age, and added to them as the result of their own higher development, and a cult of ancestors seems to have come into being. Kings of the Delta, or LOWER EGYPT, and kings of UPPER EGYPT ruled over their respective divisions of the country, and law and order up to a certain point prevailed. The objects found in the late neolithic graves show that the EGYPTIANS had learned the art of working in metals; they were acquainted with the fire drill, and they knew how to carve figures of men, women, and animals in ivory or bone, and they could cut and polish stones. But they had not acquired the art of writing, and the graves contain no inscriptions to tell us what they thought about the dead and the region where they existed. Like their remote ancestors they, seemingly, held the view that a man could be dead and alive at the same time. Their progress in the mechanical arts they probably owed to influences which came from the east by way of SYRIA and PALESTINE, but their religious convictions and their views about the dead were the result of native guesswork, and they were current in EGYPT for many, many centuries.

What these convictions and views and beliefs were we now know from the funerary inscriptions written during the dynastic period. Those now generally known as the 'Pyramid Texts'. These are found inside the pyramids of five kings, viz. the last king of the IVth dynasty, and four of the kings of the Vth dynasty, built at ṢAḲḲÂRAH. Some of these texts were composed and used during the Neolithic period, and they contain extracts from semi-magical service-books containing various offices for the dead. Two, which were composed at a later period, contain a service for the 'Opening of the Mouth' of the dead, and a Liturgy which described many scores of offerings which were made to the dead, and the formula which was spoken at the presentation of each of them. Others of this group of texts contain a long series of magical spells and compositions which must be regarded as prayers of a purely religious character, and hymns of praise which form the nuclei of many hymns of the later period, and many myths and legends of which the legend of the entrance of king UNAS into heaven may be regarded as a typical example. Most important, too, are the passages which show that the cult of the Sun and

Moon and the Stars and the Planets was the oldest form of worship known in EGYPT. Many of the texts are found in more than one pyramid, but some paragraphs are found only in one pyramid. When they first came into use cannot be said, but their literary life seems to have ended with the downfall of the VIth dynasty. Copies on papyrus of some or all of them must have been carefully kept, for we find extracts from them written on the coffins of the Middle Kingdom, and in the Theban Recensions of the *Book*

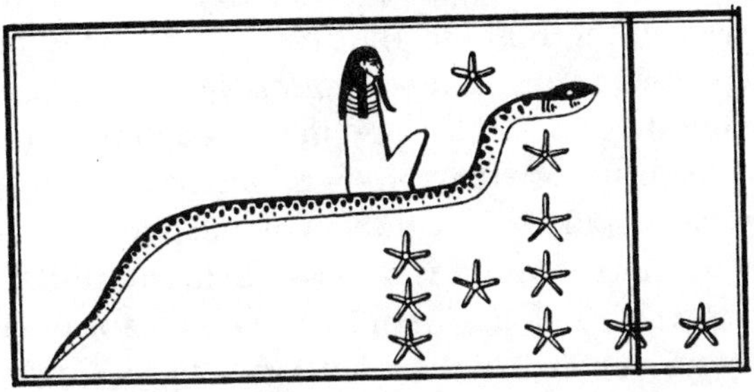

One of the gods near Orion and the god of a day of the month.

of the Dead, and in a few tombs of the late period, e.g. that of PEṬA-AMEN-APT at THEBES. A copy of several sections written during the reign of AMEN-ḤETEP III is preserved in the BRITISH MUSEUM.[1] The author, or editor, of the Pyramid Texts is unknown, and there is no mention that they were 'found' as ḤERṬAṬAF 'found' chapters XXX B and lxiv of the Theban *Book of the Dead* at HERMOPOLIS.[2] The EGYPTIAN probably assigned their authorship to THOTH, and if the GREEKS had known of them, they would have grouped them under the title of 'Hermetic Books'.

The Pyramid Texts are full of difficulties of every kind. The exact meanings of a large number of the words found in them are unknown, though in the light of later texts several of them can often be guessed at with a fair amount of success. The construction of the sentence often baffles all attempts to translate it, and when it contains wholly unknown words it becomes an unsolved riddle. It is only reasonable to suppose that these texts were often used for

1 First noticed by Birch and later by Renouf; see *Trans. Soc. Bibl. Arch.*, vol. ix, 1893, pp. 295–306.

2 See the rubrics to chapters XXX B and lxiv.

funerary purposes, but it is quite clear that the period of their use in EGYPT was little more than one hundred years. Why they were suddenly brought into use at the end of the Vth dynasty, and why they ceased to be used at the end of the VIth dynasty is inexplicable. Several passages bear evidence that the scribes who drafted the copies from which the cutters of the inscriptions worked did not understand what they were writing, and that, in consequence, they made mistakes, some of which modern Egyptologists have been able to correct. The general impression which their perusal leaves on the mind of the reader is that the priests who drafted the copies made extracts from several funerary compositions of different ages and having different contents, and that they did not trouble to arrange them in such a way as to form a connected work. In some instances the contents of one paragraph contradict those made in another and it is impossible to say which statement is the more correct. Beliefs, legends, and myths formulated by the EGYPTIANS at many stages of their development are thrown together and have become a confused mass. They show clearly that whilst the EGYPTIANS were ready and willing to adopt any belief which they thought might be of service to the dead, they found it impossible to abandon any which had been adopted by their forefathers. In such matters they forgot nothing and abandoned nothing.

The Pyramid Texts were written with one aim and object, viz. to help the kings in whose pyramids they were found to obtain everlasting life with the gods in heaven. Throughout them the kings are spoken of and described as living kings, who enter the abode of the gods with all the state and pomp with which they would enter a conquered country on earth. In fact UNAS and his successors are regarded not only as the equals of every god but as their overlords. When they sail over the waters of heaven they occupy the great boat of RĀ, and the gods, make provision for their safety, and serve as their oarsmen. They eat celestial food and drink celestial drink, and wear all the insignia which proclaims them to be the sovereign lords of the gods. Though their dead bodies lay under their tombs they were declared to be living in heaven. But having established their sovereignty in heaven how did they occupy themselves and pass their time? A remarkable passage which is found first in the pyramid of UNAS,[1] and later in the pyramid of TETA, throws much light on this point. This passage is probably one of the oldest in the Pyramid Texts, and it was probably written in very primitive times when magic was the only form of religion known to the EGYPTIANS, and when the region which the king entered after his death was inhabited by fetish spirits and not 'gods'. The variant readings which are found in the version given in the pyramid of TETA show that there were many passages in the older version of UNAS which the scribes did not understand. Why the Egyptian priests who had reached a high state of civilization under the Vth dynasty wished to represent a great king like UNAS as a brutal, cruel, licentious, and cannibalistic despot is not easily understood. Their description of his exploits in heaven is curiously like that which a scribe would write if he described what took place when an Egyptian king[2] made a great raid on the SÛDÂN. And it is possible that the priests who wrote the text for UNAS were influenced by what they must have heard of the raid of SENEFERU on the SÛDÂN about a century earlier. He slew the Blacks, and according to the PALERMO STONE, brought back to EGYPT 7,000 captives and 200,000 sheep and cattle, and left the whole country a ruin. The following is a translation of the passage describing the exploits of UNAS in heaven:

496. The heavens dissolve in a flood of water, the stars drop [like rain] out of the sky.
497. The tie-beams (?) slip from their sockets.
498. The bones (i.e. framework) of the god AKER[3] tremble. The messengers run about distractedly, when they see
499. UNAS, [who] appeareth, being endowed with a Ba like unto a god [who] liveth on his fathers and eateth
500. his mothers. This UNAS is the lord of wisdom (?), ignorant is
501. his mother of his name.[4] The augustness (or majesty) of UNAS is in heaven, his power (or strength) is in the horizon,

[1] First published with a French translation by Maspero in the earlier volumes, of the *Recueil de Travaux*, Paris, 1870 f., and later in *Les Inscriptions des Pyramides de Saqqarah*, Paris, 1894. A better text will be found in Sethe, *Pyramidentexte*, i, p. 205, Leipzig, 1898.

[2] The destruction and slaughter were always the same; see the instructive inscription on the stelae of Usertsen (Senusert) iii.

[3] The Earth-god, older than Gebb. Var. Earth-gods.

[4] i.e. Unas now belongs to the celestial hierarchy.

502. even as is that of TEM (ATEM), his father, which begot him. [ATEM] begot him, but he (i.e. UNAS) is mightier than he. The KAU[1] (male)

503. of UNAS are behind him, his ḤEMSUT (female),  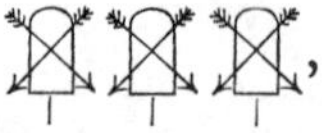, are under his feet, his gods are on him, the Cobra-goddesses are

504. on his skull, the Cobra-guide-goddess is on his forehead, seeth (?) the Soul, the blazing-goddess AAKHUT.

505. The sceptres (or powers?) of UNAS are for his protection. UNAS is the Bull[2] of the heavens, terrible in his heart, living upon the being

506. of every god. He eateth of their viscera when, with their bellies filled with magical powers ( ḤEKAU), they come from the fiery Island of SASA. This UNAS is provided

507. with the offerings (?) of his Spirits (?). UNAS riseth up like this UR (i.e. Great God), he is the lord of those who are in the position of deputy-gods. He sitteth down [with] his back near GEBB.

508. This UNAS is he who issueth decrees of judgement with the being whose name is hidden on this day of the slaying of the elders. This god is the Lord of offerings, who casteth the knotted cord (i.e. the lasso), and who himself prepareth meat and drink for his meal.

509. This UNAS devoureth men and liveth on the gods. He is the LORD of the bearers of offerings, and is the divider of offerings. AKHEM-UPT (i.e. Arranger of skulls), the dweller in KHAU, bindeth them together for UNAS.

510. DJESER-TEP (i.e. Handsome of head?) shepherdeth them and driveth them to him; ḤERI-TERUT bindeth them for him; KHENSU-METES stabs (or decapitates) them for UNAS.

511. He teareth out whatsoever is in their bellies. He (or it) is the envoy which he sendeth to meet him. SHESMU[3] slayeth them for UNAS. He cooketh parts of them in his cauldrons [which are heated] in the evenings.

[1] i.e. the powers which protect him and form his guardian angels.
[2] i.e. he is identified with one of the great stars.
[3] Later the headsman or executioner of Osiris.

512. This UNAS eateth their magic (ḤEKA), and swalloweth their noble powers (or qualities). Their great ones are [reserved] for his meal on the following day; the lesser in size are [reserved] for his evening meal; and the small ones are [reserved] for his meal at midnight.

513. Their old males and their old females [are burnt as incense] in his censers (or furnaces). The great [star]-gods who are in the north of the heavens spew out fire into the cauldrons under which the legs and thighs of their oldest ones are placed [as fuel].

514. Those who dwell in the heavens circle round about UNAS as helpers, the cauldrons are bursting (?) with the legs of their females (or women). UNAS hath gone round about through the two heavens, he hath gone round about the ATEBUI (i.e. the right and left banks of the NILE). This UNAS is the SEKHEM-UR  (i.e. the Great Power), the Power

515. among the Powers (i.e. the Greatest of the Powers). This UNAS in the ĀSHEM,[1] the ĀSHEM of the ĀSHEMU, the Great Ones. He whom he findeth on his way he devoureth forthwith (?). The position of UNAS is at the head of (or in front of)

516. all the SĀḤU (Giants?) who are dwellers in the horizon. This UNAS is the god who is older than the Old [gods]. Thousands are assigned to him, hundreds are offered up to him as sacrifices. SĀḤU (i.e. ORION), the Father of the gods, hath given unto him an authority (i.e. Patent)[2] as a SEKHEM-UR (i.e. Great Power).

517. UNAS hath risen up again as king in the heavens, he weareth the crown as 'Lord of the Horizon'. He hath dislocated the vertebrae and the ligatures of the loins. He hath seized and carried off the hearts of the gods.

518. He hath eaten the Red Crown, he hath swallowed the Green Crown. UNAS hath devoured the lungs of the wise [gods], he is replete for he is living on the hearts of the gods, and

519. likewise (?) on their ḤEKAU (i.e. magical powers). UNAS rejoiceth because he is tasting the SEBSHU which dwell in the Red Crown. He flourisheth [for] their ḤEKAU are in his belly

[1] A title, the meaning of which is unknown; probably a very old word for Chief.

[2] Compare the Paizâ of the Mongol kings.

520. and the SĀḤU of UNAS cannot be snatched away from him. UNAS hath eaten the intelligence (or wisdom) of every god. The period of life of UNAS is eternity, the boundary thereof is
521. everlastingness in this his SĀḤ. What he wisheth [to do] he will do; what he hateth [to do] he will not do: he is the dweller in the limit of the horizon—everlastingness [and] eternity.
522. Behold, their soul is in the body of UNAS, their spells are with UNAS. The offerings made to him are more numerous than
523. those made to the gods; the heat of UNAS [cometh] from their bones. Behold, their soul is with UNAS, together with their Shades and with their attributes.
524. UNAS is like unto him who riseth up [and continueth to] rise up; hidden, hidden. . . .[1]
525. The place of the heart of UNAS (i.e. the place where he wishes to dwell) is among the Living Ones in this land for ever and ever.

Thus we see that UNAS entered the Other World as a son of TEM, or ATEM, and was well received by the gods who were there. He hunts the gods, lassoes them, and slays them and eats them, and so absorbs into his person their magical powers and all their attributes; thereby he becomes immortal. He is assisted by the great Star-gods who are more powerful than the other 'gods', and ORION grants him a patent of authority to rule and to demand offerings, in the same way that thousands of years later Asiatic kings granted to their chief governors power to rule and to levy taxes. It must be noted that ORION is called the 'father of the gods', which suggests that the original form of the text in the pyramid of UNAS was drawn up at the time when the cult of the stars was predominant in EGYPT. And passages in many texts prove that in the earliest times kings and others were believed to enjoy their life of immortality in the form of stars and to join the company of the 'imperishable' stars of heaven.

From first to last there is no mention in the texts of the resurrection of the material body; indeed, we are told quite clearly, 'The AKHU (i.e. soul or spirit) to heaven, the body to earth' (Pyr. § 474). 'Thy water (i.e. essence) to heaven, thy body to earth' (Pyr. § 667).

[1] The rest of this line has baffled translators up to the present. It seems to have reference to agricultural labours which Unas will not have to perform.

And in texts of the Ptolemaic period (e.g. *The Lamentations of Isis*) we find 'Heaven holdeth thy soul, earth holdeth thy mummy'. But it is certain that it was something which had formed part of the economy of the physical body *khat*  which enjoyed the life in heaven; what was that something? On this matter the Pyramid Texts throw much light as we shall see from the following extracts:

1. 'Thou art pure, thy Ka is pure, thy Ba is pure, thy SEKHEM is pure'   (§ 837).

2. 'UNAS is happy with his Ka, UNAS liveth with his Ka'   (§ 338).

3. 'This PEPI liveth with his Ka'   (§ 908).

4. 'Thy Ba standeth among the gods'   (§ 723).

5. 'Thy Ba is equipped like the star SIRIUS'  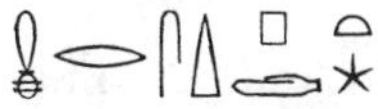; 'Thou becomest a Ba being made a Ba'   (*ibid.*).

6. 'Thy Ba is a star, behold it is the foremost of its brethren'  (§ 904).

7. 'Thy SEKHEM cometh to thee among the AAKHU' 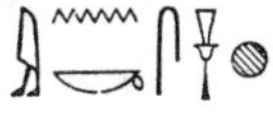  (§ 758).

8. 'Set ye his (i.e. PEPI'S) SEKHEM among the gods'   (§ 880).

9. 'Set ye his (i.e. PEPI'S) AKHU among the AKHU'  .

10. 'Behold UNAS, he cometh forth on this day in the true (or real) form of a living AKHU'   (§ 318).

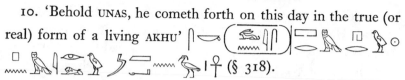

11. 'Behold thou art an AAKHU'  (§ 623); 'Thou art an AAKHU with all the AKHU'  (§ 624).

12. 'Thou hast received thy SĀḤ'  (§ 622).

13. 'The life of UNAS is everlasting, his limit is eternity in this his SĀḤ 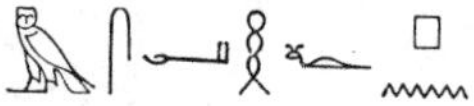 (§ 412).

14. 'Behold their (i.e. the gods') soul is under UNAS, their Shadows with their attributes' 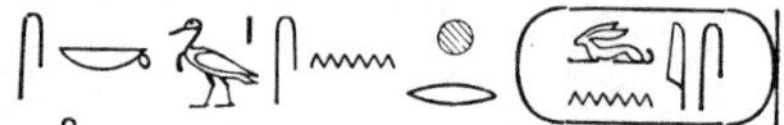  (§ 413).

15. 'This PEPI is happy with his name' 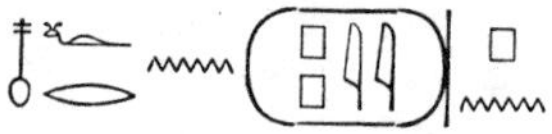 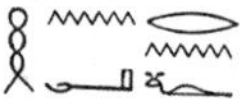 (§ 908).

Now, from the above extracts from the Pyramid Texts we learn that in addition to a physical body  *khat* a man possessed a Ka, and a Ba, a KHAIBIT, and a REN.

The Ka 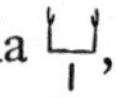, plur. Kau , , and . The exact meaning of this word is unknown, but it has been translated by 'double, image, genius, subconscious self, natural disposition, abstract personality, character, mind', &c.; all these meanings are suggested by their contexts, but the real meaning of the word has yet to be discovered. The EGYPTIANS themselves do not seem to be certain about what the Ka really was. According to the Pyramid Texts the Ka lived in heaven, and we read that 'UNAS was happy with his Ka', and 'the Ka of UNAS is [joined] to his body'; to go to one's Ka was a euphemism for dying. The belief that the Ka lived in heaven is supported by the testimony of the Memphite theologians who declared that their god PTAḤ was the creator of the Kau. The Ka of UNAS was his guide and protector in heaven, and was inseparable from him. The intimate relationship of the king and the Ka in heaven suggests that a particular Ka had been associated with the king on earth, and this is exactly what the texts of the New Kingdom prove. Summarizing the numerous statements on the subject found in the texts of the Middle and New Kingdoms we may take it for granted that a Ka from heaven was born with a man; whether it became joined to a man at the moment of his conception or at his birth cannot be said. The painted reliefs in the temples show that the Ka had the usual shape and form of the man to whom it was attached, and that it was to all intents and purposes his dual personality, in fact a double or a duplicate of him. It is possible that the Ka which lived in heaven had a double which lived on earth, and some holding this view have thought that the Ka on earth might be described as a sort of guardian angel, perhaps even a sort of Egyptian *guru*.

Now the funerary texts prove that the Ka which was born with a man did not go to heaven when he died, but lived in the tomb near his body, and subsisted on the offerings of meat, bread, fruit, flowers, vegetables, wine, milk, beer, &c. In many tombs a portion of the chamber, or hall, which was connected with the underground mummy chamber by means of a shaft, or pit, was enclosed with slabs of stone and called the 'house of the Ka' . A life-like figure or statue, seated or standing, was placed therein, and in it the Ka of the deceased, or perhaps the deceased himself, was believed to dwell. An opening in the stone partition was made, or a space between the slabs was left, so that the perfume of the incense might penetrate the Ka-chapel. Through two other small openings on the eye-line of the statue the Ka watched the performance of the ritual of offerings on days of festival and other occasions, and enjoyed the perfume of the incense. And the sight of the pouring out of libations of cool water by the 'priest (or minister) of the Ka' , and the kinsmen and friends of the deceased, refreshed the Ka. Wealthy folk handed over the care of their tombs to the Ka-priest, whose duty was to keep the tomb clean, and to arrange for a regular supply of offerings. The feeding of the Ka was a most important duty, for if the Ka was not fed, it would leave the tomb and go out and search for bread and water in the cemetery or town; and if hard pressed by hunger or thirst it might be compelled to eat filth and even to drink filthy water. It is probable that the views about the Ka held under the earlier dynasties were different from those current under the XIIth and following dynasties; under the New Empire almost every funerary text of any size or interest ends with the entreaty that sepulchral offerings may be given with unfailing regularity to the Ka of the deceased. If we are to understand that the deceased and his Ka are in heaven enjoying the food of the gods, why, we must ask, was it necessary to feed the Ka which remained on earth in the tomb?

Many passages in the Pyramid Texts mention the *Heart* of the deceased, and in § 748 it is stated that 'the heart[1] of the king shall not be carried off from him, his breast[2] shall not be removed from him'. The heart was regarded as the seat of the mind, will, wish, lust, desire, courage, sense, wisdom, intelligence, understanding, &c., and as the prime mover of the actions of the body. But it was in some way intimately connected with the Ka, as we may see from the prayer which was addressed to it by the deceased when he was in the Hall of Judgement of OSIRIS. He says, using the words as a magical prayer, 'My heart of my mother! My heart of my mother! My breast of my coming into being.[3] Resist me not during my evidence (or testifying), oppose me not before the Judges (DJADJAU), make not any turning away from me before the Keeper of the Scales (i.e. ANPU, ANUBIS). Thou art my Ka in my belly; [thou art] KHNEMU who maketh strong my members.' Later he prays that no one may make his name to stink with the SHENIT (i.e. great officials of the Hall), who make men, that men may not rise up against him, and that no lies may be told about him to the god [OSIRIS].[4] This mention of the Ka with KHNEMU, a very ancient god of the NILE and lord of the waters of heaven, is very interesting, but difficult to explain. It is clear that under the New Kingdom the Ka was a sort of guardian angel of the deceased, who expected it to bear testimony in his favour. This suggests that the heart of

1 *ab* § 748, § 311; plur. *abu* §§ 590, 1039.

2 *hat* .

3 See *Book of the Dead*, chapter XXX B.

4 See the variant 'my breast of my existence upon earth' (Papyrus of Nu, chap. XXX A).

a man might not always be in agreement with his Ka, which could be independent and be a law unto itself.

The next important spiritual element which dwelt in a man was the Ba[1] which appears in the Pyramid Texts as a bird with a tuft at its breast , but in later times as a man-headed hawk . This very ancient word has by general consent among Egyptologists been translated 'soul', but it seems certain that the meaning which the primitive EGYPTIAN gave to the word is very different from that which is given to it by scholars at the present day. The etymology of Ba is unknown.

Nebseni on his bier embraced by the Ba of Thena.

From first to last the EGYPTIANS believed in a future life, for they 'loved life and hated death', and they could not, and did not, think that the death of the body defined the period of their existence. They knew quite well that the physical body of a man could not live for ever, for they had daily proof before their eyes that the dead *did* 'see corruption'. And how could the bodies of those who were devoured by the wild beasts of the desert or by the crocodiles of the NILE, live again? Yet their faith in the future life never wavered, and they came to the conclusion that there must be in the corruptible body a something which could be separated from it and would live after the death of its body. To that something they gave the name of 'Ba', which, judging from the use of a verbal form of the word found in early texts, means 'strength', 'vital power', and the like. But how was that something, that Ba, to be obtained from the dead body which lay before them? In the earliest times the EGYPTIANS performed a series of magical ceremonies over the dead to ensure the continuance of their lives, just as many of the natives of WEST AFRICA do at the present day. But later the legend of the resurrection of OSIRIS came into being, and the medicine men (magicians) and priests did for the dead what ANUBIS, THOTH, HORUS, and ISIS had done to effect the resurrection

[1] In late texts  Bai or Bi

of OSIRIS. A legend also existed to the effect that SHU[1] opened the mouth of the gods who had died with an iron knife. Once the mouth was opened the deceased was able to breathe, and the power

Ani and his Ba leaving his tomb.

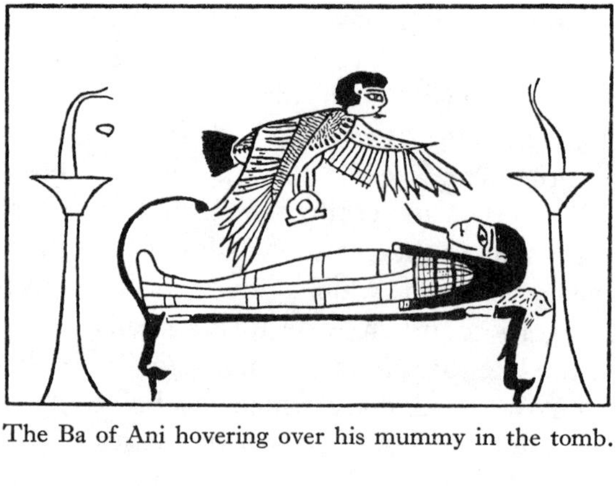

The Ba of Ani hovering over his mummy in the tomb.

to use his throat returned to him and he was able to swallow, and to move the tongue; other ceremonies were relied upon to open the eyes, ears, and nostrils. And when all these things had been done for King TETA he was able 'to weigh words, and to pass judge-

[1] Ani the scribe asked Ptaḥ to open his mouth and to remove the swathings with which Set had bound his mouth (chap. xxiii).

ment on the Two Brothers (HORUS and SET), and to give commands to one who was greater than himself' (Pyr. §§ 712, 713).

In the case of OSIRIS many gods and goddesses collected his bones, and reconstituted his flesh, and restored his head to him, and after he was mummified, HORUS 'opened his mouth with his little finger' 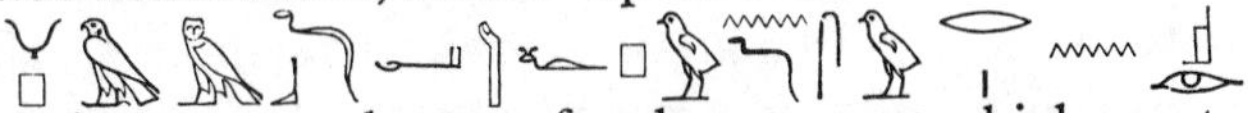 (PEPI I. 590), and so prepared OSIRIS for the great act which was to revivify his whole body and restore to him his mental faculties, and the seat of them, his heart. Next HORUS took his eye which SET had blinded and torn out of his (HORUS's) face, but which had been restored to him by THOTH, and thrust it into the newly reopened mouth of OSIRIS, and made him to live in his name of ĀNDJ-TI, . The Eye of HORUS is described as 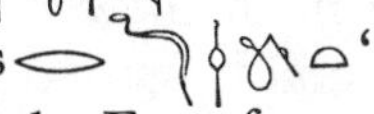 'the one which grows'.[1] Through the Eye of HORUS OSIRIS became a Ba, but he retained the form which his mummified body had, and as king and judge of the dead he is represented in the form of a mummy.

Horus and Set in a single body.

When the EGYPTIANS wished to make the Ba to develop out of the dead man they repeated the ritual and the spells which had been used by the gods to effect the revivification of OSIRIS.[2] They were unable to obtain the use of the Eye of HORUS,[3] so they called each of the long series of objects which they offered to the dead the 'Eye of HORUS', and the spell which was pronounced by the priest when he offered it was believed to transmute it into a form suitable for absorption by the Ba.

The scenes painted on the walls of the tombs and the vignettes in the funerary papyri show that the Ba was supposed to take the form of the individual from whom it proceeded, that is to say, the Ba of a man had the form of an unmummified human being, male or female. It could move about at will, could travel through the

[1] Pyr. § 614. The Horus here referred to was the Old Horus, the Sky-god, whose right eye was the sun and the left the moon.

[2] See the translation in Part II of this book, pp. 513–16.

[3] 'Eye of Horus' was the name given to the power and strength of the Sun-god which were regarded as an entirely independent god.

air, the waters, and the earth, and hunt and fish, and play draughts, and return to earth and visit its earthly body lying in the tomb. Though, of necessity, an immaterial body, it needed food and drink as we see from several passages in the funerary papyri. The whole conception of the Ba is full of difficulties, for according to the texts it was a ghost and a material body at the same time, and it possessed a kind of divine nature and character. Man, according to the legend, was formed of the water which dropped from the eyes of the Sun-god on to his members or the dust, and, as the Sun-god had a Ba, naturally each of the men he created must also have had a Ba. To evoke this Ba from the dead body was the object of every rite, and ceremony, and spell, and offering, employed for the benefit of the dead. It is quite clear that the part of man which lived after death was the Ba, or 'soul', as this word is usually translated; a better rendering would be 'ghost', or 'wraith', or 'apparition'. The Ba seems to be the equivalent of the old Sumerian *edimmu*, which I am informed by MR. SIDNEY SMITH developed itself from the *skin* of the man to whom it was related.

Many African peoples[1] have regarded the *shadow* of a man as a part of him, and believed that harm could be done to a man by stepping or walking on it. Similarly a man could protect a friend or harm a foe by causing his shadow to fall upon him. Though the Ba was a kind of spirit body the EGYPTIANS assigned to it a shadow,  *Khaibit*, and the Pyramid Texts show that the gods were supposed to cast shadows. In the Theban *Book of the Dead* (chaps. xci, xcii) the deceased prays that his Ba and his Khaibit may not be held captives in the Other World. In another place the Ba, and Akhu, and Shadow are mentioned together. In the Papyrus of NEFER-UBEN-F the Ba of the deceased is seen hovering over his shadow, which is painted black. Many other examples are given by BIRCH in his papers on the 'Shadow of the Dead', in *Trans. Soc. Bibl. Arch.*, 1885, vol. viii, p. 386 f.

The *name* of a man being equivalent to the man himself was always regarded as possessing special importance, and every EGYPTIAN took pains to have it cut and painted on the various articles of his funerary equipment. In the extract from the text of PEPI

[1] See Nassau, *Fetishism in West Africa*, pp. 65, 230; Kingsley, *West African Studies*, p. 207; Hollis, *The Nandi*, p. 41.

given above (p. 328) the NAME *ren* seems to have been associated with the Ka; as there is no mention of PEPI receiving a new name we may assume that the name in which the king was rejoicing in heaven was that which he most loved upon earth. PEPI prayed that his name might 'grow' or 'flourish' and endure as long as the names of the gods endured. His prayer, with certain necessary modifications, was in common use as a separate funerary work in

The sun rising above the tomb of Nefer-uben-f. Close by stands the Shadow of the deceased with his soul above it.

the Graeco-Roman period in EGYPT. The deceased's name endured on earth likewise as we see from the passage, 'Thy name liveth upon earth, thy name flourisheth upon earth; thou shalt not decay, thou shalt not perish for ever and ever' (Pyr. § 764). And one of PEPI's names was 'Essence renewing [its] life' (§ 767).

In the Pyramid Texts we find several passages in which the deceased is mentioned in close connexion with groups of beings who are called SEKHEMU, SĀḤU, and AAKHU (see above p. 327), and it was at one time thought that these were members of the mental and spiritual parts of a man. The SEKHEM was said to be the vital power, or rather the source of all physical strength in the body. The SĀḤ was said to be the beatified body of the man which was made for its abode in the Other World, and the AKHU was held to be a sort of ethereal, translucent, and transparent spirit-soul akin to, but somewhat different from, the Ba. But this view which was held by DÜMICHEN cannot be maintained now, for the general evidence indicates that the SEKHEMU, the SĀḤU, and the AKHU were Bau or 'Souls' who had attained to a high degree of power, glory, and knowledge. The deceased, it seems, acquired these attributes by virtue of the favour of the great gods, to which, presumably, we may add his own merit. Another view is that the SEKHEMU, SĀḤU, and AKHU were different orders of spirits, similar to the orders of angels, Thrones, Dominions, Powers, Principalities, &c., which are enumerated by ST. PAUL (Col., i. 16) and in the apocryphal literature of the Old and New Testaments.

When exactly the Ba began its beatified existence we do not know, but it was probably immediately after the funerary ceremonies had been performed. The Pyramid Texts do not describe the weighing of the heart in a pair of Scales as we find it treated at great length in chapter cxxv of the Theban *Book of the Dead*. But there are several passages in them which prove that even a king had to possess moral worth to such a degree that even the gods were satisfied on this point, and accepted his presence among them without demur. In some way the king must have justified himself, for even his 'righteousness' is referred to, but of course the degree of moral worth demanded by RĀ and his gods and goddesses under the Vth dynasty was not so great as that which a would-be denizen of heaven would have to possess before he was admitted to the kingdom of the heaven of OSIRIS under the XVIIIth dynasty. The life of the Ba in heaven was at once material and spiritual.

Though it was never forgotten that the body to which the Ba belonged lay in its tomb, and the needs of its Ka were carefully supplied, it was the life of the Ba in heaven which chiefly occupied the minds of the theologians. But in spite of this the theologians were greatly concerned about the food supply of the Ba. The offerings made to his Ka in the tomb were by means of the magical formulas recited by the priests daily transmuted into a form suitable for absorption by him, though some passages suggest that they were transported to him direct by THOTH and other star-gods. Also, as the son of the goddess NUT (who brought him forth on her two thighs), begotten by RĀ, NUT suckled him, and when necessary the other sky-goddesses assisted her as well as the two ancient Mother-goddesses NEKHEBIT and UADJIT. This took place as long as the king was a child  in heaven (Pyr. § 912), but when he grew up RĀ provided him with the 'bread which never became stale, and the beer which never went sour'.[1] But though the Ba of the king was amply provided with food and drink by the gods, and he also had the power to hunt the game of heaven, and to fish its waters, it was thought that he might still suffer from hunger and thirst, and be reduced to wandering about picking up food wherever he could find it. Moreover, it was imagined that he might even be driven to devour his own excreta and urine. And it is distinctly said that the Ba of TETA 'abominated filth, and revolted at urine, and that he would not drink it'.[2] This belief lasted for many centuries for in the Papyrus of NU, which was written early under the XVIIIth dynasty, the deceased says, 'The things which I abominate I will not eat. What I abominate is filth; I will not eat thereof. . . . Let me not fall down upon it, let it not light upon my body, let it not touch my fingers and my toes. . . . I will not tread on it with my sandals. O send not filthy water (or urine) over me.'

From the above paragraphs it will be seen that the Ba of the king is regarded both as a human and a spiritual being, and the EGYPTIANS do not appear to have noticed the absurdity and the contradictions in their funerary texts, and in the beliefs which they, and we also, could deduce from them. Again, in the earlier texts RĀ is the god and king of heaven, and the deceased becomes his son, and RĀ did not, and could not, die; in the later texts OSIRIS has usurped the position and functions of RĀ, although he had died, and the deceased then became his son. The heaven of RĀ was in the sky, a fact proved by scores of definite assertions in the Pyramid Texts, whilst the heaven of OSIRIS, or rather his kingdom, was originally in the Underworld. But there was another heaven which was older than the heavens of RĀ and OSIRIS, which was that portion of the sky in which dwelt the gods of the stars, whose cult preceded the worship of RĀ and OSIRIS. The original forms of the Pyramid Texts were written by theologians who were worshippers of RĀ.

1 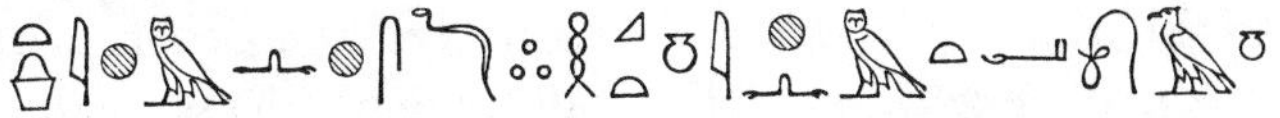 § 859.

2  Pyr. § 718.

They ignored the Star-gods, probably because the cult of them was moribund or obsolete, but traces of stellar belief crept into their writings. Then, in the century which followed the building of the pyramid of UNAS, the cult of OSIRIS, the man king who was believed to have died and risen from the dead, developed and spread with great rapidity. And the priests of RĀ were compelled to express in their texts the beliefs and tenets and dogmas of the priests of OSIRIS, who as the champion of the dead was obviously the antagonist or foe of RĀ, who could not die himself and was the almighty and everlasting god of the living. The priests found great difficulty in arranging their different views and trying to harmonize them; they failed to do so, and therefore we find many contradictions in the Pyramid Texts. But it is nevertheless clear that the life of the royal Ba after death was believed to be a happy one, and the scribes are never tired of describing its joys and delights.

The HEAVEN of the Pyramid Texts was in the eastern part of the sky, and the heaven of OSIRIS was in the west; the west from time immemorial in EGYPT was regarded as the home of the dead. The principal title of OSIRIS was 'Chief of those who are in the West', (KHENTI AMENTIU), but his priests only claimed it for their god after he had usurped the powers and attributes of the old gods of the dead of UPPER EGYPT. At one time the deceased was supposed to ascend to heaven by means of a ladder, and in the case of the royal Ba the ladder was set up by the gods and held in position by them whilst the Ba mounted it. The following brief extracts describe the delights of heaven according to the theologians of the Old Kingdom. The Ba entered heaven as a 'living soul', as one who had eaten the Eye of HORUS. He was welcomed by the gods and goddesses and by the SĀḤU and the AKHU, and the Living Ones, and the Kau and other denizens of the eastern sky. Though a spirit being, he wears crowns similar to those which he wore on earth, and he holds all the other symbols of sovereignty, his sceptre and his weapons. He is equipped with the implements of a fisherman and a hunter, and he has full use of the boats of RĀ and the divine ferryman and his boat. Every member of him is a god, he becomes a god being the son of a god, and the gods and goddesses call him 'brother'. He rules the gods, and the Great and Little Company of the gods stretch out their hands to him, and invite him to take his seat among them. In the earlier texts he is the son of RĀ and consubstantial with him; in the later texts he is HORUS, the son of OSIRIS, and does for him what HORUS did, and the gods and goddesses of the Company of OSIRIS are his brothers and sisters. He is the brother of the Moon, and the son of SOTHIS (SIRIUS); he revolves in heaven like ORION; and he rises in his place like a star, being one of the everlasting and never-setting stars of the northern sky. He is more resplendent than the AKHU, more perfect than the perfect ones, more stable than the stable gods, and he sits on the shoulders of RĀ. HORUS exchanges his Ka with him, and with his new Ka he crushes all hostile Kau. And he becomes the overlord of the Ka of the three Companies of the gods. He also becomes THOTH, the mind and wisdom of RĀ, and thus he acquires the power to judge hearts. He takes his seat with the god in his holy sanctuary. He is acclaimed as 'MAĀ-KHERU' 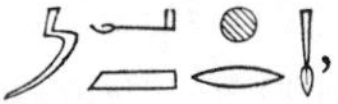, i.e. 'true of voice' (more frequently translated 'justified' or 'triumphant'), and his Ka likewise. This proves that the king had to submit to some form of judgement. He is arrayed in white apparel which is like unto the finest raiment of those who sit on the throne of living right and truth, and the framework of his iron throne is decorated with the faces of lions, and its legs have the feet of bulls. On his head he wears the great Urerit Crown.

Many paragraphs refer to his FOOD and DRINK. He neither thirsts nor hungers, for he eats what RĀ eats, and he drinks what RĀ drinks, and his food is the words which come forth from the mouth of GEBB (the Earth-god) and the gods. He sits with the great gods around the lake in the SEKHET-ḤETEP and they feed him on the 'Tree of Life'  whereon they live that he may also live. He and his Ka are washed clean and they eat bread together for ever. TEMU protects him and destroys his foes, he can never enter the earth again for his Ba hath broken the bonds of his sleep in his house upon earth. 'UNAS is in heaven, in the form of air (?), he is firmly stablished in heaven, he cannot perish, and he taketh his august seat in the bows of the Boat of RĀ. Those who row RĀ up into heaven, and those who row him under the horizon, row UNAS also. Like RĀ he entereth the west of the sky and cometh forth from the east thereof'. Notwithstanding such lofty conceptions concerning the spiritual life of the deceased, the EGYPTIANS attribute to him the passions of love and hate and speak of him as exercising the functions of the natural body; UNAS eats and drinks and voids water, and seizes women and has union with them whenever he is pleased to do so.

The texts written inside the pyramid of PEPI II prove beyond all doubt that when that king died after his very long reign of over ninety years, the priests of OSIRIS had forced the priests of RĀ to assign to their god a position in the Other World as great and powerful as that of RĀ. The god of the dead OSIRIS, whose kingdom was underground, and whose enmity to RĀ is so often referred to in the texts, had become the equal of RĀ, the king of heaven, and had usurped the powers which he, as successor to the old Sun-god HORUS, had enjoyed. The priests of RĀ gave the monopoly of heaven to the king, and the priests of OSIRIS broke it, and all sorts and conditions of men could enter into it henceforth. The cult of the stars which had preceded the cult of RĀ was absorbed into the cult of OSIRIS, and the priests of OSIRIS could offer to their congregations the choice of three heavens from which to select a 'place of abiding for eternity', viz. the 'unresting stars and the never setting stars', and the Boat of the Sun, and the subterranean ṬUAT.[1] OSIRIS was the 'lord of heaven' and the 'lord of the ṬUAT'. The priests of RĀ tried to harmonize the conflicting views, but they failed, and it is now impossible to correct the mistakes they made and to disentangle the confusions which they caused. And there are evidences in the Pyramid Texts that the scribes did not understand the meaning of some of the texts which they were adapting and drafting; in all ages copyists have made mistakes!

After the downfall of the Old Kingdom men no longer built pyramids for tombs, but they inscribed funerary texts on the walls of their rectangular stone tombs. Later, under the XIth and XIIth dynasties, they inscribed copies of these texts on the insides of huge wooden sarcophagi which took the place of the old stone-walled halls of the tombs. These texts, which are generally known as 'Coffin Texts', represent the complete fusion of the funerary

[1] Written sometimes with a star as determinative  (Pyr. § 8) and sometimes with the sign for city ⊗ as determinative  (Pyr. §§ 8, 820 *e*).

beliefs concerning RĀ as god of heaven, and OSIRIS as lord of the ṬUAT. OSIRIS has in them usurped the place of RĀ and become his overlord, and his kingdom which was in the subterranean west, and was only allowed to be near the east, has been transferred wholly to the sky. Here and there we find traces of the old star-worship, and the deceased not only becomes absorbed into the god of heaven, whether he be RĀ or OSIRIS, but has his final home in a star, e.g. ORION. In the Pyramid Texts heaven was reserved for kings only, but the Coffin Texts show that in the interval between the VIth and the XIth dynasties, scribes, high officials, and noblemen claimed a right to enter the heaven which had formerly been occupied by gods and kings only. The 'Coffin Texts' reproduce much that is found in the Pyramid Texts, but they also contain much interesting information on matters about which the older texts are silent.

In the Pyramid Texts the king is made to live a majestic but solitary life as far as parents, wife and family, and kinsfolk, and friends are concerned. But among the Coffin Texts there is a chapter[1] entitled, 'The gathering together of the ancestors of a man to him in KHERT NETER' (i.e. the Underworld) which shows that the EGYPTIANS believed that the reunion of families and the recognition of friends and acquaintances took place in the Other World. The text has been edited by M. LACAU from two coffins which were found at AL-BARSHAH in UPPER EGYPT and are now in the EGYPTIAN MUSEUM in CAIRO (Nos. 28083 and 28087). The name of the individual for whom the coffin was made was SEPI. The text reads:

'Hail, RĀ! Hail, TEM! Hail GEBB! Hail, NUT!

'Grant ye unto SEPA (or SEPI) that he may traverse the sky, that he may traverse the earth, and that he may traverse the waters. And grant that he may meet his forefathers, may meet his father, may meet his mother, may meet his sons and daughters who grew up, may meet his brethren, may meet his sisters, may meet his friends, both male and female, may meet those who have been as parents to him (uncles and aunts? foster-parents?) may meet those who have worked for him upon earth, both male and female, and may meet the concubine whom he loved and knew.

'Behold, O QEMA-UR (i.e. Great Creator), make SEPI to rejoin his grown

[1] See Lacau in *Recueil de Travaux*, Paris, 1904, pp. 67–72, and 'La réunion de la famille' by J. Baillet in *Journal Asiatique*, Xème Série, tom. iv, p. 307 f.

up sons and daughters, and his concubines who were the desire of his heart, and make SEPI to rejoin his friends, both male and female, and those who have worked for him upon earth.

'And if it should happen that his fathers should be turned aside, or oppressed, or removed, when he would appear to SEPI; or his mother when she wished to reveal herself to him, when SEPI wisheth to rejoin his forefathers, and his father, and mother, and men and women; and if it should happen that the reunion of SEPI with his young children, or brethren and sisters, or friends, or foster parents, or kinsfolk, or those who have worked for him upon earth, should be turned aside, or opposed, or done away; then, verily the heart which is equipped shall be removed from RĀ, and the oxen which have been chosen for sacrifice shall be driven away from the altars of the gods, and the bread-cakes shall not be broken, and the white loaves shall not be cut in pieces, and the meat offering shall not be sliced in the hall of sacrifice, and ropes shall not be wound, and boats shall not be manned for you.

'But, if he shall be with his father when he appeareth, and if he shall be able to receive his mother when she cometh, and if he shall be rejoined to his ancestors, and to his fathers and his mothers, and his men and his women, and his little children, and his loved ones, and his foster-parents, and his kinsfolk, and his [grown-up] sons and daughters, and his concubines, whom it is his heart's desire [to meet], and his friends, and those who have worked for him upon earth; and if he shall rejoin all his ancestors in heaven, and on earth, and in KHERT NETER, and in the sky, and in AQEB (i.e. a region of the sky), and in ḤĀPI (i.e. the NILE), and in AGEB, and in HET-UR-KAU, and in ṬEṬU, and in ṬEṬET (?), and in PA-UR, and in ĀḤAKHER, and in ABTU; then, verily the loaves shall be broken, and the white bread cakes shall be cut in pieces, and verily the meat offerings shall be cut up in the hall of sacrifice [in the tomb], and verily ropes wound, and boats shall be manned, and verily the Boat of RĀ shall journey on its way, being rowed by the mariners of the Stars that never set and the Stars that never rest; now his name is unknown, his name is unknown.

'The goddess HATHOR surroundeth SEPI with the magic which protecteth his life, but it is GEBB (the Earth-god) who equippeth him. The sister-wife of SEPI is the guardian of the wood (?) of the Great Field. And behold, the sister[-wife] of SEPI, the guardian of the wood of the Great Field, saith, "Verily thou shalt come with rejoicing, and thy heart shall be glad, and there shall be food to SEPI, and air shall be given unto thee; yea, this have thy forefathers commanded." Therefore shall SEPI come with gladness, and his heart shall rejoice, and his forefathers shall be given unto him. And the chiefs of the forefathers of SEPI shall come [to meet him] which gladness, and their hearts shall be glad, and their hearts shall be glad when they meet him. And they shall carry in their hands their staves, and their mattocks, and their tools for ploughing, and their metal weapons of the earth, and they shall deliver him from the things which the goddess . . . doeth, and from the operations of NUT, and from the mighty things which the twin Lions (i.e. SHU and TEFNUT) do to every soul and to every god. The forefathers of SEPI shall cause him to be delivered.'

The RUBRIC reads:

'And to him in KHERT NETER shall be rejoined forefathers, father, mother, kinsfolk, young children, wives, concubines, friends male and female, slaves, and the property of every kind which belongeth unto him.'

From this chapter it is clear that under the Middle Kingdom the EGYPTIANS believed in the recognition of friends and relatives and reunion with them after death. The chapter is semi-magical in character, for the deceased, like the ordinary magician, threatens the gods with penalties if they do not grant him his petition. It is interesting too to note that the friends of the dead in the Other World were believed to be ready to fight the celestial powers on behalf of their kinsman. Neither the Pyramid Texts nor the Coffin Texts tell us anything about the occupations of the denizens of the Other World other than hunting and fishing. We should expect them to spend some time daily in prayer and in the singing of hymns to RĀ and HORUS and the great solar gods who had admitted them to their company. The Pyramid Texts show (§ 855) that the deceased who knew and recited the 'Chapter of RĀ', and who performed certain ritual acts of magic 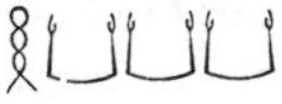 of ḤARAKHTI became a Kinsman of RĀ , and a *Smer*  (i.e. Friend) of ḤARAKHTI, and it is stated distinctly that because PEPI knew the 'Chapter', and performed the magical ritual, he attained these honours.

The oldest and longest hymn to RĀ known to us is found in the pyramid of PEPI II (§ 1587 f.) and reads:

'Homage to thee, [O] TEM!
Homage to thee, [O] KHEPRER—who came into being by himself (i.e. the self-produced).
Thou art the High One in this thy name of QAQ (i.e. Height)!
Thou didst come into being (*kheper-k*) in this thy name of KHEPRERI (i.e. Comer into being).

Homage to thee, [O] Eye of HORUS (EGYPT), which he furnished with the whole of his two arms.
He hath not allowed thee to listen (i.e. give obedience) to him of the West,
He hath not allowed thee to listen to him of the East,
He hath not allowed thee to listen to him of the South,
He hath not allowed thee to listen to him of the North,
He hath not allowed thee to listen to those who are in the middle of the land (or earth);
[But] thou hast listened to (i.e. obeyed) HORUS.
He it is who hath furnished thee,
He it is who hath built thee up,
He it is who hath made thee solid land (or given thee a foundation),
Thou hast done for him everything which he spake unto thee in every place whither he goeth.
Thou bearest to him the waters of the birds[1] which are in thee,
Thou bearest to him the waters of the birds which shall come into being in thee.
Thou bearest to him every plant (grain?) which is in thee.
Thou bearest to him every plant (grain) which shall come into being in thee.
Thou bearest to him the food and drink which are in thee,
Thou bearest to him the food and drink which are in thee, which shall come into being in thee.
Thou bearest to him the offerings which are in thee,
Thou bearest to him the offerings which shall come into being in thee.
Thou bearest to him everything which is in thee,
Thou bearest to him everything which shall come into being in thee.
Thou carriest [them] to him, to every place which his heart wisheth.
The doors that are on thee stand firm like AN-MUT-F.[2]
They do not open to those of the West,
They do not open to those of the East,
They do not open to those of the North,
They do not open to those of the South,
They do not open to the midland dwellers.
[But] they open to HORUS,
It was He who made them,
It was He who set them up,
It was He who saved them from every injury which SET worked against them,

[1] i.e. the marshes wherein birds and feathered fowl breed.

[2] A mythological being whose functions are not known. He is mentioned in the Theban *Book of the Dead*, chapters xviii; cxxxvii; cxlii. v. 7, clxxii, l. 42.

It was He who laid the foundation of thee in this thy name of "Foundation Cities".
It was He who went, He who followed bowing behind thee in this thy name of "NUT" (i.e. "The City", *par excellence*),
It was He who saved thee from every injury which SET worked upon thee.'

The next great group of texts from which much information may be obtained about the beliefs of the EGYPTIANS as to the future life is that entitled REU-ENT-PER-T EM HRU, i.e. 'The Chapters of Coming Forth by Day', or the Theban Recension of the *Book of the Dead*. It is a most valuable collection of funerary documents, and contains a number of ancient magical spells and rituals, prayers, hymns to RĀ and OSIRIS, exegetical notes and remarks, extracts from the Pyramid Texts, a series of chapters dealing with the transformations which the deceased might make, a special section dealing with the Last Judgement, and many of the chapters have long rubrics describing the use of religious spells and amulets, and religious rituals. A large number of the chapters have vignettes with short descriptions of the gods and objects which are depicted therein; these form most instructive additions to the texts. The most complete edition of the Theban Recension of the *Book of the Dead* was published by myself in 1898, for it contains a considerable number of chapters from the papyri of NU and ANI, which had not been discovered when NAVILLE published his monumental edition, *Das Todtenbuch* (vol. i, text; vol. ii, variants; and vol. iii *Einleitung*). In my edition I published 163 chapters of the Theban Recension, 14 miscellaneous chapters, and 14 of the SAÏTE Recension, with English translations and a Vocabulary. For the Bibliography of the *Book of the Dead* and all its Recensions see my *Papyrus of Ani*, LONDON, 1895, p. 371 f. The finest papyrus rolls of the *Book of the Dead*, i.e. those of NU and NEBSENI, were written at THEBES (?) under the XVIIIth dynasty, about 1600 B.C., and it is clear that the beliefs which are described in them were current among the learned scribes of that period, and perhaps also among the priests generally. The references to the ancient stellar cult are fewer in the Theban *Book of the Dead* than in the Pyramid Texts, but those which occur show that the EGYPTIANS had not entirely forgotten their old objects of worship; even the fingers of the deceased are identified with ORION. The deceased says, 'I am SAḤ travelling over his territory, marching before the stars of heaven' (chap. lxix); OSIRIS is called SAḤ (ORION, chap. cxlii); and the deceased is stablished on the sceptre of ORION (chap. clxxx). The deceased says, 'I am SEPṬ' (SOTHIS) and orders the crocodile to retreat (chap. xxxii); and he refers to the slaughtering block of SEPṬ (chap. cxxx); SOTHIS is the god of the AĀT of ATU (chap. cl), and the deceased reports to him (chap. cxlix). SOTHIS speaks his divine words to the stars (chap. cx), and the deceased becomes a star before the dweller in SOTHIS (chap. c). We find also the 'AKHEMU URTU' and the 'AKHEMU SEKU', stars of the Pyramid Texts (§§ 733, 1171), and the Morning Star  (§ 1207), and the old ferryman of RĀ, ḤER-F-ḤA-F ,[1] who has become the doorkeeper of OSIRIS  (§ 1201), and later one of the Forty-two Assessors in the Judgement Hall of OSIRIS. The ferry-boat of RĀ transported the souls of the beatified from earth to heaven, and OSIRIS used it for the same purpose. The early priests of RĀ provided a *Ladder* by which the souls of the righteous might ascend from earth to heaven.[2] The Ladder was made by RĀ and was used by him and other gods, the last god being OSIRIS who himself becomes the Ladder. In the Papyrus of ANI we have a vignette of the Ladder, and it was intended for the use of OSIRIS and his followers.

The chapters of the Theban *Book of the Dead* show that under the XVIIIth dynasty the EGYPTIAN was free to decide *where* he would spend his life after death, for some of then were intended to help him to find a home in the Boat of RĀ, and others to become a celestial being and in fact to lose his individuality in the being of the Sun-god. Other chapters and their vignettes showed him what life was like in the kingdom of OSIRIS, and that it was to all intents and purposes a continuation of the life upon earth. The vignette of chapter cx shows us the deceased in SEKHET-ḤETEP, or 'Field of Offerings' (see below, p. 352), in the form and white dress which he had upon earth. The SEKHET-ḤETEP is a district which is inter-

1  (§ 1201).

2 The *asken pet*  of § 1016 seems to have been a sort of ramp or staircase.

sected with canals, and might well be a large farm in the Delta or in the neighbourhood of THEBES. In the papyrus of ANI the deceased is accompanied by his wife and followed by THOTH. We see him seated in a boat containing a mass of offerings which he presents to the gods of the first section. In the second section we see him reaping and cattle treading out the grain; clothed in white apparel and holding the KHERṬ sceptre he kneels before two large heaps of grain, the one kind being red and the other white. In another section of the district called SEKHET-AARU, i.e. 'The Field of Reeds', he is ploughing with a yoke of oxen by the side of a stream which contains neither fish nor serpent. Its extent, or width, is unknown. A corner of the fourth section is described as the Seat of the AKHU, a group of the beatified, who are said to be seven cubits (i.e. between 11 and 12 feet) in length (i.e. height), and the grain, which is three cubits in height, is reaped by the honourable SĀḤU, another class of beatified beings. Here live the great gods. At the ends of narrow quays which project from the land are two boats, one in the form of the ordinary NILE boat, and the other with ends terminating in the heads of serpents. Each contains a seat having seven steps. They are probably the originals of the 'spirit boats' which we find mentioned in Coptic apocrypha. The scene in the Papyrus of NEBSENI is fuller in details, for we see him standing whilst a libation of cool water is being poured over him, and an attendant is bringing to him clean raiment. In the text is a prayer to OSIRIS and all the gods who live in SEKHET-ḤETEP that offerings of cakes, and beer, and oxen, and geese, and bread, and all good things, and linen garments and incense, and milk and wine may be made daily to the Ka of NEBSENI. These vignettes make it clear that at this period the Ba in the Other World had the form which its body had upon earth and that it lived upon the material offerings of food and drink which were offered daily to its Ka upon earth. It prayed for an abundant supply of the food upon which the Kau and the AKHU lived, and it says distinctly in the text of chapter cx, 'May I eat therein (i.e. SEKHET-ḤETEP), may I drink therein, may I plough and reap therein, may I fight and make love therein, may my words be mighty therein, may I never serve as a slave therein but be ever in authority'. The Ba could traverse at will the whole length and breadth of SEKHET-ḤETEP, and visit all its nomes and cities.

The beliefs current in the Ptolemaic and Roman Periods about the life of those who are in the Other World are well illustrated by the following extracts:

I. From BRIT. MUS. Papyrus, No. 10112[1] which was written for TEKHERT-PURU-ABT, the son of THENT-NUBT, who was 'justified in the judgement'.

'Thy soul liveth in heaven before RĀ. Gifts are made unto thy Ka before the gods. Thy SĀḤU is glorious among the AAKHU. Thy name is stablished upon earth before GEBB (the Earth-god). Thy body shall live for ever in KHERT-NETER. Thy house is in the possession of thy children and thy husband, who weep as they follow thee when thou goest about therein with thy children; and they are requited for what they have done for thy Ka, and concerning thy good and perfect burial. They make offerings to thy Ka in Western THEBES in the sight of thy fellow citizens and of the Lady of the Temples. The beautiful AMENTT stretcheth out her hands to receive thee according to the decree of the Lord of ABYDOS.

'Thy tomb shall never be overthrown, thy mummy bandages shall never be torn off thee, and thy body shall never be mutilated. ANUBIS[2] hath received thee in the land of the Hall of MAĀTI, and he hath made thee to be one of those favoured and honourable beings of the company of SEKER.[3] Thy soul flieth up to heaven to meet the souls of the gods, and it also hovereth over thy dead body which is in AKERT. Thou journeyest about over the earth, thou seest all that [taketh place] therein. Thou observest everything which happeneth in connexion with thy house, and thou eatest bread, as thou hast performed all the transformations which resemble those of BABA.[4] Thou goest to the city of NIFUR-T[5] at the festival of the altars on the night of the Festival of Six, and at the festival of ĀNEP. Thou goest into the city of NIFUR-T at the Festival of the Little Heat, and the festival of ANHER-T. Thou goest into the city of TATU on the festival of KA-HRA-KA (CHORAK), on the day when the ṬEṬ is set upright The breath of the wind hath made thy throat to breathe with KHENSU and SHU, the mighty one in THEBES. Thou hast abundant offerings for thy Ka every tenth day with the living image of RĀ in THEBES. Thy life is for ever and ever, and thy sovereignty is for ever, and thou shalt endure for an endless number of Henti Periods (i.e. $60 \times 2 = 120$ years).'

[1] See Birch, *Proc. Soc. Bibl. Arch.*, vol. vii, p. 49, and Lieblein, *Que mon nom fleurisse*, p. 1.

[2] A very ancient, perhaps the most ancient, god of the dead.

[3] The lord of the Memphite Underworld.

[4] Beb, Babi, Bebi, the first-born son of Osiris.

[5] A district in the nome of Abydos.

II. The OSIRIS HERTU[1] saith:

'I am RĀ in his rising. I am ATEM in his setting. I am OSIRIS KHENTI AMENTI by night and by day. . . . Accept me, O ANUBIS, HATHOR, MAĀT, doorkeeper of the ṬUAT and PER-ḤENNU,[2] gods of the ṬUAT, &c. I am your father ḤARAKHTI, HORUS, son of ISIS, HORUS the Elder, HORUS of the Two Eyes, and HORUS, lord of SEKHEM. I am THOTH, who gave a liturgy to every god.

'O Lord of Light, Thou of the Great Throne, turn thy face to me. Give me my mouth that I may speak therewith. Guide my heart at the moment [of wrath] of the devil NEBT. Fashion thou my heart that I may speak therewith before the Great God of the ṬUAT. . . . O PTAḤ, father of the gods, open thou my mouth for me as thou didst open the mouth of SEKER-OSIRIS in MEMPHIS. Make thou my name to flourish as doth that of OSIRIS KHENTI AMENTIU, and let me be recognized before the gods of the Divine Companies. . . . Let my Ka be in heaven and on the earth, and grant that I may alight on (i.e. visit) my own body [in the tomb]. . . . Let light be placed in my two eyes that I may walk by night and by day, and let me see his rays every day. . . . There is not a member of mine without a god . . . my flesh possesseth perfect life. I come forth by day. I am the master of my heart, my members, my mind, my hands, my mouth, offerings of beer, oxen and geese, water from the deeps of the river, my eyes on earth, and my eyes in the Underworld. I live on bread; by it I stand up (or subsist). I exist through milk. I drink wine. I become. I receive breath through the ERPUIT goddesses. I am the Great God who cometh from KHERT-NETER, the light of RĀ, the breath of AMEN: I am they forever. I am OSIRIS, the Great God, HORUS, the Word, I-EM-ḤETEP, born of MUT-MENU (?). RĀ, I am thy son. O THOTH, I am thine eyes. O OSIRIS, I am thy SEKHEM (i.e. Power). O ye lords of HERMOPOLIS, I am your heir (or flesh and blood), born of MAĀT.'

III. 'O KERĀSHER, thy name is permanent, thy body of flesh is stablished, thy spirit body groweth. Thy face is radiant before RĀ, thy Ba liveth before AMEN, thy body of flesh is renewed before OSIRIS. Thou breathest for ever and ever. Thy soul offereth unto thee cakes, ale, oxen, birds, and cool water daily. . . . Thy flesh is on thy bones, and thy form is ever as it was upon the earth. Thou absorbest drink into thy body, thou eatest with thy mouth, and thou receivest bread along with the rest of the gods. THOTH, the Great great god, the Lord of HERMOPOLIS, with his own fingers writeth for the THE BOOK OF BREATHINGS. Thy soul shall breathe for ever and ever, and thy form shall be made anew with life upon earth. Thou art made divine like the souls of the gods, thy heart is the heart of RĀ, and thy

[1] See Lepsius, *Denkmäler*, vi. 122; Lieblein, *Que mon nom fleurisse*, pl. 1.

[2] Temple of the Ḥennu Boat.

members are the members of the Great God. . . . AMEN cometh to thee with the breath of life, and he causeth thee to draw thy breath in thy funeral chamber. Thou appearest upon the earth each day, and the BOOK OF BREATHINGS of THOTH is a protection unto thee, for thereby dost thou draw thy breath each day, and thereby do thine eyes behold the beams of the Divine Disk.'

XV

THE ṬUAT ★ 𓅓𓏤, OR UNDERWORLD

ṬUAT is the name which the EGYPTIANS gave to the abode of the spirits and souls of the dead; it is a very old word and its exact meaning is unknown. It is commonly rendered 'Other World', or 'Underworld', and some would translate it by 'Hades' or by 'Hell'. What is quite certain is that it was regarded as the region through which the sun passed after he set, and where the spirits and souls of the dead lived. The EGYPTIANS divided the world into three parts, Heaven 𓊪𓏏 PET, Earth 𓇾 TA, and ṬUAT ★ 𓅓𓏤 ṬUAT; many of them thought that the ṬUAT was below the earth just as heaven was above it. To translate the word by 'Hell' is incorrect, for that conveys to modern peoples ideas which were wholly foreign to schools of ancient Egyptian thought. The enemies of OSIRIS and RĀ suffered punishment in the ṬUAT, but the various Books of the Dead show that there was a portion of it wherein the beatified lived happily and enjoyed immortality. The texts of the XIXth dynasty suggest that the ṬUAT was situated not below our earth, but away beyond it, and a part of it at all events ran parallel to EGYPT. The ṬUAT was supposed to be separated from this world (or EGYPT) by a range of mountains, and it seems to have had the form of a narrow valley with a river running through the whole length of it; it was separated from heaven by a range of mountains. The sun and the spirits of the dead entered it through an opening in the western range, close to Mount MANU, or the 'Mountain of the Sunset', and the sun entered this world again through an opening in the eastern range, close to Mount BAKHAU, or the 'Mountain of the Sunrise'. As heaven possessed a celestial river, and EGYPT its NILE, so the ṬUAT had a river running through it. In a vignette on the alabaster sarcophagus of SETI I in Sir JOHN SOANE'S Museum the ṬUAT is likened to the body of OSIRIS which is bent round like a hoop in such a way that his toes touch the back of his head. Thus OSIRIS under the XVIIIth dynasty was the personification of the ṬUAT, and that the ṬUAT believed to be a narrow circular valley which began where the sun sets in the west, and ended where he rose in the east.

The ṬUAT as a whole contained the ṬUATS, or Underworlds, of all the great cities of EGYPT. It was a place of difficulty and danger to all the souls who entered it and who had to traverse it in order to reach the abode of the gods and beatified souls. It was shrouded in the deepest blackness of night, and was the abode of terrible monsters of every kind and legions of devils. Each section of it contained its own special class of fiends, and offered its own formidable obstacles to the passage of souls. Under the Old Empire the priests composed long series of spells, incantations, and prayers for the use of the souls who were traversing the ṬUAT, and as time went on these were added to frequently. And the conservatism of the EGYPTIAN prevented him from rejecting even the oldest of them. Thus long after the custom of decapitating the dead and dismembering their bodies was obsolete, the spells which had been composed to prevent this happening to the dead, were carefully copied for priests and wealthy men in their funerary papyri.

The oldest funerary texts suggest that the priests who composed them professed to have exact knowledge of the various sections of the ṬUAT, and to know the names of the devils and monsters and also the barriers of every kind which barred the way of the dead therein. But we find no illustration or picture of any part of the ṬUAT before the XIth or XIIth dynasty, and even at that time it is only the 'Elysian Fields' of the EGYPTIANS which are depicted. These were called SEKHET-ḤETEP 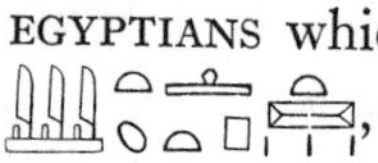, that is 'Field of Offerings', and SEKHET-AANRU , that is 'Field of Reeds (or Rushes)'. Later texts also mention a 'Field of the Grasshoppers'. Among the oldest known pictures of these regions are those which are found on the coffins of GUA-TEP, and SEN the physician, in the BRITISH MUSEUM (Nos. 30840 and 30841). On the coffin of GUA-TEP is represented a rectangular region or estate, intersected by numerous large and small canals, and containing many islands, or perhaps lakes. In one form or another this is found in all the great codices of the Theban Recension of the *Book of the Dead*, and it forms the vignette of chapter cx. A very interesting variant of it is found on the inner coffin of SEN, where special prominence is given to the magical boat which moved on the utterance of a word of power by its occupant. In the copies of the vignette made under the New Empire the deceased is seen ploughing and reaping and superintending the threshing of wheat and barley.

The 'Book of Coming Forth by Day' , which is commonly called the 'Book of the Dead', supplies much information about that part of the ṬUAT which formed the special domain of OSIRIS. According to chapter cxliv its Halls (*Ārits*) were seven in number, but only the doors by which they were entered are shown in the papyri. Each door is guarded by three gods, all of whom, with the exception of two, have the heads of sacred animals. The first god was the doorkeeper, who stayed by the door, the second was the watcher, who kept a look out and announced the arrival of visitors, and the third announced the visitor in the Hall. Each of these three gods carried a knife, and some held palm-branches (?).

Their names were:

Ārit I. 1. SEKHET ḤER-ĀSHT-ARU. 2. SEMETU. 3. HUKHERU.
Ārit II. 1. TUNPEḤTI. 2. SEQEṬ ḤER. 3. SABES.
Ārit III. 1. UNEMḤUATENTPEḤF. 2. RESHER. 3. UĀAU.
Ārit IV. 1. KHESEFḤERĀSHKHERU. 2. RESAB. 3. NETQAḤERKHESEFATU.
Ārit V. 1. ĀNKHEMFENTU. 2. ASHEBU. 3. TEBḤERKEHAUT.
Ārit VI. 1. AKENTAUKHAKHERU. 2. ANḤER. 3. METESḤERARISHE.
Ārit VII. 1. METESSEN. 2. AAKHERU. 3. KHESEFḤERKHEMIU.

Another chapter (cxlvi) states that the Secret Pylons of SEKHET-ARU, i.e. the Elysian Fields, were twenty-one in number, but in the oldest papyri the number varies from ten to fifteen. Each pylon has a name, generally a very long one, and only one gatekeeper; the names of the gatekeepers are:

Pylon I. NERI, vulture-headed, with solar disk.
" II. MES-PEḤ, lioness-headed.
" III. ERṬATSBANQA, in the form of a man. Over the pylon are the signs .

Pylon IV. NEKAU, bull-headed.

,, V. ḤENTIREQU, a goddess with the head and breasts of a hippopotamus and holding a large butcher's knife, and the sign for the fluid of life *sa*.

,, VI. SMAMTI, a god in the form of a dwarf, holding a knife and besom (?)

,, VII. AKENTI, a god with the head of the flat-horned ram of KHNEMU.

,, VIII. KHUDJETEF, a hawk wearing the Crowns of the South and North. Behind him is the *udjat*, and over the pylon two human-headed hawks and .

,, IX. DJESEF, lioness-headed and wearing a solar disk. This pylon is guarded by the Eight 'living uraei'.

,, X. SEKHENUR, ram-headed and wearing the Atef Crown.[1]

Each god, with the exception of the goddess of the Vth Pylon, holds a sort of besom. The names of the guardian gods of Pylons XI–XXI are not given. Each pylon is inscribed with a spell, which the deceased was obliged to recite if he wished to be allowed to pass through it.

In addition to the Seven Arits and the Ten (or Twenty-one) Pylons, the kingdom of the ṬUAT of OSIRIS was divided into Fourteen (or Fifteen) AATS, or States, each of which was governed by a god. The oldest list of them is given, with vignettes, in the Papyrus of NU which was written early in the XVIIIth dynasty (chaps. cxlix and cl). The AATS and their gods were called:

I. SEKHET-ARRU . Here the wheat was five cubits high, and the barley seven cubits high, and the spirits who reaped it were nine cubits high (15 feet). Its god was RĀ-ḤARAKHTI.

II. UPTENTKHET 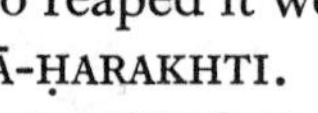, i.e. 'Brow of Fire'. Its god was FA-ĀKHU 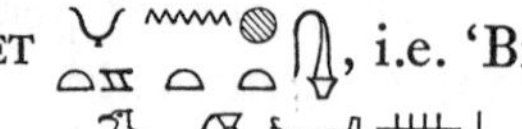.

III. ṬUQAĀT , i.e. 'Mountain, high,

[1] In the Turin Papyrus the names of the ten guardians are: Nerau, Mesptah, Beq, Hutepau, Ertahenerrequ, Samti, Amnit, Nedjses, Khudjetef, and Sekhenur. Pictures of these gods are given both in the Theban and Saïte Recensions of the *Book of the Dead* so that the deceased might identify them without difficulty.

great'; it was 300 measures long and 230 wide. Its god was SATITEMUIT, and had the form of a huge serpent.

IV. AATAAKHU. This was a region of fire surrounded with a high wall. Its god was RĀ.

V. AMMEḤT. This was a region which was difficult for the dead to pass through. It was inhabited by hostile spirits whose thighs were seven cubits long, and who lived upon the inert and feeble dead. Its god was SEKHER-REMU, or SEKHER-ĀT (?).

VI. ASEST. This was a region of blazing fires and was the home of the serpent-god REREK, whose back was seven cubits long; evil looked out from his eyes, i.e. he had the Evil Eye. His head was cut off by the goddess MAFT-Ṭ.

VII. HAḤETEP (?) (or HASERT). This region contained roaring water and was difficult to traverse. Its god was QAHAḤETEP, or FAPET.

VIII. UPTENTQAḤU, or NUTENTQAḤU. Here lived the SHADOWS who devoured the dead. Its gods were NĀU, KANUT and NEḤEBKAU.

IX. AṬU. Its god was SEPT or SOTHIS (the Dog-star).

X. UNT. Its god was SEḤETEMTBAIU.

XI. UPTENTMU. Its god was ĀASEKHEMU or the Hippopotamus-goddess.

XII. The State of KHER-ĀḤĀ. Its god was ḤĀPI the NILE-god.

XIII. ATRUENNESERFEMSHET . A region of boiling water (hot springs?).

XIV. AKESI . A region unknown even by the gods, and and its only inhabitant was the 'god, the dweller in his egg'; he was probably called MAATHTEF .

In the list of Aats given in the Papyrus of NU there is a fifteenth Aat called AMENT NEFERT , i.e. 'The Beautiful Ament', but in the text proper of the papyrus it is made to be the first of the Aats. The gods are described as eating and drinking therein, and it seems to have been their special abode in the ṬUAT. Its governor was MENU-QEṬ 'MENU the Builder' (?).

But under the New Empire the priests decided that the vignettes of the *Book of the Dead* needed supplementing, and they attempted to supply the dead with pictures of every part of the ṬUAT. In fact they compiled a sort of Guide to the ṬUAT which contained such accurate descriptions of its inhabitants, and such life-like pictures of the foes which the deceased would meet there, together with lists of their names and magical formulae, that he would find it impossible to lose his way, or be overcome by any monster. This Guide to the ṬUAT exists in two versions which are called SHĀT AMI ṬUAT , i.e. 'The Book of what is (or him that is) in the ṬUAT', and SHĀT EN SBAA . i.e. 'The Book of Gates'. Both Books were composed by the priests of AMEN-RĀ at THEBES, but they differ considerably in details. The object of both books was to prove that AMEN-RĀ was not only the god of the day, but of the night also, and that he was worshipped as the one great and absolute god by the denizens of the Underworld (ṬUAT) as well as by men on earth. The Book AMI ṬUAT practically ignores OSIRIS, and is silent even concerning the doctrines of the Judgement Hall of OSIRIS and SEKHET-ḤETEP, and in fact about all the fundamental doctrines concerning the dead according to the religion of OSIRIS, which had been universally believed throughout EGYPT for thousands of years. In the Book AMI ṬUAT AMEN-RĀ is made to pass through all the ṬUATS of EGYPT, as the overlord of all those who lived in them, and whatever refreshing or life they enjoyed in the ṬUAT was due to the light which he shed on them on his way to the region of the sunrise. Only those who were able to secure a place in the Boat of AMEN-RĀ could hope to emerge as living beings from the ṬUAT. Only to them did rebirth become possible, and only through him could they obtain new life and strength daily.

The teaching of the *Book of Gates* was very different. OSIRIS rewarded his true and loyal followers by giving them estates, or farms, or homesteads in his kingdom, where they cultivated the 'plant of truth' (or righteousness), which sprang from the body of the god, and on which they fed daily, thus becoming one body with the god. But this state of beatification could only be obtained by the OSIRIANS *because* they had worshipped OSIRIS on earth, and had not turned aside to 'wretched little gods' (i.e. false or obsolete gods), and had made all the canonical offerings, and lived righteous lives upon earth. OSIRIS rewarded his worshippers with an everlasting life of happiness upon earth, and AMEN-RĀ rewarded his followers with seats in his Boat of Millions of Years wherein as beings of light, decked out with light, they sailed over heaven with him for ever. As a whole the peoples of EGYPT in every period of their long history preferred the reward of OSIRIS to that of AMEN-RĀ.

THE BOOK AMI ṬUAT[1]

The Book AMI ṬUAT is a very lengthy work, and its sections are called 'Hours [of the Night]'. The oldest copies of the complete work are found in the tombs of AMEN-ḤETEP II, THOTHMES III, and AMEN-ḤETEP III at THEBES; the text in the tomb of the last named king is almost obliterated. The most complete copy of it is found in the tomb of THOTHMES III, and when I examined it in 1902 the hieratic text was as legible as when it was written. The best illustrated copy of it is preserved in the tomb of SETI I (XIXth dynasty) at THEBES, where we find eleven out of the twelve sections of it, and the first six sections of the short form of it which is generally known as the 'Summary', or 'Abridgement'. The Sun-god of night, like an earthly PHARAOH, made his journey through the ṬUAT in a

[1] For the texts and vignettes see the *Mémoires* of the *Mission Arch. Française* in Cairo, tom. ii, Paris, 1886, and tom. iii, Paris, 1893. For transcript of texts, translations, &c., see Budge, *The Egyptian Heaven and Hell*, London, 1925.

boat. He set out, presumably, from some place behind the mountains of Western THEBES, and sailed down the river until he reached the swamps in the north-east of the Delta. He sat in the SEKTET Boat, that is the boat in which he sailed over the sky from noon to sunset. He took the form of a ram-headed man, probably as a tribute to KHNEMU, the god of the Sources of the

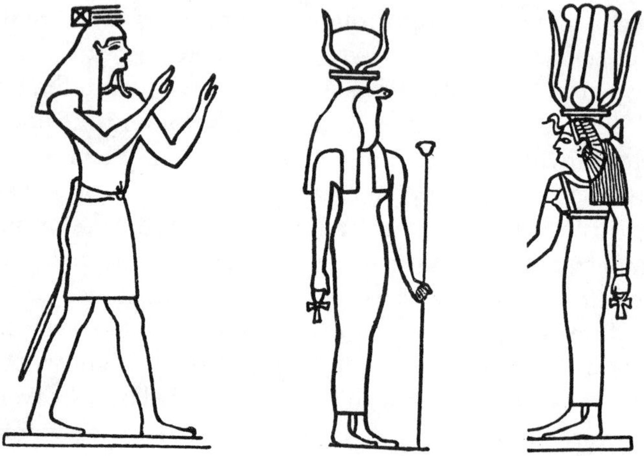

1 The god Sa. 2 Urt-ḥekau. 3 The solar Isis.

Some of the crew of the boat of the Night-sun.

NILE at ELEPHANTINE, and stood in a shrine. But he was only the body (or flesh) of RĀ, and was called AFU (or AFU-RĀ). In the boat with him are the gods UP-UATU, ḤU, SAA, ḤER-ḤEKEN, KA-SHU, NEHES, the 'look-out', KHERP, the captain, and the 'lady of the boat', who was changed every hour.

THE FIRST HOUR. Its guardian goddess was called USHMET-HATU-KHEFTIU-RĀ. The region through which AFU passed in this hour was called MAĀTI, and may be regarded as the antechamber of the ṬUAT; it was 220 *atru* in length; it was also called NET-RĀ and its guardian was ARI-NEBAUI. In it dwelt a large number of celestial beings of whose functions nothing is known, and the souls of the dead who were supposed to be waiting for an opportunity of entering the boat of AFU. This place was not Purgatory, as some have thought, for the EGYPTIANS did not believe in any intermediate state for the dead. Good souls were rewarded and bad souls were destroyed, and the enemies of RĀ or OSIRIS were cremated daily. AFU addressed the gods and dwellers in this region, and they made a suitable reply, and having conferred benefits on those of his followers who were there, and refreshed them with his light, he proceeded on his way to the entrance to the ṬUAT proper. As he left the antechamber, and darkness again settled down over it, the souls therein set up a wail. Side by side with the Boat of AFU sailed the boat containing the beetle of KHEPRI with the legend 'the coming into being of OSIRIS', i.e. OSIRIS creating himself; thus the dead sun of to-day and the embryo of the sun of to-morrow travel down the NILE together.

THE SECOND HOUR. Its guardian goddess was called SHESAT-MAKEY-NEB-S. The region passed through was 309 *atru* in length and 120 *atru* in breadth, and here lived the Souls of the ṬUAT; its name was URNES 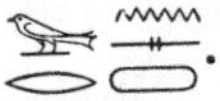. As AFU sailed down the river of the ṬUAT the gods and dwellers on both banks appeared and acclaimed him, and they made a dutiful answer full of words of homage and gratitude for the benefits which he had conferred upon them in the past. The boat of AFU now became the 'Boat of the Earth', and in it the Night-sun passed through the body of AKER, a god with the head of a bull or lion at each end of his body. AFU was preceded by four boats: (1) the 'Boat of the Full Moon'; (2) a boat with the fetish of HATHOR; (3) a boat containing an ichneumon (?) from the back of which emerge the head of OSIRIS and a White Crown; (4) the boat of the Grain-god NEPER, Multitudes of the dead lived in URNES, and when AFU shed his light upon them, and addressed them, they all sprang into life, and accepted the services of the gods their neighbours who by AFU's command provided for their wants. When AFU departed darkness fell upon them, and they set up a wail and wept bitterly.

THE THIRD HOUR. Its guardian goddess was TENT-BAIU, who piloted AFU through the region called NET-NEB-UĀ-KHEPER-AUTU. It was the duty of the gods of this region to destroy the enemies of RĀ, to make the NILE to rise and inundate the country, and to do service for the dead who were there. AFU communicated with OSIRIS, whose ministers and servants then assisted him on his journey; three boats of OSIRIS acted as a convoy for him. Among the gods of this region were the Nine Forms of OSIRIS. The dead praised AFU whilst he was with them, but their cries of joy changed to lamentations when he departed and darkness settled down on them again. The dwellers here were called 'Hidden Souls, and the section of the NILE of the ṬUAT was named NET-ASAR 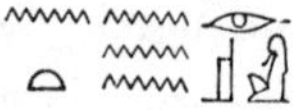 i.e. 'the stream of OSIRIS'.

THE FOURTH HOUR. Its guardian goddess was URT-SEKHEMU. The region traversed during this hour was called ĀNKHET-KHEPERU, and it was protected by a gate called AMENT-TAU. This region was known as the 'Hidden Circle of AMENT', and it included the ṬUAT of MEMPHIS, which was presided over by SEKER, the great god of the Necropolis of that city. The chief shrine was called AMMEḤET which was only reached after passing through RESTAU 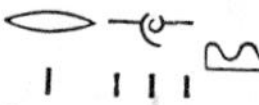, i.e. 'the entrance to the winding passages'. During the first three hours AFU passed through the ṬUATS of ABYDOS and other great cities, and then he came to a very different kind of region. It was filled with huge and fearsome snakes, (these were not gods), and the souls of the dead waited on each bank of the river to assist him; there were no beings on whom he could confer estates, and no gods to offer him a loyal address. He was obliged to leave the boat in which he sailed on the river, and to betake himself to one formed of the body of a serpent with a head at each end of his body. This boat passed through the dark and gloomy passages, guided by the light of the flames which proceeded from the mouth of the serpent which formed the boat. AFU passed the monster two-headed and three-headed serpents which guarded the domain of SEKER, and it is clear that both he and OSIRIS are subordinate to SEKER and his gods, who live on their sand, and are unseen and respond not to the words of AFU. One section of RESTAU contains the blazing fires which are shot forth from the mouth of the goddess UNEMMIT to burn up the souls of the enemies of OSIRIS, SEKER, and RĀ. One serpent has three heads, and wings, and human legs and feet; and another has two heads at one end of his body and another head terminates its tail.

THE FIFTH HOUR. The region traversed by AFU during this hour was a continuation of the domain of SEKER, which represented the

ṬUAT of MEMPHIS, and was probably the oldest abode of the dead in EGYPT; it was called AMENT.[1] Here was the 'hidden' abode of SEKER, which is in the form of a mound of sand into which the Beetle-god KHEPRI is about to enter. SEKER and KHEPRI converse together. The Land of SEKER is oval in form, is surrounded with a wall of sand, and is guarded by two sphinxes having bodies of lions with heads of men. SEKER has the form of a hawk-headed man and stands between the wings of a monster two-headed serpent. Close by him is the lake of fire in which the wicked were destroyed. As AFU the dead sun-god, is drawn over the mound of SEKER, KHEPRI, the sun-god in embryo, emerges from his abode of night, and is united with him, and AFU thus becomes potentially the sun-god of the following day. AFU next came to the region where lived the seven fire-belching gods, who consumed the dead, and the goddess who 'lived upon the blood of the dead'. Passing these AFU saw ahead of him the great Star of the 'Living God who journeyeth, and travelleth and advanceth'. This has been identified with the Morning Star, VENUS, and shows that AFU is near the region of daybreak. JÉQUIER has pointed out rightly that originally the scenes of the Fourth and Fifth Hours formed a complete Book of the ṬUAT, and that the final scene in it was the sunrise.

THE SIXTH HOUR. Having passed through the ṬUAT of MEMPHIS AFU came to the southern part of the Delta, and abandoning his serpent-boat, once more entered the SEKTET Boat, and with the gods who were in his boat when he started on his journey proceeded to enter the ṬUAT of OSIRIS in the Eastern Delta. On each bank of the river the gods of the dead and the beatified dead acclaim him, and he sends forth his light upon them, and arranges that the souls of the righteous shall provide offerings for the gods, and supply them with water daily. The name of the region traversed by AFU in this hour was MESPERIT-ARĀT-MAATU, and the great gate of it was called SEPTMETU; the goddess of the Hour was AMENT-SEMU-SET. AFU came first to the sixteen mansions of OSIRIS. In these dwelt kings of the South and kings of the North, and the ḤETEPTIU and the Spirits; AFU addressed these, arranged for their offerings, and ordered them to destroy ĀPEP, the monster of evil. Next we see

1  Ament, or Amentt, means the 'Hidden Place'.

the five-headed serpent called ĀSH-HRU  the body of which forms an irregular oval. Inside it lies AFU with his right arm raised and his hand touching the beetle of KHEPRI, the rising sun, and when RĀ spoke the word this dead god became living. Passing several groups of the companies of the gods of OSIRIS, AFU next came to the three houses of RĀ. The first had for its symbol the hind-quarters of a lion, the second a wing of HORUS (?), and the third the head of a man. Then he met the monster serpent from which sprang the heads of the Four Sons of HORUS, and next the Nine fire-spitting serpents who were armed with knives, and whose duty it was to destroy the enemies of RĀ and to hack their shadows in pieces.

THE SEVENTH HOUR. The region traversed by AFU in this hour was called TEPHET-SHETAT (i.e. the Secret Hall); the name of its gate was RUTI-ASAR, and that of its goddess was KHEFTES-ḤAU-ḤESQET-NEḤA-ḤER. AFI and his gods now found their progress obstructed by sand-banks, and at one place which is 440 cubits square, the monster serpent NEḤAḤER lay waiting to bar his way. But the Scorpion-goddess strangled him with a cord, and a god pegged his body to the ground with six huge knives. Armed with his own words of power and with those provided by OSIRIS and SER, AFU, whose shrine is now formed by the body of the serpent MEḤEN, advanced and came to the FOUR TOMBS, each of which contained a form of OSIRIS. Each tomb consists of a low mound of sand, and the souls buried under the Four Tombs are those of TEM, KHEPRI, RĀ, and OSIRIS. As the light of AFU falls on these tombs, a human head appears on each of the four corner posts; these heads represent the slaves who were killed and buried in the foundations of the buildings. As soon as AFU has passed by 'they swallow themselves', i.e. they disappear. Beyond these we see AFU-ASAR 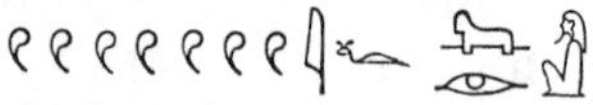 (i.e. the flesh of the seven forms of OSIRIS), seated under a canopy formed by a serpent's body, with three decapitated slaves before him. The path of AFU is now lighted up by the twelve Star-gods and the twelve goddesses of the Hours. The monster crocodile ĀB-SHE, which guarded the northern end of the region was rendered powerless by AFU's spells, and the god left the domain of OSIRIS in triumph, all the gods having promised to destroy ĀPEP.

THE EIGHTH HOUR. The name of the region which AFU, who was guarded by the serpent MEḤEN, passed through in this hour was TEBATNETRUS; its gate was called ĀḤĀNURTNEF, and the pilot goddess of the hour was NEBTUSHA. In his journey he passed Ten Circles, each of which contained a small series of gods; the names of the doors or gates of the Circles are given. AFU addressed the inhabitants of the Circles, whereupon the doors of them opened of their own accord and the gods appeared before AFU. These gods are the spirits of those who have been mummified and buried with appropriate rites and ceremonies, and at the words of AFU they all become alive, and undertake to destroy his enemies. There are five circles on each bank of the river, and the servants of OSIRIS who attend them have various inexplicable forms. The voices of the gods in the Ten Circles have different sounds, and resemble: (1) the humming of bees, (2) the wailing of women, (3) the moans of men, (4) the roaring of men and bulls who grieve, (5) the prayers of men in agony, (6) the mewing of cats, (7) the roar of the living, (8) war cries, (9) the cry of a hawk, (10) the chattering of water-fowl. Among the gods of this region are the four forms of the old Earth-god TA-TANEN; they appear as rams with flat horns, and each ram wears a special crown.

THE NINTH HOUR. The name of the region which AFU passed through in this hour was BEST-ARU-ĀNKHET-KHEPERU; its gate was called SAEMQEBH and its pilot goddess was TUATT-MAKEL-NEB-S. The spirits and souls who dwelt in this region joined their efforts to those of the sailors in the boat of AFU to help him to pass on to the Hall of the East, where the sun is to rise. The sailors in the boat of AFU ladled up water from the river with their paddles for the spirits to drink. The gods of the region helped AFU to reconstitute himself so that he may assume the form of the solar disk, and the goddesses ejected fire from their bodies, not only to light the way, but also to provide heat for the Disk and resuscitation for the body of OSIRIS. The last portion of the region contained the Elysian Fields of the Kingdom of OSIRIS.

THE TENTH HOUR. The region which AFU passed through in this hour seems to be a continuation of that described under the Ninth Hour, and it is probably the central portion of a complete work on the ṬUAT of HELIOPOLIS. The region was called METET-QA-UDJEBU, the name of its gate was ĀKHEPERU-MESARU, and the pilot goddess was TENTENIT-UHERT-KHAKABU. In this region KHEPRI, the sun-god who is about to be born, effects his mysterious union with AFU, and enters his body, and so establishes the Eye of HORUS. The sun was the right eye of the 'old god HORUS', i.e. the oldest sky-god in EGYPT, and the moon was its left eye. The devil ĀPEP and all his allies and friends were on the look out to prevent this union from taking place, and AFU called upon all the gods of the region, most of whom were of a stellar character, to sharpen their arrows, and make ready their javelins, and string their bows and to attack and defeat the powers of darkness which were waiting at the eastern end of the ṬUAT to destroy him. In one portion of this region there are shown several sheets of water, and these probably represent the great lakes and large swamps of the Delta. In these dwelt the spirits and souls of those who had been drowned, and also a long series of water-devils hostile to AFU and to RĀ. The gods of the lakes attacked these and protected AFU from their attacks, and AFU promised the dwellers in NU, or NUNU, that their members should not perish and that their flesh should not decay, and that they should be provided with everything which was necessary for them.

THE ELEVENTH HOUR. The region which AFU passed through in this hour was the last portion of the ṬUAT. It was called RENQERRT-APT-KHATU; the name of its gate was SEKHEN-TUATIU; and the pilot goddess of the hour was SEBIT, 'the Lady of the Boat, and the repeller of the SEBA fiend when he (i.e. AFU) goeth forth'. AFU stands in his boat as usual, but the sceptre which he now carries is the ordinary sceptre carried by kings, and not a serpent. On the bow of the boat there is a disk, encircled by a serpent, and its name is PESṬT 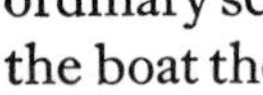. AFU now emerges from the thick or solid darkness , and enters the dusky darkness of the dawn 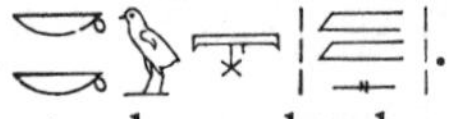. Among the gods on the banks of the river are the twelve gods who carry away the serpent MEḤEN, two cobras from the backs of which the White Crown and Red Crown spring respectively, and from these crowns human heads emerge as the god passes by. Next, in the forms of women, are the Four Forms of the goddess NEITH of SAÏS, two wearing White Crowns and two Red Crowns; these guarded the 'unknown, unseen, and invisible' gate of SAÏS. On the right bank a large number of strange beings, winged and man-headed serpents, are seen, but they only appear for a moment and then they 'swallow themselves', i.e. they dis-

The shadows of the damned being burned in the pits of fire.

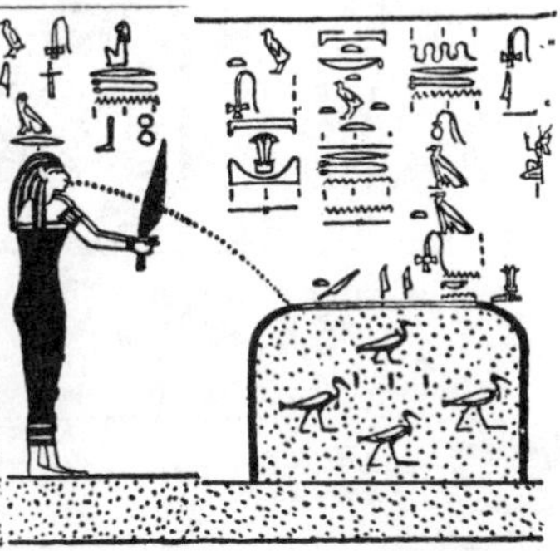

The souls of the damned being burned in the pits of fire.

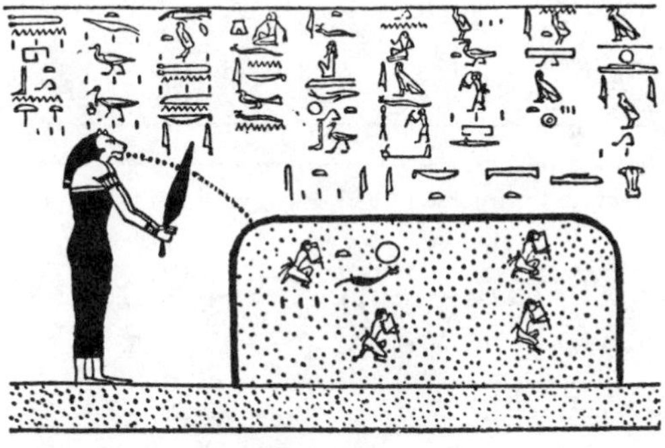

The bodies of the damned being burned in the pits of fire.

appear. Many of these were stellar gods of whose functions nothing is known. On the left bank the region is a district of blazing fire, which is ruled over by HORUS, in the form of a hawk-headed man wearing the solar disk and cobra, and holding a boomerang in his hand. This weapon is really a serpent, which when hurled at an enemy kills him and returns to the god. Before him standing on its tail is the serpent 'SET of millions of years'. Here too are the awful fire pits in which the souls, shadows, and bodies of the enemies of

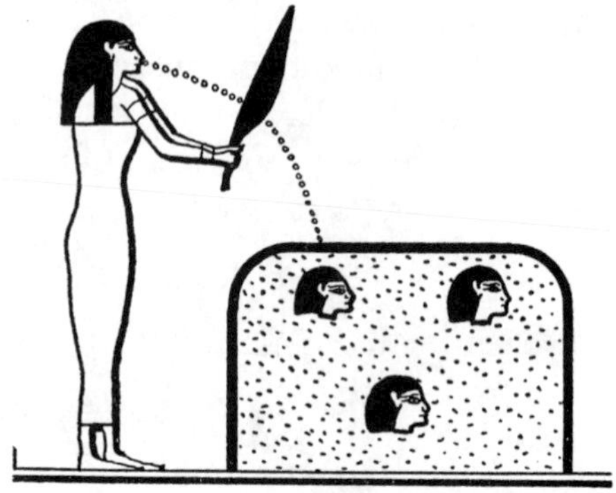

The damned immersed in the pits of fire up to their necks.

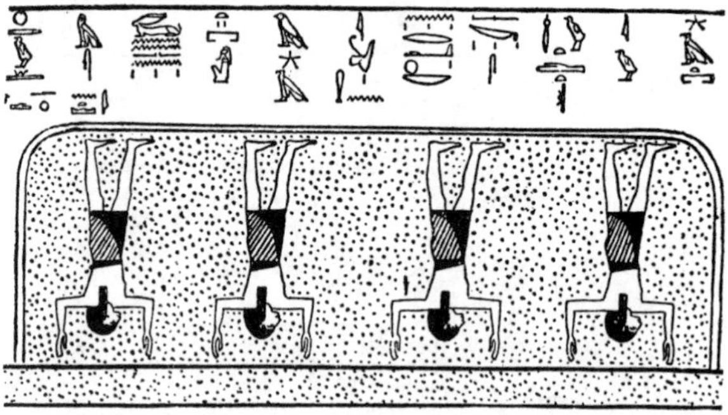

The damned immersed head downwards in the pits of fire.

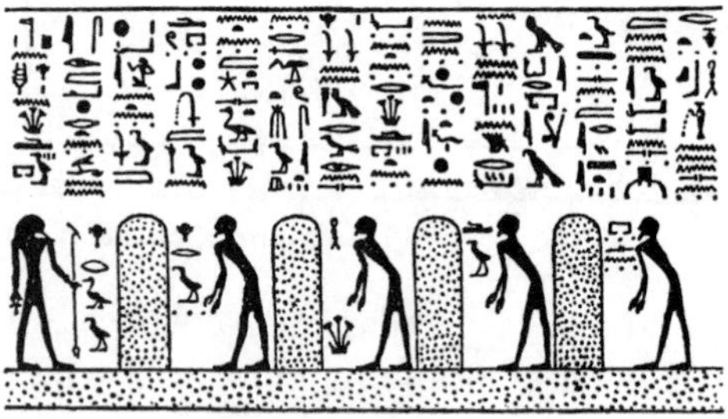

The pits of fire in which the damned are cremated.

RĀ and OSIRIS are cremated; in one pit the damned are immersed head downwards, and in another they are seen standing up to their necks in the consuming fire. The fires are maintained by goddesses who spew it out of their mouths.

THE TWELFTH HOUR. The region which AFU now entered was the antechamber of the day, and was called KHEPER-KEKU-KHĀU-MESTU; the name of its gate was THEN-NETERU, and the pilot goddess was MANEFERTRĀ. The disk PESTT is no longer on the prow of

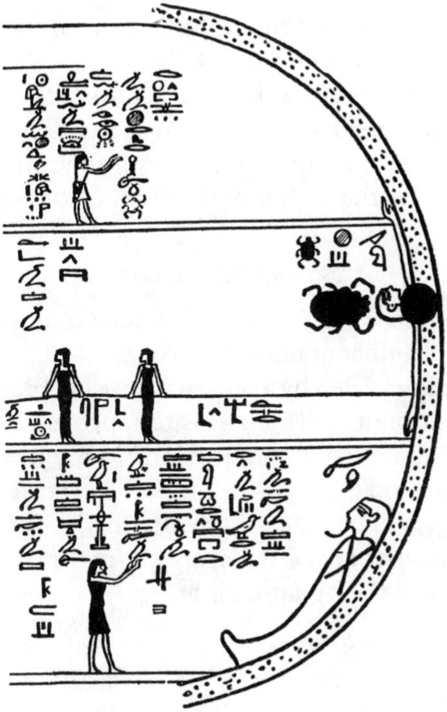

The Eastern end of the Ṭuat. The mummy of the dead Sun-god has emerged from the serpent of night and is seen lying on the lower part of the curvature. Khepri, the rising sun has appeared from out of the morning and in the form of a beetle is seen thrusting the solar disk of the new day through the end of the Ṭuat where it is received by Shu.

the boat, but the beetle of KHEPRI has taken its place in the bows. Twelve gods draw the boat, not on or over the body of the serpent KA-EN-ANKH-NETERU, but through its whole length. AFU entered the serpent in the form of a dead body, and emerged from its mouth as KHEPRI, the sun at daybreak, and SHU receives him and he takes up his position in the Eastern Horizon. Before AFU leaves the ṬUAT he casts aside his dead body, and we see it lying at the end of the ṬUAT, and the texts suggest that it represents OSIRIS.

All the gods who have witnessed and assisted the passage of the boat of AFU in the Twelfth Hour sing hymns to the rising sun and to OSIRIS.

The above is a description of the main features and contents of the Book AMI ṬUAT. It will be seen that the dead sun-god, or the sun-god of night, travelled through the ṬUAT as its king and overlord. He expected the denizens of the ṬUATS of THEBES, ABYDOS, HERAKLEOPOLIS, MEMPHIS, SAÏS, and HELIOPOLIS to assist him in every way and to render service to him as vassals.

We may now consider briefly the views about the Other World which were held by the author of the BOOK OF GATES.

THE BOOK OF GATES[1]

According to this work the ṬUAT is divided into twelve parts; the first is the antechamber of night, and the last is the antechamber of day. Each gate is guarded by a serpent of the kingdom of OSIRIS and it stands upright on its tail; it seems to represent the spirit of the leaf of a door which works on a pivot. Many of the gates have fortified walls behind the doors and these have porters or guardians in various forms. The names of the guardians of SET-AMENTT, the western antechamber or vestibule, are SET and TAT. The names of the other gates and their guardians are:

	Gate	*Serpent*		*Gate*	*Serpent*
2.	......	SAA-SET	8.	BEKHKHI	SET-ḤRA
3.	SEPTET-UAUAU	AQEBI	9.	ĀATSHEFIT	ĀBTA
4.	NEBTS-DJEFAU	DJETBI	10.	DJESERIT	SETHU(?)
5.	ARIT	TEKAḤER	11.	SHETAT-BESU	AMNETEF'
6.	NEBT-ĀḤĀ	SETEM-ARIF	12.	TESERT-BAIU	SBI, RERI
7.	PESTIT	AKHAN-MAĀT			

FIRST GATE. When the dead sun-god passed through the western antechamber he was accompanied by KHEPRI, the Beetle within a disk, which was surrounded by the convolutions of a serpent with its tail in its mouth. The Beetle was in his own boat, with SAA, the

[1] See Bonomi and Sharpe, *The Alabaster Sarcophagus of Oimenephtah*, London; *Records of the Past*, vol. x and vol. xii, London (no date); and Budge, *The Egyptian Heaven and Hell*, London, 1925; and *The Sarcophagus of Seti I* (Soane Museum), London, 1908.

god of knowledge, in the bows, and ḤEKA, the god of magic, in the stern. Thus the sun of to-morrow in embryo entered the ṬUAT with AFU-RĀ, i.e. the Body of RĀ. The funerary mountain of AMENTT served as the First Gate, and by the use of magic this was split open, and the gods of the desert and mountain lands assisted AFU to pass through the gap.

SECOND GATE. On arriving at this gate AFU called upon SAA-SET to open, and when he passed in, and the door closed, all the beings in the antechamber lamented loudly, for darkness covered them once more. AFU now assumes the form of a ram-headed man with the solar disk above the horns. The object of AFU in coming to the ṬUAT is now stated. He comes to judge the dead, to weigh words and deeds in AMENTI, to exalt the great god above the little god in the ṬUAT, to set the beatified upon their thrones, to assign places to the damned in the judgement and to destroy their bodies. SAA and ḤEKA are called upon to help him, and he awards to those who are towing along his boat righteous rewards. On his right are the ḤETEPTIU gods, i.e. the truth-speakers or loyal worshippers, and with them the MAĀTIU or doers of the Law in the ṬUAT. Because these served their god faithfully, and cursed ĀPEP, cool water and offerings and security of life and possessions are granted to them. On the left hand of AFU are the bowed and prostrate figures of the NENIU, i.e. the Apostates, who when on earth cursed RĀ and lied in their words and deeds. The god TEM stands by and pronounces their doom. They are to be fettered, and their arms tied together behind their backs. Never again shall they see the light of RĀ for their bodies shall be hacked in pieces, and their souls annihilated.

THIRD GATE. This is a very strong gate. Behind the door is a sort of double wall which is guarded by two gods in mummy form. A cobra or fire-spitting serpent rises at the two angles of the wall, behind which are the Nine Gods of the Second Company. As AFU approaches, the door of AQEBI opens and the god is towed in by eight gods who draw it *through* the body of the 'Boat of the Earth', which is a sort of tunnel each end of which terminates in the head of a bull. The text states that the SOUL of RĀ has been absorbed by the Earth-god, and he who is in the Boat of the Earth is holy. As AFU passes on he sees on the right twelve funerary shrines over the tops of which a huge serpent stretches itself at full length. The serpent's name is SETI. AFU cries out to the gods in the shrines, and the doors open, and the gods themselves come forth to rejoice in the light of AFU and to enjoy the fresh air which he has brought with him. They invite him to come to the Boiling Lake , which is close by, and when he comes there he sees a company of gods seated around it, and plants like small trees growing on the edge (?) of the lake. The water of the lake is boiling hot, and the birds do not settle round about it but betake themselves to flight because of the horrible stench which rises from its waters. AFU exhorts the gods of the lake, to cultivate the plants, and to live upon them, and he promises them that when they partake of the water it shall be cool and refreshing and not scalding to their throats. On the left we see TEM standing over the Archdevil ĀPEP, and the nine DJADJAU, or Assessors, who have assisted TEM in reducing him to helplessness. TEM cast a spell upon him and then his head was slit open, and his body slashed in pieces, and finally the fire of RĀ consumed him utterly. Another group of nine gods assist the Assessors to destroy the devils SEBA 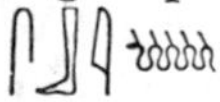 and AF 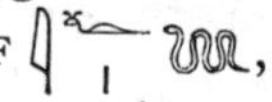, and to shut the door of the ṬUAT against ĀPEP, and to open the gates of KHENTI AMENTI to AFU. As a reward they live on the meat of RĀ and the cakes of KHENTI AMENTI. AFU's departure is lamented by these gods.

FOURTH GATE. On the approach of AFU this gate opens, and all the gods of the Third Company acclaim him, and bring him safely through the stream of fire which guards the gate. Here are the sepulchres of the gods of the Company of OSIRIS, and here, standing on a divided mound, are the goddesses of the Twelve Hours. In the space between the two groups of the goddesses is coiled up a monster serpent called ḤERRET 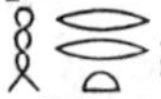; it spawns twelve serpents which the twelve hours devour. Next come a group of the gods who carry their Kau, the Twelve jackal-headed gods of the Lake of Life, and the Ten Living Cobras, which stand by the Lake of the Cobras. AFU addresses all these, and confirms their offerings, &c., in return for their loyal service to him. On the left, standing in a chamber with a vaulted dome, is the god KHENTI AMENTI, in mummied form; he wears the Crown of the South and stands on a serpent. He was in very ancient times the local god of ABYDOS, whose position and attributes were usurped by OSIRIS when the cult of OSIRIS was established in UPPER EGYPT. In front of the shrine is the Cobra-goddess NESERT. Then we have ḤER-UR, the Old HORUS, and twenty-four gods, twelve who stand before, and twelve who stand behind the shrine. Close by are the four fire pits in which the enemies of OSIRIS were destroyed. Having confirmed the offerings of all these gods, and received from them words of homage AFU continues his journey.

FIFTH GATE. The serpent guardian, and the gods of the Fourth Company, acclaim AFU as he enters the abode of the 'Souls who dwell in the ṬUAT'. The first group of gods hold the serpent NUDJI, whose functions are not known, and then AFU comes to the souls of the men who acted and spoke truthfully, and praised RĀ when on the earth. They are under the direction of a god called ḤERI-QENBET-F. On the right are the singers of hymns, and near them are the gods who hold the rope which is used in measuring out estates for the righteous; their work is directed by the ḤENBIU gods. On the left of the boat of AFU are the regions which are set apart for the souls of the various peoples known to the EGYPTIANS. The first region is occupied by 'MEN', i.e. EGYPTIANS; the second by the ĀAMU, or the people who live in the countries to the east of EGYPT and in PALESTINE and SYRIA; the third by the NEHESU, or the black-skinned races of the SÛDÂN; and the fourth by the THEMHU, or the fair-skinned LIBYANS. This shows that the EGYPTIANS did not believe in an international heaven. The explanatory text says that the REMTHU or 'Men' came into being from the tears of the Eye of RĀ, and that the BLACKS were the result of the masturbation of RĀ. The next groups of gods are the Timekeepers of OSIRIS and his chief judges, the DJADJAU. These last decide how long souls are to remain in this part of the ṬUAT, and the Timekeepers keep the tally. All these gods are confirmed in their appointments and duties by AFU, who assigns to each and all offerings of meat and drink of a celestial character.

SIXTH GATE. The vignettes show us the Gate and its guardians and the Judgement Hall of OSIRIS. The god is seated on a chair of state placed on a pedestal with nine steps, on each of which stands a god of the Company of OSIRIS. The god is in mummy form, and wears the double crown and *menat*, and holds 𓋾 and ☥ in his hands. Before him are the Great Scales, and a baboon is seen driving away the black pig of SET. The explanatory texts are written in what the early Egyptologists called the 'enigmatic' script, and they have not as yet been satisfactorily explained. The region through which AFU is towed in this part of the ṬUAT cannot be described fully, because the cover of the sarcophagus of SETI I on which it was cut is broken. But the fragments of it which remain show that the Elysian Fields of OSIRIS formed the subjects of the vignettes. On these we see the beatified engaged in agricultural labours. At intervals fetish poles appear, and some of the beatified beings are engaged in reaping, and others are tending the plants, and others are carrying loads of them on their heads. The plant is called *maāt*, and on it all who are there live; but the god SER, or SAR, i.e. OSIRIS, is himself the plant, and thus the followers of the god live on the body of their god. OSIRIS says to 'those whose Kau have been washed': 'Ye are MAĀT of MAĀT. Be at peace, O ye who have the forms of my followers, and who dwell in the house of him whose souls are holy.' In these fields wheat is grown, and the grain of the Corn-god NEPRA becometh ripe through the light of RĀ. Thus even the followers of OSIRIS in the ṬUAT obtain their sustenance through RĀ, the overlord of OSIRIS. The SET-headed fetish poles which are seen in the upper register destroy the enemies who attempt to hinder the work of the planters and reapers in the Fields of OSIRIS.

SEVENTH GATE. This gate PESṬIT is guarded by the Seventh Company of the gods, but they and the other gods acclaim AFU and admit him into this section of the ṬUAT. The first group of beings seen by AFU are the 'mysterious gods whose arms are hidden'; they serve RĀ in ḤET-BENBEN, or the temple which contains the sacred Benben Stone, in which the Spirit of RĀ dwells. Next come the 'gods of the temples', and the SENNU gods, who serve outside ḤET-BENBEN, and the gods who are armed with metal weapons, and whose duty it is to fight the great and evil WORM called MAMU.

We have now reached that part of the ṬUAT where the powers of evil congregate in order to obstruct the boat of AFU. Chief among these was SEBA ĀPEP who took the form of a huge serpent, and who made twelve heads to appear from out of his body; these the gods crush and devour. Another adversary was ĀQEN, who appeared in the form of a mummy. The gods of the twelve hours bring a double rope, and twist it round his neck and strangle him. Beyond this are the biers of the gods 'who are asleep in the body of OSIRIS'. To these the god HORUS-ṬUATI speaks, and he orders them to cast off their wigs (or head-dresses) and throw open their mummy swathings, and open their eyes and look on the light sent out by AFU. He also said, 'gather up your flesh, collect your bones, gird up your members, and make ye yourselves complete bodies. There is sweet (i.e. fresh) air for your nostrils'. NEHEP assists them on their way to SEKHET-ḤETEP. Beyond these biers lies the Pool of Fire, which is

Horus-Ṭuati and Khepri with the double cobra body.

guarded by a fiery serpent, and the gods and souls of the earth cannot descend into it because of the deadly fire of this serpent. The text makes the mysterious statement, 'The water of this pool is OSIRIS, and this water is KHENTI-ṬUAT; and he liveth therein'.

EIGHTH GATE. The serpent SET-ḤRA, and the Ninth Company of the gods, and the fiery cobras open the Gate and admit AFU, who is towed along by the usual four gods into the waters of NUNU, or NU, the primeval ocean. In front of them stands 'the Dweller in NUNU', with bowed shoulders, leaning on a staff. In the lake or sea(?) are four groups of beings, the HERPIU, AGIU, NEBIU, and KHEPAIU, i.e. Bathers, Floaters, Swimmers, and Divers, to whom the Dweller in NU says, 'Rise up, O beings of time, regard ye RĀ, for he ordereth your destinies'. AFU addresses them, and gives breath to their nostrils, and tells them that offerings shall be made to their souls which are upon earth. It seems that these beings represent the men who died by drowning. Beyond these waters we come to the gods who feed the souls which are in the fiery Lake of SERSER 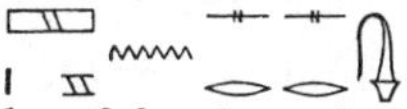. AFU confirms the arrangements for their supply of food, and accepts their praises and homage. Next come the enemies of OSIRIS who are to be burnt in the fire. HORUS the Aged watches them as they stand with their arms bound in agonizing positions before the monster fire-spitting serpent KHETI. To him HORUS says, 'O my serpent KHETI, thou Mighty Fire, open thy mouth, distend thy jaws, belch thy fire on the enemies of my father OSIRIS; burn their bodies and consume their souls.'

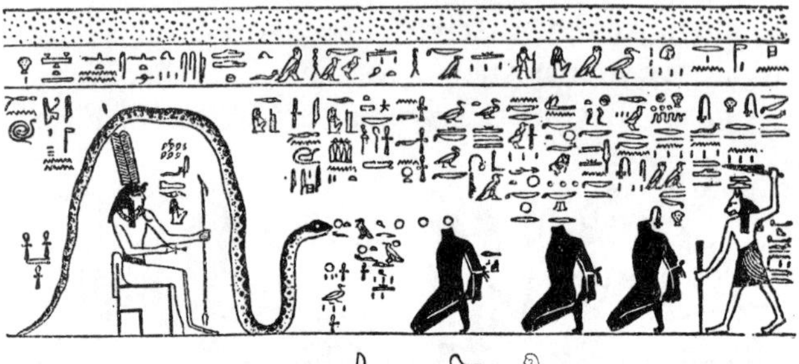

The 'Flesh of Osiris' wearing the plumes of Amen seated under a canopy formed by the body of the serpent Meḥen who blasts away with fire the heads of kneeling fettered captives.

Men, baboons, and women weaving spells with nets.

NINTH GATE. Having passed through this Gate AFU finds himself in the region where the Powers of Evil hold sway, and he finds it necessary to summon to his help all the powers of all the loyal gods to enable him to pass onwards into the eastern part of the sky. First there appear groups of men, baboons, and women with nets, and these are preceded by three gods who are armed with long harpoons. The six men with the nets are 'masters of magical spells', the baboons are SAIU, i.e. 'makers of spells by means of cords', and the women SAIT do the same. The ĀBBIU or men with the harpoons hold a rope which passes over the body and head of a prostrate naked god and is grasped by him with both hands. The name of the prostrate god is AAI, and he has on his head the solar disk from which project two objects which resemble the ears of an ass. The position of the god suggests that he has either raised himself by pulling the rope, or has been raised up by the pulling of the cord by the ĀBBIU. The meaning of this scene is obscure. If the objects with the disk are intended to represent the ears of an ass, we must regard the figure as that of the Ass-god, who was a form of the Sun-god, or of SET, or of HORUS. If of the last named, the disk and the objects with it probably represent the winged disk 𓂀. Facing AAI is the serpent ĀPEP, and above him is the crocodile SHESSHES, the tail of which terminates in a serpent. What ever he may represent, or whoever he may be, it seems clear that he was defending the road on which AFU was to travel. AFU passed on and came to the place where the gods of the White and Red Crowns were preparing his crowns for the morrow. There too was 'HORUS in his boat', who had the form of a hawk-headed lion with the head of a man above his haunches. On the lion's back stood the god HORUS-SET, with his hands resting on two White Crowns. Next come the eight-headed serpent SHEMTI and the serpent BATA, with their warders UPU and ABETH, and then the Boat of AFU, who now becomes KHEPRI, is towed along by the Souls of AMENT and the Followers of RĀ, HORUS, and KHEPRI. The last gods in this Gate are Serpent KHEPRI, with two cobras springing from his body and the Hawk of HORUS of the ṬUAT perched on him, and the Eight Powers who tow KHEPRI.

Horus-Set, lion in the boat.

TENTH GATE. Having passed through this Gate AFU comes to the region where all the gods and goddesses are ready to assist him to become the Sun-god of to-morrow. The star-gods and goddesses, who represent the planets and the other great stars, prepare for AFU a new disk and supply it with heat and light. Among the strange forms are the winged serpent SEMI; and BESI, the bull-headed fetish pole; and ĀNKH; and a serpent with two human bodies placed back to back; and HORUS–SET on the magical bow MEHEN, with six serpents. Beyond these the fight between ĀPEP and the protectors of AFU is being enacted. ĀPEP is lying on the ground and is prevented from advancing by a big chain which is held tightly by the STEFIU and other gods. Above his head is the Scorpion of the god-

The gods of the eastern sky preparing and equipping the sun which is to rise on the following morning:

1. Equipping the Disk with spirit and power.

2. Kindling the fire for the sun and arranging the hours of his course, and 'He who hath two faces' (Horus-Set) arranging the balance between day and night.

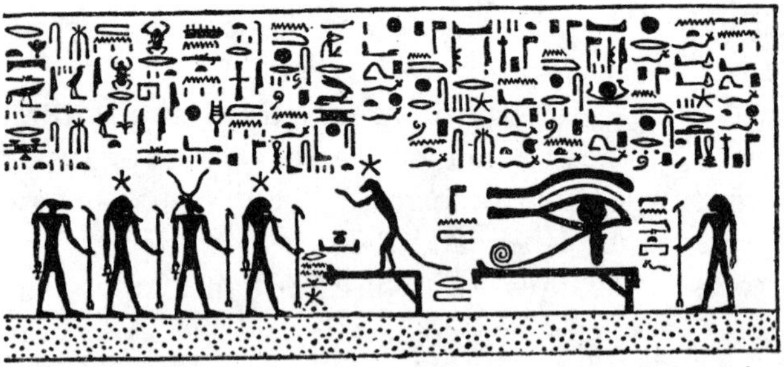

3. The constellations and the morning stars standing ready to assist the sun to rise. The Udjat or Eye of the Sun on a standard and 'the master of his home of flame' ready to fill it with flame.

dess SERQET, who is effecting his strangulation. His progress is further hampered by the ANTIU and ḤENATIU gods, each of whom is armed with a staff and a knife. The latter are represented in human form but each of them has four serpents in the place of a head. The strength of ĀPEP was very great, and another group of gods, the 'Strong-armed', grasped the rope which held ĀPEP, and a

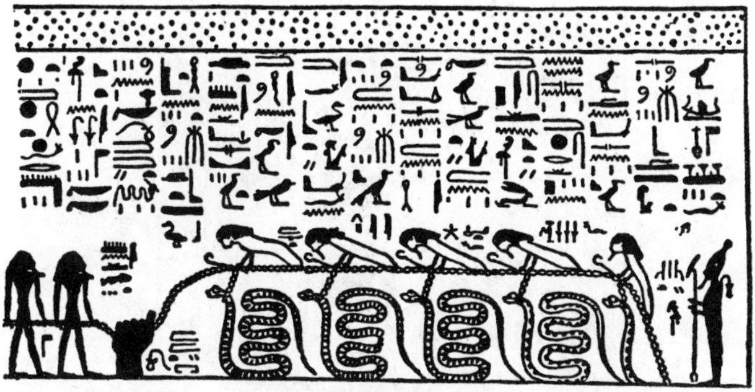

Osiris Khenti Amenti watching the fettering of the Uamemti confederation of serpents, the forces of Āpep.

mighty HAND is seen pulling down the rope. ĀPEP was supported by a group of serpent-gods called UAMEMTIU, and these are being seized by the necks by the Earth-god GEBB and the Four Sons of HORUS. These lie along the rope just behind the HAND. The UAMEMTI are the MESU-BEṬSHU or, 'Children of Revolt', who are often mentioned in the *Book of the Dead*, and OSIRIS KHENTI AMENTI stands looking on. But AFU has other helpers, namely the gods of the 'stars which never set', and of the groups of stars which are seen in the eastern sky before sunrise. With them are the star-goddesses of the twelve hours, and the gods of the great constellations, and the Ape-god of SYRIA. Beyond these is the Eye of HORUS, or RĀ, on a stand, waiting to be united to the face of the solar disk.

ELEVENTH GATE. The gods of this Gate welcome the arrival of the Boat of AFU, and when it closes after his entrance the gods on the battlements wail. During this hour AFU witnesseth the final overthrow of ĀPEP. The god 'whose name is hidden' [hieroglyphs] hath produced himself from out of the waters of NU, and hath opened the Gate by which AFU has entered NUT, the sky of this world. He now sees his everlasting and implacable enemy lying at full length helpless, and his body is tied to five stakes with chains. The Sons of HORUS hack him to pieces with their knives, and the venom

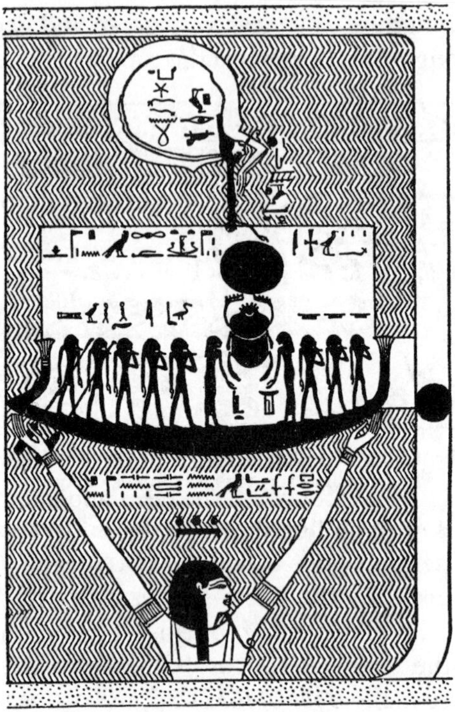

The boat containing Khepri with the solar disk above him being raised up out of the primeval ocean by Nunu. Khepri receives the disk from Osiris, whose body forms the Ṭuat. The three gods without names are the god Ḥeka (magician), the pilot and the lookout. The five gods with names are Gebb, Thoth, Horus of Ḥeken, Ḥu, and Sia.

which drops from him falls down into AMENTI. Then the celestial Baboons who praise the rising sun, and the gods who bring disks and stars, and the gods who bring offerings, and the goddesses who sing (i.e. the celestial choir), and the gods who establish the White and Red Crowns, and the gods who drive away SET, arrange themselves on both sides of the Boat of AFU, and with loud cries of joy and hymns of praise they escort the god to the Gate from which he will emerge at sunrise. The EGYPTIAN text here embodies the sense of the words, 'When the morning stars sang together, and all the sons of God shouted for joy' (Job xxxviii. 7).

TWELFTH GATE. On arriving at this Gate AFU completes his journey through the ṬUAT. Each of the doors of this Gate is guarded by a serpent, which welcomes AFU, and the doors close and the gods and souls who are once more left in the darkness of the ṬUAT lament bitterly. By the doors are the cobras of ISIS and NEPHTHYS. Instead of the company of gods who usually stand by the Gate we see on poles the head of KHEPRI with a beetle above it, and the head of TEM, with the solar disk above it; these gods represent the morning sun and the evening sun, and AFU is now about to unite these forms of the Sun-god to himself. When AFU passes through this Gate he enters NUT, or the sky of this world. And he finds awaiting him the MÂṬET (or MANDJET) Boat, i.e. the boat of the morning sun in which he sails over the sky from sunrise until noon. As AFU emerges from the eastern end of the ṬUAT, or the 'womb of the morning', the Sky-goddess NUT receives him. The vignette cut on the sarcophagus of SETI I illustrates the birth of the Sun-god daily. Here we see the head and shoulders and arms of NU, the god of the celestial ocean, thrusting upwards from the waters, and in his hands he bears the boat of the Sun-god. The Beetle of KHEPRI is in the boat and is pushing upwards the solar disk, and ISIS and NEPHTHYS are supporting him with their hands. The explanatory texts read: 'These arms come forth from the water, and they raise up this god'; 'This god rests in the MATET Boat and the gods who are in it'; 'NUT receiveth RĀ'. The goddess NUT stands on the head of OSIRIS, whose body is bent round and forms the ṬUAT.

The journey of AFU through the ṬUAT lasted from the time of sunset of one day to the time of sunrise of the next, and the reader will note the differences which exist between the Book AMI ṬUAT and the Book of Gates. It is impossible to describe the functions of all the various gods and groups of gods which are found in both works, but it is quite clear that one Book represents a system of theology which is very different from that of the other. AMI ṬUAT represents that favoured by the Court and nobles and high officials, and the Book of Gates gives that which was favoured by the people generally.

APPENDIX

Passages describing the power and attributes of God, the One God, the Creator of the universe (see above, p. 15)

1. God is One and Alone and no other [existeth] with him. God is the One, the One who hath made everything.

2. God is a Spirit, a hidden spirit, the Spirit of spirits, the great Spirit of EGYPT, the divine Spirit (or God-Spirit).

3. God is from the beginning, he hath been from the beginning, he is the primeval one and existed when nothing else was. He existed when nothing else existed, and he created what is after he came into being. He is the Father of Beginnings.

4. God is the Eternal One, he is everlasting and is without end. He is everlasting and eternal. He endureth for time without end, and he will exist to all eternity.

5. God is hidden, no man knoweth his form. No man hath searched out his similitude. He is hidden to gods and men. He is a secret (or mystery) to all his creatures.

6. No man knoweth a name by which to call him. His name remains hidden. His name is a secret to his children. His names are without numbers, his names are many, no man knoweth the number thereof.

7. God is MAĀT (i.e. Truth, or the Law). He liveth through Truth, he feedeth himself thereon. He is the King of Truth, whose Truth maketh free the tongue. He resteth on Truth, he createth the Truth, and setteth it up over the world.

8. God is life, and only through him doth one live. He poureth out life on men, he breatheth the breath of life into the nostrils.

9. God is father and mother. The Father of fathers and the Mother of mothers (i.e. the original ancestor). God begetteth and is not begotten, he bringeth forth and is not brought forth. He begot himself and brought himself forth. He fashions and is not fashioned. He is the Creator of his own form and the sculptor of his own body.

10. God himself is existence. He subsisteth in all things, he remaineth in all things. He is the subsistent element which increaseth without perishing. He is the One who multiplieth him-

self a million-fold, endowed with many forms, endowed with many members.

11. God hath made everything. He is the Creator of all which now is, the Creator of whatsoever is in this world. He is the Creator of whatsoever was, of whatsoever is, and of that which doth not yet exist. He is the Creator of the world. It was he who fashioned the world with his hands in primeval time, and he provided it with that which proceeded from himself. He is the Creator of the heavens and the earth, the Creator of heaven, earth, and the deep, the Creator of heaven, earth, the deep, the waters, and the mountains. God suspended the heavens from above, and laid the foundations of the solid earth. God made the heaven, fashioned the earth; he made the waters to gush forth, and formed the massive mountains.

12. Whatsoever his heart (or mind) planned came into being forthwith, and when once he had uttered the word it came into actual being for all time.

13. God is the Father, the Mother, the old-time Father of all the gods. He sent forth his voice and the gods came into being. The gods came into being through the utterance of his mouth. He fashioned men and gave forms to the gods. He is the Great Master, the Potter of olden time, who made men and the gods to proceed from his hands, the Potter who shaped men and the gods upon [his] potter's wheel.

14. The heavens rest upon his head, and the earth beareth his feet. Heaven hideth his spirit, the earth hideth his form, and the deep envelopeth his hidden mystery. His body is like the air (or wind), the heavens rest upon his head, and NILE-flood shroudeth his form.

15. God is compassionate towards his worshippers. He heareth the man who appealeth to him. He protecteth the weak against the strong. God heareth the crying of him who is in dire distress, he is compassionate towards the man who appealeth to him, he protecteth those who are in distress against the arrogant and truculent, and he is the Judge between those who are powerful and those who are weak. God recognizeth the man who acknowledgeth him; and rewardeth him that serveth him, and protecteth him that followeth in his way.

PART II

HYMNS TO THE GODS, LITANIES, ETC.

A HYMN OF THANKSGIVING TO THE NILE

[The hieratic text is preserved in two papyri in the BRITISH MUSEUM (SALLIER II and ANATASI VII), photographic facsimiles of which were published by BUDGE, *Hieratic Papyri in the British Museum*, Second Series, LONDON, 1924. The poem has been translated by several scholars. See MASPERO, *Hymne au Nil*, CAIRO, 1912.]

I. Homage to thee O ḤĀPI (NILE, appearing in this land, coming to vivify EGYPT). Thou art the Hidden One, the Leader of the Darkness, on the day in which he is pleased to be the Leader (?). Thou makest green the plantations which RĀ hath created to give life unto all the beasts of the field. Thou makest the desert lands to drink, being [remote] from water [that is] the dew; thou descendest from heaven. Lover of GEBU (Earth-god), Director of NEPRA (Grain-god). Thou makest prosperous the workshop of PTAḤ (the Artificer-god).

II. Thou art the lord of fish. Thou makest thy way up among the lands which thou floodest, the geese cannot alight on them. Thou art the maker of grain. Thou makest the barley to grow, thou makest the temples to keep [their] festivals. Idleness of the fingers is repugnant to him. Hundreds of thousands of men are made beggars,[1] the gods in heaven are brought low, men suffer calamity.

III. He maketh the whole earth available (?) for the cattle. Princes and peasants rest, men and women answer when he returneth. His form is [made] by KHNEMU.[2] When he riseth the earth rejoiceth, every man is filled with joy, every bone receiveth sustenance, every tooth sinketh into food.

IV. Thou art the bringer of food, thou art the great [lord] of meat and drink, and the creator of all that giveth happiness. Thou art the August (or Holy) One, the generous [Giver] of chosen sacrifices, through thee offerings are made. He maketh the green herb for the cattle, and provideth sacrifices for every god, the [perfume] of incense is with him when he taketh possession of

[1] If he be idle, i.e. fail to rise.

[2] The god who fashioned men on his potter's wheel.

the Two Lands (EGYPT). He filleth the storehouses, he maketh proud the granaries, and he taketh care for the destitute.

V. He maketh vegetation to grow sufficient for every one who desireth, and he (or no one) suffereth poverty. . . . He is not hewn in stone [figures] with the White Crown on them. He is unseen, service cannot be rendered to him, gifts cannot be given to him, he cannot be approached in the secret places in the sanctuaries, his abode is unknown, he is not to be found in inscribed shrines.

VI. No habitation containeth him. None directeth his heart. Thou makest the youths and maidens of thy children to rejoice, they salute thee as King. Thou art stablished (or permanent) by Law when thou comest forth before the South and the North. Every man drinketh of him, he giveth [his water] lavishly.

VII. . . . is glad, every heart rejoiceth. SEBEK (Crocodile-god), the son of NEITH, is glad (?), and the Company of the gods[1] (or the Nine gods) who are in thee is glorious. Thou pourest out water, and floodest the fields, [thereby] strengthening men. Drinking (?) [the water] one man loveth another. None can make a decision (or law) for thee.

VIII. He is the Light-giver, appearing from out of the darkness . . . his flocks and herds. His strength produceth everything.

[The text of the rest of this paragraph is corrupt, and though several words can be read, it is difficult to get a general sense out of them.]

IX. [The text of this paragraph also is corrupt. In the latter part of it reference seems to be made to the NILE-flood. When it appears in the THEBAÏD and the Delta men rush out with their tools to strengthen the river banks. Rich and poor alike go forth, the former without their ornaments, and the latter naked.]

X. He establisheth the Right (MAĀT). [The garbled text goes on to mention the GREAT GREEN, i.e. the MEDITERRANEAN SEA, and seems to suggest that men do not make offerings to it as to the NILE, because it gives them no benefit. Then mention is made of gold and silver and lapis lazuli which are of far less value to the EGYPTIANS than barley and millet.]

[1] The god Rā, head of the Divine Nine and their great Ancestor, sprang from the primeval abyss of water, from which the celestial Nile derives itself, and the source of the Nile of Egypt is the celestial Nile.

XI. Songs to thee are begun on the harp, the people praise thee with [clapping of] the hand; young men and maidens, who are thy children, rejoice greatly in thee. Thou hast repaid [their] toil. The August (or Holy) One cometh and maketh the earth beautiful, and maketh thee . . . to flourish before men. He maketh to live the hearts that are in the women who are with child. He loveth the multitudes of beasts of every kind.

XII. Thou risest in the city of the HEQ (i.e. the king of EGYPT), [all] men are satisfied with things of beauty . . . lilies (lotus flowers) . . . all things . . . garden herbs for all thy children. In times of scarcity, joy leaveth the houses, ruin covereth the land.

XIII. During the Inundation offerings are made unto thee, oxen are sacrificed unto thee, and great festivals are celebrated in thine honour. Geese are fattened for thee, wild animals (gazelles?) are entrapped in the desert and on the mountains. . . . Offerings are made to every god as to ḤĀPI (NILE), incense ascendeth to heaven, oxen, bulls, and geese are burned. A sanctuary hath been made to the NILE in THEBES, and his name will be unknown (henceforth) in the TUAT.

XIV. O mortals, exalt ye the Company of the gods, and him the lord of awe, who hath made NEB-ER-DJER (i.e. the Lord of the Universe) his son, to cover with vegetation the banks of the river. Flourish thou! Flourish thou, O NILE! who makest men to live on his cattle, and his cattle on [his] herbage.

A HYMN TO RĀ WHEN HE RISETH

[From the Papyrus of ANI (BRITISH MUSEUM No. 10470, sheet 1) XVIIIth or XIXth dynasty.]

Homage to thee, O thou who hast come as KHEPERI, KHEPERI, the Creator of the gods. Thou risest, thou shinest, thou lightenest thy mother [NUT]; thou art crowned King of the gods. Mother NUT payeth homage to thee, with both her hands [drooped]. MANU (the West) receiveth thee with satisfaction, MAĀT embraceth thee both at morn and at eve.

Hail, all ye gods of the Temple of the Soul, who weigh heaven and earth in the balance, and provide funerary offerings in abundance!

Hail, TA TUNEN,[1] thou ONE, Creator of mankind, Maker of the plasm of the gods of the South and of the North, of the West and of the East.

Hail, come ye and acclaim RĀ, the Lord of Heaven, the Prince (life, health, and strength be to him!),[2] Creator of the gods, and adore ye him in his beautiful form when he riseth in the ĀTET (or MĀTET) Boat.

Those who dwell in the heights, and those who dwell in the depths worship thee. THOTH[3] and MĀAT[4] write down for thee the plan of thy course, daily and every day.

Thine enemy the Serpent [UAMEMTI] hath been hurled into the fire, the Serpent SEBAU hath stumbled and fallen; his arms are bound in fetters, and RĀ hath hacked off his legs. The MESU BEṬSHU (i.e. sons of malicious revolt) shall never again raise themselves up. The Temple of the Aged One (i.e. RĀ of HELIOPOLIS) keepeth festival, and the voices of those who rejoice are heard in the mighty dwelling. The gods rejoice when they see RĀ rising, when his beams flood the world with light. The Majesty of the Holy God goeth forth and advanceth even unto the land of MANU (the West). He maketh the earth brilliant at his birth each day; he journeyeth on to the place where he was yesterday.

[Many pious scribes added personal to their official prayers, and as an example of these the following is quoted from the Papyrus of ANI.]

'O be thou at peace with me and let me behold thy beauties. May I journey forth upon earth. May I smite the [eater of] the Ass. May I crush the serpent SEBAU. May I destroy ĀPEP in his hour.[5] May I see the Abṭu[6] Fish in his season, and the Ant Fish[6] [piloting] the Boat in its waters. May I see HORUS as steersman, with THOTH and MAĀT one on each side of him. May I grasp the bows of the SEKTET Boat and the stern of the ĀTET Boat.[7]

[1] A very ancient Earth-god.

[2] A pious exclamation usually uttered on behalf of the reigning king.

[3] The divine intelligence of Rā, scribe of the gods, inventor of the arts and sciences.

[4] Associate of Thoth; the equivalent of Wisdom in Ecclesiasticus.

[5] i.e. at the time of his furious attack.

[6] These were mythological fishes. They swam by the bows of the Boat of Rā and warned him of the approach or attacks of evil spirits from the water.

[7] So that he might reach the stern of the Morning Boat from the bows of the Evening Boat.

'May RĀ grant the Ka of the OSIRIS ANI to behold the Disk of the Sun, and to see the Moon-god without ceasing each and every day. May my soul come forth and walk hither and thither and whithersoever it pleaseth. May my name be proclaimed, and may it be found upon the board of the table of offerings. May offerings be made before me even as to the followers of HORUS. May there be prepared for me a seat in the Boat of RĀ on the day when he goeth forth. May I be received into the presence of OSIRIS in the land of victory.'

A HYMN TO RĀ WHEN HE RISETH

[From the Papyrus of HU-NEFER (BRITISH MUSEUM No. 9001, sheet 1) XIXth dynasty.]

Homage to thee, O thou who art RĀ when thou risest and TEMU when thou settest.

Thou risest, thou risest,
Thou shinest, thou shinest.
O thou who art crowned King of the Gods.

Thou art the Lord of heaven, and the Lord of the earth; thou art the Creator of those who dwell in the heights and of those who dwell in the depths.

Thou art the ONE god, who came into being in the beginning of time.

Thou didst create the earth. Thou didst fashion men, thou didst make the watery abyss of the sky, thou didst form ḤĀPI (the NILE) and [his] ocean, and thou dost give life unto all that therein is. Thou hast knit together the mountains, thou hast made mankind and the beasts of the field to come into being, thou hast made the heavens and the earth. Worshipped be thou whom the goddess MAĀT embraceth at morn and at eve.

Thou dost travel across the sky, thy heart swelling with joy, and the Lake TESTES (heaven?) becometh contented thereat. The serpent-fiend NAK hath fallen and his two arms are cut off. The SEKTET Boat hath fair winds, and the heart of him who is seated in the shrine (or cabin) thereof rejoiceth. Thou art crowned the

Prince of Heaven, the ONE who is dowered with all sovereignty, who comest forth from the sky. RĀ triumpheth!

Hail Divine Youth, heir of eternity, self-begotten!
Hail to thee! Thou gavest birth to thyself!
Hail, ONE, Mighty ONE, of myriad forms and aspects!
Hail, King of the World, Prince of ON (HELIOPOLIS)!
Hail, Lord of Eternity, Ruler everlasting!

The Company of the gods rejoice when thou risest and when thou sailest across the sky.

Hail, Exalted One in the SEKTET Boat!

Homage to thee, O AMEN-RĀ, who restest upon MAĀT, who traversest heaven, every face (i.e. all men) beholding thee! As thou advancest thy Majesty increaseth; thy rays are upon all faces. Thou art unknown (unknowable?), no tongue is capable of declaring thy similitude; thyself alone [can do this]. Thou art One, even as is the bringer of the TENA basket. Men praise thee in thy name, they swear oaths by thee, for thou art lord over them. Thou hearest with thine ears, and seest with thine eyes.

Millions of years have passed; I cannot declare the number of those through which thou hast passed. Thy heart decreed a day of happiness in thy name of 'Traveller'. Thou traversest distances untellable, of myriads and millions of years, thou journeyest in peace. Thou steerest thy way across the waters to the place which thou lovest. This thou doest in one little moment, and then thou dost sink down and dost make an end of the hours.

Hail, my Lord, traverser of eternity, whose being is everlasting!

Hail, thou Disk, Lord of beams of light, thou risest and makest all men live!

A HYMN TO RĀ WHEN HE RISETH

[Papyrus of ANI, sheet 20. XVIIIth or XIXth dynasty.]

Hail, thou Disk, thou lord of rays, who risest on the horizon day by day. Homage to thee, O HARMAKHIS, who art KHEPRI, the self-created.

When thou risest on the horizon and sheddest thy beams of light upon the Lands of the North and of the South, thou art beautiful, yea beautiful, and all the gods rejoice when they behold thee, the King of heaven.

NEBT-UNNUT (i.e. the goddess of the hour) is stablished upon thy head; her uraei (cobras) of the South and North are upon thy brow, and she taketh her place before thee. THOTH is stablished in the bows of thy boat to destroy utterly all thine enemies. The dwellers in the ṬUAT come forth to meet thee, they do homage to thee as they advance to behold thy beautiful form. [Here comes a personal prayer of ANI.]

Homage to thee! Thou risest in thy horizon as RĀ, thou restest upon MAĀT (Law), thou traversest the sky, and every face watcheth thee and thy course, for thou hast been hidden from their sight. Thou appearest at dawn and eventide day by day. The SEKTET boat of thy Majesty advanceth vigorously; thy beams are on all faces, thy red and yellow rays cannot be known, and thy beams cannot be depicted. When thou risest above the sky thou art the one ONE. . . . In one little moment thou dost pass over spaces of millions of years and dost rest. Thou countest the hours of the night, and dost end them. And the earth becometh light. . . .

Thou art crowned with the majesty of thy beauties. Thou fashionest thy members as thou advancest, and thou givest birth to them painlessly in the form of RĀ, as thou risest into the upper air. [Here follows a further prayer of ANI.]

A HYMN TO RĀ WHEN HE SETTETH

[For the text see NAVILLE, *Todtenbuch*, i. 19.]

Homage to thee, O RĀ, who settest as TEM HARMAKHIS, thou divine god, thou self-created being, thou primeval matter (plasm ?). When thou appearest in the bows of thy bark men shout for joy at thee, O Maker of the gods! Thou didst stretch out the heavens wherein thy Two Eyes (i.e. the Sun and Moon) might travel, thou didst make the earth to be a vast abode for the Spirits so that each may know the other. The SEKTET Boat is glad, and the MĀTET Boat rejoiceth, and they greet thee with exaltation as thou journeyest. The god NU (Sky-god) is content, and thy mariners are satisfied. The Uraeus-goddess hath overthrown thine enemies, and thou hast carried off the legs of ĀPEP.

Thou art beautiful, O RĀ, each day, and thy mother NUT embraceth thee.[1] Thou settest in beauty, thy heart is glad in the horizon of MANU,[2] and the holy beings therein rejoice. Thou shinest there with thy beams, O thou great god OSIRIS,[3] the everlasting Prince.

The lords of the zones of the ṬUAT in their habitations stretch out their hands in adoration before thy Ka (i.e. the visible emblem of thy vital strength), and they cry out to thee, and they all come forth in thy train (or company) shining brilliantly. The hearts of the Lords of the ṬUAT are glad when thou sendest forth thy glorious light in AMENTET. Their eyes are turned towards thee, they press forward to see thee, and their hearts rejoice when they can gaze upon thee. Thou hearest the acclamations of those who are in their chests (i.e. coffins and sarcophagi), thou doest away their helplessness, and drivest away the evil influences (or beings) which are round about them. Thou givest breath in their nostrils, and they grasp the bows of thy Boat in the horizon of MANU (i.e. the West). Thou art beautiful, O RĀ, each day.

A HYMN TO RĀ WHEN HE SETTETH

[From the Papyrus of NEKHTU-AMEN (NAVILLE, op. cit., ii. 23).]

A Hymn of praise to RĀ at eventide when he setteth a living being in RAAKHA (read MANU ?). Praise be unto thee. O RĀ, praise be unto thee, O TEM in thy splendid progress. Thou didst rise and didst put on strength, and thou setteth like a living being amid thy glories in the horizon of AMENTET, in thy domain which is in MANU (the West). Thy Uraeus is behind thee; thy Uraeus is behind thee. Hail to thee, in peace; hail to thee, in peace.

Thou joinest thyself unto the Eye of HORUS, and thou hidest thyself within its secret place. It destroyeth for thee all the convulsions (?) of thy face, it maketh thee strong with life, and thou livest. It bindeth its protecting amulets behind thy members. Thou sailest forth over heaven, and thou stablishest the earth; thou joinest thyself unto the upper heaven, O thou Luminary!

[1] The goddess receives him in her arms morning and evening.

[2] i.e. the West.

[3] In the kingdom of the dead Rā identifies himself with the god of the dead, Osiris.

The lands of the East and West adore thee, they bow in homage before thee, and they praise thee day by day. The gods of AMENTET rejoice in thy splendid beauties. The hidden sanctuaries adore thee, the Aged Gods make offerings unto thee, and they create protecting powers for thee. The gods who dwell in the Eastern and Western Horizons bear thee along, and those who are in the SEKTET Boat (i.e. the Evening Boat) row thee onwards.

The Souls of AMENTET address thee, and when they meet thy Majesty (Life, Health, and Strength be to thee!) they say unto thee, 'All hail, all hail'. When thou appearest in peace shouts of delight go up before thee. O thou Lord of Heaven, Prince of AMENTT. Thy mother ISIS embraceth thee, and in thee she recognizeth her son, the lord of fear, the mighty one of terror. Thou settest as a living being within the dark portal. Thy father TA TUNEN taketh thee up, and stretcheth out his two hands behind thee; thou becomest a diving being in the earth. Thou wakest as thou settest, and thy habitation is in MANU (i.e. the West). The fear of thee is great, thy forms are majestic, and the love of thee is great among those who are in the Underworld.

THE SEVENTY-FIVE PRAISES OF RĀ[1]

[The texts are found on the north of the royal tombs at THEBES (ed. NAVILLE).]

1. Praise be unto thee, O RĀ, exalted Power, lord of the hidden Circles, producer of beings with forms. Thou reposest in secret habitation and performest thy creative works as the god TAMT .

2. Praise be unto thee, O RĀ, exalted Power, Creator, . Thou spreadest out thy wings, thou restest in the ṬUAT (i.e. Other World or Underworld), thou givest form to the things which come forth from thy divine members.

3. Praise be unto thee, O RĀ, exalted Power, TA-TENEN, the begetter of the gods [of his Company]. Thou guardest what is in them, thou performest thy acts of creation as Governor of thy Circle.

4. Praise be unto thee, O RĀ, exalted Power, who lookest on the

[1] Note the omission of an address to Osiris.

earth and brightenest AMENTET (the West, the Underworld). Thou art he whose attributes () are his own creations; thou performest thy acts of creation in thy Great Disk.

5. Praise be unto thee, O RĀ, exalted Power, thou Word-soul who resteth on his high place. Thou strengthenest thy hidden AAKHIU, and they have their forms from thee.

6. Praise be unto thee, O RĀ, exalted Power, mighty one, bold of face, who dost knit together thine own body. Thou dost gather together the gods of thy company when thou goest into thy Hidden Circle.

7. Praise be unto thee, O RĀ, exalted Power. Thou callest to thine Eye, thou speakest to thy head, thou givest breath to the souls in their places; they receive it and have their forms in him (i.e. thee).

8. Praise be unto thee, O RĀ, exalted Power, the destroyer of thine enemies; thou dost decree destruction for the dead ( ).

9. Praise be unto thee, O RĀ, exalted Power. Thou sendest light unto thy Circle, thou makest darkness to be in thy Circle, and coverest those who are therein [therewith].

10. Praise be unto thee, O RĀ, exalted Power, the illuminer of bodies in the horizon; thou enterest thy Circle.

11. Praise be unto thee, O RĀ, exalted Power, supporter (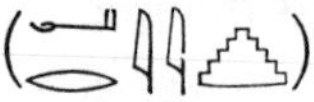) of the Circles of AMENTET; thou art the body of the god TEMU ().

12. Praise be unto thee, O RĀ, exalted Power, the hidden supporter of ANPU (); thou art the body of KHEPRI ().

13. Praise be unto thee, O RĀ, exalted Power, whose existence is longer than that of her whose forms are hidden. Truly thou art the bodies of SHU (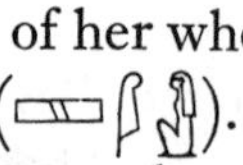).

14. Praise be unto thee, O RĀ, exalted Power, the leader (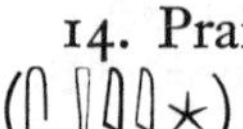) of RĀ to his members. Truly thou art the bodies of TEFNUT ().

15. Praise be unto thee, O RĀ, exalted Power, who dost make

abundant the things of RĀ in their seasons; truly thou art GEBB .

16. Praise be unto thee, O RĀ, exalted Power, thou mighty one, who keepest count of the things which are in him (i.e. thee). Truly thou art the bodies of NUT .

17. Praise be unto thee, O RĀ, exalted Power, thou lord who advancest; truly thou art ISIS .

18. Praise be unto thee, O RĀ, exalted Power, whose head shineth more than what is in front of him; truly thou art the bodies of NEPHTHYS 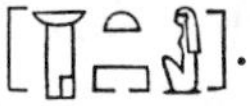.

19. Praise be unto thee, O RĀ, exalted Power, who art united in thy members, One, who collectest all seed; truly thou art the bodies of HORUS .

20. Praise be unto thee, O RĀ, exalted Power, thou shining one, who dost send forth light upon the waters of heaven. Truly thou art the bodies of NU (NUNU) .

21. Praise be unto thee, O RĀ, exalted Power, the avenger of NU, who comest forth from what is in him. Truly thou art the bodies of the god REMI .

22. Praise be unto thee, O RĀ, exalted Power. Thou art the two Uraei (Cobras) who bear their two feathers [on their heads]. Truly thou art the bodies of the Two HUAITI gods  .

23. Praise be unto thee, O RĀ, exalted Power. Thou goest in and comest out, thou comest out and goest in to thy hidden Circle. Truly thou art the bodies of ĀAṬU .

24. Praise be unto thee, O RĀ, exalted Power, the Soul who departeth at his appointed time. Truly thou art the bodies of NETHERT 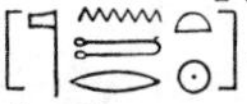.

25. Praise be unto thee, O RĀ, exalted Power, who standeth up, the Soul One, who avengeth his children. Truly thou art the bodies of NETUTI .

26. Praise be unto thee, O RĀ, exalted Power. Thou raisest

thy head, and makest thy brow strong, thou Ram, strengthener of creatures.

27. Praise be unto thee, O RĀ, exalted Power, thou light of SHU, prince of AGERT 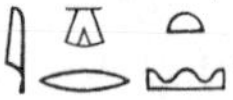. Truly thou art the bodies of AMENT (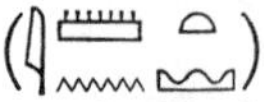).

28. Praise be unto thee, O RĀ, exalted Power, the Soul that seeth, the governor of AMENT. Truly thou art the bodies of the Double Circle ().

29. Praise be unto thee, O RĀ, exalted Power. Thou art the Soul that mourneth and the god that weepeth. Truly thou art the bodies of AAKEBI ().

30. Praise be unto thee, O RĀ, exalted Power. Thou makest thy hand to pass, and praisest thine Eye. Truly thou art the bodies of the god whose limbs are hidden (AMEN-ḤĀU 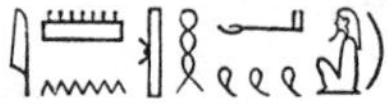).

31. Praise be unto thee, O RĀ, exalted Power. Thou art the Exalted Soul in SHETATI (). Truly thou art KHENTI AMENTI (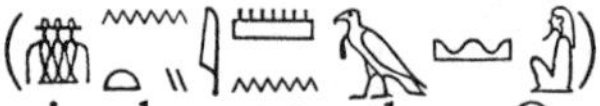).

32. Praise be unto thee, O RĀ, exalted Power, of manifold forms (?) in the Holy House. Truly thou art the bodies of the god KHEPRER ().

33. Praise be unto thee, O RĀ, exalted Power. Thou placest thine enemies in their strong fetters. Truly thou art the bodies of MATI ().

34. Praise be unto thee, O RĀ, exalted Power. Thou givest light in the hidden place. Truly thou art the bodies of the god of generation (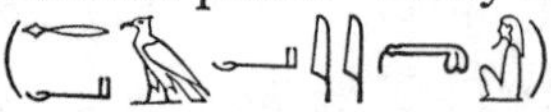).

35. Praise be unto thee, O RĀ, exalted Power, vivifier of bodies, making throats to inhale breath. Truly thou art the bodies of TEBATI ().

36. Praise be unto thee, O RĀ, exalted Power, assembler of bodies in the ṬUAT, and they acquire living forms. Thou destroyest foul humours. Truly thou art the bodies of SERQI () [the Scorpion god].

37. Praise be unto thee, O RĀ, exalted Power, Hidden-face

SESHEM NETHERT (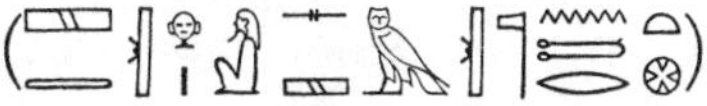). Truly thou art the bodies of SHAI ().

38. Praise be unto thee, O RĀ, exalted Power, lord of might, embracer of the ṬUAT. Truly thou art the bodies of SEKHEN-BA ().

39. Praise be unto thee, O RĀ, exalted Power, hiding thy body in what is in thee. Truly thou art the bodies of AMEN-KHAT (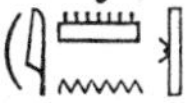 ).

40. Praise be unto thee, O RĀ, exalted Power, stronger of heart than thy followers, sender of fire into the house of destruction. Truly thou art the bodies of REKḤI ().

41. Praise be unto thee, O RĀ, exalted Power. Thou sendest forth destruction, and makest beings to live by thy creations in the ṬUAT. Truly thou art the bodies of ṬUATI (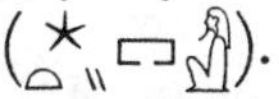).

42. Praise be unto thee, O RĀ, exalted Power, BUA-TEP ( ), governor of his Eye, the sender forth of light into the hidden place. Truly thou art the bodies of SHEPI ().

43. Praise be unto thee, O RĀ, exalted Power, TEMT-HĀTU, stablisher of AMI-TA (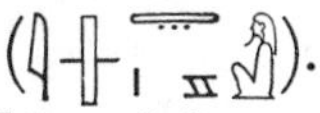). Truly thou art the bodies of ṬEMṬ-ḤĀTU (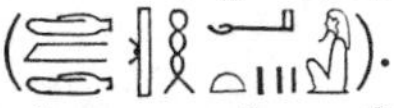).

44. Praise be unto thee, O RĀ, exalted Power, creator of hidden things, generator of bodies. Truly thou art the bodies of SESHTAI (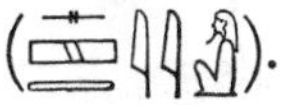).

45. Praise be unto thee, O RĀ, exalted Power, providing those who are in the ṬUAT with their necessaries in the hidden Circles. Truly thou art the bodies of ĀPER-TA (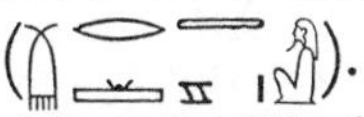).

46. Praise be unto thee, O RĀ, exalted Power. Thy limbs rejoice when they see thy body, O UASH-BA (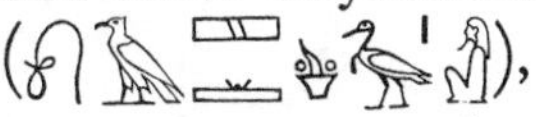), when thou enterest thy body. Truly thou art the bodies of ḤĀI (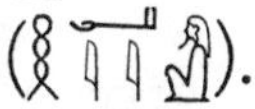).

47. Praise be unto thee, O RĀ, exalted Power. Thou art the Aged One of the pupil (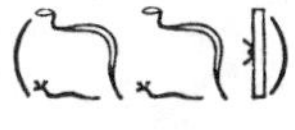) of the UDJAT, BAI ().

Thou makest full thy splendours and thou art indeed the bodies of THENTI ().

48. Praise be unto thee, O RĀ, exalted Power. Thou makest straight paths in the ṬUAT, and openest up roads in the hidden places. Truly thou art the bodies of MAĀ-UATU ().

49. Praise be unto thee, O RĀ, exalted Power, thou Soul who advancest and hasteneth thy steps. Truly thou art the bodies of AKHPA (?) ().

50. Praise be unto thee, O RĀ, exalted Power. Thou sendest out thy stars and lighteneth the darkness in the Circles of those whose forms are hidden. Truly thou art the bodies of ḤEDJIU ().

51. Praise be unto thee, O RĀ, exalted Power, maker of the Circles, maker of creatures by thine own creative force. Thou, O RĀ, hast created things existent and things non-existent, the dead, the gods, and the spirits. Truly thou art the Body that createth KHATIU .

52. Praise be unto thee, O RĀ, exalted Power, hidden and secret god twofold. The Souls go where thou leadest, and thy followers thou makest to enter in. Truly thou art the bodies of AMENI (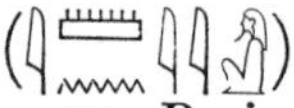).

53. Praise be unto thee, O RĀ, exalted Power, UBEN-AN (
) of AMENT. The light of the lock of hair on thee. . . . Truly thou art the bodies of UBEN.

54. Praise be unto thee, O RĀ, exalted Power, Aged One of forms who goest through the ṬUAT, to whom the Souls in their Circles ascribe praises. Truly thou art the bodies of THEN-ARU ().

55. Praise be unto thee, O RĀ, exalted Power. When thou unitest thyself to the Beautiful AMENT the gods of the ṬUAT rejoice at the sight of thee. Truly thou art the bodies of AĀI (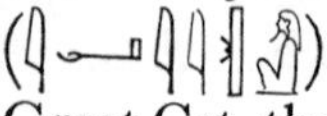).

56. Praise be unto thee, O RĀ, exalted Power, the Great Cat, the avenger of the gods, the judge of words [and deeds], President of the Assessors, and Governor of the Holy Circle. Truly thou art the bodies of the Great Cat ().

57. Praise be unto thee, O RĀ, exalted Power. When thou fillest thine Eye, and speakest to the pupil thereof, the divine dead shed tears. Truly thou art the body of METU-AAKHUT-F ( ).

58. Praise be unto thee, O RĀ, exalted Power. Thou art the Soul on high and thy bodies are hidden. Thou sendest forth light and seest thy hidden things. Truly thou art the bodies of ḤER-BA (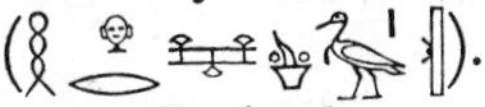).

59. Praise be unto thee, O RĀ, exalted Power, exalted of Soul, destroyer of thine enemies, sender of fire on the wicked. Truly thou art the bodies of QA-BA ().

60. Praise be unto thee, O RĀ, exalted Power. AUAIU, hider in purity. Thou art the master of the souls of the gods. Truly thou art the bodies of AUAIU ().

61. Praise be unto thee, O RĀ, exalted Power, Oldest One (), Great One, governor of the ṬUAT, KHEPRI. Thou art the creator of the SEDJTI (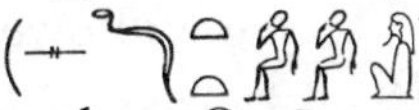), whose bodies truly thou art.

62. Praise be unto thee, O RĀ, exalted Power, Mighty One of travels. Thou orderest thy goings by MAĀT. Thou art the Soul that doest good to the body. Thou art SENK-ḤRA () (i.e. STI-ḤRA, Face of Light). Truly thou art his body.

63. Praise be unto thee, O RĀ, exalted Power. Thou protectest thy body, and holdest the balance among the gods on the hidden AMA and AM-TA. Truly thou art the bodies of AMA AMTA ().

64. Praise be unto thee, O RĀ, exalted Power, Lord of the fetters of thine enemies, One, Prince of the Baboons (). Truly thou art the bodies of ANTETU ().

65. Praise be unto thee, O RĀ, exalted Power. Thou sendest fire into thy furnaces, and cuttest off the heads of those who are to be destroyed truly thou art the bodies of KETUITI ().

66. Praise be unto thee, O RĀ, exalted Power, god of generation, destroyer of thine offspring, One, stablisher of EGYPT by thy strength. Truly thou art the bodies of TA-THENEN ().

67. Praise be unto thee, O RĀ, exalted Power, Stablisher of the gods who watch the hours (URSHIU) on their standards, and are invisible and secret. Truly thou art the bodies of the URSHIU ().

68. Praise be unto thee, O RĀ, exalted Power, thou DJENTI  of heaven, Gate of the ṬUAT, and BESI () and his spirit bodies . Truly thou art the bodies of BESI.

69. Praise be unto thee; O RĀ, exalted Power. Thou art the Apes () . . . the true creative Power of divine attributes (). Truly thou art the bodies of the Ape-god in the ṬUAT.

70. Praise be unto thee, O RĀ, exalted Power, renewer of the earth, opener of the way for that which is therein, Soul giving names unto his limbs. Truly thou art the bodies of SMA-TA ().

71. Praise be unto thee, O RĀ, exalted Power, NEHI, burning up thine enemies, SEDJTI 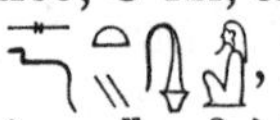, burner of fetters. Truly thou art the bodies of NEḤI (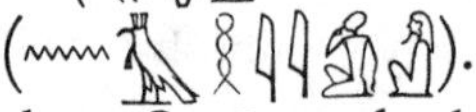).

72. Praise be unto thee, O RĀ, exalted Power, god of motion, god of light, traveller bringing on darkness after the light. Truly thou art the bodies of SHEMTI (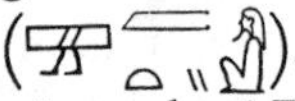).

73. Praise be unto thee, O RĀ, exalted Power, lord of souls who art in the house of thine obelisk (), chief of the gods who are governors of their shrines. Truly thou art the bodies of NEB-BAIU , Lord of Souls.

74. Praise be unto thee, O RĀ, exalted Power, Sphinx-god, Obelisk-god, Raiser of his two Eyes. Truly thou art the bodies of ḤUAITI (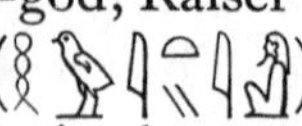).

75. Praise be unto thee, O RĀ, exalted Power, Lord of Light, Declarer of hidden things, Soul who holdest converse with the gods in their Circles. Truly thou art the bodies of NEB-SENKU (i.e. NEB-STI, Lord of Light, 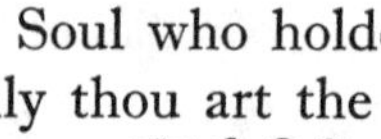).

A HYMN TO RĀ–TEM

[From the Papyrus of MUT-ḤETEP (BRITISH MUSEUM No. 10010, sheet 5.]

Hail RĀ–TEM in thy splendid progress! Thou risest, and thou settest as a living being in the glories of the western horizon; thou settest in thy territory which is in the Mount of Sunset (MANU). Thy uraeus is behind thee, thy uraeus is behind thee. Homage to thee, O thou who art in peace; homage to thee, O thou who art in peace. Thou art joined unto the EYE OF TEM, and it chooseth its powers of protection [to place them] behind thy members. Thou traversest heaven, thou travellest over the earth, and thou journeyest onwards.

O thou LIGHT, the northern and southern heavens come to thee, they prostrate themselves before thee, and do homage to thee day by day. The gods of the AMENTIU rejoice in thy beauties, and unseen places sing hymns of praise unto thee. The dwellers in the SEKTET Boat go round about thee, the Souls of the East do homage to thee, and when they meet thy Majesty they cry: 'Come in peace!' (i.e. Welcome!) Lord of heaven, governor of AMENTT, thou art welcomed with a shout of joy.

Thou art acknowledged by ISIS who seeth her son in thee, the lord who is feared, the lord who is held in awe. Thou settest as a living being in the secret place. Thy father [TA-]TUNEN placing his hands behind thee raiseth thee up; thy members of earth become endowed with divine attributes, thou rousest thyself in peace and settest in MANU.

O grant thou that I may become a being honoured before OSIRIS, and that I may come to thee, O RĀ–TEM. I have worshipped thee, therefore do thou for me that which I wish. Grant thou that I may be victorious in the presence of the Company of the Gods.

Thou art beautiful, O RĀ, in thy western horizon of AMENTET, thou lord of MAĀT, thou who art greatly feared, whose attributes are majestic. Thou art greatly beloved by those who dwell in the ṬUAT (Underworld), thou shinest with thy beams upon the beings who are therein perpetually, and thou sendest forth thy light upon the path of RE-STAU.[1] Thou openest up the path of the two Lion-

[1] A portion of the domain of Seker, the god of the Underworld of Memphis.

gods,[1] thou settest the gods upon [their] standards, and the Spirits[2] in their abiding places. The heart of NAARERF[3] is content when RĀ setteth.

Hail, O ye gods of the land of AMENTT, who make offerings and oblations unto RĀ–TEM, ascribe ye glory [unto him when] ye meet him. Grasp ye your weapons and overthrow ye the fiend SEBA on behalf of RĀ, and repulse the fiend NEBT on behalf of OSIRIS. The gods of the land of AMENTT rejoice, they lay hold upon the rigging of the SEKTET Boat, and they advance in peace. The gods of the SHETAT (Secret House) who dwell in AMENTT triumph.

A HYMN TO ATEN BY AMEN–ḤETEP IV

[For the text see Mr. N. DE G. DAVIES, *Rock Tombs*, vol. iv, pls. 32 and 33.]

A HYMN OF PRAISE TO THE LIVING HORUS OF THE TWO HORIZONS, WHO REJOICETH IN THE HORIZON IN HIS NAME OF 'SHU, WHO IS IN THE ATEN (DISK)', THE GIVER OF LIFE FOR EVER AND EVER, BY THE KING WHO LIVETH IN TRUTH, THE LORD OF THE TWO LANDS, (NEFER-KHEPERU-RĀ, UĀ-EN-RĀ), SON OF RĀ, WHO LIVETH IN TRUTH, LORD OF THE CROWNS (AAKHUNATEN), GREAT IN THE DURATION OF HIS LIFE, GIVER OF LIFE FOR EVER AND EVER.

He saith:

Thou risest gloriously, O thou Living ATEN, Lord of Eternity!
Thou art sparkling (or coruscating), beautiful, [and] mighty.
Thy love is mighty and great . . . thy light
Of diverse colours leadeth captive (or bewitcheth) all faces.
Thy skin shineth brightly to make all hearts to live.
Thou fillest the Two Lands (i.e. UPPER and LOWER EGYPT) with thy love, O thou god, who did[st] build [thy]self.
Maker of every land, Creator of whatsoever there is upon it.
Men and women, cattle, beasts of every kind, and trees of every kind that grow on the land live when thou shinest upon them.
Thou art the father and mother of what thou hast made,
Their eyes, when thou risest, turn their gaze upon thee.

[1] Shu and Tefent (?).
[2] i.e. the beatified dead.
[3] Or An-rut-f, the 'place where nothing groweth'; a region in the Underworld of Herakleopolis.

Thy rays at dawn light up the whole earth.
Every heart beateth high at the sight of thee, for thou risest as their Lord.
Thou settest in the western horizon of heaven,
[Men] lie down in the same way as those who are dead.
Their heads are wrapped up in cloth, their nostrils are blocked,
Until thy rising taketh place at dawn in the eastern horizon of heaven.
Then are their hands lifted up in adoration of thy KA (or Person);
Thou vivifiest hearts with thy beauties (or beneficent acts) which are life,
Thou sendest forth thy beams, every land is in festival,
Singing men, singing women, [and] men of the chorus make joyful noises in the Hall of the House of the Benben Obelisk, [and] in every temple in the city of AAKHUT-ATEN, the Seat of Truth, wherewith thy heart is satisfied.
Within it are dedicated offerings of rich food (?).
Thy son (i.e. the king) is sanctified (i.e. ceremonially pure)
To perform the things which thou willest, O thou ATEN,
When he showeth himself in the appointed processions.
Every creature that thou hast made boundeth towards thee.
Thy honoured (or august) son [rejoiceth], his heart is glad,
O thou Living ATEN, who [appearest] in heaven every day.
He hath brought forth his honoured son UA-EN-RĀ.
In his own similitude, never ceasing so to do.
The son of RĀ (i.e. the king) exalteth his beauties (or beneficent acts).

(NEFER-KHEPERU-RĀ UĀ-EN-RĀ) (i.e. AMEN-ḤETEP IV) saith:

I am thy son, satisfying thee, exalting thy name.
Thy strength [and] thy power are established in my heart.
Thou art the Living Disk, from thee emanateth eternity.
Thou hast made the heavens to be afar off so that thou
Mightest shine therein, and gaze upon everything which thou hast made.
Thou thyself art ONE, but there are millions of
[Powers of] life in thee to make them (i.e. thy creatures) live,
It is the breath of life in [their] nostrils to see thy beams,

[Withered] buds burst into flower (?), [and] the bush plants which grow on the wastelands of the deserts send up shoots at thy rising; they drink themselves drunk therewith before thy face.

All the beasts frisk about and caper [on their feet;

All the feathered fowl, as they rise up out of their nests, flap their wings with joy, and fly round in circles in praise of the LIVING ATEN].[1]

HYMN TO ATEN BY AI, OVERSEER OF THE HORSE OF AAKHUN-ATEN

[The best edition of the text is that of Mr. N. DE G. DAVIES, who published it in his *Rock Tombs of El-Amarna*, vol. vi, pl. 27.]

1. A HYMN OF PRAISE OF ḤER-AAKHUTI, THE LIVING ONE, EXALTED IN THE EASTERN HORIZON IN HIS NAME OF 'SHU WHO IS IN THE ATEN' WHO LIVETH FOR EVER AND EVER, THE LIVING AND GREAT ATEN, HE WHO IS ADORED IN THE SET FESTIVAL, THE LORD OF ALL THAT THE SUN ENCIRCLETH, THE LORD OF THE DISK, THE LORD OF HEAVEN, THE LORD OF EARTH, THE LORD OF THE HOUSE OF THE ATEN IN AAKHUT-ATEN, OF THE KING OF THE SOUTH AND THE NORTH, WHO LIVETH IN TRUTH, LORD OF THE TWO LANDS (i.e. UPPER AND LOWER EGYPT) (NEFER-KHEPERU-RĀ UĀ-EN-RĀ), THE SON OF RĀ, WHO LIVETH IN TRUTH, LORD OF CROWNS, (AAKHUN-ATEN) GREAT IN THE PERIOD OF HIS LIFE, [AND OF] THE GREAT ROYAL WOMAN (OR WIFE), WHOM HE LOVETH, THE LADY OF THE TWO LANDS (NEFER-NEFERU-ATEN, NEFERTITI), MAY SHE LIVE IN HEALTH AND YOUTH FOR EVER AND EVER.

2. He (i.e. AI, a fan-bearer and the Master of the King's Horse) saith:

Thy rising [is] beautiful in the horizon of heaven, O ATEN, ordainer of life!

Thou dost shoot up in the horizon of the East.

Thou fillest every land with thy beneficence.

[1] The passage in brackets is added from another copy of the Shorter or King's Hymn to Aten, viz. that of Tutu, which is also given by Mr. N. de G. Davies.

Thou art beautiful and great and sparkling, and exalted above every land.
Thy arrows (i.e. rays) envelop (or penetrate) everywhere all the lands which thou hast made.

3. Thou art as RĀ. Thou bringest [them] according to their number,
Thou subduest them for thy beloved son.
Thou thyself art afar off, but thy beams are upon the earth;
Thou art in their faces, they [admire] thy goings.
Thou settest in the horizon of the West.
The earth is in darkness, in the form of death.
Men lie down in a booth wrapped up in cloths; one eye cannot see its fellow.
If all their possessions, which are under their heads, be carried away they perceive it not.

4. Every lion emergeth from his lair,
All the creeping things (or reptiles) bite.
Darkness [is] a warm retreat (?).
The land is in silence; he who made them hath set in his horizon.
The earth becometh light, thou shootest up in the horizon,
Shining in the ATEN in the day, thou scatterest the darkness.
Thou sendest out thine arrows (i.e. rays).
The Two Lands make festival;
[Men] wake up, stand upon their feet,
It is thou who raisest them up.
They wash their bodies (or members), they take

5. [Their apparel] and array themselves therein.
Their hands are [raised] in praise at thy rising.
Throughout the land they carry on their affairs.
Beasts and cattle of all kinds settle down upon the pastures,
Shrubs and green plants flourish,
The feathered fowl fly about over their marshes,
Their feathers giving praise to thy Ka (i.e. Person).
All the cattle rise up on their legs,
Creatures that fly and insects of all kinds

6. Spring into life when thou risest upon them.
Boats, drop down and sail up the river.
Every road showeth its direction at thy rising.
The fish in the river swim towards thy face.
Thy beams are in the depths of the GREAT GREEN (i.e. the MEDITERRANEAN SEA)
Thou makest offspring to take form in women,
Thou createst seed in men,
Thou makest the son to live in the womb of his mother,
Thou makest him so that he crieth not out.

7. Thou art a nurse in the womb,
Giving breath to make live everything thou hast made.[1]
He descendeth from the womb on [the stones] on the day of his birth,
Thou openest his mouth in the normal manner.
Thou providest him with the means for his sustenance.
The young bird in the egg speaketh inside the shell,
Thou givest breath to him inside it to maintain its life;
Thou makest his form mature,
So that being fully grown inside the egg
He can crack the shell.
He cometh forth from the egg
He chirpeth with all his might;
When he hath come forth from it (the egg)
He walketh about on his two feet.
O how many are the things which thou hast made!
They are hidden from thy face, O thou One God,

8. Like whom there is no other.
Thou didst create the earth by thy heart (or Will)
When thou didst exist by thyself (or alone), and men and women,
And cattle and the beasts of every kind that are on the earth,
[And] that move upon feet (or legs),
[And] all the creatures in the sky that fly with their wings.
[And] the deserts of SYRIA, KESH (KÛSH or NUBIA) and KARUT (EGYPT)

[1] Literally 'everything which he hath made'.

Thou hast set every person in his place.
Thou providest their daily food,
Every man with the portion destined for him,
Thou dost compute the duration of his life,
Their tongues are different in speech,

9. And their characters and their skins likewise.
Thou givest distinguishing marks to the dweller in foreign lands.
Thou makest ḤĀPI (NILE) in the ṬUAT (Other World).
Thou bringest it when thou wishest to make mortals to live,
Inasmuch as thou hast made them for thyself.
Thou art their Lord, supporting them to the uttermost;
O thou Lord of every land, thou shinest upon them.
O ATEN of the day, thou great one of majesty.
Thou makest all distant foreign lands [into a highway], they live;
Thou settest ḤĀPI (NILE) in heaven, he descendeth to them.

10. He maketh a pool of water on the mountains like the GREAT GREEN SEA,
He watereth their fields in their villages.
How beneficent are thy plans, O Lord of Eternity!
Thou art the NILE in heaven for the dwellers on the hills,
[And] for all the beasts of the plain which move on legs.
ḤĀPI (NILE) cometh from the ṬUAT to TA-MERA (EGYPT).
Thy beams nourish every plantation.
Thou risest up, they live, they germinate for thee.
Thou makest the Seasons to cause everything which thou hast made to take form.

11. The Season of PERT (Nov. 16–March 16) that they may enjoy coolness (or refresh themselves);
The Season of HEP (March 16–Nov. 16) so that [men] may taste him[1]
Thou hast made the heaven which is afar off
That thou mayest rise therein and look on everything thou hast made.

[1] i.e. feel the heat of Shu who is in the Disk (Aten).

Thou art the One who is Alone, rising up among the creatures thou hast formed as the LIVING ATEN, rising up, shining, departing afar off, returning (?).
Thou hast made millions of forms from thyself being One,
Towns, villages, plantations (or settlements), road [and] river.
Every eye (i.e. all men) beholdeth thee facing them.
Thou art like ATEN of the day at its zenith (?)

12. At thy departure . . .
Thou art in my heart. There is none other who knoweth thee
Except thy son (NEFER-KHEPERU-RĀ UĀ-EN-RĀ).
Thou hast given him wisdom to understand thy plans [and] thy power.
The earth took form on thy hand,
Even as thou didst make them (i.e. men?)
Thou risest up, they live;
Thou settest, they die.
As for thee there is continuous life in thy members; there is the power of life in thee.

13. [All] eyes (i.e. men) gaze upon thy beauties at thy setting, all labours being accomplished.
Thou settest in the West, thou risest, making to flourish . . . for the king,
Every being on every leg (or foot) since thou didst lay the foundation of the earth.
Thou didst raise up for thy son, who came forth from thy members,
The king of the South and of the North,
The Liver in Truth, the Lord of the Two Lands (i.e. EGYPT)
(NEFER-KHEPERU-RĀ UA-EN-RĀ), the son of RĀ,
The Liver in Truth, the Lord of Crowns,
(AAKHUNATEN), great in his duration of life.
[And] the king's woman, Great Lady of Majesty,
Lady of the Two lands (NEFER-NEFERN-ATEU NEFERTITI)
Living [and] renewing youth for ever and ever.

HYMN TO AMEN-RĀ

[For the hieratic text see MARIETTE, *Les Papyrus Égyptiens*, pls. 11–13.]

Hymn to AMEN-RĀ, the Bull in HELIOPOLIS, president of all the gods, beneficent god, beloved one, the giver of the warmth of life to all beautiful cattle.

Hail to thee, AMEN-RĀ, Lord of the thrones of the Two Lands in the APTS (THEBES), Bull of his mother, chief of his fields, long of stride, head of the land of the South (i.e. NUBIA), lord of the MADJAU peoples, Prince of ARABIA, lord of the sky, eldest son of the earth, lord of the things which exist, establisher of things, establisher of all things, One in his times among the gods, beautiful Bull of the company of the gods, president of all the gods, lord of MAĀT (Law), father of the gods, maker of men, creator of beasts and cattle, lord of the things which exist, creator of the staff of life, master of the herbage whereon cattle live, Form made by PTAḤ, beautiful child, beloved one.

The gods adore him, the maker of things which are below, and of things which are above. He shineth on the Two Lands sailing over the sky in peace.

King of the South and North, RĀ, whose word is true (or law), prince of the world! The mighty one of valour, the lord of terror, who maketh the earth like unto himself. How much more numerous are his forms than those of any (other) god. The gods rejoice in his beauties, and they praise him in the two great horizons, and at his risings in the House of Fire. The gods love the smell of him when he, the first-born of the dew,[1] cometh from ARABIA, traversing the land of the MADJAU,[2] the beautiful face coming from the Land of the God.[3] The gods cast themselves down before his feet when they see in His Majesty their lord, the lord of fear, the mighty of Will (or Souls), the master of crowns, the verdifier of vegetation, the maker of food.

Adorations be to thee, O thou maker of the gods, who hast stretched out the heavens and founded the earth. [Thou art] the untiring watcher. MENU-AMEN lord of eternity, maker of everlastingness, adored lord in the APTS (i.e. KARNAK), established with two horns, beautiful in appearance, lord of the Uraeus Crown,

[1] Compare Psalm cx. 3. [2] The peoples of East Africa. [3] Arabia Felix.

exalted of plumes, beautiful of tiara, exalted one of the White Crown. The serpent MEHEN and the two Uraei (cobras?) are by his face; the double crown, helmet, and cap are his decorations in [his] temple. Beautiful of face, he receiveth the Atef Crown; beloved of the South and North he is master of the Sekhti Crown. He receiveth the sceptre of MENU, and is lord of the . . . and the whip (?). [Thou art] the Beautiful Prince, rising with the White Crown, the lord of rays, the creator of light. The gods acclaim him and he stretcheth his hands to him that loveth him. The flame maketh his enemies fall, his Eye overthroweth the rebels, and it driveth its spear into NUT (the sky), and maketh NAK vomit what it hath swallowed.[1]

Hail to thee, RĀ, Lord of MAĀT, whose shrine is hidden; master of the gods, KHEPRI in his boat. Through the utterance of his word the gods sprang into being. Hail ATMU,[2] maker of mortals. He maketh all kinds of creatures to live, however many kinds of them there be, and he maketh the colour of one man different from that of his neighbour.

He heareth the prayer of him that is oppressed, he is kind of heart to him that invoketh him, he delivereth him that is afraid from him that is violent of heart, he judgeth between the strong and the weak.

He is the lord of wisdom, the utterance of his mouth is knowledge. The NILE cometh at his will, the greatly beloved lord of the palm tree cometh to make mankind live. He maketh every work to progress, he worketh in the sky, and he maketh the sweet things of the daylight to come into being; the gods rejoice in his beauties, and their hearts live when they see him.

O RĀ, adored in the APTS, thou mighty one of risings in the shrine!

O ANI, lord of the festival of the new moon, thou makest the six day's festival, and the festival of the last quarter of the moon.

O Prince—life, health, and strength [be to thee]!—thou art the Lord of all the gods, whose appearances are in the horizon, thou

[1] According to one legend the fiend swallowed the crescent moon, and according to another, he swallowed all the water of the celestial ocean so that the Boat of Rā might be unable to move; in each case the spear thrust of the Sun-god made him vomit what he had swallowed.

[2] The evening sun.

president of the ancestors of AUKER-T,[1] thy name is hidden from his children in his (i.e. thy) name of 'AMEN' (i.e. the Hidden One).

Hail to thee, O thou who art in peace, lord of joy, crowned form, lord of the Urr-t Crown, whose plumes are lofty, whose tiara is beautiful, whose White Crown is lofty, the gods love to look upon thee. The double Crown of UPPER and LOWER EGYPT is established on thy brow. Thou art beautiful as thou passest through the Two Lands, in rising thou sendest forth rays from thy two beautiful eyes. The PĀT (i.e. the dead) are in raptures of delight when thou shinest; the cattle become languid when thou shinest [upon them] in full strength. Thou art loved when thou art in the southern sky, and art esteemed pleasant when thou art in the northern sky. Thy beauties seize and captivate all hearts, the love of thee maketh the arms to drop, and thy beautiful form maketh the hands tremble, and hearts to melt at the sight of thee.

O Form, ONE, creator of all things, O Only ONE, maker of things which exist. Men came forth from his two eyes, and the gods sprang into being at the utterance of his mouth. He maketh the herbage whereon cattle live, and the staff of life (i.e. the wheat plant) for man. He maketh the fish to live in the rivers, and the feathered fowl in the sky. He giveth the breath of life in the egg, he maketh birds of all kinds to live, and the reptiles which creep and fly. He causeth the rats (or mice) to live in their holes, and the birds that are on every green twig. Hail to thee, O maker of all these things, thou Only ONE!

He is of many forms in his might! He watcheth over all those who sleep, he seeketh the good for his brute creation. O AMEN, establisher of all things, ATANU and ḤARMAKHIS, all people adore thee, saying, 'Praise be unto thee because thou restest among us, homage to thee because thou hast created us'. All creatures say, 'Hail to thee!' and all lands praise thee. From the highest height of the sky, to the whole breadth of the earth, and to the depths of the sea thou art praised.

The gods bow down before Thy Majesty to exalt the Will of their creator. They rejoice when they meet their begetter, and say unto thee, 'Come in peace, O father of the fathers of all the gods, who hast spread out the sky, and founded the earth. Thou art the

[1] The necropolis of Heliopolis.

maker of the things which are, and creator of the things which exist. Prince, life, health, strength! President of the gods. We adore thy Will, inasmuch as thou hast made us, thou hast made us and given us birth, and we give praise to thee by reason of thy resting with us.'

Hail to thee maker of all things, lord of MAĀT, father of the gods, maker of men, creator of animals, lord of grain making to live the beasts of the hills. Hail, AMEN, Bull, Beautiful Face, beloved of the APTS, mighty of risings in the shrine, twice crowned in HELIOPOLIS, thou judge of HORUS and SET in the Great Hall! President of the Great Company of the gods, Only ONE, without a second at the head of the APTS, and the head of the Company of his gods, living by MAĀT, every day, the double-horizoned HORUS of the East. He hath created the earth, the silver, and the gold, and the real lapis lazuli at his Will.

Incense and fresh myrrh are prepared for thy nose. O Beautiful Face, coming from the land of the MADJAU, AMEN-RĀ, Lord of the thrones of the Two Lands, dweller in the APTS. ANI, dweller in his shrine. King, ONE among the gods, myriad are his names, so many are they that they are unknowable. Rising in the eastern horizon and setting in the western horizon, overthrowing his enemies by his birth at dawn every day. THOTH exalteth his two eyes, and maketh him to set in splendour. The gods rejoice in his beauties, which those who are in his train (?) exalt. O Lord of the SEKTI Boat[1] and of the ĀTET Boat[2] which travel over the sky for thee in peace, thy sailors rejoice when they see NAK overthrown, with his arms gashed with the knife, and the fire consuming him, and his foul soul beaten out of his body and his feet carried away. The gods rejoice, RĀ is satisfied. HELIOPOLIS is glad, the enemies of RĀ are overthrown, and the heart of the Lady of Life (i.e. ISIS) is happy because the enemies of her lord are vanquished. The gods of KHERI-ĀḤĀ rejoice, the dwellers in the shrines make obeisance when they see him mighty in his strength. Creation of the gods of MAĀT (Law), lord of the APTS in thy name of 'Maker of MAĀT' (the Law). Lord of provisions, Bull [mighty] in the name of 'AMEN, the Bull of his mother'. Maker of mortals, making creatures to exist, maker of

[1] The boat in which he sails from noon to sunset.

[2] The boat in which he sails from dawn to noon.

all the things that are in thy name of ATMU KHEPERI, Mighty MAĀT, making the body to rejoice, Beautiful of Face, making the breast glad. Creator with the lofty crown, the two URAEI (cobras) rear up by his forehead. The hearts of the dead go forth to him, and unborn generations turn to him. By his coming he maketh the Two Lands festal. Hail to thee, AMEN–RĀ, lord of the thrones of the Two Lands! His city loveth his shining.

HYMN TO AMEN—EXTRACTS FROM A PAPYRUS AT LEYDEN

[See ALAN GARDINER in *Aegyptische Zeitschrift*, Band xli. 2, 1905, pp. 12–42.]

He (i.e. AMEN) driveth away evils and scattereth diseases.
He is the physician who healeth the eye without medicaments,
He openeth the eyes, he driveth away inflammation (ophthalmia?).
He delivereth whom he pleaseth, even from the ṬUAT (Hell).
He saveth a man from what is his lot at the dictates of his heart.
To him belong both eyes and ears, on every path of him whom he loveth.
He heareth the petitions of him that appealeth to him.
To him that calleth [him] he cometh straightway (or instantly).
He lengtheneth life, he cutteth it short.
To him whom he loveth he giveth more than hath been decreed for him.
[When] AMEN casteth a spell on the water, and his name is on the waters, if this name of his be uttered, the crocodile (?) loses power. The winds are driven back, the hurricane is repulsed.
At the remembrance of him the wrath of the angry man dieth down,
He speaketh the gentle word at the moment of strife.
He is a pleasant breeze to him that appealeth to him.
He delivereth the helpless one.
He is the wise (?) god whose plans are beneficent.
He is more helpful than millions to the man who hath set him in his heart.
One warrior [who fighteth] under his name is better than hundreds of thousands.
Indeed he is the beneficent strong one.

He is perfect [and] seizeth his moment; he is irresistible.

All the gods are three, AMEN, RĀ, and PTAḤ, and there are none like unto them. He whose name is hidden is AMEN. RĀ belongeth to him as his face, and his body is PTAḤ. Their cities are established on the earth for ever, [viz.] THEBES, ANU (HELIOPOLIS), and HEKAPTAH (MEMPHIS).

When a message is sent from heaven it is heard in ANU, and is repeated in MEMPHIS to the Beautiful Face (i.e. PTAḤ). It is done into writing, in the letters of THOTH (hieroglyphs), and dispatched to the city of AMEN (i.e. THEBES) with their things. The matters are answered in THEBES.

His heart is Understanding, his lips are Taste, his Kau are all the things that are in his mouth.

He entereth, the two caverns are beneath his feet. The NILE appeareth from the hollow beneath his sandals. His soul is SHU, his heart is TEFNUT. He is HORUS of the two horizons in the upper heaven.

His right eye is day. His left eye is night. He is the leader of faces on every path. His body is NU. The dweller in it is the NILE, producing everything that is, nourishing all that is.

He breatheth breath into all nostrils.

The Luck and the Destiny of every man are with him.

His wife is the Earth, he uniteth with her.

His seed is the wheat plant, his effluxes are the grain.

A HYMN TO AMEN AND ATEN

[From a stele in the BRITISH MUSEUM (No. 475), XVIIIth dynasty. Published by PIERRET, *Recueil*, tome i, p. 20; BIRCH, *Trans. Soc. Bibl. Arch.*, vol. viii, pp. 143 ff.; and BUDGE, *Tutānkhamen*, p. 44.]

A Hymn of Praise to AMEN when he riseth as HORUS of the Two Horizons, by SUTI, Overseer of the Works of AMEN, and by ḤER (HORUS), Overseer of the Works of AMEN. They say:

Homage to thee, RĀ, beneficent One of every day! Thou shootest up at dawn without fail, KHEPRI, Great One of Works. Thy radiance is in thy face, [O thou] who canst not be known. Silver-gold, is not to be compared [in brilliance] with thy splendours. Having fashioned thyself thou didst mould thy members. [Thou]

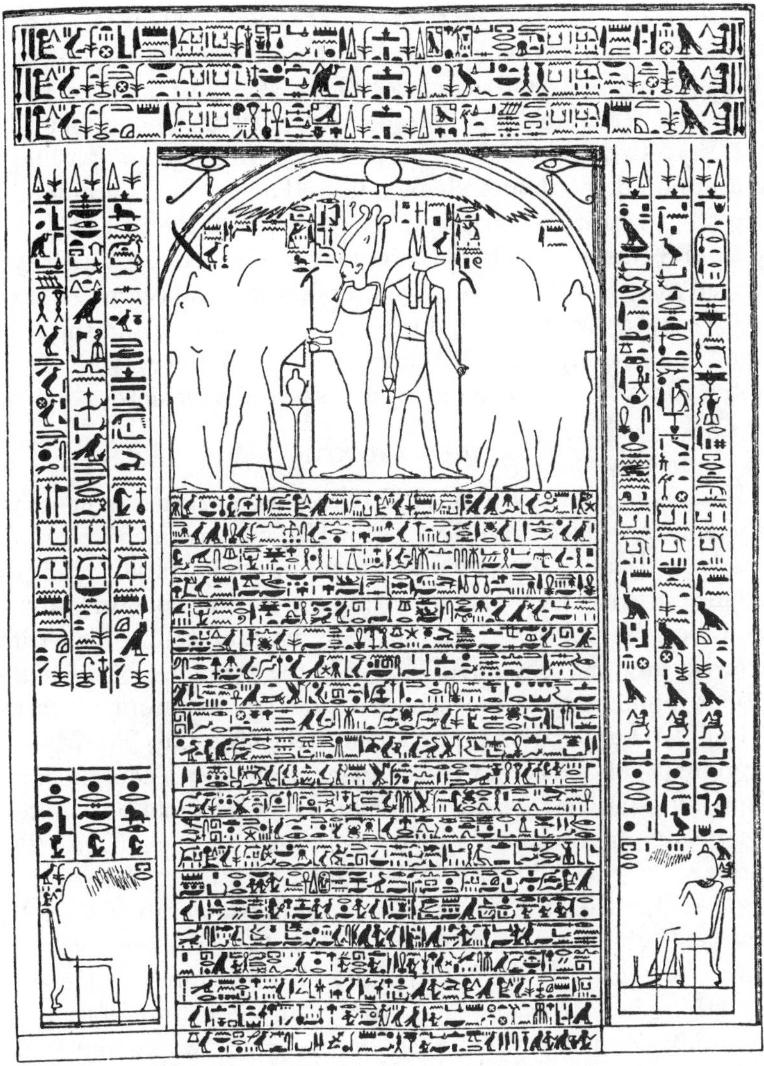

Stele of Horus and Set Horus who were architects and clerks-of-the-works at Thebes, inscribed with a hymn to Amen for one brother, and a hymn to Aten for the other. (British Museum.)

who givest birth wast not thyself born. One by himself by reason of his abilities. Traverser of eternity, he is the Chief of the roads of millions of years, maintaining his divine form. As are the beauties of the celestial regions even so are thy beauties. More brilliant is thy complexion than that of heaven. Thou sailest over the heavens and every face watcheth thee as thou goest, but thou thyself art hidden from their faces. Thou showedst thyself at break of day in beams of light. Strong is thy SEKTET Boat under Thy Majesty. In one short day thou journeyest over a road of millions and hundreds of thousands of miles. Thou passest through thy day, thou settest. Thou dost make the hours of the night likewise to fulfil themselves. There is no interruption of thy toil. All eyes (i.e. all mankind) fasten their gaze upon thee, and cease not to do so. Thy Majesty settest and thou dost hasten to rise in the ṬUAT (the Underworld). Thy sparkling rays bewitch the eyes (?). Thou settest in MANU (the West) and [men] sleep like the dead.

[HYMN TO ATEN]

Hail to thee, O ATEN of the day! Creator of mortals, maker of that whereon they live. Hail thou Great Hawk of the many coloured plumage. [Hail] KHEPRI (or Creator) who didst raise thyself up [from non-existence]. He created himself, he was not born. HORUS the Elder, dweller in NUT (the sky). At his rising and at his setting likewise men cry out joyfully. He is the fashioner of what the ground produceth, KHNEM and AMEN of the HENMEMET.[1] Master of the Two Lands, from the great one to the little one. The Mother supreme (?) of gods and men. Worker, expert, exceedingly great, flourishing in what she doeth. [His] cattle (?) cannot be counted, the mighty herdsmen herding his animals to their byre. The springer up traversing swiftly the course of KHEPRI. His birth is wonderful, raising up his beautiful form in the womb of NUT. He illumineth the Two Lands with his disk. He is the primeval substance (or plasma) of the Two Lands. He made himself. He seeth everything he hath made, the Lord ONE, bringing into captivity (?) [countless] lands every day, observing those who walk about on the earth. He shooteth up into the sky with transformations like RĀ. He maketh the seasons of the year with (?) the months. [It is] hot at his pleasure, it is cold at his pleasure. He maketh the body to be relaxed (or to droop) and he embraceth (or oppresseth) every land. The baboons cry out to him in adoration when he riseth daily.

[1] A class of celestial beings.

This hymn is followed by the interesting biographical note here given:

SUTI (SET) and ḤER (HORUS) each say: 'I was the director of thy throne and Overseer of the Works of thy sanctuary, which as was right, thy beloved son, the Lord of the Two Lands NEBMAĀTRĀ (AMEN-ḤETEP III), to whom life hath been given, made for thee. My Lord appointed me to be in charge of thy monuments, well knowing my vigilance. I worked diligently, I served the office of director of thy monuments strenuously, acting rightly according to thy heart (or wish). I knew that thou didst thyself rest upon what was right, and that thou didst magnify him that did the right upon earth. I did it and thou didst magnify me. Thou didst give praise to me on earth in the APTS (THEBES) when I was among the followers of thee at the time when thou didst ascend the throne (or appear publicly). I am [a man of] Truth, whose abomination is sin (i.e. false words and deeds). I never took pleasure in any converse wherein were words of exaggeration and lies. I only took pleasure in the affairs of my brother, who was like myself, and who came forth from the womb [of his mother] on the same day as myself.'

SUTI, Overseer of the Works of AMEN in the Southern APT (i.e. LUXOR), and ḤER, Overseer of Works in the Northern APT (KARNAK), say:

'I was Overseer of Works on the west bank of the NILE, and he was Overseer of Works on the eastern bank. We two were Overseers of the great buildings (or monuments) in the two APTS, but more particularly (?) of those round about (?) THEBES, the City of AMEN.

'[O AMEN], grant thou to me an old age in thy city. Let me look upon thy beauties, and let me be buried in AMENTT (the West), the seat of rest of heart. Let me join myself to the favoured ones who journey [thither] in peace. Grant thou unto me the sweet wind of thy town, . . . and let me wear (?) bandlets on the day of the festival of UG.'

HYMN TO SHU

[The text of this Hymn is found in a papyrus in the BRITISH MUSEUM. (Magical Papyrus), HARRIS, No. 501.]

Homage to thee, O flesh and bone of RĀ, thou first-born son who didst proceed from his members, who wast chosen to be the chief of those who were brought forth, thou mighty One, thou divine form, who art endowed with strength as the lord of transformations.

Thou overthrowest the SEBAU fiends each day.

[Thy] divine boat hath a [favourable] wind, thy heart is glad.

Those who are in the Morning Boat of RĀ (ĀNTTI) utter loud cries of joy when they see SHU, the sun of RĀ, triumphantly driving his spear in the serpent fiend NEKAU.

RĀ setteth out to sail over the heavens at dawn daily.

The goddess TEFNUT is seated on thy head, she hurleth her flames of fire against thy enemies, and maketh them to be destroyed utterly.

Thou art equipped by RĀ, thou art mighty through his magic (or words of power); thou art the heir of thy father upon his throne, and thy Kau (i.e. characters, or persons) rest in the Kau of RĀ, even as the taste of what hath been in the mouth remaineth therein.

A testament (or will) hath been done into writing by the Lord of KHEMENU (HERMOPOLIS)—THOTH, the scribe of the Library of RĀ-ḤARMAKHIS in the hall of the god-house of ANU (HELIOPOLIS), certain, perfected and made permanent in the letters of the god (hieroglyphs) under the feet of RĀ ḤARMAKHIS, and he shall transmit it to his son for ever and ever.

Homage to thee, O son of RĀ, who was begotten by TEMU himself.

Thou didst create thyself, and thou hadst no mother.

Thou art Truth, the lord of Truth, thou art the Power, the ruling power of the gods.

Thou art the Leader of the Eye of thy father RĀ.

They give gifts unto thee into thine own hands.

Thou makest the Great Goddess to be at peace when storms are passing over her. Thou didst stretch out the heavens on high, and dost make them stable with thine own hands.

Every god boweth in homage before thee, thou king of the South, thou king of the North, SHU, son of RĀ! Life, strength, health [be] unto thee!

Thou, O great god PAUTTI, art furnished with the brilliance of the Eye [of RĀ] in HELIOPOLIS, to overthrow the SEBAU fiends on behalf of thy father.

Thou makest the divine boat to sail onwards in peace.

The rowers who are therein exult, and all the gods shout for joy when they hear thy divine name.

Greater, yea greater (i.e. twice great), art thou than the gods in thy name of SHU, the son of RĀ.

THOTH'S LITANY FOR HORUS

[For the hieroglyphic text see GOLENISCHEFF, *Metternichstele*, LEIPZIG, 1877, ll. 138 ff.]

I am THOTH, I have come from heaven to protect HORUS, and to drive away the poison of the scorpion which is in every member of HORUS.

Thy head is to thee, HORUS; it shall be stable under the Urret Crown.

Thine eye is to thee, HORUS; for thou art HORUS, the son of GEBB, the Lord of the two eyes (i.e. sun and moon) in the plasma [of the gods].

Thy nose is to thee, HORUS; thou art HORUS the Elder, and thou shalt not inhale the fiery wind.

Thy bowels are to thee, HORUS; great is thy strength to slaughter the enemies of thy father.

Thy two thighs (or perhaps forearms) are to thee, HORUS; thou hast received the rank of thy father OSIRIS, and PTAḤ hath balanced for thee thy mouth on the day whereon thou wast born.

Thy breast (or heart) is to thee, HORUS; and ATEN (the Disk) maketh thy protection.

Thine Eye is to thine, HORUS; thy right eye is as SHU, and thy left eye as TEFNUT, who are the children of RĀ.

Thy belly is to thee, HORUS; children of the gods are those who are in it, and they shall not receive [into themselves] the fluid (i.e. venom) of the scorpion.

Thy strength to thee, HORUS; and the strength of SET shall not prevail against thee.

Thy phallus is to thee, HORUS; thou art the Bull of his mother, and the Avenger of his father, who providest food for his children in the course of every day.

Thy two legs are to thee, HORUS; thy strength shall destroy the enemies of thy father.

Thy two shins are to thee, HORUS; KHNEMU hath builded [them], and ISIS hath covered them over with flesh.

The soles of thy feet are to thee, HORUS; the nations who fight with the bow shall fall under thy feet. Thou rulest the South, the North, the West, and the East. Thou shalt be gazed at like RĀ, [Say four times—and likewise him that is under the knife].

I. HYMN TO OSIRIS CONTAINING A SUMMARY OF HIS HISTORY

[For the text see LEDRAIN, *Monuments Égyptiens*, Pls. XXII ff.; and for the first translation of it see CHABAS, *Revue Archéologique*, 1857, pp. 65 ff.]

Homage to thee, OSIRIS, Lord of Eternity, King of the gods! [Thou hast] many names, thou art splendid in [thy] forms. Thou art the mystery being of the things done (i.e. the miracle place) in the temples.

He the dweller in ṬEṬU (BUSIRIS) is the holy Ka, whose possessions (or wealth) are great in SEKHEM (LETOPOLIS). The lord to whom praises are sung in the nome of BUSIRIS, and is the possessor (?) of offerings of food in ON (HELIOPOLIS). He is the lord of whom mention is made in MAĀTI (?), the Hidden (or Secret) Soul, the lord of QERRT,[1] the holy one in White Wall (i.e. MEMPHIS), the Soul of RĀ, his very body.

He it is who set[2] in the city of HENSU[3] (HERAKLEOPOLIS), he is praised superlatively in the NĀRET tree which existeth to support his Soul.

He is the Lord of the Great House [of THOTH] in KHEMENU (HERMOPOLIS), he is the mighty one of terrors[4] in SHAS-ḤETEP.

[1] City of the Circles?

[2] i.e. set like the Sun.

[3] The Hanes of the Bible.

[4] He inspires abject terror.

He is the Lord of Eternity, the dweller in ABYDOS; he sitteth upon his throne in TA-DJESER.[1]

His name was firmly established in the mouth of men [dwelling] in the Two Lands (i.e. EGYPT) in the earliest times. He supplied [to the full] the offerings and food in the Companies of the gods. He is the beneficent Spirit among the Spirits (AAKHU).

NU[2] (or NENU) hath drawn off as a gift his waters, the north wind bloweth upstream for him, the sky giveth birth to air for his nostrils, to make content (or satisfy) his heart.

Plants sprout at his will, and the . . . bringeth forth herbage for him. The heights of heaven and the stars hear [i.e. obey] him, and the great gates [of the sky] throw themselves open to him. He is acclaimed as the Lord in the southern heaven, and adoration is paid to him in the northern heaven. The stars that never set (i.e. the circumpolar) are under the seat of his face (i.e. his direction), and the stars that never rest [serve] as abodes for him.

Offerings appear before him at the word (or command, or decree) of GEBB,[3] and the Company of the gods make thanksgiving to him. The gods (or stars) of the ṬUAT smell the earth[4] [before him], and those who are on the boundaries (?) bow low with bent backs in homage. [The regions?] rejoice when they see him, and the august ones there (i.e. the dead) are afraid of him. The whole of [the people of] the Two Lands ascribe praise unto His Majesty when they meet him.

The glorious SĀHU (i.e. Chief or Master) at the head of the SĀHU, endowed with a lasting appointment and established governorship, Beneficent Power (or Master) of the Company of the gods, gracious of face, beloved by those who see him.

He hath set the fear of him in all countries, with the desire that they all might proclaim his name prominently [when] all [people] made gifts to him.[5] The Lord who is commemorated in heaven and upon earth. Many people shout [in his honour] in the UAG Festival. The Two Lands together hail him with cries of joy. He is pre-eminently the Chief of his brethren, the Prince of the Company of the gods.

[1] The western suburb of Abydos.
[2] The god of the primeval celestial abyss.
[3] The Earth-god.
[4] i.e. kiss the ground.
[5] Translation doubtful and meaning obscure.

He established the right (or the Law) throughout the Two Lands, and set the son upon the great throne of his Father GEBB. He is beloved of his mother NUT.

The great one of strength he overthrew SEBA, raised of arm he slaughtered his Enemy. He set the fear of him in his Enemy, he carried away (?) the boundaries of those who revolted evilly (or talked sedition). Bold of heart he trampled on those who rose up [against him].

[He is] the heir of GEBB [and of] the sovereignty of the Two Lands. GEBB perceived his great capability [to rule], and he delivered to him the leadership of the countries straightway to prosperous times.

He set this country in his hand, the water thereof, the wind thereof, the vegetation thereof, all the cattle thereof. All the feathered fowl thereof, all the creatures thereof that hover, [all] the reptiles thereof and the wild animals of the desert were transferred rightly to the son of NUT; the Two Lands rejoice to make him to ascend the throne of his father, like RĀ when he riseth in the horizon to give light to him that is in the darkness.

He sendeth forth light from his two plumes, and floodeth [with light the Two Lands, like ATHEN (Sun-god) at early dawn.

His crown pierceth the heavens and is a companion of the stars. He is the Guide of every god, beneficent in command. He is the favoured one of the Great Company of the gods, and beloved by the Little Company of the gods.

[HERE BEGINNETH THE HISTORY OF OSIRIS]

His sister [ISIS] worked protection for him, she drove away the enemies. She turned aside evil happenings (or ill luck), pronouncing mightily (?) the word (or spell) with the splendid utterance of her mouth, skilled in her tongue, whose river remaineth without effect, beneficent in giving commands.

The word of ISIS is most mighty. She protected her brother, seeking after him unwearyingly, going round and round about through the land uttering cries of grief, and she gave herself no rest until she had found him.

She made a shade (i.e. screen) [for him] with her feathers, and produced air by [the fluttering of] her wings. She made joyful outcry [when] she drew her brother to the river bank.

She stirred up the inertness of him whose heart rested, she drew into herself his seed, she made an heir, she suckled the child in loneliness, the place where he was being unknown [to any], and she brought him forward when his arm was mighty into the abode of GEBB.

The Company of the gods rejoice, they rejoice, [saying]:

'Come, Come, OSIRIS'S son HORUS!
Stable of heart, true of word.
Son of ISIS, heir of OSIRIS.'

The judges of MAĀT (i.e. the Law) gathered together to him, and the Company of the gods, and the Lord of the Universe himself, the lords of MAĀT who were collected therein, verily they repulsed sin. They seated themselves in the Hall of GEBB, to give the position [of king] to its rightful owner, and the sovereignty to him to whom it belonged legally.

They found that the word of HORUS was true, and the rank of his father was given unto him. He appeared and by the command of GEBB was crowned. He received the overlordship of the eastern and western banks [of the NILE] and the crown was stablished firmly on his head.

The earth was allotted to him as his property, and the heavens and the earth were to be governed by him. Men, high, low, rich and poor, were handed over to him, and he was made to be the ruler of EGYPT and Lords of the North (i.e. the GREEKS) and whatsoever the Sun encircled in his course, and the north wind, and the river, and the Inundation and trees and herbs.

The Grain-god (NEPRI) yielded his growth and food for the Spirit, [who] brought offerings and distributed them in all the lands (or throughout the world).

All men were made happy, their spirits were joyful and their hearts were glad.

The people shouted for joy and all men were thankful for his beneficence, [saying], 'Great is our love for him'. His loving kindness pierceth all hearts, and the love of all folks for him is great. [They say:]

The enemies of the son of ISIS have been delivered over to him, and evil hath befallen [the rebel]. The son of ISIS hath protected (or avenged) his father and his name is exalted and famous. Power hath taken its rightful position, and under its influence there is abundance. The roads have been made apparent, and the paths have been opened out.

The Two Lands are satisfied. Sin hath departed and evil is no more. The Country rejoiceth under its lord. The right is established for the owner thereof, and the wrong is disregarded.

Let thy heart rejoice, O UN-NEFER! The son of ISIS hath put on the crown, and the rank of his father hath been delivered to him in the House of GEBB. RĀ hath spoken, THOTH hath registered, and the judges have agreed [about their verdict] therein. Thy father GEBB issued the decree on thy behalf, and what he spake hath been carried into effect.

II. A HYMN TO OSIRIS UN-NEFER

[From the Papyrus of ANI (BRITISH MUSEUM No. 10470, sheet 2), XVIIIth or XIXth dynasty.]

Glory be to OSIRIS UN-NEFER, the great god in ABTU (ABYDOS), King of Eternity, Lord of Everlastingness, whose existence is that of millions of years. The eldest son of the womb of NUT, begotten by GEBB, the ERPĀT, Lord of the Crowns of the North and South. Lord of the lofty White Crown, he hath received the crook, and the whip (?) and the rank of his divine fathers.

Let thy heart in the Mountain of AMENT be content, for thy son HORUS is established upon thy throne. Thou art crowned lord of ṬEṬU (BUSIRIS), and governor in ABYDOS.

Through thee the world waxeth green in triumph before the might of the Lord of the Universe.

He is the leader of that which is, and of that which is not yet [in being] in his name of 'TAHERSTANEF'; he toweth the earth by MAĀT in his name of 'SEKER'; he is exceedingly mighty and most terrible in his name of 'OSIRIS'; he endureth for ever and ever in his name of 'UN-NEFER'.

Homage to thee, King of kings, Lord of lords, Prince of princes, who from the womb of NUT hath ruled all the world and AKERT (the Other World). Thy body is of bright and shining metal, thy head is of azure blue, and the brilliance of the turquoise encircleth thee.

III. A HYMN TO OSIRIS WITH LITANY

[From the Papyrus of ANI, sheet 19.]

Praise be unto thee, O OSIRIS, Lord of Eternity, UN-NEFER, ḤARMAKHIS, whose forms are manifold, and whose worship (?) is majestic, PTAḤ–SEKER–TEM in ON (HELIOPOLIS), the Lord of the hidden shrine, the Creator of HET-KA-PTAḤ[1] and the gods [thereof] the Guide of the Other World (ṬUAT), who art glorious when thou settest in NUT. ISIS embraceth thee in peace, and she driveth away the fiends from the mouth of thy paths. Thou turnest thy face towards AMENTT, and thou makest the earth to shine like silver-gold. Those who are lying dead rise up to see thee, they breathe the air, and they look upon thy face when the Disk (ATEN) riseth in the horizon. Their hearts are content because they behold thee, O thou, who art Eternity and Everlastingness.

LITANY

1. Homage to thee, [Lord of] the starry gods in ON, and of the heavenly beings in KHERI-ĀḤĀ,[2] thou god UNTI, who art more glorious than the gods who are hidden in HELIOPOLIS.

2. Homage to thee, O AN in ANTES (?), ḤARMAKHIS, with long strides thou stridest over heaven O ḤER-AKHUTI.

3. Homage to thee, O everlasting Soul, thou Soul that dwellest in ṬEṬU, UN-NEFER, son of NUT; thou art the lord of AKERT.

4. Homage to thee in thy dominion over ṬEṬU; the Urret crown is established on thy head; thou One who providest the power which protecteth thee. Thou dwellest in peace in ṬEṬU.

5. Homage to thee, O lord of the Acacia Tree. The SEKER Boat is set upon its sledge. Thou repulsest the Fiend, the worker of evil, and thou makest the *Udjat* to rest upon its seat.

6. Homage to thee, Mighty One in thine hour, great and mighty Prince in ANRUṬF, lord of eternity, creator of everlastingness. Thou art the lord of HENSU (HÂNÊS, HERAKLEOPOLIS).

7. Homage to thee, O thou who restest upon MAĀT. Thou art the lord of ABYDOS, and thy limbs are joined into TA-DJESERT. Thou art he to whom fraud and guile are hateful.

[1] i.e. 'House of the Ka of Ptaḥ', a name of Memphis.

[2] A city which stood between Babylon of Egypt and Heliopolis.

8. Homage to thee, O thou who art in thy boat. Thou bringest HĀPI (NILE) forth from his sources. The light shineth upon thy body, and thou art the dweller in NEKHEN.

9. Homage to thee, Creator of the gods, King of the North and South, OSIRIS, victorious One, ruler of the world in thy gracious seasons. Thou art the lord of the two ATEBUI (i.e. the eastern and western banks of celestial NILE).

[Then comes the following petition which was recited by the deceased after each of the nine addresses given above.]

'O grant thou unto me a path whereover I may pass in peace, for I am just and true. I have not spoken lies wittingly nor have I done aught with deceit.'

IV. A HYMN TO OSIRIS UN-NEFER

[From the Papyrus of HU-NEFER (BRITISH MUSEUM No. 9901, sheet 3.]

The steward HU-NEFER praiseth OSIRIS, and acclaimeth him, and doeth homage unto UN-NEFER, and boweth down before the lord of the Land of Holiness,[1] and exalteth those who are upon his sand, saying:

I have come unto thee, O son of NUT, OSIRIS, Prince of Everlastingness; I am a follower of the god THOTH, and I have rejoiced at everything which he did for thee.

He hath brought unto thee sweet air for thy nose, and life and strength to thy beautiful face, and the north wind which cometh forth from TEM for thy nostrils. O lord of the Land of Holiness.

He hath made SHU to shine upon thy body.

He hath illumined thy path with rays of splendour.

He hath destroyed for thee all the defects which attached to thy members by the magical power of the words of his utterance.

He hath reconciled for thee the Two Horus Brethren.

He hath destroyed the storm-wind and the hurricane.

He hath made the Two Combatants (REHUI) to be gracious unto thee, and the Two Lands (EGYPT) to be at peace before thee.

He hath put away the wrath which was in their hearts and each is reconciled to his brother.

[1] Ta-Djesert, the great cemetery of Abydos.

Thy son HORUS is triumphant before the whole company of the gods.
Sovereignty over the world hath been given unto him,
And his dominion is in the uttermost parts of the earth.

The throne of the god GEBB hath been adjudged unto him, and the rank which was founded by TEMU, and hath been established by a decree in the Chamber of Books.[1] This hath been inscribed upon an iron tablet according to the command of thy father PTAḤ-TENEN [on] the great throne.

He hath set his brother upon that which SHU supporteth[2]—to spread out the waters over the mountains (or deserts), to make to spring up what groweth on the hills, and the grain which germinateth in the earth, and to give increase by water and by land.

Gods celestial and gods terrestrial have devoted themselves to the service of thy son HORUS, and they followed him into his hall [where] the decree was passed that he was to be their lord; and they accepted it straightway.

Thy heart shall rejoice, O lord of the gods, thy heart shall rejoice greatly. The Black Land (i.e. the Delta) and the Red Land (i.e. the desert of UPPER EGYPT) are at peace, and serve humbly under thy sovereign power.

The temples are established upon their own lands (or estates), and cities and nomes are in secure possession of the properties which are [registered] in their names. We will make to thee the offerings which we are required to make by statute, and offer up sacrifices to thy Name for ever. Thy Name shall be acclaimed, libations shall be poured out to thy Ka, the AKHU (Spirits) shall follow with sepulchral meals, and water shall be sprinkled . . . souls of the dead in this land. Everything which was ordered for thee by RĀ in the beginning hath been performed.

Now art thou crowned, O son of NUT, like NEB-ER-DJER (the Lord of the Universe) at his rising.

Thou livest and art stablished, thou renewest thy youth, thou art true and perfect; thy father RĀ strengtheneth thy members, and the Company of the gods acclaim thee.

[1] i.e. the Chancery of the gods.
[2] Heaven and the sky rested on the four pillars of Shu.

ISIS is with thee and leaveth thee never; thou art not overthrown by thine enemies.

The lords of all lands praise thy beauties even as they praise RĀ when he riseth at dawn each day. Thou risest up on thy standard like a governor; thy beauty exalteth the face and lengtheneth the stride.

The sovereignty of thy father GEBB hath been given unto thee, and MUT, thy mother and bearer of the gods, brought thee forth as the firstborn of five gods, and created thy beauty and fashioned thy members.

Thou art a king established! The White Crown is upon thy head, and the crook and the whip (?) are grasped by thy hands. Whilst thou was still in the womb and hadst not yet appeared upon the earth, thou wert crowned Lord of the Two Lands, and the Atef crown of RĀ was upon thy brow. The gods come to thee bowing themselves down to the ground, and they hold thee in fear. When they see that thou possessest the terror of RĀ, they withdraw and depart, and the triumph of thy Majesty is in their hearts.

THE DRAMATIC ASPECTS OF CERTAIN EGYPTIAN MYTHS

By SIDNEY SMITH, M.A., F.S.A., ETC.

AMONG the classes of myths established by students of Comparative Religion, two are particularly common in Egypt, the one closely connected with ritual and the other called aetiological. 'The Book of Overthrowing APEPI' and the myth of the destruction of mankind may be quoted as clear instances of the former class, as is sufficiently shown by the 'rubrics' in the texts; the myth of HORUS of EDFÛ proclaims itself a member of the latter class.

The division of these two classes is useful theoretically for the modern student; it does not correspond to any real distinction in ancient conceptions, nor even, probably, to any essential difference in origin, though here decisive proof is necessarily lacking so far as EGYPT is concerned. The presumptive root of both classes lies in magic. This is more clearly shown in some Babylonian examples, which may be properly compared in this aspect, as L. W. KING rightly pointed out in his Schweich Lectures, because the fundamental conceptions are the same. The Babylonian text which illustrates the close connexion of the ritual myths and the aetiological class is that called the 'Legend of the Worm', translated in CAMPBELL THOMPSON's work, *Devils and Evil Spirits of Babylonia*, vol. ii, pp. 161–3. There the incantation to be recited over a potion of beer and oil to be put on an aching tooth takes the form of a myth, which tells how, after the sky-god ANU had created heaven and earth and natural features of the earth resulted, the worm from the marshes appealed to the sun-god SHAMASH and the god of magic, EA, that it might draw sustenance from gums and teeth. The priestly doctor is then to say, 'Worm, may EA smite thee with his strong fist'. The text opens like an aetiological myth, to explain the existence of the worm, and closes as a true ritual. But the purpose is one; explanation of origin and ritual words said to action alike help to cure the complaint.

Certain Egyptian myths, more especially those only preserved in Late Egyptian or Ptolemaic texts, are best read from this point of view, with a realization that whether they be formally 'aetiological or 'ritual', they were essentially magical and were attended by action. Thus while the 'Book of Overthrowing APEPI' was read, a dummy replica of APEPI was mangled into a shapeless mass, as the colophon informs us. But apparently an essential part of the book was a myth of creation, which, as the text stands, seems to have only a slight relation to the spells against APEPI; the relation is in fact the same as in the Babylonian text just described, and we may suppose that the direct speech used throughout in the creation story given in the APEPI book is really due to a primitive drama, in which the priest spoke as the god RĀ and recounted the 'becomings' which gave him power over the typhonic beast. The incoherence of the text as a story depends upon its dramatic use; to those present at the performance, not everything needed to be said.

Incoherence is also a marked feature of the myth of HORUS of EDFÛ. Incident succeeds incident rapidly, and the explanations of the situations actually given are very scanty. The text is rather a series of explanatory comments on things done than an ordered account of beliefs about the origins of things. Direct speech, mostly in dialogue form, again points to impersonation of the gods. When narrative intervenes, that is generally because it deals with matters that cannot be dramatically represented. We may suppose that this myth really relates to a procession, during which at various halting-places ritual actions accompanied by speech were performed, the whole representing the victorious progress of HORUS through the places named in the text.

A Babylonian parallel may again be adduced for this. It is known that at the festival of the New Year at BABYLON the Creation Epic was recited twice, accompanied by mimetic actions in which the god BEL was represented sometimes by a priest and sometimes by his statue. Such ritual drama is, of course, very common, and is known to have existed in EGYPT owing to SETHE's study, *Dramatische Texte*. Some objection to the word 'drama' in this connexion has, it is true, been raised by Professor FURLANI in his work on Babylonian Religion, but rightly understood it need not mislead. The Egyptian and Babylonian ritual dramas had not even the form of a medieval miracle play; certainly not of Greek drama as we know it. But AESCHYLUS and his contemporaries were preceded by ritual 'drama' performed 'from a wagon', and there a true comparison may be found. For tragedy and comedy in GREECE were differentiated out from the same kind of religious shows. And to the end the Old Comedy retained coarse features only explicable by its origin.

To the dramatic aspect of some Egyptian myths must indeed be attributed, in my opinion, some of their most repellent points. The myth of SETH and HORUS recently published by Dr. GARDINER contains a relation of incidents which, if regarded in themselves, are totally at variance with Egyptian religion of the time to which the text belongs. We may compare the Parade of the leather Penis[1] in ARISTOPHANES. Such incidents are fossilized ritual acts, enacted in civilized periods through the power of inertia which lies in ritual. Originally they were part of a fertility *juju*; engulfed by the greater religious developments connected with the names of gods, they were connected with RĀ or HORUS, and had to find a part in the stories connected with those gods. Masturbation, connexion with himself—anything can be predicated of the divinity. But it is essential to remember that the myth which includes such incidents is not reflecting the social customs or religious ideas of the time; it is linking up ritual acts, some of them dating from remotest antiquity in a dramatic, though often still incoherent, series.

As I have previously said, a theory such as is outlined here cannot be proved. Its probability must depend on a study of comparative religion, and on that ground must be reckoned high. Readers who will take the trouble to compare the myths of this type in EGYPT with say similar examples from Babylonia, where on the whole the evidence is better, will be able to interpret the myths in the light of this 'dramatic' aspect.

Such settings do not cease in EGYPT with the end of the Egyptian

[1] The penis made of whipcord or leather, and several feet in length, is still a prominent feature at all the great festivals in Egypt, and especially in the Delta. I have seen strolling players wield it to the vast delight of crowds at Bûlâḳ Daḳrûr, close to Cairo, and the police were amused spectators and did nothing to stop the performances. On such occasions two young women appear, the one with a gander for her husband and the other a young donkey, and although every respectable man and woman revolts at the obscenities which follow their appearance they laugh and regard it as a 'part of the show'. Such revels are consecrated by their antiquity. —E. A. WALLIS BUDGE.

dynasties. Magical texts continue to use them in the Christian period. The Coptic magical texts published by Father Kropp are in many cases 'dramatic' in this same primitive sense. They deal mainly with love magic. The lover and his beloved are turned into divine figures, and an appropriate little drama is enacted to meet the particular case. As stories the myths are as unsatisfactory and incoherent as the old Egyptian myths; the sequence of situations, not the story, is the important point.

LEGENDS OF THE GODS

THE LEGEND OF THE CREATION OF THE WORLD BY NEB-ER-DJER

[Two versions of this History are found in BRITISH MUSEUM Papyrus, No. 10188, col. xxvi, ll. 22 ff. and col. xxviii, ll. 20 ff.]

THE BOOK OF KNOWING HOW RĀ CAME INTO BEING AND OF OVERTHROWING ĀPEP

[These are] the words which the Lord of All (NEB-ER-DJER) spake after he came into being:

Version A

I am he who came into being as KHEPRI.
[When] I had come into being [other] beings became formed.
All the beings which were formed came into being after I myself had come into being.
Many were the forms [taken by the beings] in coming forth from my mouth.[1]
Heaven had not come into being,
The earth had not come into being,
The creatures of the earth[2] [and] the reptiles had not been made in that place.
I lifted myself up from among them, out of the watery mass, out of inertness (or immobility)
I did not find a place (or spot) whereon I could stand,
I made strong my heart (or took courage).
I laid a foundation in . . .
I made every kind of [material] form,
I was alone (or one by myself),
I had not yet evacuated in the form of SHU,
I had not yet micturated in the form of TEFNUT,
None other had come into being to work with me,
I made a foundation in my own heart.
Very many beings came into being (or assumed forms),

[1] i.e. the God of all spake the words, and as they left his mouth the beings named by it appeared.

[2] Literally 'sons of earth', or animals large and small.

Beings from the beings of the children of the beings[1] of their children.
I, even I, cohabited with my fist.
I obtained the joys of love with my shadow,
I ejected seed from my own mouth.
I evacuated in the form of SHU,
I micturated in the form of TEFNUT.
My father NU (i.e. the watery abyss) made them to rest,
My Eye followed (?) them through long periods of times,
They went away from me
After I came into being as the One (or Only) God,
Three gods proceeded from me when I took form on this earth,
SHU and TEFNUT rejoiced in the inert waters in which they were,
They brought back my Eye which followed after them.

Now after this I gathered together my members,
I shed tears upon them.
Men [and women] arose from the tears which came forth from my Eye.
After it had come back (i.e. my Eye) growled (or raged like a panther) at me when it found that I had made another [Eye, the Moon?] in its place, and that I had endowed it with splendour.
I made it to have a prominent place in my face later.
So that it governed the whole extent of this land,

Their moment [of calamity] fell on their plants (bushes of the eyes?)
I gave back what it took therefrom,
I came forth from the plants,
I created the reptiles (or creeping things) every being (or form) among them.

SHU and TEFNUT gave birth [to GEBB] and NUT,
GEBB and NUT gave birth to OSIRIS, HORUS, the dweller without eyes (i.e. the Blind HORUS), SET, ISIS, NEPHTHYS, from the belly, one after the other.
And their children have become many on this earth.

[1] In some passages of this text the word *Khepri* 'forms', or 'beings' can be well rendered by 'generations'.

Version B

The God of All saith:

I came into being, making beings to come into being.
I came into being in the form of KHEPRI.
Coming into being in primeval time (or at the first time)
I came into being in the form of KHEPRI.
[I am] KHEPRI, maker of beings who came into being.
I produced myself from the matter [which] I made.
I produced myself in the matter;
My name [is] AUSARES (?) matter of matters.
I have worked all [my] will (or desire) in this earth,
I have made myself to permeate it,
I lifted up my hand,
I was alone; they were not born.
I had not evacuated in the form of SHU,
I had not micturated in the form of TEFNUT.
I brought forth [from] my mouth my own name—a magical spell.
I am he who became [various] forms,
I came into being in the form of KHEPRI.
I came into being out of the primeval matter.
Taking many (or manifold) forms from the beginning,
No form whatsoever had come into being in this earth.
I made everything which was made.
I was alone, there was not another who worked with me in that place.
I made forms therein by means of that Divine Soul.
I raised myself up therein out of the primeval abyss of water (NUNU), out of inertness (or immobility).
I found no place whereon I could stand.
I made strong my heart, I laid a foundation for myself (or before me),
I made everything that was made,
I was alone, I laid a foundation in my heart,
I fashioned (or created) many other forms, the forms of KHEPRI.

Their children came into being from the forms of their children.
I evacuated as SHU,
I micturated as TEFNUT,
From being one god I became three gods from myself.
They came into being on this earth.
Thereupon SHU [and] TEFNUT rejoiced in the primeval abyss of water wherein they were.
Behold (?) my Eye, I brought them, after *hentiu* periods of time they came to me.
I collected my members, they came forth there from me after I had companied with my fist.
My heart came to me from out of my hand; the seed fell from my mouth.

[What follows are repetitions of sentences which are translated above; they give nothing new, and seem to have been added inadvertently by the scribe.]

Hitherto no illustrations of the events of the Creation have been found with the exception of that given on p. 378. But the idea of the union of the Earth-god GEBB and the Sky-goddess NUT appealed strongly to the scribes or writers of the group of texts known as Solar Litanies which we find in the short papyri buried with the priests of AMEN-RĀ at THEBES. These are painted in bright colours, and among the Vignettes of the marriage of the Earth and Sky we have the following:

1. The goddess NUT in the form of a woman covering with her body the Earth-god who is depicted in the form of a snake-headed man.

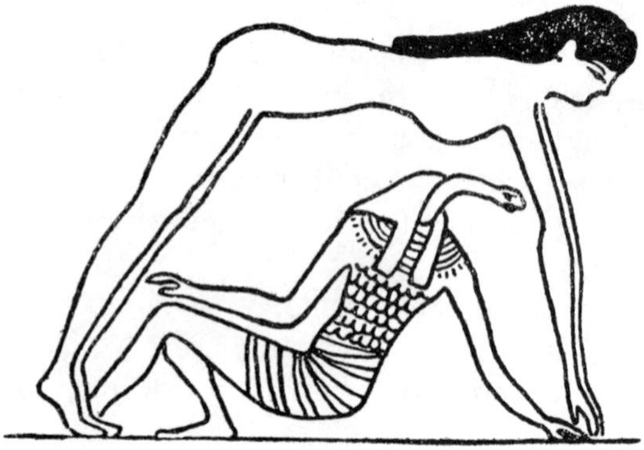

2. The goddess NUT in the form of a woman with a star-spangled body, being raised up by the god SHU from the recumbent figure of the Earth-god.

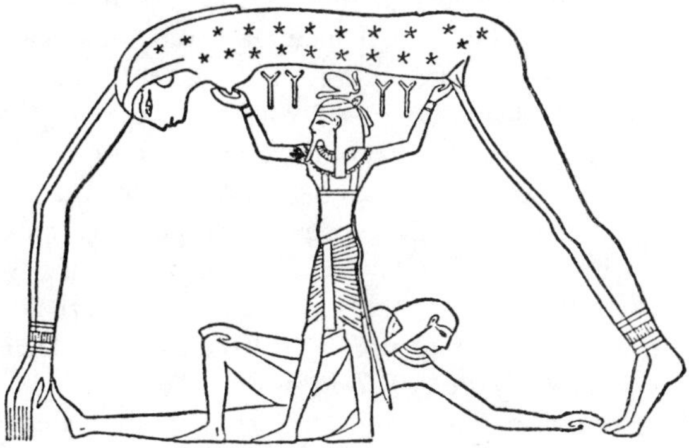

3. The sky. Beneath is the winged beetle, with horns on his head and the triple sign for good luck between his hind legs. ISIS standing on the right presenting one of the solar eyes, and NEPHTHYS on the left presenting the other. In front of NEPHTHYS is the head of the ram of KHNEMU, a very ancient god of Creation and, in later times, a form of AMEN-RĀ. Below the figure of the goddess NUT is seen covering the body of GEBB, under whose head is the beetle of KHEPRI.

LEGEND OF SHU AND GEBB WHEN THEY REIGNED AS KINGS UPON EARTH

[The original hieroglyphic text of this ancient legend is found inscribed upon a black granite shrine, with pointed top, which was made in the Ptolemaic period; the shrine is 4 feet high, 2 feet 7 inches broad, and 2 feet from back to front. It was dedicated to the old War-god SEPT, who was regarded as the Warden of the eastern frontier and marsh lands of EGYPT, and was set up at QES, or QESEM, the sanctuary of the XXth nome of LOWER EGYPT; it was transported to AL-'ARÎSH, probably when Christianity triumphed over paganism. The priests of QES called their sanctuary 'AAT-NEBES'; QESEM has been identified with the GOSHEN of the Bible. The text was first copied, translated, and published by F. LL. GRIFFITH in *The Antiquities of Tell el-Yahûdîyeh*, LONDON, 1890, and G. ROEDER has published a German translation, after a collation of the text, in *Urkunden*, p. 150. The shrine is now in the Museum of the SUEZ CANAL COMPANY at ISMÂ'ILÎYAH.]

The Majesty of SHU was as a good king, [king] of heaven, the earth, the ṬUAT, the water, the winds, NUNU (the primeval abyss), the mountains, and the [Great] Green sea [and he passed] all instructions (or decrees) upon the throne of his father RĀ ḤARMAKHIS triumphantly. And the Majesty of SHU was in his [palace] in MEMPHIS, and His Majesty said unto the Great Company of the gods who were accompanying him, 'Now come, let us go to the [horizon of] the East to my palace in AAT-NEBES, and see our father RĀ ḤARMAKHIS in the Eastern Horizon. We will travel [thither by the canal] and pass over (?) the Great Water, and the pretty country (?) to our palace in AAT-NEBES.' And they did everything according as His Majesty commanded. . . . His Majesty betook himself to his palace in the House (or Temple) of ART. Then every door (or gate) of HET-NEBES built [strongly] like heaven upon its four pillars. And the Temple of SEPṬ was built anew for the Majesty of SHU, for it was the temple which he loved. The doors were fixed with all their fittings as regardeth direction to the south, and the north, and the west, and the east. The temples were built on the sites whereon they had originally stood, every one of them, everywhere. Eight halls were constructed on the west, eight on the east, and eight in the large forecourt of the eastern horizon. These temples were erected to the Majesty of SHU in his name of SEPṬ the Lord of the East. The front of [each] chapel faced its neighbour. Doors were provided for the Great Company of the gods, and the Little Company of the gods, and the gods who are in the train of RĀ, and the gods who are in the train of SHU. And shrines were built [for SHU] round about his temple. The frontage of this temple was towards the east, where RĀ riseth. The gods who were in the train of SHU and who were distributed about in the nomes [had been brought] into this temple, and if any portion of the temple which represented a nome became ruined, this circumstance was reported to the nome. And moreover if there be a shrine of the lord of HET-NEBES which is to the north of HET-NEBES, the front thereof faceth the south. There is also a house of gods in the region of HET-NEBES and the front thereof faceth the east. There is a lake to the south of it and a lake to the north of it, and a great . . . facing this temple, extending to the Temple of AART.

[THE BUILDINGS OF SHU AT AAT-NEBES]

And the Majesty of SHU went to AAT-[NEBES] and came (?) to the divine region of AAT-NEBES, which was to the south of the Temple of AART. Gods and goddesses, men, princes, and [people] might not enter therein and look upon the mysteries of the horizon; this was given (i.e. ordered) from the time of RĀ. A great wall had been built and stood in its neighbourhood. It was . . . cubits long on each of the four sides thereof, it was twenty cubits high and fifteen cubits thick. The lake of the god at AAT-NEBES lay to the north. . . . of AAT-NEBES. SHU himself had excavated it in the time of RĀ. Its size and shape (?) cannot be seen, and it is invisible to passers by and men and cattle. The whole length of the girdle wall which was built about the temple on that site was 190 cubits, and it was 102 in cubits breadth, . . . cubits in height, and 15 cubits in thickness. The workmen (or servants) brought in the gifts and offerings to that temple secretly and unseen [by the people]. The Majesty of the god SHU erected AAT-NEBES that it might endure like the sky, and all the chambers (or chapels) like the horizon.

[SHU'S BUILDINGS WRECKED BY DESERT HORDES]

And it came to pass [when SHU] was king of the gods in AAT-NEBES, and was established upon the throne of RĀ ḤARMAKHIS, the sons of ĀPEP, enemies [of the gods of the Temple of] ART, and dwellers in the red lands (i.e. deserts), set out on the road and came to AAT-NEBES, to make an attack upon EGYPT by night (?) . . . . EGYPT, wherever they came they destroyed everything. Every place—they came by water and by land—and all the people [were overthrown] wherever they came. These enemies came into the eastern hills, and on all the roads of AAT-NEBES. Then the Majesty of SHU, and the gods who are in the train of RĀ, and the gods who are in the train [of SHU], fortified all the sacred buildings which were in the neighbourhood of AAT-NEBES. These were sacred places since the time of RĀ, when the Majesty of RĀ dwelt in AAT-NEBES . . . to AAT-NEBES. These were the great walls of EGYPT which blocked the way of the enemy when ĀPEP [wished to invade] EGYPT. Now, the gods who dwelt in them were the watch-dogs (?) (or defences?) of this land. They (i.e. the sanctuaries) were the four pillars of heaven, which watch over the . . . of the Eternal Horizon, that is the sanctuary of SHU in the Temple of NEBES. Now those who dwell in the sanctuaries (i.e. the gods) which are in AAT-NEBES are those who smite the earth. . . . [Those who dwell in the Temple of] SEPṬ are the Souls of the East who are with RĀ ḤARMAKHIS. They raise up RĀ into the heavens from the ṬUAT [in the eastern part] of heaven, and they are the lords of the eastern hills who deliver RĀ from ĀPEP.

[Here is] a list of all [the sanctuaries] which are in the district of the Temple of NEBES, and of [all] the gods who dwell in them. The sanctuary of TESTES is in AAT-NEBES, [with] a sacred lake to the east of the Temple of NEBES, and on this the Majesty of RĀ travelled when he engaged in battle with the associates of ĀPEP. [The sanctuary of] . . . is in AAT-NEBES is to the east of the Temple of NEBES, the sacred lake . . . the Temple of NEBES. [The names of the other sanctuaries are wanting.]

[GEBB FORCES HIS MOTHER TEFENT AND SEIZES THE THRONE]

[Then the Majesty] of SHU [reigned] over all the earth, no one could resist him, and [the name of] no other god was in the mouth of his people (?). [Then sickness seized] his members, and disease obtained the mastery over his eyes. His Court became unruly, and calamity invaded this land. Great strife broke out in the palace, and a revolt broke out among the associates of SHU. Then GEBB looked upon his mother [TEFENT] and he loved her greatly. His heart yearned for her, and because of this he wandered about the land suffering greatly. The majesty of SHU had gone up into heaven together with his followers, and TEFENT was in the place where she appeared [to the people] in MEMPHIS. She made a journey to the palace of SHU at the time of noon, whilst the Great Company of the gods were on their eternal course, on the road of their father RĀ ḤARMAKHIS. And the Majesty of [GEBB met her], and he found her in the place called PKHARTI, and he laid hands upon her with great violence, and a very great commotion took place in the palace. Now SHU had gone up into heaven, and no one came out of the palace for a period of nine days. And during these [nine days] there were blackness (clouds?) and winds [in EGYPT], and no man and none of the gods was able to see the face of his neighbour. And the Majesty of the god GEBB was seen on the place (or throne) of his father, and all those who were in the palace smelt the earth before him.

[GEBB GOES TO AAT-NEBES]

And after seventy-five days GEBB set out on a journey to the North Land (KHEB-CHEMMIS?) SHU having fled from the earth to heaven before him. The prince of the eastern hills [came against him]. He did not go to ANNU (HELIOPOLIS) with the men of the hills carrying the staff (?) who are called the 'TEGAIU', [because] they live on things which are an abomination to the gods, but he went to the east of USHER, and entered the Temple of AART, by the eastern gate of AAT-NEBES. He held converse concerning the affairs of this city with the gods who were in his train, and they informed him concerning all the arrangements which RĀ had brought into being in AAT-NEBES, viz., the battle of TEM–RĀ in this place, and the valorous deeds of SHU in this city, and the things which SHU had done in . . . of ĀNKHET (i.e. the serpent) of the Majesty of RĀ which was with him, and the splendid deeds of the Majesty of SHU when he fought the enemy, and placed it (i.e. the serpent) on his head.

[GEBB AND THE SERPENT AART]

And the Majesty of GEBB said, 'I will set [the serpent] on my head as my father SHU did. And GEBB went into the Temple of AART together with the gods who were with him. Then GEBB put forth his hand to uncover the chest wherein [the serpent] was. And the 'Son of the earth' (i.e. the serpent came forth, and he breathed forth his breath against the Majesty of GEBB with his very deadly venom (?), and those who were in his train died, and the Majesty [of GEBB] was burned by the heat. Then His Majesty went forth to the north of AAT-NEBES with the fever caused by the serpent on him, and His Majesty came to the Field of the Ḥenna plants, and the venom did not depart [from his body]. And the gods who were in his following said unto him. 'Let the AART of RĀ be carried thither, and let Thy Majesty go and look upon its mysteries, and [Thy] Majesty shall receive healing [of the burns] which are upon thee.' Then the Majesty of GEBB had the AART in the Temple of AART to be set upon his head, and he caused a great coffer of real stone to be made for it. It was hidden in a [secret] place in the Temple of AART near the divine AART of the Majesty of RĀ. And the burning heat flowed forth from the body of the Majesty of GEBB.

[THE TRANSFORMATION OF THE AART]

After the passage of several years this AART of the Majesty of GEBB was placed in the Temple of AART in AAT-NEBES, and it was taken to the great sacred lake of the Temple of AART which is called AAT-TESTES so that it might be washed (or bathed). And this AART transformed itself into a crocodile, and it glided into the water, and became the Crocodile-god SEBEK in AAT-NEBES. And behold, when His Majesty RĀ ḤARMAKHIS [was fighting] against [his] enemies in this Lake of AAT-TESTES they were unable to gain any advantage over His Majesty. And His Majesty rushed into the aforenamed Lake of AAT-TESTES, and his legs (?) became those of a crocodile, [and his head] the head of a hawk, and he had the two horns of a bull on his head. Thus he smote [his] enemies in the Lake of AAT-TESTES in the Temple of NEBES, and because of this the AART of the Majesty of GEBB took this form subsequently.

[THE BUILDINGS AND IRRIGATION WORKS OF SHU]

And behold the Majesty of GEBB appeared in the sanctuaries of SEBEK, and SEBEK–RĀ, and SHU, and GEBB, and OSIRIS, and RĀ upon the throne of his father SHU as king of the gods, and . . ., and men, and every being of flesh (?) in heaven, and earth, and the ṬUAT, and NUNU (NU), and mountains, and winds, and seas and storms. And His Majesty was in his palace of the Conqueror of the Two Lands in the land of the Ḥenna plants, and he had sent messengers to bring to him the peoples of ASIA from their Two Lands. And behold, the Majesty of GEBB said unto the Great Company of the gods who were in his train, 'What did my father [the Majesty of SHU] do in days of old when he appeared upon the throne of his father ATEM, when the Majesty of SHU was in his palace in AAT-NEBES?' And this Company of the gods spake unto the Majesty of GEBB, saying, 'When thy father SHU [appeared on the throne in the palace] of his father ATEM, he smote (or killed) all the enemies of his father ATEM, and he slaughtered the MESU BEṬSHU (i.e. sons of rebellion), and he destroyed utterly all the enemies of his father RĀ. Then after SHU [had gotten] the overlordship of the Two Lands, and of gods, and of men, and of the followers of ATEM, the Lord of ANNU-SHEMĀ (i.e. HERMONTHIS, but read HELIOPOLIS), he irrigated the towns, and the settlements and the nomes, and he erected the walls of EGYPT and built temples in the Land of the South and the Land of the North.'

[THE ANCIENT TEMPLE REGISTERS ARE READ BEFORE GEBB]

And the Majesty of GEBB said unto these gods, 'Tell me what sanctuaries existed in the time of RĀ, and which His Majesty had constructed on the earth. And tell me also the nomes in which the Majesty of SHU carried out building operations during his reign. I will proclaim [to you the names of] the sanctuaries in the time of the Majesty of RĀ, in all the nomes wherein the Majesty of [SHU] had erected buildings. These I am [determined] to rebuild, and I greatly desire to effect their prosperity during my reign.' Then [the priests, or scribes] read out extracts in the presence of the Majesty of GEBB from the words of the god (i.e. the hieroglyphic texts) and informed him of the hundreds of thousands of sanctuaries which the Majesty of RĀ had called into being in all the nomes, and in which the Majesty of SHU had built. These had been entered in the registers in the time of the Majesty of ATEM when he [was king], before SHU rose up on the throne of his father RĀ, and before GEBB appeared on the throne of his father SHU. Here we give the names of the sanctuaries and the nomes.

[Here] begin the nomes in which the Majesty of RĀ erected buildings.

[Here follow the names of about thirty-five towns and cities in UPPER and LOWER EGYPT and the FÂYYÛM, and among them are mentioned those of ABU (ELEPHANTINE), NEKHEN (EILEITHYASPOLIS). BEḤṬ (EDFÛ), ANNU of the South (HERMONTHIS) ABṬU (ABYDOS), ḤENSU (HERAKLEOPOLIS), and ANNU (HELIOPOLIS).]

SUMMARY OF THE LEGEND OF THE CONTENDINGS OF HORUS AND SET AS CONTAINED IN THE CHESTER BEATTY PAPYRUS NO. I

The original hieratic text is edited with a hieroglyphic transcript, translation and notes *by* DR. ALAN GARDINER.

The narrative sets forth that the child HORUS is seated in court before the company of the gods who are presided over by NEB-ER-DJER,[1] and he is claiming the sovereignty which was possessed by his father OSIRIS, who is here called the son of PTAḤ, the great god of MEMPHIS. At the same time THOTH, the scribe of the gods, presents the Eye, an important symbolic act of religious or legal import to the Mighty Prince (i.e. ATEM, a form of the Sun-god) in HELIOPOLIS. SHU, the son of RĀ, voted that the petition of HORUS be granted, and THOTH agreed wholeheartedly. Hearing this ISIS, the mother of HORUS, rejoiced greatly and she cried out to the north wind and ordered it to blow to the west and to carry the glad tidings to UN-NEFER, i.e. OSIRIS, the father of HORUS and lord of AMENTI. NEB-ER-DJER seems to demur at this rapid decision, whereupon the Nine Gods of HELIOPOLIS, the descendants of RĀ–ATEM, point out that it is futile to object to this decision because HORUS had already adopted the royal name [enclosed in a cartouche] 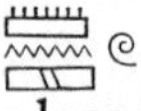, and the White Crown [of OSIRIS] has already been placed on his head. NEB-ER-DJER was displeased and held his peace.

At this juncture SET, the son of NUT, spoke and appealed to the court to cast HORUS out with him so that he might show his power over HORUS before the Nine-Gods, and he seems to add that this was the only way of taking from HORUS what he already had. THOTH answered that the gods would be unable to decide the point by

[1] 'the lord to the limit', i.e. Rā Ḥarakhti, the Sun-god of Heliopolis.

this proceeding, and asked the gods if they imagined that it would be an act of justice to give the inheritance (or heirship) of OSIRIS to SET whilst HORUS, the son of OSIRIS, was still alive? Then was RĀ ḤARAKHTI furiously angry, for he was prejudiced in favour of SET, and AN-ḤERT, a god of the nome of ABYDOS, who was evidently a friend of HORUS, cried out anxiously, 'What can we do?' since RĀ ḤARAKHTI is against us. Then ATEM (i.e. the Sun-god of HELIOPOLIS), ordered that BA-NEB-ṬEṬET, the goat-god of MENDES, be summoned, so that he might decide the matter. BA-NEB-ṬEṬET was brought and with him came PTAḤ-TANEN, an earth-god, who had once taken the form of BA-NEB-ṬEṬET, and ATEM ordered them to decide forthwith the case between HORUS and SET. The form of his speech shows that the gods were bored to death with the squabbles between the rival gods, which, as we learn later, had gone on for eighty years. But BA-NEB-ṬEṬET refused to make a decision, because of his ignorance of the facts of the case, and he advised the gods to write a letter to NEITH, the great goddess of SAÏS in the Western Delta and mother of RĀ, and to state the case to her and to abide by her decision. The Nine Gods then inform BA-NEB-ṬEṬET that the case between HORUS and SET was decided by the gods in 'prehistoric times in the Hall UĀ-MAĀTI'.[1] No details of this judgement are given, and the allusion may be to the trial at which OSIRIS was proved to be a speaker of the truth and SET a liar.

Thereupon the Nine-Gods order THOTH to write a letter to NEITH in the name of NEB-ER-DJER. THOTH did so, and after a brief expression of concern about the health and well-being of NEITH, the mother of RĀ, the god RĀ–ATEM tells her that whilst he passes anxious nights in thinking about OSIRIS, and laborious days in consultation with EGYPT, her son SEBEK flourishes. And he adds, 'What are we to do with these two beings who for the past eighty years have plagued the Court? None of us knows how to judge rightly concerning them. Prithee write and tell us what to do.' The goddess NEITH made answer to the Nine Gods and told them to give the office of OSIRIS to his son HORUS, and not to commit deeds of wickedness (i.e. injustice) which should have no place in this case, otherwise 'I shall be wroth, and the sky will fall on the earth.

1 

Moreover, command NEB-ER-DJER, the Bull in HELIOPOLIS, saying, "'I increase the possessions (or property) of SET twofold, and give unto him thy two daughters ĀNTHAT (ĀNAT) and ĀSTARTE,[1] and place HORUS on the throne of his father OSIRIS."' The advice of NEITH shows that SET was regarded as a lascivious god, to whom these two Syrian harlot-goddesses would appeal specially, and the goddess knew that with these and increased wealth in his possession he would view the loss of the office of OSIRIS with equanimity. In due course the letter of NEITH reached the Nine Gods in the Hall, ḤERU-KHENTI-ĀBIU,[2] and it was placed in the hand of THOTH. THOTH read it to NEB-ER-DJER and the whole company of the Nine Gods, and they declared with one voice that NEITH was right.

Again was NEB-ER-DJER displeased, and he was angry with HORUS, and he reviled him, saying, 'Thou art a miserable and feeble child, and art deformed in thy body. The office [of kingship] is far too great a thing for thee to have, thou wretched weakling whose mouth hath a bad taste.'[3] This abuse of HORUS stirred up AN-ḤERT to fury, and provoked the wrath of the entire company of the Nine Gods, it did even the Thirty Judges of EGYPT, but none of them attempted to gainsay the words of NEB-ER-DJER. But in the company was the god BABA or BABAI  or   (also written ), and he rose up and said to RĀ ḤARAKHTI, 'Thy shrine is empty', i.e. thy office is vacant, an equivalent of 'thou art dismissed from thy office'. In the Theban *Book of the Dead* (xvii. 44) he is said to be the 'watcher at the Bight of AMENTI', and to be the eldest son of OSIRIS (lxiii A. 3), and to live on the entrails of the great ones (cxxv, part 3, l. 6), and his phallus is mentioned (xcix, Introd., l. 17).[4] In the Pyramid Texts (PEPI,

1 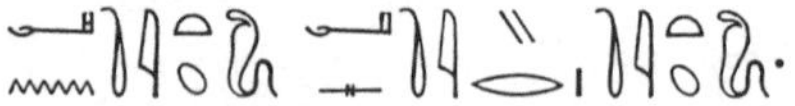

2 

3 The Greeks said that Harpokrates, the Horus here referred to, was born prematurely, and that his legs were weak. See Plutarch, *De Iside*, § 19.

4 Traditions about the genitalia of Set have found their way into some Christian apocryphal works, i.e. 'The Book of the Mysteries of Heaven and Earth', where he is said to be 1,700 cubits of the angels in height; his mouth was 40 cubits, his hand 70 cubits, his feet 7,000 cubits, and his phallus 100 cubits ነፍስቶሁ፡ ፻፡ በእመት፡

l. 604) he is called BABUI , and he is said to have a 'red ear and striped buttocks', . RĀ ḤARAKHTI was greatly irritated at this impudent remark of BABAI, and he lay down on his back with bitterness in his heart. The Nine Gods also were angry with BABAI, and they told him that he had sinned grievously and promptly ordered him to 'get outside'. The Nine Gods felt that there was nothing else to be done then, and so they withdrew to their tents.

RĀ ḤARAKHTI lay on his back alone in the court of his house for a whole day, with bitterness in his heart, and after a time HATHOR, daughter of NEB-ER-DJER, the Lady of the Sycamore of the South, came in, stood up before her father, and, apparently, with the view of cheering him up, stripped herself naked; and the great god smiled at her. Then he got up and went and took his seat with the Nine Gods and called upon HORUS and SET to plead their cause. SET said, 'I am SET, I am the strongest of the Nine Gods. As I am daily in the front of the Boat of Millions of Years I slay the enemy of RĀ daily, and no other god can do this. Therefore I am entitled to the office of OSIRIS.' The Nine Gods said, 'SET is right'. Forthwith AN-ḤERT and THOTH cried out, 'Shall the office be given to a maternal brother whilst a son of the body is actually alive?' And BA-NEB-ṬEṬET countered this remark with an opposite opinion, saying, 'Shall the office be given to this weakling whilst SET his elder brother is actually alive?' Here there is a confusion of myths. HORUS and SET were equal but opposing gods; it was OSIRIS and SET who were brothers, and HORUS, the son of ISIS, the son of OSIRIS, was the *nephew* only of his mother's brother SET. The Nine Gods cried out before NEB-ER-DJER, 'What kind of words are these which thou hast spoken? They are not fit to be listened to'.

Then HORUS, the son of ISIS, said, 'Verily it is not meet that I should be defrauded in the very presence of the Nine Gods, and that the office of my father should be filched from me'. Thereupon ISIS was furious with the Nine Gods, and she swore an oath by NEITH and PTAḤ-TANEN before them that their words should be set before ATEM, the great Prince in HELIOPOLIS, and before KHEPRI, 'who dwelleth in his boat'.[1] The anger of ISIS made her forget that

[1] A vignette in the *Book of the Dead* (chap. xvii) shows the Beetle-god Khepri in his boat.

ATEM and KHEPRI were *forms* of the Sun-god, and not two distinct gods. The Nine Gods entreated her to abandon her wrath, and told her that the rightful heir should get his rights, and that all she had said should be done. This speech of the Nine Gods made SET angry, and he threatened them that he would take his 'sceptre [weighing] four thousand five hundred *nemes*',[1] and kill one of them daily. And then he swore an oath that he would cease to plead as long as ISIS formed a member of the Court. Then RĀ ḤARAKHTI said to the Nine Gods, 'Come over to the Island in the midst of [the river?] where ye will be able to pass judgement on them. And tell ĀNTI[2] the ferryman not to ferry over to it any woman who is like ISIS.' Then the Nine Gods crossed over to the Island and partook of a meal.

Then ISIS in the form of a bent and aged woman came to ĀNTI the ferryman as he sat by his boat, and asked him to carry her over to the Island so that she might give the boy who had been herding some cattle on it for the last five days the jar of flour which she had with her because he would be hungry. ĀNTI told her that he had received orders not to ferry any woman over to the Island. ISIS asked him if this order did not refer to ISIS, thereby suggesting that he could never confuse an old and bent woman like herself with ISIS. ĀNTI asked her what she would give him to ferry her across to the Island? And ISIS said, 'I will give thee this loaf of bread'. ĀNTI's answer may be paraphrased, What is your loaf to me? Seeing that I have been ordered not to ferry any woman across to the Island, dost thou imagine that I am going to ferry thee over for a miserable loaf of bread? Then ISIS told him that she would give him the gold ring which she was wearing on her finger; and he said, 'Give me the gold ring'. And she gave it to him, and he ferried her over.

As ISIS was walking under the trees she saw the Nine Gods sitting and eating bread before NEB-ER-DJER in his bower, and SET

[1]  nems-t (?), a stone or metal weight.

[2] An ancient hawk-god with a cult in the XIIth nome of Upper Egypt. Ānti  was confused with  Antiui, i.e. Horus and Set of the Xth nome of Upper Egypt. This is proved by Sethe, *Urgeschichte*, § 51 f.

caught sight of her whilst she was some distance from him. This ISIS perceived, and making use of one of her magical spells she transformed herself into a most beautiful maiden, the like of whom did not exist in all the land; and SET fell deeply in love with her at first sight. SET rose up and went and ate bread with the Nine Gods, and then he set out to overtake her; now none of the gods except SET had seen her. SET stood behind a tree and he cried out to her, saying, 'I am waiting for thee, O lovely girl'. And she said to him: 'Not so (i.e. in vain) my great lord. I was the wife of a cattle-keeper, and I bore him a man child. My husband died, and the youth became herd of his father's cattle. Then a certain man who was an alien came and sat down in my byre, and thus spake he to my son: "I will beat thee, I will carry off the cattle of thy father, I will cast thee out." That is what he said to him. It is in my heart to make thee act for him as a strong deliverer.' And SET said unto her, 'Shall the cattle be given to aliens while the son of a farmer existeth?' Then ISIS transformed herself into a *djeri* bird, the form which she was in the habit of taking in times of stress, and she flew up and alighted on the top of a tree and cried out to SET, saying: 'Weep for thyself. Behold it is thine own mouth which hath pronounced [thy doom], it is thine own astuteness which hath brought the judicial decision. What is there for thee to do next?' He stood up, he wept, and he went to the place where RĀ ḤARAKHTI was [still] weeping.

RĀ ḤARAKHTI spake unto him, saying: 'What is there for thee to do next?' (or 'How now?') SETH complained that that wicked woman (ISIS) had come to him again so that she might once again deceive him, and she transformed herself into a [lovely] maiden before his very face; and then he related to the god, practically word for word, what she had said to him. RĀ ḤARAKHTI asked him what reply he had made, and he said, 'I asked if the cattle should be given to the alien whilst the son of the farmer existeth, and then I told her that one shall beat the face of the alien with a stick, and that he should be cast outside [the farm], and that her son should be set in his father's place'. Then RĀ ḤARAKHTI said to him, 'But consider now, for verily thou thyself hast passed judgement on thyself. What is there for thee to do next?' SET said unto him: 'Let ĀNTI the ferryman be brought hither and be thoroughly well beaten, and let him be asked why he let the woman cross over to the Island.' Thereupon ĀNTI the ferryman was brought and he was bastinadoed until the soles of his feet disappeared. ĀNTI cursed gold before the Nine Gods, because it had proved a successful bribe. [The meaning of the rest of the paragraph is not clear.]

The Nine Gods then journeyed over to the Western Delta and sat down on a hill. In the evening RĀ ḤARAKHTI and ATEM sent a message to them asking them why they were sitting there doing nothing, and suggesting that they (i.e. the Nine Gods) wanted HORUS and SET to spend their lives in their Court. Then came the Command, 'Set the White Crown on the head of HORUS, and stablish him in the office of his father OSIRIS.' Hearing this SET became furiously angry. And the Nine Gods rebuked him and reminded him that they were obliged to do what ATEM and RĀ ḤARAKHTI had commanded them, and forthwith they set the White Crown on the head of HORUS. At this the anger of SET did not diminish, and he cried out to the Nine Gods in his rage: 'Is the office to be given to my young brother whilst I, his elder brother, am in being?' Then he swore an oath, saying that the White Crown should be removed from the head of HORUS, and that he should be cast into water where he would fight him for the office of OSIRIS. All this RĀ ḤARAKHTI agreed to and carried out.

And SET proposed to HORUS that each of them should transform himself into a hippopotamus, and then cast himself into the sea, and that he who came out of the water before the end of three months was *ipso facto* disqualified from the office of OSIRIS. So each took the form of a hippopotamus and entered the sea. Then ISIS began to weep saying: 'SET hath killed my son HORUS', and she set to work to find a means of saving him. She fetched a hank of flax (or fibre?) and plaited (or twisted) it into a rope. And she fetched a lump of copper [weighing] a *teben*, and she beat and moulded it into a marine weapon, and having tied the rope to it she hurled it into the water at the place where HORUS and SET had entered the sea. The harpoon struck HORUS, and he cried out to ISIS to make it drop from him; and ISIS did so. A second time she hurled the harpoon, and this time it struck SET, and he cried out to ISIS as his maternal sister to make the harpoon drop from him. ISIS was sorry for him, and when SET entreated her not to bear enmity against her maternal brother, she commanded the harpoon to drop from his body, and it did so forthwith. Then HORUS was wroth with ISIS, and he became like a panther of the SÛDÂN. He had his axe in his hand [now it weighed sixteen *teben*], and he hacked off the head of his mother ISIS, and clasping it to his bosom he went up into a mountain. Forthwith ISIS transformed herself into a flint statue which had no head. Seeing this, RĀ ḤARAKHTI said to THOTH, 'What is this headless thing which hath come?' and THOTH told him that it was ISIS, the mother of HORUS, who had hacked off her head. RĀ ḤARAKHTI cried out with a loud voice to the Nine Gods, saying, 'Let us hasten and punish him severely', and he and the Nine Gods went up into the mountains to seek for HORUS, the son of ISIS.

Now behold HORUS was lying down under a tree with dense foliage in the country of UAHET (i.e. the Oasis KHÂRGAH-DÂKHLAH[1]). There SET found him and he seized him, and he threw him upon his back on the stony ground. He gouged out his two *Udjats* (i.e. eyes) from their sockets, and he fastened them on the stony ground to light up the earth, and the rims (literally, the outsides) of his two eyes became two balls (?) *skharer-t* , and they grew (or sprouted) into lotuses. Then SET went back and lied to RĀ ḤARAKHTI, saying, 'I could not find HORUS'.

The goddess HATHOR having, presumably, knowledge of what had happened, went and found HORUS lying on the stony ground weeping. She caught a gazelle and milked it, and told HORUS to open his eyes so that she might pour in milk. At her command HORUS opened his eyes, first the right and then the left, and when she looked at them she found that HORUS had recovered his sight. She went to RĀ ḤARAKHTI and told him that she had found HORUS whose eyes SET had carried away, and that she had restored them, and added, 'Behold, he hath come.' Thereupon the Nine Gods ordered that HORUS and SET be cited to appear that sentence may be passed on them. When they appeared before the Nine Gods NEB-ER-DJER addressed HORUS and SET, saying, 'O get ye gone, and let there be

[1] It seems as if the gods wished to go to the Oasis because Set had jurisdiction over the district. Under the XXIInd dynasty Sutekh, i.e. Set, was the 'great god' of the Oasis and was appealed to as the judge of the claim to a certain well by Nesubast. See Spiegelberg in the *Recueil*, tom. 21, pp. 12–21.

heard by you what I am about to say to you: Eat ye, drink ye, [but] we would be at peace. Stop ye from the contention in which ye indulge every day.' Then SET suggested that they should pass a happy time together (i.e. keep a feast) in his house, and HORUS said unto him, 'Assuredly I will do so; of course I will'; and the two went to SET's house. When evening came a *dîwân*, or couch, was prepared for them to sleep on, and the two laid themselves down on it.

The description of what followed this effort of the gods to reconcile the two irreconcilables forms the coarsest chapter in Egyptian literature, but it is probably very old, and it certainly deals with a very old pagan custom of very early times in ancient EGYPT. Here only a paraphrase of it is given, but a fairly literal translation of the passage is given by Dr. GARDINER in his work already mentioned (p. 21).

During the night SET became excited sexually and attempted to violate[1] HORUS and failed because HORUS caught the efflux of SET in one of his hands. HORUS went to ISIS and showed her his hand and its contents, and seizing her knife she hacked off the polluted hand of HORUS and threw it into the water, and then fashioned a hand for him as useful as that which she had cut off. Then she fetched some sweet smelling unguent and smeared the phallus of HORUS with it. This she made to swell up, and when she had placed it in a vessel HORUS made his emission to fall into it. In the morning ISIS took the efflux of HORUS and went to the garden of SET, and asked the gardener which plant SET was in the habit of eating as an aphrodisiac. The gardener replied that the only herb there under his charge which SET ate was the *āb-t* , which some believe to have been a kind of lettuce.[2]

[1] It is clear that in primitive times in Egypt the conqueror sometimes violated the person whom he had conquered, whether man or woman. This custom was known to the writers of the Pyramid Texts (§ 651) where we read, 'Hail, Osiris Teta! Wake up! Horus causeth Thoth to bring to thee thine enemy, he setteth thee on his back, he shall not defile thee. Make thy seat upon him. Come forth, sit upon him, he shall not violate thee.' What the last sentence means is made quite clear by the text  which appears in pyramids of Teta, Pepi, and Mer-en-Rā. The king is placed in such a position that Set cannot commit an act of paederasty on him. See Maspero, *Les Pyramides*, p. 126, note 2, and Wiedemann, *Sphinx*, Varia iii, tom. xiv, p. 39. About the meaning of  i.e.  there can be no possible doubt.

[2] See Keimer, *Aeg. Zeit.*, Bd. lix, p. 140.

Then ISIS poured the efflux of HORUS over these plants, and SET came day by day according to his wont, and ate them; the text adds the astonishing remark that SET became with child by the seed of HORUS.[1] This, of course, means that SET was believed to be a bisexual god like TEMU or RĀ.[2] The allusion to pregnancy caused by swallowing mentioned in the *Tale of the Two Brothers* does not help us, for the person who swallowed the two splinters of wood was a woman who could conceive and not a man who could not.

Then SET went and told HORUS that he wished to go into Court and plead against him, and as HORUS was willing they both went and stood before the Nine Gods, who straightway ordered them to make their pleadings. SET stood up and claimed the office of OSIRIS because he had performed on HORUS, who was there present, the deed of the victorious warrior (i.e. he claimed to have violated HORUS). The Nine Gods believed his lie and retched and spat in (or in front of) the face of HORUS. HORUS laughed at them, and then swore an oath by God that what SET had said was a lie. And he demanded that the seed of SET and his own seed should be summoned as witnesses, so that they might see from whence each seed would respond. On this THOTH laid his hand on the arm of HORUS, saying, 'Come forth, O seed of SET', and it made answer to him from the water in the marsh. Then THOTH laid his hand on the arm of SET, and he said, 'Come forth, O seed of HORUS.' The seed answered, 'Where shall I come forth?' and THOTH said, 'From his ear.' The seed said, 'Must I, being a divine essence, come forth from his ear?' And THOTH said, 'Come forth from the crown of his head.' And it came forth as a Disk[3] of Gold (i.e. the solar disk) on the head of SET. At this SET was wroth and he reached out his hand to lay hold on the Gold Disk, but THOTH snatched it away from him and set it as a diadem upon his own head.[4]

The Nine Gods who had been watching these acts decided that

1 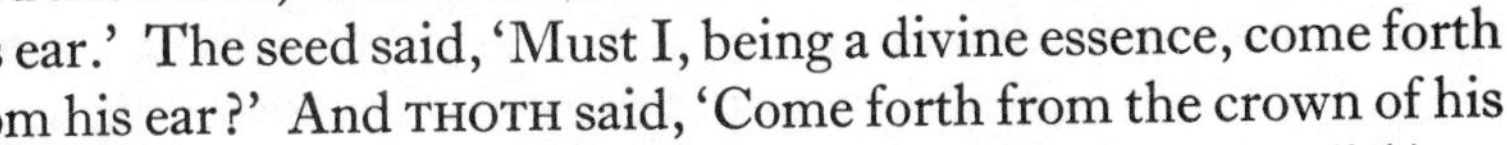

2 See the description of the origin of Shu and Tefnut, p. 142.

3 *Atennu* 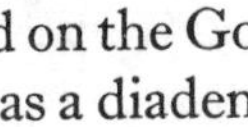.

4 The writer of this work has mixed up two or three legends, as he has done elsewhere in it. The noteworthy point about them is their great antiquity.

HORUS was in the right and SET in the wrong, and when they delivered their judgement according to their opinion SET raged, and he swore an oath and refused to accept it until he had made another attempt to defeat HORUS. Then SET proposed that he and HORUS should make boats of stone and sail about in them, and that he who sunk his rival's boat should receive the office of OSIRIS. HORUS agreed to this and went and hewed out a boat of cedar wood, and plastered it all over with *qadja*,[1] and he launched it on the river (?) at eventide, and no one in the district knew anything about it. SET saw the boat and thought that it was made of stone, and he went to a mountain and cut off a spur of it, and of this he hewed out a boat one hundred and thirty-eight cubits in length. SET and HORUS went each to his boat whilst the Nine Gods were looking on, and the boat of SET promptly sank, presumably whilst he was in it. To escape drowning SET transformed himself into a hippopotamus, and after the manner of the actual beast, charged the boat of HORUS and sank it. Then HORUS cast his harpoon at SET, and the Nine Gods told him not to attack him. Obediently HORUS collected the weapons which were used in fighting on water and put them in his boat—which must somehow have recovered its buoyancy!—and set out for SAÏS so that he might hold converse with NEITH. When he arrived he appealed to her to settle the dispute between SET and himself, a dispute which had been dragging on for eighty years, no god knowing how to settle it. HORUS went on to say that whereas SET had never once been declared to be in the right, he (HORUS) had been in the right a thousand times. Moreover SET will not accept the ruling of the Nine Gods. HORUS then enumerates the principal occasions when he was declared to be in the right: in the hall UAT-MAĀTI, in the hall ḤERU-KHENTI-ĀBIU, in the hall SEKHET-ANRE, and in the hall SHE-EN-SEKHET. And the Nine Gods spake to SHU, saying, 'All that HORUS, the son of ISIS, says is true'.

Then THOTH said unto NEB-ER-DJER, 'Let a letter be sent to OSIRIS that he may decide the case of HORUS and SET', and RĀ said, 'What THOTH hath said to the Nine Gods is right a million times over.' Straightway NEB-ER-DJER said to THOTH, 'Sit down and write a letter to OSIRIS and let us hear what he has got to say.' He

[1] A bituminous substance (?) which prevented the entrance of water through the seams.

began his letter by enumerating the five 'strong names' of RĀ as (1) The Bull name, (2) The NEBTI name, (3) The HORUS of NUBIT (OMBOS) name, (4) The NESU-BAT name, and (5) The son of PTAḤ name; and after these came the petition, 'Write unto us and [tell] us what we are to do in the case of HORUS and SET, so that we may not act with insufficient knowledge'. In due course the letter reached the 'King, the son of RĀ', and when the envoy had read it to him, he groaned aloud, and without the least delay[1] dictated his answer, which he sent to the place where NEB-ER-DJER and the Nine gods were assembled. In it OSIRIS said, 'Inasmuch as it is I who give you strength, and it is I who have created barley and *dhura* (millet) to feed the gods, likewise the [sacred] beasts and cattle, and no other god and no other goddess had the power to do this, why should my son HORUS be defrauded of his rights?'

The letter of OSIRIS reached RĀ ḤARAKHTI when he was seated with the Nine Gods at the White (?) . . .[2] in the city of KHASAUU,[3] and it was read to him and the Nine Gods by the envoy. And RĀ ḤARAKHTI said, 'Draft a letter immediately to OSIRIS, and with reference to his letter say thus: 'Even if thou hadst never been fashioned, even if thou hadst never been born, the barley and the *dhura* (millet) would have come into being just the same.'[4] And this letter of NEB-ER-DJER reached OSIRIS, and one read it before him.

Then OSIRIS sent [a reply] to RĀ ḤARAKHTI, saying, 'Good, very good is everything which thou hast done, thou real discoverer of the Nine Gods, but Truth hath been made to become submerged in the depths of the ṬUAT (i.e. hell).[5] But do thou consider matters for thyself.[6] The land wherein I am is filled with messengers [having] fierce-eyed faces[7] and they are not afraid of any god or any

[1] Literally 'in the greatest possible haste' .

[2]  I. To me the determinative suggests place and not time.

[3] A town or city usually identified with Xoïs, and the Arabic Sakhâ, a very ancient town in the province of Ghârbîyah, in the district of Kafr ash-Shaykh. Amelineau, *Géographie*, p. 410.

[4] The great Grain-god was Neper , but Osiris was a form of him.

[5] Meaning, It is all very good what thou hast done, but whilst thou hast been engaged in constructing gods the Truth hath been drowned in Hell.

[6] Without reference to the Nine Gods.

[7] See the vignette to chapter xxviii of the *Book of the Dead* in the Papyrus of Nefer-aben-f, where a picture of the great gorilla of the African forest (Pongo, or

goddess whatsoever. I will cause them to sally out and they will bring back the heart of every one who committeth evil acts, and they shall become stationary (i.e. remain) with me. What is the good of my remaining seated at peace over AMENTET whilst each and every one and all of you are outside? Who among you is mightier than I? But verily they have in fact [only] found fraud and lies. Behold, at the time when PTAḤ, the Great One, South of his wall, the Lord of ĀNKH-TAUI, made heaven, did he not say unto the stars which are therein: 'Make ye [your] settings in AMENTET (i.e. the western land) every night in the place where OSIRIS is. And following the gods, gentle and simple shall indeed sink to rest in the place wherein thou art. This was what [he said] to me.'

[Many days] after these happenings the letter of OSIRIS reached the place where NEB-ER-DJER was with the Nine Gods, and THOTH read it before them. When they had heard it they said, OSIRIS is in the right. But SET petitioned to be allowed to have one more fight, and when it had taken place on the island mentioned above HORUS was declared to be the victor, and SET was made a prisoner by ISIS. ATEM ordered ISIS to bring SET before him, and when she did so he asked SET why he had refused to accept the judgement of the gods and had seized the office of OSIRIS. SET replied that such was not the fact, and he agreed that HORUS should have his father's office. HORUS was brought forthwith, and the White Crown was placed on his head, and he was set in the place of OSIRIS. The gods acclaimed him as the good king of TA-MERA (EGYPT), and the good lord of every land for ever. ISIS rejoiced at the triumph of her son. Then PTAḤ asked what was to be done to SET, and RĀ ḤARAKHTI decreed that SET should live with him and be as a son to him, and that his occupation would be to thunder in the heavens and terrify men. The gods told RĀ ḤARAKHTI that HORUS had become governor, and he rejoiced and he ordered the Nine Gods to 'rejoice down to the ground' before HORUS, the son of ISIS. ISIS said, 'HORUS standeth

Mpungu) is given. In chapter xvii Nebseni prays to be delivered from the 'Watchers who bear slaughtering knives, and who have cruel fingers', and the vignettes to the chapters dealing with the Ārits and Halls of the kingdom of Osiris contain many examples of the terrible messengers whom Osiris sent out to bring to him the hearts of the wicked. The frightful monsters which are mentioned in Coptic martyrdoms and were believed to lie in wait to seize the soul of the dying man all had their prototypes in ancient Egyptian funerary papyri.

as ḤEQ (i.e. the hereditary Governor of EGYPT), the Nine Gods celebrate a festival, heaven rejoiceth'. Forthwith they placed garlands of flowers on their heads. The Nine Gods and all the earth were content when they saw HORUS, the son of OSIRIS of ṬEṬU, made Governor.

Thus ends this remarkable story of the Contendings of HORUS and SET.

THE EYE LEGEND OF HORUS AND THE BLACK PIG

This legend is made known to us by chapter cxii of the *Book of the Dead*. The chapter is entitled 'Chapter of knowing the Souls of the city of P[E]', and its vignette contains seated figures of HORUS (hawk-headed), and two of his sons, MESTA and ḤĀPI (human-headed). The ancient name of P[E] 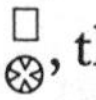, the city called BUTO by the GREEKS, was DJBĀUT 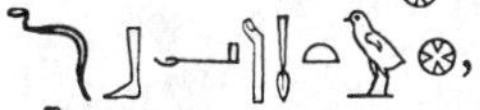, and its god was a heron or some kind of hawk, . Though the old name of the city occurs in the Pyramid Texts and on monuments of the Old Kingdom, the Theban *Book of the Dead* calls the city P[E], a word or name which means something like 'seat', 'throne', and shows that it was a royal city. And the text shows that the cult of HORUS had ousted that of the old god of the city. In chapter xciii the other two sons of HORUS, TUA-MUT-F and QEBḤ-SENU-F, form with HORUS the Souls of NEKHEN or HIERAKONPOLIS in UPPER EGYPT, a fact which indicates that the kingdom of HORUS extended from P[E] to NEKHEN. But under the Old Kingdom P[E] and ANNU (HELIOPOLIS) marked the limits of his kingdom. Chapter cxii throws an interesting light on the history of HORUS. In the opening lines some one asks the dwellers in P[E] if they know why the city of P[E] hath been given to HORUS, and says, 'I know the reason though ye know it not. This is the reason. Behold, RĀ gave it to him as a reward for the injury in his eye'. HORUS, it seems was suffering from some injury in his eye, and he betook himself to RĀ, who said to him, 'Let me look at this that hath happened in thine eye to-day'; and he looked at it. Then RĀ said to HORUS, 'Look, [canst thou see] that black pig?' And HORUS looked and forthwith he was smitten with a blow on his eye, [producing] violent pain. Then HORUS said to RĀ, 'Verily my eye [is now hurt] as it was [formerly] when SUTI (SET) inflicted that blow on my eye.' The text continues, 'He', presumably HORUS, 'ate his heart', i.e. he became angry and sorry (?). It seems natural to think that the blow in the eye of HORUS mentioned above was the second which SUTI, or SET, had inflicted upon HORUS. If so, it is possible, as SETHE suggests, that the first blow was delivered on HORUS in the great battle between him and SET, when HORUS established his sovereignty at HELIOPOLIS. The second blow was, then, delivered when HORUS seized and conquered DJBĀUT, or P[E]. This legend, which seems to have an historical foundation, must not be confounded with that which makes SET swallow the crescent moon, i.e. an eclipse took place. In that case the Sun-god drove a harpoon into the body of SET, and the monster having vomited the moon was placed under restraint (see chap. cviii).

When RĀ, the great physician as well as creator, had looked at the smitten eye of HORUS he told these gods (i.e. his company), 'Place ye him on his bed and he shall come forth healed'. Then comes the explanation, 'It is SUTI who had done what had happened to him (i.e. HORUS), in the form of a black pig; that blow in the eye of HORUS [produced] inflammation (?)'. And RĀ said unto these gods: 'The pig shall be an abominable thing to HORUS. Nevertheless HORUS shall be healed, and the pig shall be an abomination to HORUS.' Then the gods who were followers of HORUS when he was in the form of his own child, [decreed that one should give] sacrifices of his cattle, and his herds, and his pigs. The father of MESTI, ḤĀPI, TUA-MUT-F, and QEBḤ-SENU-F is HORUS, and their mother is ISIS. HORUS said unto RĀ, 'Give me two brethren in the city of P[E], and two brethren in the city of NEKHEN, who [have sprung] from my body, and who shall be with me in the guise of everlasting judges. Then shall the earth become green, and rains be dried up.' And the name of HORUS became 'He who is on his Uadj' (i.e. green stone), but the greenness implied is that of young vegetation.

The last part of the chapter seems to imply that if it were recited when storms were raging in the sky, and a man offered up sacrifices of cattle and sheep and pigs, the storms which were, of course, caused by SET, would cease, and the water floods be dried up.

The black pig mentioned above appears in the VIth section of the *Book of Gates*. OSIRIS is seated on his throne with the Great

Scales before him. Close to these is a boat in which stands the black pig who is being beaten by a baboon, the associate of THOTH. Apparently any kind of pig was unclean, for the rubric of chapter cxxvi says that the text must not be written on a tile on which a pig has trodden.

In many texts another town is mentioned with P[E], viz. that of ṬEP, which stood on the opposite side of the river, and to all intents and purposes P[E] and ṬEP were regarded as one city. The Greeks called it 'BUTO'.[1] It was famous under the Old Kingdom, and it is mentioned in the Pyramid Texts (§§ 1111 and 1117), and was the seat of the cult of the goddess UADJET, or simply. This death-dealing serpent, or cobra, was a personification of the deadly heat of the sun, or of his eye, and had its place on the forehead of the Sun-god in order to destroy all those who attacked him. It is also seen on the forehead of HORUS and SET, and a model of it in gold was fastened over the brow of the king of EGYPT. The hieroglyph with which her name is written is the stem of the papyrus plant, and she appears to be the goddess of this plant, which grew in abundance in the Delta. In the earliest times she was merely a local goddess, but of importance because her city was the first capital of LOWER EGYPT. Later she became the chief goddess of the whole Delta, and whether she is represented as a cobra or as a woman[2] she wears the Crown of LOWER EGYPT. Sometimes a cobra is coiled round the papyrus stem, which as a woman, she holds as a sceptre. As the 'Lady of heaven, and queen of all the gods' her cobra wears the Crown of the North, and stands on a basket or bowl with a cluster of papyrus plants below it.

THE LEGEND OF THE POISONING OF RĀ BY ISIS

[For the hieratic text see PLEYTE and ROSSI, *Papyrus de Turin*, pls. 31, 77, 131–8. Translated by LEFÉBURE, *Aeg. Zeit.*, 1883, p. 27; BUDGE, *First Steps in Egyptian*, LONDON, 1895, pp. 241–56.]

A chapter (i.e. legend) of the divine god, the self-created Being, the creator of the heaven and the earth, and the breath of life and

[1] Buto represents the Egyptian P-Udja, i.e. the 'House of Udja', and the Greeks called both the goddess and her city by this name.

[2] See Lanzone, Pls. LVIII–LX.

fire, and gods and men, and beasts and cattle, and reptiles, feathered fowl and fish. [He is] the King of men and gods, in one form, and aeons of time are to him as years. He hath many unknown names, which are not known [even] to the gods.

Now ISIS had taken the form of a woman. And she was very cunning in speech and seductive in words. She was sick at heart with the millions of mankind; she preferred the millions of gods, and esteemed highly the millions of the shining spirits. She pondered in her heart and wondered if it would be possible for her to become as RĀ in heaven and earth, and to make herself the landlady of the earth and goddesses. And she debated within herself whether she could not become so by knowing the NAME of the holy god (i.e. RĀ).

And behold RĀ came into [heaven] each day at the head of [his] sailors, and stablished himself upon the double throne of the horizons (i.e. sunset and sunrise). The divine one had grown old. He dribbled at his mouth, and he shot forth emissions from him upon the earth, and what he spat out (i.e. his spittle) fell upon the ground. This and the dust which was on it ISIS kneaded into a paste in her hand, and she fashioned it in the form of a holy viper (or cobra) making it to resemble a dart. It did not move and it remained lifeless in her presence. And she set the inert thing down on the path over which the god went according to his wish throughout the Two Lands (i.e. EGYPT).

The holy god rose, with his gods of the Great House behind him—life, strength, health [be to him]!, and he strode on according to his daily wont. And the holy cobra thrust its fang into him, and the fire of life went forth from his body, and [the cobra] smote the 'Dweller between the Cedars'. The divine god opened his mouth, and the cry of His Majesty, life strength, health [be to him]! echoed through heaven. His Company of the gods [said], 'What is it?' And the gods in his train asked, 'What is it?' And the god was unable, through weakness, to answer concerning it. His jaws knocked together, his whole body quaked, and the poison took possession of his members just as the NILE in his course taketh possession [of EGYPT].

The mighty god made strong his heart, and he cried out to those [gods] who were in his train, saying, 'Come ye hither to me, O ye who came into being from my members, ye gods who proceeded from me, and I will make you to know what hath happened. I have been wounded by a deadly thing; my heart knoweth it. Mine eyes, never looked upon it, my hand never made it. I know not any one who would have done this to me. I have never before felt pain like unto it, and there is no other pain like unto it for severity.

'I am a Prince, the son of a Prince, the seed produced by a god. I am a Great One, the son of a Great One. My father invented my NAME. I am of many names, of many forms. My being existeth in every god. My NAME hath been uttered by TEMU and HORUS, the gods who give names. My father and my mother spoke my NAME. It was hidden in my body by my begetter so that no one should ever have the power to enchant (or bewitch) me by the use of magical spells. I had come forth from [my] shrine to see what I had made (or had to do). I was making my progress through the Two Lands (i.e. EGYPT), which I created, when some one aimed a blow at me with a knife (?) but who it was [that aimed it] I know not. Can it be fire? Can it be water? My heart containeth fire, my limbs tremble and my flesh containeth the children of quakings (i.e. shivers). I pray you to cause to be brought to me my children, the gods, whose words possess magical powers, whose mouths are expert in speech, and whose might penetrates the heavens.'

Then his children came to him, every god was there and was weeping. And the goddess ISIS came with her magical power, and her mouth having the breath of life; her incantations destroy evils (or sicknesses) and her spells make dead throats to live. She said: 'What is this, O divine father? Explain [to me]. Is it a cobra which hath driven sickness into thee, a thing which thou hast fashioned, hath it lifted up its head against thee? Verily it shall be destroyed by means of beneficent spells. I can make it to depart in the sight of thy rays.'

The holy god opened his mouth, saying: 'I was journeying on the road, traversing the Two Lands of my territory, for my heart wished to look upon what I had created, when I was bitten by a cobra [which] I did not see. It is not fire. It is not water. I am colder than water, I am hotter than fire. All my limbs are drenched with sweat. I shiver. Mine eye is unsteady and I cannot see the heavens. Water oozeth out of my face as in the time of Summer.'

ISIS said unto RĀ: 'O father divine, tell me thy NAME.'

[And RĀ answered and said]: 'I am the maker of heaven and earth. I have tied together the mountains and created the things which exist thereon. I am the maker of water, making to come into being MEḤIT-URIT.[1] I acted as the "Bull of his mother",[2] the creator of the joys of love. I have made heaven. I have decked out the two horizons, and I have placed the splendour of the gods therein. I am he who when he openeth his two eyes light cometh, and when he shutteth his two eyes darkness superveneth. I am he who when he giveth the order the NILE riseth. I am he whose NAME the gods know not. I am the maker of the hours, the creator of days. I am the opener of the festivals of the year. I am the creator of the streams of water. I am the maker of the fire of life which causeth the works of all the houses (kitchens?) to be done. I am KHEPRI at dawn, RĀ at noon-day, and TEMU in the evening.' But the poison was not stopped in its passage [in the body of RĀ], and the great god obtained no relief.

ISIS said unto RĀ: 'Thy NAME is not mentioned among all the things which thou hast said unto me. O tell me what it is, and the venom shall come forth from thee. He who declareth his NAME liveth.' Meanwhile the venom burned with fiery fierceness [in the body of RĀ], and it was mightier than the flame of fire.

Then the Majesty of RĀ said: 'I declare myself over to ISIS that she may search me; my name shall come forth from my body into her body.'

And the divine god hid himself from the gods, and the throne in the Boat of Millions of Years was empty. When the time came for the coming forth of the heart ISIS said unto her son HORUS, 'The god hath bound himself with an oath sworn by the god, that the god will give up his two eyes [to thee].' [RĀ swore the oath] and the NAME of the great god was taken from him.

Then ISIS, the great mistress of words of magical power, said: 'Spew thyself out, [O] poison! Come forth from RĀ. O Eye of HORUS, come forth from the god, and fashion thyself on his mouth, I, even I, have worked. Fall down, descend to the ground, the venom hath been conquered. Behold, the NAME of the great god

[1] The great celestial lake of heaven.

[2] 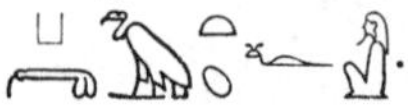.

hath been taken from him. RĀ liveth, the venom dieth; the venom dieth, RĀ liveth.' RUBRICAL DIRECTION: Let so-and-so, the son of so-and-so, [say] 'He liveth, the venom dieth'. Thus said ISIS, the mighty lady, the queen of the gods, who knew RĀ by his own name. Recite this over a figure of TEMU and HORUS of HEKEN (?) and over an image of ISIS and an image of HORUS.

LEGEND OF THE DESTRUCTION OF MANKIND BY RĀ

[For the hieroglyphic text see NAVILLE in *Trans. Soc. Bibl. Arch.*, vol. iv, pp. 1 ff.; LEFÉBURE, *Trans. Soc. Bibl. Arch.*, vol. viii, pp. 412 ff.] See also a German translation by ROEDER (*Urkunden*, pp. 142 ff.).

[Here is the legend of RĀ], the self-created god, after he had assumed the sovereignty over men, and women, and gods, and things, the ONE god.

Now men and women were plotting evil, saying, 'His Majesty—life, strength, and health be to him!—hath grown old, and his bones have become silver, and his members (or body) hath turned into gold, and his hair is like unto real lapis-lazuli'.

And His Majesty heard the words of evil which men and women were saying, and he said unto those who were in his train, 'Cry out, and bring to me my Eye, and SHU and TEFNUT, and GEBB and NUT, and the Father-gods and the Mother-gods who were with me when I was in NUNU[1] (or NU), together with my god NUN himself. Let these be brought hither to me secretly, so that men and women may not see them [coming hither], and may not therefore be stricken with fear in their hearts. Come then [O NUN] with them to the Great House, and let them declare their plans (or counsels). As for me, I will go from NUNU into the place wherein I caused myself to come into being, and let those gods be brought unto me there.'

Thereupon those gods were brought in, and they were drawn up on each side of RĀ, and they bowed down before His Majesty until their foreheads touched the ground, and in the presence of the Father of the First-born Gods, the maker of men, the king of the REKHIT,[2] spake the things which he had to say.

[1] i.e. the primeval Ocean out of which Rā appeared.
[2] A class of men, or a title of mankind in general.

And the gods spake in the presence of His Majesty saying, 'Speak unto us for we are [waiting] to hear them (i.e. thy words)'.

And RĀ spake unto NUN saying, 'O thou first-born god from whom I came into being, O ye gods of primeval time, my ancestors, take ye good heed to what men are [plotting], for behold, those who were created by my Eye are planning evil in respect of me. Tell me what ye would do in the matter? Consider this thing for me. [Meanwhile] I will search out the affair, for I will not slay them until I have heard what ye shall say to me concerning it.'

Then the Majesty of NUN spake unto RĀ, saying, 'O my son RĀ, thou art the god who art mightier than the god who made thee, thou art the CHIEF of those who were created with thee. Sit thee down [upon] thy throne. The fear of thee is great. Let thine Eye go against those who are planning evil against thee.'

And the Majesty of RĀ said, 'Behold, they have betaken themselves to flight into the mountainous deserts for their hearts have become stricken with fear because of the words which they have uttered'.

And the gods spake in the presence of His Majesty, saying, 'Let thine Eye go forth and let it destroy for thee those who speak words of evil against thee, for there is no eye whatever that can vanquish it and resist thee. Let it journey forth in the form of HATHOR.'

Thereupon this goddess went forth and slew men and women in the mountainous desert. And the Majesty of this god said, 'Come, Come in peace (i.e. Welcome!), O HATHOR, for the work which I sent thee forth to do is accomplished'.

Then this goddess said, '[I swear by] thy life that when I gained the mastery over men and women it was very gratifying to my heart'. And the Majesty of RĀ said, 'I myself will gain the mastery over them and will make them few in number'. Thus SEKHMIT[1] came into being. [She devoured] the food of the night (i.e. the evening meal), so that she might wade about in their (i.e. the slaughtered men's) blood, beginning from HENSU (i.e. HERAKLEOPOLIS, in UPPER EGYPT).

Then the Majesty of RĀ spake [unto the gods in his train], saying, 'Cry out, and summon to me swift and speedy messengers who

[1] Originally a bloodthirsty destroying goddess of Sûdânî origin, but here identified with the aspect of Hathor which represented the Eye of Rā.

are capable of travelling as fast as the shadow of the body'; and straightway messengers of this [kind] were brought unto him. And the Majesty of this god spake, saying, 'Let these messengers go to ĀBU[1] and bring me a large quantity of pomegranates (?).[2]' And when these pomegranates (?) were brought to him the Majesty of this god gave them to SEKTET (?) who is in ANNU (HELIOPOLIS) so that he might rub down these pomegranates (?) in a mortar. And when the women servants had crushed the barley (or *dhura*, i.e. millet) for [making] beer, these pomegranates (?) were mixed with the crushed grain in the pots, and it (i.e. mixture) was like the blood of men and women. And seven thousand pots of beer were made.

Then the Majesty of the King of the South and North, RĀ, came together with these gods (i.e. those in his train) to look upon these pots of beer. And behold, the day broke on which the goddess was to slay men and women on the days when they were coming up. And the Majesty of the King of the South and North said, 'They (i.e. the pots) are indeed good: I will protect men and women by means of it (i.e. the beer)'. And [the Majesty of] RĀ said, 'Carry them to the place where the goddess hath determined to slay men and women'.

Then His Majesty, the King of the South and North, RĀ, early in the darkness of the night, caused this soporific beer to be poured out from the pots. And the fields were covered all over with liquid to the height of four spans through the Souls (i.e. Will) of the Majesty of this god.

And the goddess set out at daybreak, and she found all the ground flooded with liquid. Her face looked lovely there, and then she drank [the beer], and her heart was glad, and she became drunk, and she gave no further attention to men and women.

Then the Majesty of this god said unto this goddess, 'Come in peace, come in peace (i.e. welcome! welcome!), O thou goddess AMIT'. And thus the name of beautiful women came to exist in the city of AMIT. And the Majesty of this god said unto this goddess, 'There shall be made for thee vessels of the beer which induceth sleep at every holy time and festival of the year and they shall be

[1] The city of the elephant, i.e. Elephantine, on island in the First Cataract, opposite to Aswân (Syene).

[2] *Tatait* was formerly translated by 'mandrakes'; 'haematite' has also been proposed.

in number according to the number of the serving women'. And thus was established in primeval times the custom of making on the occasions of the festivals of HATHOR, pots of this soporific beer equal in number to the number of the handmaidens of RĀ. And the Majesty of RĀ spake unto this goddess, saying, 'The pain of a burning sickness. . . .'

And the Majesty of RĀ said, 'It is true that I am alive, but my heart hath become exceedingly weary of living (?) with them. I would gladly have slain them all so that they might no longer exist, but my arm hath not been equal to [dealing with] them.' Then the gods who were in his train said unto him, 'Be not dismayed notwithstanding thy weariness, for thou hast the power to do that which thou wishest to do'.

Then the Majesty of this god said unto the Majesty of NUN, 'My members have suffered pain since primeval time, and I shall not recover until another period cometh'. And the Majesty of NUN said, 'My son SHU, let thine eye [look] upon [thy] father and protect him. My daughter NUT, set him [upon thy back].' And NUT said, 'My father NUN, how can this be done?' Thus spake NUT. . . . And the goddess NUT changed herself into a cow, and the Majesty of RĀ found himself seated upon her back.

[And when these things were done] men and women looked and [saw] him upon the back of a cow. Then these men said unto him, 'We [will protect thee], and we will cast down thine enemies.' . . . And his Majesty departed to Great House [on the back] of this cow, and all the company of the gods were with him. Then was the earth in darkness. And when it became day again these men came out with their bows . . . and they shot arrows at the enemies. Then the Majesty of this god [RĀ] said, 'Take good heed and consider, for the enemies who are on the battle field are. . . .' So the slaughtering [for sacrifice] came into being.

[The remainder of the text has nothing to do with the destruction of mankind. We find RĀ seated on the back of the Cow of heaven, and as a result of the puns which he makes various things come into being, e.g. the SEKHET-ḤETEP, the SEKHET AARU, and the stars. The Cow NUT becomes dizzy and totters because of the height, and therefore the Bearer-gods come into being, and the god SHU sets himself under the body of the Cow and supports her.

A long paragraph contains rubrical directions for making the drawing of the Cow, and the colours to be used. Nine stars are to be painted on the body, and a figure of SET is to be drawn by her hind legs. There must be also a boat with a steering pole, and a shrine of RĀ therein. RĀ also gives commands to GEBB, the Earth-god, that the serpents in the earth are to be protected, and their maintenance to be provided for. THOTH is appointed to be the scribe or secretary of RĀ, and is to superintend the lighting of the ṬUAT and the Island of BABA. THOTH is also, in the form of the moon, to act as deputy to RĀ, and men shall adore him as a god. Next follow directions concerning the recital of the texts. The priest is to use natron and incense, his garments are to be new, he must wash in the water of the inundation of the NILE, his sandals are to be white, a figure of MAĀT (Truth) must be painted on his tongue with green pigment, and when he intends to recite the text he must purify himself with a ninefold purification, lasting three days. The words of power of RĀ are his soul, the soul of SHU is KHNEMU, the soul of HEH (Eternity) is AM, the soul of KEK (Darkness) is the night. The soul of NU (the primeval abyss of water) is RĀ. The soul of OSIRIS is the Ram of MENDES. The souls of SEBEK are the crocodiles, and the souls of the gods dwell in the snakes and serpents. The soul of RĀ lives in all the land, but the soul of SET only lives in the Mountain of the East. The priest who recites this text is to use a spell in which he declares that he is the magician who is in the mouth and body of RĀ. He is also to make the figure of a woman and to paint on it a goddess and a serpent standing on its tail. On the first and fifteenth days of the month he must pray to be delivered from the gods who dwell in the East, and the recital of the whole text will give him life in the Underworld.]

THE LEGEND OF HORUS OF BEḤUṬ-T (EDFÛ) AND THE WINGED DISK

The hieroglyphic text of this legend and the reliefs which illustrate various portions of the narrative are cut on the walls of the temple of HORUS of EDFÛ in UPPER EGYPT. Both text and reliefs have been published by NAVILLE, *Textes relatifs au Mythe d'Horus*, GENEVA, 1870. German translations of it have been published by BRUGSCH, 'Die Saga von der geflügelten Sonnenscheibe' (in *Abh. Ges. Wissen.*, GÖTTINGEN, 1869);

WIEDEMANN, *Die Religion der alten Ägypter*, MÜNSTER, 1890; and ROEDER, *Urkunden*, JENA, 1923, pp. 121 ff.; and SCHÄFER in *Klio*, 1904. French translations by MASPERO have appeared in *Bibl. Égyptol.*, tom. ii, PARIS, 1893, and in *Histoire Ancienne*, tom. i, PARIS, 1895; and English translations by WIEDEMANN (in the English edition of his book) and by BUDGE, with the hieroglyphic text, in *Legends of the Gods*, LONDON, 1912, pp. 52 ff.]

TRANSLATION

In the three hundred and sixty-third year of the King of the South and of the North, RĀ ḤARAKHTI, who liveth for ever and for ever, His Majesty was in TA-STI (i.e. the Land of the Bow, or NUBIA) and his soldiers, who were innumerable, were with him. [The people] began to talk sedition (or conspire) against their lord, and the land was called WAWA-T (UAUA-T) to this day.[1] RĀ sailed down the river in his boat and his followers were with him. He arrived in the nome of UTHES-ḤER (APOLLINOPOLIS, the modern EDFÛ), in the western part thereof, and east of the canal PA-KHENU, which is called the 'Stream of RĀ' to this day. And HORUS of BEḤUṬ-T was in the boat of RĀ, and he said unto his father RĀ ḤARAKHTI, 'I see enemies conspiring against their lord. Let the serpent (cobra) on thy forehead gain the mastery over them. . . .'

Then the Majesty of RĀ ḤARAKHTI said, '. . . thy Ka, HORUS of BEḤUṬ-Ṭ, son of RĀ, exalted one, who didst proceed from me, overthrow the enemies who are before thee straightway'. And HORUS of BEḤUṬ-T flew up into the horizon in the form of a great Winged Sun-Disk, for which reason he is called 'Great god, lord of heaven', to this day. And when he saw the enemies in the heights of heaven, he set out to chase them in the form of a great Winged Sun-Disk. And he attacked with such terrific force those who opposed him that they could neither see with their eyes, nor hear with their ears. Each one killed his neighbour in a moment of time, and there was not a single head (i.e. being) who was left alive. Then HORUS of BEḤUṬ-T as a hawk-god of many colours in the form of a great Winged Sun-Disk came back to the boat of RĀ ḤARAKHTI.

And THOTH said unto RĀ, 'Lord of the gods, BEḤUṬ-[T] hath come in the divine form of the great Winged Sun-Disk [which is victorious?]', and for this reason he is called 'HORUS of BEḤUṬ-T' to this day. THOTH said, '. . . .'. Therefore he is called 'HORUS of

[1] Note the pun on *uaua* 'to conspire' and the name of Nubia.

BEḤUṬ-T' to this day, and 'HORUS of ṬEBA' (EDFÛ). And RĀ embraced his form and said unto HORUS of BEḤUṬ-T, 'Thou hast put grapes into the stream which cometh forth from it; there let thine heart rejoice'. Therefore the water from it is called 'Water of HORUS of BEḤUṬ-T' to this day, [and that god is called] 'Many coloured Image' [to this day].

HORUS of BEḤUṬ-T said, 'Advance (or hasten), O RĀ, and look thou upon thine enemies who are lying on this land beneath thee'. Thereupon the Majesty of RĀ set out on the way, and the goddess ĀSTARTE was with him, and he saw the enemies lying overthrown on the ground their heads having been cut off.

Then RĀ said unto HORUS of BEḤUṬ-T, 'There is happy life in this State', and because of this the Great House (or Palace) of HORUS of BEḤUṬ-T is called 'Happy Life' to this day.

RĀ said unto THOTH, '[Here was] the slaughter of mine enemies,' and for this reason the name of this nome is called 'ṬEBA' to this day.

THOTH said unto HORUS of BEḤUṬ-T, 'Thou art a great protector.' For this reason the Boat of HORUS of BEḤUṬ-T was called 'MĀK-Ā' (i.e. Great Protector) to this day.

Then RĀ said unto the gods who were in his following, 'Come now, let us sail in our Boat on the water (or canal), for our heart is glad because our enemies have been overthrown on the earth'. And the water whereon the great god sailed is called 'P-KHENU' to this day.

And behold, the enemies of RĀ having transformed themselves into crocodiles and hippopotami hurled themselves into the water. And whilst RĀ ḤARAKHTI was seated [in his Boat] and sailing over the water, the crocodiles and the hippopotami came nigh, and opened wide their jaws in order to destroy their enemy RĀ ḤARAKHTI. Then HORUS of BEḤUṬ-T made haste and came up, with his followers behind him, armed with metal weapons, each one by name having an axe, a spear (or harpoon), and a chain to [his] hand. They speared the crocodiles and the hippopotami, and there were brought in forthwith six (?) hundred and fifty-one rebel-fiends, and they were slain opposite to the city of EDFÛ.

RĀ ḤARAKHTI said unto HORUS of BEḤUṬ-T, 'My Image in the Land of the South, and a Victor of the Great House [art thou]'; for this reason the Palace of HORUS of BEḤUṬ-T is called 'Victory Palace' to this day.

THOTH, after he had looked upon the enemies which were lying upon the ground, spake, saying, 'Let your hearts rejoice, O ye gods of heaven! Let your hearts rejoice, O ye gods who are on the earth! The Young HORUS cometh in peace, and he hath made manifest on his journey deeds of mighty valour, which he hath performed according to the "Book of Slaying the Hippopotamus".' And to this day the armed [followers] of HORUS of BEḤUṬ-T exist.

[Then] HORUS of BEḤUṬ-T took upon himself the form of the Winged Sun-Disk, and he placed himself upon the bows of the Boat of RĀ. And he set by his side the goddess NEKHEBIT and the goddess UADJIT in the form of two serpents (cobras), so that they might make the enemies to quake (or be terrified) in [all] their members, [when they appeared] in the form of crocodiles and hippopotami, in every place wherein he came in the Land of the South and in the Land of the North. Then those enemies rose up and made their escape from before him, and their faces were [turned] to the Land of the South, and their hearts (i.e. courage) drooped through fear of him.

And HORUS of BEḤUṬ-T was behind them in this Boat of RĀ, and there were in his hands a metal spear and a chain, and with their lord were the armed [followers] who were equipped for fighting with metal spears and chains. And he saw them (i.e. the enemies) in a region to the south-east of UAS-T (THEBES) two miles (?) distant. RĀ said unto THOTH, 'O these enemies! let their persons be destroyed'. THOTH said unto RĀ, 'This place shall be called DJTM-T'.[1]

HORUS of BEḤUṬ-T made a great massacre of them, and RĀ said, 'Stand still, HORUS of BEḤUṬ-T, and let me look'. And for this reason that State (or place) is called 'House of RĀ'; the god who dwelleth therein is HORUS–BEḤUṬ-T–RĀ–MENU (or MIN).

[Then] those enemies rose up to make their escape from before him—now the face of the god was towards the Land of the North—their hearts quailed through the fear of him. HORUS of BEḤUṬ-T was behind them in the Boat of RĀ, and those who were his followers had spears of metal and chains of metal in their hands, and the god himself was equipped with weapons of war, with a spear and

[1] Here is a play on *djetba* and *djetem-t*.

a chain, and armed companions were equipped (?). He passed a whole day with them, [and then] he saw them (i.e. the enemies) to the north-east of DENDERAH. RĀ said unto THOTH, 'The enemies are delaying . . . their lord'. The Majesty of RĀ ḤARAKHTI said unto HORUS of BEḤUṬ-T, 'Thou art my exalted son who didst proceed from NUT. The enemies are helpless in thy moment'.[1] [Then] HORUS of BEḤUṬ-T made a great massacre among them. THOTH said, 'This town (or State) shall be called . . . [Winged Sun-Disk] . . . and HORUS of BEḤUṬ-T shall be proclaimed (?) . . . because of its majesty (or mistress, i.e. of the State (or town)). The front thereof shall be towards the south in the name of this god. The acacia and the sycamore-fig shall be in the grove (?).'

[Then] the enemies turned aside to flee from before him. Their faces were towards [the] north, and they rushed on by the canal (*ḥen-t*) to the regions [near] the Great Green [Sea, i.e. the RED SEA ?] . . . and [their hearts quailed through their fear of him]. HORUS of BEḤUṬ-T was in the Boat of RĀ behind them with a metal axe and a metal spear in his hands, with his followers; he was provided with weapons of war, and his followers were armed likewise. He passed four days and four nights on the water with them; but he did not see one of these enemies, for the crocodiles and the hippopotami which were in the water fled before him. Then [at length] he saw them. RĀ said unto HORUS of BEḤUṬ-T of ḤEBEN, the great god, the lord of heaven, 'Spear thou them. . . .' And he hurled his spear (or harpoon) at them, and he slew them and made a great massacre of them. One hundred and forty enemies were brought to the front of the Boat of RĀ . . . and with them was a male hippopotamus, which had been among those enemies. And he hacked them in pieces with his knife (or sword), and gave their entrails to his followers; their carcasses he gave to the gods and goddesses who were in the Boat of RĀ on the river bank of the city of ḤEBEN.

RĀ said unto THOTH, 'See what mighty things HORUS of BEḤUṬ-T hath performed in his deeds against these enemies! Verily he hath smitten them. The male hippopotamus under him opened his mouth towards him, but he drove his spear through it although he was standing on his back.'

[1] Or, the courage of the enemies hath failed in a moment.

THOTH said unto RĀ, 'For this reason HORUS shall be called "Winged Sun-Disk, Great god, Smiter of the enemy, Prince of ḤEBEN" from this day, and the priest of this god, for the same reason, shall from this day have the title of "ḤERI-SA" (i.e. he who standeth on the back)'. This is what happened in the territory of ḤEBEN, in a region which measures three hundred and forty-two cords (fathoms?) on the south, and on the north, and on the west, and on the east.

The enemies rose up before him on the Lake of the North, and their faces were set towards the Great Green [Sea], which they strove to reach by sailing down the river. But the god (?) smote their hearts and they wandered about on the water, and they rushed into the waters of MERT-AMENT. And they gathered themselves together on the waters of MERT, and made haste to band themselves with those enemies [who serve] SET and who are in that place (or State). And HORUS of BEḤUṬ-T followed them being equipped with all the weapons of war. HORUS of BEḤUṬ-T travelled downstream in this Boat of RĀ, together with the Great God who sat in his Boat, together with the gods who were his followers. He pursued them with great rapidity on the Lake of the North. He sailed down the stream for a day and a night seeking them before he saw them, [for] he did not know the place where they were. He went to PER-ṚERḤU.

And the Majesty of RĀ said unto HORUS of BEḤUṬ-T, 'Behold those enemies have assembled on the western water of the nome of MERT to band themselves with the enemies [who serve] SET who are in this place (or State). And THOTH said unto RĀ, 'For this reason the nome of MERT from this day shall be called UASEB, and the water which is in it shall be called. . . .'

[Then] HORUS of BEḤUṬ-T spake before his father RĀ, saying, 'I beseech thee to let me set thy Boat against them, so that I may be able to perform what RĀ wisheth'. He did all that was ordered. Then he made an onset upon them on the Lake which was to the west of this district, and he saw them on the bank of MERT . . . motionless. And HORUS of BEḤUṬ-T made an attack upon them, and his followers, who were provided with the weapons of war, were with him. He made a great massacre among them, and three hundred and eighty-one enemies were brought here after he had slaughtered them before the Boat of RĀ. He gave one of them to each one of his followers.

And SET rose up and came forth raging horribly, and shouted out curses and revilings because of the deeds which HORUS of BEḤUṬ-T had done whilst he was in the act of slaying them.

RĀ said unto THOTH, 'Why doth this Stinking Face shriek at the top of his voice because of the things which HORUS of BEḤUṬ-T hath done against him?' THOTH said unto RĀ, 'Because of these revilings he shall be called "Stinking Face" from this day'.

And HORUS of BEḤUṬ-T waged war against the Enemy for a long time, and he hurled his metal spear at him, and he threw him down on the ground in this place (or State). And because of this it is called 'PER-RERḤU'[1] to this day. [Then] HORUS of BEḤUṬ-T came back and brought the Enemy in fetters. His spear was in his neck, his chain was round his paws and arms and the club of HORUS had fallen on his mouth and had closed it, and he took him before his father [RĀ].

RĀ said unto HORUS, the Winged Sun-Disk, 'Great, great indeed is this deed of valour which thou hast performed; thou hast purified this place (or State)'. RĀ said unto THOTH, 'Because of this thing the Palace of HORUS of BEḤUṬ-T shall from this day be called "Lord of the pure place". And because of this also the priest of this place shall from this day be called "UR-ṬENṬEN" (i.e. great one of valour).'

And RĀ said unto THOTH, 'Let the enemies and SET be delivered over to ISIS and her son HORUS, so that they may work all their hearts' desires upon them'. And ISIS and her son HORUS set themselves there with their spears driven into him whensoever there was a storm in that place. And because of this the Lake is to this day called 'Lake of fighting'.

[Then] HORUS, the son of ISIS, cut off the head of the Enemy (SET) and the heads of his followers in the presence of his father RĀ, and the Great Company of the Gods. And he dragged him by his feet round about through the State, with his spears stuck in his head and back.

RĀ said unto THOTH, 'Lo, the son of OSIRIS draggeth the miserable wretch round about in his territory'; and THOTH said, 'Because of

[1] i.e. the House of the Two Combatants (Horus and Set).

this the territory shall be called "ATEḤ",'[1] and that is its name to this day.

And ISIS, the divine lady, spake before her father RĀ, saying, 'In heaven let the Winged Sun-Disk be the magical protection of [my son] HORUS, for he hath cut off the head of the Enemy and the heads of his associates.'

[Thus] HORUS of BEḤUṬ-T and HORUS, the son of ISIS, jointly slaughtered that miserable Enemy, and his companions and the rebels. And they arrived with them at a lake which lay to the west of that district. HORUS of BEḤUṬ-T was in the form of a man of mighty strength, and he had the head of a hawk and he was crowned with the White Crown and the Red Crown. Two plumes and two cobras were on his head, he had the back of a hawk, and a metal axe, and harpoon and a chain were in his hands. And HORUS, the son of ISIS, transformed himself, and assumed the shape which HORUS of BEḤUṬ-T had taken. And together they killed the enemies which were to the west of PER-RERḤU on the bank of the water. And this god from that day sailed over the water wherein the enemies had banded themselves together against him. Now these things took place on the seventh day of the first month of the season of PER-T.

THOTH said, 'Because of this, from this day henceforth, this region shall be called "AA-T-SHEṬAT" (i.e. "Slaughter-town"). And the Lake which is close by it shall from this day have the name of "ṬEM-T". From this day, the seventh day of the first month of the season PER-T shall be called the "Festival of the sailing".'

Then SET took upon himself the form of a hissing serpent, and he entered into the earth at this place without being seen. RĀ said, 'SET hath taken upon himself the form of a hissing serpent. Let HORUS, the son of ISIS, in the form of a hawk-headed staff, set himself over the place where he is so that he may never be able to come forth again.' And THOTH said, 'HEMHEM-T[2] shall the serpent in this place [be called]', and it is so called unto this day. 'And HORUS,

[1] A play on  and .

[2] A play on  and . The usual form of the serpent's name is 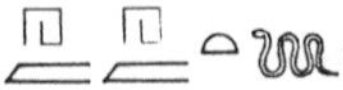.

the son of ISIS, in the form of a hawk-headed staff (or sceptre) shall stand over him (i.e. SET), and he shall remain there with his mother ISIS.'

After things had thus happened the Boat of RĀ landed at the town of PER-ĀḤĀ (i.e. Town of the Battle). The forepart thereof was made of palm wood, and the hind part of acacia wood; from that day to this the palm tree and the acacia have been sacred trees. And when the journey was ended HORUS of BEḤUṬ-T returned to the Boat of RĀ. Then RĀ said unto THOTH, 'Behold, . . . from this day the Boat of HORUS of BEḤUṬ-T shall be called "Lord of the Journey", and because of this all . . . take place in that place on this day'.

And RĀ said unto HORUS of BEḤUṬ-T, 'Behold the battle of the confederate fiends [of SET] and his mighty power (?). The fiends of SET are on the North Lake (Lake of MEḤ) . . . we will sail downstream after them.' And the Winged Sun-Disk (HORUS of BEḤUṬ-T) said: 'Whatsoever thou commandest shall take place, O RĀ, Lord of the gods. But grant that this thy Boat shall pursue them in every place whithersoever they may go, and I will do whatsoever pleaseth RĀ unto them.' And what he said was duly done. Then the Winged Sun-Disk brought this Boat of RĀ on to the waters of the Lake of MEḤ (North Lake). Then the Winged Sun-Disk took in his hands the metal [axe], and his harpoon, and all the chains [which he needed] for the fight. And he saw some of the SEBAU fiends there in one place with him (i.e. SET). He hurled his metal spears, and dragged them away together, and slaughtered them in the presence of RĀ. Thus he made an end of them, and in a moment there were no more of them left. And THOTH said, 'Because HORUS of BEḤUṬ-T hath made himself master over them (the enemies) this throne shall be called AST-AB-ḤER-T '.

And he passed six days and six nights, during which time the Boat [of RĀ] rested on the waters, without seeing one of the enemies. Then at length he saw them lying in the stream. And he stablished the town of AST-AB-ḤER-T there upon the bank of the water, and its splendid fore-front was turned towards the south. As all the rites and ceremonies of HORUS of BEḤUṬ-T were performed on the first day of the first month of the season of AKHET, and on the seventh day of the first month of the season of PER-T, and on the twenty-first and twenty-fourth days of the second month of the season of PER-T, these days are festivals in the town of AST-AB-ḤER-T to the south of AN-RUṬ-T.

And he tied up the Boat on the shore against them and watched as for a king over the Great God in AN-RUṬ-F in this town, in order to drive away the Enemy and his allies at his coming by night from the nome of MERT, to the west of this town.

HORUS of BEḤUṬ-T had the form of a man of mighty strength, with the face of a hawk. He was crowned with the White Crown and the Red Crown, and on his head were two plumes, and the Urerit Crown, and two cobras. His strong hand grasped his harpoon to slay the hippopotamus as firmly as the mountain holds the *khenem* stone which is embedded in it.

RĀ said unto THOTH, 'Verily [HORUS of] BEḤUṬ-T is a Lord of Battle in slaying his desert peoples.' THOTH said unto RĀ, 'Because of this priest of this god shall from this day be called by the name of "Lord of Battle".'

And ISIS made incantations of every kind in order to drive away the fiend from AN-RUṬ-T in this place. And THOTH said unto RĀ, 'The priestess of this god shall, because of this, be called by the name of "NEBT-ḤEKA".'

RĀ said, 'Beautiful, beautiful is this place wherein thou hast taken up thy seat, and dost keep watch in peace, as for a king, over the Great God who is in AN-RUṬ-F.' THOTH said, 'This Great House (i.e. Palace) in this place, shall from this day be called by the name of "Beautiful Place".' It standeth to the south-west of NĀR-T in a clearing four *schoinoi* square.

RĀ said unto HORUS of BEḤUṬ-T, 'Hast thou not searched through this water for the enemy?' THOTH said, 'The water of the god-house in this place shall be called "ḤEḤ-WATER".'[1]

RĀ said, 'Great is thy ship, O HORUS of BEḤUṬ-T upon the TEMIT water.' THOTH said, 'Thy ship shall be called by the name of "UR", and this water shall be called by the name of "TEMIT".'

And now as concerning the place called 'AAB'—it lieth on the shore of the water. 'AST-NEFERT' (Beautiful Place) is the name of

[1] A play on , to seek out.

the Palace, 'Lord of Battle' is the name of the priest, ['Lady of incantations'] is the name of the singing woman, 'ḤEḤ' is the name of the water, 'TEMIT' is the name of the stream. 'Palm' and 'Acacia' are the sacred trees, 'God-house' is the domain of the town. 'Great' is the name of the Boat, and the gods therein are HORUS of BEḤUṬ-T, the smiter of the desert peoples, and HORUS, the son of ISIS, the son of OSIRIS. . . .

HORUS [set out] with his armed men and his followers who were round about him, and he had his axe, and his weapons, and his dagger, and his chains. [When he reached the Land of the North his followers saw the enemies.] Through the armed men who were in the middle region he made a great massacre, and one hundred and six of the enemy were brought back, and the armed men who were in the West brought back one hundred and six of the enemy. With the armed men who were in the East HORUS of BEḤUṬ-T slaughtered the enemies in the middle regions before RĀ.

RĀ said unto THOTH, 'My heart [is satisfied] with the deeds of these armed men of HORUS of BEḤUṬ-T, and those who follow him. Images of them shall be set up in the sanctuaries, and offerings and purificatory libations shall be made to them, and a ritual of service for them shall be established. Priests who minister by the month, and priests who minister by the hour shall be appointed to serve them in every god-house (i.e. temple) whatsoever and wheresoever—as their reward because they slaughtered the enemies.'

THOTH said, 'The [central] towns (or States), shall from this day onwards be called by the name of these armed men (*mesentiu*), and HORUS of BEḤUṬ-T, the lord of armed-camps, shall from this day onward be the god in them. The whole region shall from this day onward be called "WEST MESEN". The frontage of WEST MESEN shall face the water and the place of the sunrise. This MESEN shall be called EAST MESEN from this day onwards. As concerning the double town of MESEN which [marketh] the deeds of these armed men, the frontage thereof shall be towards the south, and turned towards BEḤUṬ-T, for this is the abode of HORUS of BEḤUṬ-T. And all the rites and ceremonies of HORUS of BEḤUṬ-T shall be performed on the second day of the first month of the season of AKHET (THOTH), and on the twenty-fourth day of the fourth month of the season of

AKHET (CHOIAK), and on the seventh day of the first month of the season of PER-T (TYBI), and on the twenty-first day of the second month of the season of PER-T (MECHIR), from this day onwards. Their stream shall be called "ASTI", their Palace shall be called . . ., [their priest] shall be called "QEN-ĀḤĀ", and their Domain shall be called "KAU MESEN" from this day onwards.'

RĀ said unto HORUS of BEḤUṬ-T, 'These enemies have sailed upstream towards the eastern deserts, and the region behind ON (HELIOPOLIS) of the north, they have sailed to the east, to DJARU and the swamps thereby'. And HORUS of BEḤUṬ-T said, 'Everything which thou shalt command shall come to pass, O Lord of the gods; thou art the lord of commands'. Then they untied (or towed) the Boat of RĀ and sailed up the river towards the east. Then he looked at those enemies and saw that some of them were lying in the water, and that others were stretched out on the mountains. HORUS of BEḤUṬ-T then changed his form into that of a lion which had the face of a man, and he was wearing the triple crown with three solar disks, three pairs of plumes, two cobras and a pair of ram's horns. His paw (i.e. claw) was [sharp] like a flint knife and he compassed them about and brought back one hundred and forty-two of them, having slain them with his claws. He ripped out their tongues, and their blood flowed over the ridges of the hills, and he handed them over to his followers as their property whilst he was on the mountains.

RĀ said unto THOTH, 'Behold, HORUS of BEḤUṬ-T is like a lion on the backs of the enemies in the spot where he attacketh, and they have been forced to yield up their tongues'. And THOTH said, 'These domains shall be called "KHENT-AAB", and with DJARU shall be called by this name from this day onward, and also the tongues of land from the furthermost frontiers of DJARU shall be brought (i.e. included) in it (?). The god of DJARU shall be called "HORUS of BEḤUṬ-T" from this day onward.'

RĀ said unto HORUS of BEḤUṬ-T, 'Let us sail on the sea (?) so that we may chase out of EGYPT the enemies who are in the forms of crocodiles and hippopotami'. And HORUS of BEḤUṬ-T said, 'Thy divine KA, O RĀ, Lord of the gods'. A whirlwind rose up [and swept over] the remainder of the enemies on the sea. THOTH pronounced spells and incantations in order to protect the Boat of RĀ, and the rafts (or boats) of his armed followers, at the moment of the storm, and the sea became tranquil again.

And RĀ said unto THOTH, 'Have we not travelled over the whole land? Shall we not travel over the whole sea likewise?' And THOTH said, 'From this day onward this water shall be called "Sea of journeying".'

[HORUS OF BEḤUṬ-T RETURNS TO NUBIA]

And they set out and sailed about by day and by night, and they did not see any enemies. And they journeyed on and arrived in the country of TA-STI (NUBIA), at the town of SHAS-ḤERT; and he perceived these enemies in the country of UAUA-T (northern NUBIA), and they were conspiring against HORUS, their lord. And HORUS of BEḤUṬ-T changed his form into that of the Winged Sun-Disk, on the bows of the Boat of RĀ. He took the goddess NEKHEBIT and UADJIT in the forms of two cobras so that they might burn into their members (i.e. bodies of the enemies). Their hearts failed them because of him, they could make no resistance, and they died straightway.

Then the gods who were in the following of the Boat of RĀ ḤARAKHTI said, 'Great, great is he who hath set himself between the two cobras! He hath overthrown the enemies by means of their fear of him [alone]'. RĀ ḤARAKHTI said, 'The Great One of the two cobras, HORUS of BEḤUṬ-T, shall be called "UR UADJTI" from this day onwards'.

And RĀ ḤARAKHTI travelled on in his boat and arrived at the city of THES-ḤERU (APOLLINOPOLIS MAGNA). THOTH said, 'This being of many-coloured feathers who hath risen up out of the horizon hath smitten the enemy in this form of his, and from this day onwards he shall be called by the name of "Being of many coloured feathers who hath risen up out of the horizon".'

And RĀ ḤARAKHTI said to THOTH, 'Thou shalt make this Winged Sun-Disk to be in every place wherein I seat myself, and in the towns of the gods of the South, and in the towns of the gods of the North, and in . . ., and in the West (AMENTT) in order to keep away evil beings from their domains'.

Then THOTH made the image of the Winged Sun-Disk to be in every town, and in every temple where they now are, wherein are

[all] the gods and [all] the goddesses whoever they may be from that day to this. Now, through the Winged Sun-Disk which is on the temple buildings of all the gods and goddesses of the Land of the papyrus (South) and the Land of the Lotus (North), they shall become shrines of HORUS of BEḤUṬ-T.

HORUS of BEḤUṬ-T, the great god, the lord of heaven, the Prince in the ATER of the South, shall have a statue on the right-hand side; this is HORUS of BEḤUṬ-T with whom the goddess NEKHEBIT in the form of a cobra is placed. HORUS of BEḤUṬ-T, the great god, the lord of heaven, the lord of MESEN, the prince in the ATER of the North, shall have a statue on the left-hand side; this is HORUS of BEḤUṬ-T with whom the goddess UADJIT in the form of a cobra is placed.

HORUS of BEḤUṬ-T, the great god, the lord of heaven, the lord of MESEN, the Prince of the ATERTI, the South and the North, hath RĀ ḤARAKHTI placed in all his towns so that he may overthrow the enemies wherever they may be found. For this reason, from this day onward he shall be called the 'Prince of the two ATERTI of UPPER and LOWER EGYPT'.

A LEGEND OF KHNEMU AND OF A SEVEN YEARS' FAMINE

[The hieroglyphic text of this legend is found on one side of a large rounded block of granite nearly nine feet high which stands on the south-east portion of SÂḤAL, a little island lying in the First Cataract, about two miles to the south of ELEPHANTINE ISLAND and the modern town of ASWÂN. The inscription is not cut on the rock in the ordinary way, but was 'stunned' on it with a blunted chisel or hammer. In some lights it is invisible even to any one standing quite near the rock, unless he is aware of its existence. It is in full view of any one standing on the river-path which leads from MAHALLAH to PHILAE, and yet it escaped the notice of scores of travellers who from the days of WILKINSON, HAY, BURTON, BONOMI, LOFTIE, and others have searched the islands of the Cataract for *graffiti* and inscriptions. It was discovered accidentally on 9th February 1889 by Mr. C. E. WILBOUR, a distinguished American gentleman who in his famous house-boat *The Seven Hathors* spent many seasons in EGYPT occupying himself with archaeological research. His copy of the text and Mr. MAUDSLAY's photograph of it were sent to Dr. H. BRUGSCH who published a transcript of the text, with a German translation of it, in a work entitled *Die biblischen sieben Jahre der Hungersnoth*, LEIPZIG, 8vo. Another transcript was published by J. DE MORGAN in his *Catalogue des monuments de l'Égypte*, Série I, Tome i, 1894.]

TRANSLATION

In the eighteenth year of the HORUS. NETER-KHAT, the king of the South and the North, NETER-KHAT, the Lord of the shrines of NEKHEBIT (Vulture-goddess) and UADJIT (cobra goddess), NETER-KHAT, HORUS of NUBTI (DJESER)—to MATAR, the hereditary prince and governor of the temples (or houses) of the Land of the South, the Commander of those who dwell in ĀBU (ELEPHANTINE):

This royal decree hath been brought unto thee to inform thee that misery hath laid hold upon me, as I sit in the Great Hall of the Palace, and my heart is grievously afflicted because ḤĀPI (the NILE) hath not come forth during the period of my reign to his [proper] height for seven years. Grain is very scarce, herbs and vegetables are lacking altogether, and everything which men eat for food is of the poorest. A man now robbeth his neighbour, they go away in order not to return. The child waileth, the young man sinks down exhausted, and the hearts of the aged are crushed with despair; their legs give way under them and they sink to the ground, and their hands are [folded] inside them. The SHENNU nobles are destitute, and the storehouses are closed, and there cometh forth from them nothing but wind. Everything is in a state of ruin.

My mind hath remembered going back to a time past, that I asked for information from the ibis [of THOTH], from the KHERI ḤEB I-EM-ḤETEP,[1] the son of PTAḤ south of his Wall [saying], 'Where is the place of birth of ḤĀPI? Which is the town of the [NILE-flood?]. Who is the god to whom sacrifices should be offered up therein?' He made answer, saying (?), that it was 'necessary for me to go to the governor of ḤET-KAMT (?) (i.e. HERMOPOLIS), whose beneficence strengtheneth the hearts of all men in their duty'. Then I would go into the House of Life,[2] and I would unroll the 'Souls of RĀ' (i.e. the papyrus rolls), and I would lay my hands upon them. [The king sends to MATAR the governor.]

[1] Imouthes, the high priest and great magician of Memphis who flourished under king Djeser (IIIrd dynasty), and who was subsequently deified and made one of the chief gods of Memphis.

[2] i.e. the Hermopolitan Temple Library containing the books written by Thoth.

Then he (i.e. MATAR) set out on his journey, and he returned to me straightway. And he gave me information about the Inundation of the NILE, and everything which happened at the time. And he told me about everything which men had written concerning it, and he revealed to me secret marvels which the men of old had experienced on their way thither, the like of which no king since the time of RĀ had known. And he announced to me the following:

There is a city in the middle of the stream wherefrom ḤĀPI maketh his appearance; its name is 'ĀBU' (i.e. Elephant City, ELEPHANTINE). It is the chief (i.e. capital) city, the first city of the nome, on the way to WAWAT (NUBIA), the beginning of [that] land; it is the stairway of GEBB (the Earth-god). It is the support of RĀ where he maketh his calculation to prolong the life of every one. Its name is 'MEDJEMDJEM ĀNKH'.[1] 'The two QERTI'[2] is the name of the water, and they are the two breasts wherefrom every good thing cometh. It is the bed of ḤĀPI, wherein he reneweth his youth . . . whereby he causeth the flooding of the land. He cometh and hath union as he journeyeth, as a man hath union with a woman, and produceth offspring (?) He riseth to the height of twenty-eight cubits [at ĀBU], and in the town of SMA-BḤṬET (in the Delta) his height may be reckoned at seven cubits. The god KHNEMU is the god thereof; [it is the place of] the soles of his feet. . . . The bolt of the door is in his hand, and the double doors [of the QERTI] fall open when he wisheth it. There he is called 'SHU who dwelleth on the river banks of the district'. There he keepeth an account of all the products of the Land of the South and of the Land of the North, in order to give unto every god his proper share. He leadeth [to each] the . . . and [the precious stones, and the beasts], and the geese, and the fish and all the things on which they live. And the measuring cord and a tablet whereon registrations are made are there, and a wooden building with a door made of reeds. He is the god who dwelleth on his bank, and SHU (?) is in the heavens. His god-house (i.e. temple) hath an opening to the south-east and RĀ riseth exactly opposite thereto every day. The stream which floweth along the south side of it is unfavourable [for mariners].

[1] A name meaning something like the 'pleasure place of Life'.

[2] The two Qerti were the two underground caverns in the bowels of the granite rock through which the Nile coming from Nunu entered Egypt.

And it hath as a defence a wall between it and the people of KENS (NUBIA) on the south.

Huge mountains of stone (i.e. granite) are round about its domain on the east side, and they contain stone, and thither come the quarrymen, and people of all kinds when they seek to build any god-house (i.e. temple) in the South [and] North, or [byres] for sacred animals, or royal pyramids, or statues of every kind. They place them in the god-house and in the sanctuary chamber. And their sweet-smelling offerings are presented before the face of KHNEMU during his circuit, and so with garden herbs and flowers of every kind. The beginning [of the territory] is in ĀBU (ELEPHANTINE), and the end thereof in SUN (SYENE, ASWÂN). It (i.e. the granite) is on the east side of the river (i.e. at SYENE), and another portion is on the west side (i.e. CONTRA SYENE), and another portion is in the middle of the river. The water of the river clotheth it during a certain season of the year (i.e. during the Inundation) and it is a place of delight for every man. Work is carried on in these quarries which are on both sides of the river, which faceth immediately the city of ELEPHANTINE itself. Here is the granite, which possesseth a substance (?) very difficult to work. It is called 'stone of ĀBU'.

[Here is] a list of the names of the gods who dwell in the Temple of KHNEMU: SOTHIS (i.e. SATI), ĀNQET, ḤĀPI (NILE), SHU,[1] GEBB, NUT, OSIRIS, HORUS, ISIS, NEPHTHYS.[2]

[Here are] the names of the stones which lie in the heart of the mountains, some on the east side, some on the west side, and some [on the island] of the river of ĀBU. They are in the heart of ĀBU, they are in the country on the east bank, and in the country on the west bank, and [on the island] in the middle of the stream, namely BEHEN, MERI, ATBEKHAB, RAGES, UTSHI; these are found on the east bank. PERDJANE is found on the west bank, and TESHI in the [bed of the] river.

[Here is a list of the] names of the precious stones which are found on the upper side, and of the [metals] which are found with them for a distance of four *atru* (miles?): Gold, Silver, Copper,

[1] Tefnut is omitted by accident.

[2] There is no mention of Set. The writer gives two wives to Khnemu, viz. Sati and Ānqet, and to Osiris two, viz. Isis and Nephthys.

Iron, Lapis-lazuli, Emerald, Crystal (?), Jasper (or Ruby), Gai, Menu, Hebeqti (?), Temu. The following come forth from the fore-part of the land: Meḥi, Maki, Abheti, Iron ore (?), Gesankh, Green Eye-paint, Black Eye-paint, Herdes, Sehi, Amem, Sahpen—these are found everywhere in the district.

These were the things which I learned about it (i.e. ELEPHANTINE), and my heart was glad (?) [I] entered [the temple] in loose attire (?). I was sprinkled with water. I went into the secret places, and a great offering was made of cakes and wine, and geese, and oxen, and all good things, to the deities of ĀBU whose names are mentioned [above]. [I] lay on a couch with life and strength in my heart. I found the god standing in front of me. I made him to be at peace with me. I prayed to him and I made adoration before him and his heart was at peace with me. He made himself visible to me and he said, 'I am KHNEMU who fashioned thee. My two arms (or hands) are behind thee to make strong thy body and to give health to thy members. I [now] give thee commands. The stones in the quarries have been there from time immemorial, and yet there is no work going on in them for building the god-houses (i.e. temples) or for repairing what hath fallen into decay, or for hewing out shrines for the gods of the South and North, or for doing what [a king] ought to do for his lord. For I am the Lord of building. I am he who built (or fashioned) himself, [and] NUNU the great [Ocean], which existed in primeval time, at whose will ḤĀPI (the NILE) spilleth [over his banks]. I ordain the work which men do, and I direct all the people in their hours [of labour for me. I am] TENNU,[1] the Father of the gods, [and of] the great god SHU, the Lord of the Earth. The two openings[2] are in a chamber under me, and I have the power to let flow the Inundation. ḤĀPI (the NILE) is my kinsman. [When] he hath embraced the field-land his embrace provideth life for every nose—according to [the extent of] his embrace of the land. [With] old age [cometh weakness].

'[But] I will make the NILE rise [again] for thee, and in no year shall it fail to do so, and to produce fatness in the whole land. Herbs and trees shall flourish and shall bow their heads beneath [the

[1] i.e. Tanen, the first piece of earth which the god raised up out of Nunu, the primeval Ocean or Chaos, and on which he took his stand.

[2] i.e. the mouths of the two caverns (Qerti) through which the Nile came from the great celestial ocean into Egypt.

weight] of their produce. The goddess RENUTT[1] shall be at the head of every thing, and every product shall increase by hundreds of thousands according to the [height of the] cubit of the year [on the Nilometer]. The people shall be filled according to the desire of their hearts, and all want shall cease. And the emptiness of their granaries shall come to an end. The land of TA-MER-T (EGYPT) shall [again] be a region of cultivated land, and the fields shall be yellow (or shine) with crops of grain. And there shall be wealth and prosperity in the land among the people even as there was in days of old.'

Then I woke up in happy mind, my courage (or resolution) returned, my heart was at rest, and I promulgated the following decree concerning my father KHNEMU.

'The king giveth an offering to KHNEMU–RĀ, the Lord of QEBḤ (i.e. the First Cataract), the Governor of TA-STI[2] in return for those things which thou hast done for me.

'1. There shall be given unto thee on thy west MANU[3] and on thy east BEKHA[4] from ĀBU (ELEPHANTINE) to SAMITN (?) together with twenty measures (*schoinoi*) on the east and on the west banks, together with the plantations and the landing stage (?) everywhere throughout the region included in these [twenty *schoinoi*].

'2. From every husbandman who tilleth the ground with his peasants, and watereth the high-lying land, and the new ground which is brought into cultivation, a further contribution above that which was originally thy share shall be demanded.

'3. Whatsoever is caught by all the fishermen, and by every fowler, and by those who traffic in the waters, and by every hunter of wild game, and by the hunters of lions in the hills, of all that is brought into [the city] one tenth shall be demanded.

'4. And of all the calves which are dropped by the cows throughout the region which is here referred to, one tenth of their number shall be set apart for the byres of the temple as animals which are sealed for the burnt offerings which are offered up daily.

'5. And moreover, the gift of one tenth shall be levied upon the gold, ivory, ebony, spices, and precious stones, and woods and products of every kind whatsoever which the KHENTIU (NUBIANS)

[1] The goddess of the harvest.

[2] i.e. the 'Land of the Bow', or Northern Nubia.

[3] The land of the setting sun.

[4] The land of the rising sun.

of KHENT-ḤEN-RESU (?) (i.e. the Southern SÛDÂN) bring into EGYPT and every man [bringing] them.

'6. And every hand shall pass them, and no officer of the revenue shall issue a command outside these places, to make a levy on or to take things over and above those which are intended for thy capital city.

'7. And I will give unto thee the land containing minerals, and good land for cultivation, and nothing thereof shall be diminished or withheld. . . . And the scribes and the revenue officers shall inspect the same and be satisfied that the rendering is correct.

'8. And further I will make the masons and the hewers of ore (?) and the metal-workers, and the gold smelters, and the sculptors, and the ore crushers, and the furnace-men, and the handicraftsmen of every kind, who work in hewing and cutting and polishing stones, and in gold, and silver, and copper, and lead, and every woodsman and carpenter who worketh in wood to pay tithe on all work done.

'9. And tithe shall be paid on all natural products, and on all the precious stones and minerals which are brought down from the upper land and on all quarried stones. And there shall be an inspector over the weighing of the gold, and silver, and copper, and precious stones.

'10. And everything which the metal-workers require for the house of gold, for making images of the gods and the repairs of statues, and the workmen also shall be exempted from the tithe. And everything which hath been given [in times past] to the 'storehouse'[1] shall be given again to [their] children. And everything which is delivered to thy god-house shall be [in abundance] even as it was in times of old.

'This Decree shall be inscribed upon a stele standing in a [prominent] place in sacred characters similar to those of the [original] document [which was written] on a tablet of wood (?), and there shall also be [cut] on it a figure of this god [KHNEMU–RĀ]. [This stele] is given to inform the overseers of the priests and the overseers of all the people in that my name shall be established in the god-house of KHNEMU–RĀ, the Lord of ĀBU (ELEPHANTINE) for ever.'

[1] The building in which possessions of every kind which were royal property were stored.

A LEGEND OF KHONSU-PA-ARI-SEKHERU THE CASTER-OUT OF DEVILS

[The hieroglyphic text of this legend is found on a stele which was found in a little temple of KHONSU at THEBES, and is now preserved in the BIBLIOTHÈQUE NATIONALE in PARIS. See PRISSE D'AVENNES, *Choix de Monuments Égyptiens*, plate 24. Many translations of it have been published in English, French, and German. In the rounded portion at the top of the stele is the Winged Disk of HORUS of BEḤUṬ-T (EDFÛ) and below this are sculptured two boats containing the shrines of KHONSU-IN-THEBES-NEFER-ḤETEP, and KHONSU-PA-ARI-SEKHERU, who possessed special powers of casting out devils. The king (RAMESES II) is offering incense to the former, which is carried by six priests, and a priest is offering incense to the latter, which is carried by four priests. This legend was cut on the stele long after the reign of RAMESES II whose 'strong names' and title are given in the opening lines. These are omitted here.]

TRANSLATION

It came to pass that His Majesty USR–MAĀT–RĀ, the chosen one of RĀ, the son of RĀ (RAMESES II), the beloved of AMEN, according to his annual custom marched into NEHERN[1] and the princes of every district in the country came to do homage to him, and their backs were bent under the weight of the offerings which they brought for the Souls of His Majesty from the remotest (?) districts. Their gifts were gold, silver, lapis-lazuli, and turquoise (or, malachite); on their backs they brought precious woods and spices from the Land of God (i.e. southern ARABIA) and every one brought his neighbour. And the Prince of BEKHTEN also brought his gifts, and he placed his eldest daughter in the forefront to salute His Majesty, and obtain favour from him. Now, she was a most beautiful maiden, and she pleased His Majesty more than any other gift. And behold, he conferred upon her the title of 'Great King's woman (i.e. Queen-in-Chief) NEFERU-RĀ'.[2] And when His Majesty returned to EGYPT, she held the rank and fulfilled the duties of a Queen.

On the twenty-second day of the second month[3] of the season

[1] i.e. Bēth Nahrān, the country between the rivers, the region near the head of the River Euphrates and between the Tigris and Euphrates.

[2] A name meaning 'the beauties of Rā'.

[3] The Coptic month Paoni = May–June.

SHEMU (i.e. the season when water is lacking), in the fifteenth year of his reign, His Majesty was living in THEBES, the great city, the queen of cities, whither he had come joyfully to celebrate the worship of his father AMEN–RĀ, the Lord of APT-ASUT (KARNAK) at his splendid festival of the Apt of the South,[1] which was his favourite place of abode from the time when the world began. And one came and announced to His Majesty: 'An envoy of the Prince of BEKHTEN is here; he hath brought very many gifts for the queen.' And the envoy and the gifts were brought into the presence of His Majesty, and he bowed down and kissed the ground at the feet of His Majesty, and said: 'Adored art thou, O Sun of the Nine Nations of the bow! Grant us our life, and let us live.' And when he had finished his adoration of His Majesty, he said, 'I have come unto thee, O my sovereign Lord, on behalf of BINTHRASHIT,[2] a younger sister of Queen NEFERU-RĀ, whose members have been attacked by some dire disease. I beseech Thy Majesty to send a wise man to see her'.

His Majesty said: 'Let the scribes (or sages) of the House of Life (i.e. the Royal Library), who are resident at Court, be brought hither to me.' And forthwith they were brought into his presence. And His Majesty said: 'I have summoned you in order that ye hear these words (i.e. the envoy's). Let one of your number be brought hither to me, who is experienced in his craft and is skilful with his fingers.' Then the royal scribe DJEḤUTI-EM-ḤEB came into the presence of His Majesty, and the King commanded him to set out forthwith with the envoy for BEKHTEN.

The learned man arrived in BEKHTEN, and he found that BINTHRASHIT was possessed of a spirit [of evil], and he found, that he had not enough strength to contend with him.

And once again the Prince of BEKHTEN sent an envoy to His Majesty, saying: 'O King, my lord, let Thy Majesty command a strong god to be brought here [to fight the spirit of evil].' [This second] embassy was announced in the first month[3] of the Inundation, in the twenty-sixth year of His Majesty's reign, during the festival of AMEN, when His Majesty was in THEBES.

[1] Now known as the Temple of Luxor.
[2] A name meaning 'daughter of gladness'.
[3] The Coptic month Pakhons (April–May).

His Majesty brought the matter a second time before KHONSU-IN-THEBES-NEFER-ḤETEP, [saying]: 'Once again, my lord, I appear before thee on behalf of the daughter of the Prince of BEKHTEN.' Then KHONSU-IN-THEBES-NEFER-ḤETEP was brought before KHONSU-PA-ARI-SEKHERU, the great god who destroyeth the companies of evil spirits. His Majesty spake unto KHONSU-IN-THEBES-NEFER-ḤETEP, saying: 'O my fair lord, turn thy face to KHONSU-PA-ARI-SEKHERU, the great god who destroyeth evil spirits, and grant that he may journey to BEKHTEN.' [And the god] nodded [his head] twice vigorously[1] [meaning I consent]. And His Majesty said: 'Give him a [special] portion of magical protection, and I will permit His Majesty to go to BEKHTEN so that he may deliver the daughter of the Prince of BEKHTEN [from the spirit of evil].' And KHONSU-IN-THEBES-NEFER-ḤETEP nodded his head twice vigorously. Then he bestowed a fourfold measure of his magical power on KHONSU-PA-ARI-SEKHERU.

His Majesty commanded that KHONSU-PA-ARI-SEKHERU-IN-THEBES should be set in a large ship, with five boats as an escort [for the passage by sea], and a state wagon, and numerous horses of the West and of the East [for the journey by land]. And this god arrived in BEKHTEN after a journey of one year and five months. Then the Prince of BEKHTEN came with his soldiers and his nobles before KHONSU-PA-ARI-SEKHERU and cast themselves down on their bellies before the god, and said unto him: 'Thou hast come to us, thereby showing us an act of grace by the command of King USR–MAĀT–RĀ, the chosen of RĀ.'

Then this god went to the place where BINTHRASHIT was, and he applied[2] the protecting magic to the daughter of the Prince of BEKHTEN. And she was healed immediately. Then that spirit [of evil] which had been dwelling in her said unto KHONSU-PA-ARI-SEKHERU-IN-THEBES: 'Welcome, welcome, thou comest in peace, (i.e. thou art heartily welcome), O great god who destroyeth the companies of evil spirits, BEKHTEN is thy town, and the inhabitants thereof are thy servants: I myself also am thy servant. I would fain go back to the place from whence I came in order that thou

[1] Thus the statues of the gods in the sanctuaries had movable members.

[2] He probably made passes with his hands over the nape of her neck whereby he transferred to her body the 'fluid of life' (*sa ānkh*) which he had obtained from Khonsu-in-Thebes-Nefer-ḥetep.

mayest be happy in respect of that for which thou art come. But I beseech thy majesty to give the order to celebrate a happy day with me and the Prince.' Then this god nodded his head to his priest and informed him thereby: 'Let the Prince of BEKHTEN offer up a great offering to this spirit [of evil].'

Now whilst these things were happening between KHONSU-PA-ARI-SEKHERU-IN-THEBES, and the spirit [of evil], the Prince of BEKHTEN stood there with his soldiers and he was greatly afraid. Then he made a great offering there to KHONSU-PA-ARI-SEKHERU-IN-THEBES, and the spirit [of evil] of the Prince of BEKHTEN, and he celebrated a happy festival with him. Then the spirit went in peace to the place where he wanted to go, according to the command of KHONSU-PA-ARI-SEKHERU-IN-THEBES. And the Prince of BEKHTEN rejoiced greatly with all the people who were in BEKHTEN.

Then the Prince of BEKHTEN held counsel with his heart and said: 'This god shall be given to BEKHTEN wholly, and I will never allow him to return to EGYPT.'

And when this god had tarried for three years and nine months in BEKHTEN, the Prince of BEKHTEN, as he lay asleep on his bed, saw a vision. It seemed to him that this god came forth from his shrine in the form of a golden hawk, and that mounting up in the heavens he flew off to EGYPT. And when he awoke from his dream his whole body was quaking. And he said unto the priest of KHONSU-PA-ARI-SEKHERU-IN-THEBES: 'This god who was living here with us yesterday hath returned to EGYPT, and his chariot shall go back to EGYPT likewise.' And the Prince of BEKHTEN allowed this god to depart to EGYPT, and he gave him many gifts of all kinds of splendid (or valuable) objects, and very many soldiers and horses.

And when they had arrived safely in THEBES, KHONSU-PA-ARI-SEKHERU-IN-THEBES, went into the temple of KHONSU-IN-THEBES-NEFER-ḤETEP, and laid all the gifts and splendid objects which the Prince of BEKHTEN had given him before KHONSU-IN-THEBES-NEFER-ḤETEP, without keeping back any of them for his own temple on the nineteenth day of the second month of the season PER-T in the twenty-third year of the reign of USR–MAĀT–RĀ, the chosen of RĀ, the ever-living.

LEGEND OF THE WANDERINGS OF ISIS IN THE DELTA AND THE BIRTH OF HORUS

[From the 'Metternich Stele' which was found at ALEXANDRIA in 1828 by workmen who were making an excavation for a cistern for the Franciscan Monastery. It was made for NEKHT-ḤER-ḤEB, king of EGYPT, 378–360 B.C., and the inscription upon it was restored by NES-TEM, a divine father and prophet of the god NEBUN, son of ĀNKH-PSEMTEK, the son of a divine father and prophet and scribe of the god ḤET, and of the lady of the house TENT-ḤETNUB, who found it in the temple of OSIRIS MNEVIS. The text was published by W. GOLENISCHEFF, *Die Metternichstele*, LEIPZIG, 1877, with a translation of the greater part of it. A transcript of the hieroglyphic text was published with an English translation by BUDGE, *Egyptian Literature, Legends of the Gods*, LONDON, 1912, pp. 142 ff.]

THE NARRATIVE OF ISIS (lines 48 ff.)

I am ISIS, I have escaped from the dwelling (or prison) wherein my brother SET immured me. Behold, the god THOTH, the great god, the Prince of Justice (MAĀT = the Right) both in heaven and on the earth, said unto me: 'Prithee come, O ISIS, thou goddess. Now, it is a good thing to hearken (i.e. obey), for there is life for the man who is guided [by the advice] of another. Conceal thyself, thou and [thy] child, that he may come to us. His members shall grow, and his strength shall become fully established, and it shall come to pass that he shall be set upon the throne of his father, whom he shall avenge, and the rank of Ruler (ḤEQ) of the Two Lands (EGYPT) shall be his.'

[ISIS ESCAPES WITH HER SON HORUS]

I fled [from the prison house] at eventide, and there came forth also the Seven Scorpions following me to strike (i.e. sting) on my behalf. The two scorpions TEFEN and BEFEN were behind me; MESTET and MESTETEF were one on each side of me; PETET, THETET, and MATET went in front to prepare a way for me. I charged them strictly (or in a loud voice) and my words penetrated into their ears, [saying], 'Do not salute (?) any, make no appeal to the red men (i.e. red-haired men), pay no attention to any inferior person (?). Let your faces be turned directly towards the road (i.e. fixed on the road)'. So the guardian of the company conducted us until we arrived at the city of PER-SUI,[1] the city of the two goddesses of the Divine Sandals, at the beginning of the Papyrus Swamps and the end of the firm ground (?).

[THE SCORPIONS ATTACK A NATIVE WOMAN] (lines 55 ff.)

When I had come to the outskirts and to the houses where the men and women (or married women?) lived, a certain woman of quality [called USERT] spied me as I was travelling along the road, and she shut the door of her house in front of me, because she was terrified in her mind at the sight of the scorpions which were with me. Then the Seven Scorpions took counsel together about the matter, and they all with one consent shot out their venom on to the sting of the scorpion TEFEN. Now a swamp-woman (i.e. one of the slave women) opened her door to me, and I went into the house. And the scorpion TEFEN crawled under the leaves of the door [with me] and stung the son of the lady USERT. And a fire also broke out in the house of the lady USERT, and there was no water there to extinguish it, but the heavens rained water upon the [burning] house of USERT, although it was not the time of the year when rain fell. And behold, the heart of her who had not opened her door to me was grievously sad, because she did not know whether [her son] would live [or not]. She wandered about her town uttering cries of grief, but no one came forth at [the sound of] her lamentation. Then my heart also became grievously sad for the sake of the child, and I wished to restore to life him that was free from fault. Thereupon I cried out to the noble lady: 'Come to me, come to me! Behold my mouth beareth life upon it. I am the daughter of a city wherein I am well known, who hath the power to destroy the Fiend (or Serpent, or Worm) by the utterance [of certain words], which my father hath brought me up to know. I am his beloved daughter, the offspring of his body.'

[ISIS RESTORES THE CHILD TO LIFE] (lines 58 ff.)

Then ISIS placed her two hands on the child in order to make to live him whose throat was stopped, [and she said]:

'O poison of TEFEN, come forth, and drip upon the ground! Thou shalt not enter or penetrate [further into the child]. I am ISIS, the

[1] i.e. the House of the Crocodile.

goddess, the mistress of magic. I am accustomed to practice magic, and I know how to utter words with magical effect. Hearken unto me, O every reptile which possesseth the power to bite (or sting). O poison of MESTET fall down! Tarry, poison of MESTETEF! O poison of PETET and THETET rise not up! O poison of MATET progress not!'

[Here follows the spell against poisons given by GEBB to ISIS, and then we have:]

'Make not love, cry not out to the ṬESHERU (Red ones), turn your glances away from the noble ladies in their houses, turn your faces to the ground until we arrive at the places wherein to hide in KHEB.[1] O the child liveth and the poison dieth; RĀ liveth and the poison dieth. Verily HORUS shall be in good case for his mother ISIS. Verily he who is stricken shall be in good case likewise.'

[THE MOTHER'S GRATITUDE] (lines 66 ff.)

And the fire [in the house of USERT] was extinguished and heaven was satisfied by the spell of ISIS, the goddess. The lady [USERT] came and brought to me [some of] her possessions, and she filled [with gifts] the house of the slave woman who had opened the door to me, [when] the lady USERT was angry and on that night was irritable. She kissed the mouth of her whose son had been stung, and she brought [some of] her possessions as a recompense because she had not opened the door to me. O the child liveth and the poison dieth. Verily HORUS shall be in good case for his mother ISIS. Verily he who is stricken shall be in good case likewise.

Behold, bread made of barley driveth out the poison and it will diminish in the members, and the flame of a fire [fed with] *hedjt* leaves shall expel inflammation from the limbs (or body).[2]

[AN APPEAL TO ISIS] (lines 71 ff.)

'ISIS, ISIS, come to thy HORUS, O thou whose mouth is learned (or instructed). Come thou to thy son', said the gods in her quarter of the town (?), as for one whom a scorpion hath stung, or the scorpion UHAT hath wounded, or the animal *antesh* hath

[1] i.e. the Island of Chemmis.

[2] This short paragraph is really a rubrical direction and it indicates that the preceding paragraph is to be recited over a barley cake baked in the fire.

worried. Then ISIS came with the knife(?) on her body and she stretched out her two arms, [saying] 'Behold me, behold me, my son HORUS! Have no fear, have no fear, O son of a woman of spirit power. No evil thing of any kind whatsoever shall happen unto thee [for] there is in thee the essence (or seed) of him who hath made to exist the things which are; thou art the son of him that is in MESQET,[1] who came forth from the celestial abyss of water. Thou shalt not die through the inflammation of the poison. Thou art the great BENU[2] who was born on the balsam trees[3] which are in the House of the August One which is in ANNU (HELIOPOLIS). Thou art the brother of the ABTU Fish[4] who ordereth what is to be; thou art the nursling of the Cat[5] that dwelleth in the House of NET (NEITH of SAÏS). The goddess RERIT,[6] the goddess HAT,[7] and the god BES protect thy members. The head shall not fall to the demon who is hostile to thee. Thy members shall not receive the fire of that which is poison to thee. Thou shalt not be [driven] backwards on the land, and thou shalt not be submerged in the water. No reptile which biteth (or stingeth) shall gain the mastery over thee, and no lion that attacketh thee shall have dominion over thee. Thou art the son of the sublime god who proceeded from GEBB, thou art HORUS, and the poison shall not gain the mastery over thy members. Thou art the son of the sublime god who proceeded from GEBB, and thus likewise shall it be with those who are under the knife (i.e. those who are suffering). The four august goddesses have thy body under their protection.'

[A GLORIFICATION OF RĀ, THE SUN-GOD, AND A PRAYER]

[. . .] he who rolleth up into the sky [at dawn], and droppeth down [at eventide] into the ṬUAT; his form is in the House of QA. [When] he openeth his Eye the light cometh, and [when] he shutteth his Eye the darkness cometh. The NILE floodeth when he giveth the command; [even] the gods know not his name. [He

1 Mesqet was the name of the bull's skin in which the deceased was placed to secure for him the new life. Later it was the Underworld generally.

2 The Phoenix who kept the Book of Destiny (*Book of the Dead*, chap. xvii. 33).

3 The famous balsam of trees from which the Christians made the holy oil.

4 A mythological fish which accompanied the Boat of Rā.

5 The Cat is Rā.

6 The hippopotamus-goddess.

7 The consort of Bes.

saith], 'I light up the Two Lands (EGYPT), putting to flight darkness, rolling up [into the sky] always (?) [or unfailingly]. I am the Bull of the eastern hills, and the Lion of the western hills, traversing heaven by day and by night (or always) without being repulsed. I have come because of the cry of the son of ISIS. Behold, the blind serpent NĀ hath bitten the Bull, and the poison hath penetrated into every member of his body. I charge thee to come forth down on the ground, for he that is suffering shall not be bitten.' O thou god MENU, the Lord of COPTOS, this is the son of the White Sow which is in ANNU (HELIOPOLIS) who hath been bitten (or stung). O MENU, the Lord of COPTOS, give those breath unto him that is under the knife (i.e. the sufferer) so that breath may be given unto thee.

[NOTE BY THE RESTORER OF THE TEXT] (lines 87 ff.)

NES-ATEM, the divine father and prophet[1] of the god NEBUN, the son of the divine father, and prophet and scribe of the Inundation of the NILE ĀNKH-PSEMTEK, and of the lady of the house TENT-ḤET-NUB, hath restored this inscription which after an inspection he found in a ruined (i.e. illegible) condition in the House of OSIRIS MNEVIS, in order to keep alive (i.e. perpetuate) her [*sic*, read his?] name, and to drive away death from her [*sic*] and from every sacred animal, so that breath might be given to the servant of ATEM, and that the friends (?) of all the gods may have life. And may his Lord OSIRIS MNEVIS prolong his life with a joyful heart, and give him a fine burial after old age because of what he hath done for the House of OSIRIS MNEVIS.

[A SCORPION STINGS HORUS] (lines 89 ff.)

HORUS was bitten (i.e. stung) in SEKHET ANNU (i.e. the Field of HELIOPOLIS), to the north of ḤETEP-ḤEM (?), whilst his mother ISIS was in the celestial (or upper) houses, in order to make a libation to her brother OSIRIS. And HORUS sent forth his voice into the horizon, and those who were in the . . . heard it. And the keepers of the doors by the side of the holy ASHEṬ Tree started up at the cry of HORUS and gave vent to cries of lamentation, and heaven gave the command to heal HORUS, and give him the gift of life.

[Here come three lines, 96–8, to me untranslatable.]

[1] Literally 'minister of the god'.

Bring hither everything that thou hast to destroy the poison which is in the members of HORUS, the son of ISIS, and likewise in all the members of the sufferer.

The reliefs and inscriptions on the front of the Metternich Stele, which was made to serve as a powerful amulet against the bite of the black scorpion.

[HYMN TO HORUS] (lines 101 ff.)

A Hymn of praise to HORUS, to glorify him: to be recited over the water and over the land. THOTH speaketh and setteth free this god:

Homage to thee, God, the son of a God. Homage to thee Heir, the son of an Heir. Homage to thee, Bull, the son of a Bull, who wast brought forth by a sacred Cow (or Goddess). Homage to thee, HORUS, who didst come forth from OSIRIS, and wast brought forth by the goddess ISIS. I speak with thy magical utterance. I pronounce a spell in thine own words, which thy heart hath created, and all the words of power and incantations which have come forth from thy mouth. Thy father GEBB hath commanded thee [to recite] them, thy mother NUT hath given them to thee, the Majesty of the god of KHEM (LETOPOLIS) hath taught them to thee, in order to effect thy protection, and to continue the care of thee, to shut the mouth of all the serpents in heaven, and on earth, and in the water, to make men and women to live, to propitiate the gods, and to glorify RĀ through thy chants of praise. Come thou to me this day, quickly, quickly, as thou paddlest in the Boat of the God. Drive thou away from me every lion on the plain, and every crocodile in the waters, and every mouth which biteth in their holes. Make them to be to me like the stone of the mountain, and like the fragment of an earthenware pot which lieth about in the quarter [of the town]. Extract for me the liquid poison which riseth up in every member of the sufferer. Watch over him and let thy words destroy it. Verily thy name is invoked each day. Let thy mighty power come into being in him. Exalt thou thy magical powers. Make me to live and him whose throat is stopped up. Mankind shall give praise (or thanks) unto thee, the MAĀTI shall adore thy forms. All the gods shall invoke thee (?), and verily thy name shall be invoked this day. I am HORUS of SHEṬNU.

[A SPELL OF THOTH AGAINST POISONOUS CREATURES]
(lines 126 ff.)

O thou who art in the hole, O thou who art in the hole! O thou who art at the mouth of the hole! O thou who art on the road, O thou who art on the road! O thou who art at the mouth (i.e. entrance) of the path! MNEVIS approacheth every man, and likewise every beast. He is SEP, who is attached to ANNU (HELIOPOLIS). He is the Scorpion-god who is attached to the Great House. Bite him not, for he is RĀ; sting him not for he is THOTH. Shoot ye not your poison over him for he is NEFER-TEM. O every serpent, O every snake, O every *antesh* animal which bite with your mouths and sting with your tails, bite ye not him with your mouths, and sting ye not him with your tails! Get ye afar off from him, spray not ye your fire over him! He is the son of OSIRIS! Vomit ye, vomit ye, vomit ye, vomit ye!

[Lines 138–62 contain a Litany of THOTH; for a translation of it see p. 419.]

[A PRAYER FOR KING NECTANEBUS] (lines 163 ff.)

Mayest thou be protected, O beautiful god, (SENDJEM-AB-RĀ-SETEP-EN-AMEN) son of RĀ, (NEKHT-ḤER-ḤEBIT), whom the gods and goddesses protect, and conversely. Mayest thou be protected, O beautiful god (SENDJEM-AB-RĀ-SETEP-EN-AMEN), son of RĀ, (NEKHT-ḤER-ḤEBIT), whom HORUS of SHEṬ[NU], the great god, protecteth, and conversely.

ANOTHER CHAPTER LIKE UNTO IT (i.e. the preceding). Fear thou not, fear thou not, O BASTT, strong of heart, president of the splendid field, mighty lady among the gods! There is none who can gain the mastery over thee. Come thou outside, following my mouth (or speech), O evil poison, which is in all the members of the lion (or cat) which suffereth.

[THE NARRATIVE OF ISIS—CONTINUED] (lines 169 ff.)

I am ISIS, who conceived a child by her husband, and I became heavy with HORUS, the divine [child]. I brought forth HORUS, the son of ISIS, in a nest of papyrus plants. I rejoiced over this very very much indeed, because I saw [in him one] who would make answer for his father. I hid him and I concealed him being afraid. . . . I went (?) into the town . . . being afraid of him that would do violence (?) [to him]. I spent the whole day in attending to the child and in providing for his sustenance. I came to take HORUS into my arms (i.e. embrace him), and I found that he, HORUS, the beautiful child of gold, the helpless child, without a father, had bedewed the ground with the water from his eye and with the foam of his lips. His body was limp, his heart was motionless (or helpless), and the sinews (or muscles) of his members were still. I uttered a cry, I, even I, [saying]: 'I am deprived of a child to answer for (or avenge) me. My breasts are full [of milk], but my bosom is empty.'

[In her impassioned lament ISIS mentions the greatness of her love for the child, and the sufferings which she endured in a lonely place, the failure of the great ones to respond to her voice. She addresses her father in the ṬUAT,[1] her mother in AQERT,[1] and her great brother in the tomb (or sarcophagus): 'Think of the Enemy (i.e. SET) and how profound was the hatred of his heart against me, the Great Lady when I was in his house.' I cried out to all the people and wished that they would let their hearts turn to me? I cried out to those who dwelt in the papyrus swamps, and wished that they would come to me at once. And the slave women came out to me from their houses, they hastened to me at the sound of my voice, and they loudly bewailed with me the greatness of my affliction. But there was among them no man whose mouth could utter a command, and although every one of them lamented bitterly, there was none of them who knew how to make the child to live [again].

And there came forth unto me a woman who was very well known in her city and was famous in her quarter thereof. She came forth to me. Her mouth possessed life, and her heart was filled with understanding. [And she said] 'Fear not, fear not, [for thy] son HORUS! Be not cast down, be not cast down, O mother of the divine child, who hast conceived from her brother (?) The undergrowth hideth thee, and no enemy shall penetrate therein. The word of power (or magic) of TEM, the Father of the gods, who is in heaven, shall make thee to live. SET shall not enter this region, and he shall not make a way through KHEB (CHEMMIS), . . . and those who are in his following shall never conceal themselves therein. These things shall happen for him. HORUS shall live for his mother. By command (or at a word) a scorpion hath smitten him with his sting, the reptile (ĀUN-AB) hath wounded him.'

Then ISIS put her nose on his (i.e. HORUS's) mouth, and she knew that it [was like that of] one who was in his coffin; she probed the wound of the Divine Heir and found that there was poison therein. She took him in her arms and then leaped about with him, with quick steps, like fish which are laid upon hot coals to be roasted. [And she cried out], 'HORUS is bitten. O RĀ! Thy son is bitten [O OSIRIS]! HORUS is bitten, the flesh and blood of thine

[1] Names of the Underworld.

Heir who hath gotten the sovereignty of SHU! HORUS is bitten, the Boy of KHEB (CHEMMIS), the Child of the House of the Prince! The beautiful Child of gold is bitten, the Child who is destitute and hath no father! HORUS is bitten, the son of UN-NEFER, who was born of the Weeping Woman (?)! HORUS is bitten, he in whom there was nothing abominable, the son, the Youth among the gods! HORUS is bitten, for whose sustenance I provided abundantly; to him I looked to make answer for (or to avenge) his father! HORUS is bitten, he for whom I cared in secret, the son to whom fear was attached in the womb of his mother! HORUS is bitten, he whom I watched and looked upon (i.e. guarded), and for the life of whose heart I longed! Calamity hath befallen the Child on the water, the Child hath perished.'

[TWO GODDESSES COME TO VISIT ISIS] (lines 202 ff.)

The goddess NEPHTHYS came shedding tears and uttering cries of lamentation as she wandered about in the papyrus swamps. The goddess SERQET (i.e. the Scorpion-goddess) also came and cried out, 'What is the matter? What is the matter? What hath happened to HORUS, the son of ISIS? Now pray to heaven so that the mariners of RĀ may stop rowing for a space and that the Boat of RĀ may not pass away from the place where HORUS is [lying].'

[ISIS APPEALS TO RĀ IN HEAVEN] (lines 206 ff.)

Then ISIS sent her voice up into heaven and made supplication to the Boat of Millions of Years, and ATEN (i.e. the Sun-god) stopped in its advance and moved not from the place where it rested. Then THOTH came with his magic (or words of power), and having the Great Command of MAĀ-KHERU (i.e. unlimited power), [and he said], 'What aileth thee? What aileth thee, O ISIS thou goddess of powerful spells, whose mouth possesseth skill and knowledge? Assuredly no evil thing hath befallen thy son HORUS, [for] the Boat of RĀ hath him under its protection. This day have I come in the Divine Boat of ATEN from the place where it was yesterday. Darkness hath come and daylight is destroyed in order to heal HORUS for his mother ISIS and every person who is under the knife (i.e. suffering) likewise.'

Then ISIS, the goddess said, 'Great is thy heart, O THOTH, [but] delay attacheth to thy plan. Can it be that thou hast come [to me] without being equipped with thy magical powers, and the Great command of MAĀ-KHERU, one [spell] on the other, the number whereof is unknown? Behold, HORUS is in the grip of the poison. Evil, evil indeed is his case, death and misery to the fullest extent. The cry of his mouth is to his mother (?). I cannot [bear] to see these things following him. My heart hath rested (i.e. dwelt) on it since the beginning (?) thereof. . . .' [The rest of her speech is untranslatable to me.]

[THE ANSWER OF THOTH TO ISIS] (lines 219 ff.)

[And THOTH said] 'Be not afraid, O goddess ISIS! Be not afraid! Be not anxious, O NEPHTHYS! I have come from heaven provided with life in order to heal (?) the Child for his mother. O HORUS–RĀ (?) (or HORUS, son) let thy heart be stable that it may not be destroyed by the fire.

'The protector of HORUS is the Dweller in his Disk (i.e. the Sun-god) who lighteth up the Two Lands (i.e. EGYPT) with the splendours of his two eyes; and he protecteth likewise every sufferer.

'The protector[1] of Horus is the First-born god in heaven, who is commanded to be the Guide (or Leader) of the things which exist, and of those which do not yet exist; and he protecteth likewise every sufferer.

'The protector of HORUS is that great Dwarf who goeth round about the Two Lands in the darkness; and he protecteth likewise every sufferer.

'The protector of HORUS is the Lord (Lion?) in the night, who journeyeth from MANU (i.e. the Sunset-land, the West); and he protecteth likewise every sufferer.

'The protector of HORUS is the Great Ram who is hidden, and who goeth round about with his Eyes; and he protecteth likewise every sufferer.

'The protector of HORUS is the Great Hawk which hovereth (?) over heaven, and the earth, and the ṬUAT; and he protecteth likewise every sufferer.

'The protector of HORUS is the sacred Beetle, with great wings,

[1] Or 'the protection of Horus is in'.

at the head of NUT (the Sky); and he protecteth likewise every sufferer.

'The protector of HORUS is the Hidden Body, in his mummied form in his sarcophagus; and he protecteth likewise every sufferer.

'The protector of HORUS is the ṬUAT of the Two Lands, journeying among those who are over hidden things; and he protecteth likewise every sufferer.

'The protector of HORUS is the divine BENU (PHOENIX), which goeth before his eyes.[1]

'The protectors of HORUS are his own body and the magic of his mother.

'The protectors of HORUS are the names of his father when he leadeth in the nomes.

'The protectors of HORUS are the tears of his mother and the lamentation of his brethren.

'The protectors of HORUS are his name and heart; the gods surround him to make his bier.

'Wake up, HORUS! Thy protection is permanent. Make thou happy the heart of thy mother ISIS. The words [uttered] for HORUS shall make hearts to flourish; he maketh content him that is in affliction. Let your hearts be happy, O ye who dwell in the heavens, for HORUS hath avenged his father. Get thee back, O poison. Verily thou art cursed (?) by the mouth of RĀ, and the tongue of the Great God hath repulsed thee. The Boat of RĀ standeth still, and ATEN (the Sun-god) will not sail from the place wherein he was yesterday until HORUS is restored to health for his mother ISIS, and the sufferer is restored to health for his mother.

'Descend to earth, come O Boat, row ye mariners of heaven, transport provisions . . .

[In the four following lines the Boat and the heavens are called upon to do certain things until HORUS and every sufferer are restored to health, and the meaning of this difficult passage does not become clear until we reach line 245.]

'Come to earth, O poison! Let hearts rejoice and let radiance diffuse itself. I am THOTH, the first-born god, the son of RĀ, whom TEM and the company of the gods [have sent] to restore HORUS

[1] In this paragraph and the four following paragraphs I omit the allusion to the sufferer.

in health to his mother, and every sufferer likewise. O HORUS, O HORUS, thy KA protecteth thee, and thy Image worketh protection for thee. The poison is as the daughter of fire, it was destroyed through its wounding the son of the strong one (?). Depart to your houses [for] HORUS liveth for his mother, and the sufferer likewise.'

Then the goddess ISIS said: 'Set then his face towards those who dwell in the land of the swamps (ATEḤ), and the nurses who dwell in the double city of PE and ṬEP (BUTO). They have made very large offerings in order to cause the child to be made strong for his mother, and also for the sufferer. Do not allow them to recognize [my] KA in the land of the swamps; [I will be] a visitor (?) in their city.'

Then THOTH spake unto the gods who dwell in the land of the swamps, saying, 'O ye nurses who dwell in PE, who struck with your hands, and toiled with your arms for that Great One who came forth from among you, weep for the SEKTET Boat[1] in order that the ĀTET Boat[2] may come! HORUS is to you, ye have counted him [among] the living, [ye have] declared that he is a living being. I will make to be joyful those who are in the SEKTET Boat, and I will make the mariners to resume their work of rowing. [For] HORUS liveth for his mother ISIS, and the sufferer likewise. As for the poison, it is a thing that is powerless . . . in his hour to cast back a report to him who sent it. . . . O RĀ ḤARMAKHIS, be glad of heart, for thy son HORUS is counted [among the] living. The face of this Child is the face of eternity (?). He shall oppose the faces and block the ways of the SEBAU fiends, and shall take possession of the throne of the Two Lands. RĀ in heaven shall answer for him, his father shall watch over him, the spells of his mother shall protect him. He shall travel whithersoever he pleaseth, and set his . . . over them. . . .

THE MYSTERIES OF THE RESURRECTION OF OSIRIS

It will be noticed that I-KHERT-NEFERT says nothing about the embalmment of OSIRIS or of the means by which he was restored to life and able to enter his palace as a living being (see pp. 275–6). The people were permitted to take part in the acts of the Drama of the murder and death of OSIRIS, for these were symbolic representa-

[1] The Boat of the Sun in the afternoon and evening.
[2] The Boat of the Sun from sunrise to noon.

tions, commonly called 'Mysteries', which all sorts and conditions of men were allowed to see. The mummification and resurrection of OSIRIS were 'Secret Mysteries'  *shetaiu*, which were performed in specially prepared places attached to the temples, wherein none save the priests, and members of the family, and specially qualified members of the laity might enter. The formulae which were pronounced by the priests during the performance of the magical, that is to say symbolic, rites and ceremonies were originally handed on from generation to generation orally, but when writing became better known they were written on papyri. A papyrus so inscribed might well be described as the 'book of words' or the text of a ritual, or even 'Office'. The ceremonies connected with the mummification and resurrection of OSIRIS at ABYDOS were of a very complicated and elaborate character, and were famous throughout EGYPT, just as the ceremonies performed annually in connexion with the deaths of HASAN and HUSÊN are famous throughout the Muhammadan world in our own day.

The body of OSIRIS having been brought into a special place in the temple, was next taken to the chamber in which his resurrection was to take place. But it was thought that devils and evil spirits might attack the body, and in addition to the priests who were in the chamber always ready to protect the body, a guard of gods was established to ward off evil influences and the attacks of devils. This divine guard watched the body all day and all night, and it was changed every hour, so that every god and goddess had a turn of duty during the twenty-four hours. The watchers by night came on duty at sunset or as we may say at 6 p.m., and ended their duty at sunrise the following morning, say 6 a.m. The watchers by day kept guard from 6 a.m. to 6 p.m. This watching of the body formed a very important part of the Mysteries of OSIRIS, and the priests treated it dramatically, and the whole Drama consisted of twenty-four distinct acts, though each was complete in itself. The priests at DENDERAH, EDFÛ, and PHILAE sculptured representations of all the acts on the walls of the temples in these places, and added inscriptions containing the speeches of all the actors.[1] These show that

[1] These have been published by H. Junker, *Die Stundenwachen in den Osiris-mysterien, nach den Inschriften von Dendera, Edfu und Philae* (in the *Denkschr d. Akad. Wien, phil.-hist. Kl.* 54), Wien, 1910.

OSIRIS lay on his bier and that ISIS and NEPHTHYS, the 'two widows', sang songs of lamentation to him. Every hour one of the gods came in and addressed words to OSIRIS. And the priests came in and performed ceremonies with unguents and medicaments, and water for washing the dead, and libations, and incense. The scenes sculptured on the walls show which god came in, and the number of the hour in which he came, and the accompanying inscriptions record each god's speech to OSIRIS. The following extracts will make this clear.

As every festival day began at sunset the previous day, even as is the case at the present time, we begin with the first hour of the night, say 6 p.m.

NIGHT

FIRST HOUR. THOTH and ANUBIS enter; the protecting god is AMSET. The UTPU priest sprinkles water and tells the gods that their KA, which rose out of the primeval abyss (NUNU) cometh. The servant of the god brings a vessel of water and announces that he is THOTH, and that OSIRIS is endowed with life. The SEM priest also brings water, and says, 'This is thy cool water, O OSIRIS, which is poured out by HORUS. I bring you the Eye of HORUS to refresh thy heart.' The UTPU brings incense and bids the god put this Eye of HORUS in its right place. Then the two widows declare that they have purified themselves and have censed themselves with burning incense. Then the KHERI ḤEB, or master of the ceremonies, says four times, 'Heaven and earth join.' One of the women says four times, 'Rejoicing of heaven upon earth.' The KHERI ḤEB says four times, 'The god cometh! Genuflexion.' The woman says four times, 'Rejoicing of heaven upon earth', and she strikes her tambourine. Then the two say together four times, 'Heaven and earth rejoice and are glad. Our lord is in his house, he need fear nothing.' Then the KHERI ḤEB says: 'GEBB bringeth thy sisters ISIS and NEPHTHYS to thy side; ISIS speaketh to thee, NEPHTHYS saluteth thee, they lift up thy face. Thou shalt be justified, O KHENTI AMENTIU. AMSET cometh to gaze upon thee, he will drive away thine enemies from thy right side.' After a few words of the KHERI ḤEB a woman says, 'I weep for the god whom I love. . . . Rest in thy house and remain in thy tomb. Fall down, O evil doer, but come thou in peace [O OSIRIS].'

SECOND HOUR. ANUBIS and UP-UATU enter, to look on the god in his secret form; the protecting god is ḤĀPI. The SEM priest brings water, and says, 'O OSIRIS KHENTI AMENTIU, this thy water which is in this land and which produceth all living things is brought unto thee so that thou mayest live thereby, and become sound thereby, and breathe its air.' The UTPU brings incense, and says, 'How beautiful it is to see thee! How comforting to gaze upon thee! How beautiful it is to see the fire!—Sprinkle incense and water.' The KHERI ḤEB says, 'O OSIRIS KHENTI AMENTIU, wake up and raise thyself up on thy right and left sides. Thy father GEBB joineth thee together. He tieth thy head to thy bones, he openeth thy blind eyes, he stretcheth out thy fettered legs. O OSIRIS, thou art purified front and back.' ANUBIS says, 'Behold these four gods before the house of OSIRIS, with NEKHEBET on thy south side, and UADJIT on thy north side. They protect thy KA. . . . Thou shalt be justified, O OSIRIS, ḤĀPI cometh to see thee. He hurleth all thine enemies down before thee.' The KHERI ḤEB says, 'Where is he? Where art thou?' The woman says, 'I weep because he was forsaken. I invoke heaven and I cry to the beings in the Underworld. I clothed the naked and dressed the divine body. The great ones lament thee . . . they mourn for thee as their god. I weep for thee that thou mayest not die—thy KA shall live. The gods lament thy coming, when thou goest whither thou wishest. I bewail thee, because thou art forsaken.'

THIRD HOUR. HORUS and THOTH come in to arrange the chamber, and the god on watch is ṬUA-MUT-F. The SEM priest brings in water, and says, 'O Father of the PHARAOH, OSIRIS, thy water which thou hast made and hast produced together with the gods is brought to thee.' The UTPU priest brings incense, and says, 'Rise up in peace, the incense riseth in peace.' The KHERI ḤEB says, 'O OSIRIS, KHENTI AMENTI, rise up, raise thyself and stand up in NETIT. Thy son HORUS greeteth thee with life and happiness, thou remaining among the gods, O OSIRIS; thou hatest sleep, thou lovest not darkness, to thee it is horrible to die; it is the thing abominated by thy KA. Thou shalt be justified, thou shalt be justified. ṬUA-MUT-F cometh to inspect thee, and he will hurl down thine enemies on thy left side.' . . . The woman says, 'I have travelled through the land, and traversed NUNU, and searched the stream. I lament with tears because thou wast forsaken, and I clothed the naked one on that dyke of NETIT. The two mourning women, the two sisters, lament for thee, their wings are over thee. I mourn because thou art forsaken.'

FOURTH HOUR. HORUS and his mother ISIS come. They bring the matter which came forth from the members of the god. They set the god upright in his [proper] form. The god who protects OSIRIS in this hour is QEBḤ-SENU-F. The SEM brings water, and says, 'I bring the eye of HORUS to thee, and pour out water for thee. . . . The UTPU brings incense, and says, 'Watch in peace, ye gods, a group about OSIRIS. . . . Lay your hands upon the noble emanation which cometh forth from the horizon. His perfume cometh to you, the perfume of the Eye of Horus is to you.' The KHERI ḤEB says, 'O OSIRIS KHENTI AMENTI. . . . The four gods, AMSET, ḤĀPI, ṬUA-MUT-F, and QEBḤ-SENU-F, who sit upon the walls of thy chamber, say unto thee, "Hail! OSIRIS KHENTI AMENTI." They protect thy KA, and ward off the enemy from the place where thou art. . . . Thy Mother NUT uniteth herself unto thee that she may drive away thy sorrow. She passeth the whole day in lamenting thee, she endeth the night in glorifying thee. She hideth thy abode before the great and glorious gods and the dwellers in the horizon. She layeth her arms on thee and embraceth thee. . . . Thou shalt be justified, O OSIRIS KHENTI AMENTI. QEBḤ-SENU-F cometh to inspect thee, and he chaseth away the fiends who come behind thee.' [The rest is wanting.]

FIFTH HOUR. NEPHTHYS weeps in this hour when the god is placed in the shrine; the god on guard is ḤEKA. The UTPU sprinkleth water, and says, 'OSIRIS KHENTI AMENTI, PHARAOH cometh to thee to bring thee NUNU and what hath gone forth from it. He poureth himself out and hurrieth through the Two Lands, he causeth the NILE to rise up to thee in his course, and he maketh haste and floodeth thine altar.' . . . The servant of the god brings water and says, 'Thy head is brought to thee, the Eye of HORUS is extended to thee. I bring unto thee that which hath gone forth from NUNU, and the choicest things which have gone forth from ATUM in her name of Water-pot.' He says four times, 'OSIRIS KHENTI AMENTI is pure, is pure.' The SEM brings water, and says, 'O OSIRIS KHENTI AMENTI, this thy cool water, is brought to thee, thy cool water, by HORUS in thy name, he who went forth from cool water.' . . . The

UTPU brings incense, and says, 'O OSIRIS KHENTI AMENTI, the Eye of HORUS is brought to thee, its perfume draweth towards thee. . . . The KHERI ḤEB says, 'The son cometh and protecteth his father, so say the gods with joyful heart. HORUS cometh and protecteth his father OSIRIS, so say the Nine Gods, their hearts being glad. Thou shalt be justified. ḤEKA cometh to inspect thee, he shall drive away the enemies from thy right side. I mourn for my lord, and I lament for my lord, whom I love.' The woman says, 'I mourn weeping. I am thy sister, sad of heart. I am thy wife who is sick from suffering. . . . Let us weep for him and make him glad with our moanings and share the hours of service in the night with him.'

SIXTH HOUR. SHU and GEBB enter to see the god in his purification; the protecting god in this hour is ARMAWI. The SEM brings cool water, and says, 'PHARAOH cometh to thee, O OSIRIS. He is HORUS who protecteth his father. He bringeth to thee NUNU in a water-pot, he sprinkleth thee with that which came forth from thy members. . . .' The UTPU brings incense and says, 'PHARAOH cometh to thee, O OSIRIS. He bringeth to thee the Eye of HORUS as incense, and he censeth thee with what went forth from thee. . . .' The KHERI ḤEB says, 'I glorify thee, my father; thou endurest for ever. Thy countenance, O great god, is fully equipped. The weeping goddesses lament thee, they both smite thee with their hands, they sing to thee, they chant dirges to thee and mourn before thee so that thy soul may be glad. They lament to thee so that thy KA may glorify itself therewith. . . . Thou shalt be justified, OSIRIS KHENTI AMENTI. ARMAWI cometh to inspect thee, he hurleth to the ground thine enemies before thee.' [Speech of KHERI ḤEB wanting.] The weeping woman says, 'I came and sought the feeble one. I mourn for my lord and I weep bitterly. . . . My heart is grieved because my brother is motionless. I weep because he is alone.'

SEVENTH HOUR. THOTH and ANUBIS come to bring gifts. The protecting god of this hour is MAI-TEF-F. [Text wanting.]

EIGHTH HOUR. HORUS and his company come and overthrow the enemy at the door of the shrine. The protecting god of this hour is called, 'Creator of his own name.' The women say, 'Behold, we lament thee. Behold, we glorify thee. Behold, we weep for thee. Raise thyself up, OSIRIS KHENTI AMENTI. Thou art equipped . . . [the rest of the text is wanting].

NINTH HOUR. HORUS and THOTH enter and bring in the enemies of OSIRIS so that their flesh may be hacked from their bodies. The protecting god of this hour is called NEDJEDJ. [The text is wanting.]

TENTH HOUR. HORUS and his company come in to slay the enemy of OSIRIS. The protecting god of this hour is called ḲEDEK. The women say, 'O OSIRIS KHENTI AMENTI, ISIS healeth thee, NEPHTHYS embraceth thee. Thou art the glorious god between them and dost possess . . . [the rest is wanting].

ELEVENTH HOUR. The gods make merry when they see the beauty of the god in the shrine. The protecting god in this hour is called, 'His fire is not quenched.' [The text is wanting.]

TWELFTH HOUR. OSIRIS is saluted by his son HORUS and his father GEBB, when they see the hearts of the gods turn to him in their hour. The protecting god in this hour is SHESMU. [They say?], 'Verily, thou continuest to subsist upon thy throne. O OSIRIS KHENTI AMENTI, thou art alone, and dost rest' [on thy bier?].

DAY

FIRST HOUR. The opening of the . . . in the shrine taketh place in this hour. RĀ goeth out from the tomb of the god, and HORUS of the gods cometh to sacrifice to OSIRIS. The protecting god in this hour is AMSET. The KHERI ḤEB and the SEM say four times, 'The magical cobra is extended. My mouth is in contact with it, my mouth will be consecrated by it, my mouth will be opened by it.' SHU, the son of ATUM, says, '. . . this thy son is OSIRIS, ATUM hath provided him with what he needeth. Thou openest the mouth for him, thou dost consecrate his mouth, thou makest him to be pure and alive. Thou shalt be justified, O OSIRIS KHENTI AMENTI, thou shalt be justified. AMSET cometh to look upon thee, and he will hurl to the ground thine enemy on the right side. The SHESMU[1] brings myrrh, and says, 'OSIRIS KHENTI AMENTI, accept the spice which comes from PUNT, so that thy flesh may be sound and thy bones strong—through its name ĀNTI.' The wailing woman says, 'The solar disk of ḤARAKHTI greeteth thee. . . . I come and weep before thee, my heart will never tire of weeping for thee. . . . My heir cometh to greet thee, having made to rejoice the faces of the Company of gods. Verily thou art alive, O my lord, but thy heart is

[1] He was the executioner of the enemies of Osiris.

sorely troubled. Stand up, and in very truth thy heart shall be glad straightway. Thou shalt be justified, my lord, thou shalt become one who is justified. Verily thine enemies are lying on the ground.'

SECOND HOUR. RĀ ascendeth over the body of the god. The gods who stand behind the bier do him reverence. The protecting god in this hour is ḤĀPI. The KHERI ḤEB and the SEM say four times, 'Life and health will be given, and the god shall unite himself thereto.' [Recite]: I am HORUS, I, even I, have ascended from the horizon. I come, and I bring to the Prince (i.e. OSIRIS) life and health. The gods rejoice, O OSIRIS. The two mighty children, the children of ATUM, bring thee refreshment, they knit together thy bones, they gather thy flesh together, and they join together thy members. Thou knowest it not they are SHU and TEFNUT (or TEFENT). They place their arms round thee and protect thee from the assault of SET. . . . Thou shalt be justified, O OSIRIS KHENTI AMENTI; thou shalt be justified. ḤĀPI cometh to inspect thee, and he will hurl to the ground before thee thine enemies.' AMSET brings oil, and says, 'OSIRIS KHENTI AMENTI, I open thine eyes for thee, I open thine ears for thee so that thou mayest in the morning be uninjured like RĀ in his name of BAK (i.e. oil).' ISIS saith, 'Hail to thee! . . . O OSIRIS. I am thy sister, I am thy widow ISIS. . . . RĀ glorifieth thee, and the gods of heaven mourn for thee.'

THIRD HOUR. The nobles come to present gifts to OSIRIS. The protecting god in this hour is ṬUA-MUT-F. The KHERI ḤEB says, 'OSIRIS KHENTI AMENTI, denizen of the horizon, lord of the horizon, thou comest out through the first door of thy house. . . . The enemy is driven away from thy house, and the Adversary from thy throne. Thou shalt be justified. ṬUA-MUT-F cometh to inspect thee, and he hurleth away from thy left side the enemies [who attack thee]. ḤĀPI brings incense and says, 'O OSIRIS KHENTI AMENTI, accept the precious stuff which came out from thy father GEBB . . . in his name of "Incense".' The wailing woman saith, 'Raise thyself up! ANUBIS standeth there, oil cometh forth from his eyes. Raise thyself up! Thy mother embraceth thee, she presenteth life to thee. Raise thyself up! The two children lead the gods hither so that they may lament for thee. Raise thyself up! Thy two widows glorify thee, the two friendly companions grieve at thine appearance. Raise thyself up! HORUS protecteth thy KA, and the gods rejoice when they see it.

FOURTH HOUR. The goddess NEITH and the Two Sisters go into the shrine of the Majesty of OSIRIS. The protecting god of OSIRIS in this hour is QEBḤ-SENU-F. The KHERI ḤEB says, 'O OSIRIS KHENTI AMENTI, the gods rejoice over thee. . . . the Two Sisters make merry when the primeval Lord cometh. Thou shalt be justified. O OSIRIS KHENTI AMENTI, thou shalt be justified. QEBḤ-SENU-F cometh to inspect thee, he turneth aside the Adversary who cometh behind thee.' ṬUA-MUT-F bringeth an unguent, and says, 'Thou shalt be justified, O OSIRIS KHENTI AMENTI, thou shalt be justified. Take thou the unguent in its name of Unguent.' The weeping women say, '. . . Hail to thee! The gods of the town are behind thee, as thy KA is before thee. Thou art the lord. Raise thyself up! Thy heart shall not become tired, and thou shalt be justified.'

FIFTH HOUR. The beasts brought for sacrifice are slaughtered at the door of the shrine by ANUBIS and the Sons of HORUS. The god protecting OSIRIS in this hour is ḤEKA. The KHERI ḤEB says, 'O OSIRIS KHENTI AMENTI, wake up, raise thyself up, so that thou mayest make thyself a living being. OSIRIS KHENTI AMENTI, HORUS bringeth to thee his sons and ANUBIS that they may slay thine enemies for thee. Thou shalt be justified. ḤEKA cometh to inspect thee, and he hurleth to the ground the enemies who are on thy right side.' QEBḤ-SENU-F brings the oil of festival, and says, 'O OSIRIS KHENTI AMENTI, thy oil of festival maketh the festive in its name of Oil of Festival.' The weeping woman says, 'My lord, raise thyself up. Behold, I come and protect thee. Thy mother [NUT] extendeth herself over thee in her name of Outspread Heaven. I mourn for thee in this my name of Mourner. I made thy form to be more ornamented than the bodies of the other gods. I will exalt thy throne above [the thrones of] the glorified ones.'

SIXTH HOUR. HORUS and his followers appear, and they slaughter the bull which is to be the sacrifice at the door of the shrine. The god who protecteth OSIRIS in this hour is ARMAWI. The KHERI-ḤEB says, 'OSIRIS KHENTI AMENTI, thou art the Eye which RĀ–ATUM loveth, thou art his KA. . . . Hail to thee, O OSIRIS SEPṬ (i.e. SOTHIS) in the heavens, who arrivest happily in his lands, when he travelleth among the stars. . . . Raise thyself up, O thou Bull, thou Governor of the Nine Gods, the lord of the Underworld. Thou shalt become justified, OSIRIS KHENTI AMENTI. ARMAWI cometh to inspect thee, he hurleth down before thee thine enemy in his name of god.' ḤEKA brings oil, and says, 'I come, O OSIRIS, and I glorify thee; the Four Gods (i.e. the sons of HORUS) carry thee on their arms, in his name of Oil.' The weeping woman says, 'Hail to thee, I greet thee, O my lord, come to me, so that I may glorify thee as my lord, and that I may see thee, I, the beloved one, whom thou lovest. I am the only one who possesseth divine attributes, the wife of her husband. Come to me, descend, O my lord. . . . Hail to thee, my lord in peace, raise thyself up [for] thine enemies are driven away.'

SEVENTH HOUR. In this hour ISIS ariseth and protects the limbs of OSIRIS. The protecting god in this hour is MAI-TEF-F. [ISIS says], 'O OSIRIS KHENTI AMENTI, behold thy sister ISIS hath come to thee rejoicing in her love for thee, and she envelops thee in her magical protection.'

EIGHTH HOUR. NEPHTHYS comes as protectress of the bier of OSIRIS. The god in this hour who protects OSIRIS is 'Creator of his name' (KHEPER-REN-F). [NEPHTHYS says,] 'Behold, thy sister NEPHTHYS cometh to thee so that she may destroy the evil which is on thy members. ISIS cometh to thee, and the two of [us] protect thee. Raise thyself up, O OSIRIS KHENTI AMENTI.'

NINTH HOUR. In this hour HORUS and his followers enter, they are the gods who protect the shrine. The god in this hour who protects OSIRIS is NEDJEDJ. The KHERI ḤEB says, 'HORUS cometh and his sons AMSET, ḤĀPI, ṬUA-MUT-F, and QEBḤ-SENU-F. I am HORUS who protecteth his father OSIRIS, and ye shall protect him against his enemies. THOTH cometh and bringeth to thee [the sons of KHENTI NIUTI (i.e. HORUS)], namely ḤEKA, ARMAWI, MAI-TEF-F, and KHEPER-REN-F.

TENTH HOUR. In this hour OSIRIS is adored and his beauty praised by the gods who stand behind the bier. The god who protects OSIRIS in this hour is KEDKA. [The gods say], 'Wake in peace! The god of the nome of BUSIRIS awaketh in peace. Thou awakest joyfully. Wake in peace, OSIRIS waketh in peace. Wake in peace, the god awaketh in peace. Thou wakest joyfully. Wake in peace, OSIRIS, the great god, the lord of ABATON, waketh in peace. Thou wakest joyfully.'

ELEVENTH HOUR. HORUS and his followers come in this hour. His followers go round and adore the god at the western corner of the shrine. The god who protects OSIRIS in his hour is [called] 'He hath not quenched his fire'. [To be recited]: 'PHARAOH cometh to thee, OSIRIS. He is HORUS who protecteth his father. He cometh to thee, thou Bull of the Nine Gods. He prayeth to thee, O thou eldest son of GEBB and his mother [NUT]. He maketh these two sisters who are [the most] beautiful of women to mount up to thee. PHARAOH cometh to thee, OSIRIS; thy son HORUS bringeth to thee a funerary offering.'

TWELFTH HOUR. This is the hour in which the lamps are lighted and brought, and the doors are closed. This god is purified by HORUS and the gods who watch the bier. Hail to thee, God! Hail to thee, Soul of the gods. Hail to thee, OSIRIS KHENTI AMENTI. Raise thyself up, O Lord! How beautiful are these songs (dirges ?)! How good these women are to thy KA! How beautiful in thy repose! O thou Living God, thy women of pleasure embrace thee. Thy son HARENDOTES bringeth to thee the sons of HORUS, namely, AMSET, ḤĀPI, ṬUA-MUT-F, and QEBḤ-SENU-F.'

From the translations of the texts accompanying the scenes of the OSIRIS Dramas given above it is clear that during the twenty-four hours of the night and day the members of the body were washed ceremonially, and anointed and joined together in such a way that the body of the god was reconstituted. It now remained to revivify OSIRIS, and this great work was performed by HORUS, as we see from passages in the Pyramid Texts (TETA, ll. 264–71, &c.): 'HORUS cometh, he hath counted thee with the gods. HORUS loveth thee. He hath filled thee with his Eye, he hath joined his Eye to thee. HORUS hath opened thine eye that thou mayest see therewith. . . . HORUS departeth not from thee, behold his KA. He resteth on thee that livest. HORUS hath found thee, he hath performed the ceremonies for thee. HORUS hath brought the gods to thee, they illumine thy face. He hath set thee before the gods he hath made thee to take possession of every diadem. HORUS hath given thee life in thy name of ĀNDJI. He hath given thee his Eye which flourisheth lastingly. He hath given thee thy weapon, thou hast conquered all thine enemies. HORUS maketh thee to be a complete being, there is no defect in thee HORUS maketh thee to stand up without support.' It was through the Eye of HORUS, which entered the body of OSIRIS, that OSIRIS was revivified and continued to live.

Another text (TETA, ll. 170 ff.; UNAS, ll. 267 ff.) says:

'GEBB hath seated thee on thy throne. He hath set his sandal on the head of thine enemy [saying], "Get thee back". HORUS hath smitten him. He hath delivered his Eye from him (i.e. SET), he hath given it to thee, thou obtained a soul through it, through it thou makest thyself master at the head of the Spirits (AAKHU). . . . HORUS hath seized SET, he hath set him under thee, he hath lifted thee up above SET, who is is helpless under thee. HORUS hath made thee to seize him by the middle of his body; he shall not escape from thy hands. HORUS hath made thee to hold him in the palm of thy hand wherefrom he shall not emerge. [OSIRIS], thou hast eaten the Eye, thy body is fortified thereby. Thy son HORUS seized it for thee, thou livest thereby.' The Pyramid Texts make it quite clear that HORUS came to the dead body of OSIRIS, and embraced it. By this embrace he transferred to it his own KA or vital energy, or a portion of it. In all cases of creation or revivification the embrace plays a very important part. When ISIS revivified OSIRIS she took his flesh in her arms, and bound up his hands and embraced  him (PEPI II, l. 868). NEPHTHYS, in the character of the goddess SESHAT  put her arms about his body and embraced it (TETA, l. 268). When KHEPRI, the primeval Sun-god, wished to vivify the forms of SHU and TEFNUT which he had created, he took their forms in his arms and they became 'living gods' (Papyrus of NESI-AMSU, col. xxvii). If the king embraced the statue of a god he absorbed the god's life (MORET, *Rituel*, p. 80 f.). RĀ and OSIRIS became one god after each had embraced the other in ṬEṬU (*Book of the Dead*, chap. xvii).

The Mysteries of OSIRIS performed at DENDERAH were of a very elaborate character.[1] The body of OSIRIS was assumed to have been hacked into sixteen pieces, and a model of each piece was made of wheat mixed with a paste made of ingredients possessing magical properties, and sent to the town in which that piece of the body

[1] For the texts and sculptured scenes in the temple of Osiris at Denderah see Brugsch and Dümichen, *Recueil*, i. 15, 16, and iv. 1–27; Dümichen, *Résultats*; Mariette, *Dendérah*, tom. iv, plates 35–9; Lauth, *Aeg. Zeit.*, 1866, pp. 64 ff.; Loret, *Recueil*, tom. iii, pp. 43 ff.; tom. iv, pp. 21 ff.; tom. v, pp. 85 ff.

was believed to have been found originally. A gold mould was made, and moistened wheat mixed with incense was pressed into it and a figure of OSIRIS KHENTI AMENTI in two pieces was produced. This wheaten figure was taken from the mould, and together with figures of the other gods, and many lamps, were placed in boats and taken to the tomb of OSIRIS. Four bands of papyrus were tied round the wheaten figure. The ceremonies of embalmment were performed over in the chamber appointed for the purpose and then the figure was buried. A detailed description of the rites and ceremonies performed at DENDERAH will be found in BUDGE, *Osiris and the Egyptian Resurrection*, vol. ii, pp. 21 ff. The EGYPTIANS believed that the Ancestor-god OSIRIS was remade in the earth, and that the pieces of his body were woven together a second time through the words and ceremonies of the gods whose effigies were carried in the thirty-four boats with the three hundred and sixty-five lamps, during the procession on the water. And all evil was warded off from his body by the one hundred and four amulets which were placed in it and on it. And there was not the smallest action on the part of any member of the men and women who acted the OSIRIS Drama, and not a sentence in the Liturgy, which did not refer to some historical happening of vital significance to the follower of OSIRIS. Many of these happenings dated from the dawn of the cult of OSIRIS, and the EGYPTIANS of the Dynastic period, not knowing exactly what they were, followed tradition blindly.

The OSIRIS Drama was performed at PHILAE for some centuries after the decay of ABYDOS, and the great temple, together with its obligatory and voluntary offerings, was maintained in a flourishing state certainly until the end of the fifth century of our era. OSIRIS was not buried on the island on which the temple stood, but in a neighbouring island at the southern end of the First Cataract, which the GREEKS called 'ABATON' because no ordinary person was allowed to set foot upon it. This site has not been identified, but there is no doubt that it was regarded as a most holy place, and offerings were carried thither by ISIS whilst the OSIRIS Drama was being performed on the island of PHILAE and at ABATON. Tradition declared that it was set apart at the creation of the world as the resting-place of the body of OSIRIS. The soul of OSIRIS was believed to come and alight on the body in the form of a 'divine hawk' with the face and beard of a man. Sometimes it alighted on a branch of the sacred MENTU-TREE, whilst ISIS and NEPHTHYS stood by the body and AMEN–RĀ and THOTH prayed to it. 'HORUS the avenger of his father' (HOR-NEDJ-TEF-F, called by the GREEKS 'HARENDOTES') and the god ARI-HES-NEFER (, called by the GREEKS 'ARSNUPHIS'), were also present. During the days of the great celebration of the 'Mysteries' no man or woman might play a tambourine (or drum) or flute, or sing to the harp. Furthermore absolute silence was to be maintained, and no shouting or noise caused by any man's voice was permitted to be heard. The text printed by Dr. H. JUNKER shows that during the last centuries of the cult of OSIRIS at PHILAE the character of the god had entirely changed. He was no longer the passive Dead-God, or God of the Dead, and the attributes ascribed to his soul were those of ATUM and KHEPRI and others of the great gods of the Creation. At PHILAE and ELEPHANTINE and in the islands of the First Cataract he was called the great self-created, self-existent god, the creator of every being and thing, and the primeval god of the souls in the Underworld. RĀ and his son SHU, and his grandson GEBB, subscribed to all the regulations made concerning his worship and his temples and tomb, which were written in the writing of THOTH, i.e. hieroglyphs. OSIRIS was buried in an island tomb, perhaps in deference to a Nubian custom, for many of the kings of ETHIOPIA were buried in islands in Lake ṢÂNÂ (or TÂNÂ as it is called in some dialects).

THE BURNING OF THE DEVIL ĀPEPI, THE ARCH-ENEMY OF RĀ

[Translated from BRITISH MUSEUM Papyrus, 10188, in the *British Museum*, Series I, London 1910. See Budge, *Hieratic Papyri*, vol. i, and *Archaeologia*, vol. lii.

The greatest god of evil known to the EGYPTIANS was called SET, or SUTI, and there is little doubt that the dynastic EGYPTIANS inherited him from their savage or half-civilized ancestors. He had legions of devils and fiends in his service, and among these was the monster ĀPEPI, who appeared sometimes under the form of a serpent and sometimes under that of a crocodile. In physical nature he was the essence of darkness and the blackest part of the night, and day by day he lay in wait in the darkest part of the eastern sky at the darkest moment of black night, to prevent the sun rising and to destroy the god of day. It is not so stated, but he must have been one of the powers of darkness and evil who had lived before time was in the great abyss of waters out of which the sun rose. These powers loved inertness and inaction, and were bitterly opposed to the sun-god and his followers who were planning the creation of the heavens and the earth, and of man and beast, and movement and motion. Whether ĀPEPI attempted day by day to swallow the sun, as SET swallowed the crescent moon, cannot be said, but it is certain that a fight took place between RĀ and ĀPEPI daily, and that RĀ triumphed. How RĀ beat off his foe or disposed of him we know not, but whether he paralysed him by reciting a spell, or whether he burnt him up with his fiery rays, his victory was neither decisive nor final, for on the following morning ĀPEPI was again waiting for him and ready to renew his attack.

On dark and foggy mornings the priests on duty in the temples of RĀ must have awaited the appearance of the sun in the sky with impatient anxiety, and with the view of assisting RĀ to overcome his foe they prepared a special liturgy, and believed that the recital of it accompanied by the performance of symbolic ceremonies, would destroy ĀPEPI and assist RĀ.

This liturgy was called 'The Book of the overthrowing of ĀPEPI', or 'The Book of knowing the evolutions (or generations) of RĀ, and the overthrowing of ĀPEPI'. The name of its author is unknown, but we may rightly assume that it was one of the most important of the books of magic written by THOTH himself. In col. xxix, l. 16, it is described as a 'secret book in the hall of the temple, and no eye must look upon the secret Book of overthrowing ĀPEPI; it is a house (or treasury) of words of magical power.' The rubrics order the making of a wax figure of the crocodile of ĀPEPI, and of every fiend or devil with whom he is associated, and whom it is necessary to destroy. The name ĀPEPI shall be cut upon the wax crocodile and filled in with green paint. On a piece of new papyrus a figure of ĀPEPI shall be drawn, and this shall be folded up and made into a case or wrapper into which the wax crocodile is to be inserted. The case is to be tied round with black hairs. The wax ĀPEPI is then placed on the ground, and the priest shall stamp upon it with his left foot until it becometh a shapeless mass. Then he shall make gashes in it with a flint knife, as if he was dearticulating it, and then he shall throw it into a fire made of *khesau* herbs, which shall be ultimately extinguished by pouring upon it the urine of a crocodile. Another rubric tells us when these ceremonies were to be performed, viz. at morning, noon, and night, and at certain times and seasons which are duly specified. If tempests were raging in the sky, or if heavy black-red clouds were stealing over the sky to obscure the sun's disk, or if heavy rain had set in, to make these pass away it was necessary to burn several such figures, and to recite these chapters over them whilst they were burning. And further the rubric assures us that it is a meritorious act for a man to perform these acts, and that it is good for him upon this earth and good for him in the nether world; they will enable him to attain to dignities which are above him, and he will be delivered from all evil things. Following this comes what appears to be a note by the scribe, 'May I see these things happen to me'.

The first six sections of the Book of ĀPEPI are: (1) The Chapter of spitting upon ĀPEPI; here the act of spitting is equivalent to uttering a curse. (2) The Chapter of defiling ĀPEPI with the left foot. (3) The Chapter of taking a spear to spear ĀPEPI. (4) The Chapter of putting fetters upon ĀPEPI. (5) The Chapter of taking a flint to hack ĀPEPI in pieces. (6) The Chapter of putting fire upon ĀPEPI. Here follow extracts from the spells which were recited by the KHERI ḤEB:

Down upon thy face, ĀPEPI, thou enemy of RĀ; get back, retreat, fiend! SEBAU (the Devil) is deprived of arms and legs; thy nose shall be split; such things shall befall thee. Thou art cast down and overthrown. RĀ HARMAKHIS overthroweth thee, he destroyeth thee, he damneth thee, he driveth hooks into thy body. ISIS saith in mighty speech: 'Thy soul is hacked to pieces, thy vertebrae are severed.' HORUS hammereth thee, the Sons of HORUS smash thee with their blows, thou art destroyed by their violence.

Get thee back, retreat, retreat, thou fallest backwards, as thou retreatest ĀPEPI. The Great Company of the gods in HELIOPOLIS turn the back. HORUS repulseth thy crocodile, SUT destroyeth thy opportunity. ISIS repulseth thee. NEPHTHYS hacketh thee in pieces. The Company of the Great Gods who are in the bows of the Boat of RĀ driveth thee back. The chain of SUT is on thy neck, the Sons of HORUS spear thee, the gods of the portals repulse thee, and the flame of their fire cometh against thee.

Cursed thou art! Destroyed thou art! Repulsed thou art at thy moment of ill-luck. Tripped up thou art! Turned back are thy accursed soul and body! Flayed art thou! Blows are rained on thee, dismemberment and slaughter are performed on thee; thy crocodile is destroyed. Thou are earless and flayed, thy soul is wrenched from its shade, thy name is destroyed, thy spells are impotent, destroyed art thou, overthrown art thou; never more shalt thou emerge from thy den! Thy opportunity for escape hath been done away.

Damned are thy accursed soul and shade.

The Eye of HORUS eateth into the flesh of thy face.

Down upon thy face, ĀPEPI, enemy of RĀ! For the flame of the Eye of HORUS is coming to thee, and it bringeth death to thy soul, thy *aakhu*, thy magical forms, thy body, and thy shade.

Get thee back, O one hacked in pieces! Thy soul is shrivelled up, thy name is buried in oblivion, yea, under threefold oblivion, silence covereth it, and it is cast aside. An end to thee! An end to thee! Never shalt thou enjoy the pleasures of love, never shalt thou have offspring.

RĀ triumpheth over thee, ĀPEPI. [*Repeat four times: a rubrical direction.*]

OSIRIS triumpheth over his enemies. [*Repeat four times.*]

HORUS triumpheth over his enemies. [*Repeat four times.*]

Taste death, thou fiend SEBAU. [*These words are to be said by a person who is ceremonially pure.*]

O ye multitudinous enemies of RĀ who have rebelled, ye malicious fiends, ye spawn of inertness, ye impotent rebels, ye nameless filth, for whom pits of blazing fires have been prepared by the command of RĀ, down upon your faces! Ye are overthrown, your heads are crushed in, ye are destroyed, annihilated, gashed with flints, made an end of; your windpipes are cut, the joints of your backs are rent apart.

The fire of the Eye of HORUS is on you, burning you, grilling you, scorching you, frizzling you, stabbing you, spearing you, eating into you, consuming you, roasting you, setting you on fire, burning you to ashes, destroying every trace of you. UNEMI, the Devouring Fire, consumeth you, SEKHMIT, the blasting fire from the desert, maketh an end of you, and UPS-UR adjudgeth you to destruction. Flame, Fire, Spark, pulverize you.

Your souls, shades, bodies, and lives, shall never rise up again, your heads shall never rejoin your bodies, and even the words of power of the god THOTH[1] [the lord of spells] shall never enable you to rise up again.

[The above spells destroyed every enemy of RĀ, HORUS, AMEN–RĀ of KARNAK, PTAḤ of MEMPHIS, ATMU, THOTH, lord of HERMOPOLIS, TUSĀSET, Lady of ON, HATHOR, Lady of ḤETEP–HEMT, HORUS–KHENTI–KHAT of KAKAM, KHUAUT, BAST of BUBASTIS, OSIRIS of ṬEṬU, BA–NEB–TET, ANHER–SHU, HORUS–TEMAM, AMEN–RĀ of SMA–BEHTI, ANUBIS, lord of SIUT, HORUS of the East, HORUS of the Two Eyes, HORUS–SMA–TAIU, HORUS in PE, UADJIT in ṬEP, and HORUS the Aged.]

Down upon thy face, ĀPEPI, enemy of RĀ. Be drowned, be drowned, be vomited upon! KHNEMU taketh thy children to the block of slaughter. Be sick over thyself at the mention of thy name.

I slice his flesh from his bones. I fetter his feet. I cut off his hands and arms. I stop up his mouth and lips. I smash his teeth. I cut out his tongue. I carry away his speech. I block up his eyes. I remove his ears. I tear out his heart. He, his name, his offspring, his kinsfolk and friends, his heir, his seed, his bones, and his skin shall never exist again.

SEKHMIT teareth out his bowels and casteth them into the fire with her left foot. She filleth his cavernous belly with fire. UADJIT shutteth him in the fire pit. SEKHMIT splitteth his tongue.

The gods of the South, the North, the West, the East overthrow him. The starry gods of Orion in the South and the Great Bear in the North turn him back, and the gods of the [Thirty-six] Decans fetter him. Never more shall he breathe or smell; and neither his house nor his tomb shall exist. He shall drive his teeth into his own body![2]

Fall down under the knife of the god, for a net is cast over thy

[1] He spake the word which caused creation to come into being. He defended Osiris and his words procured his acquittal in the Hall of Judgement, and his words could raise the dead, but not the damned enemies of the Sun-god.

[2] In col. xxix, line 20, we read: 'When Rā heareth this book recited his heart is fortified, his boat is made to advance in peace.'

head, the spear is in thy belly, and the arrows of RĀ are in thee. Sexual pleasure, or emission of seed, shall never be thine, never shalt thou have male offspring, never shall thine egg grow. Thou art overthrown, destroyed, ended, chopped, hacked in pieces, slaughtered, butchered. RĀ maketh THOTH to slay thee.

HERE ENDETH THE BOOK OF NEB-ER-DJER

Then follow the twenty-eight accursed names of ĀPEPI, one for each of the days of a lunar month. The last rubric gives instructions for making wax figures of the enemies of RĀ, some with the heads of cats, some with the heads of ducks, or geese, and each of them is to have a knife stuck in its back.

THE LAMENTS OF ISIS AND NEPHTHYS

[From BRITISH MUSEUM Papyrus No. 10188 published in facsimile with a hieroglyphic transcript and English translation in BUDGE, *Hieratic Papyri in the British Museum*, Series I, LONDON, 1910.]

The rubric orders that these verses be sung in the temple of OSIRIS KHENTI AMENTIU, the Great God, the Lord of ABYDOS, on the 22nd to the 26th days of the fourth month of the season AKHET by two priestesses. These women were virgins, and they were ceremonially pure; their bodies were shaved and they wore garlands of ram's hair and held tambourines in their hands. On the shoulders of one was written the name ISIS and on the shoulders of the other NEPHTHYS, and they sang the verses among which were the following before this god [OSIRIS]. They began by chanting 'Hail lord OSIRIS', four times, and when the KHERI ḤEB, i.e. the officiating high priest, had recited a short formula four times, 'the women with the flowing hair sang:

Beautiful Youth, come to thy house at once; we see thee not.

Hail, Beautiful Boy, come to thy house, draw nigh after thy separation from us.

Hail, Beautiful Youth, pilot of time, who groweth except at his hour.

Holy Image of his father TENN,[1] mysterious essence proceeding from ATEM[2]

[1] An ancient god of creation.

[2] The god of the setting sun.

The Lord, the Lord! how much more wonderful is he than his father, the first-born son of the womb of his mother.
Come thou back to us in thy actual form; we will embrace thee.
Depart not from us, thou Beautiful Face, dearly beloved one,
The Image (or counterpart) of TENN, Male, Master of love joys.
Come thou in peace, our lord, we would see thee.
Thy two sisters will join together thy members,[1] no pain shall touch thee, they will make the injury to thee to be as if it had never happened. Our heads are turned backwards.
Great Mighty One among the gods, the road which thou travellest cannot be described.
The Babe, the Child at morn and at eve, except when thou encirclest the heavens and the earth with bodily form.
Thou art the Bull of the Two Sisters (ISIS and NEPHTHYS).
Come, thou, Babe, growing young when setting, our Lord, we would see thee,
Come thou in peace, Babe Great of his father, thou art stablished in thy house.
Fear not, thy son HORUS avengeth thee.

NEKA (the Devil) shall be carried off and thrust in his cavern of fire every day; his name shall be hacked to pieces (or slain[2]) among all the gods; TEBHA (the Devil) shall become stinking corruption.

Thou art in thy house; fear not. SUT (SET, the Devil) is suffering all the evil which he hath committed; what NUT sent hath speared him.[3]

Come, Youth of the Saffron-coloured Face, thou ONE who growest young, whose two eyes are beautiful.

I am thy sister ISIS, the darling of thy heart. Because of my love for thee, thou being absent, I water the earth with my tears this day.

Whilst thou travellest thou art hymned by us, and life springeth up for us out of thy nothingness. O our Lord, come in peace, let us see thee. Hail, Prince, come in peace, drive away the fire which is in our houses.

[1] An allusion to the dismemberment of the god by Set.

[2] To kill the name was equivalent to killing its owner; the name was the being.

[3] Set swallowed the crescent moon, but the Sky-goddess Nut speared him and made him vomit the moon.

Hail, Bull of those in AMENTI,[1] ONE, immovable, how much more marvellous than the gods is the Babe, the Male, the mighty heir of GEBB,[2] who was born God among gods.

Come thou to thy Two Widows. The whole of the Company of the gods encircle thee that they may repulse SET—cursed be his name!—when he cometh behind the shrine before thy father RĀ, who shooteth out [fire] and repulseth the SEBAU devils.

Come, thy kinsfolk await thee; drive away sorrow from our houses.

Come, thy kinsfolk await thee; there is none more stable than thee, O dweller in solitude.

The throne of our Lord is in peace. The Victor, he is greater than his long-suffering when the Lock fiend alighteth on his enemies.

O Soul who dost live again, the two sisters unite thy members.

I hid myself among the bushes[3] to conceal thy son that he might answer for thee, for separation from thee was a time of sore distress. Did she (i.e. I) not gather up thy members? I went on alone, I crept round about among the vegetation. A very large crocodile came after thy son—a female with the face of a male—but I knew, and ANUBIS (?); and I went round and retraced my way for my brother leaping clear from the evil one.

Hail, Beautiful Boy, come to thy exalted house, thy exalted house; let thy back be to thy house. The gods are upon their thrones. Hail! Come in peace, KING. Come in peace. Thy son HORUS is avenging thee. Thou causest great grief to thy Two Queens, we weep for thee at thy shrines (or sepulchres). Babe! How lovely it is to see thee! Come, come to us, O great one, glorify our love. Come thou to thy house, fear not.

O ye gods who are in heaven.

O ye gods who are on the earth.

O ye gods who are in the ṬUAT (Underworld).

O ye gods who are in the abyss.

O ye gods who are in the service of the deep.

We follow the lord, the lord of love.

[1] The Hidden Underworld (Hades).

[2] The earth-god, husband of Nut the Sky.

[3] An allusion to her bringing forth Horus among the swamps of the Delta.

I traverse the roads that thy love may come to me. I fly over the earth, I rest not in seeking thee. A flame of thy love is to me. The perfume of thy body is [that of] PUNT (i.e. the spice land).

The Cow (ISIS) weeps for thee with her voice. She avengeth thee. She sets thy nose on thy face, she collecteth thy bones for thee.

Thy mother NUT cometh to thee with holy offerings. She buildeth thee up with the life of her body. Thou art endowed with soul, thou art endowed with soul. Thou art established, thou art established.

Thy hair is turquoise on thy body when thou enterest the fields of turquoise. Thy hair is lapis-lazuli; thou art more lapis-lazuli than thy hair. Thy skin and limbs are alabaster of the south. Thy bones are silver. Thy teeth are turquoise, or the unguent of thy hair is liquid *ānti* (myrrh). Thy skull is lapis-lazuli.

SONGS OF THE HARPER

I. A SONG IN PRAISE OF DEATH

[The hieroglyphic text is found on a wall of the tomb of NEFER–ḤETEP, a 'divine father' of AMEN at THEBES. Published by A. H. GARDINER, with an English translation, in *Proc. Soc. Bibl. Arch.*, 1913, pp. 165 ff. XVIIIth dynasty. And see Roeder, *Urkunden*, JENA, 1923, p. 60.]

Thus speaketh the harpist of the Divine Father of AMEN–ḤETEP, triumphant.

[O honourable chiefs [and]
The Company of the gods of the Lady of Life (the necropolis),
Hear ye what action is praised for the Divine Father,
In the worship of his beneficent soul of an honourable chief,
Who is as a god living for ever,
 magnified in AMENT (i.e. the West)
[That] they may become a memorial for [comers] after
 every one who cometh [and] passeth by.
I have heard these songs
Which are in the sepulchres of the olden times, [and]
What they declare in magnifying [existance] on the earth,
And in belittling KHERT-NETER (i.e. the necropolis).
Why then [is this]?—doing the same concerning the land of eternity?

The just and exact and free from terrors,
Strife is an abomination thereto,
There is none who armeth himself against his neighbour,
This land hath none hostile to it,
All our kinsfolk are settled therein since the very first period of time.
Of those who shall exist millions of millions of them shall come to it.
There is no [chance] of tarrying in the Land of the Inundation (EGYPT).
There is no one who doth not set out for it.
The whole period of things done on the earth is but the period of a dream.

It is said to him that arriveth in the Great Land 'Strength and health [to thee]'.

II. ANOTHER SONG OF THE HARPER

[From the *Guide to the Fourth, Fifth, and Sixth Egyptian Rooms* (*British Museum*), LONDON, 1922, p. 209.]

O good Prince, it is a decree,
And what hath been ordered by this decree is good;
That the bodies of men shall pass away and disappear,
Whilst others remain [to succeed them].
I have heard the words of IMḤETEP[1] and ḤERṬAṬAF,[2]
Which are treasured above everything because they wrote them.
Consider what hath become of their tombs, and how their walls have been thrown down.
Their places are no more; it is just as if they had never existed.

[1] A great scribe, architect, and physician who flourished under the IIIrd dynasty.
[2] A son of Cheôps, the builder of the Great Pyramid of Gîzah, IVth dynasty.

None cometh from where they are to describe to us their state (or condition),
or to tell us of their surroundings,
or to comfort our hearts,
or to serve as our guide to the place whereunto they have departed.
Anoint thy head with scented unguents,
Array thyself in apparel made of byssus,
Immerse thyself in precious perfumes
Which are the veritable products of the gods,
Occupy thyself with thy pleasure daily, and cease not to find enjoyment for thyself.
A man is not permitted to carry away his possessions with him,
Never hath there been one who, having departed, was able to return to earth again.
Follow thine heart's desire and seek thy happiness.
Order thy surroundings on earth in such a way that they may minister to the desire of thine heart.
For at length the day of lamentation shall come.
He whose heart is still shall not hear the laments,
And cries of grief shall never make to beat again the heart of the man who is in the grave,
Comfort thine heart, forget these things;
The best thou canst do for thyself is to seek the desire of thine heart as long as thou livest.

A BLESSING AND A CURSE

The famous papyrus No. 10188 in the BRITISH MUSEUM was written for a highly placed and very important priest in the service of many gods called NESI-AMSU, or NESI-MENU, a scribe of AMEN, and the son of the prophet PEṬA-AMEN-ENSU-TAIU, by the lady TA-SHERE a sistrum bearer in the temple of AMEN. It is dated in the fourth month of the season AKHET in the twelfth year of ALEXANDER (IV), the son of ALEXANDER [the Great], who began to reign about 317 B.C., according to the Canon of PTOLEMY. ALEXANDER IV was murdered six years later, say in 311. PTOLEMY SOTER did not begin to reign until 305, and it seems therefore that the scribe either did not know of the murder, or that he added the years of the interregnum to those of the young king's actual reign. The colophon to this papyrus, which contains the 'Book of the Overthrowing of ĀPEPI' (see p. 141), gives a detailed list of the offices held by NESI-AMSU—who was certainly a pluralist!—and at the end of this come a blessing and a curse. The text says that 'their names', i.e. those of the priests who recite this book, 'are established, and permanent, and shall never be destroyed before OSIRIS, HORUS, ISIS, NEPHTHYS, and the gods and goddesses who [written] on this book, in the presence of all the gods and all the goddesses who are in the Underworld, and in the secret pylons which are in the Underworld, and their names shall be made to appear in the honourable ṬUAT. Thy name shall be proclaimed in the Boat of RĀ. Funerary offerings shall be given by them on the table of the Great God throughout each day. Cool water and incense shall be offered by them as to the honourable kings of the South and North who are in the Other World. They will grant exit and entrance among the favoured ones of OSIRIS KHENTI AMENTIU. And the rays of the Disk (i.e. the Sun) shall be made to fall upon their bodies every day.'

THE CURSE

'If any man belonging to any foreign land, whether he be Black, or Nubian (Kushite), or Syrian, removeth this book, or any thief steal it and carry it away,

Funerary offerings shall not be made to their bodies (i.e. mummies).
They shall never plunge themselves in cool water.
They shall never snuff the breezes [of the north wind].
Neither son nor daughter shall arise from their seed,
Their names shall never be commemorated upon earth by means of children.
They shall never see the beams of light of the Disk.'

THE BLESSING

'Whosoever seeth this book, and acteth in such wise that my KA and my NAME become permanent among the favoured ones [of OSIRIS], the selfsame thing shall be done for him after his death in return for what he hath done for me.'

INDEX

Aāḥ, the moon-god, 152
Aāḥ Djḥuti, 238
Aaḥes, the god, 63, 107, 255
Aakhu, the, 327, 335–6
Aaron's rod, 31, 41 *n.*, 171
Aats of the Ṭuat, the, 354–6
Āatshefit gate, the, 368, 374–5
ābebutiu, harpooners, 127
abṭ fish, cult of the, 98
Ābta, mythological serpent, 96
Ābta serpent, the, 368, 374–5
abu, elephant, 83
Abu, Elephantine, 174–6
Abydos, 107; the cult of Osiris at, 22, 274–7; the mysteries of, 25
Address of thanksgiving, the, 13
Aelian on Apis, 67, 73; on Mnevis, 74; on Bkha, 75; on the vulture, 91
Afu's passage through Ṭuat, 358–79
Agert, the underworld, 37
aḥ, (Aāḥ) moon, 6
Aḥi, 219
Ai, hymn by, 404–8
Aker, the god, 89
Akhan-Maāt serpent, the, 368, 372–3
ākhem, a cultus figure, 103
Akhemu, the never-setting stars, 241
Ākheperu-Mesaru gate, the, 363
Akhunaten. *See* Amen-Ḥetep IV
Al-Kâb, 51
Alexander the Great, 42
Alexander IV, 141, 326
All-god, the magician's, 132–3, 136
Allâh, the 99 beautiful names of, 16
ām ab, the heart, i.e. repent, 316
Ām-Mit, the eater of the dead, 38, 295
Ām-Mitu, a crocodile-lion, 103
Āmamu, the Coffin of, 4 *n.* 1
Amasis I, 248
Amen, 40, 106, 133; the bisexual nature of, 10; Amen and Ptaḥ, 17–18; the cult of, 154–5, 163–71; and his company of gods, 162; and his fetish, 162; hymns to, 413–16
Amen-em-Ḥet, king, 164
Amen-en-apt, 46
Amen-Ḥetep II, 357
Amen-Ḥetep III, 184, 357
Amen-Ḥetep IV, 11, 139, 167–8; hymn by, 402–4
Amen-neb, the papyrus of, 297 *n.* 4
Amen-Rā, the god, 18, 91, 109, 138, 139, 165–70, 233, 237; hymn to, 409–13
Amen-Rā Nesu Neteru ('King of the gods'), 166
Amen-Ren-t, 163
Amenet, the goddess, 171
Amenit, the goddess, 199
Ament, the god, 154
Ament, Ṭuat, 360–1
Ament-Semu-Set, 361–2
Ament-Tau gate, the, 360
Amenti, the Underworld, 123
Ami Ṭuat, the Book, 356–68
Amit, the goddess, 251
Ammi-as, priest, the, 30
Ammi-Khent, priest, the, 30
Ammi Ṭuat, the book of, 105, 166
Amnetef serpent, the, 368, 377–9
Amset, the god, 206
Ammt, 111 *n.*
Āmu, the, 144
Amu-Khent, Bubastus, 111
Amu-Peḥu, Tanis, 111

amulets, the use of, 125–6
Ān, the repulser, 243
An-Ḥer (Anouris), the god, 110, 134, 153, 257
Ānat, the goddess, 252
ancestor-worship, 554
Āndj-Ti, the god, 110, 184–6, 187–8 189–90, 268 *n.*
Andjet, the dweller in, 146
Aneb-Hedj, Memphis, 109, 158–9
Anhai, the papyrus of, 294, 295 *n.*, 303, 305
Ani, 332; the papyrus of, cited or quoted, 6, 19, 21 *n.*, 37, 39, 42 *n.* 2, 65, 66, 78, 119, 138, 158, 185, 190, 197, 213, 236, 238, 303–7, 387–9, 390–1, 424–6
animal cults, 9–10, 42, 67–100; gods, 29–30; models used in magic, 136–8
animal-men, 101
animals, fabulous, 103–5
animism, 55–6
Anit, the goddess, 60
ānkh, life, 33, 64, 149
ānkham plants, 65
Ānkhet-Kheperu, Ṭuat, 360
Anpu. *See* Anubis
anpu, dog, 77
Ānqet, the goddess, 176, 256
ant fish, cult of the, 98
Antaioupolites, 108
Āntat, the goddess, 251
anthropomorphization of fetishes, the, 100–2
Ānti, the ferryman, 24, 108
Āntiui, the god, 107
Anu. *See* Heliopolis
Anubis, god of the dead, 27, 29, 31, 37, 39 *n.*, 101, 147, 156; the cult of, 77, 78, 211–15
Anubis-Horus, 108, 109
Ap-t Asut, the temple of, 164
Āpep, the serpent, (Apophis), 78, 126–7, 140 *n.* 2, 141, 209, 433–6; the book of overthrowing, 429–30, 516–21. Variants Apepa, Apepi
Apesh, turtle-god, 92
Apet, the goddess, 84
Aphroditopolis, 107 *n.* 2, 109
Apis, the bull, 42, 73, 74, 194
Apit, the goddess, 150, 208
Apollinopolis Magna, 106
āpshait, a kind of beetle, 99
Apuleius, on the mysteries, 24; on Isis, 203–4; on Anubis, 215
Aqebi, mythological serpent, 96, 368, 369–70
Arabia, 111
Ari–Ḥems–Nefer, god, of Nubia, 149, 255
Arit gate, the, 368, 371
Ārits of the Ṭuat, the, 353
Aṣ-Ṣamad, the eternal, 139
Asar, Osiris, forms of, 192
Asar-bakha, 75
Asar-Ḥap. *See* Serapis
Asari, Marduk (?), 188–9
aser tree, the, 99
asfet, sin, 281
Asfettiu, the, 281
ashêrâh, 185
asheṭ, the persea tree, 99
Ashur, 185–6, 187–8
Āsit, the goddess, 252
Asna, 98
asp cult, the, 94
ass cult, the, 78
Assa, king, 254
Assyrians, the, 40
Asṭen (Asṭes), 83
Asthart, the goddess, 251–2
astronomy, Egyptian, 41–2, 240–7
Asyûṭ (Saut), 78
Atef crown, the, 152, 189, 245
Atef neter, father of the god, the, 30
Atem. *See* Temu

Ḥap. See Apis
Haphap, a star-god, 245
Ḥāpi, the Nile-god, 10, 29, 145, 190, 206, 256; the cult of, 235–7; hymn to, 385–7; the representation of, 23, 101
Ḥāp-Ur, 174
Ḥarakhti, 101
hare cult, the, 77
harper, songs of the, 524–6
Harpokrates, 152, 218–19; the begetting of, 45 *n.*, 122
Harris papyrus, the, 130, 236, 418–19
Ḥāt-Meḥit, the dolphin-goddess, 76–7, 98, 110
Hathor, the cow-goddess, 24, 35, 107, 108, 109; her abode, 99; the cult of, 228–34; her development from fetishism, 58, 59–60; the forms of, 10, 59, 150, 229–31; a representation of, 73
hawk, Osiris in the form of a, 6–7; Rā in the form of a, 6; Seker incarnate in a species of, 18, 19; -gods, 30, 147; of Horus, 73; the soul as a, 78; the cult of the 90–1, 106, 112
ḥayy bil-ḳurûn, the horned viper, 94
Ḥe-t Ka Ptaḥ, Memphis, 159
Heaven, the Egyptian, 338–9
Hebnu (Hibiu), 108
hedgehog cult, the, 81
Ḥedj-Par, the dweller in, 146
Ḥedjui, 239
Ḥeḥu, the god, 154
Ḥeḥut, the god, 154
ḥeka, magic, 32–3, 113–19, 156
Ḥeka, god of magic, 96, 113–19
ḥekau, magician, 65, 113
Heliopolis, 110–11; the nine gods of, 9; the cult of Rā at, 10; the bull of, 73; the theology of, 144–51
Ḥemaka, chancellor of Semti, 20
Ḥemsut-spirits, the, 15
Ḥen-t, 87
Ḥenkhisesui, 239
henotheism, 5
Ḥenu boat of Seker, the, 20–1, 27
Ḥeq-Āndj, Heliopolis, 110
Ḥeqa-p-Khart̥, 219
Ḥeqes, a star-god, 245
Ḥeqet, frog-goddess, 97–8, 175
Ḥeqit, the goddess, 150
Ḥer (Ḥur, Ḥor), the sun as a god, 6, 140
Ḥer and Suti, the hymn to Amen, 10
Ḥer-Akhti, 220
Ḥer-An-Mut-f, 219
Ḥer-Beḥut-t, 106, 220
Her-Em-Khent-En-Ariti, 6
Ḥer-f-Ḥa-f, 242, 272
Ḥer-Ḥekenu, 220
Ḥer-Ḥennu, 219
Ḥer-Khenti-An-Ariti, 219
Ḥer-Kenti-Khat, 219
Ḥer-Merti, 219
Ḥer-Nedj-Ḥer-Tef-f, 6, 205; the coffin of, 247
Ḥer-Netj-Ḥer-At-f, 222
Ḥer-Pa-Khart̥, Harpokrates, 45 *n.*, 122, 218, 219
Ḥer-Rā-P-Khart̥, 219
Ḥer-Sa-Ast-Sa-Asar, 221-2
Ḥer-Spt̥, 222
Ḥer-Shefit, the god, 109
Ḥeru-Shemsu, servants of Horus, 225
Ḥer-Shu-P-Khart̥-P-Ā, 219
Ḥer-Smai-Taui, 220
ḥer-t, what is above, 215
Ḥer-Ur, Horus the aged, 6, 27, 109, 218
Herakleopolis, 109
Ḥeri sesheta, 'He who is over the mysteries', 30
Hermes, 39

A CATALOG OF SELECTED DOVER BOOKS IN ALL FIELDS OF INTEREST

STICKLEY CRAFTSMAN FURNITURE CATALOGS, Gustav Stickley and L. & J. G. Stickley. Beautiful, functional furniture in two authentic catalogs from 1910. 594 illustrations, including 277 photos, show settles, rockers, armchairs, reclining chairs, bookcases, desks, tables. 183pp. 6½ × 9¼. 23838-5 Pa. $8.95

AMERICAN LOCOMOTIVES IN HISTORIC PHOTOGRAPHS: 1858 to 1949, Ron Ziel (ed.). A rare collection of 126 meticulously detailed official photographs, called "builder portraits," of American locomotives that majestically chronicle the rise of steam locomotive power in America. Introduction. Detailed captions. xi + 129pp. 9 × 12. 27393-8 Pa. $12.95

AMERICA'S LIGHTHOUSES: An Illustrated History, Francis Ross Holland, Jr. Delightfully written, profusely illustrated fact-filled survey of over 200 American lighthouses since 1716. History, anecdotes, technological advances, more. 240pp. 8 × 10¾. 25576-X Pa. $10.95

TOWARDS A NEW ARCHITECTURE, Le Corbusier. Pioneering manifesto by founder of "International School." Technical and aesthetic theories, views of industry, economics, relation of form to function, "mass-production split" and much more. Profusely illustrated. 320pp. 6⅛ × 9¼. (USO) 25023-7 Pa. $8.95

HOW THE OTHER HALF LIVES, Jacob Riis. Famous journalistic record, exposing poverty and degradation of New York slums around 1900, by major social reformer. 100 striking and influential photographs. 233pp. 10 × 7⅞. 22012-5 Pa $10.95

FRUIT KEY AND TWIG KEY TO TREES AND SHRUBS, William M. Harlow. One of the handiest and most widely used identification aids. Fruit key covers 120 deciduous and evergreen species; twig key 160 deciduous species. Easily used. Over 300 photographs. 126pp. 5⅜ × 8½. 20511-8 Pa. $2.95

COMMON BIRD SONGS, Dr. Donald J. Borror. Songs of 60 most common U.S. birds: robins, sparrows, cardinals, bluejays, finches, more—arranged in order of increasing complexity. Up to 9 variations of songs of each species. Cassette and manual 99911-4 $8.95

ORCHIDS AS HOUSE PLANTS, Rebecca Tyson Northen. Grow cattleyas and many other kinds of orchids—in a window, in a case, or under artificial light. 63 illustrations. 148pp. 5⅜ × 8½. 23261-1 Pa. $3.95

MONSTER MAZES, Dave Phillips. Masterful mazes at four levels of difficulty. Avoid deadly perils and evil creatures to find magical treasures. Solutions for all 32 exciting illustrated puzzles. 48pp. 8¼ × 11. 26005-4 Pa. $2.95

MOZART'S DON GIOVANNI (DOVER OPERA LIBRETTO SERIES), Wolfgang Amadeus Mozart. Introduced and translated by Ellen H. Bleiler. Standard Italian libretto, with complete English translation. Convenient and thoroughly portable—an ideal companion for reading along with a recording or the performance itself. Introduction. List of characters. Plot summary. 121pp. 5¼ × 8½. 24944-1 Pa. $2.95

TECHNICAL MANUAL AND DICTIONARY OF CLASSICAL BALLET, Gail Grant. Defines, explains, comments on steps, movements, poses and concepts. 15-page pictorial section. Basic book for student, viewer. 127pp. 5⅜ × 8½. 21843-0 Pa. $3.95

BRASS INSTRUMENTS: Their History and Development, Anthony Baines. Authoritative, updated survey of the evolution of trumpets, trombones, bugles, cornets, French horns, tubas and other brass wind instruments. Over 140 illustrations and 48 music examples. Corrected and updated by author. New preface. Bibliography. 320pp. 5⅜ × 8½. 27574-4 Pa. $9.95

HOLLYWOOD GLAMOR PORTRAITS, John Kobal (ed.). 145 photos from 1926–49. Harlow, Gable, Bogart, Bacall; 94 stars in all. Full background on photographers, technical aspects. 160pp. 8⅜ × 11¼. 23352-9 Pa. $9.95

MAX AND MORITZ, Wilhelm Busch. Great humor classic in both German and English. Also 10 other works: "Cat and Mouse," "Plisch and Plumm," etc. 216pp. 5⅜ × 8½. 20181-3 Pa. $5.95

THE RAVEN AND OTHER FAVORITE POEMS, Edgar Allan Poe. Over 40 of the author's most memorable poems: "The Bells," "Ulalume," "Israfel," "To Helen," "The Conqueror Worm," "Eldorado," "Annabel Lee," many more. Alphabetic lists of titles and first lines. 64pp. 5$\frac{3}{16}$ × 8¼. 26685-0 Pa. $1.00

SEVEN SCIENCE FICTION NOVELS, H. G. Wells. The standard collection of the great novels. Complete, unabridged. First Men in the Moon, Island of Dr. Moreau, War of the Worlds, Food of the Gods, Invisible Man, Time Machine, In the Days of the Comet. Total of 1,015pp. 5⅜ × 8½. (USO) 20264-X Clothbd. $29.95

AMULETS AND SUPERSTITIONS, E. A. Wallis Budge. Comprehensive discourse on origin, powers of amulets in many ancient cultures: Arab, Persian, Babylonian, Assyrian, Egyptian, Gnostic, Hebrew, Phoenician, Syriac, etc. Covers cross, swastika, crucifix, seals, rings, stones, etc. 584pp. 5⅜ × 8½. 23573-4 Pa. $10.95

RUSSIAN STORIES/PYCCKNE PACCKA3bl: A Dual-Language Book, edited by Gleb Struve. Twelve tales by such masters as Chekhov, Tolstoy, Dostoevsky, Pushkin, others. Excellent word-for-word English translations on facing pages, plus teaching and study aids, Russian/English vocabulary, biographical/critical introductions, more. 416pp. 5⅜ × 8½. 26244-8 Pa. $7.95

PHILADELPHIA THEN AND NOW: 60 Sites Photographed in the Past and Present, Kenneth Finkel and Susan Oyama. Rare photographs of City Hall, Logan Square, Independence Hall, Betsy Ross House, other landmarks juxtaposed with contemporary views. Captures changing face of historic city. Introduction. Captions. 128pp. 8¼ × 11. 25790-8 Pa. $9.95

AIA ARCHITECTURAL GUIDE TO NASSAU AND SUFFOLK COUNTIES, LONG ISLAND, The American Institute of Architects, Long Island Chapter, and the Society for the Preservation of Long Island Antiquities. Comprehensive, well-researched and generously illustrated volume brings to life over three centuries of Long Island's great architectural heritage. More than 240 photographs with authoritative, extensively detailed captions. 176pp. 8¼ × 11. 26946-9 Pa. $14.95

NORTH AMERICAN INDIAN LIFE: Customs and Traditions of 23 Tribes, Elsie Clews Parsons (ed.). 27 fictionalized essays by noted anthropologists examine religion, customs, government, additional facets of life among the Winnebago, Crow, Zuni, Eskimo, other tribes. 480pp. 6⅛ × 9¼. 27377-6 Pa. $10.95

MY BONDAGE AND MY FREEDOM, Frederick Douglass. Born a slave, Douglass became outspoken force in antislavery movement. The best of Douglass' autobiographies. Graphic description of slave life. 464pp. 5⅜ × 8½. 22457-0 Pa. $7.95

FOLLOWING THE EQUATOR: A Journey Around the World, Mark Twain. Fascinating humorous account of 1897 voyage to Hawaii, Australia, India, New Zealand, etc. Ironic, bemused reports on peoples, customs, climate, flora and fauna, politics, much more. 197 illustrations. 720pp. 5⅜ × 8½. 26113-1 Pa. $15.95

THE PEOPLE CALLED SHAKERS, Edward D. Andrews. Definitive study of Shakers: origins, beliefs, practices, dances, social organization, furniture and crafts, etc. 33 illustrations. 351pp. 5⅜ × 8½. 21081-2 Pa. $7.95

THE MYTHS OF GREECE AND ROME, H. A. Guerber. A classic of mythology, generously illustrated, long prized for its simple, graphic, accurate retelling of the principal myths of Greece and Rome, and for its commentary on their origins and significance. With 64 illustrations by Michelangelo, Raphael, Titian, Rubens, Canova, Bernini and others. 480pp. 5⅜ × 8½. 27584-1 Pa. $9.95

PSYCHOLOGY OF MUSIC, Carl E. Seashore. Classic work discusses music as a medium from psychological viewpoint. Clear treatment of physical acoustics, auditory apparatus, sound perception, development of musical skills, nature of musical feeling, host of other topics. 88 figures. 408pp. 5⅜ × 8½. 21851-1 Pa. $8.95

THE PHILOSOPHY OF HISTORY, Georg W. Hegel. Great classic of Western thought develops concept that history is not chance but rational process, the evolution of freedom. 457pp. 5⅜ × 8½. 20112-0 Pa. $8.95

THE BOOK OF TEA, Kakuzo Okakura. Minor classic of the Orient: entertaining, charming explanation, interpretation of traditional Japanese culture in terms of tea ceremony. 94pp. 5⅜ × 8½. 20070-1 Pa. $2.95

LIFE IN ANCIENT EGYPT, Adolf Erman. Fullest, most thorough, detailed older account with much not in more recent books, domestic life, religion, magic, medicine, commerce, much more. Many illustrations reproduce tomb paintings, carvings, hieroglyphs, etc. 597pp. 5⅜ × 8½. 22632-8 Pa. $9.95

SUNDIALS, Their Theory and Construction, Albert Waugh. Far and away the best, most thorough coverage of ideas, mathematics concerned, types, construction, adjusting anywhere. Simple, nontechnical treatment allows even children to build several of these dials. Over 100 illustrations. 230pp. 5⅜ × 8½. 22947-5 Pa. $5.95

DYNAMICS OF FLUIDS IN POROUS MEDIA, Jacob Bear. For advanced students of ground water hydrology, soil mechanics and physics, drainage and irrigation engineering, and more. 335 illustrations. Exercises, with answers. 784pp. 6⅛ × 9¼. 65675-6 Pa. $19.95

SONGS OF EXPERIENCE: Facsimile Reproduction with 26 Plates in Full Color, William Blake. 26 full-color plates from a rare 1826 edition. Includes "The Tyger," "London," "Holy Thursday," and other poems. Printed text of poems. 48pp. 5¼ × 7. 24636-1 Pa. $3.95

OLD-TIME VIGNETTES IN FULL COLOR, Carol Belanger Grafton (ed.). Over 390 charming, often sentimental illustrations, selected from archives of Victorian graphics—pretty women posing, children playing, food, flowers, kittens and puppies, smiling cherubs, birds and butterflies, much more. All copyright-free. 48pp. 9¼ × 12¼. 27269-9 Pa. $5.95

PIANO TUNING, J. Cree Fischer. Clearest, best book for beginner, amateur. Simple repairs, raising dropped notes, tuning by easy method of flattened fifths. No previous skills needed. 4 illustrations. 201pp. 5⅜ × 8½. 23267-0 Pa. $4.95

A SOURCE BOOK IN THEATRICAL HISTORY, A. M. Nagler. Contemporary observers on acting, directing, make-up, costuming, stage props, machinery, scene design, from Ancient Greece to Chekhov. 611pp. 5⅜ × 8½. 20515-0 Pa. $10.95

THE COMPLETE NONSENSE OF EDWARD LEAR, Edward Lear. All nonsense limericks, zany alphabets, Owl and Pussycat, songs, nonsense botany, etc., illustrated by Lear. Total of 320pp. 5⅜ × 8½. (USO) 20167-8 Pa. $5.95

VICTORIAN PARLOUR POETRY: An Annotated Anthology, Michael R. Turner. 117 gems by Longfellow, Tennyson, Browning, many lesser-known poets. "The Village Blacksmith," "Curfew Must Not Ring Tonight," "Only a Baby Small," dozens more, often difficult to find elsewhere. Index of poets, titles, first lines. xxiii + 325pp. 5⅜ × 8¼. 27044-0 Pa. $7.95

DUBLINERS, James Joyce. Fifteen stories offer vivid, tightly focused observations of the lives of Dublin's poorer classes. At least one, "The Dead," is considered a masterpiece. Reprinted complete and unabridged from standard edition. 160pp. 5³⁄₁₆ × 8¼. 26870-5 Pa. $1.00

THE HAUNTED MONASTERY and THE CHINESE MAZE MURDERS, Robert van Gulik. Two full novels by van Gulik, set in 7th-century China, continue adventures of Judge Dee and his companions. An evil Taoist monastery, seemingly supernatural events; overgrown topiary maze hides strange crimes. 27 illustrations. 328pp. 5⅜ × 8½. 23502-5 Pa. $7.95

THE BOOK OF THE SACRED MAGIC OF ABRAMELIN THE MAGE, translated by S. MacGregor Mathers. Medieval manuscript of ceremonial magic. Basic document in Aleister Crowley, Golden Dawn groups. 268pp. 5⅜ × 8½. 23211-5 Pa. $7.95

NEW RUSSIAN-ENGLISH AND ENGLISH-RUSSIAN DICTIONARY, M. A. O'Brien. This is a remarkably handy Russian dictionary, containing a surprising amount of information, including over 70,000 entries. 366pp. 4½ × 6⅛. 20208-9 Pa. $8.95

HISTORIC HOMES OF THE AMERICAN PRESIDENTS, Second, Revised Edition, Irvin Haas. A traveler's guide to American Presidential homes, most open to the public, depicting and describing homes occupied by every American President from George Washington to George Bush. With visiting hours, admission charges, travel routes. 175 photographs. Index. 160pp. 8¼ × 11. 26751-2 Pa. $10.95

NEW YORK IN THE FORTIES, Andreas Feininger. 162 brilliant photographs by the well-known photographer, formerly with *Life* magazine. Commuters, shoppers, Times Square at night, much else from city at its peak. Captions by John von Hartz. 181pp. 9¼ × 10¾. 23585-8 Pa. $12.95

INDIAN SIGN LANGUAGE, William Tomkins. Over 525 signs developed by Sioux and other tribes. Written instructions and diagrams. Also 290 pictographs. 111pp. 6⅛ × 9¼. 22029-X Pa. $3.50

CATALOG OF DOVER BOOKS

ANATOMY: A Complete Guide for Artists, Joseph Sheppard. A master of figure drawing shows artists how to render human anatomy convincingly. Over 460 illustrations. 224pp. 8⅜ × 11¼. 27279-6 Pa. $9.95

MEDIEVAL CALLIGRAPHY: Its History and Technique, Marc Drogin. Spirited history, comprehensive instruction manual covers 13 styles (ca. 4th century thru 15th). Excellent photographs; directions for duplicating medieval techniques with modern tools. 224pp. 8⅜ × 11¼. 26142-5 Pa. $11.95

DRIED FLOWERS: How to Prepare Them, Sarah Whitlock and Martha Rankin. Complete instructions on how to use silica gel, meal and borax, perlite aggregate, sand and borax, glycerine and water to create attractive permanent flower arrangements. 12 illustrations. 32pp. 5⅜ × 8½. 21802-3 Pa. $1.00

EASY-TO-MAKE BIRD FEEDERS FOR WOODWORKERS, Scott D. Campbell. Detailed, simple-to-use guide for designing, constructing, caring for and using feeders. Text, illustrations for 12 classic and contemporary designs. 96pp. 5⅜ × 8½. 25847-5 Pa. $2.95

OLD-TIME CRAFTS AND TRADES, Peter Stockham. An 1807 book created to teach children about crafts and trades open to them as future careers. It describes in detailed, nontechnical terms 24 different occupations, among them coachmaker, gardener, hairdresser, lacemaker, shoemaker, wheelwright, copper-plate printer, milliner, trunkmaker, merchant and brewer. Finely detailed engravings illustrate each occupation. 192pp. 4⅝ × 6. 27398-9 Pa. $4.95

THE HISTORY OF UNDERCLOTHES, C. Willett Cunnington and Phyllis Cunnington. Fascinating, well-documented survey covering six centuries of English undergarments, enhanced with over 100 illustrations: 12th-century laced-up bodice, footed long drawers (1795), 19th-century bustles, 19th-century corsets for men, Victorian "bust improvers," much more. 272pp. 5⅝ × 8¼. 27124-2 Pa. $9.95

ARTS AND CRAFTS FURNITURE: The Complete Brooks Catalog of 1912, Brooks Manufacturing Co. Photos and detailed descriptions of more than 150 now very collectible furniture designs from the Arts and Crafts movement depict davenports, settees, buffets, desks, tables, chairs, bedsteads, dressers and more, all built of solid, quarter-sawed oak. Invaluable for students and enthusiasts of antiques, Americana and the decorative arts. 80pp. 6½ × 9¼. 27471-3 Pa. $7.95

HOW WE INVENTED THE AIRPLANE: An Illustrated History, Orville Wright. Fascinating firsthand account covers early experiments, construction of planes and motors, first flights, much more. Introduction and commentary by Fred C. Kelly. 76 photographs. 96pp. 8¼ × 11. 25662-6 Pa. $7.95

THE ARTS OF THE SAILOR: Knotting, Splicing and Ropework, Hervey Garrett Smith. Indispensable shipboard reference covers tools, basic knots and useful hitches; handsewing and canvas work, more. Over 100 illustrations. Delightful reading for sea lovers. 256pp. 5⅜ × 8½. 26440-8 Pa. $6.95

FRANK LLOYD WRIGHT'S FALLINGWATER: The House and Its History, Second, Revised Edition, Donald Hoffmann. A total revision—both in text and illustrations—of the standard document on Fallingwater, the boldest, most personal architectural statement of Wright's mature years, updated with valuable new material from the recently opened Frank Lloyd Wright Archives. "Fascinating"—*The New York Times.* 116 illustrations. 128pp. 9¼ × 10¾. 27430-6 Pa. $10.95

PHOTOGRAPHIC SKETCHBOOK OF THE CIVIL WAR, Alexander Gardner. 100 photos taken on field during the Civil War. Famous shots of Manassas, Harper's Ferry, Lincoln, Richmond, slave pens, etc. 244pp. 10⅝ × 8¼.
22731-6 Pa. $9.95

FIVE ACRES AND INDEPENDENCE, Maurice G. Kains. Great back-to-the-land classic explains basics of self-sufficient farming. The one book to get. 95 illustrations. 397pp. 5⅜ × 8½. 20974-1 Pa. $6.95

SONGS OF EASTERN BIRDS, Dr. Donald J. Borror. Songs and calls of 60 species most common to eastern U.S.: warblers, woodpeckers, flycatchers, thrushes, larks, many more in high-quality recording. Cassette and manual 99912-2 $8.95

A MODERN HERBAL, Margaret Grieve. Much the fullest, most exact, most useful compilation of herbal material. Gigantic alphabetical encyclopedia, from aconite to zedoary, gives botanical information, medical properties, folklore, economic uses, much else. Indispensable to serious reader. 161 illustrations. 888pp. 6½ × 9¼. 2-vol. set. (USO) Vol. I: 22798-7 Pa. $9.95
Vol. II: 22799-5 Pa. $9.95

HIDDEN TREASURE MAZE BOOK, Dave Phillips. Solve 34 challenging mazes accompanied by heroic tales of adventure. Evil dragons, people-eating plants, bloodthirsty giants, many more dangerous adversaries lurk at every twist and turn. 34 mazes, stories, solutions. 48pp. 8¼ × 11. 24566-7 Pa. $2.95

LETTERS OF W. A. MOZART, Wolfgang A. Mozart. Remarkable letters show bawdy wit, humor, imagination, musical insights, contemporary musical world; includes some letters from Leopold Mozart. 276pp. 5⅜ × 8½. 22859-2 Pa. $6.95

BASIC PRINCIPLES OF CLASSICAL BALLET, Agrippina Vaganova. Great Russian theoretician, teacher explains methods for teaching classical ballet. 118 illustrations. 175pp. 5⅜ × 8½. 22036-2 Pa. $3.95

THE JUMPING FROG, Mark Twain. Revenge edition. The original story of The Celebrated Jumping Frog of Calaveras County, a hapless French translation, and Twain's hilarious "retranslation" from the French. 12 illustrations. 66pp. 5⅜ × 8½.
22686-7 Pa. $3.50

BEST REMEMBERED POEMS, Martin Gardner (ed.). The 126 poems in this superb collection of 19th- and 20th-century British and American verse range from Shelley's "To a Skylark" to the impassioned "Renascence" of Edna St. Vincent Millay and to Edward Lear's whimsical "The Owl and the Pussycat." 224pp. 5⅜ × 8½.
27165-X Pa. $3.95

COMPLETE SONNETS, William Shakespeare. Over 150 exquisite poems deal with love, friendship, the tyranny of time, beauty's evanescence, death and other themes in language of remarkable power, precision and beauty. Glossary of archaic terms. 80pp. $5\frac{3}{16}$ × 8¼. 26686-9 Pa. $1.00

BODIES IN A BOOKSHOP, R. T. Campbell. Challenging mystery of blackmail and murder with ingenious plot and superbly drawn characters. In the best tradition of British suspense fiction. 192pp. 5⅜ × 8½. 24720-1 Pa. $5.95